ALL GLORY TO ŚRĪ GURU AND GAURĀṄGA

ŚRĪMAD BHĀGAVATAM

of

KṚṢṆA-DVAIPĀYANA VYĀSA

एवं विदिततत्त्वस्य प्रकृतिर्मयि मानसम् ।
युञ्जतो नापकुरुत आत्मारामस्य कर्हिचित् ॥२६॥

evaṁ vidita-tattvasya
prakṛtir mayi mānasam
yuñjato nāpakuruta
ātmārāmasya karhicit

(p. 543)

BOOKS by
His Divine Grace
A. C. Bhaktivedanta Swami Prabhupāda

Bhagavad-gītā As It Is
Śrīmad-Bhāgavatam, cantos 1-10 (12 vols.)
Śrī Caitanya-caritāmṛta (17 vols.)
Teachings of Lord Caitanya
The Nectar of Devotion
The Nectar of Instruction
Śrī Īśopaniṣad
Easy Journey to Other Planets
Kṛṣṇa Consciousness: The Topmost Yoga System
Kṛṣṇa, The Supreme Personality of Godhead (3 vols.)
Perfect Questions, Perfect Answers
Teachings of Lord Kapila, the Son of Devahūti
Transcendental Teachings of Prahlāda Mahārāja
Dialectic Spiritualism—A Vedic View of Western Philosophy
Teachings of Queen Kuntī
Kṛṣṇa, the Reservoir of Pleasure
The Science of Self-Realization
The Path of Perfection
Search for Liberation
Life Comes from Life
The Perfection of Yoga
Beyond Birth and Death
On the Way to Kṛṣṇa
Geetār-gan (Bengali)
Vairāgya-vidyā (Bengali)
Buddhi-yoga (Bengali)
Bhakti-ratna-boli (Bengali)
Rāja-vidyā: The King of Knowledge
Elevation to Kṛṣṇa Consciousness
Kṛṣṇa Consciousness: The Matchless Gift
Back to Godhead magazine (founder)

A complete catalog is available upon request.

Bhaktivedanta Book Trust
3764 Watseka Avenue
Los Angeles, California 90034

Bhaktivedanta Book Trust
P.O. Box 262
Botany
N. S. W. 2019, Australia

ŚRĪMAD BHĀGAVATAM

Third Canto
"The Status Quo"

(Part Two—Chapters 17-33)

With the Original Sanskrit Text,
Its Roman Transliteration, Synonyms,
Translation and Elaborate Purports

by

His Divine Grace
A.C. Bhaktivedanta Swami Prabhupāda
Founder-*Ācārya* of the International Society for Krishna Consciousness

THE BHAKTIVEDANTA BOOK TRUST
Los Angeles · London · Stockholm · Bombay · Sydney

Readers interested in the subject matter of this book are invited by the International Society for Krishna Consciousness to correspond with its Secretary at either of the following addresses:

International Society for Krishna Consciousness
P. O. Box 262
Botany
N. S. W. 2019
Australia

International Society for Krishna Consciousness
3764 Watseka Avenue
Los Angeles, California 90034

First Printing, 1987: 5,000 copies

Printed in Singapore

Library of Congress Cataloging in Publication Data (Revised)

Purāṇas. Bhāgavatapurāṇa. English and Sanskrit.
Śrīmad-Bhāgavatam: with the original Sanskrit text, its roman transliteration, synonyms, translation and elaborate purports.

In English and Sanskrit.
Translation of: Bhāgavatapurāṇa
Includes index.
Contents: 1st canto. Creation—2nd canto. The cosmic manifestation—3rd canto. The status quo (2 v)—4th canto. The creation of the fourth order (2 v)—5th canto. The creative impetus—6th canto. Prescribed duties for mankind—7th canto. The science of God—8th canto. Withdrawal of the cosmic creations—9th canto. Liberation—10th canto. The summum bonum (4 v)—11th canto. General history (2 v)—12th canto. The age of deterioration.
Cantos 10 (v 2-4), 11 and 12 by Hridayananda dāsa Goswami, completing the great work of His Divine Grace A. C. Bhaktivedanta Swami Prabhupāda; Sanskrit editing by Gopīparāṇadhana dāsa Adhikārī.
1. Purāṇas. Bhāgavatapurāṇa—Criticism, interpretation, etc. I. Bhaktivedanta Swami, A. C., 1896-1977. II. Title.
BL1140.4.B432E5 1987 294.5'925 87-25585
ISBN 0-89213-253-1 (v. 4)

Table of Contents

CHAPTER TWENTY
Conversation Between Maitreya and Vidura 89

CHAPTER TWENTY-ONE
Conversation Between Manu and Kardama 139

Preface

We must know the present need of human society. And what is that need? Human society is no longer bounded by geographical limits to particular countries or communities. Human society is broader than in the Middle Ages, and the world tendency is toward one state or one human society. The ideals of spiritual communism, according to *Śrīmad-Bhāgavatam,* are based more or less on the oneness of the entire human society, nay, of the entire energy of living beings. The need is felt by great thinkers to make this a successful ideology. *Śrīmad-Bhāgavatam* will fill this need in human society. It begins, therefore, with an aphorism of Vedānta philosophy, *janmādy asya yataḥ,* to establish the ideal of a common cause.

Human society, at the present moment, is not in the darkness of oblivion. It has made rapid progress in the fields of material comforts, education and economic development throughout the entire world. But there is a pinprick somewhere in the social body at large, and therefore there are large-scale quarrels, even over less important issues. There is need of a clue as to how humanity can become one in peace, friendship and prosperity with a common cause. *Śrīmad-Bhāgavatam* will fill this need, for it is a cultural presentation for the respiritualization of the entire human society.

Śrīmad-Bhāgavatam should be introduced also in the schools and colleges, for it is recommended by the great student-devotee Prahlāda Mahārāja in order to change the demoniac face of society.

kaumāra ācaret prājño
dharmān bhāgavatān iha
durlabhaṁ mānuṣaṁ janma
tad apy adhruvam artha-dam
(*Bhāg.* 7.6.1)

Disparity in human society is due to lack of principles in a godless civilization. There is God, or the Almighty One, from whom everything emanates, by whom everything is maintained and in whom everything is merged to rest. Material science has tried to find the ultimate source of creation very insufficiently, but it is a fact that there is one ultimate source of everything that be. This ultimate source is explained rationally and authoritatively in the beautiful *Bhāgavatam,* or *Śrīmad-Bhāgavatam.*

Śrīmad-Bhāgavatam is the transcendental science not only for knowing the ultimate source of everything but also for knowing our relation with Him and our duty toward perfection of the human society on the basis of this perfect knowledge. It is powerful reading matter in the Sanskrit language, and it is now rendered into English elaborately so that simply by a careful reading one will know God perfectly well, so much so that the reader will be sufficiently educated to defend himself from the onslaught of atheists. Over and above this, the reader will be able to convert others to accepting God as a concrete principle.

Śrīmad-Bhāgavatam begins with the definition of the ultimate source. It is a bona fide commentary on the *Vedānta-sūtra* by the same author, Śrīla Vyāsadeva, and gradually it develops into nine cantos up to the highest state of God realization. The only qualification one needs to study this great book of transcendental knowledge is to proceed step by step cautiously and not jump forward haphazardly as with an ordinary book. It should be gone through chapter by chapter, one after another. The reading matter is so arranged with the original Sanskrit text, its English transliteration, synonyms, translation and purports so that one is sure to become a God-realized soul at the end of finishing the first nine cantos.

The Tenth Canto is distinct from the first nine cantos because it deals directly with the transcendental activities of the Personality of Godhead, Śrī Kṛṣṇa. One will be unable to capture the effects of the Tenth Canto without going through the first nine cantos. The book is complete in twelve cantos, each independent, but it is good for all to read them in small installments one after another.

I must admit my frailties in presenting *Śrīmad-Bhāgavatam,* but still I am hopeful of its good reception by the thinkers and leaders of society on the strength of the following statement of *Śrīmad-Bhāgavatam* (1.5.11):

tad-vāg-visargo janatāgha-viplavo
yasmin prati-ślokam abaddhavaty api

nāmāny anantasya yaśo 'ṅkitāni yac
chṛṇvanti gāyanti gṛṇanti sādhavaḥ

"On the other hand, that literature which is full of descriptions of the transcendental glories of the name, fame, form and pastimes of the unlimited Supreme Lord is a transcendental creation meant for bringing about a revolution in the impious life of a misdirected civilization. Such transcendental literature, even though irregularly composed, is heard, sung and accepted by purified men who are thoroughly honest."

Oṁ tat sat

A. C. Bhaktivedanta Swami

Introduction

"This *Bhāgavata Purāṇa* is as brilliant as the sun, and it has arisen just after the departure of Lord Kṛṣṇa to His own abode, accompanied by religion, knowledge, etc. Persons who have lost their vision due to the dense darkness of ignorance in the age of Kali shall get light from this *Purāṇa*." (*Śrīmad-Bhāgavatam* 1.3.43)

The timeless wisdom of India is expressed in the *Vedas*, ancient Sanskrit texts that touch upon all fields of human knowledge. Originally preserved through oral tradition, the *Vedas* were first put into writing five thousand years ago by Śrīla Vyāsadeva, the "literary incarnation of God." After compiling the *Vedas*, Vyāsadeva set forth their essence in the aphorisms known as *Vedānta-sūtras*. *Śrīmad-Bhāgavatam* (*Bhāgavata Purāṇa*) is Vyāsadeva's commentary on his own *Vedānta-sūtras*. It was written in the maturity of his spiritual life under the direction of Nārada Muni, his spiritual master. Referred to as "the ripened fruit of the tree of Vedic literature," *Śrīmad-Bhāgavatam* is the most complete and authoritative exposition of Vedic knowledge.

After compiling the *Bhāgavatam*, Vyāsa imparted the synopsis of it to his son, the sage Śukadeva Gosvāmī. Śukadeva Gosvāmī subsequently recited the entire *Bhāgavatam* to Mahārāja Parīkṣit in an assembly of learned saints on the bank of the Ganges at Hastināpura (now Delhi). Mahārāja Parīkṣit was the emperor of the world and was a great *rājarṣi* (saintly king). Having received a warning that he would die within a week, he renounced his entire kingdom and retired to the bank of the Ganges to fast until death and receive spiritual enlightenment. The *Bhāgavatam* begins with Emperor Parīkṣit's sober inquiry to Śukadeva Gosvāmī: "You are the spiritual master of great saints and devotees. I am therefore begging you to show the way of perfection for all persons, and especially for one who is about to die. Please let me know what a man should hear, chant, remember and worship, and also what he should not do. Please explain all this to me."

Śukadeva Gosvāmī's answer to this question, and numerous other questions posed by Mahārāja Parīkṣit, concerning everything from the nature of the self to the origin of the universe, held the assembled sages in rapt attention continuously for the seven days leading up to the king's death. The sage Sūta Gosvāmī, who was present in that assembly when Śukadeva Gosvāmī first recited *Śrīmad-Bhāgavatam*, later repeated the *Bhāgavatam* before a gathering of sages in the forest of Naimiṣāraṇya. Those sages, concerned about the spiritual welfare of the people in general, had gathered to perform a long, continuous chain of sacrifices to counteract the degrading influence of the incipient age of Kali. In response to the sages' request that he speak the essence of Vedic wisdom, Sūta Gosvāmī repeated from memory the entire eighteen thousand verses of *Śrīmad-Bhāgavatam*, as spoken by Śukadeva Gosvāmī to Mahārāja Parīkṣit.

The reader of *Śrīmad-Bhāgavatam* hears Sūta Gosvāmī relate the questions of Mahārāja Parīkṣit and the answers of Śukadeva Gosvāmī. Also, Sūta Gosvāmī sometimes responds directly to questions put by Śaunaka Ṛṣi, the spokesman for the sages gathered at Naimiṣāraṇya. One therefore simultaneously hears two dialogues: one between Mahārāja Parīkṣit and Śukadeva Gosvāmī on the bank of the Ganges, and another at Naimiṣāraṇya between Sūta Gosvāmī and the sages at Naimiṣāraṇya forest, headed by Śaunaka Ṛṣi. Furthermore, while instructing King Parīkṣit, Śukadeva Gosvāmī often relates historical episodes and gives accounts of lengthy philosophical discussions between such great souls as Nārada Muni and Vasudeva. With this understanding of the history of the *Bhāgavatam*, the reader will easily be able to follow its intermingling of dialogues and events from various sources. Since philosophical wisdom, not chronological order, is most important in the text, one need only be attentive to the subject matter of *Śrīmad-Bhāgavatam* to appreciate fully its profound message.

The translators of this edition compare the *Bhāgavatam* to sugar candy—wherever you taste it, you will find it equally sweet and relishable. Therefore, to taste the sweetness of the *Bhāgavatam*, one may begin by reading any of its volumes. After such an introductory taste, however, the serious reader is best advised to go back to the First Canto and then proceed through the *Bhāgavatam*, canto after canto, in its natural order.

This edition of the *Bhāgavatam* is the first complete English translation of this important text with an elaborate commentary, and it is the first widely available to the English-speaking public. The first twelve volumes (Canto One through Canto Ten, Part One) are the product of the scholarly and devotional effort of His Divine Grace A. C. Bhaktivedanta Swami Prabhupāda, the founder-*ācārya* of the International

Society for Krishna Consciousness and the world's most distinguished teacher of Indian religious and philosophical thought. His consummate Sanskrit scholarship and intimate familiarity with Vedic culture and thought as well as the modern way of life combine to reveal to the West a magnificent exposition of this important classic. After the departure of Śrīla Prabhupāda from this world in 1977, his monumental work of translating and annotating *Śrīmad-Bhāgavatam* has been continued by his disciples Hridayananda dāsa Goswami and Gopīparāṇadhana dāsa.

Readers will find this work of value for many reasons. For those interested in the classical roots of Indian civilization, it serves as a vast reservoir of detailed information on virtually every one of its aspects. For students of comparative philosophy and religion, the *Bhāgavatam* offers a penetrating view into the meaning of India's profound spiritual heritage. To sociologists and anthropologists, the *Bhāgavatam* reveals the practical workings of a peaceful and scientifically organized Vedic culture, whose institutions were integrated on the basis of a highly developed spiritual world view. Students of literature will discover the *Bhāgavatam* to be a masterpiece of majestic poetry. For students of psychology, the text provides important perspectives on the nature of consciousness, human behavior and the philosophical study of identity. Finally, to those seeking spiritual insight, the *Bhāgavatam* offers simple and practical guidance for attainment of the highest self-knowledge and realization of the Absolute Truth. The entire multivolume text, presented by the Bhaktivedanta Book Trust, promises to occupy a significant place in the intellectual, cultural and spiritual life of modern man for a long time to come.

—The Publishers

CHAPTER SEVENTEEN

Victory of Hiraṇyākṣa Over All the Directions of the Universe

TEXT 1

मैत्रेय उवाच
निशम्यात्मभुवा गीतं कारणं शङ्कयोज्झिताः ।
ततः सर्वे न्यवर्तन्त त्रिदिवाय दिवौकसः ॥ १ ॥

maitreya uvāca
niśamyātma-bhuvā gītaṁ
kāraṇaṁ śaṅkayojjhitāḥ
tataḥ sarve nyavartanta
tridivāya divaukasaḥ

maitreyaḥ—the sage Maitreya; *uvāca*—said; *niśamya*—upon hearing; *ātma-bhuvā*—by Brahmā; *gītam*—explanation; *kāraṇam*—the cause; *śaṅkayā*—from fear; *ujjhitāḥ*—freed; *tataḥ*—then; *sarve*—all; *nyavartanta*—returned; *tri-divāya*—to the heavenly planets; *diva-okasaḥ*—the demigods (who inhabit the higher planets).

TRANSLATION

Śrī Maitreya said: The demigods, the inhabitants of the higher planets, were freed from all fear upon hearing the cause of the darkness explained by Brahmā, who was born from Viṣṇu. Thus they all returned to their respective planets.

PURPORT

The demigods, who are denizens of higher planets, are also very much afraid of incidents such as the universe's becoming dark, and so they consulted Brahmā. This indicates that the quality of fear exists for every living entity in the material world. The four principal activities of material existence are eating, sleeping, fearing and mating. The fear element exists also in the demigods. On every planet, even in the higher planetary systems, including the moon and the sun, as well as on this earth, the same principles of animal life exist. Otherwise, why are the demigods also afraid of the darkness? The difference between the demigods and ordinary human beings is that the demigods approach authority, whereas the inhabitants of this earth defy authority. If people would only approach the authority, then every adverse condition in this universe could be rectified. Arjuna was also disturbed on the Battlefield of Kurukṣetra, but he approached the authority, Kṛṣṇa, and his problem was solved. The conclusive instruction of this incident is that we may be disturbed by some material condition, but if we approach the authority who can actually explain the matter, then our problem is solved. The demigods approached Brahmā for the meaning of the disturbance, and after hearing from him they were satisfied and returned home peacefully.

TEXT 2

दितिस्तु भर्तुरादेशादपत्यपरिशङ्किनी ।
पूर्णे वर्षशते साध्वी पुत्रौ प्रसुषुवे यमौ ॥ २ ॥

ditis tu bhartur ādeśād
apatya-pariśaṅkinī
pūrṇe varṣa-śate sādhvī
putrau prasuṣuve yamau

ditiḥ—Diti; *tu*—but; *bhartuḥ*—of her husband; *ādeśāt*—by the order; *apatya*—from her children; *pariśaṅkinī*—being apprehensive of trouble; *pūrṇe*—full; *varṣa-śate*—after one hundred years; *sādhvī*—the virtuous lady; *putrau*—two sons; *prasuṣuve*—begot; *yamau*—twins.

TRANSLATION

The virtuous lady Diti had been very apprehensive of trouble to the gods from the children in her womb, and her husband pre-

dicted the same. She brought forth twin sons after a full one hundred years of pregnancy.

TEXT 3

उत्पाता बहवस्तत्र निपेतुर्जायमानयोः ।
दिवि भुव्यन्तरिक्षे च लोकस्योरुभयावहाः ॥ ३ ॥

utpātā bahavas tatra
nipetur jāyamānayoḥ
divi bhuvy antarikṣe ca
lokasyoru-bhayāvahāḥ

utpātāḥ—natural disturbances; *bahavaḥ*—many; *tatra*—there; *nipetuḥ*—occurred; *jāyamānayoḥ*—on their birth; *divi*—in the heavenly planets; *bhuvi*—on the earth; *antarikṣe*—in outer space; *ca*—and; *lokasya*—to the world; *uru*—greatly; *bhaya-āvahāḥ*—causing fear.

TRANSLATION

On the birth of the two demons there were many natural disturbances, all very fearful and wonderful, in the heavenly planets, the earthly planets and in between them.

TEXT 4

सहाचला भुवश्चेलुर्दिशः सर्वाः प्रजज्वलुः ।
सोल्काश्चाशनयः पेतुः केतवश्चार्तिहेतवः ॥ ४ ॥

sahācalā bhuvaś celur
diśaḥ sarvāḥ prajajvaluḥ
solkāś cāśanayaḥ petuḥ
ketavaś cārti-hetavaḥ

saha—along with; *acalāḥ*—the mountains; *bhuvaḥ*—of the earth; *celuḥ*—shook; *diśaḥ*—directions; *sarvāḥ*—all; *prajajvaluḥ*—blazed like fire; *sa*—with; *ulkāḥ*—meteors; *ca*—and; *aśanayaḥ*—thunderbolts;

petuḥ—fell; *ketavaḥ*—comets; *ca*—and; *ārti-hetavaḥ*—the cause of all inauspiciousness.

TRANSLATION

There were earthquakes along the mountains on the earth, and it appeared that there was fire everywhere. Many inauspicious planets like Saturn appeared, along with comets, meteors and thunderbolts.

PURPORT

When natural disturbances occur on a planet, one should understand that a demon must have taken birth there. In the present age the number of demoniac people is increasing; therefore natural disturbances are also increasing. There is no doubt about this, as we can understand from the statements of the *Bhāgavatam.*

TEXT 5

ववौ वायुः सुदुःस्पर्शः फूत्कारानीरयन्मुहुः ।
उन्मूलयन्नगपतीन्वात्यानीको रजोध्वजः ॥५॥

vavau vāyuḥ suduḥsparśaḥ
phūt-kārān īrayan muhuḥ
unmūlayan naga-patīn
vātyānīko rajo-dhvajaḥ

vavau—blew; *vāyuḥ*—the winds; *su-duḥsparśaḥ*—unpleasant to touch; *phūt-kārān*—hissing sounds; *īrayan*—giving out; *muhuḥ*—again and again; *unmūlayan*—uprooting; *naga-patīn*—gigantic trees; *vātyā*—cyclonic air; *anīkaḥ*—armies; *rajaḥ*—dust; *dhvajaḥ*—ensigns.

TRANSLATION

There blew winds which were most uninviting to the touch, hissing again and again and uprooting gigantic trees. They had storms for their armies and clouds of dust for their ensigns.

PURPORT

When there are natural disturbances like blowing cyclones, too much heat or snowfall, and uprooting of trees by hurricanes, it is to be understood that the demoniac population is increasing and so the natural disturbance is also taking place. There are many countries on the globe, even at the present moment, where all these disturbances are current. This is true all over the world. There is insufficient sunshine, and there are always clouds in the sky, snowfall and severe cold. These assure that such places are inhabited by demoniac people who are accustomed to all kinds of forbidden, sinful activity.

TEXT 6

उद्धसत्तडिदम्भोदघटया नष्टभागणे ।
व्योम्नि प्रविष्टतमसा न स्म व्यादृश्यते पदम् ॥ ६ ॥

uddhasat-taḍid-ambhoda-
ghaṭayā naṣṭa-bhāgaṇe
vyomni praviṣṭa-tamasā
na sma vyādṛśyate padam

uddhasat—laughing loudly; *taḍit*—lightning; *ambhoda*—of clouds; *ghaṭayā*—by masses; *naṣṭa*—lost; *bhā-gaṇe*—the luminaries; *vyomni*—in the sky; *praviṣṭa*—enveloped; *tamasā*—by darkness; *na*—not; *sma vyādṛśyate*—could be seen; *padam*—any place.

TRANSLATION

The luminaries in the heavens were screened by masses of clouds, in which lightning sometimes flashed as though laughing. Darkness reigned everywhere, and nothing could be seen.

TEXT 7

चुक्रोश विमना वार्धिरुदूर्मिः क्षुभितोदरः ।
सोदपानाश्च सरितश्चुक्षुभुः शुष्कपङ्कजाः ॥ ७ ॥

cukrośa vimanā vārdhir
udūrmiḥ kṣubhitodaraḥ
sodapānāś ca saritaś
cukṣubhuḥ śuṣka-paṅkajāḥ

cukrośa—wailed aloud; *vimanāḥ*—stricken with sorrow; *vārdhiḥ*—the ocean; *udūrmiḥ*—high waves; *kṣubhita*—agitated; *udaraḥ*—the creatures inside; *sa-udapānāḥ*—with the drinking water of the lakes and the wells; *ca*—and; *saritaḥ*—the rivers; *cukṣubhuḥ*—were agitated; *śuṣka*—withered; *paṅkajāḥ*—lotus flowers.

TRANSLATION

The ocean with its high waves wailed aloud as if stricken with sorrow, and there was a commotion among the creatures inhabiting the ocean. The rivers and lakes were also agitated, and lotuses withered.

TEXT 8

मुहुः परिधयोऽभूवन् सराह्वोः शशिसूर्ययोः ।
निर्घाता रथनिर्ह्रादा विवरेभ्यः प्रजज्ञिरे ॥ ८ ॥

muhuḥ paridhayo 'bhūvan
sarāhvoḥ śaśi-sūryayoḥ
nirghātā ratha-nirhrādā
vivarebhyaḥ prajajñire

muhuḥ—again and again; *paridhayaḥ*—misty halos; *abhūvan*—appeared; *sa-rāhvoḥ*—during eclipses; *śaśi*—of the moon; *sūryayoḥ*—of the sun; *nirghātāḥ*—claps of thunder; *ratha-nirhrādāḥ*—sounds like those of rattling chariots; *vivarebhyaḥ*—from the mountain caves; *prajajñire*—were produced.

TRANSLATION

Misty halos appeared around the sun and the moon during solar and lunar eclipses again and again. Claps of thunder were heard

even without clouds, and sounds like those of rattling chariots emerged from the mountain caves.

TEXT 9

अन्तर्ग्रामेषु मुखतो वमन्त्यो वह्निमुल्बणम् ।
सृगालोलूकटङ्कारैः प्रणेदुरशिवं शिवाः ॥ ९ ॥

antar-grāmeṣu mukhato
vamantyo vahnim ulbaṇam
sṛgālolūka-ṭaṅkāraiḥ
praṇedur aśivaṁ śivāḥ

antaḥ—in the interior; *grāmeṣu*—in the villages; *mukhataḥ*—from their mouths; *vamantyaḥ*—vomiting; *vahnim*—fire; *ulbaṇam*—fearful; *sṛgāla*—jackals; *ulūka*—owls; *ṭaṅkāraiḥ*—with their cries; *praṇeduḥ*—created their respective vibrations; *aśivam*—portentously; *śivāḥ*—the she-jackals.

TRANSLATION

In the interior of the villages she-jackals yelled portentously, vomiting strong fire from their mouths, and jackals and owls also joined them with their cries.

TEXT 10

सङ्गीतवद्रोदनवदुन्नमय्य शिरोधराम् ।
व्यमुञ्चन् विविधा वाचो ग्रामसिंहास्ततस्ततः ॥१०॥

saṅgītavad rodanavad
unnamayya śirodharām
vyamuñcan vividhā vāco
grāma-siṁhās tatas tataḥ

saṅgīta-vat—like singing; *rodana-vat*—like wailing; *unnamayya*—raising; *śirodharām*—the neck; *vyamuñcan*—uttered; *vividhāḥ*—various; *vācaḥ*—cries; *grāma-siṁhāḥ*—the dogs; *tataḥ tataḥ*—here and there.

TRANSLATION

Raising their necks, dogs cried here and there, now in the manner of singing and now of wailing.

TEXT 11

खराश्च कर्कशैः क्षत्तः खुरैर्घ्नन्तो धरातलम् ।
खार्काररभसा मत्ताः पर्यधावन् वरूथशः ॥११॥

kharāś ca karkaśaiḥ kṣattaḥ
khurair ghnanto dharā-talam
khārkāra-rabhasā mattāḥ
paryadhāvan varūthaśaḥ

kharāḥ—asses; *ca*—and; *karkaśaiḥ*—hard; *kṣattaḥ*—O Vidura; *khuraiḥ*—with their hooves; *ghnantaḥ*—striking; *dharā-talam*—the surface of the earth; *khāḥ-kāra*—braying; *rabhasāḥ*—wildly engaged in; *mattāḥ*—mad; *paryadhāvan*—ran hither and thither; *varūthaśaḥ*—in herds.

TRANSLATION

O Vidura, the asses ran hither and thither in herds, striking the earth with their hard hooves and wildly braying.

PURPORT

Asses also feel very respectable as a race, and when they run in flocks hither and thither in so-called jollity, it is understood to be a bad sign for human society.

TEXT 12

रुदन्तो रासभत्रस्ता नीडादुदपतन् खगाः ।
घोषेऽरण्ये च पशवः शकृन्मूत्रमकुर्वत ॥१२॥

rudanto rāsabha-trastā
nīḍād udapatan khagāḥ

ghoṣe 'raṇye ca paśavaḥ
śakṛn-mūtram akurvata

rudantaḥ—shrieking; *rāsabha*—by the asses; *trastāḥ*—frightened; *nīḍāt*—from the nest; *udapatan*—flew up; *khagāḥ*—birds; *ghoṣe*—in the cowshed; *araṇye*—in the woods; *ca*—and; *paśavaḥ*—the cattle; *śakṛt*—dung; *mūtram*—urine; *akurvata*—passed.

TRANSLATION

Frightened by the braying of the asses, birds flew shrieking from their nests, while cattle in the cowsheds as well as in the woods passed dung and urine.

TEXT 13

गावोऽत्रसन्नसृग्दोहास्तोयदाः पूयवर्षिणः ।
व्यरुदन्देवलिङ्गानि द्रुमाः पेतुर्विनानिलम् ॥१३॥

gāvo 'trasann asṛg-dohās
toyadāḥ pūya-varṣiṇaḥ
vyarudan deva-liṅgāni
drumāḥ petur vinānilam

gāvaḥ—the cows; *atrasan*—were frightened; *asṛk*—blood; *dohāḥ*—yielding; *toyadāḥ*—clouds; *pūya*—pus; *varṣiṇaḥ*—raining; *vyarudan*—shed tears; *deva-liṅgāni*—the images of the gods; *drumāḥ*—trees; *petuḥ*—fell down; *vinā*—without; *anilam*—a blast of wind.

TRANSLATION

Cows, terrified, yielded blood in place of milk, clouds rained pus, the images of the gods in the temples shed tears, and trees fell down without a blast of wind.

TEXT 14

ग्रहान् पुण्यतमानन्ये भगणांश्चापि दीपिताः ।
अतिचेरुर्वक्रगत्या युयुधुश्च परस्परम् ॥१४॥

grahān puṇyatamān anye
bhagaṇāṁś cāpi dīpitāḥ
aticerur vakra-gatyā
yuyudhuś ca parasparam

grahān—planets; *puṇya-tamān*—most auspicious; *anye*—others (the ominous planets); *bha-gaṇān*—luminaries; *ca*—and; *api*—also; *dīpitāḥ*—illuminating; *aticeruḥ*—overlapped; *vakra-gatyā*—taking retrograde courses; *yuyudhuḥ*—came into conflict; *ca*—and; *paraḥ-param*—with one another.

TRANSLATION

Ominous planets such as Mars and Saturn shone brighter and surpassed the auspicious ones such as Mercury, Jupiter and Venus as well as a number of lunar mansions. Taking seemingly retrograde courses, the planets came in conflict with one another.

PURPORT

The entire universe is moving under the three modes of material nature. Those living entities who are in goodness are called the pious species—pious lands, pious trees, etc. It is similar with the planets also; many planets are considered pious, and others are considered impious. Saturn and Mars are considered impious. When the pious planets shine very brightly, it is an auspicious sign, but when the inauspicious planets shine very brightly, this is not a very good sign.

TEXT 15

दृष्ट्वान्यांश्च महोत्पातानतत्तत्त्वविदः प्रजाः ।
ब्रह्मपुत्रानृते भीता मेनिरे विश्वसम्प्लवम् ॥१५॥

dṛṣṭvānyāṁś ca mahotpātān
atat-tattva-vidaḥ prajāḥ
brahma-putrān ṛte bhītā
menire viśva-samplavam

His Divine Grace
A. C. Bhaktivedanta Swami Prabhupāda
Founder-Ācārya of the International Society for Krishna Consciousness

PLATE ONE: The demon Hiraṇyākṣa quickly sprang upon the Lord and swung his powerful mace at Him. But by moving slightly aside, the Lord dodged the blow, just as an accomplished *yogī* would elude death. (*p. 42*)

PLATE TWO: Under the guidance of Lord Viṣṇu, Brahmā brought his intelligence to bear and began creating the universe out of the various parts of his physical and mental bodies. (*p. 105*)

PLATE THREE: Seeking to please Devahūti, Kardama Muni employed his yogic power and instantly produced an aerial mansion that could travel anywhere at his will. (*p. 264*)

PLATE FOUR: Within Lake Bindu-sarovara, the maidservants of Devahūti very respectfully bathed her with valuable oils and ointments and then gave her fine, spotless cloth to cover her body. (*p. 274*)

PLATE FIVE: Appearing at Kardama Muni's hermitage, Lord Brahmā said, "My dear Kardama, your nine thin-waisted daughters are certainly very chaste, and I am sure they will expand the creation with their descendants. Therefore, today please give away your daughters to these foremost sages, with due regard for the girls' temperaments

and likings, and thereby spread your fame all over the universe." Then Brahmā told Devahūti about the incarnation of God in her womb: "My dear daughter of Manu, the Supreme Lord is now within your womb. He will cut all the knots of your ignorance and doubt." (*p. 319*)

PLATE SIX: After receiving instructions on self-realization from his son, Kapila, Kardama Muni circumambulated Him and then at once left for the forest. (*p. 340*)

PLATE SEVEN: Describing the path of *sāṅkhya-yoga* meditation to His mother, Lord Kapila said, "Always eager to bestow His blessings upon His devotees, the Lord is most charming to look at, for His serene aspect gladdens the eyes and souls of those who behold Him in the ecstatic trance of meditation." (*p. 569*)

PLATE EIGHT: In the course of meditation the *yogī* must fix in his heart the activities of Lakṣmī, the goddess of fortune, who is worshiped by all the demigods and who is the mother of Brahmā. With her lustrous fingers she always carefully massages the feet of Lord

Nārāyaṇa as He reclines on the thousand-headed serpent Śeṣa Nāga in the Garbha Ocean. As the source of all opulences, Lakṣmī is attractive to everyone. (*p. 579*)

PLATE NINE: A man bereft of spiritual knowledge dies most painfully and pathetically. Then the wrathful Yamadūtas come before him, and in great fear he passes stool and urine. As a criminal is arrested for punishment by the state constables, so a person who has engaged in

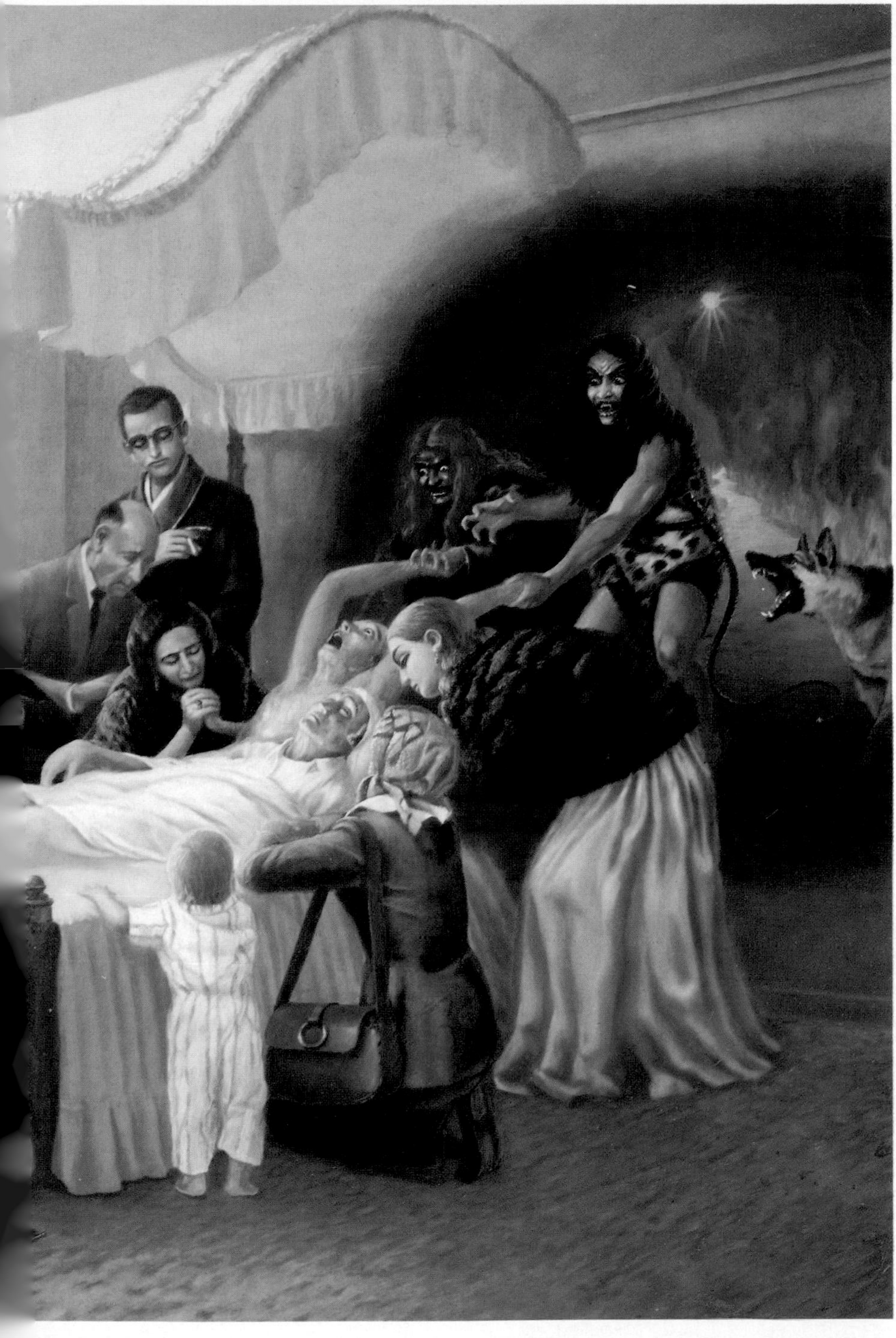

criminal sense gratification is similarly arrested by the Yamadūtas, who bind him by the neck with a strong rope and cover his subtle body so that he may undergo severe punishment. (*p. 687*)

PLATE TEN: After judgment, the sinner is at once engaged in the torturous punishment he is destined to suffer—either being forced to watch his own disembowelment while being burned alive, or being thrown off a cliff, or being torn asunder by elephants, or being forced to eat others' flesh and have his own eaten, etc. (*p. 691*)

PLATE ELEVEN: The first step in Kapiladeva's *sāṅkhya-yoga* system is to understand the difference between the soul and the body, and how the soul passes through various bodies by the process of reincarnation. (*p. 705*)

PLATE TWELVE: Devahūti said to her son, Kapila: "My Lord, at the end of the millennium You lie down on a banyan leaf, and just like a small baby You lick the toe of Your lotus foot. So it is not very wonderful that You can lie down in the abdomen of my body." (*p. 824*)

dṛṣṭvā—having seen; *anyān*—others; *ca*—and; *mahā*—great; *utpātān*—evil omens; *a-tat-tattva-vidaḥ*—not knowing the secret (of the portents); *prajāḥ*—people; *brahma-putrān*—the sons of Brahmā (the four Kumāras); *ṛte*—except; *bhītāḥ*—being fearful; *menire*—thought; *viśva-samplavam*—the dissolution of the universe.

TRANSLATION

Marking these and many other omens of evil times, everyone but the four sage-sons of Brahmā, who were aware of the fall of Jaya and Vijaya and of their birth as Diti's sons, was seized with fear. They did not know the secrets of these potents and thought that the dissolution of the universe was at hand.

PURPORT

According to *Bhagavad-gītā*, Seventh Chapter, the laws of nature are so stringent that it is impossible for the living entity to surpass their enforcement. It is also explained that only those who are fully surrendered to Kṛṣṇa in Kṛṣṇa consciousness can be saved. We can learn from the description of the *Śrīmad-Bhāgavatam* that it is because of the birth of two great demons that there were so many natural disturbances. It is to be indirectly understood, as previously described, that when there are constant disturbances on the earth, that is an omen that some demoniac people have been born or that the demoniac population has increased. In former days there were only two demons—those born of Diti—yet there were so many disturbances. At the present day, especially in this age of Kali, these disturbances are always visible, which indicates that the demoniac population has certainly increased.

To check the increase of demoniac population, the Vedic civilization enacted so many rules and regulations of social life, the most important of which is the *garbhādhāna* process for begetting good children. In *Bhagavad-gītā* Arjuna informed Kṛṣṇa that if there is unwanted population (*varṇa-saṅkara*), the entire world will appear to be hell. People are very anxious for peace in the world, but there are so many unwanted children born without the benefit of the *garbhādhāna* ceremony, just like the demons born from Diti. Diti was so lusty that she forced her husband to copulate at a time which was inauspicious, and therefore the demons were born to create disturbances. In having sex life to beget children, one should observe the process for begetting nice children; if each and every householder in every family observes the Vedic system, then there are nice children, not demons, and automatically there is peace in the world. If we do not follow regulations in life for social tranquillity, we cannot expect peace. Rather, we will have to undergo the stringent reactions of natural laws.

TEXT 16

तावादिदैत्यौ सहसा व्यज्यमानात्मपौरुषौ ।
ववृधातेऽश्मसारेण कायेनाद्रिपती इव ॥१६॥

tāv ādi-daityau sahasā
vyajyamānātma-pauruṣau
vavṛdhāte 'śma-sāreṇa
kāyenādri-patī iva

tau—those two; *ādi-daityau*—demons in the beginning of creation; *sahasā*—quickly; *vyajyamāna*—being manifest; *ātma*—own; *pauruṣau*—prowess; *vavṛdhāte*—grew; *aśma-sāreṇa*—steellike; *kāyena*—with bodily frames; *adri-patī*—two great mountains; *iva*—like.

TRANSLATION

These two demons who appeared in ancient times soon began to exhibit uncommon bodily features; they had steellike frames which began to grow just like two great mountains.

PURPORT

There are two classes of men in the world; one is called the demon, and the other is called the demigod. The demigods concern themselves with the spiritual upliftment of human society, whereas the demons are concerned with physical and material upliftment. The two demons born of Diti began to make their bodies as strong as iron frames, and they were so tall that they seemed to touch outer space. They were decorated with valuable ornaments, and they thought that this was success in life. Originally it was planned that Jaya and Vijaya, the two doorkeepers of

Vaikuṇṭha, were to take birth in this material world, where, by the curse of the sages, they were to play the part of always being angry with the Supreme Personality of Godhead. As demoniac persons, they became so angry that they were not concerned with the Supreme Personality of Godhead, but simply with physical comforts and physical upliftment.

TEXT 17

दिविस्पृशौ हेमकिरीटकोटिभि-
निरुद्धकाष्ठौ स्फुरदङ्गदाभुजौ ।
गां कम्पयन्तौ चरणैः पदे पदे
कट्या सुकाञ्च्यार्कमतीत्य तस्थतुः ॥१७॥

divi-spṛśau hema-kirīṭa-koṭibhir
niruddha-kāṣṭhau sphurad-aṅgadā-bhujau
gāṁ kampayantau caraṇaiḥ pade pade
kaṭyā sukāñcyārkam atītya tasthatuḥ

divi-spṛśau—touching the sky; *hema*—golden; *kirīṭa*—of their helmets; *koṭibhiḥ*—with the crests; *niruddha*—blocked; *kāṣṭhau*—the directions; *sphurat*—brilliant; *aṅgadā*—bracelets; *bhujau*—on whose arms; *gām*—the earth; *kampayantau*—shaking; *caraṇaiḥ*—with their feet; *pade pade*—at every step; *kaṭyā*—with their waists; *su-kāñcyā*—with beautiful decorated belts; *arkam*—the sun; *atītya*—surpassing; *tasthatuḥ*—they stood.

TRANSLATION

Their bodies became so tall that they seemed to kiss the sky with the crests of their gold crowns. They blocked the view of all directions and while walking shook the earth at every step. Their arms were adorned with brilliant bracelets, and they stood as if covering the sun with their waists, which were bound with excellent and beautiful girdles.

PURPORT

In the demoniac way of civilization, people are interested in getting a body constructed in such a way that when they walk on the street the earth will tremble and when they stand it will appear that they cover the sun and the vision of the four directions. If a race appears strong in body, their country is materially considered to be among the highly advanced nations of the world.

TEXT 18

प्रजापतिर्नाम तयोरकार्षीद्
यः प्राक् स्वदेहाद्यमयोरजायत ।
तं वै हिरण्यकशिपुं विदुः प्रजा
यं तं हिरण्याक्षमसूत साग्रतः ॥१८॥

prajāpatir nāma tayor akārṣīd
yaḥ prāk sva-dehād yamayor ajāyata
taṁ vai hiraṇyakaśipuṁ viduḥ prajā
yaṁ taṁ hiraṇyākṣam asūta sāgrataḥ

prajāpatiḥ—Kaśyapa; *nāma*—names; *tayoḥ*—of the two; *akārṣīt*—gave; *yaḥ*—who; *prāk*—first; *sva-dehāt*—from his body; *yamayoḥ*—of the twins; *ajāyata*—was delivered; *tam*—him; *vai*—indeed; *hiraṇyakaśipum*—Hiraṇyakaśipu; *viduḥ*—know; *prajāḥ*—people; *yam*—whom; *tam*—him; *hiraṇyākṣam*—Hiraṇyākṣa; *asūta*—gave birth to; *sā*—she (Diti); *agrataḥ*—first.

TRANSLATION

Kaśyapa, Prajāpati, the creator of the living entities, gave his twin sons their names; the one who was born first he named Hiraṇyākṣa, and the one who was first conceived by Diti he named Hiraṇyakaśipu.

PURPORT

There is an authoritative Vedic literature called *Piṇḍa-siddhi* in which the scientific understanding of pregnancy is very nicely described. It is stated that when the male secretion enters the menstrual flux in the uterus in two successive drops, the mother develops two embryos in her womb, and she brings forth twins in a reverse order to that in which they were first conceived; the child conceived first is born later, and the one conceived later is brought forth first. The first child conceived in the womb lives behind the second child, so when birth takes place the second child appears first, and the first child appears second. In this case it is understood that Hiraṇyākṣa, the second child conceived, was delivered first, whereas Hiraṇyakaśipu, the child who was behind him, having been conceived first, was born second.

TEXT 19

चक्रे हिरण्यकशिपुर्दोर्भ्यां ब्रह्मवरेण च ।
वशे सपालाँल्लोकांस्त्रीनकुतोमृत्युरुद्धतः ॥१९॥

cakre hiraṇyakaśipur
dorbhyāṁ brahma-vareṇa ca
vaśe sa-pālāl̐ lokāṁs trīn
akuto-mṛtyur uddhataḥ

cakre—made; *hiraṇyakaśipuḥ*—Hiraṇyakaśipu; *dorbhyām*—by his two arms; *brahma-vareṇa*—by the benediction of Brahmā; *ca*—and; *vaśe*—under his control; *sa-pālān*—along with their protectors; *lokān*—the worlds; *trīn*—three; *akutaḥ-mṛtyuḥ*—fearing death from no one; *uddhataḥ*—puffed up.

TRANSLATION

The elder child, Hiraṇyakaśipu, was unafraid of death from anyone within the three worlds because he received a benediction from Lord Brahmā. He was proud and puffed up due to this benediction and was able to bring all three planetary systems under his control.

PURPORT

As will be revealed in later chapters, Hiraṇyakaśipu underwent severe austerity and penance to satisfy Brahmā and thus receive a benediction of immortality. Actually, it is impossible even for Lord Brahmā to give anyone the benediction of becoming immortal, but indirectly Hiraṇyakaśipu received the benediction that no one within this material world would be able to kill him. In other words, because he originally came from the abode of Vaikuṇṭha, he was not to be killed by anyone within this material world. The Lord desired to appear Himself to kill him. One may be very proud of his material advancement in knowledge, but he cannot be immune to the four principles of material existence, namely birth, death, old age and disease. It was the Lord's plan to teach people that even Hiraṇyakaśipu, who was so powerful and strongly built, could not live more than his destined duration of life. One may become as strong and puffed up as Hiraṇyakaśipu and bring under his control all the three worlds, but there is no possibility of continuing life eternally or keeping the conquered booty forever. So many emperors have ascended to power, and they are now lost in oblivion; that is the history of the world.

TEXT 20

हिरण्याक्षोऽनुजस्तस्य प्रियः प्रीतिकृदन्वहम् ।
गदापाणिर्दिवं यातो युयुत्सुर्मृगयन् रणम् ॥२०॥

hiraṇyākṣo 'nujas tasya
priyaḥ prīti-kṛd anvaham
gadā-pāṇir divaṁ yāto
yuyutsur mṛgayan raṇam

hiraṇyākṣaḥ—Hiraṇyākṣa; *anujaḥ*—younger brother; *tasya*—his; *priyaḥ*—beloved; *prīti-kṛt*—ready to please; *anu-aham*—every day; *gadā-pāṇiḥ*—with a club in hand; *divam*—to the higher planets; *yātaḥ*—traveled; *yuyutsuḥ*—desirous to fight; *mṛgayan*—seeking; *raṇam*—combat.

TRANSLATION

His younger brother, Hiraṇyākṣa, was always ready to satisfy his elder brother by his activities. Hiraṇyākṣa took a club on his shoulder and traveled all over the universe with a fighting spirit just to satisfy Hiraṇyakaśipu.

PURPORT

The demoniac spirit is to train all family members to exploit the resources of this universe for personal sense gratification, whereas the godly spirit is to engage everything in the service of the Lord. Hiraṇyakaśipu was himself very powerful, and he made his younger brother, Hiraṇyākṣa, powerful to assist him in fighting with everyone and lording it over material nature as long as possible. If possible, he wanted to rule the universe eternally. These are demonstrations of the spirit of the demoniac living entity.

TEXT 21

तं वीक्ष्य दुःसहजवं रणत्काञ्चननूपुरम् ।
वैजयन्त्या स्रजा जुष्टमंसन्यस्तमहागदम् ॥२१॥

taṁ vīkṣya duḥsaha-javaṁ
raṇat-kāñcana-nūpuram
vaijayantyā srajā juṣṭam
aṁsa-nyasta-mahā-gadam

tam—him; *vīkṣya*—having seen; *duḥsaha*—difficult to control; *javam*—temper; *raṇat*—tinkling; *kāñcana*—gold; *nūpuram*—anklets; *vaijayantyā srajā*—with a *vaijayantī* garland; *juṣṭam*—adorned; *aṁsa*—on his shoulder; *nyasta*—rested; *mahā-gadam*—a huge mace.

TRANSLATION

Hiraṇyākṣa's temper was difficult to control. He had anklets of gold tinkling about his feet, he was adorned with a gigantic garland, and he rested his huge mace on one of his shoulders.

TEXT 22

मनोवीर्यवरोत्सिक्तमसृण्यमकुतोभयम् ।
भीता निलिल्यिरे देवास्तार्क्ष्यत्रस्ता इवाहयः ॥२२॥

mano-vīrya-varotsiktam
asṛṇyam akuto-bhayam
bhītā nililyire devās
tārkṣya-trastā ivāhayaḥ

manaḥ-vīrya—by mental and bodily strength; *vara*—by the boon; *utsiktam*—proud; *asṛṇyam*—not able to be checked; *akutaḥ-bhayam*—fearing no one; *bhītāḥ*—frightened; *nililyire*—hid themselves; *devāḥ*—the demigods; *tārkṣya*—Garuḍa; *trastāḥ*—frightened of; *iva*—like; *ahayaḥ*—snakes.

TRANSLATION

His mental and bodily strength as well as the boon conferred upon him had made him proud. He feared death at the hands of no one, and there was no checking him. The gods, therefore, were seized with fear at his very sight, and they hid themselves even as snakes hide themselves for fear of Garuḍa.

PURPORT

The *asuras* are generally strongly built, as described here, and therefore their mental condition is very sound, and their prowess is also extraordinary. Hiraṇyākṣa and Hiraṇyakaśipu, having received the boon that they would not be killed by any other living entity within this universe, were almost immortal, and thus they were completely fearless.

TEXT 23

स वै तिरोहितान् दृष्ट्वा महसा स्वेन दैत्यराट् ।
सेन्द्रान्देवगणान् क्षीबानपश्यन् व्यनदद् भृशम् ॥२३॥

sa vai tirohitān dṛṣṭvā
mahasā svena daitya-rāṭ
sendrān deva-gaṇān kṣībān
apaśyan vyanadad bhṛśam

saḥ—he; *vai*—indeed; *tirohitān*—vanished; *dṛṣṭvā*—having seen; *mahasā*—by might; *svena*—his own; *daitya-rāṭ*—the chief of the Daityas (demons); *sa-indrān*—along with Indra; *deva-gaṇān*—the demigods; *kṣībān*—intoxicated; *apaśyan*—not finding; *vyanadat*—roared; *bhṛśam*—loudly.

TRANSLATION

On not finding Indra and the other demigods, who had previously been intoxicated with power, the chief of the Daityas, seeing that they had all vanished before his might, roared loudly.

TEXT 24

ततो निवृत्तः क्रीडिष्यन् गम्भीरं भीमनिस्वनम् ।
विजगाहे महासत्त्वो वार्धिं मत्त इव द्विपः ॥२४॥

tato nivṛttaḥ krīḍiṣyan
gambhīraṁ bhīma-nisvanam
vijagāhe mahā-sattvo
vārdhiṁ matta iva dvipaḥ

tataḥ—then; *nivṛttaḥ*—returned; *krīḍiṣyan*—for the sake of sport; *gambhīram*—deep; *bhīma-nisvanam*—making a terrible sound; *vijagāhe*—dived; *mahā-sattvaḥ*—the mighty being; *vārdhim*—in the ocean; *mattaḥ*—in wrath; *iva*—like; *dvipaḥ*—an elephant.

TRANSLATION

After returning from the heavenly kingdom, the mighty demon, who was like an elephant in wrath, for the sake of sport dived into the deep ocean, which was roaring terribly.

TEXT 25

तस्मिन् प्रविष्टे वरुणस्य सैनिका
यादोगणाः सन्नधियः ससाध्वसाः ।
अहन्यमाना अपि तस्य वर्चसा
प्रधर्षिता दूरतरं प्रदुद्रुवुः ॥२५॥

tasmin praviṣṭe varuṇasya sainikā
yādo-gaṇāḥ sanna-dhiyaḥ sasādhvasāḥ
ahanyamānā api tasya varcasā
pradharṣitā dūrataraṁ pradudruvuḥ

tasmin praviṣṭe—when he entered the ocean; *varuṇasya*—of Varuṇa; *sainikāḥ*—the defenders; *yādaḥ-gaṇāḥ*—the aquatic animals; *sanna-dhiyaḥ*—depressed; *sa-sādhvasāḥ*—with fear; *ahanyamānāḥ*—not being hit; *api*—even; *tasya*—his; *varcasā*—by splendor; *pradharṣitāḥ*—stricken; *dūra-taram*—far away; *pradudruvuḥ*—they ran fast.

TRANSLATION

On his entering the ocean, the aquatic animals who formed the host of Varuṇa were stricken with fear and ran far away. Thus Hiraṇyākṣa showed his splendor without dealing a blow.

PURPORT

Materialistic demons sometimes appear to be very powerful and are seen to establish their supremacy throughout the world. Here also it appears that Hiraṇyākṣa, by his demoniac strength, actually established his supremacy throughout the universe, and the demigods were afraid of his uncommon power. Not only were the demigods in space afraid of the demons Hiraṇyakaśipu and Hiraṇyākṣa, but so also were the aquatic animals within the sea.

TEXT 26

स वर्षपूगानुदधौ महाबल-
श्चरन्महोर्मीञ्छ्वसनेरितान्मुहुः ।
मौर्व्याभिजघ्ने गदया विभावरी-
मासेदिवांस्तात पुरीं प्रचेतसः ॥२६॥

sa varṣa-pūgān udadhau mahā-balaś
caran mahormīñ chvasaneritān muhuḥ
maurvyābhijaghne gadayā vibhāvarīm
āsedivāṁs tāta purīṁ pracetasaḥ

saḥ—he; *varṣa-pūgān*—for many years; *udadhau*—in the ocean; *mahā-balaḥ*—mighty; *caran*—moving; *mahā-ūrmīn*—gigantic waves; *śvasana*—by the wind; *īritān*—tossed; *muhuḥ*—again and again; *maurvyā*—iron; *abhijaghne*—he struck; *gadayā*—with his mace; *vibhāva-*

rīm—Vibhāvarī; *āsedivān*—reached; *tāta*—O dear Vidura; *purīm*—the capital; *pracetasaḥ*—of Varuṇa.

TRANSLATION

Moving about in the ocean for many, many years, the mighty Hiraṇyākṣa smote the gigantic wind-tossed waves again and again with his iron mace and reached Vibhāvarī, the capital of Varuṇa.

PURPORT

Varuṇa is supposed to be the predominating deity of the waters, and his capital, which is known as Vibhāvarī, is within the watery kingdom.

TEXT 27

तत्रोपलभ्यासुरलोकपालकं
यादोगणानामृषभं प्रचेतसम् ।
स्मयन् प्रलब्धुं प्रणिपत्य नीचव-
ज्जगाद मे देह्यधिराज संयुगम् ॥२७॥

tatropalabhyāsura-loka-pālakaṁ
yādo-gaṇānām ṛṣabhaṁ pracetasam
smayan pralabdhuṁ praṇipatya nīcavaj
jagāda me dehy adhirāja saṁyugam

tatra—there; *upalabhya*—having reached; *asura-loka*—of the regions where the demons reside; *pālakam*—the guardian; *yādaḥ-gaṇānām*—of the aquatic creatures; *ṛṣabham*—the lord; *pracetasam*—Varuṇa; *smayan*—smiling; *pralabdhum*—to make fun; *praṇipatya*—having bowed down; *nīca-vat*—like a lowborn man; *jagāda*—he said; *me*—to me; *dehi*—give; *adhirāja*—O great lord; *saṁyugam*—battle.

TRANSLATION

Vibhāvarī is the home of Varuṇa, lord of the aquatic creatures and guardian of the lower regions of the universe, where the

demons generally reside. There Hiraṇyākṣa fell at Varuṇa's feet like a lowborn man, and to make fun of him he said with a smile, "Give me battle, O Supreme Lord!"

PURPORT

The demoniac person always challenges others and tries to occupy others' property by force. Here these symptoms are fully displayed by Hiraṇyākṣa, who begged war from a person who had no desire to fight.

TEXT 28

त्वं लोकपालोऽधिपतिर्बृहच्छ्रवा
वीर्यापहो दुर्मदवीरमानिनाम् ।
विजित्य लोकेऽखिलदैत्यदानवान्
यद्राजसूयेन पुरायजत्प्रभो ॥२८॥

tvaṁ loka-pālo 'dhipatir bṛhac-chravā
vīryāpaho durmada-vīra-māninām
vijitya loke 'khila-daitya-dānavān
yad rājasūyena purāyajat prabho

tvam—you (Varuṇa); *loka-pālaḥ*—guardian of the planet; *adhipatiḥ*—a ruler; *bṛhat-śravāḥ*—of wide fame; *vīrya*—the power; *apahaḥ*—diminished; *durmada*—of the proud; *vīra-māninām*—thinking themselves very big heroes; *vijitya*—having conquered; *loke*—in the world; *akhila*—all; *daitya*—the demons; *dānavān*—the Dānavas; *yat*—whence; *rāja-sūyena*—with a Rājasūya sacrifice; *purā*—formerly; *ayajat*—worshiped; *prabho*—O lord.

TRANSLATION

You are the guardian of an entire sphere and a ruler of wide fame. Having crushed the might of arrogant and conceited warriors and having conquered all the Daityas and Dānavas in the world, you once performed a Rājasūya sacrifice to the Lord.

TEXT 29

स एवमुत्सिक्तमदेन विद्विषा
दृढं प्रलब्धो भगवानपां पतिः ।
रोषं समुत्थं शमयन् स्वया धिया
व्यवोचदङ्गोपशमं गता वयम् ॥२९॥

sa evam utsikta-madena vidviṣā
dṛḍhaṁ pralabdho bhagavān apāṁ patiḥ
roṣaṁ samutthaṁ śamayan svayā dhiyā
vyavocad aṅgopaśamaṁ gatā vayam

saḥ—Varuṇa; *evam*—thus; *utsikta*—puffed up; *madena*—with vanity; *vidviṣā*—by the enemy; *dṛḍham*—deeply; *pralabdhaḥ*—mocked; *bhagavān*—worshipful; *apām*—of the waters; *patiḥ*—the lord; *roṣam*—anger; *samuttham*—sprung up; *śamayan*—controlling; *svayā dhiyā*—by his reason; *vyavocat*—he replied; *aṅga*—O dear one; *upaśamam*—desisting from warfare; *gatāḥ*—gone; *vayam*—we.

TRANSLATION

Thus mocked by an enemy whose vanity knew no bounds, the worshipful lord of the waters waxed angry, but by dint of his reason he managed to curb the anger that had sprung up in him, and he replied: O dear one, we have now desisted from warfare, having grown too old for combat.

PURPORT

As we see, warmongering materialists always create fighting without reason.

TEXT 30

पश्यामि नान्यं पुरुषात्पुरातनाद्
यः संयुगे त्वां रणमार्गकोविदम् ।

आराधयिष्यत्यसुरर्षभेहि तं
मनस्विनो यं गृणते भवादृशाः ॥३०॥

paśyāmi nānyaṁ puruṣāt purātanād
yaḥ saṁyuge tvāṁ raṇa-mārga-kovidam
ārādhayiṣyaty asurarṣabhehi taṁ
manasvino yaṁ gṛṇate bhavādṛśāḥ

paśyāmi—I see; *na*—not; *anyam*—other; *puruṣāt*—than the person; *purātanāt*—most ancient; *yaḥ*—who; *saṁyuge*—in battle; *tvām*—to you; *raṇa-mārga*—in the tactics of war; *kovidam*—very much skilled; *ārādhayiṣyati*—will give satisfaction; *asura-ṛṣabha*—O chief of the *asuras; ihi*—approach; *tam*—Him; *manasvinaḥ*—heroes; *yam*—whom; *gṛṇate*—praise; *bhavādṛśāḥ*—like you.

TRANSLATION

You are so skilled in war that I do not see anyone else but the most ancient person, Lord Viṣṇu, who can give satisfaction in battle to you. Therefore, O chief of the asuras, approach Him, whom even heroes like you mention with praise.

PURPORT

Aggressive materialistic warriors are actually punished by the Supreme Lord for their policy of unnecessarily disturbing world peace. Therefore Varuṇa advised Hiraṇyākṣa that the right course to satisfy his fighting spirit would be to seek to fight with Viṣṇu.

TEXT 31

तं वीरमारादभिपद्य विस्मयः
शयिष्यसे वीरशये श्वभिर्वृतः ।
यस्त्वद्विधानामसतां प्रशान्तये
रूपाणि धत्ते सदनुग्रहेच्छया ॥३१॥

taṁ vīram ārād abhipadya vismayaḥ
śayiṣyase vīra-śaye śvabhir vṛtaḥ

yas tvad-vidhānām asatāṁ praśāntaye
rūpāṇi dhatte sad-anugrahecchayā

tam—Him; *vīram*—the great hero; *ārāt*—quickly; *abhipadya*—on reaching; *vismayaḥ*—rid of pride; *śayiṣyase*—you will lie down; *vīra-śaye*—on the battlefield; *śvabhiḥ*—by dogs; *vṛtaḥ*—surrounded; *yaḥ*—He who; *tvat-vidhānām*—like you; *asatām*—of wicked persons; *praśān-taye*—for the extermination; *rūpāṇi*—forms; *dhatte*—He assumes; *sat*—to the virtuous; *anugraha*—to show His grace; *icchayā*—with a desire.

TRANSLATION

Varuṇa continued: On reaching Him you will be rid of your pride at once and will lie down on the field of battle, surrounded by dogs, for eternal sleep. It is in order to exterminate wicked fellows like you and to show His grace to the virtuous that He assumes His various incarnations like Varāha.

PURPORT

Asuras do not know that their bodies consist of the five elements of material nature and that when they fall they become objects of pastimes for dogs and vultures. Varuṇa advised Hiraṇyākṣa to meet Viṣṇu in His boar incarnation so that his hankering for aggressive war would be satisfied and his powerful body would be vanquished.

Thus end the Bhaktivedanta purports of the Third Canto, Seventeenth Chapter, of the Śrīmad-Bhāgavatam, *entitled "Victory of Hiraṇyākṣa Over All the Directions of the Universe."*

CHAPTER EIGHTEEN

The Battle Between Lord Boar and the Demon Hiraṇyākṣa

TEXT 1

मैत्रेय उवाच
तदेवमाकर्ण्य जलेशभाषितं
महामनास्तद्विगणय्य दुर्मदः ।
हरेर्विदित्वा गतिमङ्ग नारदाद्
रसातलं निर्विविशे त्वरान्वितः ॥ १ ॥

maitreya uvāca
tad evam ākarṇya jaleśa-bhāṣitaṁ
mahā-manās tad vigaṇayya durmadaḥ
harer viditvā gatim aṅga nāradād
rasātalaṁ nirviviśe tvarānvitaḥ

maitreyaḥ—the great sage Maitreya; *uvāca*—said; *tat*—that; *evam*—thus; *ākarṇya*—hearing; *jala-īśa*—of the controller of water, Varuṇa; *bhāṣitam*—words; *mahā-manāḥ*—proud; *tat*—those words; *vigaṇayya*—having paid little heed to; *durmadaḥ*—vainglorious; *hareḥ*—of the Supreme Personality of Godhead; *viditvā*—having learned; *gatim*—the whereabouts; *aṅga*—O dear Vidura; *nāradāt*—from Nārada; *rasātalam*—to the depths of the ocean; *nirviviśe*—entered; *tvarā-anvitaḥ*—with great speed.

TRANSLATION

Maitreya continued: The proud and falsely glorious Daitya paid little heed to the words of Varuṇa. O dear Vidura, he learned from Nārada the whereabouts of the Supreme Personality of Godhead and hurriedly betook himself to the depths of the ocean.

PURPORT

Materialistic warmongers are not even afraid to fight with their mightiest enemy, the Personality of Godhead. The demon was very encouraged to learn from Varuṇa that there was one fighter who could actually combat him, and he was very enthusiastic to search out the Supreme Personality of Godhead just to give Him a fight, even though it was predicted by Varuṇa that by fighting with Viṣṇu he would become prey for dogs, jackals and vultures. Since demoniac persons are less intelligent, they dare to fight with Viṣṇu, who is known as Ajita, or one who has never been conquered.

TEXT 2

ददर्श तत्राभिजितं धराधरं
प्रोन्नीयमानावनिमग्रदंष्ट्रया ।
मुष्णन्तमक्ष्णा स्वरुचोऽरुणश्रिया
जहास चाहो वनगोचरो मृगः ॥ २ ॥

dadarśa tatrābhijitaṁ dharā-dharaṁ
pronnīyamānāvanim agra-daṁṣṭrayā
muṣṇantam akṣṇā sva-ruco 'ruṇa-śriyā
jahāsa cāho vana-gocaro mṛgaḥ

dadarśa—he saw; *tatra*—there; *abhijitam*—the victorious; *dharā*—the earth; *dharam*—bearing; *pronnīyamāna*—being raised upward; *avanim*—the earth; *agra-daṁṣṭrayā*—by the tip of His tusk; *muṣṇantam*—who was diminishing; *akṣṇā*—with His eyes; *sva-rucaḥ*—Hiraṇyākṣa's own splendor; *aruṇa*—reddish; *śriyā*—radiant; *jahāsa*—he laughed; *ca*—and; *aho*—oh; *vana-gocaraḥ*—amphibious; *mṛgaḥ*—beast.

TRANSLATION

He saw there the all-powerful Personality of Godhead in His boar incarnation, bearing the earth upward on the ends of His tusks and robbing him of his splendor with His reddish eyes. The demon laughed: Oh, an amphibious beast!

PURPORT

In a previous chapter we have discussed the incarnation of the Supreme Personality of Godhead as Varāha, the boar. While Varāha, with His tusks, engaged in uplifting the submerged earth from the depths of the waters, this great demon Hiraṇyākṣa met Him and challenged Him, calling Him a beast. Demons cannot understand the incarnations of the Lord; they think that His incarnations as a fish or boar or tortoise are big beasts only. They misunderstand the body of the Supreme Personality of Godhead, even in His human form, and they deride His descent. In the Caitanya-sampradāya there is sometimes a demoniac misconception about the descent of Nityānanda Prabhu. Nityānanda Prabhu's body is spiritual, but demoniac persons consider the body of the Supreme Personality to be material, just like ours. *Avajānanti māṁ mūḍhāḥ:* persons who have no intelligence deride the transcendental form of the Lord as material.

TEXT 3

आहैनमेह्यज्ञ महीं विमुञ्च नो
रसौकसां विश्वसृजेयमर्पिता ।
न स्वस्ति यास्यस्यनया ममेक्षतः
सुराधमासादितसूकराकृते ॥ ३ ॥

āhainam ehy ajña mahīṁ vimuñca no
rasaukasāṁ viśva-sṛjeyam arpitā
na svasti yāsyasy anayā mamekṣataḥ
surādhamāsādita-sūkarākṛte

āha—Hiraṇyākṣa said; *enam*—to the Lord; *ehi*—come and fight; *ajña*—O fool; *mahīm*—the earth; *vimuñca*—give up; *naḥ*—to us; *rasā-okasām*—of the inhabitants of the lower regions; *viśva-sṛjā*—by the creator of the universe; *iyam*—this earth; *arpitā*—entrusted; *na*—not; *svasti*—well-being; *yāsyasi*—You will go; *anayā*—with this; *mama īkṣataḥ*—while I am seeing; *sura-adhama*—O lowest of the demigods; *āsādita*—having taken; *sūkara-ākṛte*—the form of a boar.

TRANSLATION

The demon addressed the Lord: O best of the demigods, dressed in the form of a boar, just hear me. This earth is entrusted to us, the inhabitants of the lower regions, and You cannot take it from my presence and not be hurt by me.

PURPORT

Śrīdhara Svāmī, commenting on this verse, states that although the demon wanted to deride the Personality of Godhead in the form of a boar, actually he worshiped Him in several words. For example, he addressed Him as *vana-gocaraḥ,* which means "one who is a resident of the forest," but another meaning of *vana-gocaraḥ* is "one who lies on the water." Viṣṇu lies on the water, so the Supreme Personality of Godhead can be properly addressed in this way. The demon also addressed Him as *mṛgaḥ,* indicating, unintentionally, that the Supreme Personality is sought after by great sages, saintly persons and transcendentalists. He also addressed Him as *ajña.* Śrīdhara Svāmī says that *jña* means "knowledge," and there is no knowledge which is unknown to the Supreme Personality of Godhead. Indirectly, therefore, the demon said that Viṣṇu knows everything. The demon addressed Him as *surādhama. Sura* means "the demigods," and *adhama* means "Lord of all there is." He is Lord of all the demigods; therefore He is the best of all demigods, or God. When the demon used the phrase "in my presence," the implied meaning was, "In spite of my presence, You are completely able to take away the earth." *Na svasti yāsyasi:* "Unless You kindly take this earth from our custody, there can be no good fortune for us."

TEXT 4

त्वं नः सपत्नैरभवाय किं भृतो
यो मायया हन्त्यसुरान् परोक्षजित् ।
त्वां योगमायाबलमल्पपौरुषं
संस्थाप्य मूढ प्रमृजे सुहृच्छुचः ॥ ४ ॥

tvaṁ naḥ sapatnair abhavāya kiṁ bhṛto
yo māyayā hanty asurān parokṣa-jit

tvāṁ yogamāyā-balam alpa-pauruṣaṁ
saṁsthāpya mūḍha pramṛje suhṛc-chucaḥ

tvam—You; *naḥ*—us; *sapatnaiḥ*—by our enemies; *abhavāya*—for killing; *kim*—is it that; *bhṛtaḥ*—maintained; *yaḥ*—He who; *māyayā*—by deception; *hanti*—kills; *asurān*—the demons; *parokṣa-jit*—who conquered by remaining invisible; *tvām*—You; *yogamāyā-balam*—whose strength is bewildering power; *alpa-pauruṣam*—whose power is meager; *saṁsthāpya*—after killing; *mūḍha*—fool; *pramṛje*—I shall wipe out; *suhṛt-śucaḥ*—the grief of my kinsmen.

TRANSLATION

You rascal, You have been nourished by our enemies to kill us, and You have killed some demons by remaining invisible. O fool, Your power is only mystic, so today I shall enliven my kinsmen by killing You.

PURPORT

The demon used the word *abhavāya*, which means "for killing." Śrīdhara Svāmī comments that this "killing" means liberating, or, in other words, killing the process of continued birth and death. The Lord kills the process of birth and death and keeps Himself invisible. The activities of the Lord's internal potency are inconceivable, but by a slight exhibition of this potency, the Lord, by His grace, can deliver one from nescience. *Śucaḥ* means "miseries"; the miseries of material existence can be extinguished by the Lord by His potential energy of internal *yogamāyā*. In the *Upaniṣads* (*Śvetāśvatara Up.* 6.8) it is stated, *parāsya śaktir vividhaiva śrūyate*. The Lord is invisible to the eyes of the common man, but His energies act in various ways. When demons are in adversity, they think that God is hiding Himself and is working by His mystic potency. They think that if they can find God they can kill Him just by seeing Him. Hiraṇyākṣa thought that way, and he challenged the Lord: "You have done tremendous harm to our community, taking the part of the demigods, and You have killed our kinsmen in so many ways, always keeping Yourself hidden. Now I see You face to face, and I am not going to let You go. I shall kill You and save my kinsmen from Your mystic misdeeds."

Not only are demons always anxious to kill God with words and philosophy, but they think that if one is materially powerful he can kill God with materially fatal weapons. Demons like Kaṁsa, Rāvaṇa and Hiraṇyakaśipu thought themselves powerful enough to kill even God. Demons cannot understand that God, by His multifarious potencies, can work so wonderfully that He can be present everywhere and still remain in His eternal abode, Goloka Vṛndāvana.

TEXT 5

त्वयि संस्थिते गदया शीर्णशीर्ष-
ण्यस्मद्भुजच्युतया ये च तुभ्यम् ।
बलिं हरन्त्यृषयो ये च देवाः
स्वयं सर्वे न भविष्यन्त्यमूलाः ॥ ५ ॥

tvayi saṁsthite gadayā śīrṇa-śīrṣaṇy
asmad-bhuja-cyutayā ye ca tubhyam
baliṁ haranty ṛṣayo ye ca devāḥ
svayaṁ sarve na bhaviṣyanty amūlāḥ

tvayi—when You; *saṁsthite*—are killed; *gadayā*—by the mace; *śīrṇa*—smashed; *śīrṣaṇi*—skull; *asmat-bhuja*—from my hand; *cyutayā*—released; *ye*—those who; *ca*—and; *tubhyam*—to You; *balim*—presentations; *haranti*—offer; *ṛṣayaḥ*—sages; *ye*—those who; *ca*—and; *devāḥ*—demigods; *svayam*—automatically; *sarve*—all; *na*—not; *bhaviṣyanti*—will exist; *amūlāḥ*—without roots.

TRANSLATION

The demon continued: When You fall dead with Your skull smashed by the mace hurled by my arms, the demigods and sages who offer You oblations and sacrifice in devotional service will also automatically cease to exist, like trees without roots.

PURPORT

Demons are very much disturbed when devotees worship the Lord in the prescribed ways recommended in the scriptures. In the Vedic scriptures, the neophyte devotees are advised to engage in nine kinds of devotional service, such as to hear and chant the holy name of God, to remember Him always, to chant on beads Hare Kṛṣṇa, Hare Kṛṣṇa, Kṛṣṇa Kṛṣṇa, Hare Hare/ Hare Rāma, Hare Rāma, Rāma Rāma, Hare Hare, to worship the Lord in the form of His Deity incarnation in the temples, and to engage in various activities of Kṛṣṇa consciousness to increase the number of godly persons for perfect peace in the world. Demons do not like such activity. They are always envious of God and His devotees. Their propaganda not to worship in the temple or church but simply to make material advancement for satisfaction of the senses is always current. The demon Hiraṇyākṣa, upon seeing the Lord face to face, wanted to make a permanent solution by killing the Personality of Godhead with his powerful mace. The example of an uprooted tree mentioned here by the demon is very significant. Devotees accept that God is the root of everything. Their example is that just as the stomach is the source of energy of all the limbs of the body, God is the original source of all energy manifested in the material and spiritual worlds; therefore, as supplying food to the stomach is the process to satisfy all the limbs of the body, Kṛṣṇa consciousness, or developing love of Kṛṣṇa, is the sublime method for satisfying the source of all happiness. The demon wants to uproot this source because if the root, God, were to be checked, the activities of the Lord and the devotees would automatically stop. The demon would be very much satisfied by such a situation in society. Demons are always anxious to have a godless society for their sense gratification. According to Śrīdhara Svāmī, this verse means that when the demon would be deprived of his mace by the Supreme Personality of Godhead, not only the neophyte devotees but also the ancient sagacious devotees of the Lord would be very much satisfied.

TEXT 6

स तुद्यमानोऽरिदुरुक्ततोमरै-
दंष्ट्राग्रगां गामुपलक्ष्य भीताम् ।
तोदं मृषन्निरगादम्बुमध्याद्
ग्राहाहतः सकरेणुर्यथेभः ॥ ६ ॥

sa tudyamāno 'ri-durukta-tomarair
daṁṣṭrāgra-gāṁ gām upalakṣya bhītām
todaṁ mṛṣan niragād ambu-madhyād
grāhāhataḥ sa-kareṇur yathebhaḥ

saḥ—He; *tudyamānaḥ*—being pained; *ari*—of the enemy; *durukta*—by the abusive words; *tomaraiḥ*—by the weapons; *daṁṣṭra-agra*—on the ends of His tusks; *gām*—situated; *gām*—the earth; *upalakṣya*—seeing; *bhītām*—frightened; *todam*—the pain; *mṛṣan*—bearing; *niragāt*—He came out; *ambu-madhyāt*—from the midst of the water; *grāha*—by a crocodile; *āhataḥ*—attacked; *sa-kareṇuḥ*—along with a she-elephant; *yathā*—as; *ibhaḥ*—an elephant.

TRANSLATION

Although the Lord was pained by the shaftlike abusive words of the demon, He bore the pain. But seeing that the earth on the ends of His tusks was frightened, He rose out of the water just as an elephant emerges with its female companion when assailed by an alligator.

PURPORT

The Māyāvādī philosopher cannot understand that the Lord has feelings. The Lord is satisfied if someone offers Him a nice prayer, and similarly, if someone decries His existence or calls Him by ill names, God is dissatisfied. The Supreme Personality of Godhead is decried by the Māyāvādī philosophers, who are almost demons. They say that God has no head, no form, no existence and no legs, hands or other bodily limbs. In other words, they say that He is dead or lame. All these misconceptions of the Supreme Lord are a source of dissatisfaction to Him; He is never pleased with such atheistic descriptions. In this case, although the Lord felt sorrow from the piercing words of the demon, He delivered the earth for the satisfaction of the demigods, who are ever His devotees. The conclusion is that God is as sentient as we are. He is satisfied by our prayers and dissatisfied by our harsh words against Him. In order to give protection to His devotee, He is always ready to tolerate insulting words from the atheists.

TEXT 7

तं निःसरन्तं सलिलादनुद्रुतो
हिरण्यकेशो द्विरदं यथा झषः ।
करालदंष्ट्रोऽशनिनिस्वनोऽब्रवीद्
गतह्रियां किं त्वसतां विगर्हितम् ॥ ७ ॥

taṁ niḥsarantaṁ salilād anudruto
hiraṇya-keśo dviradaṁ yathā jhaṣaḥ
karāla-daṁṣṭro 'śani-nisvano 'bravīd
gata-hriyāṁ kiṁ tv asatāṁ vigarhitam

tam—Him; *niḥsarantam*—coming out; *salilāt*—from the water; *anudrutaḥ*—chased; *hiraṇya-keśaḥ*—having golden hair; *dviradam*—an elephant; *yathā*—as; *jhaṣaḥ*—a crocodile; *karāla-daṁṣṭraḥ*—having fearful teeth; *aśani-nisvanaḥ*—roaring like thunder; *abravīt*—he said; *gata-hriyām*—for those who are shameless; *kim*—what; *tu*—indeed; *asatām*—for the wretches; *vigarhitam*—reproachable.

TRANSLATION

The demon, who had golden hair on his head and fearful tusks, gave chase to the Lord while He was rising from the water, even as an alligator would chase an elephant. Roaring like thunder, he said: Are You not ashamed of running away before a challenging adversary? There is nothing reproachable for shameless creatures!

PURPORT

When the Lord was coming out of the water, taking the earth in His arms to deliver it, the demon derided Him with insulting words, but the Lord did not care because He was very conscious of His duty. For a dutiful man there is nothing to fear. Similarly, those who are powerful have no fear of derision or unkind words from an enemy. The Lord had nothing to fear from anyone, yet He was merciful to His enemy by neglecting him. Although apparently He fled from the challenge, it was just to protect the earth from calamity that He tolerated Hiraṇyākṣa's deriding words.

TEXT 8

स गामुदस्तात्सलिलस्य गोचरे
विन्यस्य तस्यामदधात्स्वसत्त्वम् ।
अभिष्टुतो विश्वसृजा प्रसूनै-
रापूर्यमाणो विबुधैः पश्यतोऽरेः ॥ ८ ॥

sa gām udastāt salilasya gocare
vinyasya tasyām adadhāt sva-sattvam
abhiṣṭuto viśva-sṛjā prasūnair
āpūryamāṇo vibudhaiḥ paśyato 'reḥ

saḥ—the Lord; *gām*—the earth; *udastāt*—on the surface; *salilasya*—of the water; *gocare*—within His sight; *vinyasya*—having placed; *tasyām*—to the earth; *adadhāt*—He invested; *sva*—His own; *sattvam*—existence; *abhiṣṭutaḥ*—praised; *viśva-sṛjā*—by Brahmā (the creator of the universe); *prasūnaiḥ*—by flowers; *āpūryamāṇaḥ*—becoming satisfied; *vibudhaiḥ*—by the demigods; *paśyataḥ*—while looking on; *areḥ*—the enemy.

TRANSLATION

The Lord placed the earth within His sight on the surface of the water and transferred to her His own energy in the form of the ability to float on the water. While the enemy stood looking on, Brahmā, the creator of the universe, extolled the Lord, and the other demigods rained flowers on Him.

PURPORT

Those who are demons cannot understand how the Supreme Personality of Godhead floated the earth on water, but to devotees of the Lord this is not a very wonderful act. Not only the earth but many, many millions of planets are floating in the air, and this floating power is endowed upon them by the Lord; there is no other possible explanation. The materialists can explain that the planets are floating by the law of gravitation, but the law of gravitation works under the control or direction of the Supreme Lord. That is the version of *Bhagavad-gītā*, which confirms, by the Lord's statement, that behind the material laws or nature's laws and behind the growth, maintenance, production and evolution of all the planetary systems—behind everything—is the Lord's direction. The Lord's activities could be appreciated only by the demigods, headed by Brahmā, and therefore when they saw the uncommon prowess of the Lord in keeping the earth on the surface of the water, they showered flowers on Him in appreciation of His transcendental activity.

TEXT 9

परानुषक्तं तपनीयोपकल्पं
महागदं काञ्चनचित्रदंशम् ।
मर्माण्यभीक्ष्णं प्रतुदन्तं दुरुक्तैः
प्रचण्डमन्युः प्रहसंस्तं बभाषे ॥ ९ ॥

parānuṣaktaṁ tapanīyopakalpaṁ
mahā-gadaṁ kāñcana-citra-daṁśam
marmāṇy abhīkṣṇaṁ pratudantaṁ duruktaiḥ
pracaṇḍa-manyuḥ prahasaṁs taṁ babhāṣe

parā—from behind; *anuṣaktam*—who followed very closely; *tapanīya-upakalpam*—who had a considerable amount of gold ornaments; *mahā-gadam*—with a great mace; *kāñcana*—golden; *citra*—beautiful; *daṁśam*—armor; *marmāṇi*—the core of the heart; *abhīkṣṇam*—constantly; *pratudantam*—piercing; *duruktaiḥ*—by abusive words; *pracaṇḍa*—terrible; *manyuḥ*—anger; *prahasan*—laughing; *tam*—to him; *babhāṣe*—He said.

TRANSLATION

The demon, who had a wealth of ornaments, bangles and beautiful golden armor on his body, chased the Lord from behind with a great mace. The Lord tolerated his piercing ill words, but in order to reply to him, He expressed His terrible anger.

PURPORT

The Lord could have chastised the demon immediately while the demon was deriding the Lord with ill words, but the Lord tolerated him to please the demigods and to show that they should not be afraid of demons while discharging their duties. Therefore His toleration was displayed mainly to drive away the fears of the demigods, who should know that the Lord is always present to protect them. The demon's derision of the Lord was just like the barking of dogs; the Lord did not care about it, since He was doing His own work in delivering the earth from the midst of the water. Materialistic demons always possess large amounts of gold in various shapes, and they think that a large amount of gold, physical strength and popularity can save them from the wrath of the Supreme Personality of Godhead.

TEXT 10

श्रीभगवानुवाच
सत्यं वयं भो वनगोचरा मृगा
युष्मद्विधान्मृगये ग्रामसिंहान् ।
न मृत्युपाशैः प्रतिमुक्तस्य वीरा
विकत्थनं तव गृह्णन्त्यभद्र ॥१०॥

śrī-bhagavān uvāca
satyaṁ vayaṁ bho vana-gocarā mṛgā
yuṣmad-vidhān mṛgaye grāma-siṁhān
na mṛtyu-pāśaiḥ pratimuktasya vīrā
vikatthanaṁ tava gṛhṇanty abhadra

śrī-bhagavān uvāca—the Supreme Personality of Godhead said; *satyam*—indeed; *vayam*—We; *bhoḥ*—O; *vana-gocarāḥ*—dwelling in the forest; *mṛgāḥ*—creatures; *yuṣmat-vidhān*—like you; *mṛgaye*—I am searching to kill; *grāma-siṁhān*—dogs; *na*—not; *mṛtyu-pāśaiḥ*—by the bonds of death; *pratimuktasya*—of one who is bound; *vīrāḥ*—the heroes; *vikatthanam*—loose talk; *tava*—your; *gṛhṇanti*—take notice of; *abhadra*—O mischievous one.

TRANSLATION

The Personality of Godhead said: Indeed, We are creatures of the jungle, and We are searching after hunting dogs like you. One who is freed from the entanglement of death has no fear from the loose talk in which you are indulging, for you are bound up by the laws of death.

PURPORT

Demons and atheistic persons can go on insulting the Supreme Personality of Godhead, but they forget that they are subjected to the laws of birth and death. They think that simply by decrying the existence of the Supreme Lord or defying His stringent laws of nature, one can be freed from the clutches of birth and death. In *Bhagavad-gītā* it is said that simply by understanding the transcendental nature of God one can go back home, back to Godhead. But demons and atheistic persons do not try to understand the nature of the Supreme Lord; therefore they remain in the entanglement of birth and death.

TEXT 11

एते वयं न्यासहरा रसौकसां
गतह्रियो गदया द्रावितास्ते ।
तिष्ठामहेऽथापि कथञ्चिदाजौ
स्थेयं क्व यामो बलिनोत्पाद्य वैरम् ॥११॥

ete vayaṁ nyāsa-harā rasaukasāṁ
gata-hriyo gadayā drāvitās te
tiṣṭhāmahe 'thāpi kathañcid ājau
stheyaṁ kva yāmo balinotpādya vairam

ete—Ourselves; *vayam*—We; *nyāsa*—of the charge; *harāḥ*—thieves; *rasā-okasām*—of the inhabitants of Rasātala; *gata-hriyaḥ*—shameless; *gadayā*—by the mace; *drāvitāḥ*—chased; *te*—your; *tiṣṭhāmahe*—We shall stay; *atha api*—nevertheless; *kathañcit*—somehow; *ājau*—on the battlefield; *stheyam*—We must stay; *kva*—where; *yāmaḥ*—can We go;

balinā—with a powerful enemy; *utpādya*—having created; *vairam*—enmity.

TRANSLATION

Certainly We have stolen the charge of the inhabitants of Rasātala and have lost all shame. Although bitten by your powerful mace, I shall stay here in the water for some time because, having created enmity with a powerful enemy, I now have no place to go.

PURPORT

The demon should have known that God cannot be driven out of any place, for He is all-pervading. Demons think of their possessions as their property, but actually everything belongs to the Supreme Personality of Godhead, who can take anything at any time He likes.

TEXT 12

त्वं पद्रथानां किल यूथपाधिपो
घटस्व नोऽस्वस्तय आश्वनूहः ।
संस्थाप्य चास्मान् प्रमृजाश्रु स्वकानां
यः स्वां प्रतिज्ञां नातिपिपर्त्यसभ्यः ॥१२॥

tvaṁ pad-rathānāṁ kila yūthapādhipo
ghaṭasva no 'svastaya āśv anūhaḥ
saṁsthāpya cāsmān pramṛjāśru svakānāṁ
yaḥ svāṁ pratijñāṁ nātipiparty asabhyaḥ

tvam—you; *pad-rathānām*—of foot soldiers; *kila*—indeed; *yūthapa*—of the leaders; *adhipaḥ*—the commander; *ghaṭasva*—take steps; *naḥ*—Our; *asvastaye*—for defeat; *āśu*—promptly; *anūhaḥ*—without consideration; *saṁsthāpya*—having killed; *ca*—and; *asmān*—Us; *pramṛja*—wipe away; *aśru*—tears; *svakānām*—of your kith and kin; *yaḥ*—he who; *svām*—his own; *pratijñām*—promised word; *na*—not; *atipiparti*—fulfills; *asabhyaḥ*—not fit to sit in an assembly.

TRANSLATION

You are supposed to be the commander of many foot soldiers, and now you may take prompt steps to overthrow Us. Give up all your foolish talk and wipe out the cares of your kith and kin by slaying Us. One may be proud, yet he does not deserve a seat in an assembly if he fails to fulfill his promised word.

PURPORT

A demon may be a great soldier and commander of a large number of infantry, but in the presence of the Supreme Personality of Godhead he is powerless and is destined to die. The Lord, therefore, challenged the demon not to go away, but to fulfill his promised word to kill Him.

TEXT 13

मैत्रेय उवाच

सोऽधिक्षिप्तो भगवता प्रलब्धश्च रुषा भृशम् ।
आजहारोल्बणं क्रोधं क्रीड्यमानोऽहिराडिव ॥१३॥

maitreya uvāca
so 'dhikṣipto bhagavatā
pralabdhaś ca ruṣā bhṛśam
ājahārolbaṇaṁ krodhaṁ
krīḍyamāno 'hi-rāḍ iva

maitreyaḥ—the great sage Maitreya; *uvāca*—said; *saḥ*—the demon; *adhikṣiptaḥ*—having been insulted; *bhagavatā*—by the Personality of Godhead; *pralabdhaḥ*—ridiculed; *ca*—and; *ruṣā*—angry; *bhṛśam*—greatly; *ājahāra*—collected; *ulbaṇam*—great; *krodham*—anger; *krīḍyamānaḥ*—being played with; *ahi-rāṭ*—a great cobra; *iva*—like.

TRANSLATION

Śrī Maitreya said: The demon, being thus challenged by the Personality of Godhead, became angry and agitated, and he trembled in anger like a challenged cobra.

PURPORT

A cobra is very fierce before ordinary persons, but before an enchanter who can play with him, he is a plaything. Similarly, a demon may be very powerful in his own domain, but before the Lord he is insignificant. The demon Rāvaṇa was a fierce figure before the demigods, but when he was before Lord Rāmacandra he trembled and prayed to his deity, Lord Śiva, but to no avail.

TEXT 14

सृजन्नमर्षितः श्वासान्मन्युप्रचलितेन्द्रियः ।
आसाद्य तरसा दैत्यो गदयान्यहनद्धरिम् ॥१४॥

sṛjann amarṣitaḥ śvāsān
manyu-pracalitendriyaḥ
āsādya tarasā daityo
gadayā nyahanad dharim

sṛjan—giving out; *amarṣitaḥ*—being angry; *śvāsān*—breaths; *manyu*—by wrath; *pracalita*—agitated; *indriyaḥ*—whose senses; *āsādya*—attacking; *tarasā*—quickly; *daityaḥ*—the demon; *gadayā*—with his mace; *nyahanat*—struck; *harim*—Lord Hari.

TRANSLATION

Hissing indignantly, all his senses shaken by wrath, the demon quickly sprang upon the Lord and dealt Him a blow with his powerful mace.

TEXT 15

भगवांस्तु गदावेगं विसृष्टं रिपुणोरसि ।
अवञ्चयत्तिरश्चीनो योगारूढ इवान्तकम् ॥१५॥

bhagavāṁs tu gadā-vegaṁ
visṛṣṭaṁ ripuṇorasi
avañcayat tiraścīno
yogārūḍha ivāntakam

bhagavān—the Lord; *tu*—however; *gadā-vegam*—the blow of the mace; *visṛṣṭam*—thrown; *ripuṇā*—by the enemy; *urasi*—at His breast; *avañcayat*—dodged; *tiraścīnaḥ*—aside; *yoga-ārūḍhaḥ*—an accomplished *yogī; iva*—like; *antakam*—death.

TRANSLATION

The Lord, however, by moving slightly aside, dodged the violent mace-blow aimed at His breast by the enemy, just as an accomplished yogī would elude death.

PURPORT

The example is given herein that the perfect *yogī* can overcome a deathblow although it is offered by the laws of nature. It is useless for a demon to beat the transcendental body of the Lord with a powerful mace, for no one can surpass His prowess. Those who are advanced transcendentalists are freed from the laws of nature, and even a deathblow cannot act on them. Superficially it may be seen that a *yogī* is attacked by a deathblow, but by the grace of the Lord he can overcome many such attacks for the service of the Lord. As the Lord exists by His own independent prowess, by the grace of the Lord the devotees also exist for His service.

TEXT 16

पुनर्गदां स्वामादाय भ्रामयन्तमभीक्ष्णशः ।
अभ्यधावद्धरिः क्रुद्धः संरम्भाद्दष्टदच्छदम् ॥१६॥

punar gadāṁ svām ādāya
bhrāmayantam abhīkṣṇaśaḥ
abhyadhāvad dhariḥ kruddhaḥ
saṁrambhād daṣṭa-dacchadam

punaḥ—again; *gadām*—mace; *svām*—his; *ādāya*—having taken; *bhrāmayantam*—brandishing; *abhīkṣṇaśaḥ*—repeatedly; *abhyadhāvat*—rushed to meet; *hariḥ*—the Personality of Godhead; *kruddhaḥ*—angry; *saṁrambhāt*—in rage; *daṣṭa*—bitten; *dacchadam*—his lip.

TRANSLATION

The Personality of Godhead now exhibited His anger and rushed to meet the demon, who bit his lip in rage, took up his mace again and began to repeatedly brandish it about.

TEXT 17

ततश्च गदयारातिं दक्षिणस्यां भ्रुवि प्रभुः ।
आजघ्ने स तु तां सौम्य गदया कोविदोऽहनत् ॥१७॥

tataś ca gadayārātiṁ
dakṣiṇasyāṁ bhruvi prabhuḥ
ājaghne sa tu tāṁ saumya
gadayā kovido 'hanat

tataḥ—then; *ca*—and; *gadayā*—with His mace; *arātim*—the enemy; *dakṣiṇasyām*—on the right; *bhruvi*—on the brow; *prabhuḥ*—the Lord; *ājaghne*—struck; *saḥ*—the Lord; *tu*—but; *tām*—the mace; *saumya*—O gentle Vidura; *gadayā*—with his mace; *kovidaḥ*—expert; *ahanat*—he saved himself.

TRANSLATION

Then with His mace the Lord struck the enemy on the right of his brow, but since the demon was expert in fighting, O gentle Vidura, he protected himself by a maneuver of his own mace.

TEXT 18

एवं गदाभ्यां गुर्वीभ्यां हर्यक्षो हरिरेव च ।
जिगीषया सुसंरब्धावन्योन्यमभिजघ्नतुः ॥१८॥

evaṁ gadābhyāṁ gurvībhyāṁ
haryakṣo harir eva ca
jigīṣayā susaṁrabdhāv
anyonyam abhijaghnatuḥ

evam—in this way; *gadābhyām*—with their maces; *gurvībhyām*—huge; *haryakṣaḥ*—the demon Haryakṣa (Hiraṇyākṣa); *hariḥ*—Lord

Hari; *eva*—certainly; *ca*—and; *jigīṣayā*—with a desire for victory; *susaṁrabdhau*—enraged; *anyonyam*—each other; *abhijaghnatuḥ*—they struck.

TRANSLATION

In this way, the demon Haryakṣa and the Lord, the Personality of Godhead, struck each other with their huge maces, each enraged and seeking his own victory.

PURPORT

Haryakṣa is another name for Hiraṇyākṣa, the demon.

TEXT 19

तयोः स्पृधोस्तिग्मगदाहताङ्गयोः
क्षतास्रवघ्राणविवृद्धमन्य्वोः ।
विचित्रमार्गांश्चरतोर्जिगीषया
व्यभादिलायामिव शुष्मिणोर्मृधः ॥१९॥

tayoḥ spṛdhos tigma-gadāhatāṅgayoḥ
kṣatāsrava-ghrāṇa-vivṛddha-manyvoḥ
vicitra-mārgāṁś carator jigīṣayā
vyabhād ilāyām iva śuṣmiṇor mṛdhaḥ

tayoḥ—them; *spṛdhoḥ*—the two combatants; *tigma*—pointed; *gadā*—by the maces; *āhata*—injured; *aṅgayoḥ*—their bodies; *kṣata-āsrava*—blood coming out from the injuries; *ghrāṇa*—smell; *vivṛddha*—increased; *manyvoḥ*—anger; *vicitra*—of various kinds; *mārgān*—maneuvers; *caratoḥ*—performing; *jigīṣayā*—with a desire to win; *vyabhāt*—it looked like; *ilāyām*—for the sake of a cow (or the earth); *iva*—like; *śuṣmiṇoḥ*—of two bulls; *mṛdhaḥ*—an encounter.

TRANSLATION

There was keen rivalry between the two combatants; both had sustained injuries on their bodies from the blows of each other's pointed maces, and each grew more and more enraged at the smell of blood on his person. In their eagerness to win, they performed

maneuvers of various kinds, and their contest looked like an encounter between two forceful bulls for the sake of a cow.

PURPORT

Here the earth planet is called *ilā*. This earth was formerly known as Ilāvṛta-varṣa, and when Mahārāja Parīkṣit ruled the earth it was called Bhārata-varṣa. Actually, Bhārata-varṣa is the name for the entire planet, but gradually Bhārata-varṣa has come to mean India. As India has recently been divided into Pakistan and Hindustan, similarly the earth was formerly called Ilāvṛta-varṣa, but gradually as time passed it was divided by national boundaries.

TEXT 20

दैत्यस्य यज्ञावयवस्य माया-
गृहीतवाराहतनोर्महात्मनः ।
कौरव्य मह्यां द्विषतोर्विमर्दनं
दिदृक्षुरागादृषिभिर्वृतः स्वराट् ॥२०॥

daityasya yajñāvayavasya māyā-
gṛhīta-vārāha-tanor mahātmanaḥ
kauravya mahyāṁ dviṣator vimardanaṁ
didṛkṣur āgād ṛṣibhir vṛtaḥ svarāṭ

daityasya—of the demon; *yajña-avayavasya*—of the Personality of Godhead (of whose body *yajña* is a part); *māyā*—through His potency; *gṛhīta*—was assumed; *vārāha*—of a boar; *tanoḥ*—whose form; *mahā-ātmanaḥ*—of the Supreme Lord; *kauravya*—O Vidura (descendant of Kuru); *mahyām*—for the sake of the world; *dviṣatoḥ*—of the two enemies; *vimardanam*—the fight; *didṛkṣuḥ*—desirous to see; *āgāt*—came; *ṛṣibhiḥ*—by the sages; *vṛtaḥ*—accompanied; *svarāṭ*—Brahmā.

TRANSLATION

O descendant of Kuru, Brahmā, the most independent demigod of the universe, accompanied by his followers, came to see the terrible fight for the sake of the world between the demon and the Personality of Godhead, who appeared in the form of a boar.

PURPORT

The fight between the Lord, the Supreme Personality of Godhead, and the demon is compared to a fight between bulls for the sake of a cow. The earth planet is also called *go*, or cow. As bulls fight between themselves to ascertain who will have union with a cow, there is always a constant fight between the demons and the Supreme Lord or His representative for supremacy over the earth. Here the Lord is significantly described as *yajñāvayava.* One should not consider the Lord to have the body of an ordinary boar. He can assume any form, and He possesses all such forms eternally. It is from Him that all other forms have emanated. This boar form is not to be considered the form of an ordinary hog; His body is actually full of *yajña,* or worshipful offerings. *Yajña* (sacrifices) are offered to Viṣṇu. *Yajña* means the body of Viṣṇu. His body is not material; therefore He should not be taken to be an ordinary boar.

Brahmā is described in this verse as *svarāṭ.* Actually, full independence is exclusive to the Lord Himself, but as part and parcel of the Supreme Lord, every living entity has a minute quantity of independence. Each and every one of the living entities within this universe has this minute independence, but Brahmā, being the chief of all living entities, has a greater potential of independence than any other. He is the representative of Kṛṣṇa, the Supreme Personality of Godhead, and has been assigned to preside over universal affairs. All other demigods work for him; therefore he is described here as *svarāṭ.* He is always accompanied by great sages and transcendentalists, all of whom came to see the bullfight between the demon and the Lord.

TEXT 21

आसन्नशौण्डीरमपेतसाध्वसं
कृतप्रतीकारमहार्यविक्रमम् ।
विलक्ष्य दैत्यं भगवान् सहस्रणी-
र्जगाद नारायणमादिसूकरम् ॥२१॥

āsanna-śauṇḍīram apeta-sādhvasaṁ
kṛta-pratīkāram ahārya-vikramam

vilakṣya daityaṁ bhagavān sahasra-ṇīr
jagāda nārāyaṇam ādi-sūkaram

āsanna—attained; *śauṇḍīram*—power; *apeta*—devoid of; *sādhvasam*—fear; *kṛta*—making; *pratīkāram*—opposition; *ahārya*—unopposable; *vikramam*—having power; *vilakṣya*—having seen; *daityam*—the demon; *bhagavān*—the worshipful Brahmā; *sahasra-nīḥ*—the leader of thousands of sages; *jagāda*—addressed; *nārāyaṇam*—Lord Nārāyaṇa; *ādi*—the original; *sūkaram*—having the form of a boar.

TRANSLATION

After arriving at the place of combat, Brahmā, the leader of thousands of sages and transcendentalists, saw the demon, who had attained such unprecedented power that no one could fight with him. Brahmā then addressed Nārāyaṇa, who was assuming the form of a boar for the first time.

TEXTS 22–23

ब्रह्मोवाच
एष ते देव देवानामङ्घ्रिमूलमुपेयुषाम् ।
विप्राणां सौरभेयीणां भूतानामप्यनागसाम् ॥२२॥
आगस्कृद्भयकृद्दुष्कृदस्मद्राद्धवरोऽसुरः ।
अन्वेषन्नप्रतिरथो लोकानटति कण्टकः ॥२३॥

brahmovāca
eṣa te deva devānām
aṅghri-mūlam upeyuṣām
viprāṇāṁ saurabheyīṇāṁ
bhūtānām apy anāgasām

āgas-kṛd bhaya-kṛd duṣkṛd
asmad-rāddha-varo 'suraḥ
anveṣann apratiratho
lokān aṭati kaṇṭakaḥ

brahmā uvāca—Lord Brahmā said; *eṣaḥ*—this demon; *te*—Your; *deva*—O Lord; *devānām*—to the demigods; *aṅghri-mūlam*—Your feet; *upeyuṣām*—to those having obtained; *viprāṇām*—to the *brāhmaṇas; saurabheyīṇām*—to the cows; *bhūtānām*—to ordinary living entities; *api*—also; *anāgasām*—innocent; *āgaḥ-kṛt*—an offender; *bhaya-kṛt*—a source of fear; *duṣkṛt*—wrongdoer; *asmat*—from me; *rāddha-varaḥ*—having attained a boon; *asuraḥ*—a demon; *anveṣan*—searching; *apratirathaḥ*—having no proper combatant; *lokān*—all over the universe; *aṭati*—he wanders; *kaṇṭakaḥ*—being a pinprick for everyone.

TRANSLATION

Lord Brahmā said: My dear Lord, this demon has proved to be a constant pinprick to the demigods, the brāhmaṇas, the cows and innocent persons who are spotless and always dependent upon worshiping Your lotus feet. He has become a source of fear by unnecessarily harassing them. Since he has attained a boon from me, he has become a demon, always searching for a proper combatant, wandering all over the universe for this infamous purpose.

PURPORT

There are two classes of living entities; one is called *sura*, or the demigods, and the other is called *asura*, or the demons. Demons are generally fond of worshiping the demigods, and there are evidences that by such worship they get extensive power for their sense gratification. This later proves to be a cause of trouble to the *brāhmaṇas*, demigods and other innocent living entities. Demons habitually find fault with the demigods, *brāhmaṇas* and innocent, to whom they are a constant source of fear. The way of the demon is to take power from the demigods and then tease the demigods themselves. There is an instance of a great devotee of Lord Śiva who obtained a boon from Lord Śiva that the head of whomever he touched with his hand would come off its trunk. As soon as the boon was offered to him, the demon wanted to touch the very head of Lord Śiva. That is their way. The devotees of the Supreme Personality of Godhead do not, however, ask any favor for sense gratification. Even if they are offered liberation, they refuse it. They are happy simply engaging in the transcendental loving service of the Lord.

TEXT 24

मैनं मायाविनं दृप्तं निरङ्कुशमसत्तमम् ।
आक्रीड बालवद्देव यथाशीविषमुत्थितम् ॥२४॥

mainaṁ māyāvinaṁ dṛptaṁ
niraṅkuśam asattamam
ākrīḍa bālavad deva
yathāśīviṣam utthitam

mā—do not; *enam*—him; *māyā-vinam*—skilled in conjuring tricks; *dṛptam*—arrogant; *niraṅkuśam*—self-sufficient; *asat-tamam*—most wicked; *ākrīḍa*—play with; *bāla-vat*—like a child; *deva*—O Lord; *yathā*—as; *āśīviṣam*—a serpent; *utthitam*—aroused.

TRANSLATION

Lord Brahmā continued: My dear Lord, there is no need to play with this serpentine demon, who is always very skilled in conjuring tricks and is arrogant, self-sufficient and most wicked.

PURPORT

No one is unhappy when a serpent is killed. It is a practice among village boys to catch a serpent by the tail and play with it for some time and then kill it. Similarly, the Lord could have killed the demon at once, but He played with him in the same way as a child plays with a snake before killing it. Brahmā requested, however, that since the demon was more wicked and undesirable than a serpent, there was no need to play with him. It was his wish that he be killed at once, without delay.

TEXT 25

न यावदेष वर्धेत स्वां वेलां प्राप्य दारुणः ।
स्वां देव मायामास्थाय तावज्जह्यघमच्युत ॥२५॥

na yāvad eṣa vardheta
svāṁ velāṁ prāpya dāruṇaḥ

svāṁ deva māyām āsthāya
tāvaj jahy agham acyuta

na yāvat—before; *eṣaḥ*—this demon; *vardheta*—may increase; *svām*—his own; *velām*—demoniac hour; *prāpya*—having reached; *dāruṇaḥ*—formidable; *svām*—Your own; *deva*—O Lord; *māyām*—internal potency; *āsthāya*—using; *tāvat*—at once; *jahi*—kill; *agham*—the sinful one; *acyuta*—O infallible one.

TRANSLATION

Brahmā continued: My dear Lord, You are infallible. Please kill this sinful demon before the demoniac hour arrives and he presents another formidable approach favorable to him. You can kill him by Your internal potency without doubt.

TEXT 26

एषा घोरतमा सन्ध्या लोकच्छम्बट्करी प्रभो ।
उपसर्पति सर्वात्मन् सुराणां जयमावह ॥२६॥

eṣā ghoratamā sandhyā
loka-cchambaṭ-karī prabho
upasarpati sarvātman
surāṇāṁ jayam āvaha

eṣā—this; *ghora-tamā*—darkest; *sandhyā*—evening time; *loka*—the world; *chambaṭ-karī*—destroying; *prabho*—O Lord; *upasarpati*—is approaching; *sarva-ātman*—O Soul of all souls; *surāṇām*—to the demigods; *jayam*—victory; *āvaha*—bring.

TRANSLATION

My Lord, the darkest evening, which covers the world, is fast approaching. Since You are the Soul of all souls, kindly kill him and win victory for the demigods.

TEXT 27

अधुनैषोऽभिजिन्नाम योगो मौहूर्तिको ह्यगात् ।
शिवाय नस्त्वं सुहृदामाशु निस्तर दुस्तरम् ॥२७॥

adhunaiṣo 'bhijin nāma
yogo mauhūrtiko hy agāt
śivāya nas tvaṁ suhṛdām
āśu nistara dustaram

adhunā—now; *eṣaḥ*—this; *abhijit nāma*—called *abhijit; yogaḥ*—auspicious; *mauhūrtikaḥ*—moment; *hi*—indeed; *agāt*—has almost passed; *śivāya*—for the welfare; *naḥ*—of us; *tvam*—You; *suhṛdām*—of Your friends; *āśu*—quickly; *nistara*—dispose of; *dustaram*—the formidable foe.

TRANSLATION

The auspicious period known as abhijit, which is most opportune for victory, commenced at midday and has all but passed; therefore, in the interest of Your friends, please dispose of this formidable foe quickly.

TEXT 28

दिष्ट्या त्वां विहितं मृत्युमयमासादितः स्वयम् ।
विक्रम्यैनं मृधे हत्वा लोकानाधेहि शर्मणि ॥२८॥

diṣṭyā tvāṁ vihitaṁ mṛtyum
ayam āsāditaḥ svayam
vikramyainaṁ mṛdhe hatvā
lokān ādhehi śarmaṇi

diṣṭyā—by fortune; *tvām*—to You; *vihitam*—ordained; *mṛtyum*—death; *ayam*—this demon; *āsāditaḥ*—has come; *svayam*—of his own accord; *vikramya*—exhibiting Your prowess; *enam*—him; *mṛdhe*—in the duel; *hatvā*—killing; *lokān*—the worlds; *ādhehi*—establish; *śarmaṇi*—in peace.

TRANSLATION

This demon, luckily for us, has come of his own accord to You, his death ordained by You; therefore, exhibiting Your ways, kill him in the duel and establish the worlds in peace.

Thus end the Bhaktivedanta purports of the Third Canto, Eighteenth Chapter, of the Śrīmad-Bhāgavatam, *entitled "The Battle Between Lord Boar and the Demon Hiraṇyākṣa."*

CHAPTER NINETEEN

The Killing of the Demon Hiraṇyākṣa

TEXT 1

मैत्रेय उवाच
अवधार्य विरिञ्चस्य निर्व्यलीकामृतं वचः ।
प्रहस्य प्रेमगर्भेण तदपाङ्गेन सोऽग्रहीत् ॥ १ ॥

maitreya uvāca
avadhārya viriñcasya
nirvyalīkāmṛtaṁ vacaḥ
prahasya prema-garbheṇa
tad apāṅgena so 'grahīt

maitreyaḥ uvāca—Maitreya said; *avadhārya*—after hearing; *viriñcasya*—of Lord Brahmā; *nirvyalīka*—free from all sinful purposes; *amṛtam*—nectarean; *vacaḥ*—words; *prahasya*—heartily laughing; *prema-garbheṇa*—laden with love; *tat*—those words; *apāṅgena*—with a glance; *saḥ*—the Supreme Personality of Godhead; *agrahīt*—accepted.

TRANSLATION

Śrī Maitreya said: After hearing the words of Brahmā, the creator, which were free from all sinful purposes and as sweet as nectar, the Lord heartily laughed and accepted his prayer with a glance laden with love.

PURPORT

The word *nirvyalīka* is very significant. The prayers of the demigods or devotees of the Lord are free from all sinful purposes, but the prayers of demons are always filled with sinful purposes. The demon Hiraṇyākṣa became powerful by deriving a boon from Brahmā, and after attaining that boon he created a disturbance because of his sinful intentions. The prayers of Brahmā and other demigods are not to be compared to the prayers of the demons. Their purpose is to please the Supreme Lord; therefore the Lord smiled and accepted the prayer to kill the demon. Demons, who are never interested in praising the Supreme Personality of Godhead because they have no information of Him, go to the demigods, and in *Bhagavad-gītā* this is condemned. Persons who go to the demigods and pray for advancement in sinful activities are considered to be bereft of all intelligence. Demons have lost all intelligence because they do not know what is actually their self-interest. Even if they have information of the Supreme Personality of Godhead, they decline to approach Him; it is not possible for them to get their desired boons from the Supreme Lord because their purposes are always sinful. It is said that the dacoits in Bengal used to worship the goddess Kālī for fulfillment of their sinful desires to plunder others' property, but they never went to a Viṣṇu temple because they might have been unsuccessful in praying to Viṣṇu. Therefore the prayers of the demigods or the devotees of the Supreme Personality of Godhead are always untinged by sinful purposes.

TEXT 2

ततः सपत्नं मुखतश्चरन्तमकुतोभयम् ।
जघानोत्पत्य गदया हनावसुरमक्षजः ॥ २ ॥

tataḥ sapatnaṁ mukhataś
carantam akuto-bhayam
jaghānotpatya gadayā
hanāv asuram akṣajaḥ

tataḥ—then; *sapatnam*—enemy; *mukhataḥ*—in front of Him; *carantam*—stalking; *akutaḥ-bhayam*—fearlessly; *jaghāna*—struck; *utpatya*—after springing up; *gadayā*—with His mace; *hanau*—at the chin; *asuram*—the demon; *akṣa-jaḥ*—the Lord, who was born from the nostril of Brahmā.

TRANSLATION

The Lord, who had appeared from the nostril of Brahmā, sprang and aimed His mace at the chin of His enemy, the Hiraṇyākṣa demon, who was stalking fearlessly before Him.

TEXT 3

सा हता तेन गदया विहता भगवत्करात् ।
विघूर्णितापतद्रेजे तदद्भुतमिवाभवत् ॥ ३ ॥

sā hatā tena gadayā
vihatā bhagavat-karāt
vighūrṇitāpatad reje
tad adbhutam ivābhavat

sā—that mace; *hatā*—struck; *tena*—by Hiraṇyākṣa; *gadayā*—with his mace; *vihatā*—slipped; *bhagavat*—of the Supreme Personality of Godhead; *karāt*—from the hand; *vighūrṇitā*—whirling; *apatat*—fell down; *reje*—was shining; *tat*—that; *adbhutam*—miraculous; *iva*—indeed; *abhavat*—was.

TRANSLATION

Struck by the demon's mace, however, the Lord's mace slipped from His hand and looked splendid as it fell down whirling. This was miraculous, for the mace was blazing wonderfully.

TEXT 4

स तदा लब्धतीर्थोऽपि न बबाधे निरायुधम् ।
मानयन् स मृधे धर्मं विष्वक्सेनं प्रकोपयन् ॥ ४ ॥

sa tadā labdha-tīrtho 'pi
na babādhe nirāyudham
mānayan sa mṛdhe dharmaṁ
viṣvaksenaṁ prakopayan

saḥ—that Hiraṇyākṣa; *tadā*—then; *labdha-tīrthaḥ*—having gained an excellent opportunity; *api*—although; *na*—not; *babādhe*—attacked; *nirāyudham*—having no weapon; *mānayan*—respecting; *saḥ*—Hiraṇyākṣa; *mṛdhe*—in battle; *dharmam*—the code of combat; *viṣvak-senam*—the Supreme Personality of Godhead; *prakopayan*—making angry.

TRANSLATION

Even though the demon had an excellent opportunity to strike his unarmed foe without obstruction, he respected the law of single combat, thereby kindling the fury of the Supreme Lord.

TEXT 5

गदायामपविद्धायां हाहाकारे विनिर्गते ।
मानयामास तद्धर्मं सुनाभं चास्मरद्विभुः ॥ ५ ॥

gadāyām apaviddhāyāṁ
hāhā-kāre vinirgate
mānayām āsa tad-dharmaṁ
sunābhaṁ cāsmarad vibhuḥ

gadāyām—as His mace; *apaviddhāyām*—fell; *hāhā-kāre*—a cry of alarm; *vinirgate*—arose; *mānayām āsa*—acknowledged; *tat*—of Hiraṇyākṣa; *dharmam*—righteousness; *sunābham*—the Sudarśana *cakra;* *ca*—and; *asmarat*—remembered; *vibhuḥ*—the Supreme Personality of Godhead.

TRANSLATION

As the Lord's mace fell to the ground and a cry of alarm arose from the witnessing crowd of gods and ṛṣis, the Personality of Godhead acknowledged the demon's love of righteousness and therefore invoked His Sudarśana discus.

TEXT 6

तं व्यग्रचक्रं दितिपुत्राधमेन
स्वपार्षदमुख्येन विषज्जमानम् ।
चित्रा वाचोऽतद्विदां खेचराणां
तत्र स्मासन् स्वस्ति तेऽमुं जहीति ॥ ६ ॥

taṁ vyagra-cakraṁ diti-putrādhamena
sva-pārṣada-mukhyena viṣajjamānam

citrā vāco 'tad-vidāṁ khe-carāṇāṁ
tatra smāsan svasti te 'muṁ jahīti

tam—unto the Personality of Godhead; *vyagra*—revolving; *cakram*—whose discus; *diti-putra*—son of Diti; *adhamena*—vile; *sva-pārṣada*—of His associates; *mukhyena*—with the chief; *viṣajjamānam*—playing; *citrāḥ*—various; *vācaḥ*—expressions; *a-tat-vidām*—of those who did not know; *khe-carāṇām*—flying in the sky; *tatra*—there; *sma āsan*—occurred; *svasti*—fortune; *te*—unto You; *amum*—him; *jahi*—please kill; *iti*—thus.

TRANSLATION

As the discus began to revolve in the Lord's hands and the Lord contended at close quarters with the chief of His Vaikuṇṭha attendants, who had been born as Hiraṇyākṣa, a vile son of Diti, there issued from every direction strange expressions uttered by those who were witnessing from airplanes. They had no knowledge of the Lord's reality, and they cried, "May victory attend You! Pray dispatch him. Play no more with him."

TEXT 7

स तं निशाम्यात्तरथाङ्गमग्रतो
व्यवस्थितं पद्मपलाशलोचनम् ।
विलोक्य चामर्षपरिप्लुतेन्द्रियो
रुषा स्वदन्तच्छदमादशच्छ्वसन् ॥ ७ ॥

sa taṁ niśāmyātta-rathāṅgam agrato
vyavasthitaṁ padma-palāśa-locanam
vilokya cāmarṣa-pariplutendriyo
ruṣā sva-danta-cchadam ādaśac chvasan

saḥ—that demon; *tam*—the Supreme Personality of Godhead; *niśāmya*—after seeing; *ātta-rathāṅgam*—armed with the Sudarśana disc; *agrataḥ*—before him; *vyavasthitam*—standing in position; *padma*—lotus flower; *palāśa*—petals; *locanam*—eyes; *vilokya*—after seeing; *ca*—and; *amarṣa*—by indignation; *paripluta*—overpowered; *indriyaḥ*—his senses; *ruṣā*—with great resentment; *sva-danta-chadam*—his own lip; *ādaśat*—bit; *śvasan*—hissing.

TRANSLATION

When the demon saw the Personality of Godhead, who had eyes just like lotus petals, standing in position before him, armed with His Sudarśana discus, his senses were overpowered by indignation. He began to hiss like a serpent, and he bit his lip in great resentment.

TEXT 8

करालदंष्ट्रश्चक्षुर्भ्यां सञ्चक्षाणो दहन्निव ।
अभिप्लुत्य स्वगदया हतोऽसीत्याहनद्धरिम् ॥ ८ ॥

karāla-daṁṣṭraś cakṣurbhyāṁ
sañcakṣāṇo dahann iva
abhiplutya sva-gadayā
hato 'sīty āhanad dharim

karāla—fearful; *daṁṣṭraḥ*—having tusks; *cakṣurbhyām*—with both eyes; *sañcakṣāṇaḥ*—staring; *dahan*—burning; *iva*—as if; *abhiplutya*—attacking; *sva-gadayā*—with his own club; *hataḥ*—slain; *asi*—You are; *iti*—thus; *āhanat*—struck; *harim*—at Hari.

TRANSLATION

The demon, who had fearful tusks, stared at the Personality of Godhead as though to burn Him. Springing into the air, he aimed his mace at the Lord, exclaiming at the same time, "You are slain!"

TEXT 9

पदा सव्येन तां साधो भगवान् यज्ञसूकरः ।
लीलया मिषतः शत्रोः प्राहरद्वातरंहसम् ॥ ९ ॥

padā savyena tāṁ sādho
bhagavān yajña-sūkaraḥ
līlayā miṣataḥ śatroḥ
prāharad vāta-raṁhasam

padā—with His foot; *savyena*—left; *tām*—that mace; *sādho*—O Vidura; *bhagavān*—the Supreme Personality of Godhead; *yajña-sūkaraḥ*—in His boar form, the enjoyer of all sacrifices; *līlayā*—playfully; *miṣataḥ*—looking on; *śatroḥ*—of His enemy (Hiraṇyākṣa); *prāharat*—knocked down; *vāta-raṁhasam*—having the force of a tempest.

TRANSLATION

O saintly Vidura, while His enemy looked on, the Lord in His boar form, the enjoyer of all sacrificial offerings, playfully knocked down the mace with His left foot, even as it came upon Him with the force of a tempest.

TEXT 10

आह चायुधमाधत्स्व घटस्व त्वं जिगीषसि ।
इत्युक्तः स तदा भूयस्ताडयन् व्यनदद् भृशम् ॥१०॥

āha cāyudham ādhatsva
ghaṭasva tvaṁ jigīṣasi
ity uktaḥ sa tadā bhūyas
tāḍayan vyanadad bhṛśam

āha—He said; *ca*—and; *āyudham*—weapon; *ādhatsva*—take up; *ghaṭasva*—try; *tvam*—you; *jigīṣasi*—are eager to conquer; *iti*—thus; *uktaḥ*—challenged; *saḥ*—Hiraṇyākṣa; *tadā*—at that time; *bhūyaḥ*—again; *tāḍayan*—striking at; *vyanadat*—roared; *bhṛśam*—loudly.

TRANSLATION

The Lord then said: "Take up your weapon and try again, eager as you are to conquer Me." Challenged in these words, the demon aimed his mace at the Lord and once more loudly roared.

TEXT 11

तां स आपततीं वीक्ष्य भगवान् समवस्थितः ।
जग्राह लीलया प्राप्तां गरुत्मानिव पन्नगीम् ॥११॥

tāṁ sa āpatatīṁ vīkṣya
bhagavān samavasthitaḥ
jagrāha līlayā prāptāṁ
garutmān iva pannagīm

tām—that mace; *saḥ*—He; *āpatatīm*—flying toward; *vīkṣya*—after seeing; *bhagavān*—the Supreme Personality of Godhead; *samavasthitaḥ*—stood firmly; *jagrāha*—caught; *līlayā*—easily; *prāptām*—entered into His presence; *garutmān*—Garuḍa; *iva*—as; *pannagīm*—a serpent.

TRANSLATION

When the Lord saw the mace flying toward Him, He stood firmly where He was and caught it with the same ease as Garuḍa, the king of birds, would seize a serpent.

TEXT 12

स्वपौरुषे प्रतिहते हतमानो महासुरः ।
नैच्छद्गदां दीयमानां हरिणा विगतप्रभः ॥१२॥

sva-pauruṣe pratihate
hata-māno mahāsuraḥ
naicchad gadāṁ dīyamānāṁ
hariṇā vigata-prabhaḥ

sva-pauruṣe—his valor; *pratihate*—frustrated; *hata*—destroyed; *mānaḥ*—pride; *mahā-asuraḥ*—the great demon; *na aicchat*—desired not (to take); *gadām*—the mace; *dīyamānām*—being offered; *hariṇā*—by Hari; *vigata-prabhaḥ*—reduced in splendor.

TRANSLATION

His valor thus frustrated, the great demon felt humiliated and was put out of countenance. He was reluctant to take back the mace when it was offered by the Personality of Godhead.

TEXT 13

जग्राह त्रिशिखं शूलं ज्वलज्ज्वलनलोलुपम् ।
यज्ञाय धृतरूपाय विप्रायाभिचरन् यथा ॥१३॥

jagrāha tri-śikhaṁ śūlaṁ
jvalaj-jvalana-lolupam
yajñāya dhṛta-rūpāya
viprāyābhicaran yathā

jagrāha—took up; *tri-śikham*—three-pointed; *śūlam*—trident; *jvalat*—flaming; *jvalana*—fire; *lolupam*—rapacious; *yajñāya*—at the enjoyer of all sacrifices; *dhṛta-rūpāya*—in the form of Varāha; *viprāya*—unto a *brāhmaṇa; abhicaran*—acting malevolently; *yathā*—as.

TRANSLATION

He now took a trident which was as rapacious as a flaming fire and hurled it against the Lord, the enjoyer of all sacrifices, even as one would use penance for a malevolent purpose against a holy brāhmaṇa.

TEXT 14

तदोजसा दैत्यमहाभटार्पितं
चकासदन्तःख उदीर्णदीधिति ।
चक्रेण चिच्छेद निशातनेमिना
हरिर्यथा तार्क्ष्यपतत्रमुज्झितम् ॥१४॥

tad ojasā daitya-mahā-bhaṭārpitaṁ
cakāsad antaḥ-kha udīrṇa-dīdhiti
cakreṇa ciccheda niśāta-neminā
harir yathā tārkṣya-patatram ujjhitam

tat—that trident; *ojasā*—with all his strength; *daitya*—among the demons; *mahā-bhaṭa*—by the mighty fighter; *arpitam*—hurled; *cakāsat*—shining; *antaḥ-khe*—in the middle of the sky; *udīrṇa*—increased; *dīdhiti*—illumination; *cakreṇa*—by the Sudarśana disc; *ciccheda*—He cut to pieces; *niśāta*—sharpened; *neminā*—rim; *hariḥ*—

Indra; *yathā*—as; *tārkṣya*—of Garuḍa; *patatram*—the wing; *ujjhitam*—abandoned.

TRANSLATION

Hurled by the mighty demon with all his strength, the flying trident shone brightly in the sky. The Personality of Godhead, however, tore it to pieces with His discus Sudarśana, which had a sharp-edged rim, even as Indra cut off a wing of Garuḍa.

PURPORT

The context of the reference given herein regarding Garuḍa and Indra is this. Once upon a time, Garuḍa, the carrier of the Lord, snatched away a nectar pot from the hands of the demigods in heaven in order to liberate his mother, Vinatā, from the clutches of his stepmother, Kadrū, the mother of the serpents. On learning of this, Indra, the King of heaven, hurled his thunderbolt against Garuḍa. With a view to respect the infallibility of Indra's weapon, Garuḍa, though otherwise invincible, being the Lord's own mount, dropped one of his wings, which was shattered to pieces by the thunderbolt. The inhabitants of higher planets are so sensible that even in the process of fighting they observe the preliminary rules and regulations of gentleness. In this case, Garuḍa wanted to show respect for Indra; since he knew that Indra's weapon must destroy something, he offered his wing.

TEXT 15

वृक्णे स्वशूले बहुधारिणा हरेः
प्रत्येत्य विस्तीर्णमुरो विभूतिमत् ।
प्रवृद्धरोषः स कठोरमुष्टिना
नदन् प्रहृत्यान्तरधीयतासुरः ॥१५॥

vṛkṇe sva-śūle bahudhāriṇā hareḥ
pratyetya vistīrṇam uro vibhūtimat
pravṛddha-roṣaḥ sa kaṭhora-muṣṭinā
nadan prahṛtyāntaradhīyatāsuraḥ

vṛkṇe—when cut; *sva-śūle*—his trident; *bahudhā*—to many pieces; *ariṇā*—by the Sudarśana *cakra; hareḥ*—of the Supreme Personality of Godhead; *pratyetya*—after advancing toward; *vistīrṇam*—broad; *uraḥ*—chest; *vibhūti-mat*—the abode of the goddess of fortune; *pravṛddha*—having been increased; *roṣaḥ*—anger; *saḥ*—Hiraṇyākṣa; *kaṭhora*—hard; *muṣṭinā*—with his fist; *nadan*—roaring; *prahṛtya*—after striking; *antaradhīyata*—disappeared; *asuraḥ*—the demon.

TRANSLATION

The demon was enraged when his trident was cut to pieces by the discus of the Personality of Godhead. He therefore advanced toward the Lord and, roaring aloud, struck his hard fist against the Lord's broad chest, which bore the mark of Śrīvatsa. Then he went out of sight.

PURPORT

Śrīvatsa is a curl of white hair on the chest of the Lord which is a special sign of His being the Supreme Personality of Godhead. In Vaikuṇṭhaloka or in Goloka Vṛndāvana, the inhabitants are exactly of the same form as the Personality of Godhead, but by this Śrīvatsa mark on the chest of the Lord He is distinguished from all others.

TEXT 16

तेनेत्थमाहतः क्षत्तर्भगवानादिसूकरः ।
नाकम्पत मनाक् क्वापि स्रजा हत इव द्विपः ॥१६॥

tenettham āhataḥ kṣattar
bhagavān ādi-sūkaraḥ
nākampata manāk kvāpi
srajā hata iva dvipaḥ

tena—by Hiraṇyākṣa; *ittham*—thus; *āhataḥ*—struck; *kṣattaḥ*—O Vidura; *bhagavān*—the Supreme Personality of Godhead; *ādi-sūkaraḥ*—the first boar; *na akampata*—did not feel quaking; *manāk*—even slightly; *kva api*—anywhere; *srajā*—by a garland of flowers; *hataḥ*—struck; *iva*—as; *dvipaḥ*—an elephant.

TRANSLATION

Hit in this manner by the demon, O Vidura, the Lord, who had appeared as the first boar, did not feel the least quaking in any part of His body, any more than an elephant would when struck with a wreath of flowers.

PURPORT

As previously explained, the demon was originally a servitor of the Lord in Vaikuṇṭha, but somehow or other he fell as a demon. His fight with the Supreme Lord was meant for his liberation. The Lord enjoyed the striking on His transcendental body, just like a fully grown-up father fighting with his child. Sometimes a father takes pleasure in having a mock fight with his small child, and similarly the Lord felt Hiraṇyākṣa's striking on His body to be like flowers offered for worship. In other words, the Lord desired to fight in order to enjoy His transcendental bliss; therefore He enjoyed the attack.

TEXT 17

अथोरुधासृजन्मायां योगमायेश्वरे हरौ ।
यां विलोक्य प्रजास्त्रस्ता मेनिरेऽस्योपसंयमम् ॥१७॥

athorudhāsṛjan māyāṁ
yoga-māyeśvare harau
yāṁ vilokya prajās trastā
menire 'syopasaṁyamam

atha—then; *urudhā*—in many ways; *asṛjat*—he cast; *māyām*—conjuring tricks; *yoga-māyā-īśvare*—the Lord of *yogamāyā; harau*—at Hari; *yām*—which; *vilokya*—after seeing; *prajāḥ*—the people; *trastāḥ*—fearful; *menire*—thought; *asya*—of this universe; *upasaṁyamam*—the dissolution.

TRANSLATION

The demon, however, employed many conjuring tricks against the Personality of Godhead, who is the Lord of yogamāyā. At the sight of this the people were filled with alarm and thought that the dissolution of the universe was near.

PURPORT

The fighting enjoyment of the Supreme Lord with His devotee, who had been converted into a demon, appeared severe enough to bring about the dissolution of the universe. This is the greatness of the Supreme Personality of Godhead; even the wavering of His little finger appears to be a great and very dangerous movement in the eyes of the inhabitants of the universe.

TEXT 18

प्रववुर्वायवश्चण्डास्तमः पांसवमैरयन् ।
दिग्भ्यो निपेतुर्ग्रावाणः क्षेपणैः प्रहिता इव ॥१८॥

pravavur vāyavaś caṇḍās
tamaḥ pāṁsavam airayan
digbhyo nipetur grāvāṇaḥ
kṣepaṇaiḥ prahitā iva

pravavuḥ—were blowing; *vāyavaḥ*—winds; *caṇḍāḥ*—fierce; *tamaḥ*—darkness; *pāṁsavam*—caused by dust; *airayan*—were spreading; *digbhyaḥ*—from every direction; *nipetuḥ*—came down; *grāvāṇaḥ*—stones; *kṣepaṇaiḥ*—by machine guns; *prahitāḥ*—thrown; *iva*—as if.

TRANSLATION

Fierce winds began to blow from all directions, spreading darkness occasioned by dust and hail storms; stones came in volleys from every corner, as if thrown by machine guns.

TEXT 19

द्यौर्नष्टभगणाभ्रौघैः सविद्युत्स्तनयित्नुभिः ।
वर्षद्भिः पूयकेशासृग्विण्मूत्रास्थीनि चासकृत् ॥१९॥

dyaur naṣṭa-bhagaṇābhraughaiḥ
sa-vidyut-stanayitnubhiḥ
varṣadbhiḥ pūya-keśāsṛg-
viṇ-mūtrāsthīni cāsakṛt

dyauḥ—the sky; *naṣṭa*—having disappeared; *bha-gaṇa*—luminaries; *abhra*—of clouds; *oghaiḥ*—by masses; *sa*—accompanied by; *vidyut*—lightning; *stanayitnubhiḥ*—and thunder; *varṣadbhiḥ*—raining; *pūya*—pus; *keśa*—hair; *asṛk*—blood; *viṭ*—stool; *mūtra*—urine; *asthīni*—bones; *ca*—and; *asakṛt*—again and again.

TRANSLATION

The luminaries in outer space disappeared due to the sky's being overcast with masses of clouds, which were accompanied by lightning and thunder. The sky rained pus, hair, blood, stool, urine and bones.

TEXT 20

गिरयः प्रत्यदृश्यन्त नानायुधमुचोऽनघ ।
दिग्वाससो यातुधान्यः शूलिन्यो मुक्तमूर्धजाः ॥२०॥

girayaḥ pratyadṛśyanta
nānāyudha-muco 'nagha
dig-vāsaso yātudhānyaḥ
śūlinyo mukta-mūrdhajāḥ

girayaḥ—mountains; *pratyadṛśyanta*—appeared; *nānā*—various; *āyudha*—weapons; *mucaḥ*—discharging; *anagha*—O sinless Vidura; *dik-vāsasaḥ*—naked; *yātudhānyaḥ*—demonesses; *śūlinyaḥ*—armed with tridents; *mukta*—hanging loose; *mūrdhajāḥ*—hair.

TRANSLATION

O sinless Vidura, mountains discharged weapons of various kinds, and naked demonesses armed with tridents appeared with their hair hanging loose.

TEXT 21

बहुभिर्यक्षरक्षोभिः पत्त्यश्वरथकुञ्जरैः ।
आततायिभिरुत्सृष्टा हिंस्रा वाचोऽतिवैशसाः ॥२१॥

bahubhir yakṣa-rakṣobhiḥ
patty-aśva-ratha-kuñjaraiḥ
ātatāyibhir utsṛṣṭā
hiṁsrā vāco 'tivaiśasāḥ

bahubhiḥ—by many; *yakṣa-rakṣobhiḥ*—Yakṣas and Rākṣasas; *patti*—marching on foot; *aśva*—on horses; *ratha*—on chariots; *kuñjaraiḥ*—or on elephants; *ātatāyibhiḥ*—ruffians; *utsṛṣṭāḥ*—were uttered; *hiṁsrāḥ*—cruel; *vācaḥ*—words; *ati-vaiśasāḥ*—murderous.

TRANSLATION

Cruel and savage slogans were uttered by hosts of ruffian Yakṣas and Rākṣasas, who all either marched on foot or rode on horses, elephants or chariots.

TEXT 22

प्रादुष्कृतानां मायानामासुरीणां विनाशयत् ।
सुदर्शनास्त्रं भगवान् प्रायुङ्क्त दयितं त्रिपात् ॥२२॥

prāduṣkṛtānāṁ māyānām
āsurīṇāṁ vināśayat
sudarśanāstraṁ bhagavān
prāyuṅkta dayitaṁ tri-pāt

prāduṣkṛtānām—displayed; *māyānām*—the magical forces; *āsurīṇām*—displayed by the demon; *vināśayat*—desiring to destroy; *sudarśana-astram*—the Sudarśana weapon; *bhagavān*—the Supreme Personality of Godhead; *prāyuṅkta*—threw; *dayitam*—beloved; *tri-pāt*—the enjoyer of all sacrifices.

TRANSLATION

The Lord, the personal enjoyer of all sacrifices, now discharged His beloved Sudarśana, which was capable of dispersing the magical forces displayed by the demon.

PURPORT

Even famous *yogīs* and demons can sometimes enact very magical feats by their mystic power, but in the presence of the Sudarśana *cakra*, when it is let loose by the Lord, all such magical jugglery is dispersed. The instance of the quarrel between Durvāsā Muni and Mahārāja Ambarīṣa is a practical example in this matter. Durvāsā Muni wanted to display many magical wonders, but when the Sudarśana *cakra* appeared, Durvāsā himself was afraid and fled to various planets for his personal protection. The Lord is described here as *tri-pāt*, which means that He is the enjoyer of three kinds of sacrifices. In *Bhagavad-gītā* the Lord confirms that He is the beneficiary and enjoyer of all sacrifices, penances and austerities. The Lord is the enjoyer of three kinds of *yajña*. As further described in *Bhagavad-gītā*, there are sacrifices of goods, sacrifices of meditation and sacrifices of philosophical speculation. Those on the paths of *jñāna*, *yoga* and *karma* all have to come in the end to the Supreme Lord because *vāsudevaḥ sarvam iti*—the Supreme Lord is the ultimate enjoyer of everything. That is the perfection of all sacrifice.

TEXT 23

तदा दितेः समभवत्सहसा हृदि वेपथुः ।
स्मरन्त्या भर्तुरादेशं स्तनाच्चासृक् प्रसुस्रुवे ॥२३॥

tadā diteḥ samabhavat
sahasā hṛdi vepathuḥ
smarantyā bhartur ādeśaṁ
stanāc cāsṛk prasusruve

tadā—at that moment; *diteḥ*—of Diti; *samabhavat*—occurred; *sahasā*—suddenly; *hṛdi*—in the heart; *vepathuḥ*—a shudder; *smarantyāḥ*—recalling; *bhartuḥ*—of her husband, Kaśyapa; *ādeśam*—the words; *stanāt*—from her breast; *ca*—and; *asṛk*—blood; *prasusruve*—flowed.

TRANSLATION

At that very moment, a shudder suddenly ran through the heart of Diti, the mother of Hiraṇyākṣa. She recalled the words of her husband, Kaśyapa, and blood flowed from her breasts.

PURPORT

At Hiraṇyākṣa's last moment, his mother, Diti, remembered what her husband had said. Although her sons would be demons, they would have the advantage of being killed by the Personality of Godhead Himself. She remembered this incident by the grace of the Lord, and her breasts flowed blood instead of milk. In many instances we find that when a mother is moved by affection for her sons, milk flows from her breasts. In the case of the demon's mother, the blood could not transform into milk, but it flowed down her breasts as it was. Blood transforms into milk. To drink milk is auspicious, but to drink blood is inauspicious, although they are one and the same thing. This formula is applicable in the case of cow's milk also.

TEXT 24

विनष्टासु स्वमायासु भूयश्चाव्रज्य केशवम् ।
रुषोपगूहमानोऽमुं ददृशेऽवस्थितं बहिः ॥२४॥

vinaṣṭāsu sva-māyāsu
bhūyaś cāvrajya keśavam
ruṣopagūhamāno 'muṁ
dadṛśe 'vasthitaṁ bahiḥ

vinaṣṭāsu—when dispelled; *sva-māyāsu*—his magic forces; *bhūyaḥ*—again; *ca*—and; *āvrajya*—after coming into the presence; *keśavam*—the Supreme Personality of Godhead; *ruṣā*—full of rage; *upagūhamānaḥ*—embracing; *amum*—the Lord; *dadṛśe*—saw; *avasthitam*—standing; *bahiḥ*—outside.

TRANSLATION

When the demon saw his magic forces dispelled, he once again came into the presence of the Personality of Godhead, Keśava, and, full of rage, tried to embrace Him within his arms to crush Him. But to his great amazement he found the Lord standing outside the circle of his arms.

PURPORT

In this verse the Lord is addressed as Keśava because He killed the demon Keśī in the beginning of creation. Keśava is also a name of Kṛṣṇa.

Kṛṣṇa is the origin of all incarnations, and it is confirmed in *Brahma-saṁhitā* that Govinda, the Supreme Personality of Godhead, the cause of all causes, exists simultaneously in His different incarnations and expansions. The demon's attempt to measure the Supreme Personality of Godhead is significant. The demon wanted to embrace Him with his arms, thinking that with his limited arms he could capture the Absolute by material power. He did not know that God is the greatest of the great and the smallest of the small. No one can capture the Supreme Lord or bring Him under his control. But the demoniac person always attempts to measure the length and breadth of the Supreme Lord. By His inconceivable potency the Lord can become the universal form, as explained in *Bhagavad-gītā*, and at the same time He can remain within the box of His devotees as their worshipable Deity. There are many devotees who keep a statue of the Lord in a small box and carry it with them everywhere; every morning they worship the Lord in the box. The Supreme Lord, Keśava, or the Personality of Godhead, Kṛṣṇa, is not bound by any measurement of our calculation. He can remain with His devotee in any suitable form, yet He is unapproachable by any amount of demoniac activities.

TEXT 25

तं मुष्टिभिर्विनिघ्नन्तं वज्रसारैरधोक्षजः ।
करेण कर्णमूलेऽहन् यथा त्वाष्ट्रं मरुत्पतिः ॥२५॥

taṁ muṣṭibhir vinighnantaṁ
vajra-sārair adhokṣajaḥ
kareṇa karṇa-mūle 'han
yathā tvāṣṭraṁ marut-patiḥ

tam—Hiraṇyākṣa; *muṣṭibhiḥ*—with his fists; *vinighnantam*—striking; *vajra-sāraiḥ*—as hard as a thunderbolt; *adhokṣajaḥ*—Lord Adhokṣaja; *kareṇa*—with the hand; *karṇa-mūle*—at the root of the ear; *ahan*—struck; *yathā*—as; *tvāṣṭram*—the demon Vṛtra (son of Tvaṣṭā); *marut-patiḥ*—Indra (lord of the Maruts).

TRANSLATION

The demon now began to strike the Lord with his hard fists, but Lord Adhokṣaja slapped him in the root of the ear, even as Indra, the lord of the Maruts, hit the demon Vṛtra.

PURPORT

The Lord is explained here to be *adhokṣaja*, beyond the reach of all material calculation. *Akṣaja* means "the measurement of our senses," and *adhokṣaja* means "that which is beyond the measurement of our senses."

TEXT 26

स आहतो विश्वजिता ह्यवज्ञया
परिभ्रमद्गात्र उदस्तलोचनः ।
विशीर्णबाह्वङ्घ्रिशिरोरुहोऽपतद्
यथा नगेन्द्रो लुलितो नभस्वता ॥२६॥

sa āhato viśva-jitā hy avajñayā
paribhramad-gātra udasta-locanaḥ
viśīrṇa-bāhv-aṅghri-śiroruho 'patad
yathā nagendro lulito nabhasvatā

saḥ—he; *āhataḥ*—having been struck; *viśva-jitā*—by the Supreme Personality of Godhead; *hi*—though; *avajñayā*—indifferently; *paribhramat*—wheeling; *gātraḥ*—body; *udasta*—bulged out; *locanaḥ*—eyes; *viśīrṇa*—broken; *bāhu*—arms; *aṅghri*—legs; *śiraḥ-ruhaḥ*—hair; *apatat*—fell down; *yathā*—like; *naga-indraḥ*—a gigantic tree; *lulitaḥ*—uprooted; *nabhasvatā*—by the wind.

TRANSLATION

Though struck indifferently by the Lord, the conqueror of all, the demon's body began to wheel. His eyeballs bulged out of their sockets. His arms and legs broken and the hair on his head scattered, he fell down dead, like a gigantic tree uprooted by the wind.

PURPORT

It does not take even a moment for the Lord to kill any powerful demon, including Hiraṇyākṣa. The Lord could have killed him long before, but He allowed the demon to display the full extent of his magical feats. One may know that by magical feats, by scientific advancement of knowledge or by material power one cannot become the equal of the

Supreme Personality of Godhead. His one signal is sufficient to destroy all our attempts. His inconceivable power, as displayed here, is so strong that the demon, despite all his demoniac maneuvers, was killed by the Lord when the Lord desired, simply by one slap.

TEXT 27

क्षितौ शयानं तमकुण्ठवर्चसं
करालदंष्ट्रं परिदष्टदच्छदम् ।
अजादयो वीक्ष्य शशंसुरागता
अहो इमां को नु लभेत संस्थितिम् ॥२७॥

kṣitau śayānaṁ tam akuṇṭha-varcasaṁ
karāla-daṁṣṭraṁ paridaṣṭa-dacchadam
ajādayo vīkṣya śaśaṁsur āgatā
aho imaṁ ko nu labheta saṁsthitim

kṣitau—on the ground; *śayānam*—lying; *tam*—Hiraṇyākṣa; *akuṇṭha*—unfaded; *varcasam*—glow; *karāla*—fearful; *daṁṣṭram*—teeth; *paridaṣṭa*—bitten; *dat-chadam*—lip; *aja-ādayaḥ*—Brahmā and others; *vīkṣya*—having seen; *śaśaṁsuḥ*—admiringly said; *āgatāḥ*—arrived; *aho*—oh; *imam*—this; *kaḥ*—who; *nu*—indeed; *labheta*—could meet; *saṁsthitim*—death.

TRANSLATION

Aja [Brahmā] and others arrived on the spot to see the fearfully tusked demon lying on the ground, biting his lip. The glow of his face was yet unfaded, and Brahmā admiringly said: Oh, who could meet such blessed death?

PURPORT

Although the demon was dead, his bodily luster was unfaded. This is very peculiar because when a man or animal is dead, the body immediately becomes pale, the luster gradually fades, and decomposition takes place. But here, although Hiraṇyākṣa lay dead, his bodily luster was unfaded because the Lord, the Supreme Spirit, was touching his body. One's bodily luster remains fresh only as long as the spirit soul is present. Although the demon's soul had departed his body, the Supreme Spirit touched the body, and therefore his bodily luster did not fade. The individual soul is different from the Supreme Personality of Godhead. One who sees the Supreme Personality of Godhead when he quits his body is certainly very fortunate, and therefore personalities like Brahmā and the other demigods eulogized the death of the demon.

TEXT 28

यं योगिनो योगसमाधिना रहो
ध्यायन्ति लिङ्गादसतो मुमुक्षया ।
तस्यैष दैत्यऋषभः पदाहतो
मुखं प्रपश्यंस्तनुमुत्ससर्ज ह ॥२८॥

yaṁ yogino yoga-samādhinā raho
dhyāyanti liṅgād asato mumukṣayā
tasyaiṣa daitya-ṛṣabhaḥ padāhato
mukhaṁ prapaśyaṁs tanum utsasarja ha

yam—whom; *yoginaḥ*—the *yogīs; yoga-samādhinā*—in mystic trance; *rahaḥ*—in seclusion; *dhyāyanti*—meditate upon; *liṅgāt*—from the body; *asataḥ*—unreal; *mumukṣayā*—seeking freedom; *tasya*—of Him; *eṣaḥ*—this; *daitya*—son of Diti; *ṛṣabhaḥ*—the crest jewel; *padā*—by a foot; *āhataḥ*—struck; *mukham*—countenance; *prapaśyan*—while gazing on; *tanum*—the body; *utsasarja*—he cast off; *ha*—indeed.

TRANSLATION

Brahmā continued: He was struck by a forefoot of the Lord, whom yogīs, seeking freedom from their unreal material bodies, meditate upon in seclusion in mystic trance. While gazing on His countenance, this crest jewel of Diti's sons has cast off his mortal coil.

PURPORT

The process of *yoga* is very clearly described in this verse of *Śrīmad-Bhāgavatam.* It is said here that the ultimate end of the *yogīs* and mystics who perform meditation is to get rid of this material body. Therefore they meditate in secluded places to attain yogic trance. *Yoga* has to be performed in a secluded place, not in public or in a demonstration on stage, as nowadays practiced by many so-called *yogīs*. Real *yoga* aims at ridding one of the material body. *Yoga* practice is not intended to keep the body fit and young. Such advertisements of so-called *yoga* are not approved by any standard method. Particularly mentioned in this verse is the word *yam*, or "unto whom," indicating that meditation should be targeted on the Personality of Godhead. Even if one concentrates his mind on the boar form of the Lord, that is also *yoga*. As confirmed in *Bhagavad-gītā*, one who concentrates his mind constantly in meditation upon the Personality of Godhead in one of His many varieties of forms is the first-class *yogī*, and he can very easily attain trance simply by meditating upon the form of the Lord. If one is able to continue such meditation on the Lord's form at the time of one's death, one is liberated from this mortal body and is transferred to the kingdom of God. This opportunity was given to the demon by the Lord, and therefore Brahmā and other demigods were astonished. In other words, the perfection of *yoga* practice can be attained by a demon also if he is simply kicked by the Lord.

TEXT 29

एतौ तौ पार्षदावस्य शापाद्यातावसद्गतिम् ।
पुनः कतिपयैः स्थानं प्रपत्स्येते ह जन्मभिः ॥२९॥

etau tau pārṣadāv asya
śāpād yātāv asad-gatim
punaḥ katipayaiḥ sthānaṁ
prapatsyete ha janmabhiḥ

etau—these two; *tau*—both; *pārṣadau*—personal assistants; *asya*—of the Personality of Godhead; *śāpāt*—because of being cursed; *yātau*—have gone; *asat-gatim*—to take birth in a demoniac family; *punaḥ*—again; *katipayaiḥ*—a few; *sthānam*—own place; *prapatsyete*—will get back; *ha*—indeed; *janmabhiḥ*—after births.

TRANSLATION

These two personal assistants of the Supreme Lord, having been cursed, have been destined to take birth in demoniac families. After a few such births, they will return to their own positions.

TEXT 30

देवा ऊचुः
नमो नमस्तेऽखिलयज्ञतन्तवे
स्थितौ गृहीतामलसत्त्वमूर्तये ।
दिष्ट्या हतोऽयं जगतामरुन्तुद-
स्त्वत्पादभक्त्या वयमीश निर्वृताः ॥३०॥

devā ūcuḥ
namo namas te 'khila-yajña-tantave
sthitau gṛhītāmala-sattva-mūrtaye
diṣṭyā hato 'yaṁ jagatām aruntudas
tvat-pāda-bhaktyā vayam īśa nirvṛtāḥ

devāḥ—the demigods; *ūcuḥ*—said; *namaḥ*—obeisances; *namaḥ*—obeisances; *te*—unto You; *akhila-yajña-tantave*—the enjoyer of all sacrifices; *sthitau*—for the purpose of maintaining; *gṛhīta*—assumed; *amala*—pure; *sattva*—goodness; *mūrtaye*—form; *diṣṭyā*—fortunately; *hataḥ*—slain; *ayam*—this; *jagatām*—to the worlds; *aruntudaḥ*—causing torment; *tvat-pāda*—to Your feet; *bhaktyā*—with devotion; *vayam*—we; *īśa*—O Lord; *nirvṛtāḥ*—have attained happiness.

TRANSLATION

The demigods addressed the Lord: All obeisances unto You! You are the enjoyer of all sacrifices, and You have assumed the form of a boar, in pure goodness, for the purpose of maintaining the world. Fortunately for us, this demon, who was a torment to the worlds, has been slain by You, and we too, O Lord, are now at ease, in devotion to Your lotus feet.

PURPORT

The material world consists of three modes—goodness, passion and ignorance—but the spiritual world is pure goodness. It is said here that the form of the Lord is pure goodness, which means that it is not material. In the material world there is no pure goodness. In the *Bhāgavatam* the stage of pure goodness is called *sattvaṁ viśuddham. Viśuddham* means "pure." In pure goodness there is no contamination by the two inferior qualities, namely passion and ignorance. The form of the boar, therefore, in which the Lord appeared, is nothing of the material world. There are many other forms of the Lord, but none of them belong to the material qualities. Such forms are nondifferent from the Viṣṇu form, and Viṣṇu is the enjoyer of all sacrifices.

The sacrifices which are recommended in the *Vedas* are meant to please the Supreme Personality of Godhead. In ignorance only, people try to satisfy many other agents, but the real purpose of life is to satisfy the Supreme Lord, Viṣṇu. All sacrifices are meant to please the Supreme Lord. The living entities who know this perfectly well are called demigods, godly or almost God. Since the living entity is part and parcel of the Supreme Lord, it is his duty to serve the Lord and please Him. The demigods are all attached to the Personality of Godhead, and for their pleasure the demon, who was a source of trouble to the world, was killed. Purified life is meant to please the Lord, and all sacrifices performed in purified life are called Kṛṣṇa consciousness. This Kṛṣṇa consciousness is developed by devotional service, as clearly mentioned here.

TEXT 31

मैत्रेय उवाच

एवं हिरण्याक्षमसह्यविक्रमं
स सादयित्वा हरिरादिसूकरः ।
जगाम लोकं स्वमखण्डितोत्सवं
समीडितः पुष्करविष्टरादिभिः ॥३१॥

maitreya uvāca
evaṁ hiraṇyākṣam asahya-vikramaṁ
sa sādayitvā harir ādi-sūkaraḥ

jagāma lokaṁ svam akhaṇḍitotsavaṁ
samīḍitaḥ puṣkara-viṣṭarādibhiḥ

maitreyaḥ uvāca—Śrī Maitreya said; *evam*—thus; *hiraṇyākṣam*—Hiraṇyākṣa; *asahya-vikramam*—very powerful; *saḥ*—the Lord; *sādayitvā*—after killing; *hariḥ*—the Supreme Personality of Godhead; *ādi-sūkaraḥ*—the origin of the boar species; *jagāma*—returned; *lokam*—to His abode; *svam*—own; *akhaṇḍita*—uninterrupted; *utsavam*—festival; *samīḍitaḥ*—being praised; *puṣkara-viṣṭara*—lotus seat (by Lord Brahmā, whose seat is a lotus); *ādibhiḥ*—and the others.

TRANSLATION

Śrī Maitreya continued: After thus killing the most formidable demon Hiraṇyākṣa, the Supreme Lord Hari, the origin of the boar species, returned to His own abode, where there is always an uninterrupted festival. The Lord was praised by all the demigods, headed by Brahmā.

PURPORT

The Lord is spoken of herewith as the origin of the boar species. As stated in the *Vedānta-sūtra* (1.1.2), the Absolute Truth is the origin of everything. Therefore it is to be understood that all 8,400,000 species of bodily forms originate from the Lord, who is always *ādi*, or the beginning. In *Bhagavad-gītā* Arjuna addresses the Lord as *ādyam*, or the original. Similarly, in the *Brahma-saṁhitā* the Lord is addressed as *ādi-puruṣam*, the original person. Indeed, in *Bhagavad-gītā* (10.8) the Lord Himself declares, *mattaḥ sarvaṁ pravartate:* "From Me everything proceeds."

In this situation the Lord assumed the shape of a boar to kill the demon Hiraṇyākṣa and pick up the earth from the Garbha Ocean. Thus He became *ādi-sūkara*, the original boar. In the material world a boar or pig is considered most abominable, but the *ādi-sūkara*, the Supreme Personality of Godhead, was not treated as an ordinary boar. Even Lord Brahmā and the other demigods praised the Lord's form as a boar.

This verse confirms the statement in *Bhagavad-gītā* that the Lord appears as He is from His transcendental abode for the sake of killing the miscreants and saving the devotees. By killing the demon Hiraṇyākṣa He fulfilled His promise to kill the demons and always protect the demigods headed by Brahmā. The statement that the Lord returned to His own abode indicates that He has His own particular transcendental residence. Since He is full of all energies, He is all-pervasive in spite of His residing in Goloka Vṛndāvana, just as the sun, although situated in a particular place within the universe, is present by its sunshine throughout the universe.

Although the Lord has His particular abode in which to reside, He is all-pervasive. The impersonalists accept one aspect of the Lord's features, the all-pervasive aspect, but they cannot understand His localized situation in His transcendental abode, where He always engages in fully transcendental pastimes. Especially mentioned in this verse is the word *akhaṇḍitotsavam. Utsava* means "pleasure." Whenever some function takes place to express happiness, it is called *utsava. Utsava,* the expression of complete happiness, is always present in the Vaikuṇṭhalokas, the abode of the Lord, who is worshipable even by demigods like Brahmā, to say nothing of other, less important entities such as human beings.

The Lord descends from His abode to this world, and therefore He is called *avatāra,* which means "one who descends." Sometimes *avatāra* is understood to refer to an incarnation who assumes a material form of flesh and bone, but actually *avatāra* refers to one who descends from higher regions. The Lord's abode is situated far above this material sky, and He descends from that higher position; thus He is called *avatāra.*

TEXT 32

मया यथानूक्तमवादि ते हरेः
कृतावतारस्य सुमित्र चेष्टितम् ।
यथा हिरण्याक्ष उदारविक्रमो
महामृधे क्रीडनवन्निराकृतः ॥३२॥

mayā yathānūktam avādi te hareḥ
kṛtāvatārasya sumitra ceṣṭitam
yathā hiraṇyākṣa udāra-vikramo
mahā-mṛdhe krīḍanavan nirākṛtaḥ

mayā—by me; *yathā*—as; *anūktam*—told; *avādi*—was explained; *te*—to you; *hareḥ*—of the Supreme Personality of Godhead; *kṛta-avatārasya*—who assumed the incarnation; *sumitra*—O dear Vidura; *ceṣṭitam*—the activities; *yathā*—as; *hiraṇyākṣaḥ*—Hiraṇyākṣa; *udāra*—very extensive; *vikramaḥ*—prowess; *mahā-mṛdhe*—in a great fight; *krīḍana-vat*—like a plaything; *nirākṛtaḥ*—was killed.

TRANSLATION

Maitreya continued: My dear Vidura, I have explained to you the Personality of Godhead's coming down as the first boar incarnation and killing in a great fight a demon of unprecedented prowess as if he were just a plaything. This has been narrated by me as I heard it from my predecessor spiritual master.

PURPORT

Here the sage Maitreya admits that he explained the incident of the killing of Hiraṇyākṣa by the Supreme Personality of Godhead as a straight narration; he did not manufacture anything or add interpretation, but explained whatever he had heard from his spiritual master. Thus he accepted as bona fide the system of *paramparā*, or receiving the transcendental message in disciplic succession. Unless received by this bona fide process of hearing from a spiritual master, the statement of an *ācārya* or preceptor cannot be valid.

It is also stated here that although the demon Hiraṇyākṣa was unlimited in prowess, he was just like a doll for the Lord. A child breaks so many dolls without real endeavor. Similarly, although a demon may be very powerful and extraordinary in the eyes of an ordinary man in the material world, to the Lord, killing such a demon is no difficulty. He can kill millions of demons as simply as a child plays with dolls and breaks them.

TEXT 33

सूत उवाच

इति कौषारवाख्यातामाश्रुत्य भगवत्कथाम् ।
क्षत्तानन्दं परं लेभे महाभागवतो द्विज ॥३३॥

sūta uvāca
iti kauṣāravākhyātām
āśrutya bhagavat-kathām
kṣattānandaṁ paraṁ lebhe
mahā-bhāgavato dvija

sūtaḥ—Sūta Gosvāmī; *uvāca*—said; *iti*—thus; *kauṣārava*—from Maitreya (son of Kuṣāru); *ākhyātām*—told; *āśrutya*—having heard; *bhagavat-kathām*—the narration about the Lord; *kṣattā*—Vidura; *ānandam*—bliss; *param*—transcendental; *lebhe*—achieved; *mahā-bhāgavataḥ*—the great devotee; *dvija*—O *brāhmaṇa* (Śaunaka).

TRANSLATION

Śrī Sūta Gosvāmī continued: My dear brāhmaṇa, Kṣattā [Vidura] the great devotee of the Lord achieved transcendental bliss by hearing the narration of the pastimes of the Supreme Personality of Godhead from the authoritative source of the sage Kauṣārava [Maitreya], and he was very pleased.

PURPORT

If anyone wants to derive transcendental pleasure by hearing the pastimes of the Lord, he must hear from the authoritative source, as explained here. Maitreya heard the narration from his bona fide spiritual master, and Vidura also heard from Maitreya. One becomes an authority simply by presenting whatever he has heard from his spiritual master, and one who does not accept a bona fide spiritual master cannot be an authority. This is clearly explained here. If one wants to have transcendental pleasure, he must find a person with authority. It is also stated in the *Bhāgavatam* that simply by hearing from an authoritative source, with the ear and the heart, one can relish the pastimes of the Lord, otherwise it is not possible. Sanātana Gosvāmī, therefore, has especially warned that one should not hear anything about the personality of the Lord from the lips of a nondevotee. Nondevotees are considered to be like serpents; as milk is poisoned by a serpent's touch, so, although the narration of the pastimes of the Lord is as pure as milk, when administered by serpentlike nondevotees it becomes poisonous. Not only does it have no effect in transcendental pleasure, but it is dangerous also. Lord Caitanya Mahāprabhu has warned that no description of the pastimes of the Lord should be heard from the Māyāvāda, or impersonalist, school. He has clearly said, *māyāvādi-bhāṣya śunile haya sarva nāśa:* if anyone hears the Māyāvādīs' interpretation of the pastimes of the Lord, or their interpretation of *Bhagavad-gītā, Śrīmad-Bhāgavatam* or any other Vedic literature, then he is doomed. Once one is associated with impersonalists, he can never understand the personal feature of the Lord and His transcendental pastimes.

Sūta Gosvāmī was speaking to the sages headed by Śaunaka, and therefore he addressed them in this verse as *dvija,* twice-born. The sages assembled in Naimiṣāraṇya hearing *Śrīmad-Bhāgavatam* from Sūta Gosvāmī were all *brāhmaṇas,* but to acquire the qualifications of a *brāhmaṇa* is not everything. Merely to be twice-born is not perfection. Perfection is attained when one hears the pastimes and activities of the Lord from a bona fide source.

TEXT 34

अन्येषां पुण्यश्लोकानामुद्दामयशसां सताम् ।
उपश्रुत्य भवेन्मोदः श्रीवत्साङ्कस्य किं पुनः ॥३४॥

anyeṣāṁ puṇya-ślokānām
uddāma-yaśasāṁ satām
upaśrutya bhaven modaḥ
śrīvatsāṅkasya kiṁ punaḥ

anyeṣām—of others; *puṇya-ślokānām*—of pious reputation; *uddāma-yaśasām*—whose fame is spread everywhere; *satām*—of the devotees; *upaśrutya*—by hearing; *bhavet*—may arise; *modaḥ*—pleasure; *śrīvatsa-aṅkasya*—of the Lord, who bears the mark Śrīvatsa; *kim punaḥ*—what to speak of.

TRANSLATION

What to speak of hearing the pastimes of the Lord, whose chest is marked with Śrivatsa, people may take transcendental pleasure

even in hearing of the works and deeds of the devotees, whose fame is immortal.

PURPORT

Bhāgavatam literally means the pastimes of the Lord and the Lord's devotees. For example, there are pastimes of Lord Kṛṣṇa and narrations of devotees like Prahlāda, Dhruva and Mahārāja Ambarīṣa. Both pastimes pertain to the Supreme Personality of Godhead because the devotees' pastimes are in relation with Him. The *Mahābhārata*, for example, the history of the Pāṇḍavas and their activities, is sacred because the Pāṇḍavas had a direct relationship with the Supreme Personality of Godhead.

TEXT 35

यो गजेन्द्रं झषग्रस्तं ध्यायन्तं चरणाम्बुजम् ।
क्रोशन्तीनां करेणूनां कृच्छ्रतोऽमोचयद् द्रुतम् ॥३५॥

yo gajendraṁ jhaṣa-grastaṁ
dhyāyantaṁ caraṇāmbujam
krośantīnāṁ kareṇūnāṁ
kṛcchrato 'mocayad drutam

yaḥ—He who; *gaja-indram*—the king of elephants; *jhaṣa*—an alligator; *grastam*—attacked by; *dhyāyantam*—meditating upon; *caraṇa*—feet; *ambujam*—lotus; *krośantīnām*—while crying; *kareṇūnām*—the female elephants; *kṛcchrataḥ*—from danger; *amocayat*—delivered; *drutam*—quickly.

TRANSLATION

The Personality of Godhead delivered the king of the elephants, who was attacked by an alligator and who meditated upon the lotus feet of the Lord. At that time the female elephants who accompanied him were crying, and the Lord saved them from the impending danger.

PURPORT

The example of the elephant in danger who was saved by the Supreme Lord is especially cited here because even if one is an animal he can approach the Personality of Godhead in devotional service, whereas even a demigod cannot approach the Supreme Person unless he is a devotee.

TEXT 36

तं सुखाराध्यमृजुभिरनन्यशरणैर्नृभिः ।
कृतज्ञः को न सेवेत दुराराध्यमसाधुभिः ॥३६॥

taṁ sukhārādhyam ṛjubhir
ananya-śaraṇair nṛbhiḥ
kṛtajñaḥ ko na seveta
durārādhyam asādhubhiḥ

tam—unto Him; *sukha*—easily; *ārādhyam*—worshiped; *ṛjubhiḥ*—by the unpretentious; *ananya*—no other; *śaraṇaiḥ*—who take shelter; *nṛbhiḥ*—by men; *kṛta-jñaḥ*—grateful soul; *kaḥ*—what; *na*—not; *seveta*—would render service; *durārādhyam*—impossible to be worshiped; *asādhubhiḥ*—by the nondevotees.

TRANSLATION

What grateful soul is there who would not render his loving service to such a great master as the Personality of Godhead? The Lord can be easily pleased by spotless devotees who resort exclusively to Him for protection, though the unrighteous man finds it difficult to propitiate Him.

PURPORT

Every living entity, especially persons in the human race, must feel grateful for the benedictions offered by the grace of the Supreme Lord. Anyone, therefore, with a simple heart of gratefulness must be Kṛṣṇa conscious and offer devotional service to the Lord. Those who are actually thieves and rogues do not recognize or acknowledge the benedictions offered to them by the Supreme Lord, and they cannot render Him devotional service. Ungrateful persons are those who do not understand how much benefit they are deriving by the arrangement of the Lord. They enjoy the sunshine and moonshine, and they get water free of charge, yet they do not feel grateful, but simply go on enjoying these gifts of the Lord. Therefore, they must be called thieves and rogues.

TEXT 37

यो वै हिरण्याक्षवधं महाद्भुतं
विक्रीडितं कारणसूकरात्मनः ।
शृणोति गायत्यनुमोदतेऽञ्जसा
विमुच्यते ब्रह्मवधादपि द्विजाः ॥३७॥

yo vai hiraṇyākṣa-vadhaṁ mahādbhutaṁ
vikrīḍitaṁ kāraṇa-sūkarātmanaḥ
śṛṇoti gāyaty anumodate 'ñjasā
vimucyate brahma-vadhād api dvijāḥ

yaḥ—he who; *vai*—indeed; *hiraṇyākṣa-vadham*—of the killing of Hiraṇyākṣa; *mahā-adbhutam*—most wonderful; *vikrīḍitam*—pastime; *kāraṇa*—for reasons like raising the earth from the ocean; *sūkara*—appearing in the form of a boar; *ātmanaḥ*—of the Supreme Personality of Godhead; *śṛṇoti*—hears; *gāyati*—chants; *anumodate*—takes pleasure; *añjasā*—at once; *vimucyate*—becomes freed; *brahma-vadhāt*—from the sin of killing a *brāhmaṇa; api*—even; *dvijāḥ*—O *brāhmaṇas.*

TRANSLATION

O brāhmaṇas, anyone who hears, chants, or takes pleasure in the wonderful narration of the killing of the Hiraṇyākṣa demon by the Lord, who appeared as the first boar in order to deliver the world, is at once relieved of the results of sinful activities, even the killing of a brāhmaṇa.

PURPORT

Since the Personality of Godhead is in the absolute position, there is no difference between His pastimes and His personality. Anyone who hears about the pastimes of the Lord associates with the Lord directly, and one who associates directly with the Lord is certainly freed from all sinful activities, even to the extent of the killing of a *brāhmaṇa*, which is considered the most sinful activity in the material world. One should be very eager to hear about the activities of the Lord from the bona fide source, the pure devotee. If one simply gives aural reception to the narration and accepts the glories of the Lord, then he is qualified. The impersonalist philosophers cannot understand the activities of the Lord. They think that all His activities are *māyā;* therefore they are called Māyāvādīs. Since everything to them is *māyā,* these narrations are not for them. Some impersonalists are reluctant to hear *Śrīmad-Bhāgavatam,* although many of them are now taking an interest in it just for monetary gain. Actually, however, they have no faith. On the contrary, they describe it in their own way. We should not hear, therefore, from the Māyāvādīs. We have to hear from Sūta Gosvāmī or Maitreya, who actually present the narrations as they are, and only then can we relish the pastimes of the Lord; otherwise the effects on the neophyte audience will be poisonous.

TEXT 38

एतन्महापुण्यमलं पवित्रं
धन्यं यशस्यं पदमायुराशिषाम् ।
प्राणेन्द्रियाणां युधि शौर्यवर्धनं
नारायणोऽन्ते गतिरङ्ग शृण्वताम् ॥३८॥

etan mahā-puṇyam alaṁ pavitraṁ
dhanyaṁ yaśasyaṁ padam āyur-āśiṣām
prāṇendriyāṇāṁ yudhi śaurya-vardhanaṁ
nārāyaṇo 'nte gatir aṅga śṛṇvatām

etat—this narrative; *mahā-puṇyam*—conferring great merit; *alam*—very; *pavitram*—sacred; *dhanyam*—conferring wealth; *yaśasyam*—bearing fame; *padam*—the receptacle; *āyuḥ*—of longevity; *āśiṣām*—of the objects of one's desire; *prāṇa*—of the vital organs; *indriyāṇām*—of the organs of action; *yudhi*—on the field of battle; *śaurya*—the strength; *vardhanam*—increasing; *nārāyaṇaḥ*—Lord Nārāyaṇa; *ante*—at the end of life; *gatiḥ*—shelter; *aṅga*—O dear Śaunaka; *śṛṇvatām*—of those who listen.

TRANSLATION

This most sacred narrative confers extraordinary merit, wealth, fame, longevity, and all the objects of one's desire. On the field of battle it promotes the strength of one's vital organs and organs of action. One who listens to it at the last moment of his life is transferred to the supreme abode of the Lord, O dear Śaunaka.

PURPORT

Devotees are generally attracted by the narratives of the pastimes of the Lord, and even though they do not prosecute austerities or meditation, this very process of *hearing* attentively about the pastimes of the Lord will endow them with innumerable benefits, such as wealth, fame, longevity and other desirable aims of life. If one continues to hear *Śrīmad-Bhāgavatam*, which is full of narratives of the pastimes of the Lord, at the end of this life, one is sure to be transferred to the eternal, transcendental abode of the Lord. Thus hearers are benefited both ultimately and for as long as they are in the material world. That is the supreme, sublime result of engaging in devotional service. The beginning of devotional service is to spare some time and listen to *Śrīmad-Bhāgavatam* from the right source. Lord Caitanya Mahāprabhu also recommended five items of devotional service, namely to serve the devotees of the Lord, to chant Hare Kṛṣṇa, to hear *Śrīmad-Bhāgavatam*, to worship the Deity of the Lord and to live in a place of pilgrimage. Just performing these five activities can deliver one from the miserable condition of material life.

Thus end the Bhaktivedanta purports of the Third Canto, Nineteenth Chapter, of the Śrīmad-Bhāgavatam, *entitled "The Killing of the Demon Hiraṇyākṣa."*

CHAPTER TWENTY

Conversation Between Maitreya and Vidura

TEXT 1

शौनक उवाच

महीं प्रतिष्ठामध्यस्य सौते स्वायम्भुवो मनुः ।
कान्यन्वतिष्ठद् द्वाराणि मार्गायावरजन्मनाम् ॥ १ ॥

śaunaka uvāca
mahīṁ pratiṣṭhām adhyasya
saute svāyambhuvo manuḥ
kāny anvatiṣṭhad dvārāṇi
mārgāyāvara-janmanām

śaunakaḥ—Śaunaka; *uvāca*—said; *mahīm*—the earth; *pratiṣṭhām*—situated; *adhyasya*—having secured; *saute*—O Sūta Gosvāmī; *svāyambhuvaḥ*—Svāyambhuva; *manuḥ*—Manu; *kāni*—what; *anvatiṣṭhat*—performed; *dvārāṇi*—ways; *mārgāya*—to get out; *avara*—later; *janmanām*—of those to be born.

TRANSLATION

Śrī Śaunaka inquired: O Sūta Gosvāmī, after the earth was again situated in its orbit, what did Svāyambhuva Manu do to show the path of liberation to persons who were to take birth later on?

PURPORT

The appearance of the Lord as the first boar incarnation occurred during the time of Svāyambhuva Manu, whereas the present age is in the period of Vaivasvata Manu. Each Manu's period lasts seventy-two times the cycle of four ages, and one cycle of ages equals 4,320,000 solar years. Thus 4,320,000 X 72 solar years is the reign of one Manu. In each

Manu's period there are many changes in many ways, and there are fourteen Manus within one day of Brahmā. It is understood here that Manu creates scriptural regulations for the salvation of the conditioned souls, who come to the material world for material enjoyment. The Lord is so kind that any soul who wants to enjoy in this material world is given full facility for enjoyment, and at the same time he is shown the path of salvation. Śaunaka Ṛṣi, therefore, inquired from Sūta Gosvāmī: "What did Svāyambhuva Manu do after the reinstatement of the earth in its orbital situation?"

TEXT 2

क्षत्ता महाभागवतः कृष्णस्यैकान्तिकः सुहृत् ।
यस्तत्याजाग्रजं कृष्णे सापत्यमघवानिति ॥ २ ॥

kṣattā mahā-bhāgavataḥ
kṛṣṇasyaikāntikaḥ suhṛt
yas tatyājāgrajaṁ kṛṣṇe
sāpatyaṁ aghavān iti

kṣattā—Vidura; *mahā-bhāgavataḥ*—a great devotee of the Lord; *kṛṣṇasya*—of Lord Kṛṣṇa; *ekāntikaḥ*—unalloyed devotee; *suhṛt*—intimate friend; *yaḥ*—he who; *tatyāja*—abandoned; *agra-jam*—his elder brother (King Dhṛtarāṣṭra); *kṛṣṇe*—toward Kṛṣṇa; *sa-apatyam*—along with his one hundred sons; *agha-vān*—offender; *iti*—thus.

TRANSLATION

Śaunaka Ṛṣi inquired about Vidura, who was a great devotee and friend of Lord Kṛṣṇa and who gave up the company of his elder brother because the latter, along with his sons, played tricks against the desires of the Lord.

PURPORT

The incident referred to here is that Vidura left the protection of his elder brother Dhṛtarāṣṭra, went traveling everywhere to sacred places and met Maitreya at Hardwar. Śaunaka Ṛṣi here inquires about the topics of the conversation between Maitreya Ṛṣi and Vidura. Vidura's qualification was that he was not only a friend of the Lord but also a great devotee. When Kṛṣṇa tried to stop the war and mitigate the misunderstanding between the cousin-brothers, they refused to accept His counsel; therefore Kṣattā, or Vidura, was unsatisfied with them, and he left the palace. As a devotee, Vidura showed by example that anywhere that Kṛṣṇa is not honored is a place unfit for human habitation. A devotee may be tolerant regarding his own interests, but he should not be tolerant when there is misbehavior toward the Lord or the Lord's devotee. Here the word *aghavān* is very significant, for it indicates that the Kauravas, Dhṛtarāṣṭra's sons, lost the war because of being sinful in disobeying the instructions of Kṛṣṇa.

TEXT 3

द्वैपायनादनवरो महित्वे तस्य देहजः ।
सर्वात्मना श्रितः कृष्णं तत्परांश्चाप्यनुव्रतः ॥ ३ ॥

dvaipāyanād anavaro
mahitve tasya dehajaḥ
sarvātmanā śritaḥ kṛṣṇaṁ
tat-parāṁś cāpy anuvrataḥ

dvaipāyanāt—from Vyāsadeva; *anavaraḥ*—in no way inferior; *mahitve*—in greatness; *tasya*—his (Vyāsa's); *deha-jaḥ*—born of his body; *sarva-ātmanā*—with all his heart; *śritaḥ*—took shelter; *kṛṣṇam*—Lord Kṛṣṇa; *tat-parān*—those devoted to Him; *ca*—and; *api*—also; *anuvrataḥ*—followed.

TRANSLATION

Vidura was born from the body of Vedavyāsa and was not less than he. Thus he accepted the lotus feet of Kṛṣṇa wholeheartedly and was attached to His devotees.

PURPORT

The history of Vidura is that he was born of a *śūdra* mother, but his seminal father was Vyāsadeva; thus he was not less than Vyāsadeva in any respect. Since he was born of a great father, who was supposed to be an incarnation of Nārāyaṇa and who composed all the Vedic literatures, Vidura was also a great personality. He accepted Kṛṣṇa as his worshipable Lord and followed His instructions wholeheartedly.

TEXT 4

किमन्वपृच्छन्मैत्रेयं विरजास्तीर्थसेवया ।
उपगम्य कुशावर्त आसीनं तत्त्ववित्तमम् ॥ ४ ॥

kim anvapṛcchan maitreyaṁ
virajās tīrtha-sevayā
upagamya kuśāvarta
āsīnaṁ tattva-vittamam

kim—what; *anvapṛcchat*—inquired; *maitreyam*—from the sage Maitreya; *virajāḥ*—Vidura, who was without material contamination; *tīrtha-sevayā*—by visiting sacred places; *upagamya*—having met; *kuśāvarte*—at Kuśāvarta (Haridvāra, or Hardwar); *āsīnam*—who was abiding; *tattva-vit-tamam*—the foremost knower of the science of spiritual life.

TRANSLATION

Vidura was purified of all passion by wandering in sacred places, and at last he reached Hardwar, where he met the great sage who knew the science of spiritual life, and he inquired from him. Śaunaka Ṛṣi therefore asked: What more did Vidura inquire from Maitreya?

PURPORT

Here the words *virajās tīrtha-sevayā* refer to Vidura, who was completely cleansed of all contamination by traveling to places of pilgrimage. In India there are hundreds of sacred places of pilgrimage, of which Prayāga, Hardwar, Vṛndāvana and Rāmeśvaram are considered principal. After leaving his home, which was full of politics and diplomacy, Vidura wanted to purify himself by traveling to all the sacred places, which are so situated that anyone who goes there automatically becomes purified. This is especially true in Vṛndāvana; any person may go there, and even if he is sinful he will at once contact an atmosphere of spiritual life and will automatically chant the names of Kṛṣṇa and Rādhā. That we have actually seen and experienced. It is recommended in the *śāstras* that after retiring from active life and accepting the *vānaprastha* (retired) order, one should travel everywhere to places of pilgrimage in order to purify himself. Vidura completely discharged this duty, and at last he reached Kuśāvarta, or Hardwar, where the sage Maitreya was sitting.

Another significant point is that one must go to sacred places not only to take bath there but to search out great sages like Maitreya and take instructions from them. If one does not do so, his traveling to places of pilgrimage is simply a waste of time. Narottama dāsa Ṭhākura, a great *ācārya* of the Vaiṣṇava sect, has, for the present, forbidden us to go to such places of pilgrimage because in this age, the times having so changed, a sincere person may have a different impression on seeing the behavior of the present residents of the pilgrimage sites. He has recommended that instead of taking the trouble to travel to such places, one should concentrate his mind on Govinda, and that will help him. Of course, to concentrate one's mind on Govinda in any place is a path meant for those who are the most spiritually advanced; it is not for ordinary persons. Ordinary persons may still derive benefit from traveling to holy places like Prayāga, Mathurā, Vṛndāvana and Hardwar.

It is recommended in this verse that one find a person who knows the science of God, or a *tattva-vit. Tattva-vit* means "one who knows the Absolute Truth." There are many pseudotranscendentalists, even at places of pilgrimage. Such men are always present, and one has to be intelligent enough to find the actual person to be consulted; then one's attempt to progress by traveling to different holy places will be successful. One has to be freed from all contamination, and at the same time he has to find a person who knows the science of Kṛṣṇa. Kṛṣṇa helps a sincere person; as stated in the *Caitanya-caritāmṛta, guru-kṛṣṇa-prasāde:* by the mercy of the spiritual master and Kṛṣṇa, one attains the path of salvation, devotional service. If one sincerely searches for spiritual salvation, then Kṛṣṇa, being situated in everyone's heart, gives him the intelligence to find a suitable spiritual master. By the grace of a spiritual master like Maitreya, one gets the proper instruction and advances in his spiritual life.

TEXT 5

तयोः संवदतोः सूत प्रवृत्ता ह्यमलाः कथाः ।
आपो गाङ्गा इवाघघ्नीर्हरेः पादाम्बुजाश्रयाः ॥ ५ ॥

tayoḥ saṁvadatoḥ sūta
pravṛttā hy amalāḥ kathāḥ
āpo gāṅgā ivāgha-ghnīr
hareḥ pādāmbujāśrayāḥ

tayoḥ—while the two (Maitreya and Vidura); *saṁvadatoḥ*—were conversing; *sūta*—O Sūta; *pravṛttāḥ*—arose; *hi*—certainly; *amalāḥ*—spotless; *kathāḥ*—narrations; *āpaḥ*—waters; *gāṅgāḥ*—of the River Ganges; *iva*—like; *agha-ghnīḥ*—vanquishing all sins; *hareḥ*—of the Lord; *pāda-ambuja*—the lotus feet; *āśrayāḥ*—taking shelter.

TRANSLATION

Śaunaka inquired about the conversation between Vidura and Maitreya: There must have been many narrations of the spotless pastimes of the Lord. The hearing of such narrations is exactly like bathing in the water of the Ganges, for it can free one from all sinful reactions.

PURPORT

The water of the Ganges is purified because it pours forth from the lotus feet of the Lord. Similarly, *Bhagavad-gītā* is as good as the water of the Ganges because it is spoken from the mouth of the Supreme Lord. So it is with any topic on the pastimes of the Lord or the characteristics of His transcendental activities. The Lord is absolute; there is no difference between His words, His perspiration or His pastimes. The water of the Ganges, the narrations of His pastimes and the words spoken by Him are all on the absolute platform, and thus taking shelter of any one of them is equally good. Śrīla Rūpa Gosvāmī has enunciated that anything in relationship with Kṛṣṇa is on the transcendental platform. If we can dovetail all our activities in relationship with Kṛṣṇa, then we do not stand on the material platform, but always on the spiritual platform.

TEXT 6

ता नः कीर्तय भद्रं ते कीर्तन्योदारकर्मणः ।
रसज्ञः को नु तृप्येत हरिलीलामृतं पिबन् ॥ ६ ॥

tā naḥ kīrtaya bhadraṁ te
kīrtanyodāra-karmaṇaḥ
rasajñaḥ ko nu tṛpyeta
hari-līlāmṛtaṁ piban

tāḥ—those talks; *naḥ*—to us; *kīrtaya*—narrate; *bhadram te*—may all good come unto you; *kīrtanya*—should be chanted; *udāra*—liberal; *karmaṇaḥ*—activities; *rasa-jñaḥ*—a devotee who can appreciate mellow tastes; *kaḥ*—who; *nu*—indeed; *tṛpyeta*—would feel satisfied; *hari-līlā-amṛtam*—the nectar of the pastimes of the Lord; *piban*—drinking.

TRANSLATION

O Sūta Gosvāmī, all good fortune to you! Please narrate the activities of the Lord, which are all magnanimous and worth glorifying. What sort of devotee can be satiated by hearing the nectarean pastimes of the Lord?

PURPORT

The narration of the pastimes of the Lord, which are always enacted on the transcendental platform, should be received with all respect by devotees. Those who are actually on the transcendental platform are never satiated by hearing the continuous narration of the pastimes of the Lord. For example, if any self-realized soul reads from *Bhagavad-gītā*, he will never feel satiated. The narrations of *Bhagavad-gītā* and *Śrīmad-Bhāgavatam* may be read thousands and thousands of times, and still, without fail, new aspects of the subject matter will be relished by the devotee.

TEXT 7

एवमुग्रश्रवाः पृष्ट ऋषिभिर्नैमिषायनैः ।
भगवत्यर्पिताध्यात्मस्तानाह श्रूयतामिति ॥ ७ ॥

evam ugraśravāḥ pṛṣṭa
ṛṣibhir naimiṣāyanaiḥ
bhagavaty arpitādhyātmas
tān āha śrūyatām iti

evam—thus; *ugraśravāḥ*—Sūta Gosvāmī; *pṛṣṭaḥ*—being asked; *ṛṣibhiḥ*—by the sages; *naimiṣa-ayanaiḥ*—who were assembled in the forest of Naimiṣa; *bhagavati*—unto the Lord; *arpita*—dedicated; *adhyātmaḥ*—his mind; *tān*—to them; *āha*—said; *śrūyatām*—just hear; *iti*—thus.

TRANSLATION

On being asked to speak by the great sages of Naimiṣāraṇya, the son of Romaharṣaṇa, Sūta Gosvāmī, whose mind was absorbed in the transcendental pastimes of the Lord, said: Please hear what I shall now speak.

TEXT 8

सूत उवाच
हरेर्धृतक्रोडतनोः स्वमायया
निशम्य गोरुद्धरणं रसातलात् ।
लीलां हिरण्याक्षमवज्ञया हतं
सञ्जातहर्षो मुनिमाह भारतः ॥ ८ ॥

sūta uvāca
harer dhṛta-kroḍa-tanoḥ sva-māyayā
niśamya gor uddharaṇaṁ rasātalāt
līlāṁ hiraṇyākṣam avajñayā hataṁ
sañjāta-harṣo munim āha bhārataḥ

sūtaḥ uvāca—Sūta said; *hareḥ*—of the Lord; *dhṛta*—who had assumed; *kroḍa*—of a boar; *tanoḥ*—body; *sva-māyayā*—by His divine potency; *niśamya*—having heard; *goḥ*—of the earth; *uddharaṇam*—uplifting; *rasātalāt*—from the bottom of the ocean; *līlām*—sport; *hiraṇyākṣam*—the demon Hiraṇyākṣa; *avajñayā*—neglectfully;

hatam—killed; *sañjāta-harṣaḥ*—being overjoyed; *munim*—to the sage (Maitreya); *āha*—said; *bhārataḥ*—Vidura.

TRANSLATION

Sūta Gosvāmī continued: Vidura, the descendant of Bharata, was delighted to hear the story of the Lord, who, having assumed by His own divine potency the form of a boar, had enacted the sport of lifting the earth from the bottom of the ocean and indifferently killing the demon Hiraṇyākṣa. Vidura then spoke to the sage as follows.

PURPORT

It is stated here that the Lord assumed the form of a boar by His own potency. His form is not actually the form of a conditioned soul. A conditioned soul is forced to accept a particular type of body by the higher authority of material laws, but here it is clearly said that the Lord was not forced to accept the form of a boar by the external power. In *Bhagavad-gītā* the same fact is confirmed; when the Lord descends to this earth, He assumes a form by His own internal potency. The form of the Lord, therefore, can never consist of material energy. The Māyāvāda version that when Brahman assumes a form the form is accepted from *māyā* is not acceptable, because although *māyā* is superior to the conditioned soul, she is not superior to the Supreme Personality of Godhead; she is under the control of the Supreme Godhead, as confirmed in *Bhagavad-gītā. Māyā* is under His superintendence; *māyā* cannot overcome the Lord. The Māyāvāda idea that the living entity is the Supreme Absolute Truth but has become covered by *māyā* is invalid, because *māyā* cannot be so great that it can cover the Supreme. The covering capacity can be employed on the part and parcel of Brahman, not on the Supreme Brahman.

TEXT 9

विदुर उवाच

प्रजापतिपतिः सृष्ट्वा प्रजासर्गे प्रजापतीन् ।
किमारभत मे ब्रह्मन् प्रब्रूह्यव्यक्तमार्गवित् ॥ ९ ॥

vidura uvāca
prajāpati-patiḥ sṛṣṭvā
prajā-sarge prajāpatīn
kim ārabhata me brahman
prabrūhy avyakta-mārga-vit

viduraḥ uvāca—Vidura said; *prajāpati-patiḥ*—Lord Brahmā; *sṛṣṭvā*—after creating; *prajā-sarge*—for the purpose of creating living beings; *prajāpatīn*—the Prajāpatis; *kim*—what; *ārabhata*—started; *me*—to me; *brahman*—O holy sage; *prabrūhi*—tell; *avyakta-mārga-vit*—knower of that which we do not know.

TRANSLATION

Vidura said: Since you know of matters inconceivable to us, tell me, O holy sage, what did Brahmā do to create living beings after evolving the Prajāpatis, the progenitors of living beings?

PURPORT

Significant here is the word *avyakta-mārga-vit*, "one who knows that which is beyond our perception." To know matters beyond one's perception, one has to learn from a superior authority in the line of disciplic succession. Just to know who is our father is beyond our perception. For that, the mother is the authority. Similarly, we have to understand everything beyond our perception from the authority who actually knows. The first *avyakta-mārga-vit*, or authority, is Brahmā, and the next authority in disciplic succession is Nārada. Maitreya Ṛṣi belongs to that disciplic succession, so he also is *avyakta-mārga-vit.* Anyone in the bona fide line of disciplic succession is *avyakta-mārga-vit*, a personality who knows that which is beyond ordinary perception.

TEXT 10

ये मरीच्यादयो विप्रा यस्तु स्वायम्भुवो मनुः ।
ते वै ब्रह्मण आदेशात्कथमेतदभावयन् ॥१०॥

ye marīcy-ādayo viprā
yas tu svāyambhuvo manuḥ
te vai brahmaṇa ādeśāt
katham etad abhāvayan

ye—those; *marīci-ādayaḥ*—great sages headed by Marīci; *viprāḥ*—*brāhmaṇas; yaḥ*—who; *tu*—indeed; *svāyambhuvaḥ manuḥ*—and Svāyambhuva Manu; *te*—they; *vai*—indeed; *brahmaṇaḥ*—of Lord Brahmā; *ādeśāt*—by the order; *katham*—how; *etat*—this universe; *abhāvayan*—evolved.

TRANSLATION

Vidura inquired: How did the Prajāpatis [such progenitors of living entities as Marīci and Svāyambhuva Manu] create according to the instruction of Brahmā, and how did they evolve this manifested universe?

TEXT 11

सद्वितीयाः किमसृजन् स्वतन्त्रा उत कर्मसु ।
आहोस्वित्संहताः सर्व इदं स्म समकल्पयन् ॥११॥

sa-dvitīyāḥ kim asṛjan
svatantrā uta karmasu
āho svit saṁhatāḥ sarva
idaṁ sma samakalpayan

sa-dvitīyāḥ—with their wives; *kim*—whether; *asṛjan*—created; *svatantrāḥ*—remaining independent; *uta*—or; *karmasu*—in their actions; *āho svit*—or else; *saṁhatāḥ*—jointly; *sarve*—all the Prajāpatis; *idam*—this; *sma samakalpayan*—produced.

TRANSLATION

Did they evolve the creation in conjunction with their respective wives, did they remain independent in their action, or did they all jointly produce it?

TEXT 12

मैत्रेय उवाच
दैवेन दुर्वितर्क्येण परेणानिमिषेण च ।
जातक्षोभाद्भगवतो महानासीद् गुणत्रयात् ॥१२॥

maitreya uvāca
daivena durvitarkyeṇa
pareṇānimiṣeṇa ca
jāta-kṣobhād bhagavato
mahān āsīd guṇa-trayāt

maitreyaḥ uvāca—Maitreya said; *daivena*—by superior management known as destiny; *durvitarkyeṇa*—beyond empiric speculation; *pareṇa*—by Mahā-Viṣṇu; *animiṣeṇa*—by the potency of eternal time; *ca*—and; *jāta-kṣobhāt*—the equilibrium was agitated; *bhagavataḥ*—of the Personality of Godhead; *mahān*—the total material elements (the *mahat-tattva*); *āsīt*—were produced; *guṇa-trayāt*—from the three modes of nature.

TRANSLATION

Maitreya said: When the equilibrium of the combination of the three modes of nature was agitated by the unseen activity of the living entity, by Mahā-Viṣṇu and by the force of time, the total material elements were produced.

PURPORT

The cause of the material creation is described here very lucidly. The first cause is *daiva*, or the destiny of the conditioned soul. The material creation exists for the conditioned soul who wanted to become a false lord for sense enjoyment. One cannot trace out the history of when the conditioned soul first desired to lord it over material nature, but in Vedic literature we always find that the material creation is meant for the sense enjoyment of the conditioned soul. There is a nice verse which says that the sum and substance of the conditioned soul's sense enjoyment is that as soon as he forgets his primary duty, to render service to the Lord, he creates an atmosphere of sense enjoyment, which is called *māyā;* that is the cause of material creation.

Another word used here is *durvitarkyeṇa*. No one can argue about when and how the conditioned soul became desirous of sense enjoyment, but the cause is there. Material nature is an atmosphere meant only for the sense enjoyment of the conditioned soul, and it is created by the Personality of Godhead. It is mentioned here that in the beginning of the creation the material nature, or *prakṛti*, is agitated by the Personality of Godhead, Viṣṇu. There are three Viṣṇus mentioned. One is Mahā-Viṣṇu, another is Garbhodakaśāyī Viṣṇu, and the third is Kṣīrodakaśāyī Viṣṇu. The First Canto of *Śrīmad-Bhāgavatam* discusses all these three Viṣṇus, and here also it is confirmed that Viṣṇu is the cause of creation. From *Bhagavad-gītā* also we learn that *prakṛti* begins to work and is still working under Kṛṣṇa's, or Viṣṇu's, glance of superintendence, but the Supreme Personality of Godhead is unchangeable. One should not mistakenly think that because the creation emanates from the Supreme Personality of Godhead, He has therefore transformed into this material cosmic manifestation. He exists in His personal form always, but the cosmic manifestation takes place by His inconceivable potency. The workings of that energy are difficult to comprehend, but it is understood from Vedic literature that the conditioned soul creates his own destiny and is offered a particular body by the laws of nature under the superintendence of the Supreme Personality of Godhead, who always accompanies him as Paramātmā.

TEXT 13

रजःप्रधानान्महतस्त्रिलिङ्गो दैवचोदितात् ।
जातः ससर्ज भूतादिर्वियदादीनि पञ्चशः ॥१३॥

rajaḥ-pradhānān mahatas
tri-liṅgo daiva-coditāt
jātaḥ sasarja bhūtādir
viyad-ādīni pañcaśaḥ

rajaḥ-pradhānāt—in which the element of *rajas*, or passion, predominates; *mahataḥ*—from the *mahat-tattva; tri-liṅgaḥ*—of three kinds; *daiva-coditāt*—impelled by superior authority; *jātaḥ*—was born; *sasarja*—evolved; *bhūta-ādiḥ*—the false ego (origin of the material elements); *viyat*—the ether; *ādīni*—beginning with; *pañcaśaḥ*—in groups of five.

TRANSLATION

As impelled by the destiny of the jīva, the false ego, which is of three kinds, evolved from the mahat-tattva, in which the element of rajas predominates. From the ego, in turn, evolved many groups of five principles.

PURPORT

The primordial matter, or *prakṛti*, material nature, consisting of three modes, generates four groups of five. The first group is called elementary and consists of earth, water, fire, air and ether. The second group of five is called *tan-mātra*, referring to the subtle elements (sense objects): sound, touch, form, taste and smell. The third group is the five sense organs for acquiring knowledge: eyes, ears, nose, tongue and skin. The fourth group is the five working senses: speech, hands, feet, anus and genitals. Some say that there are five groups of five. One group is the sense objects, one is the five elements, one is the five sense organs for acquiring knowledge, another is the senses for working, and the fifth group is the five deities who control these divisions.

TEXT 14

तानि चैकैकशः स्रष्टुमसमर्थानि भौतिकम् ।
संहत्य दैवयोगेन हैममण्डमवासृजन् ॥१४॥

tāni caikaikaśaḥ sraṣṭum
asamarthāni bhautikam
saṁhatya daiva-yogena
haimam aṇḍam avāsṛjan

tāni—those elements; *ca*—and; *eka-ekaśaḥ*—separately; *sraṣṭum*—to produce; *asamarthāni*—unable; *bhautikam*—the material universe; *saṁhatya*—having combined; *daiva-yogena*—with the energy of the Supreme Lord; *haimam*—shining like gold; *aṇḍam*—globe; *avāsṛjan*—produced.

TRANSLATION

Separately unable to produce the material universe, they combined with the help of the energy of the Supreme Lord and were able to produce a shining egg.

TEXT 15

सोऽशयिष्टाब्धिसलिले आण्डकोशो निरात्मकः ।
साग्रं वै वर्षसाहस्रमन्ववात्सीत्तमीश्वरः ॥१५॥

so 'śayiṣṭābdhi-salile
āṇḍakośo nirātmakaḥ
sāgraṁ vai varṣa-sāhasram
anvavātsīt tam īśvaraḥ

saḥ—it; *aśayiṣṭa*—lay; *abdhi-salile*—on the waters of the Causal Ocean; *āṇḍa-kośaḥ*—egg; *nirātmakaḥ*—in an unconscious state; *sa-agram*—a little more than; *vai*—in fact; *varṣa-sāhasram*—a thousand years; *anvavātsīt*—became situated; *tam*—in the egg; *īśvaraḥ*—the Lord.

TRANSLATION

For over one thousand years the shiny egg lay on the waters of the Causal Ocean in the lifeless state. Then the Lord entered it as Garbhodakaśāyī Viṣṇu.

PURPORT

From this verse it appears that all the universes are floating in the Causal Ocean.

TEXT 16

तस्य नाभेरभूत्पद्मं सहस्रार्कोरुदीधिति ।
सर्वजीवनिकायौको यत्र स्वयमभूत्स्वराट् ॥१६॥

tasya nābher abhūt padmaṁ
sahasrārkoru-dīdhiti

sarva-jīvanikāyauko
yatra svayam abhūt svarāṭ

tasya—of the Lord; *nābheḥ*—from the navel; *abhūt*—sprouted up; *padmam*—a lotus; *sahasra-arka*—a thousand suns; *uru*—more; *dīdhiti*—with dazzling splendor; *sarva*—all; *jīva-nikāya*—resting place of conditioned souls; *okaḥ*—place; *yatra*—where; *svayam*—himself; *abhūt*—emanated; *sva-rāṭ*—the omnipotent (Lord Brahmā).

TRANSLATION

From the navel of the Personality of Godhead Garbhodakaśāyī Viṣṇu sprouted a lotus flower effulgent like a thousand blazing suns. This lotus flower is the reservoir of all conditioned souls, and the first living entity who came out of the lotus flower was the omnipotent Brahmā.

PURPORT

It appears from this verse that the conditioned souls who rested within the body of the Personality of Godhead after the dissolution of the last creation came out in the sum total form of the lotus. This is called *hiraṇyagarbha.* The first living entity to come out was Lord Brahmā, who is independently able to create the rest of the manifested universe. The lotus is described here as effulgent as the glare of a thousand suns. This indicates that the living entities, as parts and parcels of the Supreme Lord, are also of the same quality, since the Lord also diffuses His bodily glare, known as *brahmajyoti.* The description of Vaikuṇṭhaloka, as stated in *Bhagavad-gītā* and other Vedic literatures, is confirmed herewith. In Vaikuṇṭha, the spiritual sky, there is no need of sunshine, moonshine, electricity or fire. Every planet there is self-effulgent like the sun.

TEXT 17

सोऽनुविष्टो भगवता यः शेते सलिलाशये ।
लोकसंस्थां यथापूर्वं निर्ममे संस्थया स्वया ॥१७॥

so 'nuviṣṭo bhagavatā
yaḥ śete salilāśaye

loka-saṁsthāṁ yathā pūrvaṁ
nirmame saṁsthayā svayā

saḥ—Lord Brahmā; *anuviṣṭaḥ*—was entered; *bhagavatā*—by the Lord; *yaḥ*—who; *śete*—sleeps; *salila-āśaye*—on the Garbhodaka Ocean; *loka-saṁsthām*—the universe; *yathā pūrvam*—as previously; *nirmame*—created; *saṁsthayā*—by intelligence; *svayā*—his own.

TRANSLATION

When that Supreme Personality of Godhead who is lying on the Garbhodaka Ocean entered the heart of Brahmā, Brahmā brought his intelligence to bear, and with the intelligence invoked he began to create the universe as it was before.

PURPORT

At a certain time, the Personality of Godhead, Kāraṇodakaśāyī Viṣṇu, lies in the Kāraṇa Ocean and produces many thousands of universes from His breathing; then He enters again into each and every universe as Garbhodakaśāyī Viṣṇu and fills up half of each universe with His own perspiration. The other half of the universe remains vacant, and that vacant region is called outer space. Then the lotus flower sprouts from His abdomen and produces the first living creature, Brahmā. Then again, as Kṣīrodakaśāyī Viṣṇu, the Lord enters into the heart of every living entity, including Brahmā. This is confirmed in *Bhagavad-gītā*, Fifteenth Chapter. The Lord says, "I am seated in everyone's heart, and by Me are remembrance and forgetfulness made possible." As the witness of the activities of the individual entities, the Lord gives each one remembrance and intelligence to act according to his desire at the time he was annihilated in his last birth in the last millennium. This intelligence is invoked according to one's own capacity, or by the law of *karma.*

Brahmā was the first living entity, and he was empowered by the Supreme Lord to act in charge of the mode of passion; therefore, he was given the required intelligence, which is so powerful and extensive that he is almost independent of the control of the Supreme Personality of Godhead. Just as a highly posted manager is almost as independent as the owner of a firm, Brahmā is described here as independent because, as the Lord's representative to control the universe, he is almost as powerful and independent as the Supreme Personality of Godhead. The Lord, as the Supersoul within Brahmā, gave him the intelligence to create. The creative power, therefore, of every living entity is not his own; it is by the grace of the Lord that one can create. There are many scientists and great workers in this material world who have wonderful creative force, but they act and create only according to the direction of the Supreme Lord. A scientist may create many wonderful inventions by the direction of the Lord, but it is not possible for him to overcome the stringent laws of material nature by his intelligence, nor is it possible to acquire such intelligence from the Lord, for the Lord's supremacy would then be hampered. It is stated in this verse that Brahmā created the universe as it was before. This means that he created everything by the same name and form as in the previous cosmic manifestation.

TEXT 18

ससर्ज च्छाययाविद्यां पञ्चपर्वाणमग्रतः ।
तामिस्रमन्धतामिस्रं तमो मोहो महातमः ॥१८॥

sasarja cchāyayāvidyāṁ
pañca-parvāṇam agrataḥ
tāmisram andha-tāmisraṁ
tamo moho mahā-tamaḥ

sasarja—created; *chāyayā*—with his shadow; *avidyām*—ignorance; *pañca-parvāṇam*—five varieties; *agrataḥ*—first of all; *tāmisram*—*tāmisra; andha-tāmisram*—*andha-tāmisra; tamaḥ*—*tamas; mohaḥ*—*moha; mahā-tamaḥ*—*mahā-tamas*, or *mahā-moha.*

TRANSLATION

First of all, Brahmā created from his shadow the coverings of ignorance of the conditioned souls. They are five in number and are called tāmisra, andha-tāmisra, tamas, moha and mahā-moha.

PURPORT

Thc conditioned souls, or living entities who come to the material world to enjoy sense gratification, are covered in the beginning by five different conditions. The first condition is a covering of *tāmisra,* or anger. Constitutionally, each and every living entity has minute independence; it is misuse of that minute independence for the conditioned soul to think that he can also enjoy like the Supreme Lord or to think, "Why shall I not be a free enjoyer like the Supreme Lord?" This forgetfulness of his constitutional position is due to anger or envy. The living entity, being eternally a part-and-parcel servitor of the Supreme Lord, can never, by constitution, be an equal enjoyer with the Lord. When he forgets this, however, and tries to be one with Him, his condition is called *tāmisra.* Even in the field of spiritual realization, this *tāmisra* mentality of the living entity is hard to overcome. In trying to get out of the entanglement of material life, there are many who want to be one with the Supreme. Even in their transcendental activities, this lower-grade mentality of *tāmisra* continues.

Andha-tāmisra involves considering death to be the ultimate end. The atheists generally think that the body is the self and that everything is therefore ended with the end of the body. Thus they want to enjoy material life as far as possible during the existence of the body. Their theory is: "As long as you live, you should live prosperously. Never mind whether you commit all kinds of so-called sins. You must eat sumptuously. Beg, borrow and steal, and if you think that by stealing and borrowing you are being entangled in sinful activities for which you will have to pay, then just forget that misconception because after death everything is finished. No one is responsible for anything he does during his life." This atheistic conception of life is killing human civilization, for it is without knowledge of the continuation of eternal life.

This *andha-tāmisra* ignorance is due to *tamas.* The condition of not knowing anything about the spirit soul is called *tamas.* This material world is also generally called *tamas* because ninety-nine percent of its living entities are ignorant of their identity as soul. Almost everyone is thinking that he is this body; he has no information of the spirit soul. Guided by this misconception, one always thinks, "This is my body, and anything in relationship with this body is mine." For such misguided living entities, sex life is the background of material existence. Actually, the conditioned souls, in ignorance in this material world, are simply guided by sex life, and as soon as they get the opportunity for sex life, they become attached to so-called home, motherland, children, wealth and opulence. As these attachments increase, *moha*, or the illusion of the bodily concept of life, also increases. Thus the idea that "I am this body, and everything belonging to this body is mine" also increases, and as the whole world is put into *moha*, sectarian societies, families and nationalities are created, and they fight with one another. *Mahā-moha* means to be mad after material enjoyment. Especially in this age of Kali, everyone is overwhelmed by the madness to accumulate paraphernalia for material enjoyment. These definitions are very nicely given in *Viṣṇu Purāṇa*, wherein it is said:

tamo 'viveko mohaḥ syād
antaḥ-karaṇa-vibhramaḥ
mahā-mohas tu vijñeyo
grāmya-bhoga-sukhaiṣaṇā

maraṇaṁ hy andha-tāmisraṁ
tāmisraṁ krodha ucyate
avidyā pañca-parvaiṣā
prādurbhūtā mahātmanaḥ

TEXT 19

विससर्जात्मनः कायं नाभिनन्दंस्तमोमयम् ।
जगृहुर्यक्षरक्षांसि रात्रिं क्षुत्तृट्समुद्भवाम् ॥१९॥

visasarjātmanaḥ kāyaṁ
nābhinandaṁs tamomayam
jagṛhur yakṣa-rakṣāṁsi
rātriṁ kṣut-tṛṭ-samudbhavām

visasarja—threw off; *ātmanaḥ*—his own; *kāyam*—body; *na*—not; *abhinandan*—being pleased; *tamaḥ-mayam*—made of ignorance; *jagṛhuḥ*—took possession; *yakṣa-rakṣāṁsi*—the Yakṣas and Rākṣasas; *rātrim*—night; *kṣut*—hunger; *tṛṭ*—thirst; *samudbhavām*—the source.

TRANSLATION

Out of disgust, Brahmā threw off the body of ignorance, and taking this opportunity, Yakṣas and Rākṣasas sprang for possession of the body, which continued to exist in the form of night. Night is the source of hunger and thirst.

TEXT 20

क्षुत्तृड्भ्यामुपसृष्टास्ते तं जग्धुमभिदुद्रुवुः ।
मा रक्षतैनं जक्षध्वमित्यूचुः क्षुत्तृडर्दिताः ॥२०॥

kṣut-tṛdbhyām upasṛṣṭās te
taṁ jagdhum abhidudruvuḥ
mā rakṣatainaṁ jakṣadhvam
ity ūcuḥ kṣut-tṛḍ-arditāḥ

kṣut-tṛḍbhyām—by hunger and thirst; *upasṛṣṭāḥ*—were overcome; *te*—the demons (Yakṣas and Rākṣasas); *tam*—Lord Brahmā; *jagdhum*—to eat; *abhidudruvuḥ*—ran toward; *mā*—do not; *rakṣata*—spare; *enam*—him; *jakṣadhvam*—eat; *iti*—thus; *ūcuḥ*—said; *kṣut-tṛṭ-arditāḥ*—afflicted by hunger and thirst.

TRANSLATION

Overpowered by hunger and thirst, they ran to devour Brahmā from all sides and cried, "Spare him not! Eat him up!"

PURPORT

The representatives of the Yakṣas and Rākṣasas still exist in some countries of the world. It is understood that such uncivilized men take pleasure in killing their own grandfathers and holding a "love feast" by roasting the bodies.

TEXT 21

देवस्तानाह संविग्नो मा मां जक्षत रक्षत ।
अहो मे यक्षरक्षांसि प्रजा यूयं बभूविथ ॥२१॥

devas tān āha saṁvigno
mā māṁ jakṣata rakṣata
aho me yakṣa-rakṣāṁsi
prajā yūyaṁ babhūvitha

devaḥ—Lord Brahmā; *tān*—to them; *āha*—said; *saṁvignaḥ*—being anxious; *mā*—do not; *mām*—me; *jakṣata*—eat; *rakṣata*—protect; *aho*—oh; *me*—my; *yakṣa-rakṣāṁsi*—O Yakṣas and Rākṣasas; *prajāḥ*—sons; *yūyam*—you; *babhūvitha*—were born.

TRANSLATION

Brahmā, the head of the demigods, full of anxiety, asked them, "Do not eat me, but protect me. You are born from me and have become my sons. Therefore you are Yakṣas and Rākṣasas."

PURPORT

The demons who were born from the body of Brahmā were called Yakṣas and Rākṣasas because some of them cried that Brahmā should be eaten and the others cried that he should not be protected. The ones who said that he should be eaten were called Yakṣas, and the ones who said that he should not be protected became Rākṣasas, man-eaters. The two, Yakṣas and Rākṣasas, are the original creation by Brahmā and are represented even until today in the uncivilized men who are scattered all over the universe. They are born of the mode of ignorance, and therefore, because of their behavior, they are called Rākṣasas, or man-eaters.

TEXT 22

देवताः प्रभया या या दीव्यन् प्रमुखतोऽसृजत् ।
ते अहार्षुर्देवयन्तो विसृष्टां तां प्रभामहः ॥२२॥

devatāḥ prabhayā yā yā
dīvyan pramukhato 'sṛjat
te ahārṣur devayanto
visṛṣṭāṁ tāṁ prabhām ahaḥ

devatāḥ—the demigods; *prabhayā*—with the glory of light; *yāḥ yāḥ*—those who; *dīvyan*—shining; *pramukhataḥ*—chiefly; *asṛjat*—created; *te*—they; *ahārṣuḥ*—took possession of; *devayantaḥ*—being active; *visṛṣṭām*—separated; *tām*—that; *prabhām*—effulgent form; *ahaḥ*—daytime.

TRANSLATION

He then created the chief demigods, who were shining with the glory of goodness. He dropped before them the effulgent form of daytime, and the demigods sportingly took possession of it.

PURPORT

Demons were born from the creation of night, and the demigods were born from the creation of day. In other words, demons like the Yakṣas and Rākṣasas are born of the quality of ignorance, and demigods are born of the quality of goodness.

TEXT 23

देवोऽदेवाञ्जघनतः सृजति स्मातिलोलुपान् ।
त एनं लोलुपतया मैथुनायाभिपेदिरे ॥२३॥

devo 'devāñ jaghanataḥ
sṛjati smātilolupān
ta enaṁ lolupatayā
maithunāyābhipedire

devaḥ—Lord Brahmā; *adevān*—demons; *jaghanataḥ*—from his buttocks; *sṛjati sma*—gave birth; *ati-lolupān*—excessively fond of sex; *te*—they; *enam*—Lord Brahmā; *lolupatayā*—with lust; *maithunāya*—for copulation; *abhipedire*—approached.

TRANSLATION

Lord Brahmā then gave birth to the demons from his buttocks, and they were very fond of sex. Because they were too lustful, they approached him for copulation.

PURPORT

Sex life is the background of material existence. Here also it is repeated that demons are very fond of sex life. The more one is free from the desires for sex, the more he is promoted to the level of the demigods; the more one is inclined to enjoy sex, the more he is degraded to the level of demoniac life.

TEXT 24

ततो हसन् स भगवानसुरैर्निरपत्रपैः ।
अन्वीयमानस्तरसा क्रुद्धो भीतः परापतत् ॥२४॥

tato hasan sa bhagavān
asurair nirapatrapaiḥ
anvīyamānas tarasā
kruddho bhītaḥ parāpatat

tataḥ—then; *hasan*—laughing; *saḥ bhagavān*—the worshipful Lord Brahmā; *asuraiḥ*—by the demons; *nirapatrapaiḥ*—shameless; *anvīyamānaḥ*—being followed; *tarasā*—in great haste; *kruddhaḥ*—angry; *bhītaḥ*—being afraid; *parāpatat*—ran away.

TRANSLATION

The worshipful Brahmā first laughed at their stupidity, but finding the shameless asuras close upon him, he grew indignant and ran in great haste out of fear.

PURPORT

Sexually inclined demons have no respect even for their father, and the best policy for a saintly father like Brahmā is to leave such demoniac sons.

TEXT 25

स उपव्रज्य वरदं प्रपन्नार्तिहरं हरिम् ।
अनुग्रहाय भक्तानामनुरूपात्मदर्शनम् ॥२५॥

sa upavrajya varadaṁ
prapannārti-haraṁ harim
anugrahāya bhaktānām
anurūpātma-darśanam

saḥ—Lord Brahmā; *upavrajya*—approaching; *vara-dam*—the bestower of all boons; *prapanna*—of those taking shelter at His lotus feet; *ārti*—distress; *haram*—who dispels; *harim*—Lord Śrī Hari; *anugrahāya*—for showing mercy; *bhaktānām*—to His devotees; *anurūpa*—in suitable forms; *ātma-darśanam*—who manifests Himself.

TRANSLATION

He approached the Personality of Godhead, who bestows all boons and who dispels the agony of His devotees and of those who take shelter of His lotus feet. He manifests His innumerable transcendental forms for the satisfaction of His devotees.

PURPORT

Here the words *bhaktānām anurūpātma-darśanam* mean that the Personality of Godhead manifests His multiforms according to the desires of the devotees. For example, Hanumānjī (Vajrāṅgajī) wanted to see the form of the Lord as the Personality of Godhead Rāmacandra, whereas other Vaiṣṇavas want to see the form of Rādhā-Kṛṣṇa, and still other devotees want to see the Lord in the form of Lakṣmī-Nārāyaṇa. The Māyāvādī philosophers think that although all these forms are assumed by the Lord just as the devotees desire to see Him, actually He is impersonal. From *Brahma-saṁhitā*, however, we can understand that this is not so, for the Lord has multiforms. It is said in the *Brahma-saṁhitā, advaitam acyutam.* The Lord does not appear before the devotee because of the devotee's imagination. *Brahma-saṁhitā* further explains that the Lord has innumerable forms: *rāmādi-mūrtiṣu kalā-niyamena tiṣṭhan.* He exists in millions and millions of forms. There are 8,400,000 species of living entities, but the incarnations of the Supreme Lord are innumerable. In the *Bhāgavatam* it is stated that as the waves in the sea cannot be counted but appear and disappear continually, the incarnations and forms of the Lord are innumerable. A devotee is attached to a particular form, and it is that form which he worships. We have just described the first appearance of the boar within this universe. There are innumerable universes, and somewhere or other the boar form is now existing. All the forms of the Lord are eternal. It is the devotee's inclination to worship a particular form, and he engages in devotional service to that form. In a verse in the *Rāmāyaṇa*, Hanumān, the great devotee of Rāma, said, "I know that there is no difference between the Sītā-Rāma and Lakṣmī-Nārāyaṇa forms of the Supreme Personality of Godhead, but nevertheless, the form of Rāma and Sītā has absorbed my affection and love. Therefore I want to see the Lord in the forms of Rāma and Sītā." Similarly, the Gauḍīya Vaiṣṇava loves the forms of Rādhā and Kṛṣṇa, and Kṛṣṇa and Rukmiṇī at Dvārakā. The words *bhaktānām anurūpātma-darśanam* mean that the Lord is always pleased to favor the devotee in the particular form in which the devotee wants to worship and render service unto Him. In this verse it is stated that Brahmā approached Hari, the Supreme Personality of Godhead. This form of the Lord is Kṣīrodakaśāyī Viṣṇu. Whenever there is some trouble and Brahmā has to approach the Lord, he can approach Kṣīrodakaśāyī Viṣṇu, and it is the grace of the Lord that whenever Brahmā approaches about disturbances in the universe, the Lord gives him relief in so many ways.

TEXT 26

पाहि मां परमात्मंस्ते प्रेषणेनासृजं प्रजाः ।
ता इमा यभितुं पापा उपाक्रामन्ति मां प्रभो ॥२६॥

pāhi māṁ paramātmaṁs te
preṣaṇenāsṛjaṁ prajāḥ
tā imā yabhituṁ pāpā
upākrāmanti māṁ prabho

pāhi—protect; *mām*—me; *parama-ātman*—O Supreme Lord; *te*—Your; *preṣaṇena*—by order; *asṛjam*—I created; *prajāḥ*—living beings; *tāḥ imāḥ*—those very persons; *yabhitum*—to have sex; *pāpāḥ*—sinful beings; *upākrāmanti*—are approaching; *mām*—me; *prabho*—O Lord.

TRANSLATION

Lord Brahmā, approaching the Lord, addressed Him thus: My Lord, please protect me from these sinful demons, who were created by me under Your order. They are infuriated by an appetite for sex and have come to attack me.

PURPORT

It appears here that the homosexual appetite of males for each other is created in this episode of the creation of the demons by Brahmā. In other words, the homosexual appetite of a man for another man is demoniac and is not for any sane male in the ordinary course of life.

TEXT 27

त्वमेकः किल लोकानां क्लिष्टानां क्लेशनाशनः ।
त्वमेकः क्लेशदस्तेषामनासन्नपदां तव ॥२७॥

tvam ekaḥ kila lokānāṁ
kliṣṭānāṁ kleśa-nāśanaḥ
tvam ekaḥ kleśadas teṣām
anāsanna-padāṁ tava

tvam—You; *ekaḥ*—alone; *kila*—indeed; *lokānām*—of the people; *kliṣṭānām*—afflicted with miseries; *kleśa*—the distresses; *nāśanaḥ*—relieving; *tvam ekaḥ*—You alone; *kleśa-daḥ*—inflicting distress; *teṣām*—on those; *anāsanna*—not taken shelter; *padām*—feet; *tava*—Your.

TRANSLATION

My Lord, You are the only one capable of ending the affliction of the distressed and inflicting agony on those who never resort to Your feet.

PURPORT

The words *kleśadas teṣām anāsanna-padāṁ tava* indicate that the Lord has two concerns. The first is to give protection to persons who take shelter of His lotus feet, and the second is to give trouble to those who are always demoniac and who are inimical toward the Lord. *Māyā's* function is to give afflictions to the nondevotees. Here Brahmā said, "You are the protector of the surrendered souls; therefore I surrender unto Your lotus feet. Please give me protection from these demons."

TEXT 28

सोऽवधार्यास्य कार्पण्यं विविक्ताध्यात्मदर्शनः ।
विमुञ्चात्मतनुं घोरामित्युक्तो विमुमोच ह ॥२८॥

so 'vadhāryāsya kārpaṇyaṁ
viviktādhyātma-darśanaḥ
vimuñcātma-tanuṁ ghorām
ity ukto vimumoca ha

saḥ—the Supreme Lord, Hari; *avadhārya*—perceiving; *asya*—of Lord Brahmā; *kārpaṇyam*—the distress; *vivikta*—without a doubt; *adhyātma*—minds of others; *darśanaḥ*—one who can see; *vimuñca*—cast off; *ātma-tanum*—your body; *ghorām*—impure; *iti uktaḥ*—thus commanded; *vimumoca ha*—Lord Brahmā threw it off.

TRANSLATION

The Lord, who can distinctly see the minds of others, perceived Brahmā's distress and said to him: "Cast off this impure body of yours." Thus commanded by the Lord, Brahmā cast off his body.

PURPORT

The Lord is described here by the word *viviktādhyātma-darśanaḥ.* If anyone can completely perceive another's distress without doubt, it is the Lord Himself. If someone is in distress and wants to get relief from his friend, sometimes it so happens that his friend does not appreciate the volume of distress he is suffering. But for the Supreme Lord it is not difficult. The Supreme Lord, as Paramātmā, is sitting within the heart of every living entity, and He directly perceives the exact causes of distress. In *Bhagavad-gītā* the Lord says, *sarvasya cāhaṁ hṛdi sanniviṣṭaḥ:* "I am sitting in everyone's heart, and because of Me one's remembrance and forgetfulness occur." Thus whenever one fully surrenders unto the Supreme Lord, one finds that He is sitting within one's heart. He can give us direction how to get out of dangers or how to approach Him in devotional service. The Lord, however, asked Brahmā to give up his present body because it had created the demoniac principle. According to Śrīdhara Svāmī, Brahmā's constant dropping of his body does not refer to his actually giving up his body. Rather, he suggests that Brahmā gave up a particular mentality. Mind is the subtle body of the living entity. We may sometimes be absorbed in some thought which is sinful, but if we give up the sinful thought, it may be said that we give up the body. Brahmā's mind was not in correct order when he created the demons. It must have been full of passion because the entire creation was passionate; therefore such passionate sons were born. It follows that any father and mother should also be careful while begetting children. The mental condition of a child depends upon the mental status of his parents at the time he is conceived. According to the Vedic system, therefore, the *garbhādhāna-saṁskāra*, or the ceremony for giving birth to a child, is observed. Before begetting a child, one has to sanctify his perplexed mind. When the parents engage their minds in the lotus feet of the Lord and in such a state the child is born, naturally good devotee children come; when the society is full of such good population, there is no trouble from demoniac mentalities.

TEXT 29

तां क्वणच्चरणाम्भोजां मदविह्वललोचनाम् ।
काञ्चीकलापविलसद्दुकूलच्छन्नरोधसम् ॥२९॥

tāṁ kvaṇac-caraṇāmbhojāṁ
mada-vihvala-locanām
kāñcī-kalāpa-vilasad-
dukūla-cchanna-rodhasam

tām—that body; *kvaṇat*—tinkling with ankle bells; *caraṇa-ambhojām*—with lotus feet; *mada*—intoxication; *vihvala*—overwhelmed; *locanām*—with eyes; *kāñcī-kalāpa*—with a girdle made of golden ornaments; *vilasat*—shining; *dukūla*—by fine cloth; *channa*—covered; *rodhasam*—having hips.

TRANSLATION

The body given up by Brahmā took the form of the evening twilight, when the day and night meet, a time which kindles passion. The asuras, who are passionate by nature, dominated as they are by the element of rajas, took it for a damsel, whose lotus feet resounded with the tinkling of anklets, whose eyes were wide with intoxication and whose hips were covered by fine cloth, over which shone a girdle.

PURPORT

As early morning is the period for spiritual cultivation, the beginning of evening is the period for passion. Demoniac men are generally very fond of sex enjoyment; therefore they very much appreciate the approach of evening. The demons took the approach of the evening twilight to be a beautiful woman, and they began to adore her in various ways. They imagined the twilight to be a very beautiful woman with tinkling bangles on her feet, a girdle on her hips, and beautiful breasts, and for their sexual satisfaction they imagined the appearance of this beautiful girl before them.

TEXT 30

अन्योन्यश्लेषयोत्तुङ्गनिरन्तरपयोधराम् ।
सुनासां सुद्विजां स्निग्धहासलीलावलोकनाम् ॥३०॥

anyonya-śleṣayottuṅga-
nirantara-payodharām
sunāsāṁ sudvijāṁ snigdha-
hāsa-līlāvalokanām

anyonya—to each other; *śleṣayā*—because of clinging; *uttuṅga*—raised; *nirantara*—without intervening space; *payaḥ-dharām*—breasts; *su-nāsām*—shapely nose; *su-dvijām*—beautiful teeth; *snigdha*—lovely; *hāsa*—smile; *līlā-avalokanām*—sportful glance.

TRANSLATION

Her breasts projected upward because of their clinging to each other, and they were too contiguous to admit any intervening

space. She had a shapely nose and beautiful teeth; a lovely smile played on her lips, and she cast a sportful glance at the asuras.

TEXT 31

गूहन्तीं व्रीडयात्मानं नीलालकवरूथिनीम् ।
उपलभ्यासुरा धर्म सर्वे सम्मुमुहुः स्त्रियम् ॥३१॥

gūhantīṁ vrīḍayātmānaṁ
nīlālaka-varūthinīm
upalabhyāsurā dharma
sarve sammumuhuḥ striyam

gūhantīm—hiding; *vrīḍayā*—out of shyness; *ātmānam*—herself; *nīla*—dark; *alaka*—hair; *varūthinīm*—a bunch; *upalabhya*—upon imagining; *asurāḥ*—the demons; *dharma*—O Vidura; *sarve*—all; *sammumuhuḥ*—were captivated; *striyam*—woman.

TRANSLATION

Adorned with dark tresses, she hid herself, as it were, out of shyness. Upon seeing that girl, the asuras were all infatuated with an appetite for sex.

PURPORT

The difference between demons and demigods is that a beautiful woman very easily attracts the minds of demons, but she cannot attract the mind of a godly person. A godly person is full of knowledge, and a demoniac person is full of ignorance. Just as a child is attracted by a beautiful doll, similarly a demon, who is less intelligent and full of ignorance, is attracted by material beauty and an appetite for sex. The godly person knows that this nicely dressed and ornamented attraction of high breasts, high hips, beautiful nose and fair complexion is *māyā.* All the beauty a woman can display is only a combination of flesh and blood. Śrī Śaṅkarācārya has advised all persons not to be attracted by the interaction of flesh and blood; they should be attracted by the real beauty in spiritual life. The real beauty is Kṛṣṇa and Rādhā. One who is attracted by the beauty of Rādhā and Kṛṣṇa cannot be attracted by the false beauty of this material world. That is the difference between a demon and a godly person or devotee.

TEXT 32

अहो रूपमहो धैर्यमहो अस्या नवं वयः ।
मध्ये कामयमानानामकामेव विसर्पति ॥३२॥

aho rūpam aho dhairyam
aho asyā navaṁ vayaḥ
madhye kāmayamānānām
akāmeva visarpati

aho—oh; *rūpam*—what beauty; *aho*—oh; *dhairyam*—what self-control; *aho*—oh; *asyāḥ*—her; *navam*—budding; *vayaḥ*—youth; *madhye*—in the midst; *kāmayamānānām*—of those passionately longing for; *akāmā*—free from passion; *iva*—like; *visarpati*—walking with us.

TRANSLATION

The demons praised her: Oh, what a beauty! What rare self-control! What a budding youth! In the midst of us all, who are passionately longing for her, she is moving about like one absolutely free from passion.

TEXT 33

वितर्कयन्तो बहुधा तां सन्ध्यां प्रमदाकृतिम् ।
अभिसम्भाव्य विश्रम्भात्पर्यपृच्छन् कुमेधसः ॥३३॥

vitarkayanto bahudhā
tāṁ sandhyāṁ pramadākṛtim
abhisambhāvya viśrambhāt
paryapṛcchan kumedhasaḥ

vitarkayantaḥ—indulging in speculations; *bahudhā*—various kinds; *tām*—her; *sandhyām*—the evening twilight; *pramadā*—a young woman; *ākṛtim*—in the form of; *abhisambhāvya*—treating with great respect; *viśrambhāt*—fondly; *paryapṛcchan*—questioned; *ku-medhasaḥ*—wicked-minded.

TRANSLATION

Indulging in various speculations about the evening twilight, which appeared to them endowed with the form of a young woman, the wicked-minded asuras treated her with respect and fondly spoke to her as follows.

TEXT 34

कासि कस्यासि रम्भोरु को वार्थस्तेऽत्र भामिनि।
रूपद्रविणपण्येन दुर्भगान्नो विबाधसे ॥३४॥

kāsi kasyāsi rambhoru
ko vārthas te 'tra bhāmini
rūpa-draviṇa-paṇyena
durbhagān no vibādhase

kā—who; *asi*—are you; *kasya*—belonging to whom; *asi*—are you; *rambhoru*—O pretty one; *kaḥ*—what; *vā*—or; *arthaḥ*—object; *te*—your; *atra*—here; *bhāmini*—O passionate lady; *rūpa*—beauty; *draviṇa*—priceless; *paṇyena*—with the commodity; *durbhagān*—unfortunate; *naḥ*—us; *vibādhase*—you tantalize.

TRANSLATION

Who are you, O pretty girl? Whose wife or daughter are you, and what can be the object of your appearing before us? Why do you tantalize us, unfortunate as we are, with the priceless commodity of your beauty?

PURPORT

The mentality of the demons in being enamored by the false beauty of this material world is expressed herein. The demoniac can pay any price for the skin beauty of this material world. They work very hard all day and night, but the purpose of their hard work is to enjoy sex life. Sometimes they misrepresent themselves as *karma-yogīs*, not knowing the meaning of the word *yoga. Yoga* means to link up with the Supreme Personality of Godhead, or to act in Kṛṣṇa consciousness. A person who works very hard, no matter in what occupation, and who offers the result of the work to the service of the Supreme Personality of Godhead, Kṛṣṇa, is called a *karma-yogī.*

TEXT 35

या वा काचित्त्वमबले दिष्ट्या सन्दर्शनं तव ।
उत्सुनोषीक्षमाणानां कन्दुकक्रीडया मनः ॥३५॥

yā vā kācit tvam abale
diṣṭyā sandarśanaṁ tava
utsunoṣīkṣamāṇānāṁ
kanduka-krīḍayā manaḥ

yā—whosoever; *vā*—or; *kācit*—anyone; *tvam*—you; *abale*—O beautiful girl; *diṣṭyā*—by fortune; *sandarśanam*—seeing; *tava*—of you; *utsunoṣi*—you agitate; *īkṣamāṇānām*—of the onlookers; *kanduka*—with a ball; *krīḍayā*—by play; *manaḥ*—the mind.

TRANSLATION

Whosoever you may be, O beautiful girl, we are fortunate in being able to see you. While playing with a ball, you have agitated the minds of all onlookers.

PURPORT

Demons arrange many kinds of performances to see the glaring beauty of a beautiful woman. Here it is stated that they saw the girl playing with a ball. Sometimes the demoniac arrange for so-called sports, like tennis, with the opposite sex. The purpose of such sporting is to see the bodily construction of the beautiful girl and enjoy a subtle sex mentality. This demoniac sex mentality of material enjoyment is sometimes encouraged by so-called *yogīs* who encourage the public to enjoy sex life in different varieties and at the same time advertise that if one meditates on a certain manufactured *mantra* one can become God within six months. The public wants to be cheated, and Kṛṣṇa therefore creates such cheaters to misrepresent and delude. These so-called *yogīs* are actually enjoyers of the world garbed as *yogīs*. *Bhagavad-gītā*, however, recommends that if one wants to enjoy life, then it cannot be with these gross senses. A patient is advised by the experienced physician to refrain from ordinary enjoyment while in the diseased condition. A diseased person cannot enjoy anything; he has to restrain his enjoyment in order to get rid of the disease. Similarly, our material condition is a diseased condition. If one wants to enjoy real sense enjoyment, then one must get free of the entanglement of material existence. In spiritual life we can enjoy sense enjoyment which has no end. The difference between material and spiritual enjoyment is that material enjoyment is limited. Even if a man engages in material sex enjoyment, he cannot enjoy it for long. But when the sex enjoyment is given up, then one can enter spiritual life, which is unending. In the *Bhāgavatam* (5.5.1) it is stated that *brahma-saukhya*, spiritual happiness, is *ananta*, unending. Foolish creatures are enamored by the beauty of matter and think that the enjoyment it offers is real, but actually that is not real enjoyment.

TEXT 36

नैकत्र ते जयति शालिनि पादपद्मं
घ्नन्त्या मुहुः करतलेन पतत्पतङ्गम् ।
मध्यं विषीदति बृहत्स्तनभारभीतं
शान्तेव दृष्टिरमला सुशिखासमूहः ॥३६॥

naikatra te jayati śālini pāda-padmaṁ
ghnantyā muhuḥ kara-talena patat-pataṅgam
madhyaṁ viṣīdati bṛhat-stana-bhāra-bhītaṁ
śānteva dṛṣṭir amalā suśikhā-samūhaḥ

na—not; *ekatra*—in one place; *te*—your; *jayati*—stay; *śālini*—O beautiful woman; *pāda-padmam*—lotus feet; *ghnantyāḥ*—striking; *muhuḥ*—again and again; *kara-talena*—by the palm of the hand; *patat*—bouncing; *pataṅgam*—the ball; *madhyam*—waist; *viṣīdati*—

gets fatigued; *bṛhat*—full grown; *stana*—of your breasts; *bhāra*—by the weight; *bhītam*—oppressed; *śāntā iva*—as if fatigued; *dṛṣṭiḥ*—vision; *amalā*—clear; *su*—beautiful; *śikhā*—your hair; *samūhaḥ*—bunch.

TRANSLATION

O beautiful woman, when you strike the bouncing ball against the ground with your hand again and again, your lotus feet do not stay in one place. Oppressed by the weight of your full-grown breasts, your waist becomes fatigued, and your clear vision grows dull, as it were. Pray braid your comely hair.

PURPORT

The demons observed beautiful gestures in the woman's every step. Here they praise her full-grown breasts, her scattered hair and her movements in stepping forward and backward while playing with the ball. In every step they enjoy her womanly beauty, and while they enjoy her beauty their minds become agitated by sex desire. As moths at night surround a fire and are killed, so the demons become victims of the movements of the ball-like breasts of a beautiful woman. The scattered hair of a beautiful woman also afflicts the heart of a lusty demon.

TEXT 37

इति सायन्तनीं सन्ध्यामसुराः प्रमदायतीम् ।
प्रलोभयन्तीं जगृहुर्मत्वा मूढधियः स्त्रियम् ॥३७॥

iti sāyantanīṁ sandhyām
asurāḥ pramadāyatīm
pralobhayantīṁ jagṛhur
matvā mūḍha-dhiyaḥ striyam

iti—in this way; *sāyantanīm*—the evening; *sandhyām*—twilight; *asurāḥ*—the demons; *pramadāyatīm*—behaving like a wanton woman; *pralobhayantīm*—alluring; *jagṛhuḥ*—seized; *matvā*—thinking to be; *mūḍha-dhiyaḥ*—unintelligent; *striyam*—a woman.

TRANSLATION

The asuras, clouded in their understanding, took the evening twilight to be a beautiful woman showing herself in her alluring form, and they seized her.

PURPORT

The *asuras* are described here as *mūḍha-dhiyaḥ*, meaning that they are captivated by ignorance, just like the ass. The demons were captivated by the false, glaring beauty of this material form, and thus they embraced her.

TEXT 38

प्रहस्य भावगम्भीरं जिघ्रन्त्यात्मानमात्मना ।
कान्त्या ससर्ज भगवान् गन्धर्वाप्सरसां गणान् ॥३८॥

prahasya bhāva-gambhīraṁ
jighrantyātmānam ātmanā
kāntyā sasarja bhagavān
gandharvāpsarasāṁ gaṇān

prahasya—smiling; *bhāva-gambhīram*—with a deep purpose; *jighrantyā*—understanding; *ātmānam*—himself; *ātmanā*—by himself; *kāntyā*—by his loveliness; *sasarja*—created; *bhagavān*—the worshipful Lord Brahmā; *gandharva*—the celestial musicians; *apsarasām*—and of the heavenly dancing girls; *gaṇān*—the hosts of.

TRANSLATION

With a laugh full of deep significance, the worshipful Brahmā then evolved by his own loveliness, which seemed to enjoy itself by itself, the hosts of Gandharvas and Apsarās.

PURPORT

The musicians in the upper planetary systems are called Gandharvas, and the dancing girls are called Apsarās. After being attacked by the demons and evolving a form of a beautiful woman in the twilight, Brahmā next created Gandharvas and Apsarās. Music and dancing employed in sense gratification are to be accepted as demoniac, but the same music and dancing, when employed in glorifying the Supreme Lord as *kīrtana*, are transcendental, and they bring about a life completely fit for spiritual enjoyment.

TEXT 39

विससर्ज तनुं तां वै ज्योत्स्नां कान्तिमतीं प्रियाम् ।
त एव चाददुः प्रीत्या विश्वावसुपुरोगमाः ॥३९॥

visasarja tanuṁ tāṁ vai
jyotsnāṁ kāntimatīṁ priyām
ta eva cādaduḥ prītyā
viśvāvasu-purogamāḥ

visasarja—gave up; *tanum*—form; *tām*—that; *vai*—in fact; *jyotsnām*—moonlight; *kānti-matīm*—shining; *priyām*—beloved; *te*—the Gandharvas; *eva*—certainly; *ca*—and; *ādaduḥ*—took possession; *prītyā*—gladly; *viśvāvasu-puraḥ-gamāḥ*—headed by Viśvāvasu.

TRANSLATION

After that, Brahmā gave up that shining and beloved form of moonlight. Viśvāvasu and other Gandharvas gladly took possession of it.

TEXT 40

सृष्ट्वा भूतपिशाचांश्च भगवानात्मतन्द्रिणा ।
दिग्वाससो मुक्तकेशान् वीक्ष्य चामीलयद् दृशौ ॥४०॥

sṛṣṭvā bhūta-piśācāṁś ca
bhagavān ātma-tandriṇā
dig-vāsaso mukta-keśān
vīkṣya cāmīlayad dṛśau

sṛṣṭvā—having created; *bhūta*—ghosts; *piśācān*—fiends; *ca*—and; *bhagavān*—Lord Brahmā; *ātma*—his; *tandriṇā*—from laziness; *dik-vāsasaḥ*—naked; *mukta*—disheveled; *keśān*—hair; *vīkṣya*—seeing; *ca*—and; *amīlayat*—closed; *dṛśau*—two eyes.

TRANSLATION

The glorious Brahmā next evolved from his sloth the ghosts and fiends, but he closed his eyes when he saw them stand naked with their hair scattered.

PURPORT

Ghosts and mischievous hobgoblins are also the creation of Brahmā; they are not false. All of them are meant for putting the conditioned soul into various miseries. They are understood to be the creation of Brahmā under the direction of the Supreme Lord.

TEXT 41

जगृहुस्तद्विसृष्टां तां जृम्भणाख्यां तनुं प्रभोः ।
निद्रामिन्द्रियविक्लेदो यया भूतेषु दृश्यते ।
येनोच्छिष्टान्धर्षयन्ति तमुन्मादं प्रचक्षते ॥४१॥

jagṛhus tad-visṛṣṭāṁ tāṁ
jṛmbhaṇākhyāṁ tanuṁ prabhoḥ
nidrām indriya-vikledo
yayā bhūteṣu dṛśyate
yenocchiṣṭān dharṣayanti
tam unmādaṁ pracakṣate

jagṛhuḥ—took possession; *tat-visṛṣṭām*—thrown off by him; *tām*—that; *jṛmbhaṇa-ākhyām*—known as yawning; *tanum*—the body; *prabhoḥ*—of Lord Brahmā; *nidrām*—sleep; *indriya-vikledaḥ*—drooling; *yayā*—by which; *bhūteṣu*—among the living beings; *dṛśyate*—is observed; *yena*—by which; *ucchiṣṭān*—smeared with stool and urine; *dharṣayanti*—bewilder; *tam*—that; *unmādam*—madness; *pracakṣate*—is spoken of.

TRANSLATION

The ghosts and hobgoblins took possession of the body thrown off in the form of yawning by Brahmā, the creator of the living entities. This is also known as the sleep which causes drooling. The hobgoblins and ghosts attack men who are impure, and their attack is spoken of as insanity.

PURPORT

The disease of insanity or being haunted by ghosts takes place in an unclean state of existence. Here it is clearly stated that when a man is fast asleep and saliva flows from his mouth and he remains unclean, ghosts then take advantage of his unclean state and haunt his body. In other words, those who drool while sleeping are considered unclean and are subject to be haunted by ghosts or to go insane.

TEXT 42

ऊर्जस्वन्तं मन्यमान आत्मानं भगवानजः ।
साध्यान् गणान् पितृगणान् परोक्षेणासृजत्प्रभुः ॥४२॥

ūrjasvantaṁ manyamāna
ātmānaṁ bhagavān ajaḥ
sādhyān gaṇān pitṛ-gaṇān
parokṣeṇāsṛjat prabhuḥ

ūrjaḥ-vantam—full of energy; *manyamānaḥ*—recognizing; *ātmānam*—himself; *bhagavān*—the most worshipful; *ajaḥ*—Brahmā; *sādhyān*—the demigods; *gaṇān*—hosts; *pitṛ-gaṇān*—and the Pitās; *parokṣeṇa*—from his invisible form; *asṛjat*—created; *prabhuḥ*—the lord of beings.

TRANSLATION

Recognizing himself to be full of desire and energy, the worshipful Brahmā, the creator of the living entities, evolved from his own invisible form, from his navel, the hosts of Sādhyas and Pitās.

PURPORT

The Sādhyas and Pitās are invisible forms of departed souls, and they are also created by Brahmā.

TEXT 43

त आत्मसर्गं तं कायं पितरः प्रतिपेदिरे ।
साध्येभ्यश्च पितृभ्यश्च कवयो यद्वितन्वते ॥४३॥

ta ātma-sargaṁ taṁ kāyaṁ
pitaraḥ pratipedire
sādhyebhyaś ca pitṛbhyaś ca
kavayo yad vitanvate

te—they; *ātma-sargam*—source of their existence; *tam*—that; *kāyam*—body; *pitaraḥ*—the Pitās; *pratipedire*—accepted; *sādhyebhyaḥ*—to the Sādhyas; *ca*—and; *pitṛbhyaḥ*—to the Pitās; *ca*—also; *kavayaḥ*—those well versed in rituals; *yat*—through which; *vitanvate*—offer oblations.

TRANSLATION

The Pitās themselves took possession of the invisible body, the source of their existence. It is through the medium of this invisible body that those well versed in the rituals offer oblations to the Sādhyas and Pitās [in the form of their departed ancestors] on the occasion of śrāddha.

PURPORT

Śrāddha is a ritualistic performance observed by the followers of the *Vedas.* There is a yearly occasion of fifteen days when ritualistic religionists follow the principle of offering oblations to departed souls. Thus those fathers and ancestors who, by freaks of nature, might not have a gross body for material enjoyment can again gain such bodies due to the offering of *śrāddha* oblations by their descendants. The performance of *śrāddha,* or offering oblations with *prasāda,* is still current in India, especially at Gayā, where oblations are offered at the lotus feet of

Viṣṇu in a celebrated temple. Because the Lord is thus pleased with the devotional service of the descendants, by His grace He liberates the condemned souls of forefathers who do not have gross bodies, and He favors them to again receive a gross body for development of spiritual advancement.

Unfortunately, by the influence of *māyā*, the conditioned soul employs the body he gets for sense gratification, forgetting that such an occupation may lead him to return to an invisible body. The devotee of the Lord, or one who is in Kṛṣṇa consciousness, however, does not need to perform such ritualistic ceremonies as *śrāddha* because he is always pleasing the Supreme Lord; therefore his fathers and ancestors who might have been in difficulty are automatically relieved. The vivid example is Prahlāda Mahārāja. Prahlāda Mahārāja requested Lord Nṛsiṁhadeva to deliver his sinful father, who had so many times offended the lotus feet of the Lord. The Lord replied that in a family where a Vaiṣṇava like Prahlāda is born, not only his father but his father's father and their fathers—up to the fourteenth father back—are all automatically delivered. The conclusion, therefore, is that Kṛṣṇa consciousness is the sum total of all good work for the family, for society and for all living entities. In the *Caitanya-caritāmṛta* the author says that a person fully conversant with Kṛṣṇa consciousness does not perform any rituals because he knows that simply by serving Kṛṣṇa in full Kṛṣṇa consciousness, all rituals are automatically performed.

TEXT 44

सिद्धान् विद्याधरांश्चैव तिरोधानेन सोऽसृजत् ।
तेभ्योऽददात्तमात्मानमन्तर्धानाख्यमद्भुतम् ॥४४॥

siddhān vidyādharāṁś caiva
tirodhānena so 'sṛjat
tebhyo 'dadāt tam ātmānam
antardhānākhyam adbhutam

siddhān—the Siddhas; *vidyādharān*—Vidyādharas; *ca eva*—and also; *tirodhānena*—by the faculty of remaining hidden from vision; *saḥ*—Lord Brahmā; *asṛjat*—created; *tebhyaḥ*—to them; *adadāt*—gave;

tam ātmānam—that form of his; *antardhāna-ākhyam*—known as the Antardhāna; *adbhutam*—wonderful.

TRANSLATION

Then Lord Brahmā, by his ability to be hidden from vision, created the Siddhas and Vidyādharas and gave them that wonderful form of his known as the Antardhāna.

PURPORT

Antardhāna means that these living creatures can be perceived to be present, but they cannot be seen by vision.

TEXT 45

स किन्नरान् किम्पुरुषान् प्रत्यात्म्येनासृजत्प्रभुः ।
मानयन्नात्मनात्मानमात्माभासं विलोकयन् ॥४५॥

sa kinnarān kimpuruṣān
pratyātmyenāsrjat prabhuḥ
mānayann ātmanātmānam
ātmābhāsaṁ vilokayan

saḥ—Lord Brahmā; *kinnarān*—the Kinnaras; *kimpuruṣān*—the Kimpuruṣas; *pratyātmyena*—from his reflection (in water); *asṛjat*—created; *prabhuḥ*—the lord of the living beings (Brahmā); *mānayan*—admiring; *ātmanā ātmānam*—himself by himself; *ātma-ābhāsam*—his reflection; *vilokayan*—seeing.

TRANSLATION

One day, Brahmā, the creator of the living entities, beheld his own reflection in the water, and admiring himself, he evolved Kimpuruṣas as well as Kinnaras out of that reflection.

TEXT 46

ते तु तज्जगृहू रूपं त्यक्तं यत्परमेष्ठिना ।
मिथुनीभूय गायन्तस्तमेवोषसि कर्मभिः ॥४६॥

te tu taj jagṛhū rūpaṁ
tyaktaṁ yat parameṣṭhinā
mithunī-bhūya gāyantas
tam evoṣasi karmabhiḥ

te—they (the Kinnaras and Kimpuruṣas); *tu*—but; *tat*—that; *jagṛhuḥ*—took possession of; *rūpam*—that shadowy form; *tyaktam*—given up; *yat*—which; *parameṣṭhinā*—by Brahmā; *mithunī-bhūya*—coming together with their spouses; *gāyantaḥ*—praise in song; *tam*—him; *eva*—only; *uṣasi*—at daybreak; *karmabhiḥ*—with his exploits.

TRANSLATION

The Kimpuruṣas and Kinnaras took possession of that shadowy form left by Brahmā. That is why they and their spouses sing his praises by recounting his exploits at every daybreak.

PURPORT

The time early in the morning, one and a half hours before sunrise, is called *brāhma-muhūrta.* During this *brāhma-muhūrta,* spiritual activities are recommended. Spiritual activities performed early in the morning have a greater effect than in any other part of the day.

TEXT 47

देहेन वै भोगवता शयानो बहुचिन्तया ।
सर्गेऽनुपचिते क्रोधादुत्ससर्ज ह तद्वपुः ॥४७॥

dehena vai bhogavatā
śayāno bahu-cintayā
sarge 'nupacite krodhād
utsasarja ha tad vapuḥ

dehena—with his body; *vai*—indeed; *bhogavatā*—stretching out full length; *śayānaḥ*—lying fully stretched; *bahu*—great; *cintayā*—with concern; *sarge*—the creation; *anupacite*—not proceeded; *krodhāt*—out of anger; *utsasarja*—gave up; *ha*—in fact; *tat*—that; *vapuḥ*—body.

TRANSLATION

Once Brahmā lay down with his body stretched at full length. He was very concerned that the work of creation had not proceeded apace, and in a sullen mood he gave up that body too.

TEXT 48

येऽहीयन्तामुतः केशा अहयस्तेऽङ्ग जज्ञिरे ।
सर्पाः प्रसर्पतः क्रूरा नागा भोगोरुकन्धराः ॥४८॥

ye 'hīyantāmutaḥ keśā
ahayas te 'ṅga jajñire
sarpāḥ prasarpataḥ krūrā
nāgā bhogoru-kandharāḥ

ye—which; *ahīyanta*—dropped out; *amutaḥ*—from that; *keśāḥ*—hairs; *ahayaḥ*—snakes; *te*—they; *aṅga*—O dear Vidura; *jajñire*—took birth as; *sarpāḥ*—snakes; *prasarpataḥ*—from the crawling body; *krūrāḥ*—envious; *nāgāḥ*—cobras; *bhoga*—with hoods; *uru*—big; *kandharāḥ*—whose necks.

TRANSLATION

O dear Vidura, the hair that dropped from that body transformed into snakes, and even while the body crawled along with its hands and feet contracted, there sprang from it ferocious serpents and Nāgas with their hoods expanded.

TEXT 49

स आत्मानं मन्यमानः कृतकृत्यमिवात्मभूः ।
तदा मनून् ससर्जान्ते मनसा लोकभावनान् ॥४९॥

sa ātmānaṁ manyamānaḥ
kṛta-kṛtyam ivātmabhūḥ
tadā manūn sasarjānte
manasā loka-bhāvanān

saḥ—Lord Brahmā; *ātmānam*—himself; *manyamānaḥ*—considering; *kṛta-kṛtyam*—had accomplished the object of life; *iva*—as if; *ātma-bhūḥ*—born from the Supreme; *tadā*—then; *manūn*—the Manus; *sasarja*—created; *ante*—at the end; *manasā*—from his mind; *loka*—of the world; *bhāvanān*—promoting the welfare.

TRANSLATION

One day Brahmā, the self-born, the first living creature, felt as if the object of his life had been accomplished. At that time he evolved from his mind the Manus, who promote the welfare activities of the universe.

TEXT 50

तेभ्यः सोऽसृजत्स्वीयं पुरं पुरुषमात्मवान् ।
तान् दृष्ट्वा ये पुरा सृष्टाः प्रशशंसुः प्रजापतिम् ॥५०॥

tebhyaḥ so 'sṛjat svīyaṁ
puraṁ puruṣam ātmavān
tān dṛṣṭvā ye purā sṛṣṭāḥ
praśaśaṁsuḥ prajāpatim

tebhyaḥ—to them; *saḥ*—Lord Brahmā; *asṛjat*—gave; *svīyam*—his own; *puram*—body; *puruṣam*—human; *ātma-vān*—self-possessed; *tān*—them; *dṛṣṭvā*—on seeing; *ye*—those who; *purā*—earlier; *sṛṣṭāḥ*—were created (the demigods, Gandharvas, etc., who were created earlier); *praśaśaṁsuḥ*—applauded; *prajāpatim*—Brahmā (the lord of created beings).

TRANSLATION

The self-possessed creator gave them his own human form. On seeing the Manus, those who had been created earlier—the demigods, the Gandharvas and so on—applauded Brahmā, the lord of the universe.

TEXT 51

अहो एतज्जगत्स्रष्टः सुकृतं बत ते कृतम् ।
प्रतिष्ठिताः क्रिया यस्मिन् साकमन्नमदामहे ॥५१॥

aho etaj jagat-sraṣṭaḥ
sukṛtaṁ bata te kṛtam
pratiṣṭhitāḥ kriyā yasmin
sākam annam adāma he

aho—oh; *etat*—this; *jagat-sraṣṭaḥ*—O creator of the universe; *sukṛtam*—well done; *bata*—indeed; *te*—by you; *kṛtam*—produced; *pratiṣṭhitāḥ*—established soundly; *kriyāḥ*—all ritualistic performances; *yasmin*—in which; *sākam*—along with this; *annam*—the sacrificial oblations; *adāma*—we shall share; *he*—O.

TRANSLATION

They prayed: O creator of the universe, we are glad; what you have produced is well done. Since ritualistic acts have now been established soundly in this human form, we shall all share the sacrificial oblations.

PURPORT

The importance of sacrifice is also mentioned in *Bhagavad-gītā*, Third Chapter, verse 10. The Lord confirms there that in the beginning of creation Brahmā created the Manus, along with the ritualistic sacrificial method, and blessed them: "Continue these sacrificial rites, and you will be gradually elevated to your proper position of self-realization and will also enjoy material happiness." All the living entities created by Brahmā are conditioned souls and are inclined to lord it over material nature. The purpose of sacrificial rituals is to revive, gradually, the spiritual realization of the living entities. That is the beginning of life within this universe. These sacrificial rituals, however, are intended to please the Supreme Lord. Unless one pleases the Supreme Lord, or unless one is Kṛṣṇa conscious, one cannot be happy either in material enjoyment or in spiritual realization.

TEXT 52

तपसा विद्यया युक्तो योगेन सुसमाधिना ।
ऋषीनृषिर्हृषीकेशः ससर्जाभिमताः प्रजाः ॥५२॥

tapasā vidyayā yukto
yogena susamādhinā
ṛṣīn ṛṣir hṛṣīkeśaḥ
sasarjābhimatāḥ prajāḥ

tapasā—by penance; *vidyayā*—by worship; *yuktaḥ*—being engaged; *yogena*—by concentration of the mind in devotion; *su-samādhinā*—by nice meditation; *ṛṣīn*—the sages; *ṛṣiḥ*—the first seer (Brahmā); *hṛṣīkeśaḥ*—the controller of his senses; *sasarja*—created; *abhimatāḥ*—beloved; *prajāḥ*—sons.

TRANSLATION

Having equipped himself with austere penance, adoration, mental concentration and absorption in devotion, accompanied by dispassion, and having controlled his senses, Brahmā, the self-born living creature, evolved great sages as his beloved sons.

PURPORT

The ritualistic performances of sacrifice are meant for material economic development; in other words, they are meant to keep the body in good condition for cultivation of spiritual knowledge. But for actual attainment of spiritual knowledge, other qualifications are needed. What is essential is *vidyā*, or worship of the Supreme Lord. Sometimes the word *yoga* is used to refer to the gymnastic performances of different bodily postures which help mental concentration. Generally, the different bodily postures in the *yoga* system are accepted by less intelligent men to be the end of *yoga*, but actually they are meant to concentrate the mind upon the Supersoul. After creating persons for economic development, Brahmā created sages who would set the example for spiritual realization.

TEXT 53

तेभ्यश्चैकैकशः स्वस्य देहस्यांशमदादजः ।
यत्तत्समाधियोगर्द्धितपोविद्याविरक्तिमत् ॥५३॥

tebhyaś caikaikaśaḥ svasya
dehasyāṁśam adād ajaḥ

yat tat samādhi-yogarddhi-
tapo-vidyā-viraktimat

tebhyaḥ—to them; *ca*—and; *ekaikaśaḥ*—each one; *svasya*—of his own; *dehasya*—body; *aṁśam*—part; *adāt*—gave; *ajaḥ*—the unborn Brahmā; *yat*—which; *tat*—that; *samādhi*—deep meditation; *yoga*—concentration of the mind; *ṛddhi*—supernatural power; *tapaḥ*—austerity; *vidyā*—knowledge; *virakti*—renunciation; *mat*—possessing.

TRANSLATION

To each one of these sons the unborn creator of the universe gave a part of his own body, which was characterized by deep meditation, mental concentration, supernatural power, austerity, adoration and renunciation.

PURPORT

The word *viraktimat* in this verse means "possessed of the qualification of renunciation." Spiritual realization cannot be attained by materialistic persons. For those who are addicted to sense enjoyment, spiritual realization is not possible. In *Bhagavad-gītā* it is stated that those who are too attached to seeking material possessions and material enjoyment cannot reach *yoga-samādhi*, absorption in Kṛṣṇa consciousness. Propaganda that one can enjoy this life materially and at the same time spiritually advance is simply bogus. The principles of renunciation are four: (1) to avoid illicit sex life, (2) to avoid meat-eating, (3) to avoid intoxication and (4) to avoid gambling. These four principles are called *tapasya*, or austerity. To absorb the mind in the Supreme in Kṛṣṇa consciousness is the process of spiritual realization.

Thus end the Bhaktivedanta purports of the Third Canto, Twentieth Chapter, of the Śrīmad-Bhāgavatam, *entitled "Conversation Between Maitreya and Vidura."*

CHAPTER TWENTY-ONE

Conversation Between Manu and Kardama

TEXT 1

विदुर उवाच
स्वायम्भुवस्य च मनोर्वंशः परमसम्मतः ।
कथ्यतां भगवन् यत्र मैथुनेनैधिरे प्रजाः ॥ १ ॥

vidura uvāca
svāyambhuvasya ca manor
vaṁśaḥ parama-sammataḥ
kathyatām bhagavan yatra
maithunenaidhire prajāḥ

viduraḥ uvāca—Vidura said; *svāyambhuvasya*—of Svāyambhuva; *ca*—and; *manoḥ*—of Manu; *vaṁśaḥ*—the dynasty; *parama*—most; *sammataḥ*—esteemed; *kathyatām*—kindly describe; *bhagavan*—O worshipful sage; *yatra*—in which; *maithunena*—through sexual intercourse; *edhire*—multiplied; *prajāḥ*—the progeny.

TRANSLATION

Vidura said: The line of Svāyambhuva Manu was most esteemed. O worshipful sage, I beg you—give me an account of this race, whose progeny multiplied through sexual intercourse.

PURPORT

Regulated sex life to generate good population is worth accepting. Actually, Vidura was not interested in hearing the history of persons who merely engaged in sex life, but he was interested in the progeny of Svāyambhuva Manu because in that dynasty, good devotee kings appeared who protected their subjects very carefully with spiritual knowledge. By hearing the history of their activities, therefore, one becomes more enlightened. An important word used in this connection is *parama-sammataḥ*, which indicates that the progeny created by Svāyambhuva Manu and his sons was approved of by great authorities. In other words, sex life for creating exemplary population is acceptable to all sages and authorities of Vedic scripture.

TEXT 2

प्रियव्रतोत्तानपादौ सुतौ स्वायम्भुवस्य वै ।
यथाधर्मं जुगुपतुः सप्तद्वीपवतीं महीम् ॥ २ ॥

priyavratottānapādau
sutau svāyambhuvasya vai
yathā-dharmaṁ jugupatuḥ
sapta-dvīpavatīṁ mahīm

priyavrata—Mahārāja Priyavrata; *uttānapādau*—and Mahārāja Uttānapāda; *sutau*—the two sons; *svāyambhuvasya*—of Svāyambhuva Manu; *vai*—indeed; *yathā*—according to; *dharmam*—religious principles; *jugupatuḥ*—ruled; *sapta-dvīpa-vatīm*—consisting of seven islands; *mahīm*—the world.

TRANSLATION

The two great sons of Svāyambhuva Manu—Priyavrata and Uttānapāda—ruled the world, consisting of seven islands, just according to religious principles.

PURPORT

Śrīmad-Bhāgavatam is also a history of the great rulers of different parts of the universe. In this verse the names of Priyavrata and Uttānapāda, sons of Svāyambhuva, are mentioned. They ruled this earth, which is divided into seven islands. These seven islands are still current, as Asia, Europe, Africa, America, Australia and the North and South Poles. There is no chronological history of all the Indian kings in *Śrīmad-Bhāgavatam*, but the deeds of the most important kings, such as Priyavrata and Uttānapāda, and many others, like Lord Rāmacandra and

Mahārāja Yudhiṣṭhira, are recorded because the activities of such pious kings are worth hearing; people may benefit by studying their histories.

TEXT 3

तस्य वै दुहिता ब्रह्मन्देवहूतीति विश्रुता ।
पत्नी प्रजापतेरुक्ता कर्दमस्य त्वयानघ ॥ ३ ॥

tasya vai duhitā brahman
devahūtīti viśrutā
patnī prajāpater uktā
kardamasya tvayānagha

tasya—of that Manu; *vai*—indeed; *duhitā*—the daughter; *brahman*—O holy *brāhmaṇa; devahūti*—named Devahūti; *iti*—thus; *viśrutā*—was known; *patnī*—wife; *prajāpateḥ*—of the lord of created beings; *uktā*—has been spoken of; *kardamasya*—of Kardama Muni; *tvayā*—by you; *anagha*—O sinless one.

TRANSLATION

O holy brāhmaṇa, O sinless one, you have spoken of his daughter, known by the name Devahūti, as the wife of the sage Kardama, the lord of created beings.

PURPORT

Here we are speaking of Svāyambhuva Manu, but in *Bhagavad-gītā* we hear about Vaivasvata Manu. The present age belongs to the Vaivasvata Manu. Svāyambhuva Manu was previously ruling, and his history begins from the Varāha age, or the millennium when the Lord appeared as the boar. There are fourteen Manus in one day of the life of Brahmā, and in the life of each Manu there are particular incidents. The Vaivasvata Manu of *Bhagavad-gītā* is different from Svāyambhuva Manu.

TEXT 4

तस्यां स वै महायोगी युक्तायां योगलक्षणैः ।
ससर्ज कतिधा वीर्यं तन्मे शुश्रूषवे वद ॥ ४ ॥

tasyāṁ sa vai mahā-yogī
yuktāyāṁ yoga-lakṣaṇaiḥ
sasarja katidhā vīryaṁ
tan me śuśrūṣave vada

tasyām—in her; *saḥ*—Kardama Muni; *vai*—in fact; *mahā-yogī*—great mystic *yogī; yuktāyām*—endowed; *yoga-lakṣaṇaiḥ*—with the eightfold symptoms of yogic perfection; *sasarja*—propagated; *katidhā*—how many times; *vīryam*—offspring; *tat*—that narration; *me*—to me; *śuśrūṣave*—who am eager to hear; *vada*—tell.

TRANSLATION

How many offspring did that great yogī beget through the princess, who was endowed with eightfold perfection in the yoga principles? Oh, pray tell me this, for I am eager to hear it.

PURPORT

Here Vidura inquired about Kardama Muni and his wife, Devahūti, and about their children. It is described here that Devahūti was very much advanced in the performance of eightfold *yoga*. The eight divisions of *yoga* performance are described as (1) control of the senses, (2) strict following of the rules and regulations, (3) practice of the different sitting postures, (4) control of the breath, (5) withdrawing the senses from sense objects, (6) concentration of the mind, (7) meditation and (8) self-realization. After self-realization there are eight further perfectional stages, which are called *yoga-siddhis*. The husband and wife, Kardama and Devahūti, were advanced in *yoga* practice; the husband was a *mahā-yogī*, great mystic, and the wife was a *yoga-lakṣaṇa*, or one advanced in *yoga*. They united and produced children. Formerly, after making their lives perfect, great sages and saintly persons used to beget children, otherwise they strictly observed the rules and regulations of celibacy. *Brahmacarya* (following the rules and regulations of celibacy) is required for perfection of self-realization and mystic power. There is no recommendation in the Vedic scriptures that one can go on enjoying material sense gratification at one's whims, as one likes, and at the same time become a great meditator by paying a rascal some money.

TEXT 5

रुचिर्यो भगवान् ब्रह्मन्दक्षो वा ब्रह्मणः सुतः ।
यथा ससर्ज भूतानि लब्ध्वा भार्यां च मानवीम् ॥ ५ ॥

rucir yo bhagavān brahman
dakṣo vā brahmaṇaḥ sutaḥ
yathā sasarja bhūtāni
labdhvā bhāryāṁ ca mānavīm

ruciḥ—Ruci; *yaḥ*—who; *bhagavān*—worshipful; *brahman*—O holy sage; *dakṣaḥ*—Dakṣa; *vā*—and; *brahmaṇaḥ*—of Lord Brahmā; *sutaḥ*—the son; *yathā*—in what way; *sasarja*—generated; *bhūtāni*—offspring; *labdhvā*—after securing; *bhāryām*—as their wives; *ca*—and; *mānavīm*—the daughters of Svāyambhuva Manu.

TRANSLATION

O holy sage, tell me how the worshipful Ruci and Dakṣa, the son of Brahmā, generated children after securing as their wives the other two daughters of Svāyambhuva Manu.

PURPORT

All the great personalities who increased the population in the beginning of the creation are called Prajāpatis. Brahmā is also known as Prajāpati, as were some of his later sons. Svāyambhuva Manu is also known as Prajāpati, as is Dakṣa, another son of Brahmā. Svāyambhuva had two daughters, Ākūti and Prasūti. The Prajāpati Ruci married Ākūti, and Dakṣa married Prasūti. These couples and their children produced immense numbers of children to populate the entire universe. Vidura's inquiry was, "How did they beget the population in the beginning?"

TEXT 6

मैत्रेय उवाच
प्रजाः सृजेति भगवान् कर्दमो ब्रह्मणोदितः ।
सरस्वत्यां तपस्तेपे सहस्राणां समा दश ॥ ६ ॥

maitreya uvāca
prajāḥ sṛjeti bhagavān
kardamo brahmaṇoditaḥ
sarasvatyāṁ tapas tepe
sahasrāṇāṁ samā daśa

maitreyaḥ uvāca—the great sage Maitreya said; *prajāḥ*—children; *sṛja*—beget; *iti*—thus; *bhagavān*—the worshipful; *kardamaḥ*—Kardama Muni; *brahmaṇā*—by Lord Brahmā; *uditaḥ*—commanded: *sarasvatyām*—on the bank of the River Sarasvatī; *tapaḥ*—penance; *tepe*—practiced; *sahasrāṇām*—of thousands; *samāḥ*—years; *daśa*—ten.

TRANSLATION

The great sage Maitreya replied: Commanded by Lord Brahmā to beget children in the worlds, the worshipful Kardama Muni practiced penance on the bank of the River Sarasvatī for a period of ten thousand years.

PURPORT

It is understood herein that Kardama Muni meditated in *yoga* for ten thousand years before attaining perfection. Similarly, we have information that Vālmīki Muni also practiced *yoga* meditation for sixty thousand years before attaining perfection. Therefore, *yoga* practice can be successfully performed by persons who have a very long duration of life, such as one hundred thousand years; in that way it is possible to have perfection in *yoga*. Otherwise, there is no possibility of attaining the real perfection. Following the regulations, controlling the senses and practicing the different sitting postures are merely the preliminary practices. We do not know how people can be captivated by the bogus *yoga* system in which it is stated that simply by meditating fifteen minutes daily one can attain the perfection of becoming one with God. This age (Kali-yuga) is the age of bluffing and quarrel. Actually there is no possibility of attaining *yoga* perfection by such paltry proposals. The Vedic literature, for emphasis, clearly states three times that in this age of Kali—*kalau nāsty eva nāsty eva nāsty eva*—there is no other alternative, no other alternative, no other alternative than *harer nāma*, chanting the holy name of the Lord.

TEXT 7

ततः समाधियुक्तेन क्रियायोगेन कर्दमः ।
सम्प्रपेदे हरिं भक्त्या प्रपन्नवरदाशुषम् ॥ ७ ॥

tataḥ samādhi-yuktena
kriyā-yogena kardamaḥ
samprapede hariṁ bhaktyā
prapanna-varadāśuṣam

tataḥ—then, in that penance; *samādhi-yuktena*—in trance; *kriyā-yogena*—by *bhakti-yoga* worship; *kardamaḥ*—the sage Kardama; *samprapede*—served; *harim*—the Personality of Godhead; *bhaktyā*—in devotional service; *prapanna*—to the surrendered souls; *vara-dāśuṣam*—the bestower of all blessings.

TRANSLATION

During that period of penance, the sage Kardama, by worship through devotional service in trance, propitiated the Personality of Godhead, who is the quick bestower of all blessings upon those who flee to Him for protection.

PURPORT

The significance of meditation is described here. Kardama Muni practiced mystic *yoga* meditation for ten thousand years just to please the Supreme Personality of Godhead, Hari. Therefore, whether one practices *yoga* or speculates and does research to find God, one's efforts must be mixed with the process of devotion. Without devotion, nothing can be perfect. The target of perfection and realization is the Supreme Personality of Godhead. In the Sixth Chapter of *Bhagavad-gītā* it is clearly said that one who constantly engages in Kṛṣṇa consciousness is the topmost *yogī*. The Personality of Godhead, Hari, also fulfills the desires of His surrendered devotee. One has to surrender unto the lotus feet of the Personality of Godhead, Hari, or Kṛṣṇa, in order to achieve real success. Devotional service, or engagement in Kṛṣṇa consciousness, is the direct method, and all other methods, although recommended, are indirect. In this age of Kali the direct method is especially more feasible than the indirect because people are short-living, their intelligence is poor, and they are poverty-stricken and embarrassed by so many miserable disturbances. Lord Caitanya, therefore, has given the greatest boon: in this age one simply has to chant the holy name of God to attain perfection in spiritual life.

The words *samprapede harim* mean that in various ways Kardama Muni satisfied the Supreme Personality of Godhead, Hari, by his devotional service. Devotional service is also expressed by the word *kriyā-yogena.* Kardama Muni not only meditated but also engaged in devotional service; to attain perfection in *yoga* practice or meditation, one must act in devotional service by hearing, chanting, remembering, etc. Remembering is meditation also. But who is to be remembered? One should remember the Supreme Personality of Godhead. Not only must one remember the Supreme Person; one must hear about the activities of the Lord and chant His glories. This information is in the authoritative scriptures. After engaging himself for ten thousand years in performing different types of devotional service, Kardama Muni attained the perfection of meditation, but that is not possible in this age of Kali, wherein it is very difficult to live for as much as one hundred years. At the present moment, who will be successful in the rigid performance of the many *yoga* rules and regulations? Moreover, perfection is attained only by those who are surrendered souls. Where there is no mention of the Personality of Godhead, where is there surrender? And where there is no meditation upon the Personality of Godhead, where is the *yoga* practice? Unfortunately, people in this age, especially persons who are of a demoniac nature, want to be cheated. Thus the Supreme Personality of Godhead sends great cheaters who mislead them in the name of *yoga* and render their lives useless and doomed. In *Bhagavad-gītā,* therefore, it is clearly stated, in the Sixteenth Chapter, verse 17, that rascals of self-made authority, being puffed up by illegally collected money, perform *yoga* without following the authoritative books. They are very proud of the money they have plundered from innocent persons who wanted to be cheated.

TEXT 8

तावत्प्रसन्नो भगवान् पुष्कराक्षः कृते युगे ।
दर्शयामास तं क्षत्तः शाब्दं ब्रह्म दधद्वपुः ॥ ८ ॥

tāvat prasanno bhagavān
puṣkarākṣaḥ kṛte yuge
darśayām āsa taṁ kṣattaḥ
śābdaṁ brahma dadhad vapuḥ

tāvat—then; *prasannaḥ*—being pleased; *bhagavān*—the Supreme Personality of Godhead; *puṣkara-akṣaḥ*—lotus-eyed; *kṛte yuge*—in the Satya-yuga; *darśayām āsa*—showed; *tam*—to that Kardama Muni; *kṣattaḥ*—O Vidura; *śābdam*—which is to be understood only through the *Vedas; brahma*—the Absolute Truth; *dadhat*—exhibiting; *vapuḥ*—His transcendental body.

TRANSLATION

Then, in the Satya-yuga, the lotus-eyed Supreme Personality of Godhead, being pleased, showed Himself to that Kardama Muni and displayed His transcendental form, which can be understood only through the Vedas.

PURPORT

Here two points are very significant. The first is that Kardama Muni attained success by *yoga* practice in the beginning of Satya-yuga, when people used to live for one hundred thousand years. Kardama Muni attained success, and the Lord, being pleased with him, showed him His form, which is not imaginary. Sometimes the impersonalists recommend that one can arbitrarily concentrate one's mind on some form he imagines or which pleases him. But here it is very clearly said that the form which the Lord showed to Kardama Muni by His divine grace is described in the Vedic literature. *Śābdaṁ brahma:* the forms of the Lord are clearly indicated in the Vedic literature. Kardama Muni did not discover any imaginary form of God, as alleged by rascals; he actually saw the eternal, blissful and transcendental form of the Lord.

TEXT 9

स तं विरजमर्काभं सितपद्मोत्पलस्रजम् ।
स्निग्धनीलालकव्रातवक्त्राब्जं विरजोऽम्बरम् ॥९॥

sa taṁ virajam arkābhaṁ
sita-padmotpala-srajam

snigdha-nīlālaka-vrāta-
vaktrābjaṁ virajo 'mbaram

saḥ—that Kardama Muni; *tam*—Him; *virajam*—without contamination; *arka-ābham*—effulgent like the sun; *sita*—white; *padma*—lotuses; *utpala*—water lilies; *srajam*—garland; *snigdha*—slick; *nīla*—blackish blue; *alaka*—of locks of hair; *vrāta*—an abundance; *vaktra*—face; *abjam*—lotuslike; *virajaḥ*—spotless; *ambaram*—clothing.

TRANSLATION

Kardama Muni saw the Supreme Personality of Godhead, who is free from material contamination, in His eternal form, effulgent like the sun, wearing a garland of white lotuses and water lilies. The Lord was clad in spotless yellow silk, and His lotus face was fringed with slick dark locks of curly hair.

TEXT 10

किरीटिनं कुण्डलिनं शङ्खचक्रगदाधरम् ।
श्वेतोत्पलक्रीडनकं मनःस्पर्शस्मितेक्षणम् ॥१०॥

kirīṭinaṁ kuṇḍalinaṁ
śaṅkha-cakra-gadā-dharam
śvetotpala-krīḍanakaṁ
manaḥ-sparśa-smitekṣaṇam

kirīṭinam—adorned with a crown; *kuṇḍalinam*—wearing earrings; *śaṅkha*—conch; *cakra*—disc; *gadā*—mace; *dharam*—holding; *śveta*—white; *utpala*—lily; *krīḍanakam*—plaything; *manaḥ*—heart; *sparśa*—touching; *smita*—smiling; *īkṣaṇam*—and glancing.

TRANSLATION

Adorned with a crown and earrings, He held His characteristic conch, disc and mace in three of His hands and a white lily in the fourth. He glanced about in a happy, smiling mood whose sight captivates the hearts of all devotees.

TEXT 11

विन्यस्तचरणाम्भोजमंसदेशे गरुत्मतः ।
दृष्ट्वा खेऽवस्थितं वक्षःश्रियं कौस्तुभकन्धरम् ॥११॥

vinyasta-caraṇāmbhojam
aṁsa-deśe garutmataḥ
dṛṣṭvā khe 'vasthitaṁ vakṣaḥ-
śriyaṁ kaustubha-kandharam

vinyasta—having been placed; *caraṇa-ambhojam*—lotus feet; *aṁsa-deśe*—on the shoulders; *garutmataḥ*—of Garuḍa; *dṛṣṭvā*—having seen; *khe*—in the air; *avasthitam*—standing; *vakṣaḥ*—on His chest; *śriyam*—auspicious mark; *kaustubha*—the Kaustubha gem; *kandharam*—neck.

TRANSLATION

A golden streak on His chest, the famous Kaustubha gem suspended from His neck, He stood in the air with His lotus feet placed on the shoulders of Garuḍa.

PURPORT

The descriptions in verses 9–11 of the Lord in His transcendental, eternal form are understood to be descriptions from the authoritative Vedic version. These descriptions are certainly not the imagination of Kardama Muni. The decorations of the Lord are beyond material conception, as admitted even by impersonalists like Śaṅkarācārya: Nārāyaṇa, the Supreme Personality of Godhead, has nothing to do with the material creation. The varieties of the transcendental Lord—His body, His form, His dress, His instruction, His words—are not manufactured by the material energy, but are all confirmed in the Vedic literature. By performance of *yoga* Kardama Muni actually saw the Supreme Lord as He is. There was no point in seeing an imagined form of God after practicing *yoga* for ten thousand years. The perfection of *yoga*, therefore, does not terminate in voidness or impersonalism; on the contrary, the perfection of *yoga* is attained when one actually sees the Personality of Godhead in His eternal form. The process of Kṛṣṇa consciousness is to deliver the form of Kṛṣṇa directly. The form of Kṛṣṇa is described in the authoritative Vedic literature *Brahma-saṁhitā:* His abode is made of *cintāmaṇi* stone, and the Lord plays there as a cowherd boy and is served by many thousands of *gopīs.* These descriptions are authoritative, and a Kṛṣṇa conscious person takes them directly, acts on them, preaches them and practices devotional service as enjoined in the authoritative scriptures.

TEXT 12

जातहर्षोऽपतन्मूर्ध्ना क्षितौ लब्धमनोरथः ।
गीर्भिस्त्वभ्यगृणात्प्रीतिस्वभावात्मा कृताञ्जलिः ॥१२॥

jāta-harṣo 'patan mūrdhnā
kṣitau labdha-manorathaḥ
gīrbhis tv abhyagṛṇāt prīti-
svabhāvātmā kṛtāñjaliḥ

jāta-harṣaḥ—naturally jubilant; *apatat*—he fell down; *mūrdhnā*—with his head; *kṣitau*—on the ground; *labdha*—having been achieved; *manaḥ-rathaḥ*—his desire; *gīrbhiḥ*—with prayers; *tu*—and; *abhyagṛṇāt*—he satisfied; *prīti-svabhāva-ātmā*—whose heart is by nature always full of love; *kṛta-añjaliḥ*—with folded hands.

TRANSLATION

When Kardama Muni actually realized the Supreme Personality of Godhead in person, he was greatly satisfied because his transcendental desire was fulfilled. He fell on the ground with his head bowed to offer obeisances unto the lotus feet of the Lord. His heart naturally full of love of God, with folded hands he satisfied the Lord with prayers.

PURPORT

The realization of the personal form of the Lord is the highest perfectional stage of *yoga.* In the Sixth Chapter of *Bhagavad-gītā,* where *yoga* practice is described, this realization of the personal form of the Lord is called the perfection of *yoga.* After practicing the sitting postures and other regulative principles of the system, one finally reaches the stage of *samādhi*—absorption in the Supreme. In the *samādhi* stage one can see the Supreme Personality of Godhead in His partial form as Paramātmā, or as He is. *Samādhi* is described in authoritative *yoga* scriptures, such as the *Patañjali-sūtras*, to be a transcendental pleasure. The *yoga* system described in the books of Patañjali is authoritative, and the modern so-called *yogīs* who have manufactured their own ways, not consulting the authorities, are simply ludicrous. The Patañjali *yoga* system is called *aṣṭāṅga-yoga.* Sometimes impersonalists pollute the Patañjali *yoga* system because they are monists. Patañjali describes that the soul is transcendentally pleased when he meets the Supersoul and sees Him. If the existence of the Supersoul and the individual is admitted, then the impersonalist theory of monism is nullified. Therefore some impersonalists and void philosophers twist the Patañjali system in their own way and pollute the whole *yoga* process.

According to Patañjali, when one becomes free from all material desires he attains his real, transcendental situation, and realization of that stage is called spiritual power. In material activities a person engages in the modes of material nature. The aspirations of such people are (1) to be religious, (2) to be economically enriched, (3) to be able to gratify the senses and, at last, (4) to become one with the Supreme. According to the monists, when a *yogī* becomes one with the Supreme and loses his individual existence, he attains the highest stage, called *kaivalya.* But actually, the stage of realization of the Personality of Godhead is *kaivalya.* The oneness of understanding that the Supreme Lord is fully spiritual and that in full spiritual realization one can understand what He is—the Supreme Personality of Godhead—is called *kaivalya*, or, in the language of Patañjali, realization of spiritual power. His proposal is that when one is freed from material desires and fixed in spiritual realization of the self and the Superself, that is called *cit-śakti.* In full spiritual realization there is a perception of spiritual happiness, and that happiness is described in *Bhagavad-gītā* as the supreme happiness, which is beyond the material senses. Trance is described to be of two kinds, *samprajñāta* and *asamprajñāta*, or mental speculation and self-realization. In *samādhi* or *asamprajñāta* one can realize, by his spiritual senses, the spiritual form of the Lord. That is the ultimate goal of spiritual realization.

According to Patañjali, when one is fixed in constant realization of the supreme form of the Lord, one has attained the perfectional stage, as attained by Kardama Muni. Unless one attains this stage of perfection—beyond the perfection of the preliminaries of the *yoga* system—there is no ultimate realization. There are eight perfections in the *aṣṭāṅga-yoga* system. One who has attained them can become lighter than the lightest and greater than the greatest, and he can achieve whatever he likes. But even achieving such material success in *yoga* is not the perfection or the ultimate goal. The ultimate goal is described here: Kardama Muni saw the Supreme Personality of Godhead in His eternal form. Devotional service begins with the relationship of the individual soul and the Supreme Soul, or Kṛṣṇa and Kṛṣṇa's devotees, and when one attains it there is no question of falling down. If, through the *yoga* system, one wants to attain the stage of seeing the Supreme Personality of Godhead face to face, but is attracted instead to attainment of some material power, then he is detoured from proceeding further. Material enjoyment, as encouraged by bogus *yogīs*, has nothing to do with the transcendental realization of spiritual happiness. Real devotees of *bhakti-yoga* accept only the material necessities of life absolutely needed to maintain the body and soul together; they refrain completely from all exaggerated material sense gratification. They are prepared to undergo all kinds of tribulation, provided they can make progress in the realization of the Personality of Godhead.

TEXT 13

ऋषिरुवाच
जुष्टं बताद्याखिलसत्त्वराशेः
सांसिद्ध्यमक्ष्णोस्तव दर्शनान्नः ।
यद्दर्शनं जन्मभिरीड्य सद्भि-
राशासते योगिनो रूढयोगाः ॥१३॥

ṛṣir uvāca
juṣṭaṁ batādyākhila-sattva-rāśeḥ
sāṁsiddhyam akṣṇos tava darśanān naḥ
yad-darśanaṁ janmabhir īḍya sadbhir
āśāsate yogino rūḍha-yogāḥ

ṛṣiḥ uvāca—the great sage said; *juṣṭam*—is attained; *bata*—ah; *adya*—now; *akhila*—all; *sattva*—of goodness; *rāśeḥ*—who are the reservoir; *sāṁsiddhyam*—the complete success; *akṣṇoḥ*—of the two eyes; *tava*—of You; *darśanāt*—from the sight; *naḥ*—by us; *yat*—of whom; *darśanam*—sight; *janmabhiḥ*—through births; *īḍya*—O worshipable Lord; *sadbhiḥ*—gradually elevated in position; *āśāsate*—aspire; *yoginaḥ*—*yogīs; rūḍha-yogāḥ*—having obtained perfection in *yoga.*

TRANSLATION

The great sage Kardama said: O supreme worshipful Lord, my power of sight is now fulfilled, having attained the greatest perfection of the sight of You, who are the reservoir of all existences. Through many successive births of deep meditation, advanced yogīs aspire to see Your transcendental form.

PURPORT

The Supreme Personality of Godhead is described here as the reservoir of all goodness and all pleasure. Unless one is situated in the mode of goodness, there is no real pleasure. When, therefore, one's body, mind and activities are situated in the service of the Lord, one is on the highest perfectional stage of goodness. Kardama Muni says, "Your Lordship is the reservoir of all that can be understood by the nomenclature of goodness, and by experiencing You face to face, eye to eye, the perfection of sight has now been attained." These statements are the pure devotional situation; for a devotee, the perfection of the senses is to engage in the service of the Lord. The sense of sight, when engaged in seeing the beauty of the Lord, is perfected; the power to hear, when engaged in hearing the glories of the Lord, is perfected; the power to taste, when one enjoys by eating *prasāda*, is perfected. When all the senses engage in relationship with the Personality of Godhead, one's perfection is technically called *bhakti-yoga*, which entails detaching the senses from material indulgence and attaching them to the service of the Lord. When one is freed from all designated conditional life and fully engages in the service of the Lord, one's service is called *bhakti-yoga*. Kardama Muni admits that seeing the Lord personally in *bhakti-yoga* is the perfection of sight. The exalted perfection of seeing the Lord is not exaggerated by Kardama Muni. He gives evidence that those who are actually elevated in *yoga* aspire in life after life to see this form of the Personality of Godhead. He was not a fictitious *yogī.* Those who are actually on the advanced path aspire only to see the eternal form of the Lord.

TEXT 14

ये मायया ते हतमेधसस्त्वत्-
पादारविन्दं भवसिन्धुपोतम् ।
उपासते कामलवाय तेषां
रासीश कामान्निरयेऽपि ये स्युः ॥१४॥

ye māyayā te hata-medhasas tvat-
pādāravindaṁ bhava-sindhu-potam
upāsate kāma-lavāya teṣāṁ
rāsīśa kāmān niraye 'pi ye syuḥ

ye—those persons; *māyayā*—by the deluding energy; *te*—of You; *hata*—has been lost; *medhasaḥ*—whose intelligence; *tvat*—Your; *pāda-aravindam*—lotus feet; *bhava*—of mundane existence; *sindhu*—the ocean; *potam*—the boat for crossing; *upāsate*—worship; *kāma-lavāya*—for obtaining trivial pleasures; *teṣām*—their; *rāsi*—You bestow; *īśa*—O Lord; *kāmān*—desires; *niraye*—in hell; *api*—even; *ye*—which desires; *syuḥ*—can be available.

TRANSLATION

Your lotus feet are the true vessel to take one across the ocean of mundane nescience. Only persons deprived of their intelligence by the spell of the deluding energy will worship those feet with a view to attain the trivial and momentary pleasures of the senses, which even persons rotting in hell can attain. However, O my Lord, You are so kind that You bestow mercy even upon them.

PURPORT

As stated in *Bhagavad-gītā,* Seventh Chapter, there are two kinds of devotees—those who desire material pleasures and those who desire nothing but service to the Lord. Material pleasures can be attained even by hogs and dogs, whose condition of life is hellish. The hog also eats, sleeps and enjoys sex life to the full extent, and it is also very satisfied with such hellish enjoyment of material existence. Modern *yogīs* advise that because one has senses, one must enjoy to the fullest extent like cats and dogs, yet one can go on and practice *yoga.* This is condemned here by Kardama Muni; he says that such material pleasures are available for cats and dogs in a hellish condition. The Lord is so kind that if so-called *yogīs* are satisfied by hellish pleasures, He can give them facilities to attain all the material pleasures they desire, but they cannot attain the perfectional stage attained by Kardama Muni.

Hellish and demoniac persons do not actually know what is the ultimate attainment in perfection, and therefore they think that sense gratification is the highest goal of life. They advise that one can satisfy the senses and at the same time, by reciting some *mantra* and by some practice, can cheaply aspire for perfection. Such persons are described here as *hata-medhasaḥ,* which means "those whose brains are spoiled." They aspire for material enjoyment by perfection of *yoga* or meditation. In *Bhagavad-gītā* it is stated by the Lord that the intelligence of those who worship the demigods has been spoiled. Similarly, here too it is stated by Kardama Muni that one who aspires after material enjoyment by practice of *yoga* has spoiled his brain substance and is fool number one. Actually, the intelligent practitioner of *yoga* should aspire for nothing else but to cross over the ocean of nescience by worshiping the Personality of Godhead and to see the lotus feet of the Lord. The Lord is so kind, however, that even today persons whose brain substance is spoiled are given the benediction to become cats, dogs or hogs and enjoy material happiness from sex life and sense gratification. The Lord confirms this benediction in *Bhagavad-gītā:* "Whatever a person aspires to receive from Me, I offer him as he desires."

TEXT 15

तथा स चाहं परिवोढुकामः
समानशीलां गृहमेधधेनुम् ।
उपेयिवान्मूलमशेषमूलं
दुराशयः कामदुघाङ्घ्रिपस्य ॥१५॥

tathā sa cāhaṁ parivoḍhu-kāmaḥ
samāna-śīlāṁ gṛhamedha-dhenum
upeyivān mūlam aśeṣa-mūlaṁ
durāśayaḥ kāma-dughāṅghripasya

tathā—similarly; *saḥ*—myself; *ca*—also; *aham*—I; *parivoḍhu-kāmaḥ*—desiring to marry; *samāna-śīlām*—a girl of like disposition; *gṛha-medha*—in married life; *dhenum*—a cow of plenty; *upeyivān*—have approached; *mūlam*—the root (lotus feet); *aśeṣa*—of everything; *mūlam*—the source; *durāśayaḥ*—with lustful desire; *kāma-dugha*—yielding all desires; *aṅghripasya*—(of You) who are the tree.

TRANSLATION

Therefore, desiring to marry a girl of like disposition who may prove to be a veritable cow of plenty in my married life, to satisfy my lustful desire I too have sought the shelter of Your lotus feet, which are the source of everything, for You are like a desire tree.

PURPORT

In spite of his condemning persons who approach the Lord for material advantages, Kardama Muni expressed his material inability and desire before the Lord by saying, "Although I know that nothing material should be asked from You, I nevertheless desire to marry a girl of like disposition." The phrase "like disposition" is very significant. Formerly, boys and girls of similar dispositions were married; the similar natures of the boy and girl were united in order to make them happy. Not more than twenty-five years ago, and perhaps it is still current, parents in India used to consult the horoscope of the boy and girl to see whether there would be factual union in their psychological conditions. These considerations are very important. Nowadays marriage takes place without such consultation, and therefore, soon after the marriage, there is divorce and separation. Formerly husband and wife used to live together peacefully throughout their whole lives, but nowadays it is a very difficult task.

Kardama Muni wanted to have a wife of like disposition because a wife is necessary to assist in spiritual and material advancement. It is said that a wife yields the fulfillment of all desires in religion, economic development and sense gratification. If one has a nice wife, he is to be considered a most fortunate man. In astrology, a man is considered fortunate who has great wealth, very good sons or a very good wife. Of these three, one who has a very good wife is considered the most fortunate. Before marrying, one should select a wife of like disposition and not be enamored by so-called beauty or other attractive features for sense gratification. In the *Bhāgavatam,* Twelfth Canto, it is said that in the Kali-yuga marriage will be based on the consideration of sex life; as soon as there is deficiency in sex life, the question of divorce will arise.

Kardama Muni could have asked his benediction from Umā, for it is recommended in the scriptures that if anyone wants a good wife, he should worship Umā. But he preferred to worship the Supreme Personality of Godhead because it is recommended in the *Bhāgavatam* that everyone, whether he is full of desires, has no desire or desires liberation, should worship the Supreme Lord. Of these three classes of men, one tries to be happy by fulfillment of material desires, another wants to be happy by becoming one with the Supreme, and another, the perfect man, is a devotee. He does not want anything in return from the Personality of Godhead; he only wants to render transcendental loving service. In any case, everyone should worship the Supreme Personality of Godhead, for He will fulfill everyone's desire. The advantage of worshiping the Supreme Person is that even if one has desires for material enjoyment, if he worships Kṛṣṇa he will gradually become a pure devotee and have no more material hankering.

TEXT 16

प्रजापतेस्ते वचसाधीश तन्त्या
लोकः किलायं कामहतोऽनुबद्धः ।
अहं च लोकानुगतो वहामि
बलिं च शुक्लानिमिषाय तुभ्यम् ॥१६॥

prajāpates te vacasādhīśa tantyā
lokaḥ kilāyaṁ kāma-hato 'nubaddhaḥ

ahaṁ ca lokānugato vahāmi
baliṁ ca śuklānimiṣāya tubhyam

prajāpateḥ—who are the master of all living entities; *te*—of You; *vacasā*—under the direction; *adhīśa*—O my Lord; *tantyā*—by a rope; *lokaḥ*—conditioned souls; *kila*—indeed; *ayam*—these; *kāma-hataḥ*—conquered by lusty desires; *anubaddhaḥ*—are bound; *aham*—I; *ca*—and; *loka-anugataḥ*—following the conditioned souls; *vahāmi*—offer; *balim*—oblations; *ca*—and; *śukla*—O embodiment of religion; *animiṣāya*—existing as eternal time; *tubhyam*—to You.

TRANSLATION

O my Lord, You are the master and leader of all living entities. Under Your direction, all conditioned souls, as if bound by rope, are constantly engaged in satisfying their desires. Following them, O embodiment of religion, I also bear oblations for You, who are eternal time.

PURPORT

In the *Kaṭha Upaniṣad* it is stated that the Supreme Lord is the leader of all living entities. He is their sustainer and the awarder of all their necessities and desires. No living entity is independent; all are dependent on the mercy of the Supreme Lord. Therefore the Vedic instruction is that one should enjoy life under the direction of the supreme leader, the Personality of Godhead. Vedic literatures like *Īśopaniṣad* direct that since everything belongs to the Supreme Personality of Godhead, one should not encroach upon another's property, but should enjoy one's individual allotment. The best program for every living entity is to take direction from the Supreme Lord and enjoy material or spiritual life.

A question may be raised: Since Kardama Muni was advanced in spiritual life, why then did he not ask the Lord for liberation? Why did he want to enjoy material life in spite of his personally seeing and experiencing the Supreme Lord? The answer is that not everyone is competent to be liberated from material bondage. It is everyone's duty, therefore, to enjoy according to his present position, but under the direction of the Lord or the *Vedas*. The *Vedas* are considered to be the direct words of the Lord. The Lord gives us the opportunity to enjoy material life as we want, and at the same time He gives directions for the modes and processes of abiding by the *Vedas* so that gradually one may be elevated to liberation from material bondage. The conditioned souls who have come to the material world to fulfill their desires to lord it over material nature are bound by the laws of nature. The best course is to abide by the Vedic rules; that will help one to be gradually elevated to liberation.

Kardama Muni addresses the Lord as *śukla*, which means "the leader of religion." One who is pious should follow the rules of religion, for such rules are prescribed by the Lord Himself. No one can manufacture or concoct a religion; "religion" refers to the injunctions or laws of the Lord. In *Bhagavad-gītā* the Lord says that religion means to surrender unto Him. Therefore one should follow the Vedic regulations and surrender unto the Supreme Lord because that is the ultimate goal of perfection in human life. One should live a life of piety, follow the religious rules and regulations, marry and live peacefully for elevation to the higher status of spiritual realization.

TEXT 17

लोकांश्च लोकानुगतान् पशूंश्च
हित्वा श्रितास्ते चरणातपत्रम् ।
परस्परं त्वद्गुणवादसीधु-
पीयूषनिर्यापितदेहधर्माः ॥१७॥

lokāṁś ca lokānugatān paśūṁś ca
hitvā śritās te caraṇātapatram
parasparaṁ tvad-guṇa-vāda-sīdhu-
pīyūṣa-niryāpita-deha-dharmāḥ

lokān—worldly affairs; *ca*—and; *loka-anugatān*—the followers of worldly affairs; *paśūn*—beastly; *ca*—and; *hitvā*—having given up; *śritāḥ*—taken shelter; *te*—Your; *caraṇa*—of lotus feet; *ātapatram*—the umbrella; *parasparam*—with one another; *tvat*—Your; *guṇa*—of qualities; *vāda*—by discussion; *sīdhu*—intoxicating; *pīyūṣa*—by the nectar; *niryāpita*—extinguished; *deha-dharmāḥ*—the primary necessities of the body.

TRANSLATION

However, persons who have given up stereotyped worldly affairs and the beastly followers of these affairs, and who have taken shelter of the umbrella of Your lotus feet by drinking the intoxicating nectar of Your qualities and activities in discussions with one another, can be freed from the primary necessities of the material body.

PURPORT

After describing the necessity of married life, Kardama Muni asserts that marriage and other social affairs are stereotyped regulations for persons who are addicted to material sense enjoyment. The principles of animal life—eating, sleeping, mating and defending—are actually necessities of the body, but those who engage in transcendental Kṛṣṇa consciousness, giving up all the stereotyped activities of this material world, are freed from social conventions. Conditioned souls are under the spell of material energy, or eternal time—past, present and future—but as soon as one engages in Kṛṣṇa consciousness, he transcends the limits of past and present and becomes situated in the eternal activities of the soul. One has to act in terms of the Vedic injunctions in order to enjoy material life, but those who have taken to the devotional service of the Lord are not afraid of the regulations of this material world. Such devotees do not care for the conventions of material activities; they boldly take to that shelter which is like an umbrella against the sun of repeated birth and death.

Constant transmigration of the soul from one body to another is the cause of suffering in material existence. This conditional life in material existence is called *saṁsāra.* One may perform good work and take his birth in a very nice material condition, but the process under which birth and death take place is like a terrible fire. Śrī Viśvanātha Cakravartī Ṭhākura, in his prayer to the spiritual master, has described this. *Saṁsāra*, or the repetition of birth and death, is compared to a forest fire. A forest fire takes place automatically, without anyone's endeavor, by the friction of dried wood, and no fire department or sympathetic person can extinguish it. The raging forest fire can be extinguished only when there is a constant downpour of water from a cloud. The cloud is compared to the mercy of the spiritual master. By the grace of the spiritual master the cloud of the mercy of the Personality of Godhead is brought in, and then only, when the rains of Kṛṣṇa consciousness fall, can the fire of material existence be extinguished. This is also explained here. In order to find freedom from the stereotyped conditional life of material existence, one has to take shelter of the lotus feet of the Lord, not in the manner in which the impersonalists indulge, but in devotional service, chanting and hearing of the activities of the Lord. Only then can one be freed from the actions and reactions of material existence. It is recommended here that one should give up the conditional life of this material world and the association of so-called civilized human beings who are simply following, in a polished way, the same stereotyped principles of eating, sleeping, defending and mating. Chanting and hearing of the glories of the Lord is described here as *tvad-guṇa-vāda-sīdhu.* Only by drinking the nectar of chanting and hearing the pastimes of the Lord can one forget the intoxication of material existence.

TEXT 18

न तेऽजराक्षभ्रमिरायुरेषां
त्रयोदशारं त्रिशतं षष्टिपर्व ।
षण्नेम्यनन्तच्छदि यत्त्रिणाभि
करालस्रोतो जगदाच्छिद्य धावत् ॥१८॥

na te 'jarākṣa-bhramir āyur eṣāṁ
trayodaśāraṁ tri-śataṁ ṣaṣṭi-parva
ṣaṇ-nemy ananta-cchadi yat tri-ṇābhi
karāla-sroto jagad ācchidya dhāvat

na—not; *te*—Your; *ajara*—of imperishable Brahman; *akṣa*—on the axle; *bhramiḥ*—rotating; *āyuḥ*—span of life; *eṣām*—of the devotees; *trayodaśa*—thirteen; *aram*—spokes; *tri-śatam*—three hundred; *ṣaṣṭi*—sixty; *parva*—functions; *ṣaṭ*—six; *nemi*—rims; *ananta*—innumerable; *chadi*—leaves; *yat*—which; *tri*—three; *nābhi*—naves; *karāla-srotaḥ*—with tremendous velocity; *jagat*—the universe; *ācchidya*—cutting short; *dhāvat*—running.

TRANSLATION

Your wheel, which has three naves, rotates around the axis of the imperishable Brahman. It has thirteen spokes, 360 joints, six rims and numberless leaves carved upon it. Though its revolution cuts short the life-span of the entire creation, this wheel of tremendous velocity cannot touch the life-span of the devotees of the Lord.

PURPORT

The time factor cannot affect the span of life of the devotees. In *Bhagavad-gītā* it is stated that a little execution of devotional service saves one from the greatest danger. The greatest danger is transmigration of the soul from one body to another, and only devotional service to the Lord can stop this process. It is stated in the Vedic literatures, *harim vinā na sṛtim taranti:* without the mercy of the Lord, one cannot stop the cycle of birth and death. In *Bhagavad-gītā* it is stated that only by understanding the transcendental nature of the Lord and His activities, His appearance and disappearance, can one stop the cycle of death and go back to Him. The time factor is divided into many fractions of moments, hours, months, years, periods, seasons, etc. All the divisions in this verse are determined according to the astronomical calculations of Vedic literature. There are six seasons, called *ṛtus*, and there is the period of four months called *cāturmāsya.* Three periods of four months complete one year. According to Vedic astronomical calculations, there are thirteen months. The thirteenth month is called *adhi-māsa* or *mala-māsa* and is added every third year. The time factor, however, cannot touch the life-span of the devotees. In another verse it is stated that when the sun rises and sets it takes away the life of all living entities, but it cannot take away the life of those who are engaged in devotional service. Time is compared here to a big wheel which has 360 joints, six rims in the shape of seasons, and numberless leaves in the shape of moments. It rotates on the eternal existence, Brahman.

TEXT 19

एकः स्वयं सञ्जगतः सिसृक्षया-
द्वितीययात्मन्नधियोगमायया ।

सृजस्यदः पासि पुनर्ग्रसिष्यसे
यथोर्णनाभिर्भगवन् स्वशक्तिभिः ॥१९॥

ekaḥ svayaṁ sañ jagataḥ sisṛkṣayā-
dvitīyayātmann adhi-yogamāyayā
sṛjasy adaḥ pāsi punar grasiṣyase
yathorṇa-nābhir bhagavan sva-śaktibhiḥ

ekaḥ—one; *svayam*—Yourself; *san*—being; *jagataḥ*—the universes; *sisṛkṣayā*—with a desire to create; *advitīyayā*—without a second; *ātman*—in Yourself; *adhi*—controlling; *yoga-māyayā*—by *yogamāyā; sṛjasi*—You create; *adaḥ*—those universes; *pāsi*—You maintain; *punaḥ*—again; *grasiṣyase*—You will wind up; *yathā*—like; *ūrṇa-nābhiḥ*—a spider; *bhagavan*—O Lord; *sva-śaktibhiḥ*—by its own energy.

TRANSLATION

My dear Lord, You alone create the universes. O Personality of Godhead, desiring to create these universes, You create them, maintain them and again wind them up by Your own energies, which are under the control of Your second energy, called yogamāyā, just as a spider creates a cobweb by its own energy and again winds it up.

PURPORT

In this verse two important words nullify the impersonalist theory that everything is God. Here Kardama says, "O Personality of Godhead, You are alone, but You have various energies." The example of the spider is very significant also. The spider is an individual living entity, and by its energy it creates a cobweb and plays on it, and whenever it likes it winds up the cobweb, thus ending the play. When the cobweb is manufactured by the saliva of the spider, the spider does not become impersonal. Similarly, the creation and manifestation of the material or spiritual energy does not render the creator impersonal. Here the very prayer suggests that God is sentient and can hear the prayers and fulfill the desires of the devotee. Therefore, He is *sac-cid-ānanda-vigraha*, the form of bliss, knowledge and eternity.

TEXT 20

नैतद्बताधीश पदं तवेप्सितं
यन्मायया नस्तनुषे भूतसूक्ष्मम् ।
अनुग्रहायास्त्वपि यर्हि मायया
लसत्तुलस्या भगवान् विलक्षितः ॥२०॥

naitad batādhīśa padaṁ tavepsitaṁ
yan māyayā nas tanuṣe bhūta-sūkṣmam
anugrahāyāstv api yarhi māyayā
lasat-tulasyā bhagavān vilakṣitaḥ

na—not; *etat*—this; *bata*—indeed; *adhīśa*—O Lord; *padam*—material world; *tava*—Your; *īpsitam*—desire; *yat*—which; *māyayā*—by Your external energy; *naḥ*—for us; *tanuṣe*—You manifest; *bhūta-sūkṣmam*—the elements, gross and subtle; *anugrahāya*—for bestowing mercy; *astu*—let it be; *api*—also; *yarhi*—when; *māyayā*—through Your causeless mercy; *lasat*—splendid; *tulasyā*—with a wreath of *tulasī* leaves; *bhagavān*—the Supreme Personality of Godhead; *vilakṣitaḥ*—is perceived.

TRANSLATION

My dear Lord, although it is not Your desire, You manifest this creation of gross and subtle elements just for our sensual satisfaction. Let Your causeless mercy be upon us, for You have appeared before us in Your eternal form, adorned with a splendid wreath of tulasī leaves.

PURPORT

It is clearly stated here that the material world is not created by the personal will of the Supreme Lord; it is created by His external energy because the living entities want to enjoy it. This material world is not created for those who do not want to enjoy sense gratification, who constantly remain in transcendental loving service and who arc eternally Kṛṣṇa conscious. For them, the spiritual world is eternally existing, and thcy enjoy there. Elsewhere in the *Śrīmad-Bhāgavatam* it is stated that for those who have taken shelter of the lotus feet of the Supreme Personality of Godhead, this material world is useless; because this material world is full of danger at every step, it is not meant for the devotees but for living entities who want to lord it over the material energy at their own risk. Kṛṣṇa is so kind that He allows the sense-enjoying living entities a separate world created by Him to enjoy as they like, yet at the same time He appears in His personal form. The Lord unwillingly creates this material world, but He descends in His personal form or sends one of His reliable sons or a servant or a reliable author like Vyāsadeva to give instruction. He Himself also instructs in His speeches of *Bhagavad-gītā.* This propaganda work goes on side by side with the creation to convince the misguided living entities who are rotting in this material world to come back to Him and surrender unto Him. Therefore the last instruction of *Bhagavad-gītā* is this: "Give up all your manufactured engagements in the material world and just surrender unto Me. I shall protect you from all sinful reactions."

TEXT 21

तं त्वानुभूत्योपरतक्रियार्थं
स्वमायया वर्तितलोकतन्त्रम् ।
नमाम्यभीक्ष्णं नमनीयपाद-
सरोजमल्पीयसि कामवर्षम् ॥२१॥

taṁ tvānubhūtyoparata-kriyārthaṁ
sva-māyayā vartita-loka-tantram
namāmy abhīkṣṇaṁ namanīya-pāda-
sarojam alpīyasi kāma-varṣam

tam—that; *tvā*—You; *anubhūtyā*—by realizing; *uparata*—disregarded; *kriyā*—enjoyment of fruitive activities; *artham*—in order that; *sva-māyayā*—by Your own energy; *vartita*—brought about; *loka-tantram*—the material worlds; *namāmi*—I offer obeisances; *abhīkṣṇam*—continuously; *namanīya*—worshipable; *pāda-sarojam*—lotus feet; *alpīyasi*—on the insignificant; *kāma*—desires; *varṣam*—showering.

TRANSLATION

I continuously offer my respectful obeisances unto Your lotus feet, of which it is worthy to take shelter, because You shower all benedictions on the insignificant. To give all living entities detachment from fruitive activity by realizing You, You have expanded these material worlds by Your own energy.

PURPORT

Everyone, therefore, whether he desires material enjoyment, liberation or the transcendental loving service of the Lord, should engage himself, offering obeisances unto the Supreme Lord, because the Lord can award everyone his desired benediction. In *Bhagavad-gītā* the Lord affirms, *ye yathā māṁ prapadyante:* anyone who desires to be a successful enjoyer in this material world is awarded that benediction by the Lord, anyone who wants to be liberated from the entanglement of this material world is given liberation by the Lord, and anyone who desires to constantly engage in His service in full Kṛṣṇa consciousness is awarded that benediction by the Lord. For material enjoyment He has prescribed so many ritualistic sacrificial performances in the *Vedas*, and thus people may take advantage of those instructions and enjoy material life in higher planets or in a noble aristocratic family. These processes are mentioned in the *Vedas*, and one can take advantage of them. It is similar with those who want to be liberated from this material world.

Unless one is disgusted with the enjoyment of this material world, he cannot aspire for liberation. Liberation is for one who is disgusted with material enjoyment. *Vedānta-sūtra* says, therefore, *athāto brahma-jijñāsā:* those who have given up the attempt to be happy in this material world can inquire about the Absolute Truth. For those who want to know the Absolute Truth, the *Vedānta-sūtra* is available, as is *Śrīmad-Bhāgavatam*, the actual explanation of *Vedānta-sūtra*. Since *Bhagavad-gītā* is also *Vedānta-sūtra*, by understanding *Śrīmad-Bhāgavatam*, *Vedānta-sūtra* or *Bhagavad-gītā* one can obtain real knowledge. When one obtains real knowledge, he becomes theoretically one with the Supreme, and when he actually begins the service of Brahman, or Kṛṣṇa consciousness, he is not only liberated but situated in his spiritual life. Similarly, for those who want to lord it over material nature, there are so many departments of material enjoyment; material knowledge and material science are available, and the Lord provides for persons who want to enjoy them. The conclusion is that one should worship the Supreme Personality of Godhead for any benediction. The word *kāma-varṣam* is very significant, for it indicates that He satisfies the desires of anyone who approaches Him. But one who sincerely loves Kṛṣṇa and yet wants material enjoyment is in perplexity. Kṛṣṇa, being very kind toward him, gives him an opportunity to engage in the transcendental loving service of the Lord, and so he gradually forgets the hallucination.

TEXT 22

ऋषिरुवाच
इत्यव्यलीकं प्रणुतोऽब्जनाभ-
स्तमाबभाषे वचसामृतेन ।
सुपर्णपक्षोपरि रोचमानः
प्रेमस्मितोद्वीक्षणविभ्रमद्भ्रूः ॥२२॥

ṛṣir uvāca
ity avyalīkaṁ praṇuto 'bja-nābhas
tam ābabhāṣe vacasāmṛtena
suparṇa-pakṣopari rocamānaḥ
prema-smitodvīkṣaṇa-vibhramad-bhrūḥ

ṛṣiḥ uvāca—the great sage Maitreya said; *iti*—thus; *avyalīkam*—sincerely; *praṇutaḥ*—having been praised; *abja-nābhaḥ*—Lord Viṣṇu; *tam*—to Kardama Muni; *ābabhāṣe*—replied; *vacasā*—with words; *amṛtena*—as sweet as nectar; *suparṇa*—of Garuḍa; *pakṣa*—the shoulders; *upari*—upon; *rocamānaḥ*—shining; *prema*—of affection; *smita*—with a smile; *udvīkṣaṇa*—looking; *vibhramat*—gracefully moving; *bhrūḥ*—eyebrows.

TRANSLATION

Maitreya resumed: Sincerely extolled in these words, Lord Viṣṇu, shining very beautifully on the shoulders of Garuḍa, replied with words as sweet as nectar. His eyebrows moved gracefully as He looked at the sage with a smile full of affection.

PURPORT

The word *vacasāmṛtena* is significant. Whenever the Lord speaks, He speaks from the transcendental world. He does not speak from the material world. Since He is transcendental, His speech is also transcendental, as is His activity; everything in relation to Him is transcendental. The word *amṛta* refers to one who does not meet with death. The words and activities of the Lord are deathless; therefore they are not manufactured of this material world. The sound of this material world and that of the spiritual world are completely different. The sound of the spiritual world is nectarean and eternal, whereas the sound of the material world is hackneyed and subject to end. The sound of the holy name—Hare Kṛṣṇa, Hare Kṛṣṇa, Kṛṣṇa Kṛṣṇa, Hare Hare—everlastingly increases the enthusiasm of the chanter. If one repeats monotonous material words, he will feel exhausted, but if he chants Hare Kṛṣṇa twenty-four hours a day, he will never feel exhausted; rather, he will feel encouraged to continue chanting more and more. When the Lord replied to the sage Kardama, the word *vacasāmṛtena* is specifically mentioned, since He spoke from the transcendental world. He replied in transcendental words, and when He spoke His eyebrows moved with great affection. When a devotee praises the glories of the Lord, the Lord is very satisfied, and He bestows His transcendental benediction upon the devotee without reservation because He is always causelessly merciful toward His devotee.

TEXT 23

श्रीभगवानुवाच
विदित्वा तव चैत्यं मे पुरैव समयोजि तत् ।
यदर्थमात्मनियमैस्त्वयैवाहं समर्चितः ॥२३॥

śrī-bhagavān uvāca
viditvā tava caityaṁ me
puraiva samayoji tat
yad-artham ātma-niyamais
tvayaivāhaṁ samarcitaḥ

śrī-bhagavān uvāca—the Supreme Lord said; *viditvā*—understanding; *tava*—your; *caityam*—mental condition; *me*—by Me; *purā*—

previously; *eva*—certainly; *samayoji*—was arranged; *tat*—that; *yat-artham*—for the sake of which; *ātma*—of the mind and senses; *niyamaiḥ*—by discipline; *tvayā*—by you; *eva*—only; *aham*—I; *samar-citaḥ*—have been worshiped.

TRANSLATION

The Supreme Lord said: Having come to know what was in your mind, I have already arranged for that for which you have worshiped Me well through your mental and sensory discipline.

PURPORT

The Supreme Personality of Godhead in His Paramātmā feature is situated in everyone's heart. He knows, therefore, the past, present and future of every individual person as well as his desires, activities and everything about him. It is stated in *Bhagavad-gītā* that He is seated in the heart as a witness. The Personality of Godhead knew the heart's desire of Kardama Muni, and He had already arranged for the fulfillment of his desires. He never disappoints a sincere devotee, regardless of what he wants, but He never allows anything which will be detrimental to the individual's devotional service.

TEXT 24

न वै जातु मृषैव स्यात्प्रजाध्यक्ष मदर्हणम् ।
भवद्विधेष्वतितरां मयि संगृभितात्मनाम् ॥२४॥

na vai jātu mṛṣaiva syāt
prajādhyakṣa mad-arhaṇam
bhavad-vidheṣu atitarāṁ
mayi saṅgṛbhitātmanām

na—not; *vai*—indeed; *jātu*—ever; *mṛṣā*—useless; *eva*—only; *syāt*—it may be; *prajā*—of the living entities; *adhyakṣa*—O leader; *mat-arhaṇam*—worship of Me; *bhavat-vidheṣu*—unto persons like you; *atitarām*—entirely; *mayi*—on Me; *saṅgṛbhita*—are fixed; *ātmanām*—of those whose minds.

TRANSLATION

The Lord continued: My dear ṛṣi, O leader of the living entities, for those who serve Me in devotion by worshiping Me, especially persons like you who have given up everything unto Me, there is never any question of frustration.

PURPORT

Even if he has some desires, one engaged in the service of the Lord is never frustrated. Those engaged in His service are called *sakāma* and *akāma.* Those who approach the Supreme Personality of Godhead with desires for material enjoyment are called *sakāma,* and those devotees who have no material desires for sense gratification but serve the Supreme Lord out of spontaneous love for Him are called *akāma. Sakāma* devotees are divided into four classes—those in distress, those in need of money, the inquisitive and the wise. Someone worships the Supreme Lord because of bodily or mental distress, someone else worships the Supreme Lord because he is in need of money, someone else worships the Lord out of inquisitiveness to know Him as He is, and someone wants to know the Lord as a philosopher can know Him, by the research work of his wisdom. There is no frustration for any of these four classes of men; each is endowed with the desired result of his worship.

TEXT 25

प्रजापतिसुतः सम्राण्मनुर्विख्यातमङ्गलः ।
ब्रह्मावर्तं योऽधिवसन् शास्ति सप्तार्णवां महीम् ॥२५॥

prajāpati-sutaḥ samrāṇ
manur vikhyāta-maṅgalaḥ
brahmāvartaṁ yo 'dhivasan
śāsti saptārṇavāṁ mahīm

prajāpati-sutaḥ—the son of Lord Brahmā; *samrāṭ*—the Emperor; *manuḥ*—Svāyambhuva Manu; *vikhyāta*—well known; *maṅgalaḥ*—whose righteous acts; *brahmāvartam*—Brahmāvarta; *yaḥ*—he who; *adhivasan*—living in; *śāsti*—rules; *sapta*—seven; *arṇavām*—oceans; *mahīm*—the earth.

TRANSLATION

The Emperor Svāyambhuva Manu, the son of Lord Brahmā, who is well known for his righteous acts, has his seat in Brahmāvarta and rules over the earth with its seven oceans.

PURPORT

Sometimes it is stated that Brahmāvarta is a part of Kurukṣetra or that Kurukṣetra itself is situated in Brahmāvarta, because the demigods are recommended to perform spiritual ritualistic performances in Kurukṣetra. But in others' opinion, Brahmāvarta is a place in Brahmaloka, where Svāyambhuva ruled. There are many places on the surface of this earth which are also known in the higher planetary systems; we have places on this planet like Vṛndāvana, Dvārakā and Mathurā, but they are also eternally situated in Kṛṣṇaloka. There are many similar names on the surface of the earth, and it may be that in the Boar age Svāyambhuva Manu ruled this planet, as stated here. The word *maṅgalaḥ* is significant. *Maṅgala* means one who is elevated in every respect in the opulences of religious performances, ruling power, cleanliness and all other good qualities. *Vikhyāta* means "celebrated." Svāyambhuva Manu was celebrated for all good qualities and opulences.

TEXT 26

स चेह विप्र राजर्षिर्महिष्या शतरूपया ।
आयास्यति दिदृक्षुस्त्वां परश्वो धर्मकोविदः ॥२६॥

sa ceha vipra rājarṣir
mahiṣyā śatarūpayā
āyāsyati didṛkṣus tvāṁ
paraśvo dharma-kovidaḥ

saḥ—Svāyambhuva Manu; *ca*—and; *iha*—here; *vipra*—O holy *brāhmaṇa; rāja-ṛṣiḥ*—the saintly king; *mahiṣyā*—along with his queen; *śatarūpayā*—called Śatarūpā; *āyāsyati*—will come; *didṛkṣuḥ*—desiring to see; *tvām*—you; *paraśvaḥ*—the day after tomorrow; *dharma*—in religious activities; *kovidaḥ*—expert.

TRANSLATION

The day after tomorrow, O brāhmaṇa, that celebrated emperor, who is expert in religious activities, will come here with his queen, Śatarūpā, wishing to see you.

TEXT 27

आत्मजामसितापाङ्गीं वयःशीलगुणान्विताम् ।
मृगयन्तीं पतिं दास्यत्यनुरूपाय ते प्रभो ॥२७॥

ātmajām asitāpāṅgīṁ
vayaḥ-śīla-guṇānvitām
mṛgayantīṁ patiṁ dāsyaty
anurūpāya te prabho

ātma-jām—his own daughter; *asita*—black; *apāṅgīm*—eyes; *vayaḥ*—grown-up age; *śīla*—with character; *guṇa*—with good qualities; *an-vitām*—endowed; *mṛgayantīm*—searching for; *patim*—a husband; *dāsyati*—he will give; *anurūpāya*—who are suitable; *te*—unto you; *prabho*—My dear sir.

TRANSLATION

He has a grown-up daughter whose eyes are black. She is ready for marriage, and she has good character and all good qualities. She is also searching for a good husband. My dear sir, her parents will come to see you, who are exactly suitable for her, just to deliver their daughter as your wife.

PURPORT

The selection of a good husband for a good girl was always entrusted to the parents. Here it is clearly stated that Manu and his wife were coming to see Kardama Muni to offer their daughter because the daughter was well qualified and the parents were searching out a similarly qualified man. This is the duty of parents. Girls are never thrown into the public street to search out their husband, for when girls are grown up and are searching after a boy, they forget to consider whether the boy they select is actually sutiable for them. Out of the urge of sex desire, a girl may accept anyone, but if the husband is chosen by the parents, they can consider who is to be selected and who is not. According to the Vedic system, therefore, the girl is given over to a suitable boy by the parents; she is never allowed to select her own husband independently.

TEXT 28

समाहितं ते हृदयं यत्रेमान् परिवत्सरान् ।
सा त्वां ब्रह्मन्नृपवधूः काममाशु भजिष्यति ॥२८॥

samāhitaṁ te hṛdayaṁ
yatremān parivatsarān
sā tvāṁ brahman nṛpa-vadhūḥ
kāmam āśu bhajiṣyati

samāhitam—has been fixed; *te*—your; *hṛdayam*—heart; *yatra*—on whom; *imān*—for all these; *parivatsarān*—years; *sā*—she; *tvām*—you; *brahman*—O *brāhmaṇa; nṛpa-vadhūḥ*—the princess; *kāmam*—as you desire; *āśu*—very soon; *bhajiṣyati*—will serve.

TRANSLATION

That princess, O holy sage, will be just the type you have been thinking of in your heart for all these long years. She will soon be yours and will serve you to your heart's content.

PURPORT

The Lord awards all benedictions according to the heart's desire of a devotee, so the Lord informed Kardama Muni, "The girl who is coming to be married with you is a princess, the daughter of Emperor Svāyambhuva, and so just suitable for your purpose." Only by God's grace can one get a nice wife just as he desires. Similarly, it is only by God's grace that a girl gets a husband suitable to her heart. Thus it is said that if we pray to the Supreme Lord in every transaction of our material existence, everything will be done very nicely and just suitable to our heart's desire. In other words, in all circumstances we must take shelter of the Supreme Personality of Godhead and depend completely on His decision. Man proposes, God disposes. The fulfillment of desires, therefore, should be entrusted to the Supreme Personality of Godhead; that is the nicest solution. Kardama Muni desired only a wife, but because he was a devotee of the Lord, the Lord selected a wife for him who was the Emperor's daughter, a princess. Thus Kardama Muni got a wife beyond his expectation. If we depend on the choice of the Supreme Personality of Godhead, we will receive benedictions in greater opulence than we desire.

It is also significantly noted here that Kardama Muni was a *brāhmaṇa*, whereas Emperor Svāyambhuva was a *kṣatriya*. Therefore, intercaste marriage was current even in those days. The system was that a *brāhmaṇa* could marry the daughter of a *kṣatriya*, but a *kṣatriya* could not marry the daughter of a *brāhmaṇa*. We have evidences from the history of the Vedic age that Śukrācārya offered his daughter to Mahārāja Yayāti, but the King had to refuse to marry the daughter of a *brāhmaṇa*; only with the special permission of the *brāhmaṇa* could they marry. Intercaste marriage, therefore, was not prohibited in the olden days, many millions of years ago, but there was a regular system of social behavior.

TEXT 29

या त आत्मभृतं वीर्यं नवधा प्रसविष्यति ।
वीर्ये त्वदीये ऋषय आधास्यन्त्यञ्जसात्मनः ॥२९॥

yā ta ātma-bhṛtaṁ vīryaṁ
navadhā prasaviṣyati
vīrye tvadīye ṛṣaya
ādhāsyanty añjasātmanaḥ

yā—she; *te*—by you; *ātma-bhṛtam*—sown in her; *vīryam*—the seed; *nava-dhā*—nine daughters; *prasaviṣyati*—will bring forth; *vīrye tvadīye*—in the daughters begotten by you; *ṛṣayaḥ*—the sages; *ādhāsyanti*—will beget; *añjasā*—in total; *ātmanaḥ*—children.

TRANSLATION

She will bring forth nine daughters from the seed sown in her by you, and through the daughters you beget, the sages will duly beget children.

TEXT 30

त्वं च सम्यगनुष्ठाय निदेशं म उशत्तमः ।
मयि तीर्थीकृताशेषक्रियार्थो मां प्रपत्स्यसे ॥३०॥

tvaṁ ca samyag anuṣṭhāya
nideśaṁ ma uśattamaḥ
mayi tīrthī-kṛtāśeṣa-
kriyārtho māṁ prapatsyase

tvam—you; *ca*—and; *samyak*—properly; *anuṣṭhāya*—having carried out; *nideśam*—command; *me*—My; *uśattamaḥ*—completely cleansed; *mayi*—unto Me; *tīrthī-kṛta*—having resigned; *aśeṣa*—all; *kriyā*—of actions; *arthaḥ*—the fruits; *mām*—to Me; *prapatsyase*—you will attain.

TRANSLATION

With your heart cleansed by properly carrying out My command, resigning to Me the fruits of all your acts, you will finally attain to Me.

PURPORT

Here the words *tīrthī-kṛtāśeṣa-kriyārthaḥ* are significant. *Tīrtha* means a sanctified place where charity is given. People used to go to places of pilgrimage and give munificently in charity. This system is still current. Therefore the Lord said, "In order to sanctify your activities and the results of your actions, you will offer everything unto Me." This is also confirmed in *Bhagavad-gītā:* "Whatever you do, whatever you eat, whatever you sacrifice, the result should be given to Me only." In another place in *Bhagavad-gītā* the Lord said, "I am the enjoyer of all sacrifices, all penances and everything done for the welfare of mankind or society." All activities, therefore, whether for the welfare of family, society, country or humanity at large, must be performed in Kṛṣṇa consciousness. That is the instruction given by the Lord to Kardama Muni. Mahārāja Yudhiṣṭhira welcomed Nārada Muni: "Wherever you are present, that place becomes sanctified because the Lord Himself is always seated in your heart." Similarly, if we act in Kṛṣṇa consciousness under the direction of the Lord and His representative, then everything is sanctified. This is the indication given to Kardama Muni, who acted on it and therefore received the most excellent wife and child, as will be disclosed in later verses.

TEXT 31

कृत्वा दयां च जीवेषु दत्त्वा चाभयमात्मवान् ।
मय्यात्मानं सह जगद् द्रक्ष्यस्यात्मनि चापि माम् ॥३१॥

kṛtvā dayāṁ ca jīveṣu
dattvā cābhayam ātmavān
mayy ātmānaṁ saha jagad
drakṣyasy ātmani cāpi mām

kṛtvā—having shown; *dayām*—compassion; *ca*—and; *jīveṣu*—toward living beings; *dattvā*—having given; *ca*—and; *abhayam*—assurance of safety; *ātma-vān*—self-realized; *mayi*—in Me; *ātmānam*—yourself; *saha jagat*—along with the universe; *drakṣyasi*—you will perceive; *ātmani*—in yourself; *ca*—and; *api*—also; *mām*—Me.

TRANSLATION

Showing compassion to all living entities, you will attain self-realization. Giving assurance of safety to all, you will perceive your own self as well as all the universes in Me, and Myself in you.

PURPORT

The simple process of self-realization for every living entity is described here. The first principle to be understood is that this world is a product of the supreme will. There is an identity of this world with the Supreme Lord. This identity is accepted in a misconceived way by the impersonalists; they say that the Supreme Absolute Truth, transforming Himself into the universe, loses His separate existence. Thus they accept the world and everything in it to be the Lord. That is pantheism, wherein everything is considered to be the Lord. This is the view of the impersonalist. But those who are personal devotees of the Lord take everything to be the property of the Supreme Lord. Everything, whatever we see, is the manifestation of the Supreme Lord; therefore, everything should be engaged in the service of the Lord. This is oneness. The difference between the impersonalist and the personalist is that the impersonalist does not accept the separate existence of the Lord, but the personalist accepts the Lord; he understands that although He distributes Himself in so many ways, He has His separate personal existence. This is described in *Bhagavad-gītā:* "I am spread all over the universe in My impersonal form. Everything is resting on Me, but I am not present." There is a nice example regarding the sun and the sunshine. The sun, by its sunshine, is spread all over the universe, and all the planets rest on the sunshine. But all the planets are different from the sun planet; one cannot say that because the planets are resting on the sunshine, these planets are also the sun. Similarly, the impersonal or pantheistic view that everything is God is not a very intelligent proposal. The real position, as explained by the Lord Himself, is that although nothing can exist without Him, it is not a fact that everything *is* Him. He is different from everything. So here also the Lord says: "You will see everything in the world to be nondifferent from Me." This means that everything should be considered a product of the Lord's energy, and therefore everything should be employed in the service of the Lord. One's energy should be utilized for one's self-interest. That is the perfection of the energy.

This energy can be utilized for real self-interest if one is compassionate. A person in Kṛṣṇa consciousness, a devotee of the Lord, is always compassionate. He is not satisfied that only he himself is a devotee, but he tries to distribute the knowledge of devotional service to everyone. There are many devotees of the Lord who faced many risks in distributing the devotional service of the Lord to people in general. That should be done.

It is also said that a person who goes to the temple of the Lord and worships with great devotion, but who does not show sympathy to people in general or show respect to other devotees, is considered to be a third-class devotee. The second-class devotee is he who is merciful and compassionate to the fallen soul. The second-class devotee is always cognizant of his position as an eternal servant of the Lord; he therefore makes friendships with devotees of the Lord, acts compassionately toward the general public in teaching them devotional service, and refuses to cooperate or associate with nondevotees. As long as one is not compassionate to people in general in his devotional service to the Lord, he is a third-class devotee. The first-class devotee gives assurance to every living being that there is no fear of this material existence: "Let us live in Kṛṣṇa consciousness and conquer the nescience of material existence."

It is indicated here that Kardama Muni was directed by the Lord to be very compassionate and liberal in his householder life and to give assurance to the people in his renounced life. A *sannyāsī,* one in the renounced order of life, is meant to give enlightenment to the people. He should travel, going from home to home to enlighten. The householder, by the spell of *māyā,* becomes absorbed in family affairs and forgets his relationship with Kṛṣṇa. If he dies in forgetfulness, like the cats and dogs, then his life is spoiled. It is the duty of a *sannyāsī,* therefore, to go and awaken the forgetful souls with enlightenment of their eternal relationship with the Lord and to engage them in devotional service. The devotee should show mercy to the fallen souls and also give them the assurance of fearlessness. As soon as one becomes a devotee of the Lord, he is convinced that he is protected by the Lord. Fear itself is afraid of the Lord; therefore, what has he to do with fearfulness?

To award fearlessness to the common man is the greatest act of charity. A *sannyāsī,* or one who is in the renounced order of life, should wander from door to door, from village to village, from town to town and from country to country, all over the world as far as he is able to travel, and enlighten the householders about Kṛṣṇa consciousness. A person who is a householder but is initiated by a *sannyāsī* has the duty to spread Kṛṣṇa consciousness at home; as far as possible, he should call his friends and neighbors to his house and hold classes in Kṛṣṇa consciousness. Holding a class means chanting the holy name of Kṛṣṇa and speaking from *Bhagavad-gītā* or *Śrīmad-Bhāgavatam.* There are immense literatures for spreading Kṛṣṇa consciousness, and it is the duty of each and every householder to learn about Kṛṣṇa from his *sannyāsī* spiritual master. There is a division of labor in the Lord's service. The householder's duty is to earn money because a *sannyāsī* is not supposed to earn money but is completely dependent on the householder. The householder should earn money by business or by profession and spend at least fifty percent of his income to spread Kṛṣṇa consciousness; twenty-five percent he can spend for his family, and twenty-five percent he should save to meet emergencies. This example was shown by Rūpa Gosvāmī, so devotees should follow it.

Actually, to be one with the Supreme Lord means to be one with the interest of the Lord. Becoming one with the Supreme Lord does not imply becoming as great as the Supreme Lord. It is impossible. The part is never equal to the whole. The living entity is always a minute part. Therefore his oneness with the Lord is that he is interested in the one interest of the Lord. The Lord wants every living entity to always think about Him, to be His devotee and always worship Him. This is clearly stated in *Bhagavad-gītā: man-manā bhava mad-bhaktaḥ.* Kṛṣṇa wants everyone always to think of Him. Everyone should always offer obeisances to Kṛṣṇa. This is the will of the Supreme Lord, and devotees should try to fulfill His desire. Since the Lord is unlimited, His desire is also unlimited. There is no stoppage, and therefore the service of the devotee is also unlimited. In the transcendental world there is unlimited competition between the Lord and the servitor. The Lord wants to fulfill His desires unlimitedly, and the devotee also serves Him to fulfill His unlimited desires. There is an unlimited oneness of interest between the Lord and His devotee.

TEXT 32

सहाहं स्वांशकलया त्वद्वीर्येण महामुने ।
तव क्षेत्रे देवहूत्यां प्रणेष्ये तत्त्वसंहिताम् ॥३२॥

sahāhaṁ svāṁśa-kalayā
tvad-vīryeṇa mahā-mune
tava kṣetre devahūtyāṁ
praṇeṣye tattva-saṁhitām

saha—with; *aham*—I; *sva-aṁśa-kalayā*—My own plenary portion; *tvat-vīryeṇa*—by your semen; *mahā-mune*—O great sage; *tava kṣetre*—in your wife; *devahūtyām*—in Devahūti; *praṇeṣye*—I shall instruct; *tattva*—of the ultimate principles; *saṁhitām*—the doctrine.

TRANSLATION

O great sage, I shall manifest My own plenary portion through your wife, Devahūti, along with your nine daughters, and I shall instruct her in the system of philosophy that deals with the ultimate principles or categories.

PURPORT

Herein the word *svāṁśa-kalayā* indicates that the Lord would appear as the son of Devahūti and Kardama Muni as Kapiladeva, the first propounder of the Sāṅkhya philosophy, which is mentioned here as *tattva-saṁhitā.* The Lord foretold to Kardama Muni that He would appear in His incarnation Kapiladeva and would propagate the philosophy of Sāṅkhya. Sāṅkhya philosophy is very well known in the world as propagated by another Kapiladeva, but that Sāṅkhya philosophy is different from the Sāṅkhya which was propounded by the Lord Himself. There are two kinds of Sāṅkhya philosophy: one is godless Sāṅkhya philosophy, and the other is godly Sāṅkhya philosophy. The Sāṅkhya propagated by Kapiladeva, son of Devahūti, is godly philosophy.

There are different manifestations of the Lord. He is one, but He has become many. He divides Himself into two different expansions, one called *kalā* and the other *vibhinnāṁśa.* Ordinary living entities are called *vibhinnāṁśa* expansions, and the unlimited expansions of *viṣṇu-tattva,* such as Vāmana, Govinda, Nārāyaṇa, Pradyumna, Vāsudeva and Ananta, are called *svāṁśa-kalā. Svāṁśa* refers to a direct expansion, and *kalā* denotes an expansion from the expansion of the original Lord. Baladeva is an expansion of Kṛṣṇa, and from Baladeva the next expansion is Saṅkarṣaṇa; thus Saṅkarṣaṇa is *kalā,* but Baladeva is *svāṁśa.* There is no difference, however, among Them. This is very nicely explained in the *Brahma-saṁhitā* (5.46): *dīpārcir eva hi daśāntaram abhyupetya.* With one candle one may light a second candle, with the second a third and then a fourth, and in this way one can light up thousands of candles, and no candle is inferior to another in distributing light. Every candle has the full potential candlepower, but there is still the distinction that one candle is the first, another the second, another the third and another the fourth. Similarly, there is no difference between the immediate expansion of the Lord and His secondary expansion. The Lord's names are considered in exactly the same way; since the Lord is absolute, His name, His form, His pastimes, His paraphernalia and His quality all have the same potency. In the absolute world, the name Kṛṣṇa is the transcendental sound representation of the Lord. There is no potential difference between His quality, name, form, etc. If we chant the name of the Lord, Hare Kṛṣṇa, that has as much potency as the Lord Himself. There is no potential difference between the form of the Lord whom we worship and the form of the Lord in the temple. One should not think that one is worshiping a doll or statue of the Lord, even if others consider it to be a statue. Because there is not potential difference, one gets the same result by worshiping the statue of the Lord or the Lord Himself. This is the science of Kṛṣṇa consciousness.

TEXT 33

मैत्रेय उवाच
एवं तमनुभाष्याथ भगवान् प्रत्यगक्षजः ।
जगाम बिन्दुसरसः सरस्वत्या परिश्रितात् ॥३३॥

maitreya uvāca
evaṁ tam anubhāṣyātha
bhagavān pratyag-akṣajaḥ
jagāma bindusarasaḥ
sarasvatyā pariśritāt

maitreyaḥ uvāca—the great sage Maitreya said; *evam*—thus; *tam*—to him; *anubhāṣya*—having spoken; *atha*—then; *bhagavān*—the Lord; *pratyak*—directly; *akṣa*—by senses; *jaḥ*—who is perceived; *jagāma*—went away; *bindu-sarasaḥ*—from Lake Bindu-sarovara; *sarasvatyā*—by the River Sarasvatī; *pariśritāt*—encircled.

TRANSLATION

Maitreya went on: Thus having spoken to Kardama Muni, the Lord, who reveals Himself only when the senses are in Kṛṣṇa consciousness, departed from that lake called Bindu-sarovara, which was encircled by the River Sarasvatī.

PURPORT

One word in this verse is very significant. The Lord is stated here to be *pratyag-akṣaja.* He is imperceptible to material senses, but still He can be seen. This appears to be contradictory. We have material senses, but how can we see the Supreme Lord? He is called *adhokṣaja,* which means that He cannot be seen by the material senses. *Akṣaja* means "knowledge perceived by material senses." Because the Lord is not an object that can be understood by speculation with our material senses, He is also called *ajita;* He will conquer, but no one can conquer Him. What does it mean, then, that still He can be seen? It is explained that no one can hear the transcendental name of Kṛṣṇa, no one can understand His transcendental form, and no one can assimilate His transcendental pastimes. It is not possible. Then how is it possible that He can be seen and understood? When one is trained in devotional service and renders service unto Him, gradually one's senses are purified of material contamination. When one's senses are thus purified, then one can see, one can understand, one can hear and so on. The purification of the material senses and perception of the transcendental form, name and quality of Kṛṣṇa are combined together in one word, *pratyag-akṣaja,* which is used here.

TEXT 34

निरीक्षतस्तस्य ययावशेष-
सिद्धेश्वराभिष्टुतसिद्धमार्गः ।
आकर्णयन् पत्ररथेन्द्रपक्षै-
रुच्चारितं स्तोममुदीर्णसाम ॥३४॥

nirīkṣatas tasya yayāv aśeṣa-
siddheśvarābhiṣṭuta-siddha-mārgaḥ
ākarṇayan patra-rathendra-pakṣair
uccāritaṁ stomam udīrṇa-sāma

nirīkṣataḥ tasya—while he was looking on; *yayau*—He left; *aśeṣa*—all; *siddha-īśvara*—by liberated souls; *abhiṣṭuta*—is praised; *siddha-mārgaḥ*—the way to the spiritual world; *ākarṇayan*—hearing; *patra-ratha-indra*—of Garuḍa (king of birds); *pakṣaiḥ*—by the wings; *uccāritam*—vibrated; *stomam*—hymns; *udīrṇa-sāma*—forming the *Sāma Veda.*

TRANSLATION

While the sage stood looking on, the Lord left by the pathway leading to Vaikuṇṭha, a path extolled by all great liberated souls.

The sage stood listening as the hymns forming the basis of the Sāma Veda were vibrated by the flapping wings of the Lord's carrier, Garuḍa.

PURPORT

In the Vedic literature it is stated that the two wings of the transcendental bird Garuḍa, who carries the Lord everywhere, are two divisions of the *Sāma Veda* known as *bṛhat* and *rathāntara.* Garuḍa works as the carrier of the Lord; therefore he is considered the transcendental prince of all carriers. With his two wings Garuḍa began to vibrate the *Sāma Veda*, which is chanted by great sages to pacify the Lord. The Lord is worshiped by Brahmā, by Lord Śiva, by Garuḍa and other demigods with selected poems, and great sages worship Him with the hymns of Vedic literatures, such as the *Upaniṣads* and *Sāma Veda.* These *Sāma Veda* utterances are automatically heard by the devotee when another great devotee of the Lord, Garuḍa, flaps his wings.

It is clearly stated here that the sage Kardama began to look to the path by which the Lord was being carried to Vaikuṇṭha. It is thus confirmed that the Lord descends from His abode, Vaikuṇṭha, in the spiritual sky, and is carried by Garuḍa. The path which leads to Vaikuṇṭha is not worshiped by the ordinary class of transcendentalists. Only those who are already liberated from material bondage can become devotees of the Lord. Those who are not liberated from material bondage cannot understand transcendental devotional service. In *Bhagavad-gītā* it is clearly stated, *yatatām api siddhānām.* There are many persons who are trying to attain perfection by striving for liberation from material bondage, and those who are actually liberated are called *brahma-bhūta* or *siddha.* Only the *siddhas*, or persons liberated from material bondage, can become devotees. This is also confirmed in *Bhagavad-gītā:* anyone who is engaged in Kṛṣṇa consciousness, or devotional service, is already liberated from the influence of the modes of material nature. Here it is also confirmed that the path of devotional service is worshiped by liberated persons, not the conditioned souls. The conditioned soul cannot understand the devotional service of the Lord. Kardama Muni was a liberated soul who saw the Supreme Lord in person, face to face. There was no doubt that he was liberated, and thus he could see Garuḍa carrying the

Lord on the way to Vaikuṇṭha and hear the flapping of his wings vibrating the sound of Hare Kṛṣṇa, the essence of the *Sāma Veda.*

TEXT 35

**अथ सम्प्रस्थिते शुक्ले कर्दमो भगवानृषिः ।
आस्ते स्म बिन्दुसरसि तं कालं प्रतिपालयन् ॥३५॥**

atha samprasthite śukle
kardamo bhagavān ṛṣiḥ
āste sma bindusarasi
taṁ kālaṁ pratipālayan

atha—then; *samprasthite śukle*—when the Lord had gone; *kardamaḥ*—Kardama Muni; *bhagavān*—the greatly powerful; *ṛṣiḥ*—sage; *āste sma*—stayed; *bindu-sarasi*—on the bank of Lake Bindu-sarovara; *tam*—that; *kālam*—time; *pratipālayan*—awaiting.

TRANSLATION

Then, after the departure of the Lord, the worshipful sage Kardama stayed on the bank of Bindu-sarovara, awaiting the time of which the Lord had spoken.

TEXT 36

**मनुः स्यन्दनमास्थाय शातकौम्भपरिच्छदम् ।
आरोप्य स्वां दुहितरं सभार्यः पर्यटन्महीम् ॥३६॥**

manuḥ syandanam āsthāya
śātakaumbha-paricchadam
āropya svāṁ duhitaraṁ
sa-bhāryaḥ paryaṭan mahīm

manuḥ—Svāyambhuva Manu; *syandanam*—the chariot; *āsthāya*—having mounted; *śātakaumbha*—made of gold; *paricchadam*—the outer cover; *āropya*—putting on; *svām*—his own; *duhitaram*—daughter; *sa-bhāryaḥ*—along with his wife; *paryaṭan*—traveling all over; *mahīm*—the globe.

TRANSLATION

Svāyambhuva Manu, with his wife, mounted his chariot, which was decorated with golden ornaments. Placing his daughter on it with them, he began traveling all over the earth.

PURPORT

The Emperor Manu, as the great ruler of the world, could have engaged an agent to find a suitable husband for his daughter, but because he loved her just as a father should, he himself left his state on a golden chariot, with only his wife, to find her a suitable husband.

TEXT 37

तस्मिन् सुधन्वन्नहनि भगवान् यत्समादिशत् ।
उपायादाश्रमपदं मुनेः शान्तव्रतस्य तत् ॥३७॥

tasmin sudhanvann ahani
bhagavān yat samādiśat
upāyād āśrama-padaṁ
muneḥ śānta-vratasya tat

tasmin—on that; *su-dhanvan*—O great bowman Vidura; *ahani*—on the day; *bhagavān*—the Lord; *yat*—which; *samādiśat*—foretold; *upāyāt*—he reached; *āśrama-padam*—the holy hermitage; *muneḥ*—of the sage; *śānta*—completed; *vratasya*—whose vows of austerity; *tat*—that.

TRANSLATION

O Vidura, they reached the hermitage of the sage, who had just completed his vows of austerity on the very day foretold by the Lord.

TEXTS 38–39

यस्मिन् भगवतो नेत्रान्न्यपतन्नश्रुबिन्दवः ।
कृपया सम्परीतस्य प्रपन्नेऽर्पितया भृशम् ॥३८॥

तद्वै बिन्दुसरो नाम सरस्वत्या परिप्लुतम् ।
पुण्यं शिवामृतजलं महर्षिगणसेवितम् ॥३९॥

yasmin bhagavato netrān
nyapatann aśru-bindavaḥ
kṛpayā samparītasya
prapanne 'rpitayā bhṛśam

tad vai bindusaro nāma
sarasvatyā pariplutam
puṇyaṁ śivāmṛta-jalaṁ
maharṣi-gaṇa-sevitam

yasmin—in which; *bhagavataḥ*—of the Lord; *netrāt*—from the eye; *nyapatan*—fell down; *aśru-bindavaḥ*—teardrops; *kṛpayā*—by compassion; *samparītasya*—who was overwhelmed; *prapanne*—on the surrendered soul (Kardama); *arpitayā*—placed upon; *bhṛśam*—extremely; *tat*—that; *vai*—indeed; *bindu-saraḥ*—lake of tears; *nāma*—called; *sarasvatyā*—by the River Sarasvatī; *pariplutam*—overflowed; *puṇyam*—holy; *śiva*—auspicious; *amṛta*—nectar; *jalam*—water; *mahārṣi*—of great sages; *gaṇa*—by hosts; *sevitam*—served.

TRANSLATION

The holy Lake Bindu-sarovara, flooded by the waters of the River Sarasvatī, was resorted to by hosts of eminent sages. Its holy water was not only auspicious but as sweet as nectar. It was called Bindu-sarovara because drops of tears had fallen there from the eyes of the Lord, who was overwhelmed by extreme compassion for the sage who had sought His protection.

PURPORT

Kardama underwent austerities to gain the causeless mercy of the Lord, and when the Lord arrived there He was so compassionate that in pleasure He shed tears, which became Bindu-sarovara. Bindu-sarovara, therefore, is worshiped by great sages and learned scholars because, according to the philosophy of the Absolute Truth, the Lord and the tears from His eyes are not different. Just as drops of perspiration which fell from the toe of the Lord became the sacred Ganges, so teardrops from the transcendental eyes of the Lord became Bindu-sarovara. Both are transcendental entities and are worshiped by great sages and scholars. The water of Bindu-sarovara is described here as *śivāmṛta-jala. Śiva* means "curing." Anyone who drinks the water of Bindu-sarovara is cured of all material diseases; similarly, anyone who takes his bath in the Ganges also is relieved of all material diseases. These claims are accepted by great scholars and authorities and are still being acted upon even in this fallen age of Kali.

TEXT 40

पुण्यद्रुमलताजालैः कूजत्पुण्यमृगद्विजैः ।
सर्वर्तुफलपुष्पाढ्यं वनराजिश्रियान्वितम् ॥४०॥

puṇya-druma-latā-jālaiḥ
kūjat-puṇya-mṛga-dvijaiḥ
sarvartu-phala-puṣpāḍhyaṁ
vana-rāji-śriyānvitam

puṇya—pious; *druma*—of trees; *latā*—of creepers; *jālaiḥ*—with clusters; *kūjat*—uttering cries; *puṇya*—pious; *mṛga*—animals; *dvijaiḥ*—with birds; *sarva*—in all; *ṛtu*—seasons; *phala*—in fruits; *puṣpa*—in flowers; *āḍhyam*—rich; *vana-rāji*—of groves of trees; *śriyā*—by the beauty; *anvitam*—adorned.

TRANSLATION

The shore of the lake was surrounded by clusters of pious trees and creepers, rich in fruits and flowers of all seasons, that afforded shelter to pious animals and birds, which uttered various cries. It was adorned by the beauty of groves of forest trees.

PURPORT

It is stated here that Bindu-sarovara was surrounded by pious trees and birds. As there are different classes of men in human society, some pious and virtuous and some impious and sinful, so also among trees and birds there are the pious and the impious. Trees which do not bear nice fruit or flowers are considered impious, and birds which are very nasty, such as crows, are considered impious. In the land surrounding Bindu-sarovara there was not a single impious bird or tree. Every tree bore fruits and flowers, and every bird sang the glories of the Lord—Hare Kṛṣṇa, Hare Kṛṣṇa, Kṛṣṇa Kṛṣṇa, Hare Hare/ Hare Rāma, Hare Rāma, Rāma Rāma, Hare Hare.

TEXT 41

मत्तद्विजगणैर्घुष्टं मत्तभ्रमरविभ्रमम् ।
मत्तबर्हिनटाटोपमाह्वयन्मत्तकोकिलम् ॥४१॥

matta-dvija-gaṇair ghuṣṭaṁ
matta-bhramara-vibhramam
matta-barhi-naṭāṭopam
āhvayan-matta-kokilam

matta—overjoyed; *dvija*—of birds; *gaṇaiḥ*—by flocks; *ghuṣṭam*—resounded; *matta*—intoxicated; *bhramara*—of bees; *vibhramam*—wandering; *matta*—maddened; *barhi*—of peacocks; *naṭa*—of dancers; *āṭopam*—pride; *āhvayat*—calling one another; *matta*—merry; *kokilam*—cuckoos.

TRANSLATION

The area resounded with the notes of overjoyed birds. Intoxicated bees wandered there, intoxicated peacocks proudly danced, and merry cuckoos called one another.

PURPORT

The beauty of the pleasant sounds heard in the area surrounding Lake Bindu-sarovara is described here. After drinking honey, the black bees became maddened, and they hummed in intoxication. Merry peacocks danced just like actors and actresses, and merry cuckoos called their mates very nicely.

TEXTS 42–43

कदम्बचम्पकाशोककरञ्जबकुलासनैः ।
कुन्दमन्दारकुटजैश्चूतपोतैरलङ्कृतम् ॥४२॥
कारण्डवैः प्लवैर्हंसैः कुररैर्जलकुक्कुटैः ।
सारसैश्चक्रवाकैश्च चकोरैर्वल्गु कूजितम् ॥४३॥

kadamba-campakāśoka-
karañja-bakulāsanaiḥ
kunda-mandāra-kuṭajaiś
cūta-potair alaṅkṛtam

kāraṇḍavaiḥ plavair haṁsaiḥ
kurarair jala-kukkuṭaiḥ
sārasaiś cakravākaiś ca
cakorair valgu kūjitam

kadamba—*kadamba* flowers; *campaka*—*campaka* flowers; *aśoka*—*aśoka* flowers; *karañja*—*karañja* flowers; *bakula*—*bakula* flowers; *āsanaiḥ*—by *āsana* trees; *kunda*—*kunda; mandāra*—*mandāra; kuṭajaiḥ*—and by *kuṭaja* trees; *cūta-potaiḥ*—by young mango trees; *alaṅkṛtam*—adorned; *kāraṇḍavaiḥ*—by *kāraṇḍava* ducks; *plavaiḥ*—by *plavas; haṁsaiḥ*—by swans; *kuraraiḥ*—by ospreys; *jala-kukkuṭaiḥ*—by waterfowl; *sārasaiḥ*—by cranes; *cakravākaiḥ*—by *cakravāka* birds; *ca*—and; *cakoraiḥ*—by *cakora* birds; *valgu*—pleasing; *kūjitam*—vibration of birds' sounds.

TRANSLATION

Lake Bindu-sarovara was adorned by flowering trees such as kadamba, campaka, aśoka, karañja, bakula, āsana, kunda, mandāra, kuṭaja and young mango trees. The air was filled with the pleasing notes of kāraṇḍava ducks, plavas, swans, ospreys, waterfowl, cranes, cakravākas and cakoras.

PURPORT

For most of the trees, flowers, fruits and birds mentioned here as surrounding Bindu-sarovara Lake, English synonyms cannot be found. All the trees mentioned are very pious in that they produce a nice aromatic flower, such as the *campaka*, *kadamba* and *bakula*. The sweet sounds of waterfowl and cranes made the surrounding area as pleasant as possible and created a very suitable spiritual atmosphere.

TEXT 44

तथैव हरिणैः क्रोडैः श्वाविद्गवयकुञ्जरैः ।
गोपुच्छैर्हरिभिर्मर्कैर्नकुलैर्नाभिभिर्वृतम् ॥४४॥

tathaiva hariṇaiḥ kroḍaiḥ
śvāvid-gavaya-kuñjaraiḥ
gopucchair haribhir markair
nakulair nābhibhir vṛtam

tathā eva—likewise; *hariṇaiḥ*—by deer; *kroḍaiḥ*—by boars; *śvāvit*—porcupines; *gavaya*—a wild animal closely resembling the cow; *kuñjaraiḥ*—by elephants; *gopucchaiḥ*—by baboons; *haribhiḥ*—by lions; *markaiḥ*—by monkeys; *nakulaiḥ*—by mongooses; *nābhibhiḥ*—by musk deer; *vṛtam*—surrounded.

TRANSLATION

Its shores abounded with deer, boars, porcupines, gavayas, elephants, baboons, lions, monkeys, mongooses and musk deer.

PURPORT

Musk deer are not found in every forest, but only in places like Bindu-sarovara. They are always intoxicated by the aroma of musk secreted from their navels. *Gavayas*, the species of cow mentioned herein, bear a bunch of hair at the end of their tails. This bunch of hair is used in temple worship to fan the Deities. *Gavayas* are sometimes called *camarīs*, and they are considered very sacred. In India there are still gypsies or forest mercantile people who flourish by trading *kastūrī*, or musk, and the bunches of hair from the *camarīs*. These are always in great demand for the higher classes of Hindu population, and such business still goes on in large cities and villages in India.

TEXTS 45–47

प्रविश्य तत्तीर्थवरमादिराजः सहात्मजः ।
ददर्श मुनिमासीनं तस्मिन् हुतहुताशनम् ॥४५॥
विद्योतमानं वपुषा तपस्युग्रयुजा चिरम् ।
नातिक्षामं भगवतः स्निग्धापाङ्गावलोकनात् ।
तद्व्याहृतामृतकलापीयूषश्रवणेन च ॥४६॥
प्रांशुं पद्मपलाशाक्षं जटिलं चीरवाससम् ।
उपसंश्रित्य मलिनं यथार्हणमसंस्कृतम् ॥४७॥

praviśya tat tīrtha-varam
ādi-rājaḥ sahātmajaḥ
dadarśa munim āsīnaṁ
tasmin huta-hutāśanam

vidyotamānaṁ vapuṣā
tapasy ugra-yujā ciram
nātikṣāmaṁ bhagavataḥ
snigdhāpāṅgāvalokanāt
tad-vyāhṛtāmṛta-kalā-
pīyūṣa-śravaṇena ca

prāṁśuṁ padma-palāśākṣaṁ
jaṭilaṁ cīra-vāsasam
upasaṁśritya malinaṁ
yathārhaṇam asaṁskṛtam

praviśya—entering; *tat*—that; *tīrtha-varam*—best of sacred places; *ādi-rājaḥ*—the first monarch (Svāyambhuva Manu); *saha-ātmajaḥ*—along with his daughter; *dadarśa*—saw; *munim*—the sage; *āsīnam*—sitting; *tasmin*—in the hermitage; *huta*—being offered oblations; *huta-aśanam*—the sacred fire; *vidyotamānam*—shining brilliantly; *vapuṣā*—by his body; *tapasi*—in penance; *ugra*—terribly; *yujā*—engaged in *yoga; ciram*—for a long time; *na*—not; *atikṣāmam*—very emaciated; *bhagavataḥ*—of the Lord; *snigdha*—affectionate; *apāṅga*—sidelong;

avalokanāt—from the glance; *tat*—of Him; *vyāhṛta*—from the words; *amṛta-kalā*—moonlike; *pīyūṣa*—the nectar; *śravaṇena*—by hearing; *ca*—and; *prāṁśum*—tall; *padma*—lotus flower; *palāśa*—petal; *akṣam*—eyes; *jaṭilam*—matted locks; *cīra-vāsasam*—having rags for clothes; *upasaṁśritya*—having approached; *malinam*—soiled; *yathā*—like; *arhaṇam*—gem; *asaṁskṛtam*—unpolished.

TRANSLATION

Entering that most sacred spot with his daughter and going near the sage, the first monarch, Svāyambhuva Manu, saw the sage sitting in his hermitage, having just propitiated the sacred fire by pouring oblations into it. His body shone most brilliantly; though he had engaged in austere penance for a long time, he was not emaciated, for the Lord had cast His affectionate sidelong glance upon him and he had also heard the nectar flowing from the moonlike words of the Lord. The sage was tall, his eyes were large, like the petals of a lotus, and he had matted locks on his head. He was clad in rags. Svāyambhuva Manu approached and saw him to be somewhat soiled, like an unpolished gem.

PURPORT

Here are some descriptions of a *brahmacārī-yogī*. In the morning, the first duty of a *brahmacārī* seeking spiritual elevation is *huta-hutāśana*, to offer sacrifical oblations to the Supreme Lord. Those engaged in *brahmacarya* cannot sleep until seven or nine o'clock in the morning. They must rise early in the morning, at least one and a half hours before the sun rises, and offer oblations, or in this age, they must chant the holy name of the Lord, Hare Kṛṣṇa. As referred to by Lord Caitanya, *kalau nāsty eva nāsty eva nāsty eva gatir anyathā:* there is no other alternative, no other alternative, no other alternative, in this age, to chanting the holy name of the Lord. The *brahmacārī* must rise early in the morning and, after placing himself, should chant the holy name of the Lord. From the very features of the sage, it appeared that he had undergone great austerities; that is the sign of one observing *brahmacarya*, the vow of celibacy. If one lives otherwise, it will be manifest in the lust visible in his face and body. The word *vidyotamānam* indicates that the *brahmacārī* feature showed in his body. That is the certificate that one has undergone great austerity in *yoga.* A drunkard or smoker or sex-monger can never be eligible to practice *yoga.* Generally *yogīs* look very skinny because of their not being comfortably situated, but Kardama Muni was not emaciated, for he had seen the Supreme Personality of Godhead face to face. Here the word *snigdhāpāṅgāvalokanāt* means that he was fortunate enough to see the Supreme Lord face to face. He looked healthy because he had directly received the nectarean sound vibrations from the lotus lips of the Personality of Godhead. Similarly, one who hears the transcendental sound vibration of the holy name of the Lord, Hare Kṛṣṇa, also improves in health. We have actually seen that many *brahmacārīs* and *gṛhasthas* connected with the International Society for Krishna Consciousness have improved in health, and a luster has come to their faces. It is essential that a *brahmacārī* engaged in spiritual advancement look very healthy and lustrous. The comparison of the sage to an unpolished gem is very appropriate. Even if a gem just taken from a mine looks unpolished, the luster of the gem cannot be stopped. Similarly, although Kardama was not properly dressed and his body was not properly cleansed, his overall appearance was gemlike.

TEXT 48

अथोटजमुपायातं नृदेवं प्रणतं पुरः ।
सपर्यया पर्यगृह्णात्प्रतिनन्द्यानुरूपया ॥४८॥

athoṭajam upāyātaṁ
nṛdevaṁ praṇataṁ puraḥ
saparyayā paryagṛhṇāt
pratinandyānurūpayā

atha—then; *uṭajam*—the hermitage; *upāyātam*—approached; *nṛdevam*—the monarch; *praṇatam*—bowed down; *puraḥ*—in front; *saparyayā*—with honor; *paryagṛhṇāt*—received him; *pratinandya*—greeting him; *anurūpayā*—befitting the King's position.

TRANSLATION

Seeing that the monarch had come to his hermitage and was bowing before him, the sage greeted him with benediction and received him with due honor.

PURPORT

Emperor Svāyambhuva Manu not only approached the cottage of dried leaves possessed by the hermit Kardama but also offered respectful obeisances unto him. Similarly, it was the duty of the hermit to offer blessings to kings who used to approach his hermitage in the jungle.

TEXT 49

गृहीतार्हणमासीनं संयतं प्रीणयन्मुनिः ।
स्मरन् भगवदादेशमित्याह श्लक्ष्णया गिरा ॥४९॥

gṛhītārhaṇam āsīnaṁ
saṁyataṁ prīṇayan muniḥ
smaran bhagavad-ādeśam
ity āha ślakṣṇayā girā

gṛhīta—received; *arhaṇam*—honor; *āsīnam*—seated; *saṁyatam*—remained silent; *prīṇayan*—delighting; *muniḥ*—the sage; *smaran*—remembering; *bhagavat*—of the Lord; *ādeśam*—the order; *iti*—thus; *āha*—spoke; *ślakṣṇayā*—sweet; *girā*—with a voice.

TRANSLATION

After receiving the sage's attention, the King sat down and was silent. Recalling the instructions of the Lord, Kardama then spoke to the King as follows, delighting him with his sweet accents.

TEXT 50

नूनं चङ्क्रमणं देव सतां संरक्षणाय ते ।
वधाय चासतां यस्त्वं हरेः शक्तिर्हि पालिनी ॥५०॥

nūnaṁ caṅkramaṇaṁ deva
satāṁ saṁrakṣaṇāya te
vadhāya cāsatāṁ yas tvaṁ
hareḥ śaktir hi pālinī

nūnam—surely; *caṅkramaṇam*—the tour; *deva*—O lord; *satām*—of the virtuous; *saṁrakṣaṇāya*—for the protection; *te*—your; *vadhāya*—for killing; *ca*—and; *asatām*—of the demons; *yaḥ*—the person who; *tvam*—you; *hareḥ*—of the Supreme Personality of Godhead; *śaktiḥ*—the energy; *hi*—since; *pālinī*—protecting.

TRANSLATION

The tour you have undertaken, O lord, is surely intended to protect the virtuous and kill the demons, since you embody the protecting energy of Śrī Hari.

PURPORT

It appears from many Vedic literatures, especially histories like *Śrīmad-Bhāgavatam* and the *Purāṇas*, that the pious kings of old used to tour their kingdoms in order to give protection to the pious citizens and to chastise or kill the impious. Sometimes they used to kill animals in the forests to practice the killing art because without such practice they would not be able to kill the undesirable elements. *Kṣatriyas* are allowed to commit violence in that way because violence for a good purpose is a part of their duty. Here two terms are clearly mentioned: *vadhāya*, "for the purpose of killing," and *asatām*, "those who are undesirable." The protecting energy of the king is supposed to be the energy of the Supreme Lord. In *Bhagavad-gītā* (4.8) the Lord says, *paritrāṇāya sādhūnāṁ vināśāya ca duṣkṛtām.* The Lord descends to give protection to the pious and to kill the demons. The potency, therefore, to give protection to the pious and kill the demons or undesirables is directly an energy from the Supreme Lord, and the king or the chief executive of the state is supposed to possess such energy. In this age it is very difficult to find such a head of state who is expert in killing the undesirables. Modern heads of state sit very nicely in their palaces and try without reason to kill innocent persons.

TEXT 51

योऽर्केन्द्वग्नीन्द्रवायूनां यमधर्मप्रचेतसाम् ।
रूपाणि स्थान आधत्से तस्मै शुक्लाय ते नमः ॥५१॥

yo 'rkendv-agnīndra-vāyūnāṁ
yama-dharma-pracetasām
rūpāṇi sthāna ādhatse
tasmai śuklāya te namaḥ

yaḥ—you who; *arka*—of the sun; *indu*—of the moon; *agni*—of Agni, the fire-god; *indra*—of Indra, the lord of heaven; *vāyūnām*—of Vāyu, the wind-god; *yama*—of Yama, the god of punishment; *dharma*—of Dharma, the god of piety; *pracetasām*—and of Varuṇa, the god of the waters; *rūpāṇi*—the forms; *sthāne*—when necessary; *ādhatse*—you assume; *tasmai*—unto Him; *śuklāya*—unto Lord Viṣṇu; *te*—unto you; *namaḥ*—obeisances.

TRANSLATION

You assume, when necessary, the part of the sun-god; the moon-god; Agni, the god of fire; Indra, the lord of paradise; Vāyu, the wind-god; Yama, the god of punishment; Dharma, the god of piety; and Varuṇa, the god presiding over the waters. All obeisances to you, who are none other than Lord Viṣṇu!

PURPORT

Since the sage Kardama was a *brāhmaṇa* and Svāyambhuva was a *kṣatriya*, the sage was not supposed to offer obeisances to the King because socially his position was greater than the King's. But he offered his obeisances to Svāyambhuva Manu because as Manu, king and emperor, he was the representative of the Supreme Lord. The Supreme Lord is always worshipable, regardless of whether one is a *brāhmaṇa*, a *kṣatriya* or a *śūdra*. As the representative of the Supreme Lord, the King deserved respectful obeisances from everyone.

TEXTS 52–54

न यदा रथमास्थाय जैत्रं मणिगणार्पितम् ।
विस्फूर्जच्चण्डकोदण्डो रथेन त्रासयन्नघान् ॥५२॥
स्वसैन्यचरणक्षुण्णं वेपयन्मण्डलं भुवः ।
विकर्षन् बृहतीं सेनां पर्यटस्यंशुमानिव ॥५३॥

तदैव सेतवः सर्वे वर्णाश्रमनिबन्धनाः ।
भगवद्रचिता राजन् भिद्येरन् बत दस्युभिः ॥५४॥

na yadā ratham āsthāya
jaitraṁ maṇi-gaṇārpitam
visphūrjac-caṇḍa-kodaṇḍo
rathena trāsayann aghān

sva-sainya-caraṇa-kṣuṇṇaṁ
vepayan maṇḍalaṁ bhuvaḥ
vikarṣan bṛhatīṁ senāṁ
paryaṭasy aṁśumān iva

tadaiva setavaḥ sarve
varṇāśrama-nibandhanāḥ
bhagavad-racitā rājan
bhidyeran bata dasyubhiḥ

na—not; *yadā*—when; *ratham*—the chariot; *āsthāya*—having mounted; *jaitram*—victorious; *maṇi*—of jewels; *gaṇa*—with clusters; *arpitam*—bedecked; *visphūrjat*—twanging; *caṇḍa*—a fearful sound just to punish the criminals; *kodaṇḍaḥ*—bow; *rathena*—by the presence of such a chariot; *trāsayan*—threatening; *aghān*—all the culprits; *sva-sainya*—of your soldiers; *caraṇa*—by the feet; *kṣuṇṇam*—trampled; *vepayan*—causing to tremble; *maṇḍalam*—the globe; *bhuvaḥ*—of the earth; *vikarṣan*—leading; *bṛhatīm*—huge; *senām*—army; *paryaṭasi*—you roam about; *aṁśumān*—the brilliant sun; *iva*—like; *tadā*—then; *eva*—certainly; *setavaḥ*—religious codes; *sarve*—all; *varṇa*—of *varṇas; āśrama*—of *āśramas; nibandhanāḥ*—obligations; *bhagavat*—by the Lord; *racitāḥ*—created; *rājan*—O King; *bhidyeran*—they would be broken; *bata*—alas; *dasyubhiḥ*—by rogues.

TRANSLATION

If you did not mount your victorious jeweled chariot, whose mere presence threatens culprits, if you did not produce fierce sounds by the twanging of your bow, and if you did not roam about the world like the brilliant sun, leading a huge army whose

trampling feet cause the globe of the earth to tremble, then all the moral laws governing the varṇas and āśramas created by the Lord Himself would be broken by the rogues and rascals.

PURPORT

It is the duty of a responsible king to protect the social and spiritual orders in human society. The spiritual orders are divided into four *āśramas—brahmacarya, gṛhastha, vānaprastha* and *sannyāsa*—and the social orders, according to work and qualification, are made up of the *brāhmaṇas*, the *kṣatriyas*, the *vaiśyas* and the *śūdras*. These social orders, according to the different grades of work and qualification, are described in *Bhagavad-gītā*. Unfortunately, for want of proper protection by responsible kings, the system of social and spiritual orders has now become a hereditary caste system. But this is not the actual system. Human society means that society which is making progress toward spiritual realization. The most advanced human society was known as *ārya; ārya* refers to those who are advancing. So the question is, "Which society is advancing?" Advancement does not mean creating material "necessities" unnecessarily and thus wasting human energy in aggravation over so-called material comforts. Real advancement is advancement toward spiritual realization, and the community which acted toward this end was known as the Āryan civilization. The intelligent men, the *brāhmaṇas*, as exemplified by Kardama Muni, were engaged in advancing the spiritual cause, and *kṣatriyas* like Emperor Svāyambhuva used to rule the country and insure that all facilities for spiritual realization were nicely provided. It is the duty of the king to travel all over the country and see that everything is in order. Indian civilization on the basis of the four *varṇas* and *āśramas* deteriorated because of her dependency on foreigners, or those who did not follow the civilization of *varṇāśrama*. Thus the *varṇāśrama* system has now been degraded into the caste system.

The institution of four *varṇas* and four *āśramas* is confirmed herewith to be *bhagavad-racita*, which means "designed by the Supreme Personality of Godhead." In *Bhagavad-gītā* this is also confirmed: *cātur-varṇyaṁ mayā sṛṣṭam*. The Lord says that the institution of four *varṇas* and four *āśramas* "is created by Me." Anything created by the Lord cannot be closed or covered. The divisions of *varṇas* and *āśramas* will continue to exist, either in their original form or in degraded form, but because they are created by the Lord, the Supreme Personality of Godhead, they cannot be extinguished. They are like the sun, a creation of God, and therefore will remain. Either covered by clouds or in a clear sky, the sun will continue to exist. Similarly, when the *varṇāśrama* system becomes degraded, it appears as a hereditary caste system, but in every society there is an intelligent class of men, a martial class, a mercantile class and a laborer class. When they are regulated for cooperation among communities according to the Vedic principles, then there is peace and spiritual advancement. But when there is hatred and malpractice and mutual mistrust in the caste system, the whole system becomes degraded, and as stated herein, it creates a deplorable state. At the present moment, the entire world is in this deplorable condition because of giving rights to so many interests. This is due to the degradation of the four castes of *varṇas* and *āśramas.*

TEXT 55

अधर्मश्च समेधेत लोलुपैर्व्यङ्कुशैर्नृभिः ।
शयाने त्वयि लोकोऽयं दस्युग्रस्तो विनङ्क्ष्यति॥५५॥

adharmaś ca samedheta
lolupair vyaṅkuśair nṛbhiḥ
śayāne tvayi loko 'yaṁ
dasyu-grasto vinaṅkṣyati

adharmaḥ—unrighteousness; *ca*—and; *samedheta*—would flourish; *lolupaiḥ*—simply hankering after money; *vyaṅkuśaiḥ*—uncontrolled; *nṛbhiḥ*—by men; *śayāne tvayi*—when you lie down for rest; *lokaḥ*—world; *ayam*—this; *dasyu*—by the miscreants; *grastaḥ*—attacked; *vinaṅkṣyati*—it will perish.

TRANSLATION

If you gave up all thought of the world's situation, unrighteousness would flourish, for men who hanker only after money would be unopposed. Such miscreants would attack, and the world would perish.

PURPORT

Because the scientific division of four *varṇas* and four *āśramas* is now being extinguished, the entire world is being governed by unwanted men who have no training in religion, politics or social order, and it is in a very deplorable condition. In the institution of four *varṇas* and four *āśramas* there are regular training principles for the different classes of men. Just as, in the modern age, there is a necessity for engineers, medical practioners and electricians, and they are properly trained in different scientific institutions, similarly, in former times, the higher social orders, namely the intelligent class (the *brāhmaṇas*), the ruling class (the *kṣatriyas*) and the mercantile class (the *vaiśyas*), were properly trained. *Bhagavad-gītā* describes the duties of the *brāhmaṇas, kṣatriyas, vaiśyas* and *śūdras*. When there is no such training, one simply claims that because he is born in a *brāhmaṇa* or *kṣatriya* family, he is therefore a *brāhmaṇa* or a *kṣatriya*, even though he performs the duties of a *śūdra*. Such undue claims to being a higher-caste man make the system of scientific social orders into a caste system, completely degrading the original system. Thus society is now in chaos, and there is neither peace nor prosperity. It is clearly stated herein that unless there is the vigilance of a strong king, impious, unqualified men will claim a certain status in society, and that will make the social order perish.

TEXT 56

अथापि पृच्छे त्वां वीर यदर्थं त्वमिहागतः ।
तद्वयं निर्व्यलीकेन प्रतिपद्यामहे हृदा ॥५६॥

athāpi pṛcche tvāṁ vīra
yad-arthaṁ tvam ihāgataḥ
tad vayaṁ nirvyalīkena
pratipadyāmahe hṛdā

atha api—in spite of all this; *pṛcche*—I ask; *tvām*—you; *vīra*—O valiant King; *yat-artham*—the purpose; *tvam*—you; *iha*—here; *āgataḥ*—have come; *tat*—that; *vayam*—we; *nirvyalīkena*—without reservation; *pratipadyāmahe*—we shall carry out; *hṛdā*—with heart and soul.

TRANSLATION

In spite of all this, I ask you, O valiant King, the purpose for which you have come here. Whatever it may be, we shall carry it out without reservation.

PURPORT

When a guest comes to a friend's house, it is understood that there is some special purpose. Kardama Muni could understand that such a great king as Svāyambhuva, although traveling to inspect the condition of his kingdom, must have had some special purpose to come to his hermitage. Thus he prepared himself to fulfill the King's desire. Formerly it was customary that the sages used to go to the kings and the kings used to visit the sages in their hermitages; each was glad to fulfill the other's purpose. This reciprocal relationship is called *bhakti-kārya.* There is a nice verse describing the relationship of mutual beneficial interest between the *brāhmaṇa* and the *kṣatriya* (*kṣatraṁ dvijatvam*). *Kṣatram* means "the royal order," and *dvijatvam* means "the brahminical order." The two were meant for mutual interest. The royal order would give protection to the *brāhmaṇas* for the cultivation of spiritual advancement in society, and the *brāhmaṇas* would give their valuable instruction to the royal order on how the state and the citizens can gradually be elevated in spiritual perfection.

Thus end the Bhaktivedanta purports of the Third Canto, Twenty-first Chapter, of the Śrīmad-Bhāgavatam, *entitled "Conversation Between Manu and Kardama."*

CHAPTER TWENTY-TWO

The Marriage of Kardama Muni and Devahūti

TEXT 1

मैत्रेय उवाच

एवमाविष्कृताशेषगुणकर्मोदयो मुनिम् ।
सव्रीड इव तं सम्राडुपारतमुवाच ह ॥ १ ॥

maitreya uvāca
evam āviṣkṛtāśeṣa-
guṇa-karmodayo munim
savrīḍa iva taṁ samrāḍ
upāratam uvāca ha

maitreyaḥ—the great sage Maitreya; *uvāca*—said; *evam*—thus; *āviṣkṛta*—having been described; *aśeṣa*—all; *guṇa*—of the virtues; *karma*—of the activities; *udayaḥ*—the greatness; *munim*—the great sage; *sa-vrīḍaḥ*—feeling modest; *iva*—as though; *tam*—him (Kardama); *samrāṭ*—Emperor Manu; *upāratam*—silent; *uvāca ha*—addressed.

TRANSLATION

Śrī Maitreya said: After describing the greatness of the Emperor's manifold qualities and activities, the sage became silent, and the Emperor, feeling modesty, addressed him as follows.

TEXT 2

मनुरुवाच

ब्रह्मासृजत्स्वमुखतो युष्मानात्मपरीप्सया ।
छन्दोमयस्तपोविद्यायोगयुक्तानलम्पटान् ॥ २ ॥

manur uvāca
brahmāsṛjat sva-mukhato
yuṣmān ātma-parīpsayā
chandomayas tapo-vidyā-
yoga-yuktān alampaṭān

manuḥ—Manu; *uvāca*—said; *brahmā*—Lord Brahmā; *asṛjat*—created; *sva-mukhataḥ*—from his face; *yuṣmān*—you (*brāhmaṇas*); *ātma-parīpsayā*—to protect himself by expanding; *chandaḥ-mayaḥ*—the form of the *Vedas; tapaḥ-vidyā-yoga-yuktān*—full of austerity, knowledge and mystic power; *alampaṭān*—averse to sense gratification.

TRANSLATION

Manu replied: To expand himself in Vedic knowledge, Lord Brahmā, the personified Veda, from his face created you, the brāhmaṇas, who are full of austerity, knowledge and mystic power and are averse to sense gratification.

PURPORT

The purpose of the *Vedas* is to propagate the transcendental knowledge of the Absolute Truth. The *brāhmaṇas* were created from the mouth of the Supreme Person, and therefore they are meant to spread the knowledge of the *Vedas* in order to spread the glories of the Lord. In *Bhagavad-gītā* also Lord Kṛṣṇa says that all the *Vedas* are meant for understanding the Supreme Personality of Godhead. It is especially mentioned here (*yoga-yuktān alampaṭān*) that *brāhmaṇas* are full of mystic power and are completely averse to sense gratification. Actually there are two kinds of occupations. One occupation, in the material world, is sense gratification, and the other occupation is spiritual activity—to satisfy the Lord by His glorification. Those who engage in sense gratification are called demons, and those who spread the glorification of the Lord or satisfy the transcendental senses of the Lord are called demigods. It is specifically mentioned here that the *brāhmaṇas* are created from the face of the cosmic personality, or *virāṭ-puruṣa;* similarly the *kṣatriyas* are said to be created from His arms, the *vaiśyas* are created from His waist, and the *śūdras* are created from His legs. *Brāhmaṇas* are especially meant for austerity, learning and knowledge and arc averse to all kinds of sense gratification.

TEXT 3

तत्त्राणायासृजच्चास्मान्दोःसहस्रात्सहस्रपात् ।
हृदयं तस्य हि ब्रह्म क्षत्रमङ्गं प्रचक्षते ॥ ३ ॥

tat-trāṇāyāsṛjac cāsmān
doḥ-sahasrāt sahasra-pāt
hṛdayaṁ tasya hi brahma
kṣatram aṅgaṁ pracakṣate

tat-trāṇāya—for the protection of the *brāhmaṇas; asṛjat*—created; *ca*—and; *asmān*—us (*kṣatriyas*); *doḥ-sahasrāt*—from His thousand arms; *sahasra-pāt*—the thousand-legged Supreme Being (the universal form); *hṛdayam*—heart; *tasya*—His; *hi*—for; *brahma*—*brāhmaṇas; kṣatram*—the *kṣatriyas; aṅgam*—arms; *pracakṣate*—are spoken of.

TRANSLATION

For the protection of the brāhmaṇas, the thousand-legged Supreme Being created us, the kṣatriyas, from His thousand arms. Hence the brāhmaṇas are said to be His heart and the kṣatriyas His arms.

PURPORT

Kṣatriyas are specifically meant to maintain the *brāhmaṇas* because if the *brāhmaṇas* are protected, then the head of civilization is protected. *Brāhmaṇas* are supposed to be the head of the social body; if the head is clear and has not gone mad, then everything is in proper position. The Lord is described thus: *namo brahmaṇya-devāya go-brāhmaṇa-hitāya ca.* The purport of this prayer is that the Lord specifically protects the *brāhmaṇas* and the cows, and then He protects all other members of society (*jagad-dhitāya*). It is His will that universal welfare work depends on the protection of cows and *brāhmaṇas;* thus brahminical culture and cow protection are the basic principles for human civilization.

Kṣatriyas are especially meant to protect the *brāhmaṇas,* as is the supreme will of the Lord: *go-brāhmaṇa-hitāya ca.* As, within the body, the heart is a very important part, so the *brāhmaṇas* are also the important element in human society. The *kṣatriyas* are more like the whole body; even though the whole body is bigger than the heart, the heart is more important.

TEXT 4

अतो ह्यन्योन्यमात्मानं ब्रह्म क्षत्रं च रक्षतः ।
रक्षति स्माव्ययो देवः स यः सदसदात्मकः ॥ ४ ॥

ato hy anyonyam ātmānaṁ
brahma kṣatraṁ ca rakṣataḥ
rakṣati smāvyayo devaḥ
sa yaḥ sad-asad-ātmakaḥ

ataḥ—hence; *hi*—certainly; *anyonyam*—each other; *ātmānam*—the self; *brahma*—the *brāhmaṇas; kṣatram*—the *kṣatriyas; ca*—and; *rakṣataḥ*—protect; *rakṣati sma*—protects; *avyayaḥ*—immutable; *devaḥ*—the Lord; *saḥ*—He; *yaḥ*—who; *sat-asat-ātmakaḥ*—the form of the cause and effect.

TRANSLATION

That is why the brāhmaṇas and kṣatriyas protect each other, as well as themselves; and the Lord Himself, who is both the cause and effect and is yet immutable, protects them through each other.

PURPORT

The entire social structure of *varṇa* and *āśrama* is a cooperative system meant to uplift all to the highest platform of spiritual realization. The *brāhmaṇas* are intended to be protected by the *kṣatriyas,* and the *kṣatriyas* also are intended to be enlightened by the *brāhmaṇas.* When the *brāhmaṇas* and *kṣatriyas* cooperate nicely, the other subordinate divisions, the *vaiśyas,* or mercantile people, and the *śūdras,* or laborer class, automatically flourish. The entire elaborate system of Vedic society was therefore based on the importance of the *brāhmaṇas* and *kṣatriyas.*

The Lord is the real protector, but He is unattached to the affairs of protection. He creates *brāhmaṇas* for the protection of the *kṣatriyas*, and *kṣatriyas* for the protection of the *brāhmaṇas*. He remains aloof from all activities; therefore, He is called *nirvikāra*, "without activity." He has nothing to do. He is so great that He does not perform action personally, but His energies act. The *brāhmaṇas* and *kṣatriyas*, and anything that we see, are different energies acting upon one another.

Although individual souls are all different, the Superself, or Supersoul, is the Supreme Personality of Godhead. Individually one's self may differ from others in certain qualities and may engage in different activities, such as those of a *brāhmaṇa*, *kṣatriya* or *vaiśya*, but when there is complete cooperation among different individual souls, the Supreme Personality of Godhead as Supersoul, Paramātmā, being one in every individual soul, is pleased and gives them all protection. As stated before, the *brāhmaṇas* are produced from the mouth of the Lord, and the *kṣatriyas* are produced from the chest or arms of the Lord. If the different castes or social sections, although apparently differently occupied in different activities, nevertheless act in full cooperation, then the Lord is pleased. This is the idea of the institution of four *varṇas* and four *āśramas*. If the members of different *āśramas* and *varṇas* cooperate fully in Kṛṣṇa consciousness, then society is well protected by the Lord, without doubt.

In *Bhagavad-gītā* it is stated that the Lord is the proprietor of all different bodies. The individual soul is the proprietor of his individual body, but the Lord clearly states, "My dear Bhārata, you must know that I am also *kṣetra-jña*." *Kṣetra-jña* means "the knower or proprietor of the body." The individual soul is the proprietor of the individual body, but the Supersoul, the Personality of Godhead, Kṛṣṇa, is the proprietor of all bodies everywhere. He is the proprietor not only of human bodies but of birds, beasts and all other entities, not only on this planet but on other planets also. He is the supreme proprietor; therefore He does not become divided by protecting the different individual souls. He remains one and the same. That the sun appears on top of everyone's head when at the meridian does not imply that the sun becomes divided. One man thinks that the sun is on his head only, whereas five thousand miles away another man is thinking that the sun is only on his head. Similarly, the Supersoul, the Supreme Personality of Godhead, is one, but He appears to individually oversee each individual soul. This does not mean that the individual soul and the Supersoul are one. They are one in quality, as spirit soul, but the individual soul and Supersoul are different.

TEXT 5

तव सन्दर्शनादेवच्छिन्ना मे सर्वसंशयाः ।
यत्स्वयं भगवान् प्रीत्या धर्ममाह रिरक्षिषोः ॥ ५ ॥

tava sandarśanād eva
cchinnā me sarva-saṁśayāḥ
yat svayaṁ bhagavān prītyā
dharmam āha rirakṣiṣoḥ

tava—your; *sandarśanāt*—by sight; *eva*—only; *chinnāḥ*—resolved; *me*—my; *sarva-saṁśayāḥ*—all doubts; *yat*—inasmuch as; *svayam*—personally; *bhagavān*—Your Lordship; *prītyā*—lovingly; *dharmam*—duty; *āha*—explained; *rirakṣiṣoḥ*—of a king anxious to protect his subjects.

TRANSLATION

Now I have resolved all my doubts simply by meeting you, for Your Lordship has very kindly and clearly explained the duty of a king who desires to protect his subjects.

PURPORT

Manu described herewith the result of seeing a great saintly person. Lord Caitanya says that one should always try to associate with saintly persons because if one establishes a proper association with a saintly person, even for a moment, one attains all perfection. Somehow or other, if one meets a saintly person and achieves his favor, then the entire mission of one's human life is fulfilled. In our personal experience we have actual proof of this statement of Manu. Once we had the opportunity to meet Viṣṇupāda Śrī Śrīmad Bhaktisiddhānta Sarasvatī Gosvāmī Mahārāja, and on first sight he requested this humble self to preach his message in the Western countries. There was no preparation for this, but somehow or other he desired it, and by his grace we are now engaged in executing his order, which has given us a transcendental occupation and has saved and liberated us from the occupation of material activities. Thus it is actually a fact that if one meets a saintly person completely engaged in transcendental duties and achieves his favor, then one's life mission becomes complete. What is not possible to achieve in thousands of lives can be achieved in one moment if there is an opportunity to meet a saintly person. It is therefore enjoined in Vedic literature that one should always try to associate with saintly persons and try to disassociate oneself from the common man, because by one word of a saintly person one can be liberated from material entanglement. A saintly person has the power, because of his spiritual advancement, to give immediate liberation to the conditioned soul. Here Manu admits that all his doubts are now over because Kardama has very kindly described the different duties of individual souls.

TEXT 6

दिष्टया मे भगवान् दृष्टो दुर्दर्शो योऽकृतात्मनाम् ।
दिष्टया पादरजः स्पृष्टं शीर्ष्णा मे भवतः शिवम् ॥६॥

diṣṭyā me bhagavān dṛṣṭo
durdarśo yo 'kṛtātmanām
diṣṭyā pāda-rajaḥ spṛṣṭaṁ
śīrṣṇā me bhavataḥ śivam

diṣṭyā—by good fortune; *me*—my; *bhagavān*—all-powerful; *dṛṣṭaḥ*—is seen; *durdarśaḥ*—not easily seen; *yaḥ*—who; *akṛta-ātmanām*—of those who have not controlled the mind and senses; *diṣṭyā*—by my good fortune; *pāda-rajaḥ*—the dust of the feet; *spṛṣṭam*—is touched; *śīrṣṇā*—by the head; *me*—my; *bhavataḥ*—your; *śivam*—causing all auspiciousness.

TRANSLATION

It is my good fortune that I have been able to see you, for you cannot easily be seen by persons who have not subdued the mind

or controlled the senses. I am all the more fortunate to have touched with my head the blessed dust of your feet.

PURPORT

The perfection of transcendental life can be achieved simply by touching the holy dust of the lotus feet of a holy man. In the *Bhāgavatam* it is said, *mahat-pāda-rajo-'bhiṣekam,* which means to be blessed by the holy dust of the lotus feet of a *mahat,* a great devotee. As stated in *Bhagavad-gītā, mahātmānas tu:* those who are great souls are under the spell of spiritual energy, and their symptom is that they fully engage in Kṛṣṇa consciousness for the service of the Lord. Therefore they are called *mahat.* Unless one is fortunate enough to have the dust of the lotus feet of a *mahātmā* on one's head, there is no possibility of perfection in spiritual life.

The *paramparā* system of disciplic succession is very important as a means of spiritual success. One becomes a *mahat* by the grace of his *mahat* spiritual master. If one takes shelter of the lotus feet of a great soul, there is every possibility of one's also becoming a great soul. When Mahārāja Rahūgaṇa asked Jaḍa Bharata about his wonderful achievement of spiritual success, he replied to the King that spiritual success is not possible simply by following the rituals of religion or simply by converting oneself into a *sannyāsī* or offering sacrifices as recommended in the scriptures. These methods are undoubtedly helpful for spiritual realization, but the real effect is brought about by the grace of a *mahātmā.* In Viśvanātha Cakravartī Ṭhākura's eight stanzas of prayer to the spiritual master, it is clearly stated that simply by satisfying the spiritual master one can achieve the supreme success in life, and in spite of executing all ritualistic performances, if one cannot satisfy the spiritual master, one has no access to spiritual perfection. Here the word *akṛtātmanām* is very significant. *Ātmā* means "body," "soul," or "mind," and *akṛtātmā* means the common man, who cannot control the senses or the mind. Because the common man is unable to control the senses and the mind, it is his duty to seek the shelter of a great soul or a great devotee of the Lord and just try to please him. That will make his life perfect. A common man cannot rise to the topmost stage of spiritual perfection simply by following the rituals and religious principles. He has to take shelter of a bona fide spiritual master and work under his direction faithfully and sincerely; then he becomes perfect, without a doubt.

TEXT 7

दिष्टया त्वयानुशिष्टोऽहं कृतश्चानुग्रहो महान् ।
अपावृतैः कर्णरन्ध्रैर्जुष्टा दिष्टयोशतीर्गिरः ॥ ७ ॥

diṣṭyā tvayānuśiṣṭo 'haṁ
kṛtaś cānugraho mahān
apāvṛtaiḥ karṇa-randhrair
juṣṭā diṣṭyośatīr giraḥ

diṣṭyā—luckily; *tvayā*—by you; *anuśiṣṭaḥ*—instructed; *aham*—I; *kṛtaḥ*—bestowed; *ca*—and; *anugrahaḥ*—favor; *mahān*—great; *apāvṛtaiḥ*—open; *karṇa-randhraiḥ*—with the holes of the ears; *juṣṭāḥ*—received; *diṣṭyā*—by good fortune; *uśatīḥ*—pure; *giraḥ*—words.

TRANSLATION

I have fortunately been instructed by you, and thus great favor has been bestowed upon me. I thank God that I have listened with open ears to your pure words.

PURPORT

Śrīla Rūpa Gosvāmī has given directions, in his *Bhakti-rasāmṛta-sindhu,* on how to accept a bona fide spiritual master and how to deal with him. First, the desiring candidate must find a bona fide spiritual master, and then he must very eagerly receive instructions from him and execute them. This is reciprocal service. A bona fide spiritual master or saintly person always desires to elevate a common man who comes to him. Because everyone is under the delusion of *māyā* and is forgetful of his prime duty, Kṛṣṇa consciousness, a saintly person always desires that everyone become a saintly person. It is the function of a saintly person to invoke Kṛṣṇa consciousness in every forgetful common man.

Manu said that since he was advised and instructed by Kardama Muni, he was very much favored. He considered himself lucky to receive the message by aural reception. It is especially mentioned here that one should be very inquisitive to hear with open ears from the authorized source of the bona fide spiritual master. How is one to receive? One should receive the transcendental message by aural reception. The word *karṇa-randhraiḥ* means "through the holes of the ears." The favor of the spiritual master is not received through any other part of the body but the ears. This does not mean, however, that the spiritual master gives a particular type of *mantra* through the ears in exchange for some dollars and if the man meditates on that he achieves perfection and becomes God within six months. Such reception through the ears is bogus. The real fact is that a bona fide spiritual master knows the nature of a particular man and what sort of duties he can perform in Kṛṣṇa consciousness, and he instructs him in that way. He instructs him through the ear, not privately, but publicly. "You are fit for such and such work in Kṛṣṇa consciousness. You can act in this way." One person is advised to act in Kṛṣṇa consciousness by working in the Deities' room, another is advised to act in Kṛṣṇa consciousness by performing editorial work, another is advised to do preaching work, and another is advised to carry out Kṛṣṇa consciousness in the cooking department. There are different departments of activity in Kṛṣṇa consciousness, and a spiritual master, knowing the particular ability of a particular man, trains him in such a way that by his tendency to act he becomes perfect. *Bhagavad-gītā* makes it clear that one can attain the highest perfection of spiritual life simply by offering service according to his ability, just as Arjuna served Kṛṣṇa by his ability in the military art. Arjuna offered his service fully as a military man, and he became perfect. Similarly, an artist can attain perfection simply by performing artistic work under the direction of the spiritual master. If one is a literary man, he can write articles and poetry for the service of the Lord under the direction of the spiritual master. One has to receive the message of the spiritual master regarding how to act in one's capacity, for the spiritual master is expert in giving such instructions.

This combination, the instruction of the spiritual master and the faithful execution of the instruction by the disciple, makes the entire process perfect. Śrīla Viśvanātha Cakravartī Ṭhākura describes in his explanation of the verse in *Bhagavad-gītā, vyavasāyātmikā buddhiḥ,* that one who wants to be certain to achieve spiritual success must take the instruction from the spiritual master as to what his particular function is. He should faithfully try to execute that particular instruction and should consider that his life and soul. The faithful execution of the instruction which he receives from the spiritual master is the only duty of a disciple, and that will bring him perfection. One should be very careful to receive the message from the spiritual master through the ears and execute it faithfully. That will make one's life successful.

TEXT 8

स भवान्दुहितृस्नेहपरिक्लिष्टात्मनो मम ।
श्रोतुमर्हसि दीनस्य श्रावितं कृपया मुने ॥ ८ ॥

sa bhavān duhitṛ-sneha-
parikliṣṭātmano mama
śrotum arhasi dīnasya
śrāvitaṁ kṛpayā mune

saḥ—yourself; *bhavān*—Your Honor; *duhitṛ-sneha*—by affection for my daughter; *parikliṣṭa-ātmanaḥ*—whose mind is agitated; *mama*—my; *śrotum*—to listen; *arhasi*—be pleased; *dīnasya*—of my humble self; *śrāvitam*—to the prayer; *kṛpayā*—graciously; *mune*—O sage.

TRANSLATION

O great sage, graciously be pleased to listen to the prayer of my humble self, for my mind is troubled by affection for my daughter.

PURPORT

When a disciple is perfectly in consonance with the spiritual master, having received his message and executed it perfectly and sincerely, he has a right to ask a particular favor from the spiritual master. Generally a pure devotee of the Lord or a pure disciple of a bona fide spiritual master does not ask any favor either from the Lord or the spiritual master, but even if there is a need to ask a favor from the spiritual master, one cannot ask that favor without satisfying him fully.

Svāyambhuva Manu wanted to disclose his mind regarding the function he wanted to execute due to affection for his daughter.

TEXT 9

प्रियव्रतोत्तानपदोः स्वसेयं दुहिता मम ।
अन्विच्छति पतिं युक्तं वयःशीलगुणादिभिः ॥ ९ ॥

priyavratottānapadoḥ
svaseyaṁ duhitā mama
anvicchati patiṁ yuktaṁ
vayaḥ-śīla-guṇādibhiḥ

priyavrata-uttānapadoḥ—of Priyavrata and Uttānapāda; *svasā*—sister; *iyam*—this; *duhitā*—daughter; *mama*—my; *anvicchati*—is seeking; *patim*—husband; *yuktam*—suited; *vayaḥ-śīla-guṇa-ādibhiḥ*—by age, character, good qualities, etc.

TRANSLATION

My daughter is the sister of Priyavrata and Uttānapāda. She is seeking a suitable husband in terms of age, character and good qualities.

PURPORT

The grown-up daughter of Svāyambhuva Manu, Devahūti, had good character and was well qualified; therefore she was searching for a suitable husband just befitting her age, qualities and character. The purpose of Manu's introducing his daughter as the sister of Priyavrata and Uttānapāda, two great kings, was to convince the sage that the girl came from a great family. She was his daughter and at the same time the sister of *kṣatriyas;* she did not come from a lower-class family. Manu therefore offered her to Kardama as just suitable for his purpose. It is clear that although the daughter was mature in age and qualities, she did not go out and find her husband independently. She expressed her desire for a suitable husband corresponding to her character, age and quality, and the father himself, out of affection for his daughter, took charge of finding such a husband.

TEXT 10

यदा तु भवतः शीलश्रुतरूपवयोगुणान् ।
अशृणोन्नारदादेषा त्वय्यासीत्कृतनिश्चया ॥१०॥

yadā tu bhavataḥ śīla-
śruta-rūpa-vayo-guṇān
aśṛṇon nāradād eṣā
tvayy āsīt kṛta-niścayā

yadā—when; *tu*—but; *bhavataḥ*—your; *śīla*—noble character; *śruta*—learning; *rūpa*—beautiful appearance; *vayaḥ*—youth; *guṇān*—virtues; *aśṛṇot*—heard; *nāradāt*—from Nārada Muni; *eṣā*—Devahūti; *tvayi*—in you; *āsīt*—became; *kṛta-niścayā*—fixed in determination.

TRANSLATION

The moment she heard from the sage Nārada of your noble character, learning, beautiful appearance, youth and other virtues, she fixed her mind upon you.

PURPORT

The girl Devahūti did not personally see Kardama Muni, nor did she personally experience his character or qualities, since there was no social intercourse by which she could gain such understanding. But she heard about Kardama Muni from the authority of Nārada Muni. Hearing from an authority is a better experience than gaining personal understanding. She heard from Nārada Muni that Kardama Muni was just fit to be her husband; therefore she became fixed in her heart that she would marry him, and she expressed her desire to her father, who therefore brought her before him.

TEXT 11

तत्प्रतीच्छ द्विजाग्र्येमां श्रद्धयोपहृतां मया ।
सर्वात्मनानुरूपां ते गृहमेधिषु कर्मसु ॥११॥

tat pratīccha dvijāgryemāṁ
śraddhayopahṛtāṁ mayā

sarvātmanānurūpāṁ te
gṛhamedhiṣu karmasu

tat—therefore; *pratīccha*—please accept; *dvija-agrya*—O best of the *brāhmaṇas; imām*—her; *śraddhayā*—with faith; *upahṛtām*—offered as a presentation; *mayā*—by me; *sarva-ātmanā*—in every way; *anu-rūpām*—suitable; *te*—for you; *gṛha-medhiṣu*—in the household; *kar-masu*—duties.

TRANSLATION

Therefore please accept her, O chief of the brāhmaṇas, for I offer her with faith and she is in every respect fit to be your wife and take charge of your household duties.

PURPORT

The words *gṛhamedhiṣu karmasu* mean "in household duties." Another word is also used here: *sarvātmanānurūpām.* The purport is that a wife should not only be equal to her husband in age, character and qualities, but must be helpful to him in his household duties. The household duty of a man is not to satisfy his sense gratification, but to remain with a wife and children and at the same time attain advancement in spiritual life. One who does not do so is not a householder but a *gṛhamedhī.* Two words are used in Sanskrit literature; one is *gṛhastha,* and the other is *gṛhamedhī.* The difference between *gṛhamedhī* and *gṛhastha* is that *gṛhastha* is also an *āśrama,* or spiritual order, but if one simply satisfies his senses as a householder, then he is a *gṛhamedhī.* For a *gṛhamedhī,* to accept a wife means to satisfy the senses, but for a *gṛhastha* a qualified wife is an assistant in every respect for advancement in spiritual activities. It is the duty of the wife to take charge of household affairs and not to compete with the husband. A wife is meant to help, but she cannot help her husband unless he is completely equal to her in age, character and quality.

TEXT 12

उद्यतस्य हि कामस्य प्रतिवादो न शस्यते ।
अपि निर्मुक्तसङ्गस्य कामरक्तस्य किं पुनः ॥१२॥

udyatasya hi kāmasya
prativādo na śasyate
api nirmukta-saṅgasya
kāma-raktasya kiṁ punaḥ

udyatasya—which has come of itself; *hi*—in fact; *kāmasya*—of material desire; *prativādaḥ*—the denial; *na*—not; *śasyate*—to be praised; *api*—even; *nirmukta*—of one who is free; *saṅgasya*—from attachment; *kāma*—to sensual pleasures; *raktasya*—of one addicted; *kim punaḥ*—how much less.

TRANSLATION

To deny an offering that has come of itself is not commendable even for one absolutely free from all attachment, much less one addicted to sensual pleasure.

PURPORT

In material life everyone is desirous of sense gratification; therefore, a person who gets an object of sense gratification without endeavor should not refuse to accept it. Kardama Muni was not meant for sense gratification, yet he aspired to marry and prayed to the Lord for a suitable wife. This was known to Svāyambhuva Manu. He indirectly convinced Kardama Muni: "You desire a suitable wife like my daughter, and she is now present before you. You should not reject the fulfillment of your prayer; you should accept my daughter."

TEXT 13

य उद्यतमनादृत्य कीनाशमभियाचते ।
क्षीयते तद्यशः स्फीतं मानश्चावज्ञया हतः ॥१३॥

ya udyatam anādṛtya
kīnāśam abhiyācate
kṣīyate tad-yaśaḥ sphītaṁ
mānaś cāvajñayā hataḥ

yaḥ—who; *udyatam*—an offering; *anādṛtya*—rejecting; *kīnāśam*—from a miser; *abhiyācate*—begs; *kṣīyate*—is lost; *tat*—his; *yaśaḥ*—

reputation; *sphītam*—widespread; *mānaḥ*—honor; *ca*—and; *avajñayā*—by neglectful behavior; *hataḥ*—destroyed.

TRANSLATION

One who rejects an offering that comes of its own accord but later begs a boon from a miser thus loses his widespread reputation, and his pride is humbled by the neglectful behavior of others.

PURPORT

The general procedure of Vedic marriage is that a father offers his daughter to a suitable boy. That is a very respectable marriage. A boy should not go to the girl's father and ask for the hand of his daughter in marriage. That is considered to be humbling one's respectable position. Svāyambhuva Manu wanted to convince Kardama Muni, since he knew that the sage wanted to marry a suitable girl: "I am offering just such a suitable wife. Do not reject the offer, or else, because you are in need of a wife, you will have to ask for such a wife from someone else, who may not behave with you so well. In that case your position will be humbled."

Another feature of this incident is that Svāyambhuva Manu was the emperor, but he went to offer his qualified daughter to a poor *brāhmaṇa*. Kardama Muni had no worldly possessions—he was a hermit living in the forest—but he was advanced in culture. Therefore, in offering one's daughter to a person, the culture and quality are counted as prominent, not wealth or any other material consideration.

TEXT 14

अहं त्वाश‍ृणवं विद्वन् विवाहार्थं समुद्यतम् ।
अतस्त्वमुपकुर्वाणः प्रत्तां प्रतिगृहाण मे ॥१४॥

ahaṁ tvāśṛṇavaṁ vidvan
vivāhārthaṁ samudyatam
atas tvam upakurvāṇaḥ
prattāṁ pratigṛhāṇa me

aham—I; *tvā*—you; *aśṛṇavam*—heard; *vidvan*—O wise man; *vivāha-artham*—for the sake of marriage; *samudyatam*—prepared; *ataḥ*—hence; *tvam*—you; *upakurvāṇaḥ*—not taken a vow of perpetual celibacy; *prattām*—offered; *pratigṛhāṇa*—please accept; *me*—of me.

TRANSLATION

Svāyambhuva Manu continued: O wise man, I heard that you were prepared to marry. Please accept her hand, which is being offered to you by me, since you have not taken a vow of perpetual celibacy.

PURPORT

The principle of *brahmacarya* is celibacy. There are two kinds of *brahmacārīs.* One is called *naiṣṭhika-brahmacārī,* which means one who takes a vow of celibacy for his whole life, whereas the other, the *upakurvāṇa-brahmacārī,* is a *brahmacārī* who takes the vow of celibacy up to a certain age. For example, he may take the vow to remain celibate up to twenty-five years of age; then, with the permission of his spiritual master, he enters married life. *Brahmacarya* is student life, the beginning of life in the spiritual orders, and the principle of *brahmacarya* is celibacy. Only a householder can indulge in sense gratification or sex life, not a *brahmacārī.* Svāyambhuva Manu requested Kardama Muni to accept his daughter, since Kardama had not taken the vow of *naiṣṭhika-brahmacarya.* He was willing to marry, and the suitable daughter of a high royal family was presented.

TEXT 15

ऋषिरुवाच
बाढमुद्वोढुकामोऽहमप्रत्ता च तवात्मजा ।
आवयोरनुरूपोऽसावाद्यो वैवाहिको विधिः ॥१५॥

ṛṣir uvāca
bāḍham udvoḍhu-kāmo 'ham
aprattā ca tavātmajā

āvayor anurūpo 'sāv
ādyo vaivāhiko vidhiḥ

ṛṣiḥ—the great sage Kardama; *uvāca*—said; *bāḍham*—very well; *ud-voḍhu-kāmaḥ*—desirous to marry; *aham*—I; *aprattā*—not promised to anyone else; *ca*—and; *tava*—your; *ātma-jā*—daughter; *āvayoḥ*—of us two; *anurūpaḥ*—proper; *asau*—this; *ādyaḥ*—first; *vaivāhikaḥ*—of marriage; *vidhiḥ*—ritualistic ceremony.

TRANSLATION

The great sage replied: Certainly I have a desire to marry, and your daughter has not yet married or given her word to anyone. Therefore our marriage according to the Vedic system can take place.

PURPORT

There were many considerations by Kardama Muni before accepting the daughter of Svāyambhuva Manu. Most important is that Devahūti had first of all fixed her mind on marrying him. She did not choose to have any other man as her husband. That is a great consideration because female psychology dictates that when a woman offers her heart to a man for the first time, it is very difficult for her to take it back. Also, she had not married before; she was a virgin girl. All these considerations convinced Kardama Muni to accept her. Therefore he said, "Yes, I shall accept your daughter under religious regulations of marriage." There are different kinds of marriages, of which the first-class marriage is held by inviting a suitable bridegroom for the daughter and giving her in charity, well dressed and well decorated with ornaments, along with a dowry according to the means of the father. There are other kinds of marriage, such as *gāndharva* marriage and marriage by love, which are also accepted as marriage. Even if one is forcibly kidnapped and later on accepted as a wife, that is also accepted. But Kardama Muni accepted the first-class way of marriage because the father was willing and the daughter was qualified. She had never offered her heart to anyone else. All these considerations made Kardama Muni agree to accept the daughter of Svāyambhuva Manu.

TEXT 16

कामः स भूयान्नरदेव तेऽस्याः
पुत्र्याः समाम्नायविधौ प्रतीतः ।
क एव ते तनयां नाद्रियेत
स्वयैव कान्त्या क्षिपतीमिव श्रियम् ॥१६॥

kāmaḥ sa bhūyān naradeva te 'syāḥ
putryāḥ samāmnāya-vidhau pratītaḥ
ka eva te tanayāṁ nādriyeta
svayaiva kāntyā kṣipatīm iva śriyam

kāmaḥ—desire; *saḥ*—that; *bhūyāt*—let it be fulfilled; *nara-deva*—O King; *te*—your; *asyāḥ*—this; *putryāḥ*—of the daughter; *samāmnāya-vidhau*—in the process of the Vedic scriptures; *pratītaḥ*—recognized; *kaḥ*—who; *eva*—in fact; *te*—your; *tanayām*—daughter; *na ādriyeta*—would not adore; *svayā*—by her own; *eva*—alone; *kāntyā*—bodily luster; *kṣipatīm*—excelling; *iva*—as if; *śriyam*—ornaments.

TRANSLATION

Let your daughter's desire for marriage, which is recognized in the Vedic scriptures, be fulfilled. Who would not accept her hand? She is so beautiful that by her bodily luster alone she excels the beauty of her ornaments.

PURPORT

Kardama Muni wanted to marry Devahūti in the recognized manner of marriage prescribed in the scriptures. As stated in the Vedic scriptures, the first-class process is to call the bridegroom to the home of the bride and hand her to him in charity with a dowry of necessary ornaments, gold, furniture and other household paraphernalia. This form of marriage is prevalent among higher-class Hindus even today and is declared in the *śāstras* to confer great religious merit on the bride's father. To give a daughter in charity to a suitable son-in-law is considered to be one of the pious activities of a householder. There are eight forms of marriage mentioned in the scripture *Manu-smṛti*, but only one process of marriage, *brāhma* or *rājasika* marriage, is now current. Other kinds of marriage—by love, by exchange of garlands or by kidnapping the bride—are now forbidden in this Kali age. Formerly, *kṣatriyas* would, at their pleasure, kidnap a princess from another royal house, and there would be a fight between the *kṣatriya* and the girl's family; then, if the kidnapper was the winner, the girl would be offered to him for marriage. Even Kṛṣṇa married Rukmiṇī by that process, and some of His sons and grandsons also married by kidnapping. Kṛṣṇa's grandsons kidnapped Duryodhana's daughter, which caused a fight between the Kuru and Yadu families. Afterward, an adjustment was made by the elderly members of the Kuru family. Such marriages were current in bygone ages, but at the present moment they are impossible because the strict principles of *kṣatriya* life have practically been abolished. Since India has become dependent on foreign countries, the particular influences of her social orders have been lost; now, according to the scriptures, everyone is a *śūdra.* The so-called *brāhmaṇas, kṣatriyas* and *vaiśyas* have forgotten their traditional activities, and in the absence of these activities they are called *śūdras.* It is said in the scriptures, *kalau śūdra-sambhavaḥ.* In the age of Kali everyone will be like *śūdras.* The traditional social customs are not followed in this age, although formerly they were followed strictly.

TEXT 17

यां हर्म्यपृष्ठे क्वणदङ्घ्रिशोभां
विक्रीडतीं कन्दुकविह्वलाक्षीम् ।
विश्वावसुर्न्यपतत्स्वाद्विमाना-
द्विलोक्य सम्मोहविमूढचेताः ॥१७॥

yāṁ harmya-pṛṣṭhe kvaṇad-aṅghri-śobhāṁ
vikrīḍatīṁ kanduka-vihvalākṣīm
viśvāvasur nyapatat svād vimānād
vilokya sammoha-vimūḍha-cetāḥ

yām—whom; *harmya-pṛṣṭhe*—on the roof of the palace; *kvaṇat-aṅghri-śobhām*—whose beauty was heightened by the tinkling ornaments on her feet; *vikrīḍatīm*—playing; *kanduka-vihvala-akṣīm*—with eyes bewildered, following her ball; *viśvāvasuḥ*—Viśvāvasu; *nyapatat*—fell down; *svāt*—from his own; *vimānāt*—from the airplane; *vilokya*—seeing; *sammoha-vimūḍha-cetāḥ*—whose mind was stupefied.

TRANSLATION

I have heard that Viśvāvasu, the great Gandharva, his mind stupefied with infatuation, fell from his airplane after seeing your daughter playing with a ball on the roof of the palace, for she was indeed beautiful with her tinkling ankle bells and her eyes moving to and fro.

PURPORT

It is understood that not only at the present moment but in those days also there were skyscrapers. Herein we find the word *harmya-pṛṣṭhe*. *Harmya* means "a very big palatial building." *Svād vimānāt* means "from his own airplane." It is suggested that private airplanes or helicopters were also current in those days. The Gandharva Viśvāvasu, while flying in the sky, could see Devahūti playing ball on the roof of the palace. Ball playing was also current, but aristocratic girls would not play in a public place. Ball playing and other such pleasures were not meant for ordinary women and girls; only princesses like Devahūti could indulge in such sports. It is described here that she was seen from the flying airplane. This indicates that the palace was very high, otherwise how could one see her from an airplane? The vision was so distinct that the Gandharva Viśvāvasu was bewildered by her beauty and by hearing the sound of her ankle bangles, and being captivated by the sound and beauty, he fell down. Kardama Muni mentioned the incident as he had heard it.

TEXT 18

तां प्रार्थयन्तीं ललनाललाम-

मसेवितश्रीचरणैरदृष्टाम् ।

वत्सां मनोरुच्चपदः स्वसारं
को नानुमन्येत बुधोऽभियाताम् ॥१८॥

tāṁ prārthayantīṁ lalanā-lalāmam
asevita-śrī-caraṇair adṛṣṭām
vatsāṁ manor uccapadaḥ svasāraṁ
ko nānumanyeta budho 'bhiyātām

tām—her; *prārthayantīm*—seeking; *lalanā-lalāmam*—the ornament of women; *asevita-śrī-caraṇaiḥ*—by those who have not worshiped the feet of Lakṣmī; *adṛṣṭām*—not seen; *vatsām*—beloved daughter; *manoḥ*—of Svāyambhuva Manu; *uccapadaḥ*—of Uttānapāda; *svasāram*—sister; *kaḥ*—what; *na anumanyeta*—would not welcome; *budhaḥ*—wise man; *abhiyātām*—who has come of her own accord.

TRANSLATION

What wise man would not welcome her, the very ornament of womanhood, the beloved daughter of Svāyambhuva Manu and sister of Uttānapāda? Those who have not worshiped the gracious feet of the goddess of fortune cannot even perceive her, yet she has come of her own accord to seek my hand.

PURPORT

Kardama Muni praised the beauty and qualification of Devahūti in different ways. Devahūti was actually the ornament of all ornamented beautiful girls. A girl becomes beautiful by putting ornaments on her body, but Devahūti was more beautiful than the ornaments; she was considered the ornament of the ornamented beautiful girls. Demigods and Gandharvas were attracted by her beauty. Kardama Muni, although a great sage, was not a denizen of the heavenly planets, but it is mentioned in the previous verse that Viśvāvasu, who came from heaven, was also attracted by the beauty of Devahūti. Besides her personal beauty, she was the daughter of Emperor Svāyambhuva and sister of King Uttānapāda. Who could refuse the hand of such a girl?

TEXT 19

अतो भजिष्ये समयेन साध्वीं
यावत्तेजो बिभृयादात्मनो मे ।
अतो धर्मान् पारमहंस्यमुख्यान्
शुक्लप्रोक्तान् बहु मन्येऽविहिंस्रान् ॥१९॥

ato bhajiṣye samayena sādhvīṁ
yāvat tejo bibhṛyād ātmano me
ato dharmān pāramahaṁsya-mukhyān
śukla-proktān bahu manye 'vihiṁsrān

ataḥ—therefore; *bhajiṣye*—I shall accept; *samayena*—on the conditions; *sādhvīm*—the chaste girl; *yāvat*—until; *tejaḥ*—semen; *bibhṛyāt*—may bear; *ātmanaḥ*—from my body; *me*—my; *ataḥ*—thereafter; *dharmān*—the duties; *pāramahaṁsya-mukhyān*—of the best of the *paramahaṁsas; śukla-proktān*—spoken by Lord Viṣṇu; *bahu*—much; *manye*—I shall consider; *avihiṁsrān*—free from envy.

TRANSLATION

Therefore I shall accept this chaste girl as my wife, on the condition that after she bears semen from my body, I shall accept the life of devotional service accepted by the most perfect human beings. That process was described by Lord Viṣṇu. It is free from envy.

PURPORT

Kardama Muni expressed his desire for a very beautiful wife to Emperor Svāyambhuva and accepted the Emperor's daughter for marriage. Kardama Muni was in the hermitage practicing complete celibacy as a *brahmacārī*, and although he had the desire to marry, he did not want to be a householder for the whole span of his life because he was conversant with the Vedic principles of human life. According to Vedic principles, the first part of life should be utilized in *brahmacarya* for the development of character and spiritual qualities. In the next part of life, one may accept a wife and beget children, but one should not beget children like cats and dogs.

Kardama Muni desired to beget a child who would be a ray of the Supreme Personality of Godhead. One should beget a child who can perform the duties of Viṣṇu, otherwise there is no need to produce children. There are two kinds of children born of good fathers: one is educated in Kṛṣṇa consciousness so that he can be delivered from the clutches of *māyā* in that very life, and the other is a ray of the Supreme Personality of Godhead and teaches the world the ultimate goal of life. As will be described in later chapters, Kardama Muni begot such a child—Kapila, the incarnation of the Personality of Godhead who enunciated the philosophy of Sāṅkhya. Great householders pray to God to send His representative so that there may be an auspicious movement in human society. This is one reason to beget a child. Another reason is that a highly enlightened parent can train a child in Kṛṣṇa consciousness so that the child will not have to come back again to this miserable world. Parents should see to it that the child born of them does not enter the womb of a mother again. Unless one can train a child for liberation in that life, there is no need to marry or produce children. If human society produces children like cats and dogs for the disturbance of social order, then the world becomes hellish, as it has in this age of Kali. In this age, neither parents nor their children are trained; both are animalistic and simply eat, sleep, mate, defend, and gratify their senses. This disorder in social life cannot bring peace to human society. Kardama Muni explains beforehand that he would not associate with the girl Devahūti for the whole duration of his life. He would simply associate with her until she had a child. In other words, sex life should be utilized only to produce a nice child, not for any other purpose. Human life is especially meant for complete devotion to the service of the Lord. That is the philosophy of Lord Caitanya.

After fulfilling his responsibility to produce a nice child, one should take *sannyāsa* and engage in the perfectional *paramahaṁsa* stage. *Paramahaṁsa* refers to the most highly elevated perfectional stage of life. There are four stages within *sannyāsa* life, and *paramahaṁsa* is the highest order. The *Śrīmad-Bhāgavatam* is called the *paramahaṁsa-saṁhitā*, the treatise for the highest class of human beings. The *paramahaṁsa* is free from envy. In other stages, even in the householder stage of life, there is competition and envy, but since the activities of the human being in the *paramahaṁsa* stage are completely engaged in Kṛṣṇa consciousness, or devotional service, there is no scope for envy. In the same order as Kardama Muni, about one hundred years ago, Ṭhākura Bhaktivinoda also wanted to beget a child who could preach the philosophy and teachings of Lord Caitanya to the fullest extent. By his prayers to the Lord he had as his child Bhaktisiddhānta Sarasvatī Gosvāmī Mahārāja, who at the present moment is preaching the philosophy of Lord Caitanya throughout the entire world through his bona fide disciples.

TEXT 20

यतोऽभवद्विश्वमिदं विचित्रं
संस्थास्यते यत्र च वावतिष्ठते ।
प्रजापतीनां पतिरेष मह्यं
परं प्रमाणं भगवाननन्तः ॥२०॥

yato 'bhavad viśvam idaṁ vicitraṁ
saṁsthāsyate yatra ca vāvatiṣṭhate
prajāpatīnāṁ patir eṣa mahyaṁ
paraṁ pramāṇaṁ bhagavān anantaḥ

yataḥ—from whom; *abhavat*—emanated; *viśvam*—creation; *idam*—this; *vicitram*—wonderful; *saṁsthāsyate*—will dissolve; *yatra*—in whom; *ca*—and; *vā*—or; *avatiṣṭhate*—presently exists; *prajā-patīnām*—of the Prajāpatis; *patiḥ*—the Lord; *eṣaḥ*—this; *mahyam*—to me; *param*—highest; *pramāṇam*—authority; *bhagavān*—Supreme Lord; *anantaḥ*—unlimited.

TRANSLATION

The highest authority for me is the unlimited Supreme Personality of Godhead, from whom this wonderful creation emanates and in whom its sustenance and dissolution rest. He is the origin of all Prajāpatis, the personalities meant to produce living entities in this world.

PURPORT

Kardama Muni was ordered by his father, Prajāpati, to produce children. In the beginning of creation the Prajāpatis were meant to produce the large population which was to reside in the planets of the gigantic universe. But Kardama Muni said that although his father was Prajāpati, who desired him to produce children, actually his origin was the Supreme Personality of Godhead, Viṣṇu, because Viṣṇu is the origin of everything; He is the actual creator of this universe, He is the actual maintainer, and when everything is annihilated, it rests in Him only. That is the conclusion of *Śrīmad-Bhāgavatam.* For creation, maintenance and annihilation there are the three deities Brahmā, Viṣṇu and Maheśvara (Śiva), but Brahmā and Maheśvara are qualitative expansions of Viṣṇu. Viṣṇu is the central figure. Viṣṇu, therefore, takes charge of maintenance. No one can maintain the whole creation but He. There are innumerable entities, and they have innumerable demands; no one but Viṣṇu can fulfill the unnumerable demands of all the innumerable living entities. Brahmā is ordered to create, and Śiva is ordered to annihilate. The middle function, maintenance, is taken charge of by Viṣṇu. Kardama Muni knew very well, by his power in progressive spiritual life, that Viṣṇu, the Personality of Godhead, was his worshipable Deity. Whatever Viṣṇu desired was his duty, and nothing else. He was not prepared to beget a number of children. He would beget only one child, who would help the mission of Viṣṇu. As stated in *Bhagavad-gītā,* whenever there is a discrepancy in the discharge of religious principles, the Lord descends on the surface of the earth to protect religious principles and to annihilate the miscreants.

Marrying and begetting a child is considered to liquidate one's debts to the family in which one is born. There are many debts which are imposed upon a child just after his birth. There are debts to the family in which one is born, debts to the demigods, debts to the Pitās, debts to the *ṛṣis,* etc. But if someone engages only in the service of the Supreme Lord, the Personality of Godhead, who is actually worshipable, then even without trying to liquidate other debts, one becomes free from all obligations. Kardama Muni preferred to devote his life as a servant of the Lord in *paramahaṁsa* knowledge and to beget a child only for that purpose, not to beget numberless children to fill up the vacancies in the universe.

TEXT 21

मैत्रेय उवाच
स उग्रधन्वन्नियदेवाबभाषे
आसीच्च तूष्णीमरविन्दनाभम् ।
धियोपगृह्णन् स्मितशोभितेन
मुखेन चेतो लुलुभे देवहूत्याः ॥२१॥

maitreya uvāca
sa ugra-dhanvann iyad evābabhāṣe
āsīc ca tūṣṇīm aravinda-nābham
dhiyopagṛhṇan smita-śobhitena
mukhena ceto lulubhe devahūtyāḥ

maitreyaḥ—the great sage Maitreya; *uvāca*—said; *saḥ*—he (Kardama); *ugra-dhanvan*—O great warrior Vidura; *iyat*—this much; *eva*—only; *ābabhāṣe*—spoke; *āsīt*—became; *ca*—and; *tūṣṇīm*—silent; *aravinda-nābham*—Lord Viṣṇu (whose navel is adorned by a lotus); *dhiyā*—by thought; *upagṛhṇan*—seizing; *smita-śobhitena*—beautified by his smile; *mukhena*—by his face; *cetaḥ*—the mind; *lulubhe*—was captivated; *devahūtyāḥ*—of Devahūti.

TRANSLATION

Śrī Maitreya said: O great warrior Vidura, the sage Kardama said this much only and then became silent, thinking of his worshipable Lord Viṣṇu, who has a lotus on His navel. As he silently smiled, his face captured the mind of Devahūti, who began to meditate upon the great sage.

PURPORT

It appears that Kardama Muni was fully absorbed in Kṛṣṇa consciousness because as soon as he became silent, he at once began to think of Lord Viṣṇu. That is the way of Kṛṣṇa consciousness. Pure devotees are so absorbed in thought of Kṛṣṇa that they have no other engagement; although they may seem to think or act otherwise, they are always thinking of Kṛṣṇa. The smile of such a Kṛṣṇa conscious person is so attractive that simply by smiling he wins so many admirers, disciples and followers.

TEXT 22

सोऽनु ज्ञात्वा व्यवसितं महिष्या दुहितुः स्फुटम् ।
तस्मै गुणगणाढ्याय ददौ तुल्यां प्रहर्षितः ॥२२॥

so 'nu jñātvā vyavasitaṁ
mahiṣyā duhituḥ sphuṭam
tasmai guṇa-gaṇāḍhyāya
dadau tulyāṁ praharṣitaḥ

saḥ—he (Emperor Manu); *anu*—afterward; *jñātvā*—having known; *vyavasitam*—the fixed decision; *mahiṣyāḥ*—of the Queen; *duhituḥ*—of his daughter; *sphuṭam*—clearly; *tasmai*—to him; *guṇa-gaṇa-āḍhyāya*—who was endowed with a host of virtues; *dadau*—gave away; *tulyām*—who was equal (in good qualities); *praharṣitaḥ*—extremely pleased.

TRANSLATION

After having unmistakably known the decision of the Queen, as well as that of Devahūti, the Emperor most gladly gave his daughter to the sage, whose host of virtues was equaled by hers.

TEXT 23

शतरूपा महाराज्ञी पारिबर्हान्महाधनान् ।
दम्पत्योः पर्यदात्प्रीत्या भूषावासः परिच्छदान् ॥२३॥

śatarūpā mahā-rājñī
pāribarhān mahā-dhanān
dampatyoḥ paryadāt prītyā
bhūṣā-vāsaḥ paricchadān

śatarūpā—Empress Śatarūpā; *mahā-rājñī*—the Empress; *pāribar-hān*—dowry; *mahā-dhanān*—valuable presents; *dam-patyoḥ*—to the bride and bridegroom; *paryadāt*—gave; *prītyā*—out of affection;

bhūṣā—ornaments; *vāsaḥ*—clothes; *paricchadān*—articles for household use.

TRANSLATION

Empress Śatarūpā lovingly gave most valuable presents, suitable for the occasion, such as jewelry, clothes and household articles, in dowry to the bride and bridegroom.

PURPORT

The custom of giving one's daughter in charity with a dowry is still current in India. The gifts are given according to the position of the father of the bride. *Pāribarhān mahā-dhanān* means the dowry which must be awarded to the bridegroom at the time of marriage. Here *mahā-dhanān* means greatly valuable gifts befitting the dowry of an empress. The words *bhūṣā-vāsaḥ paricchadān* also appear here. *Bhūṣā* means "ornaments," *vāsaḥ* means "clothing," and *paricchadān* means "various household articles." All things befitting the marriage ceremony of an emperor's daughter were awarded to Kardama Muni, who was until now observing celibacy as a *brahmacārī*. The bride, Devahūti, was very richly dressed with ornaments and clothing.

In this way Kardama Muni was married with full opulence to a qualified wife and was endowed with the necessary paraphernalia for household life. In the Vedic way of marriage such a dowry is still given to the bridegroom by the father of the bride; even in poverty-stricken India there are marriages where hundreds and thousands of rupees are spent for a dowry. The dowry system is not illegal, as some have tried to prove. The dowry is a gift given to the daughter by the father to show good will, and it is compulsory. In rare cases where the father is completely unable to give a dowry, it is enjoined that he must at least give a fruit and a flower. As stated in *Bhagavad-gītā*, God can also be pleased even by a fruit and a flower. When there is financial inability and no question of accumulating a dowry by another means, one can give a fruit and flower for the satisfaction of the bridegroom.

TEXT 24

प्रत्तां दुहितरं सम्राट् सदृक्षाय गतव्यथः ।
उपगुह्य च बाहुभ्यामौत्कण्ठ्योन्मथिताशयः ॥२४॥

prattāṁ duhitaraṁ samrāṭ
sadṛkṣāya gata-vyathaḥ
upaguhya ca bāhubhyām
autkaṇṭhyonmathitāśayaḥ

prattām—who was given; *duhitaram*—daughter; *samrāṭ*—the Emperor (Manu); *sadṛkṣāya*—unto a suitable person; *gata-vyathaḥ*—relieved of his responsibility; *upaguhya*—embracing; *ca*—and; *bāhubhyām*—with his two arms; *autkaṇṭhya-unmathita-āśayaḥ*—having an anxious and agitated mind.

TRANSLATION

Thus relieved of his responsibility by handing over his daughter to a suitable man, Svāyambhuva Manu, his mind agitated by feelings of separation, embraced his affectionate daughter with both his arms.

PURPORT

A father always remains in anxiety until he can hand over his grown-up daughter to a suitable boy. A father and mother's responsibility for children continues until they marry them to suitable spouses; when the father is able to perform that duty, he is relieved of his responsibility.

TEXT 25

अशक्नुवंस्तद्विरहं मुञ्चन् बाष्पकलां मुहुः ।
आसिञ्चदम्ब वत्सेति नेत्रोदैर्दुहितुः शिखाः ॥२५॥

aśaknuvaṁs tad-virahaṁ
muñcan bāṣpa-kalāṁ muhuḥ
āsiñcad amba vatseti
netrodair duhituḥ śikhāḥ

aśaknuvan—being unable to bear; *tat-viraham*—separation from her; *muñcan*—shedding; *bāṣpa-kalām*—tears; *muhuḥ*—again and again; *āsiñcat*—he drenched; *amba*—my dear mother; *vatsa*—my dear daughter; *iti*—thus; *netra-udaiḥ*—by the water from his eyes; *duhituḥ*—of his daughter; *śikhāḥ*—the locks of hair.

TRANSLATION

The Emperor was unable to bear the separation of his daughter. Therefore tears poured from his eyes again and again, drenching his daughter's head as he cried, "My dear mother! My dear daughter!"

PURPORT

The word *amba* is significant. A father sometimes addresses his daughter in affection as "mother" and sometimes as "my darling." The feeling of separation occurs because until the daughter is married she remains the daughter of the father, but after her marriage she is no longer claimed as a daughter in the family; she must go to the husband's house, for after marriage she becomes the property of the husband. According to *Manu-saṁhitā*, a woman is never independent. She must remain the property of the father while she is not married, and she must remain the property of the husband until she is elderly and has grown-up children of her own. In old age, when the husband has taken *sannyāsa* and left home, she remains the property of the sons. A woman is always dependent, either upon the father, husband or elderly sons. That will be exhibited in the life of Devahūti. Devahūti's father handed over responsibility for her to the husband, Kardama Muni, and in the same way, Kardama Muni also left home, giving the responsibility to his son, Kapiladeva. This narration will describe these events one after another.

TEXTS 26–27

आमन्त्र्य तं मुनिवरमनुज्ञातः सहानुगः ।
प्रतस्थे रथमारुह्य सभार्यः स्वपुरं नृपः ॥२६॥
उभयोर्ऋषिकुल्यायाः सरस्वत्याः सुरोधसोः ।
ऋषीणामुपशान्तानां पश्यन्नाश्रमसम्पदः ॥२७॥

āmantrya taṁ muni-varam
anujñātaḥ sahānugaḥ

pratasthe ratham āruhya
sabhāryaḥ sva-puraṁ nṛpaḥ

ubhayor ṛṣi-kulyāyāḥ
sarasvatyāḥ surodhasoḥ
ṛṣīṇām upaśāntānāṁ
paśyann āśrama-sampadaḥ

āmantrya—taking permission to go; *tam*—from him (Kardama); *muni-varam*—from the best of sages; *anujñātaḥ*—being permitted to leave; *saha-anugaḥ*—along with his retinue; *pratasthe*—started for; *ratham āruhya*—mounting his chariot; *sa-bhāryaḥ*—along with his wife; *sva-puram*—his own capital; *nṛpaḥ*—the Emperor; *ubhayoḥ*—on both; *ṛṣi-kulyāyāḥ*—agreeable to the sages; *sarasvatyāḥ*—of the River Sarasvatī; *su-rodhasoḥ*—the charming banks; *ṛṣīṇām*—of the great sages; *upaśāntānām*—tranquil; *paśyan*—seeing; *āśrama-sampadaḥ*—the prosperity of the beautiful hermitages.

TRANSLATION

After asking and obtaining the great sage's permission to leave, the monarch mounted his chariot with his wife and started for his capital, followed by his retinue. Along the way he saw the prosperity of the tranquil seers' beautiful hermitages on both the charming banks of the Sarasvatī, the river so agreeable to saintly persons.

PURPORT

As cities are constructed in the modern age with great engineering and architectural craftsmanship, so in days gone by there were neighborhoods called *ṛṣi-kulas*, where great saintly persons resided. In India there are still many magnificent places for spiritual understanding; there are many *ṛṣis* and saintly persons living in nice cottages on the banks of the Ganges and Yamunā for purposes of spiritual cultivation. While passing through the *ṛṣi-kulas* the King and his party were very much satisfied with the beauty of thc cottages and hermitages. It is stated here, *paśyann āśrama-sampadaḥ.* The great sages had no skyscrapers, but the hermitages were so beautiful that the King was very much pleased at the sight.

TEXT 28

तमायान्तमभिप्रेत्य ब्रह्मावर्तात्प्रजाः पतिम् ।
गीतसंस्तुतिवादित्रैः प्रत्युदीयुः प्रहर्षिताः ॥२८॥

tam āyāntam abhipretya
brahmāvartāt prajāḥ patim
gīta-saṁstuti-vāditraiḥ
pratyudīyuḥ praharṣitāḥ

tam—him; *āyāntam*—who was arriving; *abhipretya*—knowing of; *brahmāvartāt*—from Brahmāvarta; *prajāḥ*—his subjects; *patim*—their lord; *gīta-saṁstuti-vāditraiḥ*—with songs, praise and instrumental music; *pratyudīyuḥ*—came forward to greet; *praharṣitāḥ*—overjoyed.

TRANSLATION

Overjoyed to know of his arrival, his subjects came forth from Brahmāvarta to greet their returning lord with songs, prayers and musical instruments.

PURPORT

It is the custom of the citizens of a kingdom's capital to receive the king when he returns from a tour. There is a similar description when Kṛṣṇa returned to Dvārakā after the Battle of Kurukṣetra. At that time He was received by all classes of citizens at the gate of the city. Formerly, capital cities were surrounded by walls, and there were different gates for regular entrance. Even in Delhi today there are old gates, and some other old cities have such gates where citizens would gather to receive the king. Here also the citizens of Barhiṣmatī, the capital of Brahmāvarta, the kingdom of Svāyambhuva, came nicely dressed to receive the Emperor with decorations and musical instruments.

TEXTS 29–30

बर्हिष्मती नाम पुरी सर्वसम्पत्समन्विता ।
न्यपतन् यत्र रोमाणि यज्ञस्याङ्गं विधुन्वतः ॥२९॥
कुशाः काशास्त एवासन् शश्वद्धरितवर्चसः ।
ऋषयो यैः पराभाव्य यज्ञघ्नान् यज्ञमीजिरे ॥३०॥

barhiṣmatī nāma purī
sarva-sampat-samanvitā
nyapatan yatra romāṇi
yajñasyāṅgaṁ vidhunvataḥ

kuśāḥ kāśās ta evāsan
śaśvad-dharita-varcasaḥ
ṛṣayo yaiḥ parābhāvya
yajña-ghnān yajñam ījire

barhiṣmatī—Barhiṣmatī; *nāma*—named; *purī*—city; *sarva-sampat*—all kinds of wealth; *samanvitā*—full of; *nyapatan*—fell down; *yatra*—where; *romāṇi*—the hairs; *yajñasya*—of Lord Boar; *aṅgam*—His body; *vidhunvataḥ*—shaking; *kuśāḥ*—*kuśa* grass; *kāśāḥ*—*kāśa* grass; *te*—they; *eva*—certainly; *āsan*—became; *śaśvat-harita*—of evergreen; *varcasaḥ*—having the color; *ṛṣayaḥ*—the sages; *yaiḥ*—by which; *parābhāvya*—defeating; *yajña-ghnān*—the disturbers of the sacrificial performances; *yajñam*—Lord Viṣṇu; *ījire*—they worshiped.

TRANSLATION

The city of Barhiṣmatī, rich in all kinds of wealth, was so called because Lord Viṣṇu's hair dropped there from His body when He manifested Himself as Lord Boar. As He shook His body, this very hair fell and turned into blades of evergreen kuśa grass and kāśa [another kind of grass used for mats], by means of which the sages worshiped Lord Viṣṇu after defeating the demons who had interfered with the performance of their sacrifices.

PURPORT

Any place directly connected with the Supreme Lord is called *pīṭha-sthāna.* Barhiṣmatī, the capital of Svāyambhuva Manu, was exalted not because the city was very rich in wealth and opulence, but because the hairs of Lord Varāha fell at this very spot. These hairs of the Lord later grew as green grass, and the sages used to worship the Lord with that grass after the time when the Lord killed the demon Hiraṇyākṣa. *Yajña* means Viṣṇu, the Supreme Personality of Godhead. In *Bhagavad-gītā, karma* is described as *yajñārtha. Yajñārtha-karma* means "work done only for the satisfaction of Viṣṇu." If something is done for sense gratification or any other purpose, it will be binding upon the worker. If one wants to be freed from the reaction of his work, he must perform everything for the satisfaction of Viṣṇu, or Yajña. In the capital of Svāyambhuva Manu, Barhiṣmatī, these particular functions were being performed by the great sages and saintly persons.

TEXT 31

कुशकाशमयं बर्हिरास्तीर्य भगवान्मनुः ।
अयजद्यज्ञपुरुषं लब्धा स्थानं यतो भुवम् ॥३१॥

kuśa-kāśamayaṁ barhir
āstīrya bhagavān manuḥ
ayajad yajña-puruṣaṁ
labdhā sthānaṁ yato bhuvam

kuśa—of *kuśa* grass; *kāśa*—and of *kāśa* grass; *mayam*—made; *barhiḥ*—a seat; *āstīrya*—having spread; *bhagavān*—the greatly fortunate; *manuḥ*—Svāyambhuva Manu; *ayajat*—worshiped; *yajña-puruṣam*—Lord Viṣṇu; *labdhā*—had achieved; *sthānam*—the abode; *yataḥ*—from whom; *bhuvam*—the earth.

TRANSLATION

Manu spread a seat of kuśas and kāśas and worshiped the Lord, the Personality of Godhead, by whose grace he had obtained the rule of the terrestrial globe.

PURPORT

Manu is the father of mankind, and therefore from *Manu* comes the word *man*, or, in Sanskrit, *manuṣya*. Those who are in a better position in the world, having sufficient wealth, should especially take lessons from Manu, who acknowledged his kingdom and opulence to be gifts from the Supreme Personality of Godhead and thus always engaged in devotional service. Similarly, the descendants of Manu, or human beings, especially those who are situated in a well-to-do condition, must consider that whatever riches they have are gifts from the Supreme Personality of Godhead. Those riches should be utilized for the service of the Lord in sacrifices performed to please Him. That is the way of utilizing wealth and opulence. No one can achieve wealth, opulence, good birth, a beautiful body or nice education without the mercy of the Supreme Lord. Therefore, those who are in possession of such valuable facilities must acknowledge their gratefulness to the Lord by worshiping Him and offering what they have received from Him. When such acknowledgment is given, either by a family, nation or society, their abode becomes almost like Vaikuṇṭha, and it becomes free from the operation of the threefold miseries of this material world. In the modern age the mission of Kṛṣṇa consciousness is for everyone to acknowledge the supremacy of Lord Kṛṣṇa; whatever one has in his possession must be considered a gift by the grace of the Lord. Everyone, therefore, should engage in devotional service through Kṛṣṇa consciousness. If one wants to be happy and peaceful in his position, either as a householder or citizen or member of human society, one must promote devotional service for the pleasure of the Lord.

TEXT 32

बर्हिष्मतीं नाम विभुर्यां निर्विश्य समावसत् ।
तस्यां प्रविष्टो भवनं तापत्रयविनाशनम् ॥३२॥

barhiṣmatīṁ nāma vibhur
yāṁ nirviśya samāvasat
tasyāṁ praviṣṭo bhavanaṁ
tāpa-traya-vināśanam

barhiṣmatīm—the city Barhiṣmatī; *nāma*—named; *vibhuḥ*—the very powerful Svāyambhuva Manu; *yām*—which; *nirviśya*—having entered; *samāvasat*—he lived in previously; *tasyām*—in that city; *praviṣṭaḥ*—entered; *bhavanam*—the palace; *tāpa-traya*—the threefold miseries; *vināśanam*—destroying.

TRANSLATION

Having entered the city of Barhiṣmatī, in which he had previously lived, Manu entered his palace, which was filled with an atmosphere that eradicated the three miseries of material existence.

PURPORT

The material world, or material existential life, is filled with threefold miseries: miseries pertaining to the body and mind, miseries pertaining to natural disturbances and miseries inflicted by other living entities. Human society is meant to create a spiritual atmosphere by spreading the spirit of Kṛṣṇa consciousness. The miseries of material existence cannot affect the status of Kṛṣṇa consciousness. It is not that the miseries of the material world completely vanish when one takes to Kṛṣṇa consciousness, but for one who is Kṛṣṇa conscious the miseries of material existence have no effect. We cannot stop the miseries of the material atmosphere, but Kṛṣṇa consciousness is the antiseptic method to protect us from being affected by the miseries of material existence. For a Kṛṣṇa conscious person, both living in heaven and living in hell are equal. How Svāyambhuva Manu created an atmosphere wherein he was not affected by material miseries is explained in the following verses.

TEXT 33

सभार्यः सप्रजः कामान् बुभुजेऽन्याविरोधतः ।
सङ्गीयमानसत्कीर्तिः सस्त्रीभिः सुरगायकैः ।
प्रत्यूषेष्वनुबद्धेन हृदा शृण्वन् हरेः कथाः ॥३३॥

sabhāryaḥ saprajaḥ kāmān
bubhuje 'nyāvirodhataḥ

saṅgīyamāna-sat-kīrtiḥ
sastrībhiḥ sura-gāyakaiḥ
praty-ūṣeṣv anubaddhena
hṛdā śṛṇvan hareḥ kathāḥ

sa-bhāryaḥ—along with his wife; *sa-prajaḥ*—along with his subjects; *kāmān*—the necessities of life; *bubhuje*—he enjoyed; *anya*—from others; *avirodhataḥ*—without disturbance; *saṅgīyamāna*—being praised; *sat-kīrtiḥ*—reputation for pious activities; *sa-strībhiḥ*—along with their wives; *sura-gāyakaiḥ*—by celestial musicians; *prati-ūṣeṣu*—at every dawn; *anubaddhena*—being attached; *hṛdā*—with the heart; *śṛṇvan*—listening to; *hareḥ*—of Lord Hari; *kathāḥ*—the topics.

TRANSLATION

Emperor Svāyambhuva Manu enjoyed life with his wife and subjects and fulfilled his desires without being disturbed by unwanted principles contrary to the process of religion. Celestial musicians and their wives sang in chorus about the pure reputation of the Emperor, and early in the morning, every day, he used to listen to the pastimes of the Supreme Personality of Godhead with a loving heart.

PURPORT

Human society is actually meant for realization of perfection in Kṛṣṇa consciousness. There is no restriction against living with a wife and children, but life should be so conducted that one may not go against the principles of religion, economic development, regulated sense enjoyment and, ultimately, liberation from material existence. The Vedic principles are designed in such a way that the conditioned souls who have come to this material existence may be guided in fulfilling their material desires and at the same time be liberated and go back to Godhead, back home.

It is understood that Emperor Svāyambhuva Manu enjoyed his household life by following these principles. It is stated here that early in the morning there were musicians who used to sing with musical instruments about the glories of the Lord, and the Emperor, with his family, personally used to hear about the pastimes of the Supreme Person. This custom is still prevalent in India in some of the royal families and temples. Professional musicians sing with *śahnāīs*, and the sleeping members of the house gradually get up from their beds in a pleasing atmosphere. During bedtime also the singers sing songs in relationship with the pastimes of the Lord, with *śahnāī* accompaniment, and the householders gradually fall asleep remembering the glories of the Lord. In every house, in addition to the singing program, there is an arrangement for *Bhāgavatam* lectures in the evening; family members sit down, hold Hare Kṛṣṇa *kīrtana*, hear narrations from *Śrīmad-Bhāgavatam* and *Bhagavad-gītā* and enjoy music before going to bed. The atmosphere created by this *saṅkīrtana* movement lives in their hearts, and while sleeping they also dream of the singing and glorification of the Lord. In such a way, perfection of Kṛṣṇa consciousness can be attained. This practice is very old, as learned from this verse of *Śrīmad-Bhāgavatam;* millions of years ago, Svāyambhuva Manu used to avail himself of this opportunity to live householder life in the peace and prosperity of a Kṛṣṇa consciousness atmosphere.

As far as temples are concerned, in each and every royal palace or rich man's house, inevitably there is a nice temple, and the members of the household rise early in the morning and go to the temple to see the *maṅgalārātrika* ceremony. The *maṅgalārātrika* ceremony is the first worship of the morning. In the *ārātrika* ceremony a light is offered in circles before the Deities, as are a conchshell and flowers and a fan. The Lord is supposed to rise early in the morning and take some light refreshment and give audience to the devotees. The devotees then go back to the house or sing the glories of the Lord in the temple. The early morning ceremony still takes place in Indian temples and palaces. Temples are meant for the assembly of the general public. Temples within palaces are especially for the royal families, but in many of these palace temples the public is also allowed to visit. The temple of the King of Jaipur is situated within the palace, but the public is allowed to assemble; if one goes there, he will see that the temple is always crowded with at least five hundred devotees. After the *maṅgalārātrika* ceremony they sit down together and sing the glories of the Lord with musical instruments and thus enjoy life. Temple worship by the royal family is also mentioned in *Bhagavad-gītā*, where it is stated that those who fail to achieve success in the *bhakti-yoga* principles within one life are given a chance to take birth in the next life in a family of rich men or in a royal family or family of learned *brāhmaṇas* or devotees. If one gets the opportunity to take birth in these families, he can achieve the facilities of a Kṛṣṇa conscious atmosphere without difficulty. A child born in that Kṛṣṇa atmosphere is sure to develop Kṛṣṇa consciousness. The perfection which he failed to attain in his last life is again offered in this life, and he can make himself perfect without fail.

TEXT 34

निष्णातं योगमायासु मुनिं स्वायम्भुवं मनुम् ।
यदाभ्रंशयितुं भोगा न शेकुर्भगवत्परम् ॥३४॥

niṣṇātaṁ yogamāyāsu
muniṁ svāyambhuvaṁ manum
yad ābhraṁśayituṁ bhogā
na śekur bhagavat-param

niṣṇātam—absorbed; *yoga-māyāsu*—in temporary enjoyment; *munim*—who was equal to a saint; *svāyambhuvam*—Svāyambhuva; *manum*—Manu; *yat*—from which; *ābhraṁśayitum*—to cause to deviate; *bhogāḥ*—material enjoyments; *na*—not; *śekuḥ*—were able; *bhagavat-param*—who was a great devotee of the Supreme Personality of Godhead.

TRANSLATION

Thus Svāyambhuva Manu was a saintly king. Although absorbed in material happiness, he was not dragged to the lowest grade of life, for he always enjoyed his material happiness in a Kṛṣṇa conscious atmosphere.

PURPORT

The kingly happiness of material enjoyment generally drags one to the lowest grade of life, namely degradation to animal life, because of unrestricted sense enjoyment. But Svāyambhuva Manu was considered as good as a saintly sage because the atmosphere created in his kingdom and home was completely Kṛṣṇa conscious. The case is similar with the conditioned souls in general; they have come into this material life for sense gratification, but if they are able to create a Kṛṣṇa conscious atmosphere, as depicted here or as prescribed in revealed scriptures, by temple worship and household Deity worship, then in spite of their material enjoyment they can make advancement in pure Kṛṣṇa consciousness without a doubt. At the present moment, modern civilization is too much attached to the material way of life, or sense gratification. Therefore, the Kṛṣṇa consciousness movement can give the people in general the best opportunity to utilize their human life in the midst of material enjoyment. Kṛṣṇa consciousness does not stop them in their propensity for material enjoyment, but simply regulates their habits in the life of sense enjoyment. In spite of their enjoying the material advantages, they can be liberated in this very life by practicing Kṛṣṇa consciousness by the simple method of chanting the holy names of the Lord—Hare Kṛṣṇa, Hare Kṛṣṇa, Kṛṣṇa Kṛṣṇa, Hare Hare/ Hare Rāma, Hare Rāma, Rāma Rāma, Hare Hare.

TEXT 35

अयातयामास्तस्यासन् यामाः स्वान्तरयापनाः ।
शृण्वतो ध्यायतो विष्णोः कुर्वतो ब्रुवतः कथाः ॥३५॥

ayāta-yāmās tasyāsan
yāmāḥ svāntara-yāpanāḥ
śṛṇvato dhyāyato viṣṇoḥ
kurvato bruvataḥ kathāḥ

ayāta-yāmāḥ—time never lost; *tasya*—of Manu; *āsan*—were; *yāmāḥ*—the hours; *sva-antara*—his duration of life; *yāpanāḥ*—bringing to an end; *śṛṇvataḥ*—hearing; *dhyāyataḥ*—contemplating; *viṣṇoḥ*—of Lord Viṣṇu; *kurvataḥ*—acting; *bruvataḥ*—speaking; *kathāḥ*—the topics.

TRANSLATION

Consequently, although his duration of life gradually came to an end, his long life, consisting of a Manvantara era, was not spent in

vain, since he ever engaged in hearing, contemplating, writing down and chanting the pastimes of the Lord.

PURPORT

As freshly prepared food is very tasteful but if kept for three or four hours becomes stale and tasteless, so the existence of material enjoyment can endure as long as life is fresh, but at the fag end of life everything becomes tasteless, and everything appears to be vain and painful. The life of Emperor Svāyambhuva Manu, however, was not tasteless; as he grew older, his life remained as fresh as in the beginning because of his continued Kṛṣṇa consciousness. The life of a man in Kṛṣṇa consciousness is always fresh. It is said that the sun rises in the morning and sets in the evening and its business is to reduce the duration of everyone's life. But the sunrise and sunset cannot diminish the life of one who engages in Kṛṣṇa consciousness. Svāyambhuva Manu's life did not become stale after some time, for he engaged himself always in chanting about and meditating upon Lord Viṣṇu. He was the greatest *yogī* because he never wasted his time. It is especially mentioned here, *viṣṇoḥ kurvato bruvataḥ kathāḥ.* When he talked, he talked only of Kṛṣṇa and Viṣṇu, the Personality of Godhead; when he heard something, it was about Kṛṣṇa; when he meditated, it was upon Kṛṣṇa and His activities.

It is stated that his life was very long, seventy-one *yugas.* One *yuga* is completed in 4,320,000 years, seventy-one of such *yugas* is the duration of the life of a Manu, and fourteen such Manus come and go in one day of Brahmā. For the entire duration of his life—4,320,000 X 71 years—Manu engaged in Kṛṣṇa consciousness by chanting, hearing, talking about and meditating upon Kṛṣṇa. Therefore, his life was not wasted, nor did it become stale.

TEXT 36

स एवं स्वान्तरं निन्ये युगानामेकसप्ततिम् ।
वासुदेवप्रसङ्गेन परिभूतगतित्रयः ॥३६॥

sa evaṁ svāntaraṁ ninye
yugānām eka-saptatim

vāsudeva-prasaṅgena
paribhūta-gati-trayaḥ

saḥ—he (Svāyambhuva Manu); *evam*—thus; *sva-antaram*—his own period; *ninye*—passed; *yugānām*—of the cycles of four ages; *eka-saptatim*—seventy-one; *vāsudeva*—with Vāsudeva; *prasaṅgena*—by topics connected; *paribhūta*—transcended; *gati-trayaḥ*—the three destinations.

TRANSLATION

He passed his time, which lasted seventy-one cycles of the four ages [71 X 4,320,000 years], always thinking of Vāsudeva and always engaged in matters regarding Vāsudeva. Thus he transcended the three destinations.

PURPORT

The three destinations are meant for persons who are under the control of the three modes of material nature. These destinations are sometimes described as the awakened, dreaming and unconscious stages. In *Bhagavad-gītā* the three destinations are described as the destinations of persons in the modes of goodness, passion and ignorance. It is stated in the *Gītā* that those who are in the mode of goodness are promoted to better living conditions in higher planets, and those who are in the mode of passion remain within this material world on the earth or on heavenly planets, but those who are in the mode of ignorance are degraded to an animal life on planets where life is lower than human. But one who is Kṛṣṇa conscious is above these three modes of material nature. It is stated in *Bhagavad-gītā* that anyone who engages in devotional service to the Lord automatically becomes transcendental to the three destinations of material nature and is situated in the *brahma-bhūta*, or self-realized, stage. Although Svāyambhuva Manu, the ruler of this material world, appeared to be absorbed in material happiness, he was neither in the mode of goodness nor in the modes of passion or ignorance, but in the transcendental stage.

Therefore, one who fully engages in devotional service is always liberated. Bilvamaṅgala Ṭhākura, a great devotee of the Lord, stated: "If I have unflinching devotion to the lotus feet of Kṛṣṇa, then Mother Liberation is always engaged in my service. The complete perfection of material enjoyment, religion and economic development is at my command." People are after *dharma*, *artha*, *kāma* and *mokṣa*. Generally they perform religious activities to achieve some material gain, and they engage in material activity for sense gratification. After being frustrated in material sense gratification, one wants to be liberated and become one with the Absolute Truth. These four principles form the transcendental path for the less intelligent. Those who are actually intelligent engage in Kṛṣṇa consciousness, not caring for these four principles of the transcendental method. They at once elevate themselves to the transcendental platform which is above liberation. Liberation is not a very great achievement for a devotee, to say nothing of the results of ritualistic performances in religion, economic development or the materialistic life of sense gratification. Devotees do not care for these. They are situated always on the transcendental platform of the *brahma-bhūta* stage of self-realization.

TEXT 37

शारीरा मानसा दिव्या वैयासे ये च मानुषाः ।
भौतिकाश्च कथं क्लेशा बाधन्ते हरिसंश्रयम् ॥३७॥

śārīrā mānasā divyā
vaiyāse ye ca mānuṣāḥ
bhautikāś ca kathaṁ kleśā
bādhante hari-saṁśrayam

śārīrāḥ—pertaining to the body; *mānasāḥ*—pertaining to the mind; *divyāḥ*—pertaining to supernatural powers (demigods); *vaiyāse*—O Vidura; *ye*—those; *ca*—and; *mānuṣāḥ*—pertaining to other men; *bhautikāḥ*—pertaining to other living beings; *ca*—and; *katham*—how; *kleśāḥ*—miseries; *bādhante*—can trouble; *hari-saṁśrayam*—one who has taken shelter of Lord Kṛṣṇa.

TRANSLATION

Therefore, O Vidura, how can persons completely under the shelter of Lord Kṛṣṇa in devotional service be put into miseries

pertaining to the body, the mind, nature, and other men and living creatures?

PURPORT

Every living entity within this material world is always afflicted by some kind of miseries, pertaining either to the body, the mind or natural disturbances. Distresses due to cold in winter and severe heat in summer always inflict miseries on the living entities in this material world, but one who has completely taken shelter of the lotus feet of the Lord in Kṛṣṇa consciousness is in the transcendental stage; he is not disturbed by any miseries, either due to the body, the mind, or natural disturbances of summer and winter. He is transcendental to all these miseries.

TEXT 38

यः पृष्टो मुनिभिः प्राह धर्मान्नानाविधाञ्छुभान् ।
नृणां वर्णाश्रमाणां च सर्वभूतहितः सदा ॥३८॥

yaḥ pṛṣṭo munibhiḥ prāha
dharmān nānā-vidhāñ chubhān
nṛṇāṁ varṇāśramāṇāṁ ca
sarva-bhūta-hitaḥ sadā

yaḥ—who; *pṛṣṭaḥ*—being questioned; *munibhiḥ*—by the sages; *prāha*—spoke; *dharmān*—the duties; *nānā-vidhān*—many varieties; *śubhān*—auspicious; *nṛṇām*—of human society; *varṇa-āśramāṇām*—of the *varṇas* and *āśramas; ca*—and; *sarva-bhūta*—for all living beings; *hitaḥ*—who does welfare; *sadā*—always.

TRANSLATION

In reply to questions asked by certain sages, he [Svāyambhuva Manu], out of compassion for all living entities, taught the diverse sacred duties of men in general and the different varṇas and āśramas.

TEXT 39

एतत्त आदिराजस्य मनोश्चरितमद्भुतम् ।
वर्णितं वर्णनीयस्य तदपत्योदयं शृणु ॥३९॥

etat ta ādi-rājasya
manoś caritam adbhutam
varṇitaṁ varṇanīyasya
tad-apatyodayaṁ śṛṇu

etat—this; *te*—unto you; *ādi-rājasya*—of the first emperor; *manoḥ*—of Svāyambhuva Manu; *caritam*—the character; *adbhutam*—wonderful; *varṇitam*—described; *varṇanīyasya*—whose reputation is worthy of description; *tat-apatya*—of his daughter; *udayam*—to the flourishing; *śṛṇu*—please listen.

TRANSLATION

I have spoken to you of the wonderful character of Svāyambhuva Manu, the original king, whose reputation is worthy of description. Please hear as I speak of the flourishing of his daughter Devahūti.

Thus end the Bhaktivedanta purports of the Third Canto, Twenty-second Chapter, of the Śrīmad-Bhāgavatam, *entitled "The Marriage of Kardama Muni and Devahūti."*

CHAPTER TWENTY-THREE

Devahūti's Lamentation

TEXT 1

मैत्रेय उवाच
पितृभ्यां प्रस्थिते साध्वी पतिमिङ्गितकोविदा ।
नित्यं पर्यचरत्प्रीत्या भवानीव भवं प्रभुम् ॥ १ ॥

maitreya uvāca
pitṛbhyāṁ prasthite sādhvī
patim iṅgita-kovidā
nityaṁ paryacarat prītyā
bhavānīva bhavaṁ prabhum

maitreyaḥ uvāca—Maitreya said; *pitṛbhyām*—by the parents; *prasthite*—at the departure; *sādhvī*—the chaste woman; *patim*—her husband; *iṅgita-kovidā*—understanding the desires; *nityam*—constantly; *paryacarat*—she served; *prītyā*—with great love; *bhavānī*—the goddess Pārvatī; *iva*—like; *bhavam*—Lord Śiva; *prabhum*—her lord.

TRANSLATION

Maitreya continued: After the departure of her parents, the chaste woman Devahūti, who could understand the desires of her husband, served him constantly with great love, as Bhavānī, the wife of Lord Śiva, serves her husband.

PURPORT

The specific example of Bhavānī is very significant. *Bhavānī* means the wife of Bhava, or Lord Śiva. Bhavānī, or Pārvatī, the daughter of the King of the Himalayas, selected Lord Śiva, who appears to be just like a beggar, as her husband. In spite of her being a princess, she undertook all kinds of tribulations to associate with Lord Śiva, who did not even have a house, but was sitting underneath the trees and passing his time in meditation. Although Bhavānī was the daughter of a very great king, she used to serve Lord Śiva just like a poor woman. Similarly, Devahūti was the daughter of an emperor, Svāyambhuva Manu, yet she preferred to accept Kardama Muni as her husband. She served him with great love and affection, and she knew how to please him. Therefore, she is designated here as *sādhvī,* which means "a chaste, faithful wife." Her rare example is the ideal of Vedic civilization. Every woman is expected to be as good and chaste as Devahūti or Bhavānī. Today in Hindu society, unmarried girls are still taught to worship Lord Śiva with the idea that they may get husbands like him. Lord Śiva is the ideal husband, not in the sense of riches or sense gratification, but because he is the greatest of all devotees. *Vaiṣṇavānāṁ yathā śambhuḥ:* Śambhu, or Lord Śiva, is the ideal Vaiṣṇava. He constantly meditates upon Lord Rāma and chants Hare Rāma, Hare Rāma, Rāma Rāma, Hare Hare. Lord Śiva has a Vaiṣṇava *sampradāya,* which is called the Viṣṇusvāmi-sampradāya. Unmarried girls worship Lord Śiva so that they can expect a husband who is as good a Vaiṣṇava as he. The girls are not taught to select a husband who is very rich or very opulent for material sense gratification; rather, if a girl is fortunate enough to get a husband as good as Lord Śiva in devotional service, then her life becomes perfect. The wife is dependent on the husband, and if the husband is a Vaiṣṇava, then naturally she shares the devotional service of the husband because she renders him service. This reciprocation of service and love between husband and wife is the ideal of a householder's life.

TEXT 2

विश्रम्भेणात्मशौचेन गौरवेण दमेन च ।
शुश्रूषया सौहृदेन वाचा मधुरया च भोः ॥ २ ॥

viśrambheṇātma-śaucena
gauraveṇa damena ca
śuśrūṣayā sauhṛdena
vācā madhurayā ca bhoḥ

viśrambheṇa—with intimacy; *ātma-śaucena*—with purity of mind and body; *gauraveṇa*—with great respect; *damena*—with control of the senses; *ca*—and; *śuśrūṣayā*—with service; *sauhṛdena*—with love; *vācā*—with words; *madhurayā*—sweet; *ca*—and; *bhoḥ*—O Vidura.

TRANSLATION

O Vidura, Devahūti served her husband with intimacy and great respect, with control of the senses, with love and with sweet words.

PURPORT

Here two words are very significant. Devahūti served her husband in two ways, *viśrambheṇa* and *gauraveṇa.* These are two important processes in serving the husband or the Supreme Personality of Godhead. *Viśrambheṇa* means "with intimacy," and *gauraveṇa* means "with great reverence." The husband is a very intimate friend; therefore, the wife must render service just like an intimate friend, and at the same time she must understand that the husband is superior in position, and thus she must offer him all respect. A man's psychology and woman's psychology are different. As constituted by bodily frame, a man always wants to be superior to his wife, and a woman, as bodily constituted, is naturally inferior to her husband. Thus the natural instinct is that the husband wants to post himself as superior to the wife, and this must be observed. Even if there is some wrong on the part of the husband, the wife must tolerate it, and thus there will be no misunderstanding between husband and wife. *Viśrambheṇa* means "with intimacy," but it must not be familiarity that breeds contempt. According to the Vedic civilization, a wife cannot call her husband by name. In the present civilization the wife calls her husband by name, but in Hindu civilization she does not. Thus the inferiority and superiority complexes are recognized. *Damena ca:* a wife has to learn to control herself even if there is a misunderstanding. *Sauhṛdena vācā madhurayā* means always desiring good for the husband and speaking to him with sweet words. A person becomes agitated by so many material contacts in the outside world; therefore, in his home life he must be treated by his wife with sweet words.

TEXT 3

विसृज्य कामं दम्भं च द्वेषं लोभमघं मदम् ।
अप्रमत्तोद्यता नित्यं तेजीयांसमतोषयत् ॥ ३ ॥

visṛjya kāmaṁ dambhaṁ ca
dveṣaṁ lobham aghaṁ madam
apramattodyatā nityaṁ
tejīyāṁsam atoṣayat

visṛjya—giving up; *kāmam*—lust; *dambham*—pride; *ca*—and; *dveṣam*—envy; *lobham*—greed; *agham*—sinful activities; *madam*—vanity; *apramattā*—sane; *udyatā*—laboring diligently; *nityam*—always; *tejīyāṁsam*—her very powerful husband; *atoṣayat*—she pleased.

TRANSLATION

Working sanely and diligently, she pleased her very powerful husband, giving up all lust, pride, envy, greed, sinful activities and vanity.

PURPORT

Here are some of the qualities of a great husband's great wife. Kardama Muni is great by spiritual qualification. Such a husband is called *tejīyāṁsam*, most powerful. Although a wife may be equal to her husband in advancement in spiritual consciousness, she should not be vainly proud. Sometimes it happens that the wife comes from a very rich family, as did Devahūti, the daughter of Emperor Svāyambhuva Manu. She could have been very proud of her parentage, but that is forbidden. The wife should not be proud of her parental position. She must always be submissive to the husband and must give up all vanity. As soon as the wife becomes proud of her parentage, her pride creates great misunderstanding between the husband and wife, and their nuptial life is ruined. Devahūti was very careful about that, and therefore it is said here that she gave up pride completely. Devahūti was not unfaithful. The most sinful activity for a wife is to accept another husband or another lover. Cāṇakya Paṇḍita has described four kinds of enemies at home. If the father is in debt he is considered to be an enemy; if the mother has selected another husband in the presence of her grown-up children, she is considered to be an enemy; if a wife does not live well with her husband but deals very roughly, then she is an enemy; and if a son is a fool, he is also an enemy. In family life, father, mother, wife and children are assets, but if the wife or mother accepts another husband in the presence of her husband or son, then, according to Vedic civilization, she is considered an enemy. A chaste and faithful woman must not practice adultery—that is a greatly sinful act.

TEXTS 4–5

स वै देवर्षिवर्यस्तां मानवीं समनुव्रताम् ।
दैवाद्गरीयसः पत्युराशासानां महाशिषः ॥ ४ ॥
कालेन भूयसा क्षामां कर्शितां व्रतचर्यया ।
प्रेमगद्गदया वाचा पीडितः कृपयाब्रवीत् ॥ ५ ॥

sa vai devarṣi-varyas tāṁ
mānavīṁ samanuvratām
daivād garīyasaḥ patyur
āśāsānāṁ mahāśiṣaḥ

kālena bhūyasā kṣāmāṁ
karśitāṁ vrata-caryayā
prema-gadgadayā vācā
pīḍitaḥ kṛpayābravīt

saḥ—he (Kardama); *vai*—certainly; *deva-ṛṣi*—of the celestial sages; *varyaḥ*—the foremost; *tām*—her; *mānavīm*—the daughter of Manu; *samanuvratām*—fully devoted; *daivāt*—than providence; *garīyasaḥ*—who was greater; *patyuḥ*—from her husband; *āśāsānām*—expecting; *mahā-āśiṣaḥ*—great blessings; *kālena bhūyasā*—for a long time; *kṣāmām*—weak; *karśitām*—emaciated; *vrata-caryayā*—by religious observances; *prema*—with love; *gadgadayā*—stammering; *vācā*—with a voice; *pīḍitaḥ*—overcome; *kṛpayā*—with compassion; *abravīt*—he said.

TRANSLATION

The daughter of Manu, who was fully devoted to her husband, looked upon him as greater even than providence. Thus she expected great blessings from him. Having served him for a long

time, she grew weak and emaciated due to her religious observances. Seeing her condition, Kardama, the foremost of celestial sages, was overcome with compassion and spoke to her in a voice choked with great love.

PURPORT

The wife is expected to be of the same category as the husband. She must be prepared to follow the principles of the husband, and then there will be happy life. If the husband is a devotee and the wife is materialistic, there cannot be any peace in the home. The wife must see the tendencies of the husband and must be prepared to follow him. From *Mahābhārata* we learn that when Gāndhārī understood that her would-be husband, Dhṛtarāṣṭra, was blind, she immediately began to practice blindness herself. Thus she covered her eyes and played the part of a blind woman. She decided that since her husband was blind, she must also act like a blind woman, otherwise she would be proud of her eyes, and her husband would be seen as inferior. The word *samanuvrata* indicates that it is the duty of a wife to adopt the special circumstances in which the husband is situated. Of course, if the husband is as great as Kardama Muni, then a very good result accrues from following him. But even if the husband is not a great devotee like Kardama Muni, it is the wife's duty to adapt herself according to his mentality. That makes married life very happy. It is also mentioned herein that by following the strict vows of a chaste woman, Princess Devahūti became very skinny, and therefore her husband became compassionate. He knew that she was the daughter of a great king and yet was serving him just like an ordinary woman. She was reduced in health by such activities, and he became compassionate and addressed her as follows.

TEXT 6

कर्दम उवाच

तुष्टोऽहमद्य तव मानवि मानदायाः
शुश्रूषया परमया परया च भक्त्या ।
यो देहिनामयमतीव सुहृत्स देहो
नावेक्षितः समुचितः क्षपितुं मदर्थे ॥ ६ ॥

kardama uvāca
tuṣṭo 'ham adya tava mānavi mānadāyāḥ
śuśrūṣayā paramayā parayā ca bhaktyā
yo dehinām ayam atīva suhṛt sa deho
nāvekṣitaḥ samucitaḥ kṣapituṁ mad-arthe

kardamaḥ uvāca—the great sage Kardama said; *tuṣṭaḥ*—pleased; *aham*—I am; *adya*—today; *tava*—with you; *mānavi*—O daughter of Manu; *māna-dāyāḥ*—who are respectful; *śuśrūṣayā*—by the service; *paramayā*—most excellent; *parayā*—highest; *ca*—and; *bhaktyā*—by the devotion; *yaḥ*—that which; *dehinām*—to the embodied; *ayam*—this; *atīva*—extremely; *suhṛt*—dear; *saḥ*—that; *dehaḥ*—body; *na*—not; *avekṣitaḥ*—taken care of; *samucitaḥ*—properly; *kṣapitum*—to expend; *mat-arthe*—on my account.

TRANSLATION

Kardama Muni said: O respectful daughter of Svāyambhuva Manu, today I am very much pleased with you for your great devotion and most excellent loving service. Since the body is so dear to embodied beings, I am astonished that you have neglected your own body to use it on my behalf.

PURPORT

It is indicated here that one's body is very dear, yet Devahūti was so faithful to her husband that not only did she serve him with great devotion, service and respect, but she did not even care for her own health. That is called selfless service. It appears that Devahūti had no sense pleasure, even with her husband, otherwise she would not have deteriorated in health. Acting to facilitate Kardama Muni's engagement in spiritual elevation, she continually assisted him, not caring for bodily comfort. It is the duty of a faithful and chaste wife to help her husband in every respect, especially when the husband is engaged in Kṛṣṇa consciousness. In this case, the husband also amply rewarded the wife. This is not to be expected by a woman who is the wife of an ordinary person.

TEXT 7

ये मे स्वधर्मनिरतस्य तपःसमाधि-
विद्यात्मयोगविजिता भगवत्प्रसादाः ।
तानेव ते मदनुसेवनयावरुद्धान्
दृष्टिं प्रपश्य वितराम्यभयानशोकान् ॥ ७ ॥

ye me sva-dharma-niratasya tapaḥ-samādhi-
vidyātma-yoga-vijitā bhagavat-prasādāḥ
tān eva te mad-anusevanayāvaruddhān
dṛṣṭiṁ prapaśya vitarāmy abhayān aśokān

ye—those which; *me*—by me; *sva-dharma*—own religious life; *niratasya*—fully occupied with; *tapaḥ*—in austerity; *samādhi*—in meditation; *vidyā*—in Kṛṣṇa consciousness; *ātma-yoga*—by fixing the mind; *vijitāḥ*—achieved; *bhagavat-prasādāḥ*—the blessings of the Lord; *tān*—them; *eva*—even; *te*—by you; *mat*—to me; *anusevanayā*—by devoted service; *avaruddhān*—obtained; *dṛṣṭim*—transcendental vision; *prapaśya*—just see; *vitarāmi*—I am giving; *abhayān*—which are free from fear; *aśokān*—which are free from lamentation.

TRANSLATION

Kardama Muni continued: I have achieved the blessings of the Lord in discharging my own religious life of austerity, meditation and Kṛṣṇa consciousness. Although you have not yet experienced these achievements, which are free from fear and lamentation, I shall offer them all to you because you are engaged in my service. Now just look at them. I am giving you the transcendental vision to see how nice they are.

PURPORT

Devahūti engaged only in the service of Kardama Muni. She was not supposed to be so advanced in austerity, ecstasy, meditation or Kṛṣṇa consciousness, but, imperceptibly, she was sharing her husband's achievements, which she could neither see nor experience. Automatically she achieved these graces of the Lord.

What are the graces of the Lord? It is stated here that the graces of the Lord are *abhaya,* free from fearfulness. In the material world, if someone accumulates a million dollars, he is always full of fear because he is always thinking, "What if the money is lost?" But the benediction of the Lord, *bhagavat-prasāda,* is never to be lost. It is simply to be enjoyed. There is no question of loss. One simply gains and enjoys gaining. *Bhagavad-gītā* also confirms this: when one achieves the grace of the Lord, the result is that *sarva-duḥkhāni,* all distresses, are destroyed. When situated in the transcendental position, one is freed from the two kinds of material diseases—hankering and lamentation. This is also stated in *Bhagavad-gītā.* After devotional life begins, we can achieve the full result of love of Godhead. Love of Kṛṣṇa is the highest perfection of *bhagavat-prasāda,* or divine mercy. This transcendental achievement is so greatly valuable that no material happiness can compare to it. Prabodhānanda Sarasvatī said that if one achieves the grace of Lord Caitanya he becomes so great that he does not care a fig even for the demigods, he thinks of monism as hellish, and for him the perfection of controlling the senses is as easy as anything. Heavenly pleasures become to him no more than stories. Actually, there is no comparison between material happiness and transcendental happiness.

By the grace of Kardama Muni, Devahūti experienced actual realization simply by serving. We get a similar example in the life of Nārada Muni. In his previous life, Nārada was a maidservant's son, but his mother was engaged in the service of great devotees. He got the opportunity to serve the devotees, and simply by eating the remnants of their foodstuff and carrying out their orders he became so elevated that in his next life he became the great personality Nārada. For spiritual achievement the easiest path is to take shelter of a bona fide spiritual master and to serve him with heart and soul. That is the secret of success. As stated by Viśvanātha Cakravartī Ṭhākura in his eight stanzas of prayer to the spiritual master, *yasya prasādād bhagavat-prasādaḥ:* by serving or receiving the grace of the spiritual master, one receives the grace of the Supreme Lord. By serving her devotee husband, Kardama Muni, Devahūti shared in his achievements. Similarly, a sincere disciple, simply by serving a bona fide spiritual master, can achieve all the mercy of the Lord and the spiritual master simultaneously.

TEXT 8

अन्ये पुनर्भगवतो भ्रुव उद्विजृम्भ-
विभ्रंशितार्थरचनाः किमुरुक्रमस्य ।
सिद्धासि भुङ्क्ष्व विभवान्निजधर्मदोहान्
दिव्यान्नरैर्दुरधिगान्नृपविक्रियाभिः ॥ ८ ॥

anye punar bhagavato bhruva udvijṛmbha-
vibhraṁśitārtha-racanāḥ kim urukramasya
siddhāsi bhuṅkṣva vibhavān nija-dharma-dohān
divyān narair duradhigān nṛpa-vikriyābhiḥ

anye—others; *punaḥ*—again; *bhagavataḥ*—of the Lord; *bhruvaḥ*—of the eyebrows; *udvijṛmbha*—by the movement; *vibhraṁśita*—annihilated; *artha-racanāḥ*—material achievements; *kim*—what use; *urukramasya*—of Lord Viṣṇu (far-stepping); *siddhā*—successful; *asi*—you are; *bhuṅkṣva*—enjoy; *vibhavān*—the gifts; *nija-dharma*—by your own principles of devotion; *dohān*—gained; *divyān*—transcendental; *naraiḥ*—by persons; *duradhigān*—difficult to obtain; *nṛpa-vikriyābhiḥ*—proud of aristocracy.

TRANSLATION

Kardama Muni continued: What is the use of enjoyments other than the Lord's grace? All material achievements are subject to be annihilated simply by a movement of the eyebrows of Lord Viṣṇu, the Supreme Personality of Godhead. By your principles of devotion to your husband, you have achieved and can enjoy transcendental gifts very rarely obtained by persons proud of aristocracy and material possessions.

PURPORT

Lord Caitanya recommended that the greatest achievement of human life is to achieve the grace of the Lord, love of God. He said, *premā pumartho mahān:* to achieve love of Godhead is the highest perfection of life. The same perfection is recommended by Kardama Muni to his wife. His wife belonged to a very aristocratic royal family. Generally, those who are very materialistic or who possess material wealth and prosperity are unable to appreciate the value of transcendental love of God. Although Devahūti was a princess coming from a very great royal family, fortunately she was under the supervision of her great husband, Kardama Muni, who offered her the best gift which can be bestowed in human life—the grace of the Lord, or love of God. This grace of the Lord was achieved by Devahūti by the good will and satisfaction of her husband. She served her husband, who was a great devotee and saintly person, with great sincerity, love, affection and service, and Kardama Muni was satisfied. He willingly gave love of God, and he recommended that she accept it and enjoy it because he had already achieved it.

Love of God is not an ordinary commodity. Caitanya Mahāprabhu was worshiped by Rūpa Gosvāmī because He distributed love of God, *kṛṣṇa-premā*, to everyone. Rūpa Gosvāmī praised Him as *mahā-vadānya*, a greatly munificent personality, because He was freely distributing to everyone love of Godhead, which is achieved by wise men only after many, many births. *Kṛṣṇa-premā*, Kṛṣṇa consciousness, is the highest gift which can be bestowed on anyone whom we presume to love.

One word used in this verse, *nija-dharma-dohān*, is very significant. Devahūti, as the wife of Kardama Muni, achieved an invaluable gift from her husband because she was very faithful to him. For a woman the first principle of religion is to be faithful to her husband. If, fortunately, the husband is a great personality, then the combination is perfect, and the lives of both the wife and the husband are at once fulfilled.

TEXT 9

एवं ब्रुवाणमबलाखिलयोगमाया-
विद्याविचक्षणमवेक्ष्य गताधिरासीत् ।
सम्प्रश्रयप्रणयविह्वलया गिरेषद्-
व्रीडावलोकविलसद्धसिताननाह ॥ ९ ॥

evaṁ bruvāṇam abalākhila-yogamāyā-
vidyā-vicakṣaṇam avekṣya gatādhir āsīt
sampraśraya-praṇaya-vihvalayā gireṣad-
vrīḍāvaloka-vilasad-dhasitānanāha

evam—thus; *bruvāṇam*—speaking; *abalā*—the woman; *akhila*—all; *yoga-māyā*—of transcendental science; *vidyā-vicakṣaṇam*—excelling in knowledge; *avekṣya*—after hearing; *gata-ādhiḥ*—satisfied; *āsīt*—she became; *sampraśraya*—with humility; *praṇaya*—and with love; *vihvalayā*—choked up; *girā*—with a voice; *īṣat*—slightly; *vrīḍā*—bashful; *avaloka*—with a glance; *vilasat*—shining; *hasita*—smiling; *ānanā*—her face; *āha*—she spoke.

TRANSLATION

Upon hearing the speaking of her husband, who excelled in knowledge of all kinds of transcendental science, innocent Devahūti was very satisfied. Her smiling face shining with a slightly bashful glance, she spoke in a choked voice because of great humility and love.

PURPORT

It is said that if one is already engaged in Kṛṣṇa consciousness and is rendering transcendental loving service to the Lord, then it can be supposed that he has finished all the recommended courses of austerity, penance, religion, sacrifice, mystic *yoga* and meditation. Devahūti's husband was so expert in the transcendental science that there was nothing for him to argue about, and when she heard him speak she was confident that since he was very much advanced in devotional service he had already surpassed all transcendental educational activities. She had no doubt about the gifts offered by her husband; she knew that he was expert in offering such gifts, and when she understood that he was offering the greatest gift, she was very satisfied. She was overwhelmed with ecstatic love, and therefore she could not reply; then, with faltering language, just like an attractive wife, she spoke the following words.

TEXT 10

देवहूतिरुवाच

राद्धं बत द्विजवृषैतदमोघयोग-

मायाधिपे त्वयि विभो तदवैमि भर्तः ।

यस्तेऽभ्यधायि समयः सकृदङ्गसङ्गो
भूयाद्गरीयसि गुणः प्रसवः सतीनाम् ॥१०॥

devahūtir uvāca
rāddhaṁ bata dvija-vṛṣaitad amogha-yoga-
māyādhipe tvayi vibho tad avaimi bhartaḥ
yas te 'bhyadhāyi samayaḥ sakṛd aṅga-saṅgo
bhūyād garīyasi guṇaḥ prasavaḥ satīnām

devahūtiḥ uvāca—Devahūti said; *rāddham*—it has been achieved; *bata*—indeed; *dvija-vṛṣa*—O best of the *brāhmaṇas; etat*—this; *amogha*—infallible; *yoga-māyā*—of mystic powers; *adhipe*—the master; *tvayi*—in you; *vibho*—O great one; *tat*—that; *avaimi*—I know; *bhartaḥ*—O husband; *yaḥ*—that which; *te*—by you; *abhyadhāyi*—was given; *samayaḥ*—promise; *sakṛt*—once; *aṅga-saṅgaḥ*—bodily union; *bhūyāt*—may be; *garīyasi*—when very glorious; *guṇaḥ*—a great quality; *prasavaḥ*—progeny; *satīnām*—of chaste women.

TRANSLATION

Śrī Devahūti said: My dear husband, O best of brāhmaṇas, I know that you have achieved perfection and are the master of all the infallible mystic powers because you are under the protection of yogamāyā, the transcendental nature. But you once made a promise that our bodily union should now fulfill, since children are a great quality for a chaste woman who has a glorious husband.

PURPORT

Devahūti expressed her happiness by uttering the word *bata*, for she knew that her husband was in a highly elevated, transcendental position and was under the shelter of *yogamāyā*. As stated in *Bhagavad-gītā*, those who are great souls, *mahātmās*, are not under the control of the material energy. The Supreme Lord has two energies, material and spiritual. The living entities are marginal energy. As marginal energy, a person may be under the control of the material energy or the spiritual energy (*yogamāyā*). Kardama Muni was a great soul, and therefore he was under the spiritual energy, which means that he was directly connected with the Supreme Lord. The symptom of this is Kṛṣṇa consciousness, constant engagement in devotional service. This was known to Devahūti, yet she was anxious to have a son by bodily union with the sage. She reminded her husband of his promise to her parents: "I will remain only until the time of Devahūti's pregnancy." She reminded him that for a chaste woman to have a child by a great personality is most glorious. She wanted to be pregnant, and she prayed for that. The word *strī* means "expansion." By bodily union of the husband and wife their qualities are expanded: children born of good parents are expansions of the parents' personal qualifications. Both Kardama Muni and Devahūti were spiritually enlightened; therefore she desired from the beginning that first she be pregnant and then she be empowered with the achievement of God's grace and love of God. For a woman it is a great ambition to have a son of the same quality as a highly qualified husband. Since she had the opportunity to have Kardama Muni as her husband, she also desired to have a child by bodily union.

TEXT 11

तत्रेतिकृत्यमुपशिक्ष यथोपदेशं
येनैष मे कर्शितोऽतिरिरंसयात्मा ।
सिद्ध्येत ते कृतमनोभवधर्षिताया
दीनस्तदीश भवनं सदृशं विचक्ष्व ॥११॥

tatreti-kṛtyam upaśikṣa yathopadeśaṁ
yenaiṣa me karśito 'tiriraṁsayātmā
siddhyeta te kṛta-manobhava-dharṣitāyā
dīnas tad īśa bhavanaṁ sadṛśaṁ vicakṣva

tatra—in that; *iti-kṛtyam*—what is necessary to be done; *upaśikṣa*—perform; *yathā*—according to; *upadeśam*—instruction in scripture; *yena*—by which; *eṣaḥ*—this; *me*—my; *karśitaḥ*—emaciated; *atiriraṁsayā*—due to intense passion not being satisfied; *ātmā*—body; *siddhyeta*—it may be rendered fit; *te*—for you; *kṛta*—excited; *manaḥ-bhava*—by emotion; *dharṣitāyāḥ*—who am struck; *dīnaḥ*—poor; *tat*—

therefore; *īśa*—O my dear lord; *bhavanam*—house; *sadṛśam*—suitable; *vicakṣva*—please think of.

TRANSLATION

Devahūti continued: My dear lord, I am struck by excited emotion for you. Therefore kindly make what arrangements must be made according to the scriptures so that my skinny body, emaciated through unsatisfied passion, may be rendered fit for you. Also, my lord, please think of a suitable house for this purpose.

PURPORT

The Vedic literatures are not only full of spiritual instruction but are also instructive in how to prosecute material existence very nicely, with the ultimate aim of spiritual perfection. Devahūti asked her husband, therefore, how to prepare herself for sex life according to the Vedic instructions. Sex life is especially meant for having good children. The circumstances for creating good children are mentioned in *kāma-śāstra*, the scripture in which suitable arrangements are prescribed for factually glorious sex life. Everything needed is mentioned in the scriptures—what sort of house and decorations there should be, what sort of dress the wife should have, how she should be decorated with ointments, scents and other attractive features, etc. With these requisites fulfilled, the husband will be attracted by her beauty, and a favorable mental situation will be created. The mental situation at the time of sex life may then be transferred into the womb of the wife, and good children can come out of that pregnancy. Here is a special reference to Devahūti's bodily features. Because she had become skinny, she feared that her body might have no attraction for Kardama. She wanted to be instructed how to improve her bodily condition in order to attract her husband. Sexual intercourse in which the husband is attracted to the wife is sure to produce a male child, but sexual intercourse based on attraction of the wife for the husband may produce a girl. That is mentioned in the *Āyur-veda*. When the passion of the woman is greater, there is a chance of a girl's being born. When the passion of the man is greater, then there is the possibility of a son. Devahūti wanted the passion of her husband to be increased by the arrangement mentioned in the *kāma-śāstra*. She wanted him to instruct her in that way, and she also requested that he arrange for a suitable house because the hermitage in which Kardama Muni was living was very simple and completely in the mode of goodness, and there was less possibility of passion's being aroused in his heart.

TEXT 12

मैत्रेय उवाच
प्रियायाः प्रियमन्विच्छन् कर्दमो योगमास्थितः ।
विमानं कामगं क्षत्तस्तर्ह्येवाविरचीकरत् ॥१२॥

maitreya uvāca
priyāyāḥ priyam anvicchan
kardamo yogam āsthitaḥ
vimānaṁ kāma-gaṁ kṣattas
tarhy evāviracīkarat

maitreyaḥ—the great sage Maitreya; *uvāca*—said; *priyāyāḥ*—of his beloved wife; *priyam*—the pleasure; *anvicchan*—seeking; *kardamaḥ*—the sage Kardama; *yogam*—yogic power; *āsthitaḥ*—exercised; *vimānam*—an airplane; *kāma-gam*—moving at will; *kṣattaḥ*—O Vidura; *tarhi*—instantly; *eva*—quite; *āviracīkarat*—he produced.

TRANSLATION

Maitreya continued: O Vidura, seeking to please his beloved wife, the sage Kardama exercised his yogic power and instantly produced an aerial mansion that could travel at his will.

PURPORT

Here the words *yogam āsthitaḥ* are significant. The sage Kardama was completely perfect in *yoga*. As the result of real *yoga* practice there are eight kinds of perfection: the *yogī* can become smaller than the smallest, greater than the greatest or lighter than the lightest, he can achieve anything he likes, he can create even a planet, he can establish influence over anyone, etc. In this way yogic perfection is achieved, and after this one can achieve the perfection of spiritual life. Thus it was not very wonderful for Kardama Muni to create a mansion in the air, according to his own desire, to fulfill the desire of his beloved wife. He at once created the palace, which is described in the following verses.

TEXT 13

सर्वकामदुघं दिव्यं सर्वरत्नसमन्वितम् ।
सर्वर्द्ध्युपचयोदर्कं मणिस्तम्भैरुपस्कृतम् ॥१३॥

sarva-kāma-dughaṁ divyaṁ
sarva-ratna-samanvitam
sarvarddhy-upacayodarkaṁ
maṇi-stambhair upaskṛtam

sarva—all; *kāma*—desires; *dugham*—yielding; *divyam*—wonderful; *sarva-ratna*—all sorts of jewels; *samanvitam*—bedecked with; *sarva*—all; *ṛddhi*—of wealth; *upacaya*—increase; *udarkam*—gradual; *maṇi*—of precious stones; *stambhaiḥ*—with pillars; *upaskṛtam*—adorned.

TRANSLATION

It was a wonderful structure, bedecked with all sorts of jewels, adorned with pillars of precious stones, and capable of yielding whatever one desired. It was equipped with every form of furniture and wealth, which tended to increase in the course of time.

PURPORT

The castle created in the sky by Kardama Muni may be called "a castle in the air," but by his mystic power of *yoga* Kardama Muni actually constructed a huge castle in the air. To our feeble imagination, a castle in the sky is an impossibility, but if we scrutinizingly consider the matter we can understand that it is not impossible at all. If the Supreme Personality of Godhead can create so many planets, carrying millions of castles in the air, a perfect *yogī* like Kardama Muni can easily construct one castle in the air. The castle is described as *sarva-kāma-dugham*, "yielding whatever one desired." It was full of jewels. Even the pillars were made of pearls and valuable stones. These valuable jewels and stones were not subject to deterioration, but were everlastingly and increasingly opulent. We sometimes hear of castles thus bedecked on the surface of this earth also. The castles constructed by Lord Kṛṣṇa for His 16,108 wives were so bedecked with jewels that there was no need of lamplight during the night.

TEXTS 14–15

दिव्योपकरणोपेतं सर्वकालसुखावहम् ।
पट्टिकाभिः पताकाभिर्विचित्राभिरलंकृतम् ॥१४॥
स्रग्भिर्विचित्रमाल्याभिर्मञ्जुशिञ्जत्षडङ्घ्रिभिः ।
दुकूलक्षौमकौशेयैर्नानावस्त्रैर्विराजितम् ॥१५॥

divyopakaraṇopetaṁ
sarva-kāla-sukhāvaham
paṭṭikābhiḥ patākābhir
vicitrābhir alaṅkṛtam

sragbhir vicitra-mālyābhir
mañju-śiñjat-ṣaḍ-aṅghribhiḥ
dukūla-kṣauma-kauśeyair
nānā-vastrair virājitam

divya—wonderful; *upakaraṇa*—with paraphernalia; *upetam*—equipped; *sarva-kāla*—in all seasons; *sukha-āvaham*—bringing happiness; *paṭṭikābhiḥ*—with festoons; *patākābhiḥ*—with flags; *vicitrābhiḥ*—of various colors and fabrics; *alaṅkṛtam*—decorated; *sragbhiḥ*—with wreaths; *vicitra-mālyābhiḥ*—with charming flowers; *mañju*—sweet; *śiñjat*—humming; *ṣaṭ-aṅghribhiḥ*—with bees; *dukūla*—fine cloth; *kṣauma*—linen; *kauśeyaiḥ*—of silk cloth; *nānā*—various; *vastraiḥ*—with tapestries; *virājitam*—embellished.

TRANSLATION

The castle was fully equipped with all necessary paraphernalia, and it was pleasing in all seasons. It was decorated all around with flags, festoons and artistic work of variegated colors. It was further embellished with wreaths of charming flowers that attracted

sweetly humming bees and with tapestries of linen, silk and various other fabrics.

TEXT 16

उपर्युपरि विन्यस्तनिलयेषु पृथक्पृथक् ।
क्षिप्तैः कशिपुभिः कान्तं पर्यङ्कव्यजनासनैः ॥१६॥

upary upari vinyasta-
nilayeṣu pṛthak pṛthak
kṣiptaiḥ kaśipubhiḥ kāntaṁ
paryaṅka-vyajanāsanaiḥ

upari upari—one upon another; *vinyasta*—placed; *nilayeṣu*—in stories; *pṛthak pṛthak*—separately; *kṣiptaiḥ*—arranged; *kaśipubhiḥ*—with beds; *kāntam*—charming; *paryaṅka*—couches; *vyajana*—fans; *āsanaiḥ*—with seats.

TRANSLATION

The palace looked charming, with beds, couches, fans and seats, all separately arranged in seven stories.

PURPORT

It is understood from this verse that the castle had many stories. The words *upary upari vinyasta* indicate that skyscrapers are not newly invented. Even in those days, millions of years ago, the idea of building many-storied houses was current. They contained not merely one or two rooms, but many different apartments, and each was completely decorated with cushions, bedsteads, sitting places and carpets.

TEXT 17

तत्र तत्र विनिक्षिप्तनानाशिल्पोपशोभितम् ।
महामरकतस्थल्या जुष्टं विद्रुमवेदिभिः ॥१७॥

tatra tatra vinikṣipta-
nānā-śilpopaśobhitam

mahā-marakata-sthalyā
juṣṭaṁ vidruma-vedibhiḥ

tatra tatra—here and there; *vinikṣipta*—placed; *nānā*—various; *śilpa*—by artistic engravings; *upaśobhitam*—extraordinarily beautiful; *mahā-marakata*—of great emeralds; *sthalyā*—with a floor; *juṣṭam*—furnished; *vidruma*—of coral; *vedibhiḥ*—with raised platforms (daises).

TRANSLATION

Its beauty was enhanced by artistic engravings here and there on the walls. The floor was of emerald, with coral daises.

PURPORT

At the present moment people are very proud of their architectural art, yet floors are generally decorated with colored cement. It appears, however, that the castle constructed by the yogic powers of Kardama Muni had floors of emerald with coral daises.

TEXT 18

द्वाःसु विद्रुमदेहल्या भातं वज्रकपाटवत् ।
शिखरेष्विन्द्रनीलेषु हेमकुम्भैरधिश्रितम् ॥१८॥

dvāḥsu vidruma-dehalyā
bhātaṁ vajra-kapāṭavat
śikhareṣv indranīleṣu
hema-kumbhair adhiśritam

dvāḥsu—in the entrances; *vidruma*—of coral; *dehalyā*—with a threshold; *bhātam*—beautiful; *vajra*—bedecked with diamonds; *kapāṭa-vat*—having doors; *śikhareṣu*—on the domes; *indra-nīleṣu*—of sapphires; *hema-kumbhaiḥ*—with gold pinnacles; *adhiśritam*—crowned.

TRANSLATION

The palace was very beautiful, with its coral thresholds at the entrances and its doors bedecked with diamonds. Gold pinnacles crowned its domes of sapphire.

TEXT 19

चक्षुष्मत्पद्मरागाग्र्यैर्वज्रभित्तिषु निर्मितैः ।
जुष्टं विचित्रवैतानैर्महार्हैर्हेमतोरणैः ॥१९॥

cakṣuṣmat padmarāgāgryair
vajra-bhittiṣu nirmitaiḥ
juṣṭaṁ vicitra-vaitānair
mahārhair hema-toraṇaiḥ

cakṣuḥ-mat—as if possessed of eyes; *padma-rāga*—with rubies; *agryaiḥ*—choicest; *vajra*—of diamond; *bhittiṣu*—on the walls; *nirmitaiḥ*—set; *juṣṭam*—furnished; *vicitra*—various; *vaitānaiḥ*—with canopies; *mahā-arhaiḥ*—greatly valuable; *hema-toraṇaiḥ*—with gates of gold.

TRANSLATION

With the choicest rubies set in its diamond walls, it appeared as though possessed of eyes. It was furnished with wonderful canopies and greatly valuable gates of gold.

PURPORT

Artistic jewelry and decorations giving the appearance of eyes are not imaginary. Even in recent times the Mogul emperors constructed their palaces with decorations of jeweled birds with eyes made of valuable stones. The stones have been taken away by the authorities, but the decorations are still present in some of the castles constructed by the Mogul emperors in New Delhi. The royal palaces were built with jewels and rare stones resembling eyes, and thus at night they would give off reflective light without need of lamps.

TEXT 20

हंसपारावतव्रातैस्तत्र तत्र निकूजितम् ।
कृत्रिमान् मन्यमानैः स्वानधिरुह्याधिरुह्य च ॥२०॥

haṁsa-pārāvata-vrātais
tatra tatra nikūjitam

kṛtrimān manyamānaiḥ svān
adhiruhyādhiruhya ca

haṁsa—of swans; *pārāvata*—of pigeons; *vrātaiḥ*—with multitudes; *tatra tatra*—here and there; *nikūjitam*—vibrated; *kṛtrimān*—artificial; *manyamānaiḥ*—thinking; *svān*—belonging to their own kind; *adhiruhya adhiruhya*—rising repeatedly; *ca*—and.

TRANSLATION

Here and there in that palace were multitudes of live swans and pigeons, as well as artificial swans and pigeons so lifelike that the real swans rose above them again and again, thinking them live birds like themselves. Thus the palace vibrated with the sounds of these birds.

TEXT 21

विहारस्थानविश्रामसंवेशप्राङ्गणाजिरैः ।
यथोपजोषं रचितैर्विस्मापनमिवात्मनः ॥२१॥

vihāra-sthāna-viśrāma-
saṁveśa-prāṅgaṇājiraiḥ
yathopajoṣaṁ racitair
vismāpanam ivātmanaḥ

vihāra-sthāna—pleasure grounds; *viśrāma*—resting chambers; *saṁveśa*—bedrooms; *prāṅgaṇa*—inner yards; *ajiraiḥ*—with outer yards; *yathā-upajoṣam*—according to comfort; *racitaiḥ*—which were designed; *vismāpanam*—causing astonishment; *iva*—indeed; *ātmanaḥ*—to himself (Kardama).

TRANSLATION

The castle had pleasure grounds, resting chambers, bedrooms and inner and outer yards designed with an eye to comfort. All this caused astonishment to the sage himself.

PURPORT

Kardama Muni, being a saintly person, was living in a humble hermitage, but when he saw the palace constructed by his yogic powers, which was full of resting rooms, rooms for sex enjoyment, and inner and outer yards, he himself was astonished. That is the way of a God-gifted person. A devotee like Kardama Muni exhibited such opulence by his yogic power at the request of his wife, but when the opulence was produced, he himself could not understand how such manifestations could be possible. When a *yogī's* power is exhibited, the *yogī* himself is sometimes astonished.

TEXT 22

ईदृग्गृहं तत्पश्यन्तीं नातिप्रीतेन चेतसा ।
सर्वभूताशयाभिज्ञः प्रावोचत्कर्दमः स्वयम् ॥२२॥

īdṛg gṛhaṁ tat paśyantīṁ
nātiprītena cetasā
sarva-bhūtāśayābhijñaḥ
prāvocat kardamaḥ svayam

īdṛk—such; *gṛham*—house; *tat*—that; *paśyantīm*—looking at; *na atiprītena*—not much pleased; *cetasā*—with a heart; *sarva-bhūta*—of everyone; *āśaya-abhijñaḥ*—understanding the heart; *prāvocat*—he addressed; *kardamaḥ*—Kardama; *svayam*—personally.

TRANSLATION

When he saw Devahūti looking at the gigantic, opulent palace with a displeased heart, Kardama Muni could understand her feelings because he could study the heart of anyone. Thus he personally addressed his wife as follows.

PURPORT

Devahūti had spent a long time in the hermitage, not taking much care of her body. She was covered with dirt, and her clothing was not very nice. Kardama Muni was surprised that he could produce such a palace, and similarly his wife, Devahūti, was also astonished. How could she live in that opulent palace? Kardama Muni could understand her astonishment, and thus he spoke as follows.

TEXT 23

निमज्ज्यास्मिन् ह्रदे भीरु विमानमिदमारुह ।
इदं शुक्लकृतं तीर्थमाशिषां यापकं नृणाम् ॥२३॥

nimajjyāsmin hrade bhīru
vimānam idam āruha
idaṁ śukla-kṛtaṁ tīrtham
āśiṣāṁ yāpakaṁ nṛṇām

nimajjya—after bathing; *asmin*—in this; *hrade*—in the lake; *bhīru*—O fearful one; *vimānam*—airplane; *idam*—this; *āruha*—ascend; *idam*—this; *śukla-kṛtam*—created by Lord Viṣṇu; *tīrtham*—sacred lake; *āśiṣām*—the desires; *yāpakam*—bestowing; *nṛṇām*—of human beings.

TRANSLATION

My dear Devahūti, you look very much afraid. First bathe in Lake Bindu-sarovara, created by Lord Viṣṇu Himself, which can grant all the desires of a human being, and then mount this airplane.

PURPORT

It is still the system to go to places of pilgrimage and take a bath in the water there. In Vṛndāvana the people take baths in the River Yamunā. In other places, such as Prayāga, they take baths in the River Ganges. The words *tīrtham āśiṣāṁ yāpakam* refer to the fulfillment of desires by bathing in a place of pilgrimage. Kardama Muni advised his good wife to bathe in Lake Bindu-sarovara so that she could revive the former beauty and luster of her body.

TEXT 24

सा तद्भर्तुः समादाय वचः कुवलयेक्षणा ।
सरजं बिभ्रती वासो वेणीभूतांश्च मूर्धजान् ॥२४॥

sā tad bhartuḥ samādāya
vacaḥ kuvalayekṣaṇā
sarajaṁ bibhratī vāso
veṇī-bhūtāṁś ca mūrdhajān

sā—she; *tat*—then; *bhartuḥ*—of her husband; *samādāya*—accepting; *vacaḥ*—the words; *kuvalaya-īkṣaṇā*—the lotus-eyed; *sa-rajam*—dirty; *bibhratī*—wearing; *vāsaḥ*—clothing; *veṇī-bhūtān*—matted; *ca*—and; *mūrdha-jān*—hair.

TRANSLATION

The lotus-eyed Devahūti accepted the order of her husband. Because of her dirty dress and the locks of matted hair on her head, she did not look very attractive.

PURPORT

It appears that Devahūti's hair had remained uncombed for many years and had become complicated in tangles. In other words, she neglected her bodily dress and comforts to engage in the service of her husband.

TEXT 25

अङ्गं च मलपङ्केन संछन्नं शबलस्तनम् ।
आविवेश सरस्वत्याः सरः शिवजलाशयम् ॥२५॥

aṅgaṁ ca mala-paṅkena
sañchannaṁ śabala-stanam
āviveśa sarasvatyāḥ
saraḥ śiva-jalāśayam

aṅgam—body; *ca*—and; *mala-paṅkena*—with dirt; *sañchannam*—covered; *śabala*—discolored; *stanam*—breasts; *āviveśa*—she entered; *sarasvatyāḥ*—of the River Sarasvatī; *saraḥ*—the lake; *śiva*—sacred; *jala*—waters; *āśayam*—containing.

TRANSLATION

Her body was coated with a thick layer of dirt, and her breasts were discolored. She dove, however, into the lake, which contained the sacred waters of the Sarasvatī.

TEXT 26

सान्तःसरसि वेश्मस्थाः शतानि दश कन्यकाः ।
सर्वाः किशोरवयसो ददर्शोत्पलगन्धयः ॥२६॥

sāntaḥ sarasi veśma-sthāḥ
śatāni daśa kanyakāḥ
sarvāḥ kiśora-vayaso
dadarśotpala-gandhayaḥ

sā—she; *antaḥ*—inside; *sarasi*—in the lake; *veśma-sthāḥ*—situated in a house; *śatāni daśa*—ten hundred; *kanyakāḥ*—girls; *sarvāḥ*—all; *kiśora-vayasaḥ*—in the prime of youth; *dadarśa*—she saw; *utpala*—like lotuses; *gandhayaḥ*—fragrant.

TRANSLATION

In a house inside the lake she saw one thousand girls, all in the prime of youth and fragrant like lotuses.

TEXT 27

तां दृष्ट्वा सहसोत्थाय प्रोचुः प्राञ्जलयः स्त्रियः ।
वयं कर्मकरीस्तुभ्यं शाधि नः करवाम किम् ॥२७॥

tāṁ dṛṣṭvā sahasotthāya
procuḥ prāñjalayaḥ striyaḥ
vayaṁ karma-karīs tubhyaṁ
śādhi naḥ karavāma kim

tām—her; *dṛṣṭvā*—seeing; *sahasā*—suddenly; *utthāya*—rising; *procuḥ*—they said; *prāñjalayaḥ*—with folded hands; *striyaḥ*—the damsels; *vayam*—we; *karma-karīḥ*—maidservants; *tubhyam*—for you; *śādhi*—please tell; *naḥ*—us; *karavāma*—we can do; *kim*—what.

TRANSLATION

Seeing her, the damsels suddenly rose and said with folded hands, "We are your maidservants. Tell us what we can do for you."

PURPORT

While Devahūti was thinking of what to do in that great palace in her dirty clothes, there were at once, by the yogic powers of Kardama Muni, one thousand maidservants prepared to serve her. They appeared before Devahūti within the water and presented themselves as her maidservants, simply awaiting her orders.

TEXT 28

स्नानेन तां महार्हेण स्नापयित्वा मनस्विनीम् ।
दुकूले निर्मले नूत्ने ददुरस्यै च मानदाः ॥२८॥

snānena tāṁ mahārheṇa
snāpayitvā manasvinīm
dukūle nirmale nūtne
dadur asyai ca mānadāḥ

snānena—with bathing oils; *tām*—her; *mahā-arheṇa*—very costly; *snāpayitvā*—after bathing; *manasvinīm*—the virtuous wife; *dukūle*—in fine cloth; *nirmale*—spotless; *nūtne*—new; *daduḥ*—they gave; *asyai*—to her; *ca*—and; *māna-dāḥ*—the respectful girls.

TRANSLATION

The girls, being very respectful to Devahūti, brought her forth, and after bathing her with valuable oils and ointments, they gave her fine, new, spotless cloth to cover her body.

TEXT 29

भूषणानि परार्ध्यानि वरीयांसि द्युमन्ति च ।
अन्नं सर्वगुणोपेतं पानं चैवामृतासवम् ॥२९॥

bhūṣaṇāni parārdhyāni
varīyāṁsi dyumanti ca
annaṁ sarva-guṇopetaṁ
pānaṁ caivāmṛtāsavam

bhūṣaṇāni—ornaments; *para-ardhyāni*—most valuable; *varīyāṁsi*—very excellent; *dyumanti*—splendid; *ca*—and; *annam*—food; *sarva-guṇa*—all good qualities; *upetam*—containing; *pānam*—beverages; *ca*—and; *eva*—also; *amṛta*—sweet; *āsavam*—intoxicating.

TRANSLATION

They then decorated her with very excellent and valuable jewels, which shone brightly. Next they offered her food containing all good qualities, and a sweet, inebriating drink called āsavam.

PURPORT

Āsavam is an Āyur-vedic medical preparation; it is not a liquor. It is especially made from drugs and is meant to improve metabolism for the healthy condition of the body.

TEXT 30

अथादर्शे स्वमात्मानं स्रग्विणं विरजाम्बरम् ।
विरजं कृतस्वस्त्ययनं कन्याभिर्बहुमानितम् ॥३०॥

athādarśe svam ātmānaṁ
sragviṇaṁ virajāmbaram
virajaṁ kṛta-svastyayanaṁ
kanyābhir bahu-mānitam

atha—then; *ādarśe*—in a mirror; *svam ātmānam*—her own reflection; *srak-viṇam*—adorned with a garland; *viraja*—unsullied; *am-*

baram—robes; *virajam*—freed from all bodily dirt; *kṛta-svasti-ayanam*—decorated with auspicious marks; *kanyābhiḥ*—by the maids; *bahu-mānitam*—very respectfully served.

TRANSLATION

Then in a mirror she beheld her own reflection. Her body was completely freed from all dirt, and she was adorned with a garland. Dressed in unsullied robes and decorated with auspicious marks of tilaka, she was served very respectfully by the maids.

TEXT 31

स्नातं कृतशिरःस्नानं सर्वाभरणभूषितम् ।
निष्कग्रीवं वलयिनं कूजत्काञ्चननूपुरम् ॥३१॥

snātaṁ kṛta-śiraḥ-snānaṁ
sarvābharaṇa-bhūṣitam
niṣka-grīvaṁ valayinaṁ
kūjat-kāñcana-nūpuram

snātam—bathed; *kṛta-śiraḥ*—including the head; *snānam*—bathing; *sarva*—all over; *ābharaṇa*—with ornaments; *bhūṣitam*—decorated; *niṣka*—a gold necklace with a locket; *grīvam*—on the neck; *valayi-nam*—with bangles; *kūjat*—tinkling; *kāñcana*—made of gold; *nū-puram*—ankle bells.

TRANSLATION

Her entire body, including her head, was completely bathed, and she was decorated all over with ornaments. She wore a special necklace with a locket. There were bangles on her wrists and tinkling anklets of gold about her ankles.

PURPORT

The word *kṛta-śiraḥ-snānam* appears here. According to the *smṛti-śāstra's* directions for daily duties, ladies are allowed to bathe daily up to the neck. The hair on the head does not necessarily have to be washed daily because the mass of wet hair may cause a cold. For ladies, therefore, taking a bath up to the neck is ordinarily prescribed, and they take a full bath only on certain occasions. On this occasion Devahūti took a full bath and washed her hair very nicely. When a lady takes an ordinary bath it is called *mala-snāna*, and when she takes a full bath, including the head, it is called *śiraḥ-snāna.* At this time she needs sufficient oil to smear on her head. That is the direction of the commentators of *smṛti-śāstra.*

TEXT 32

श्रोण्योरध्यस्तया काञ्च्या काञ्चन्या बहुरत्नया ।
हारेण च महार्हेण रुचकेन च भूषितम् ॥३२॥

śroṇyor adhyastayā kāñcyā
kāñcanyā bahu-ratnayā
hāreṇa ca mahārheṇa
rucakena ca bhūṣitam

śroṇyoḥ—on the hips; *adhyastayā*—worn; *kāñcyā*—with a girdle; *kāñcanyā*—made of gold; *bahu-ratnayā*—decorated with numerous jewels; *hāreṇa*—with a pearl necklace; *ca*—and; *mahā-arheṇa*—precious; *rucakena*—with auspicious substances; *ca*—and; *bhūṣitam*—adorned.

TRANSLATION

About her hips she wore a girdle of gold, set with numerous jewels, and she was further adorned with a precious pearl necklace and auspicious substances.

PURPORT

Auspicious substances include saffron, *kuṅkuma* and sandalwood pulp. Before taking a bath there are other auspicious substances, such as turmeric mixed with mustard seed oil, which are smeared all over the body. All kinds of auspicious substances were used to bathe Devahūti from top to toe.

TEXT 33

सुदता सुभ्रुवा श्लक्ष्णस्निग्धापाङ्गेन चक्षुषा ।
पद्मकोशस्पृधा नीलैरलकैश्च लसन्मुखम् ॥३३॥

sudatā subhruvā ślakṣṇa-
snigdhāpāṅgena cakṣuṣā
padma-kośa-spṛdhā nīlair
alakaiś ca lasan-mukham

su-datā—with beautiful teeth; *su-bhruvā*—with charming eyebrows; *ślakṣṇa*—lovely; *snigdha*—moist; *apāṅgena*—corners of eyes; *cakṣuṣā*—with eyes; *padma-kośa*—lotus buds; *spṛdhā*—defeating; *nīlaiḥ*—bluish; *alakaiḥ*—with curling hair; *ca*—and; *lasat*—shining; *mukham*—countenance.

TRANSLATION

Her countenance shone, with beautiful teeth and charming eyebrows. Her eyes, distinguished by lovely moist corners, defeated the beauty of lotus buds. Her face was surrounded by dark curling tresses.

PURPORT

According to Vedic culture, white teeth are very much appreciated. Devahūti's white teeth increased the beauty of her face and made it look like a lotus flower. When a face looks very attractive, the eyes are generally compared to lotus petals and the face to a lotus flower.

TEXT 34

यदा सस्मार ऋषभमृषीणां दयितं पतिम् ।
तत्र चास्ते सह स्त्रीभिर्यत्रास्ते स प्रजापतिः ॥३४॥

yadā sasmāra ṛṣabham
ṛṣīṇāṁ dayitaṁ patim
tatra cāste saha strībhir
yatrāste sa prajāpatiḥ

yadā—when; *sasmāra*—she thought of; *ṛṣabham*—the foremost; *ṛṣīṇām*—among the *ṛṣis; dayitam*—dear; *patim*—husband; *tatra*—there; *ca*—and; *āste*—she was present; *saha*—along with; *strībhiḥ*—the maidservants; *yatra*—where; *āste*—was present; *saḥ*—he; *prajā-patiḥ*—the Prajāpati (Kardama).

TRANSLATION

When she thought of her great husband, the best of the sages, Kardama Muni, who was very dear to her, she, along with all the maidservants, at once appeared where he was.

PURPORT

It appears from this verse that in the beginning Devahūti thought herself to be dirty and dressed in a very niggardly way. When her husband asked her to enter the lake, she saw the maidservants, and they took care of her. Everything was done within the water, and as soon as she thought of her beloved husband, Kardama, she was brought before him without delay. These are some of the powers attained by perfect *yogīs;* they can immediately execute anything they desire.

TEXT 35

भर्तुः पुरस्तादात्मानं स्त्रीसहस्रवृतं तदा ।
निशाम्य तद्योगगतिं संशयं प्रत्यपद्यत ॥३५॥

bhartuḥ purastād ātmānaṁ
strī-sahasra-vṛtaṁ tadā
niśāmya tad-yoga-gatiṁ
saṁśayaṁ pratyapadyata

bhartuḥ—of her husband; *purastāt*—in the presence; *ātmānam*—herself; *strī-sahasra*—by a thousand maids; *vṛtam*—surrounded; *tadā*—then; *niśāmya*—seeing; *tat*—his; *yoga-gatim*—yogic power; *saṁśayam pratyapadyata*—she was amazed.

TRANSLATION

She was amazed to find herself surrounded by a thousand maids in the presence of her husband and to witness his yogic power.

PURPORT

Devahūti saw everything miraculously done, yet when brought before her husband she could understand that it was all due to his great yogic mystic power. She understood that nothing was impossible for a *yogī* like Kardama Muni.

TEXTS 36–37

स तां कृतमलस्नानां विभ्राजन्तीमपूर्ववत् ।
आत्मनो बिभ्रतीं रूपं संवीतरुचिरस्तनीम् ॥३६॥
विद्याधरीसहस्रेण सेव्यमानां सुवाससम् ।
जातभावो विमानं तदारोहयदमित्रहन् ॥३७॥

sa tāṁ kṛta-mala-snānāṁ
vibhrājantīm apūrvavat
ātmano bibhratīṁ rūpaṁ
saṁvīta-rucira-stanīm

vidyādharī-sahasreṇa
sevyamānāṁ suvāsasam
jāta-bhāvo vimānaṁ tad
ārohayad amitra-han

saḥ—the sage; *tām*—her (Devahūti); *kṛta-mala-snānām*—bathed clean; *vibhrājantīm*—shining forth; *apūrva-vat*—unprecedentedly; *ātmanaḥ*—her own; *bibhratīm*—possessing; *rūpam*—beauty; *saṁvīta*—girded; *rucira*—charming; *stanīm*—with breasts; *vidyādharī*—of Gandharva girls; *sahasreṇa*—by a thousand; *sevyamānām*—being waited upon; *su-vāsasam*—dressed in excellent robes; *jāta-bhāvaḥ*—struck with fondness; *vimānam*—airplane like a mansion; *tat*—that; *ārohayat*—he put her on board; *amitra-han*—O destroyer of the enemy.

TRANSLATION

The sage could see that Devahūti had washed herself clean and was shining forth as though no longer his former wife. She had regained her own original beauty as the daughter of a prince. Dressed in excellent robes, her charming breasts duly girded, she was waited upon by a thousand Gandharva girls. O destroyer of the enemy, his fondness for her grew, and he placed her on the aerial mansion.

PURPORT

Before her marriage, when Devahūti was brought by her parents before the sage Kardama, she was the perfectly beautiful princess, and Kardama Muni remembered her former beauty. But after her marriage, when she was engaged in the service of Kardama Muni, she neglected to care for her body like a princess, since there was no means for such care; her husband was living in a cottage, and since she was always engaged in serving him, her royal beauty disappeared, and she became just like an ordinary maidservant. Now, after being bathed by the Gandharva girls by the order of Kardama Muni's yogic power, she regained her beauty, and Kardama Muni felt attracted to the beauty she had shown before the marriage. The real beauty of a young woman is her breasts. When Kardama Muni saw the breasts of his wife so nicely decorated, increasing her beauty many times, he was attracted, even though he was a great sage. Śrīpāda Śaṅkarācārya has therefore warned the transcendentalists that one who is after transcendental realization should not be attracted by the raised breasts of a woman because they are nothing but an interaction of fat and blood within the body.

TEXT 38

तस्मिन्नलुप्तमहिमा प्रिययानुरक्तो
विद्याधरीभिरुपचीर्णवपुर्विमाने ।
बभ्राज उत्कचकुमुद्गणवानपीच्य-
स्ताराभिरावृत इवोडुपतिर्नभःस्थः ॥३८॥

tasminn alupta-mahimā priyayānurakto
vidyādharībhir upacīrṇa-vapur vimāne

babhrāja utkaca-kumud-gaṇavān apīcyas
tārābhir āvṛta ivoḍu-patir nabhaḥ-sthaḥ

tasmin—in that; *alupta*—not lost; *mahimā*—glory; *priyayā*—with his beloved consort; *anuraktaḥ*—attached; *vidyādharībhiḥ*—by the Gandharva girls; *upacīrṇa*—waited upon; *vapuḥ*—his person; *vimāne*—on the airplane; *babhrāja*—he shone; *utkaca*—open; *kumut-gaṇa-vān*—the moon, which is followed by rows of lilies; *apīcyaḥ*—very charming; *tārābhiḥ*—by stars; *āvṛtaḥ*—surrounded; *iva*—as; *uḍu-patiḥ*—the moon (the chief of the stars); *nabhaḥ-sthaḥ*—in the sky.

TRANSLATION

Though seemingly attached to his beloved consort while served by the Gandharva girls, the sage did not lose his glory, which was mastery over his self. In the aerial mansion Kardama Muni with his consort shone as charmingly as the moon in the midst of the stars in the sky, which causes rows of lilies to open in ponds at night.

PURPORT

The mansion was in the sky, and therefore the comparison to the full moon and stars is very beautifully composed in this verse. Kardama Muni looked like the full moon, and the girls who surrounded his wife, Devahūti, seemed just like the stars. On a full-moon night the stars and the moon together form a beautiful constellation; similarly, in that aerial mansion in the sky, Kardama Muni with his beautiful wife and the damsels surrounding them appeared like the moon and stars on a full-moon night.

TEXT 39

तेनाष्टलोकपविहारकुलाचलेन्द्र-
द्रोणीस्वनङ्गसखमारुतसौभगासु ।
सिद्धैर्नुतो द्युधुनिपातशिवस्वनासु
रेमे चिरं धनदवल्ललनावरूथी ॥३९॥

tenāṣṭa-lokapa-vihāra-kulācalendra-
droṇīṣv anaṅga-sakha-māruta-saubhagāsu
siddhair nuto dyudhuni-pāta-śiva-svanāsu
reme ciraṁ dhanadaval-lalanā-varūthī

tena—by that airplane; *aṣṭa-loka-pa*—of the predominating deities of the eight heavenly planets; *vihāra*—the pleasure grounds; *kula-acala-indra*—of the king of the mountains (Meru); *droṇīṣu*—in the valleys; *anaṅga*—of passion; *sakha*—the companions; *māruta*—with breezes; *saubhagāsu*—beautiful; *siddhaiḥ*—by the Siddhas; *nutaḥ*—being praised; *dyu-dhuni*—of the Ganges; *pāta*—of the downfall; *śiva-svanāsu*—vibrating with auspicious sounds; *reme*—he enjoyed; *ciram*—for a long time; *dhanada-vat*—like Kuvera; *lalanā*—by damsels; *varūthī*—surrounded.

TRANSLATION

In that aerial mansion he traveled to the pleasure valleys of Mount Meru, which were rendered all the more beautiful by cool, gentle, fragrant breezes that stimulated passion. In these valleys, the treasurer of the gods, Kuvera, surrounded by beautiful women and praised by the Siddhas, generally enjoys pleasure. Kardama Muni also, surrounded by the beautiful damsels and his wife, went there and enjoyed for many, many years.

PURPORT

Kuvera is one of the eight demigods who are in charge of different directions of the universe. It is said that Indra is in charge of the eastern side of the universe, where the heavenly planet, or paradise, is situated. Similarly, Agni is in charge of the southeastern portion of the universe; Yama, the demigod who punishes sinners, is in charge of the southern portion; Nirṛti is in charge of the southwestern part of the universe; Varuṇa, the demigod in charge of the waters, is in charge of the western portion; Vāyu, who controls the air and who has wings to travel in the air, is in charge of the northwestern part of the universe; and Kuvera, the treasurer of the demigods, is in charge of the northern part of the universe. All these demigods take pleasure in the valleys of Mount Meru, which is situated somewhere between the sun and the earth. In the aerial mansion, Kardama Muni traveled throughout the eight directions controlled by the different demigods described above, and as the demigods go to Mount Meru, he also went there to enjoy life. When one is surrounded by young, beautiful girls, sex stimulation naturally becomes prominent. Kardama Muni was sexually stimulated, and he enjoyed his wife for many, many years in that part of Mount Meru. But his sex indulgence was praised by many, many Siddhas, beings who have attained perfection, because it was intended to produce good progeny for the good of universal affairs.

TEXT 40

वैश्रम्भके सुरसने नन्दने पुष्पभद्रके ।
मानसे चैत्ररथ्ये च स रेमे रामया रतः ॥४०॥

vaiśrambhake surasane
nandane puṣpabhadrake
mānase caitrarathye ca
sa reme rāmayā rataḥ

vaiśrambhake—in the Vaiśrambhaka garden; *surasane*—in Surasana; *nandane*—in Nandana; *puṣpabhadrake*—in Puṣpabhadraka; *mānase*—by the Mānasa-sarovara Lake; *caitrarathye*—in Caitrarathya; *ca*—and; *saḥ*—he; *reme*—enjoyed; *rāmayā*—by his wife; *rataḥ*—satisfied.

TRANSLATION

Satisfied by his wife, he enjoyed in that aerial mansion not only on Mount Meru but in different gardens known as Vaiśrambhaka, Surasana, Nandana, Puṣpabhadraka and Caitrarathya, and by the Mānasa-sarovara Lake.

TEXT 41

भ्राजिष्णुना विमानेन कामगेन महीयसा ।
वैमानिकानत्यशेत चरँल्लोकान् यथानिलः ॥४१॥

bhrājiṣṇunā vimānena
kāma-gena mahīyasā

vaimānikān atyaśeta
caraṁl lokān yathānilaḥ

bhrājiṣṇunā—splendid; *vimānena*—with the airplane; *kāma-gena*—which flew according to his desire; *mahīyasā*—very great; *vaimānikān*—the demigods in their airplanes; *atyaśeta*—he surpassed; *caran*—traveling; *lokān*—through the planets; *yathā*—like; *anilaḥ*—the air.

TRANSLATION

He traveled in that way through the various planets, as the air passes uncontrolled in every direction. Coursing through the air in that great and splendid aerial mansion, which could fly at his will, he surpassed even the demigods.

PURPORT

The planets occupied by the demigods are restricted to their own orbits, but Kardama Muni, by his yogic power, could travel all over the different directions of the universe without restriction. The living entities who are within the universe are called conditioned souls; that is, they are not free to move everywhere. We are inhabitants of this earthly globe; we cannot move freely to other planets. In the modern age, man is trying to go to other planets, but so far he has been unsuccessful. It is not possible to travel to any other planets because by the laws of nature even the demigods cannot move from one planet to another. But Kardama Muni, by his yogic power, could surpass the strength of the demigods and travel in space in all directions. The comparison here is very suitable. The words *yathā anilaḥ* indicate that as the air is free to move anywhere without restriction, so Kardama Muni unrestrictedly traveled in all directions of the universe.

TEXT 42

किं दुरापादनं तेषां पुंसामुद्दामचेतसाम् ।
यैराश्रितस्तीर्थपदश्चरणो व्यसनात्ययः ॥४२॥

kiṁ durāpādanaṁ teṣāṁ
puṁsām uddāma-cetasām

yair āśritas tīrtha-padaś
caraṇo vyasanātyayaḥ

kim—what; *durāpādanam*—difficult to achieve; *teṣām*—for those; *puṁsām*—men; *uddāma-cetasām*—who are determined; *yaiḥ*—by whom; *āśritaḥ*—taken refuge; *tīrtha-padaḥ*—of the Supreme Personality of Godhead; *caraṇaḥ*—feet; *vyasana-atyayaḥ*—which vanquish dangers.

TRANSLATION

What is difficult to achieve for determined men who have taken refuge of the Supreme Personality of Godhead's lotus feet? His feet are the source of sacred rivers like the Ganges, which put an end to the dangers of mundane life.

PURPORT

The words *yair āśritas tīrtha-padaś caraṇaḥ* are significant here. The Supreme Personality of Godhead is known as *tīrtha-pāda.* The Ganges is called a sacred river because it emanates from the toe of Viṣṇu. The Ganges is meant to eradicate all the material distresses of the conditioned souls. For any living entity, therefore, who has taken shelter of the holy lotus feet of the Lord, nothing is impossible. Kardama Muni is special not because he was a great mystic, but because he was a great devotee. Therefore it is said here that for a great devotee like Kardama Muni, nothing is impossible. Although *yogīs* can perform wonderful feats, as Kardama has already displayed, Kardama was more than a *yogī* because he was a great devotee of the Lord; therefore he was more glorious than an ordinary *yogī.* As it is confirmed in *Bhagavad-gītā,* "Out of the many *yogīs,* he who is a devotee of the Lord is first class." For a person like Kardama Muni there is no question of being conditioned; he was already a liberated soul and better than the demigods, who are also conditioned. Although he was enjoying with his wife and many other women, he was above material, conditional life. Therefore the word *vyasanātyayaḥ* is used to indicate that he was beyond the position of a conditioned soul. He was transcendental to all material limitations.

TEXT 43

प्रेक्षयित्वा भुवो गोलं पत्न्यै यावान् स्वसंस्थया ।
बह्वाश्चर्यं महायोगी स्वाश्रमाय न्यवर्तत ॥४३॥

prekṣayitvā bhuvo golaṁ
patnyai yāvān sva-saṁsthayā
bahv-āścaryaṁ mahā-yogī
svāśramāya nyavartata

prekṣayitvā—after showing; *bhuvaḥ*—of the universe; *golam*—the globe; *patnyai*—to his wife; *yāvān*—as much; *sva-saṁsthayā*—with its arrangements; *bahu-āścaryam*—full of many wonders; *mahā-yogī*—the great *yogī* (Kardama); *sva-āśramāya*—to his own hermitage; *nyavartata*—returned.

TRANSLATION

After showing his wife the globe of the universe and its different arrangements, full of many wonders, the great yogī Kardama Muni returned to his own hermitage.

PURPORT

All the planets are here described as *gola*, round. Every planet is round, and each planet is a different shelter, just like islands in the great ocean. Planets are sometimes called *dvīpa* or *varṣa*. This earth planet is called Bhārata-varṣa because it was ruled by King Bharata. Another significant word used in this verse is *bahv-āścaryam*, "many wonderful things." This indicates that the different planets are distributed all over the universe in the eight directions, and each and every one of them is wonderful in itself. Each planet has its particular climatic influences and particular types of inhabitants and is completely equipped with everything, including the beauty of the seasons. In the *Brahma-saṁhitā* (5.40) it is similarly stated, *vibhūti-bhinnam:* on each and every planet there are different opulences. It cannot be expected that one planet is exactly like another. By God's grace, by nature's law, each and every planet is made differently and has different wonderful features. All such wonders were personally experienced by Kardama Muni while he traveled with his wife, yet he could return again to his humble hermitage. He showed his princess-wife that although he was living in the hermitage, he had the power to go everywhere and do anything by mystic *yoga*. That is the perfection of *yoga*. One cannot become a perfect *yogī* simply by showing some sitting postures, nor by such sitting postures or so-called meditation can one become God, as is being advertised. Foolish persons are misled into believing that simply by some caricature of meditation and sitting postures one can become God within six months.

Here is the example of a perfect *yogī;* he could travel all over the universe. Similarly, there is a description of Durvāsā Muni, who also traveled in space. Actually, the perfect *yogī* can do that. But even if one can travel all over the universe and show wonderful feats like Kardama Muni, he cannot be compared to the Supreme Personality of Godhead, whose power and inconceivable energy can never be attained by any conditioned or liberated soul. By the actions of Kardama Muni we can understand that in spite of his immense mystic power, he remained a devotee of the Lord. That is the real position of every living entity.

TEXT 44

विभज्य नवधात्मानं मानवीं सुरतोत्सुकाम् ।
रामां निरमयन् रेमे वर्षपूगान्मुहूर्तवत् ॥४४॥

vibhajya navadhātmānaṁ
mānavīṁ suratotsukām
rāmāṁ niramayan reme
varṣa-pūgān muhūrtavat

vibhajya—having divided; *nava-dhā*—into nine; *ātmānam*—himself; *mānavīm*—the daughter of Manu (Devahūti); *surata*—for sex life; *utsukām*—who was eager; *rāmām*—to his wife; *niramayan*—giving pleasure; *reme*—he enjoyed; *varṣa-pūgān*—for many years; *muhūrta-vat*—like a moment.

TRANSLATION

After coming back to his hermitage, he divided himself into nine personalities just to give pleasure to Devahūti, the daughter

of Manu, who was eager for sex life. In that way he enjoyed with her for many, many years, which passed just like a moment.

PURPORT

Here the daughter of Svāyambhuva Manu, Devahūti, is described as *suratotsuka.* After traveling with her husband all over the universe, in Mount Meru and the beautiful gardens of the heavenly kingdoms, she naturally became sexually stimulated, and in order to satisfy her sexual desire, Kardama Muni expanded himself into nine forms. Instead of one, he became nine, and nine persons had sexual intercourse with Devahūti for many, many years. It is understood that the sexual appetite of a woman is nine times greater than that of a man. That is clearly indicated here. Otherwise, Kardama Muni would have had no reason to expand himself into nine. Here is another example of yogic power. As the Supreme Personality of Godhead can expand Himself in millions of forms, a *yogī* can also expand up to nine forms, but not more than that. Another example is that of Saubhari Muni; he also expanded himself into eight forms. But however powerful a *yogī* may be, he cannot expand himself into more than eight or nine forms. The Supreme Personality of Godhead, however, can expand Himself into millions of forms, *ananta-rūpa*—innumerable, countless forms—as stated in the *Brahma-saṁhitā.* No one can compare to the Supreme Personality of Godhead by any conceivable energetic manifestation of power.

TEXT 45

तस्मिन् विमान उत्कृष्टां शय्यां रतिकरीं श्रिता ।
न चाबुध्यत तं कालं पत्यापीच्येन सङ्गता ॥४५॥

tasmin vimāna utkṛṣṭāṁ
śayyāṁ rati-karīṁ śritā
na cābudhyata taṁ kālaṁ
patyāpīcyena saṅgatā

tasmin—in that; *vimāne*—airplane; *utkṛṣṭām*—excellent; *śayyām*—a bed; *rati-karīm*—increasing sexual desires; *śritā*—situated on; *na*—not;

ca—and; *abudhyata*—she noticed; *tam*—that; *kālam*—time; *patyā*—with her husband; *apīcyena*—most handsome; *saṅgatā*—in company.

TRANSLATION

In that aerial mansion, Devahūti, in the company of her handsome husband, situated on an excellent bed that increased sexual desires, could not realize how much time was passing.

PURPORT

Sex indulgence is so enjoyable for materialistic people that when they engage in such activities they forget how time is passing. Saint Kardama and Devahūti, in their sex indulgence, also forgot how time was passing by.

TEXT 46

एवं योगानुभावेन दम्पत्यो रममाणयोः ।
शतं व्यतीयुः शरदः कामलालसयोर्मनाक् ॥४६॥

evaṁ yogānubhāvena
dam-patyo ramamāṇayoḥ
śataṁ vyatīyuḥ śaradaḥ
kāma-lālasayor manāk

evam—thus; *yoga-anubhāvena*—by yogic powers; *dam-patyoḥ*—the couple; *ramamāṇayoḥ*—while enjoying themselves; *śatam*—a hundred; *vyatīyuḥ*—passed; *śaradaḥ*—autumns; *kāma*—sexual pleasure; *lālasa-yoḥ*—who were eagerly longing for; *manāk*—like a short time.

TRANSLATION

While the couple, who eagerly longed for sexual pleasure, were thus enjoying themselves by virtue of mystic powers, a hundred autumns passed like a brief span of time.

TEXT 47

तस्यामाधत्त रेतस्तां भावयन्नात्मनात्मवित् ।
नोधा विधाय रूपं स्वं सर्वसङ्कल्पविद्विभुः ॥४७॥

tasyām ādhatta retas tāṁ
bhāvayann ātmanātma-vit
nodhā vidhāya rūpaṁ svaṁ
sarva-saṅkalpa-vid vibhuḥ

tasyām—in her; *ādhatta*—he deposited; *retaḥ*—semen; *tām*—her; *bhāvayan*—regarding; *ātmanā*—as half of himself; *ātma-vit*—a knower of spirit soul; *nodhā*—into nine; *vidhāya*—having divided; *rūpam*—body; *svam*—his own; *sarva-saṅkalpa-vit*—the knower of all desires; *vibhuḥ*—the powerful Kardama.

TRANSLATION

The powerful Kardama Muni was the knower of everyone's heart, and he could grant whatever one desired. Knowing the spiritual soul, he regarded her as half of his body. Dividing himself into nine forms, he impregnated Devahūti with nine discharges of semen.

PURPORT

Since Kardama Muni could understand that Devahūti wanted many children, at the first chance he begot nine children at one time. He is described here as *vibhu*, the most powerful master. By his yogic power he could at once produce nine daughters in the womb of Devahūti.

TEXT 48

अतः सा सुषुवे सद्यो देवहूतिः स्त्रियः प्रजाः ।
सर्वास्ताश्चारुसर्वाङ्ग्यो लोहितोत्पलगन्धयः ॥४८॥

ataḥ sā suṣuve sadyo
devahūtiḥ striyaḥ prajāḥ
sarvās tāś cāru-sarvāṅgyo
lohitotpala-gandhayaḥ

ataḥ—then; *sā*—she; *suṣuve*—gave birth; *sadyaḥ*—on the same day; *devahūtiḥ*—Devahūti; *striyaḥ*—females; *prajāḥ*—progeny; *sarvāḥ*—all; *tāḥ*—they; *cāru-sarva-aṅgyaḥ*—charming in every limb; *lohita*—red; *utpala*—like the lotus; *gandhayaḥ*—fragrant.

TRANSLATION

Immediately afterward, on the same day, Devahūti gave birth to nine female children, all charming in every limb and fragrant with the scent of the red lotus flower.

PURPORT

Devahūti was too sexually excited, and therefore she discharged more ova, and nine daughters were born. It is said in the *smṛti-śāstra* as well as in the *Āyur-veda* that when the discharge of the male is greater, male children are begotten, but when the discharge of the female is greater, female children are begotten. It appears from the circumstances that Devahūti was more sexually excited, and therefore she had nine daughters at once. All the daughters, however, were very beautiful, and their bodies were nicely formed; each resembled a lotus flower and was fragrant like a lotus.

TEXT 49

पतिं सा प्रव्रजिष्यन्तं तदालक्ष्योशती बहिः ।
स्मयमाना विक्लवेन हृदयेन विदूयता ॥४९॥

patiṁ sā pravrajiṣyantaṁ
tadālakṣyośatī bahiḥ
smayamānā viklavena
hṛdayena vidūyatā

patim—her husband; *sā*—she; *pravrajiṣyantam*—going to leave home; *tadā*—then; *ālakṣya*—after seeing; *uśatī*—beautiful; *bahiḥ*—outwardly; *smayamānā*—smiling; *viklavena*—agitated; *hṛdayena*—with a heart; *vidūyatā*—being distressed.

TRANSLATION

When she saw her husband about to leave home, she smiled externally, but at heart she was agitated and distressed.

PURPORT

Kardama Muni finished his household affairs quickly by his mystic power. The building of the castle in the air, traveling all over the universe with his wife in the company of beautiful girls, and begetting of children were finished, and now, according to his promise to leave home for his real concern of spiritual realization after impregnating his wife, he was about to go away. Seeing her husband about to leave, Devahūti was very disturbed, but to satisfy her husband she was smiling. The example of Kardama Muni should be understood very clearly; a person whose main concern is Kṛṣṇa consciousness, even if he is entrapped in household life, should always be ready to leave household enticement as soon as possible.

TEXT 50

लिखन्त्यधोमुखी भूमिं पदा नखमणिश्रिया ।
उवाच ललितां वाचं निरुध्याश्रुकलां शनैः ॥५०॥

likhanty adho-mukhī bhūmiṁ
padā nakha-maṇi-śriyā
uvāca lalitāṁ vācaṁ
nirudhyāśru-kalāṁ śanaiḥ

likhantī—scratching; *adhaḥ-mukhī*—her head bent down; *bhūmim*—the ground; *padā*—with her foot; *nakha*—nails; *maṇi*—gemlike; *śriyā*—with radiant; *uvāca*—she spoke; *lalitām*—charming; *vācam*—accents; *nirudhya*—suppressing; *aśru-kalām*—tears; *śanaiḥ*—slowly.

TRANSLATION

She stood and scratched the ground with her foot, which was radiant with the luster of her gemlike nails. Her head bent down, she spoke in slow yet charming accents, suppressing her tears.

PURPORT

Devahūti was so beautiful that her toenails appeared just like pearls, and as she scratched the ground it appeared as if pearls had been thrown on the ground. When a woman scratches the ground with her foot, it is a sign that her mind is very disturbed. These signs were sometimes exhibited by the *gopīs* before Kṛṣṇa. When the *gopīs* came in the dead of night and Kṛṣṇa asked them to return to their homes, the *gopīs* also scratched the ground like this because their minds were very disturbed.

TEXT 51

देवहूतिरुवाच

सर्वं तद्भगवान्मह्यमुपोवाह प्रतिश्रुतम् ।
अथापि मे प्रपन्नाया अभयं दातुमर्हसि ॥५१॥

devahūtir uvāca
sarvaṁ tad bhagavān mahyam
upovāha pratiśrutam
athāpi me prapannāyā
abhayaṁ dātum arhasi

devahūtiḥ—Devahūti; *uvāca*—said; *sarvam*—all; *tat*—that; *bhagavān*—Your Lordship; *mahyam*—for me; *upovāha*—has been fulfilled; *pratiśrutam*—promised; *atha api*—yet; *me*—unto me; *prapannāyai*—unto one who has surrendered; *abhayam*—fearlessness; *dātum*—to give; *arhasi*—you deserve.

TRANSLATION

Śrī Devahūti said: My lord, you have fulfilled all the promises you gave me, yet because I am your surrendered soul, you should give me fearlessness too.

PURPORT

Devahūti requested her husband to grant her something without fear. As a wife, she was a fully surrendered soul to her husband, and it is the responsibility of the husband to give his wife fearlessness. How one awards fearlessness to his subordinate is mentioned in the Fifth Canto of *Śrīmad-Bhāgavatam.* One who cannot get free from the clutches of death is dependent, and he should not become a spiritual master, nor a husband, nor a kinsman, nor a father, nor a mother, etc. It is the duty of the superior to give fearlessness to the subordinate. To take charge of someone, therefore, either as father, mother, spiritual master, relative or husband, one must accept the responsibility to give his ward freedom from the fearful situation of material existence. Material existence is always fearful and full of anxiety. Devahūti is saying, "You have given me all sorts of material comforts by your yogic power, and since you are now prepared to go away, you must give me your last award so that I may get free from this material, conditional life."

TEXT 52

ब्रह्मन्दुहितृभिस्तुभ्यं विमृग्याः पतयः समाः ।
कश्चित्स्यान्मे विशोकाय त्वयि प्रव्रजिते वनम् ।।५२।।

brahman duhitṛbhis tubhyaṁ
vimṛgyāḥ patayaḥ samāḥ
kaścit syān me viśokāya
tvayi pravrajite vanam

brahman—my dear *brāhmaṇa; duhitṛbhiḥ*—by the daughters themselves; *tubhyam*—for you; *vimṛgyāḥ*—to be found out; *patayaḥ*—husbands; *samāḥ*—suitable; *kaścit*—someone; *syāt*—there should be; *me*—my; *viśokāya*—for solace; *tvayi*—when you; *pravrajite*—departed; *vanam*—to the forest.

TRANSLATION

My dear brāhmaṇa, as far as your daughters are concerned, they will find their own suitable husbands and go away to their respective homes. But who will give me solace after your departure as a sannyāsī?

PURPORT

It is said that the father himself becomes the son in another form. The father and son are therefore considered to be nondifferent. A widow who has her son is actually not a widow, because she has the representative of her husband. Similarly, Devahūti is indirectly asking Kardama Muni to leave a representative so that in his absence she might be relieved of her anxieties by a suitable son. A householder is not expected to remain at home for all his days. After getting his sons and daughters married, a householder can retire from household life, leaving his wife in the charge of the grown-up sons. That is the social convention of the Vedic system. Devahūti is indirectly asking that in his absence from home there be at least one male child to give her relief from her anxieties. This relief means spiritual instruction. Relief does not mean material comforts. Material comforts will end with the end of the body, but spiritual instruction will not end; it will go on with the spirit soul. Instruction in spiritual advancement is necessary, but without having a worthy son, how could Devahūti advance in spiritual knowledge? It is the duty of the husband to liquidate his debt to his wife. The wife gives her sincere service to the husband, and he becomes indebted to her because one cannot accept service from his subordinate without giving him something in exchange. The spiritual master cannot accept service from a disciple without awarding him spiritual instruction. That is the reciprocation of love and duty. Thus Devahūti reminds her husband, Kardama Muni, that she has rendered him faithful service. Even considering the situation on the basis of liquidating his debt toward his wife, he must give a male child before he leaves. Indirectly, Devahūti requests her husband to remain at home a few days more, or at least until a male child is born.

TEXT 53

एतावतालं कालेन व्यतिक्रान्तेन मे प्रभो ।
इन्द्रियार्थप्रसङ्गेन परित्यक्तपरात्मनः ॥५३॥

etāvatālaṁ kālena
vyatikrāntena me prabho
indriyārtha-prasaṅgena
parityakta-parātmanaḥ

etāvatā—so much; *alam*—for nothing; *kālena*—time; *vyatikrāntena*—passed by; *me*—my; *prabho*—O my lord; *indriya-artha*—sense gratification; *prasaṅgena*—in the matter of indulging; *parityakta*—disregarding; *para-ātmanaḥ*—knowledge of the Supreme Lord.

TRANSLATION

Until now we have simply wasted so much of our time in sense gratification, neglecting to cultivate knowledge of the Supreme Lord.

PURPORT

Human life is not meant to be wasted, like that of the animals, in sense gratificatory activities. Animals always engage in sense gratification—eating, sleeping, fearing and mating—but that is not the engagement of the human being, although, because of the material body, there is need of sense gratification according to a regulative principle. So, in effect, Devahūti said to her husband: "So far we have these daughters, and we have enjoyed material life in the aerial mansion, traveling all over the universe. These boons have come by your grace, but they have all been for sense gratification. Now there must be something for my spiritual advancement."

TEXT 54

इन्द्रियार्थेषु सज्जन्त्या प्रसङ्गस्त्वयि मे कृतः ।
अजानन्त्या परं भावं तथाप्यस्त्वभयाय मे ॥५४॥

indriyārtheṣu sajjantyā
prasaṅgas tvayi me kṛtaḥ
ajānantyā paraṁ bhāvaṁ
tathāpy astv abhayāya me

indriya-artheṣu—to sense gratification; *sajjantyā*—being attached; *prasaṅgaḥ*—affinity; *tvayi*—for you; *me*—by me; *kṛtaḥ*—was done; *ajānantyā*—not knowing; *param bhāvam*—your transcendent situation; *tathā api*—nonetheless; *astu*—let it be; *abhayāya*—for fearlessness; *me*—my.

TRANSLATION

Not knowing your transcendental situation, I have loved you while remaining attached to the objects of the senses. Nonetheless, let the affinity I have developed for you rid me of all fear.

PURPORT

Devahūti is lamenting her position. As a woman, she had to love someone. Somehow or other, she came to love Kardama Muni, but without knowing of his spiritual advancement. Kardama Muni could understand Devahūti's heart; generally all women desire material enjoyment. They are called less intelligent because they are mostly prone to material enjoyment. Devahūti laments because her husband had given her the best kind of material enjoyment, but she did not know that he was so advanced in spiritual realization. Her plea was that even though she did not know the glories of her great husband, because she had taken shelter of him she must be delivered from material entanglement. Association with a great personality is most important. In *Caitanya-caritāmṛta* Lord Caitanya says that *sādhu-saṅga*, the association of a great saintly person, is very important, because even if one is not advanced in knowledge, simply by association with a great saintly person one can immediately make considerable advancement in spiritual life. As a woman, as an ordinary wife, Devahūti became attached to Kardama Muni in order to satisfy her sense enjoyment and other material necessities, but actually she associated with a great personality. Now she understood this, and she wanted to utilize the advantage of the association of her great husband.

TEXT 55

सङ्गो यः संसृतेर्हेतुरसत्सु विहितोऽधिया ।
स एव साधुषु कृतो निःसङ्गत्वाय कल्पते ॥५५॥

saṅgo yaḥ saṁsṛter hetur
asatsu vihito 'dhiyā
sa eva sādhuṣu kṛto
niḥsaṅgatvāya kalpate

saṅgaḥ—association; *yaḥ*—which; *saṁsṛteḥ*—of the cycle of birth and death; *hetuḥ*—the cause; *asatsu*—with those engaged in sense gratification; *vihitaḥ*—done; *adhiyā*—through ignorance; *saḥ*—the same thing; *eva*—certainly; *sādhuṣu*—with saintly persons; *kṛtaḥ*—performed; *niḥsaṅgatvāya*—to liberation; *kalpate*—leads.

TRANSLATION

Association for sense gratification is certainly the path of bondage. But the same type of association, performed with a saintly person, leads to the path of liberation, even if performed without knowledge.

PURPORT

The association of a saintly person in any way bears the same result. For example, Lord Kṛṣṇa met many kinds of living entities, and some treated Him as an enemy, and some treated Him as an agent for sense gratification. It is generally said that the *gopīs* were attached to Kṛṣṇa for sense attractions, and yet they became first-class devotees of the Lord. Kaṁsa, Śiśupāla, Dantavakra and other demons, however, were related to Kṛṣṇa as enemies. But whether they associated with Kṛṣṇa as enemies or for sense gratification, out of fear or as pure devotees, they all got liberation. That is the result of association with the Lord. Even if one does not understand who He is, the results have the same efficacy. Association with a great saintly person also results in liberation, just as whether one goes toward fire knowingly or unknowingly, the fire will make one warm. Devahūti expressed her gratefulness, for although she wanted to associate with Kardama Muni only for sense gratification, because he was spiritually great she was sure to be liberated by his benediction.

TEXT 56

नेह यत्कर्म धर्माय न विरागाय कल्पते ।
न तीर्थपदसेवायै जीवन्नपि मृतो हि सः ।।५६।।

neha yat karma dharmāya
na virāgāya kalpate
na tīrtha-pada-sevāyai
jīvann api mṛto hi saḥ

na—not; *iha*—here; *yat*—which; *karma*—work; *dharmāya*—for perfection of religious life; *na*—not; *virāgāya*—for detachment; *kal-*

pate—leads; *na*—not; *tīrtha-pada*—of the Lord's lotus feet; *sevāyai*—to devotional service; *jīvan*—living; *api*—although; *mṛtaḥ*—dead; *hi*—indeed; *saḥ*—he.

TRANSLATION

Anyone whose work is not meant to elevate him to religious life, anyone whose religious ritualistic performances do not raise him to renunciation, and anyone situated in renunciation that does not lead him to devotional service to the Supreme Personality of Godhead, must be considered dead, although he is breathing.

PURPORT

Devahūti's statement is that since she was attached to living with her husband for sense gratification, which does not lead to liberation from material entanglement, her life was simply a waste of time. Any work one performs that does not lead to the state of religious life is useless activity. Everyone is by nature inclined to some sort of work, and when that work leads one to religious life and religious life leads one to renunciation and renunciation leads one to devotional service, one attains the perfection of work. As stated in *Bhagavad-gītā*, any work that does not lead ultimately to the standard of devotional service is a cause of bondage in the material world. *Yajñārthāt karmaṇo 'nyatra loko 'yaṁ karma-bandhanaḥ.* Unless one is gradually elevated to the position of devotional service, beginning from his natural activity, he is to be considered a dead body. Work which does not lead one to the understanding of Kṛṣṇa consciousness is considered useless.

TEXT 57

साहं भगवतो नूनं वञ्चिता मायया दृढम् ।
यत्त्वां विमुक्तिदं प्राप्य न मुमुक्षेय बन्धनात् ॥५७॥

sāhaṁ bhagavato nūnaṁ
vañcitā māyayā dṛḍham
yat tvāṁ vimuktidaṁ prāpya
na mumukṣeya bandhanāt

sā—that very person; *aham*—I am; *bhagavataḥ*—of the Lord; *nūnam*—surely; *vañcitā*—cheated; *māyayā*—by the illusory energy; *dṛḍham*—solidly; *yat*—because; *tvām*—you; *vimukti-dam*—who gives liberation; *prāpya*—having attained; *na mumukṣeya*—I have not sought liberation; *bandhanāt*—from material bondage.

TRANSLATION

My lord, surely I have been solidly cheated by the insurmountable illusory energy of the Supreme Personality of Godhead, for in spite of having obtained your association, which gives liberation from material bondage, I did not seek such liberation.

PURPORT

An intelligent man should utilize good opportunities. The first opportunity is the human form of life, and the second opportunity is to take birth in a suitable family where there is cultivation of spiritual knowledge; this is rarely obtained. The greatest opportunity is to have the association of a saintly person. Devahūti was conscious that she was born as the daughter of an emperor. She was sufficiently educated and cultured, and at last she got Kardama Muni, a saintly person and a great *yogī*, as her husband. Still, if she did not get liberation from the entanglement of material energy, then certainly she would be cheated by the insurmountable illusory energy. Actually, the illusory, material energy is cheating everyone. People do not know what they are doing when they worship the material energy in the form of goddess Kālī or Durgā for material boons. They ask, "Mother, give me great riches, give me a good wife, give me fame, give me victory." But such devotees of the goddess Māyā, or Durgā, do not know that they are being cheated by that goddess. Material achievement is actually no achievement because as soon as one is illusioned by the material gifts, he becomes more and more entangled, and there is no question of liberation. One should be intelligent enough to know how to utilize material assets for the purpose of spiritual realization. That is called *karma-yoga* or *jñāna-yoga*. Whatever we have we should use as service to the Supreme Person. It is advised in *Bhagavad-gītā, sva-karmaṇā tam abhyarcya:* one should try to worship the Supreme Personality of Godhead by one's assets. There are many forms of service to the Supreme Lord, and anyone can render service unto Him according to the best of his ability.

Thus end the Bhaktivedanta purports of the Third Canto, Twenty-third Chapter, of the Śrīmad-Bhāgavatam, *entitled "Devahūti's Lamentation."*

CHAPTER TWENTY-FOUR

The Renunciation of Kardama Muni

TEXT 1

मैत्रेय उवाच
निर्वेदवादिनीमेवं मनोर्दुहितरं मुनिः ।
दयालुः शालिनीमाह शुक्लाभिव्याहृतं स्मरन् ॥ १ ॥

maitreya uvāca
nirveda-vādinīm evaṁ
manor duhitaraṁ muniḥ
dayāluḥ śālinīm āha
śuklābhivyāhṛtaṁ smaran

maitreyaḥ—the great sage Maitreya; *uvāca*—said; *nirveda-vādinīm*—who was speaking words full of renunciation; *evam*—thus; *manoḥ*—of Svāyambhuva Manu; *duhitaram*—to the daughter; *muniḥ*—the sage Kardama; *dayāluḥ*—merciful; *śālinīm*—who was worthy of praise; *āha*—replied; *śukla*—by Lord Viṣṇu; *abhivyāhṛtam*—what was said; *smaran*—recalling.

TRANSLATION

Recalling the words of Lord Viṣṇu, the merciful sage Kardama replied as follows to Svāyambhuva Manu's praiseworthy daughter, Devahūti, who was speaking words full of renunciation.

TEXT 2

ऋषिरुवाच
मा खिदो राजपुत्रीत्थमात्मानं प्रत्यनिन्दिते ।
भगवांस्तेऽक्षरो गर्भमदूरात्सम्प्रपत्स्यते ॥ २ ॥

ṛṣir uvāca
mā khido rāja-putrīttham
ātmānaṁ praty anindite
bhagavāṁs te 'kṣaro garbham
adūrāt samprapatsyate

ṛṣiḥ uvāca—the sage said; *mā khidaḥ*—do not be disappointed; *rāja-putri*—O princess; *ittham*—in this way; *ātmānam*—yourself; *prati*—toward; *anindite*—O praiseworthy Devahūti; *bhagavān*—the Supreme Personality of Godhead; *te*—your; *akṣaraḥ*—infallible; *garbham*—womb; *adūrāt*—without delay; *samprapatsyate*—will enter.

TRANSLATION

The sage said: Do not be disappointed with yourself, O princess. You are actually praiseworthy. The infallible Supreme Personality of Godhead will shortly enter your womb as your son.

PURPORT

Kardama Muni encouraged his wife not to be sorry, thinking herself unfortunate, because the Supreme Personality of Godhead, by His incarnation, was going to come from her body.

TEXT 3

धृतव्रतासि भद्रं ते दमेन नियमेन च ।
तपोद्रविणदानैश्च श्रद्धया चेश्वरं भज ॥ ३ ॥

dhṛta-vratāsi bhadraṁ te
damena niyamena ca
tapo-draviṇa-dānaiś ca
śraddhayā ceśvaraṁ bhaja

dhṛta-vratā asi—you have undertaken sacred vows; *bhadram te*—may God bless you; *damena*—by control of the senses; *niyamena*—by religious observances; *ca*—and; *tapaḥ*—austerities; *draviṇa*—of money; *dānaiḥ*—by giving in charity; *ca*—and; *śraddhayā*—with great faith; *ca*—and; *īśvaram*—the Supreme Lord; *bhaja*—worship.

TRANSLATION

You have undertaken sacred vows. God will bless you. Hence you should worship the Lord with great faith, through sensory control, religious observances, austerities and gifts of your money in charity.

PURPORT

In order to spiritually advance or to achieve the mercy of the Lord, one must be self-controlled in the following manner: he must be restrained in sense gratification and must follow the rules and regulations of religious principles. Without austerity and penance and without sacrificing one's riches, one cannot achieve the mercy of the Supreme Lord. Kardama Muni advised his wife: "You have to factually engage in devotional service with austerity and penance, following the religious principles and giving charity. Then the Supreme Lord will be pleased with you, and He will come as your son."

TEXT 4

स त्वयाराधितः शुक्लो वितन्वन्मामकं यशः।
छेत्ता ते हृदयग्रन्थिमौदर्यो ब्रह्मभावनः ॥ ४ ॥

sa tvayārādhitaḥ śuklo
vitanvan māmakaṁ yaśaḥ
chettā te hṛdaya-granthim
audaryo brahma-bhāvanaḥ

saḥ—He; *tvayā*—by you; *ārādhitaḥ*—being worshiped; *śuklaḥ*—the Personality of Godhead; *vitanvan*—spreading; *māmakam*—my; *yaśaḥ*—fame; *chettā*—He will cut; *te*—your; *hṛdaya*—of the heart; *granthim*—knot; *audaryaḥ*—your son; *brahma*—knowledge of Brahman; *bhāvanaḥ*—teaching.

TRANSLATION

The Personality of Godhead, being worshiped by you, will spread my name and fame. He will vanquish the knot of your heart by becoming your son and teaching knowledge of Brahman.

PURPORT

When the Supreme Personality of Godhead comes to disseminate spiritual knowledge for the benefit of all people, He generally descends as the son of a devotee, being pleased by the devotee's devotional service. The Supreme Personality of Godhead is the father of everyone. No one, therefore, is His father, but by His inconceivable energy He accepts some of the devotees as His parents and descendants. It is explained here that spiritual knowledge vanquishes the knot of the heart. Matter and spirit are knotted by false ego. This identification of oneself with matter, which is called *hṛdaya-granthi*, exists for all conditioned souls, and it becomes more and more tightened when there is too much affection for sex life. The explanation was given by Lord Ṛṣabha to His sons that this material world is an atmosphere of attraction between male and female. That attraction takes the shape of a knot in the heart, and by material affection it becomes still more tight. For people who hanker after material possessions, society, friendship and love, this knot of affection becomes very strong. It is only by *brahma-bhāvana*—the instruction by which spiritual knowledge is enhanced—that the knot in the heart is cut to pieces. No material weapon is needed to cut this knot, but it requires bona fide spiritual instruction. Kardama Muni instructed his wife, Devahūti, that the Lord would appear as her son and disseminate spiritual knowledge to cut the knot of material identification.

TEXT 5

मैत्रेय उवाच

देवहूत्यपि संदेशं गौरवेण प्रजापतेः ।
सम्यक् श्रद्धाय पुरुषं कूटस्थमभजद्गुरुम् ॥ ५ ॥

maitreya uvāca
devahūty api sandeśaṁ
gauraveṇa prajāpateḥ
samyak śraddhāya puruṣaṁ
kūṭa-stham abhajad gurum

maitreyaḥ uvāca—Maitreya said; *devahūti*—Devahūti; *api*—also; *sandeśam*—the direction; *gauraveṇa*—with great respect; *prajā-*

pateḥ—of Kardama; *samyak*—complete; *śraddhāya*—having faith in; *puruṣam*—the Supreme Personality of Godhead; *kūṭa-stham*—situated in everyone's heart; *abhajat*—worshiped; *gurum*—most worshipable.

TRANSLATION

Śrī Maitreya said: Devahūti was fully faithful and respectful toward the direction of her husband, Kardama, who was one of the Prajāpatis, or generators of human beings in the universe. O great sage, she thus began to worship the master of the universe, the Supreme Personality of Godhead, who is situated in everyone's heart.

PURPORT

This is the process of spiritual realization; one has to receive instruction from a bona fide spiritual master. Kardama Muni was Devahūti's husband, but because he instructed her on how to achieve spiritual perfection, he naturally became her spiritual master also. There are many instances wherein the husband becomes the spiritual master. Lord Śiva also is the spiritual master of his consort, Pārvatī. A husband should be so enlightened that he should become the spiritual master of his wife in order to enlighten her in the advancement of Kṛṣṇa consciousness. Generally *strī,* or woman, is less intelligent than man; therefore, if the husband is intelligent enough, the woman gets a great opportunity for spiritual enlightenment.

Here it is clearly said (*samyak śraddhāya*) that with great faith one should receive knowledge from the spiritual master and with great faith execute the performance of service. Śrīla Viśvanātha Cakravartī Ṭhākura, in his commentary on *Bhagavad-gītā,* has especially stressed the instruction of the spiritual master. One should accept the instruction of the spiritual master as one's life and soul. Whether one is liberated or not liberated, one should execute the instruction of the spiritual master with great faith. It is also stated that the Lord is situated in everyone's heart. One does not have to seek the Lord outside; He is already there. One simply has to concentrate on one's worship in good faith, as instructed by the bona fide spiritual master, and one's efforts will come out successfully. It is also clear that the Supreme Personality of Godhead does not appear as an ordinary child; He appears as He is. As stated in

Bhagavad-gītā, He appears by His own internal potency, *ātma-māyā*. And how does He appear? He appears when pleased by the worship of a devotee. A devotee may ask the Lord to appear as her son. The Lord is already sitting within the heart, and if He comes out from the body of a devotee it does not mean that the particular woman becomes His mother in the material sense. He is always there, but in order to please His devotee, He appears as her son.

TEXT 6

तस्यां बहुतिथे काले भगवान्मधुसूदनः ।
कार्दमं वीर्यमापन्नो जज्ञेऽग्निरिव दारुणि ॥ ६ ॥

tasyāṁ bahu-tithe kāle
bhagavān madhusūdanaḥ
kārdamaṁ vīryam āpanno
jajñe 'gnir iva dāruṇi

tasyām—in Devahūti; *bahu-tithe kāle*—after many years; *bhagavān*—the Supreme Personality of Godhead; *madhu-sūdanaḥ*—the killer of the demon Madhu; *kārdamam*—of Kardama; *vīryam*—the semen; *āpannaḥ*—entered; *jajñe*—He appeared; *agniḥ*—fire; *iva*—like; *dāruṇi*—in wood.

TRANSLATION

After many, many years, the Supreme Personality of Godhead, Madhusūdana, the killer of the demon Madhu, having entered the semen of Kardama, appeared in Devahūti just as fire comes from wood in a sacrifice.

PURPORT

It is clearly stated here that the Lord is always the Supreme Personality of Godhead, although He appeared as the son of Kardama Muni. Fire is already present in wood, but by a certain process, fire is kindled. Similarly, God is all-pervading. He is everywhere, and since He may come out from everything, He appeared in His devotee's semen. Just as an ordinary living entity takes his birth by taking shelter of the semen of a certain living entity, the Supreme Personality of Godhead accepts the shelter of the semen of His devotee and comes out as His son. This manifests His full independence to act in any way, and it does not mean that He is an ordinary living entity forced to take birth in a certain type of womb. Lord Nṛsiṁha appeared from the pillar of Hiraṇyakaśipu's palace, Lord Varāha appeared from the nostril of Brahmā, and Lord Kapila appeared from the semen of Kardama, but this does not mean that the nostril of Brahmā or the pillar of Hiraṇyakaśipu's palace or the semen of Kardama Muni is the source of the appearance of the Lord. The Lord is always the Lord. *Bhagavān madhusūdanaḥ*—He is the killer of all kinds of demons, and He always remains the Lord, even if He appears as the son of a particular devotee. The word *kārdamam* is significant, for it indicates that the Lord had some devotional affection or relationship in devotional service with Kardama and Devahūti. But we should not mistakenly understand that He was born just like an ordinary living entity from the semen of Kardama Muni in the womb of Devahūti.

TEXT 7

अवादयंस्तदा व्योम्नि वादित्राणि घनाघनाः ।
गायन्ति तं स्म गन्धर्वा नृत्यन्त्यप्सरसो मुदा ॥ ७ ॥

avādayaṁs tadā vyomni
vāditrāṇi ghanāghanāḥ
gāyanti taṁ sma gandharvā
nṛtyanty apsaraso mudā

avādayan—sounded; *tadā*—at that time; *vyomni*—in the sky; *vāditrāṇi*—musical instruments; *ghanāghanāḥ*—the rain clouds; *gāyanti*—sang; *tam*—to Him; *sma*—certainly; *gandharvāḥ*—the Gandharvas; *nṛtyanti*—danced; *apsarasaḥ*—the Apsarās; *mudā*—in joyful ecstasy.

TRANSLATION

At the time of His descent on earth, demigods in the form of raining clouds sounded musical instruments in the sky. The celestial musicians, the Gandharvas, sang the glories of the Lord,

while celestial dancing girls known as Apsarās danced in joyful ecstasy.

TEXT 8

पेतुः सुमनसो दिव्याः खेचरैरपवर्जिताः ।
प्रसेदुश्च दिशः सर्वा अम्भांसि च मनांसि च ॥ ८ ॥

petuḥ sumanaso divyāḥ
khe-carair apavarjitāḥ
praseduś ca diśaḥ sarvā
ambhāṁsi ca manāṁsi ca

petuḥ—fell; *sumanasaḥ*—flowers; *divyāḥ*—beautiful; *khe-caraiḥ*—by the demigods who fly in the sky; *apavarjitāḥ*—dropped; *praseduḥ*—became satisfied; *ca*—and; *diśaḥ*—directions; *sarvāḥ*—all; *ambhāṁsi*—waters; *ca*—and; *manāṁsi*—minds; *ca*—and.

TRANSLATION

At the time of the Lord's appearance, the demigods flying freely in the sky showered flowers. All the directions, all the waters and everyone's mind became very satisfied.

PURPORT

It is learned herewith that in the higher sky there are living entities who can travel through the air without being hampered. Although we can travel in outer space, we are hampered by so many impediments, but they are not. We learn from the pages of *Śrīmad-Bhāgavatam* that the inhabitants of the planet called Siddhaloka can travel in space from one planet to another without impediment. They showered flowers on the earth when Lord Kapila, the son of Kardama, appeared.

TEXT 9

तत्कर्दमाश्रमपदं सरस्वत्या परिश्रितम् ।
स्वयम्भूः साकमृषिभिर्मरीच्यादिभिरभ्ययात् ॥ ९ ॥

tat kardamāśrama-padaṁ
sarasvatyā pariśritam
svayambhūḥ sākam ṛṣibhir
marīcy-ādibhir abhyayāt

tat—that; *kardama*—of Kardama; *āśrama-padam*—to the place of the hermitage; *sarasvatyā*—by the River Sarasvatī; *pariśritam*—surrounded; *svayambhūḥ*—Brahmā (the self-born); *sākam*—along with; *ṛṣibhiḥ*—the sages; *marīci*—the great sage Marīci; *ādibhiḥ*—and others; *abhyayāt*—he came there.

TRANSLATION

Brahmā, the first-born living being, went along with Marīci and other sages to the place of Kardama's hermitage, which was surrounded by the River Sarasvatī.

PURPORT

Brahmā is called Svayambhū because he is not born of any material father and mother. He is the first living creature and is born from the lotus which grows from the abdomen of the Supreme Personality of Godhead Garbhodakaśāyī Viṣṇu. Therefore he is called Svayambhū, self-born.

TEXT 10

भगवन्तं परं ब्रह्म सत्त्वेनांशेन शत्रुहन् ।
तत्त्वसंख्यानविज्ञप्त्यै जातं विद्वानजः स्वराट् ॥१०॥

bhagavantaṁ paraṁ brahma
sattvenāṁśena śatru-han
tattva-saṅkhyāna-vijñaptyai
jātaṁ vidvān ajaḥ svarāṭ

bhagavantam—the Lord; *param*—supreme; *brahma*—Brahman; *sattvena*—having an uncontaminated existence; *aṁśena*—by a plenary portion; *śatru-han*—O killer of the enemy, Vidura; *tattva-saṅkhyāna*—

the philosophy of the twenty-four material elements; *vijñaptyai*—for explaining; *jātam*—appeared; *vidvān*—knowing; *ajaḥ*—the unborn (Lord Brahmā); *sva-rāṭ*—independent.

TRANSLATION

Maitreya continued: O killer of the enemy, the unborn Lord Brahmā, who is almost independent in acquiring knowledge, could understand that a portion of the Supreme Personality of Godhead, in His quality of pure existence, had appeared in the womb of Devahūti just to explain the complete state of knowledge known as sāṅkhya-yoga.

PURPORT

In *Bhagavad-gītā*, Fifteenth Chapter, it is stated that the Lord Himself is the compiler of *Vedānta-sūtra*, and He is the perfect knower of *Vedānta-sūtra.* Similarly, the Sāṅkhya philosophy is compiled by the Supreme Personality of Godhead in His appearance as Kapila. There is an imitation Kapila who has a Sāṅkhya philosophical system, but Kapila the incarnation of God is different from that Kapila. Kapila the son of Kardama Muni, in His system of Sāṅkhya philosophy, very explicitly explained not only the material world but also the spiritual world. Brahmā could understand this fact because he is *svarāṭ*, almost independent in receiving knowledge. He is called *svarāṭ* because he did not go to any school or college to learn but learned everything from within. Because Brahmā is the first living creature within this universe, he had no teacher; his teacher was the Supreme Personality of Godhead Himself, who is seated in the heart of every living creature. Brahmā acquired knowledge directly from the Supreme Lord within the heart; therefore he is sometimes called *svarāṭ* and *aja.*

Another important point is stated here. *Sattvenāṁśena:* when the Supreme Personality of Godhead appears, He brings with Him all His paraphernalia of Vaikuṇṭha; therefore His name, His form, His quality, His paraphernalia and His entourage all belong to the transcendental world. Real goodness is in the transcendental world. Here in the material world, the quality of goodness is not pure. Goodness may exist, but there must also be some tinges of passion and ignorance. In the spiritual world thc unalloyed quality of goodness prevails; there the quality of goodness is called *śuddha-sattva*, pure goodness. Another name for *śuddha-sattva* is *vasudeva* because God is born from Vasudeva. Another meaning is that when one is purely situated in the qualities of goodness, he can understand the form, name, quality, paraphernalia and entourage of the Supreme Personality of Godhead. The word *aṁśena* also indicates that the Supreme Personality of Godhead, Kṛṣṇa, appeared as Kapiladeva in a portion of His portion. God expands either as *kalā* or as *aṁśa*. *Aṁśa* means "direct expansion," and *kalā* means "expansion of the expansion." There is no difference between the expansion, the expansion of the expansion, and the Supreme Personality of Godhead directly, as there is no difference between one candle and another—but still the candle from which the others are lit is called the original. Kṛṣṇa, therefore, is called the Parabrahman, or the ultimate Godhead and cause of all causes.

TEXT 11

सभाजयन् विशुद्धेन चेतसा तच्चिकीर्षितम् ।
प्रहृष्यमाणैरसुभिः कर्दमं चेदमभ्यधात् ॥११॥

sabhājayan viśuddhena
cetasā tac-cikīrṣitam
prahṛṣyamāṇair asubhiḥ
kardamaṁ cedam abhyadhāt

sabhājayan—worshiping; *viśuddhena*—pure; *cetasā*—with a heart; *tat*—of the Supreme Personality of Godhead; *cikīrṣitam*—the intended activities; *prahṛṣyamāṇaiḥ*—gladdened; *asubhiḥ*—with senses; *kardamam*—to Kardama Muni; *ca*—and Devahūti; *idam*—this; *abhyadhāt*—spoke.

TRANSLATION

After worshiping the Supreme Lord with gladdened senses and a pure heart for His intended activities as an incarnation, Brahmā spoke as follows to Kardama and Devahūti.

PURPORT

As explained in *Bhagavad-gītā*, Fourth Chapter, anyone who understands the transcendental activities, the appearance and the disappearance of the Supreme Personality of Godhead is to be considered liberated. Brahmā, therefore, is a liberated soul. Although he is in charge of this material world, he is not exactly like the common living entity. Since he is liberated from the majority of the follies of the common living entities, he was in knowledge of the appearance of the Supreme Personality of Godhead, and he therefore worshiped the Lord's activities, and with a glad heart he also praised Kardama Muni because the Supreme Personality of Godhead, as Kapila, had appeared as his son. One who can become the father of the Supreme Personality of Godhead is certainly a great devotee. There is a verse spoken by a *brāhmaṇa* in which he says that he does not know what the *Vedas* and what the *Purāṇas* are, but while others might be interested in the *Vedas* or *Purāṇas*, he is interested in Nanda Mahārāja, who appeared as the father of Kṛṣṇa. The *brāhmaṇa* wanted to worship Nanda Mahārāja because the Supreme Personality of Godhead, as a child, crawled in the yard of his house. These are some of the good sentiments of devotees. If a recognized devotee brings forth the Supreme Personality of Godhead as his son, how he should be praised! Brahmā, therefore, not only worshiped the incarnation of Godhead Kapila but also praised His so-called father, Kardama Muni.

TEXT 12

ब्रह्मोवाच

त्वया मेऽपचितिस्तात कल्पिता निर्व्यलीकतः ।
यन्मे सञ्जगृहे वाक्यं भवान्मानद मानयन् ॥१२॥

brahmovāca
tvayā me 'pacitis tāta
kalpitā nirvyalīkataḥ
yan me sañjagṛhe vākyaṁ
bhavān mānada mānayan

brahmā—Lord Brahmā; *uvāca*—said; *tvayā*—by you; *me*—my; *apacitiḥ*—worship; *tāta*—O son; *kalpitā*—is accomplished; *nirvyalīkataḥ*—

without duplicity; *yat*—since; *me*—my; *sañjagṛhe*—have completely accepted; *vākyam*—instructions; *bhavān*—you; *māna-da*—O Kardama (one who offers honor to others); *mānayan*—respecting.

TRANSLATION

Lord Brahmā said: My dear son Kardama, since you have completely accepted my instructions without duplicity, showing them proper respect, you have worshiped me properly. Whatever instructions you took from me you have carried out, and thereby you have honored me.

PURPORT

Lord Brahmā, as the first living entity within the universe, is supposed to be the spiritual master of everyone, and he is also the father, the creator, of all beings. Kardama Muni is one of the Prajāpatis, or creators of the living entities, and he is also a son of Brahmā. Brahmā praises Kardama because he carried out the orders of the spiritual master *in toto* and without cheating. A conditioned soul in the material world has the disqualification of cheating. He has four disqualifications: he is sure to commit mistakes, he is sure to be illusioned, he is prone to cheat others, and his senses are imperfect. But if one carries out the order of the spiritual master by disciplic succession, or the *paramparā* system, he overcomes the four defects. Therefore, knowledge received from the bona fide spiritual master is not cheating. Any other knowledge which is manufactured by the conditioned soul is cheating only. Brahmā knew well that Kardama Muni exactly carried out the instructions received from him and that he actually honored his spiritual master. To honor the spiritual master means to carry out his instructions word for word.

TEXT 13

एतावत्येव शुश्रूषा कार्या पितरि पुत्रकैः ।
बाढमित्यनुमन्येत गौरवेण गुरोर्वचः ॥१३॥

etāvaty eva śuśrūṣā
kāryā pitari putrakaiḥ
bāḍham ity anumanyeta
gauraveṇa guror vacaḥ

etāvatī—to this extent; *eva*—exactly; *śuśrūṣā*—service; *kāryā*—ought to be rendered; *pitari*—to the father; *putrakaiḥ*—by the sons; *bāḍham iti*—accepting, "Yes, sir"; *anumanyeta*—he should obey; *gauraveṇa*—with due deference; *guroḥ*—of the *guru; vacaḥ*—commands.

TRANSLATION

Sons ought to render service to their father exactly to this extent. One should obey the command of his father or spiritual master with due deference, saying, "Yes, sir."

PURPORT

Two words in this verse are very important; one word is *pitari*, and another word is *guroḥ*. The son or disciple should accept the words of his spiritual master and father without hesitation. Whatever the father and the spiritual master order should be taken without argument: "Yes." There should be no instance in which the disciple or the son says, "This is not correct. I cannot carry it out." When he says that, he is fallen. The father and the spiritual master are on the same platform because a spiritual master is the second father. The higher classes are called *dvija*, twice-born. Whenever there is a question of birth, there must be a father. The first birth is made possible by the actual father, and the second birth is made possible by the spiritual master. Sometimes the father and the spiritual master may be the same man, and sometimes they are different men. In any case, the order of the father or the order of the spiritual master must be carried out without hesitation, with an immediate yes. There should be no argument. That is real service to the father and to the spiritual master. Viśvanātha Cakravartī Ṭhākura has stated that the order of the spiritual master is the life and soul of the disciples. As a man cannot separate his life from his body, a disciple cannot separate the order of the spiritual master from his life. If a disciple follows the instruction of the spiritual master in that way, he is sure to become perfect. This is confirmed in the *Upaniṣads:* the import of Vedic instruction is revealed automatically only to one who has implicit faith in the Supreme Personality of Godhead and in his spiritual master. One may be materially considered an illiterate man, but if he has faith in the spiritual master as well as in the Supreme Personality of Godhead, then the meaning of scriptural revelation is immediately manifested before him.

TEXT 14

इमा दुहितरः सत्यस्तव वत्स सुमध्यमाः ।
सर्गमेतं प्रभावैः स्वैर्बृंहयिष्यन्त्यनेकधा ॥१४॥

imā duhitaraḥ satyas
tava vatsa sumadhyamāḥ
sargam etaṁ prabhāvaiḥ svair
bṛṁhayiṣyanty anekadhā

imāḥ—these; *duhitaraḥ*—daughters; *satyaḥ*—chaste; *tava*—your; *vatsa*—O my dear son; *su-madhyamāḥ*—thin-waisted; *sargam*—creation; *etam*—this; *prabhāvaiḥ*—by descendants; *svaiḥ*—their own; *bṛṁhayiṣyanti*—they will increase; *aneka-dhā*—in various ways.

TRANSLATION

Lord Brahmā then praised Kardama Muni's nine daughters, saying: All your thin-waisted daughters are certainly very chaste. I am sure they will increase this creation by their own descendants in various ways.

PURPORT

In the beginning of creation, Brahmā was concerned more or less with increasing the population, and when he saw that Kardama Muni had already begotten nine nice daughters, he was hopeful that through the daughters many children would come who would take charge of the creative principle of the material world. He was therefore happy to see them. The word *sumadhyamā* means "a good daughter of a beautiful woman." If she has a thin waist, a woman is considered very beautiful. All the daughters of Kardama Muni were of the same beautiful feature.

TEXT 15

अतस्त्वमृषिमुख्येभ्यो यथाशीलं यथारुचि ।
आत्मजाः परिदेह्यद्य विस्तृणीहि यशो भुवि ॥१५॥

atas tvam ṛṣi-mukhyebhyo
yathā-śīlaṁ yathā-ruci

ātmajāḥ paridehy adya
vistṛṇīhi yaśo bhuvi

ataḥ—therefore; *tvam*—you; *ṛṣi-mukhyebhyaḥ*—unto the foremost sages; *yathā-śīlam*—according to temperament; *yathā-ruci*—according to taste; *ātma-jāḥ*—your daughters; *paridehi*—please give away; *adya*—today; *vistṛṇīhi*—spread; *yaśaḥ*—fame; *bhuvi*—over the universe.

TRANSLATION

Therefore, today please give away your daughters to the foremost of the sages, with due regard for the girls' temperaments and likings, and thereby spread your fame all over the universe.

PURPORT

The nine principal *ṛṣis*, or sages, are Marīci, Atri, Aṅgirā, Pulastya, Pulaha, Kratu, Bhṛgu, Vasiṣṭha and Atharvā. All these *ṛṣis* are most important, and Brahmā desired that the nine daughters already born of Kardama Muni be handed over to them. Here two words are used very significantly—*yathā-śīlam* and *yathā-ruci.* The daughters should be handed over to the respective *ṛṣis*, not blindly, but according to the combination of character and taste. That is the art of combining a man and woman. Man and woman should not be united simply on the consideration of sex life. There are many other considerations, especially character and taste. If the taste and character differ between the man and woman, their combination will be unhappy. Even about forty years ago, in Indian marriages, the taste and character of the boy and girl were first of all matched, and then they were allowed to marry. This was done under the direction of the respective parents. The parents used to astrologically determine the character and tastes of the boy and girl, and when they corresponded, the match was selected: "This girl and this boy are just suitable, and they should be married." Other considerations were less important. The same system was also advised in the beginning of the creation by Brahmā: "Your daughters should be handed over to the *ṛṣis* according to taste and character."

According to astrological calculation, a person is classified according to whether he belongs to the godly or demoniac quality. In that way the spouse was selected. A girl of godly quality should be handed over to a boy of godly quality. A girl of demoniac quality should be handed over to a boy of demoniac quality. Then they will be happy. But if the girl is demoniac and the boy is godly, then the combination is incompatible; they cannot be happy in such a marriage. At the present moment, because boys and girls are not married according to quality and character, most marriages are unhappy, and there is divorce.

It is foretold in the Twelfth Canto of the *Bhāgavatam* that in this age of Kali married life will be accepted on the consideration of sex only; when the boy and girl are pleased in sex, they get married, and when there is deficiency in sex, they separate. That is not actual marriage, but a combination of men and women like cats and dogs. Therefore, the children produced in the modern age are not exactly human beings. Human beings must be twice-born. A child is first born of a good father and mother, and then he is born again of the spiritual master and the *Vedas*. The first mother and father bring about his birth into the world; then the spiritual master and the *Vedas* become his second father and mother. According to the Vedic system of marriage for producing children, every man and woman was enlightened in spiritual knowledge, and at the time of their combination to produce a child, everything was scrutinizingly and scientifically done.

TEXT 16

वेदाहमाद्यं पुरुषमवतीर्णं स्वमायया ।
भूतानां शेवधिं देहं बिभ्राणं कपिलं मुने ॥१६॥

vedāham ādyaṁ puruṣam
avatīrṇaṁ sva-māyayā
bhūtānāṁ śevadhiṁ dehaṁ
bibhrāṇaṁ kapilaṁ mune

veda—know; *aham*—I; *ādyam*—the original; *puruṣam*—enjoyer; *avatīrṇam*—incarnated; *sva-māyayā*—by His own internal energy; *bhūtānām*—of all the living entities; *śevadhim*—the bestower of all desired, who is just like a vast treasure; *deham*—the body; *bibhrāṇam*—assuming; *kapilam*—Kapila Muni; *mune*—O sage Kardama.

TRANSLATION

O Kardama, I know that the original Supreme Personality of Godhead has now appeared as an incarnation by His internal energy. He is the bestower of all desired by the living entities, and He has now assumed the body of Kapila Muni.

PURPORT

In this verse we find the words *puruṣam avatīrṇaṁ sva-māyayā.* The Supreme Personality of Godhead is everlastingly, eternally the form of *puruṣa,* the predominator or enjoyer, and when He appears He never accepts anything of this material energy. The spiritual world is a manifestation of His personal, internal potency, whereas the material world is a manifestation of His material, or differentiated, energy. The word *sva-māyayā,* "by His own internal potency," indicates that whenever the Supreme Personality of Godhead descends, He comes in His own energy. He may assume the body of a human being, but that body is not material. In *Bhagavad-gītā,* therefore, it is clearly stated that only fools and rascals, *mūḍhas,* consider the body of Kṛṣṇa to be the body of a common human being. The word *śevadhim* means that He is the original bestower of all the necessities of life upon the living entities. In the *Vedas* also it is stated that He is the chief living entity and that He bestows all the desired necessities of other living entities. Because He is the bestower of the necessities of all others, He is called God. The Supreme is also a living entity; He is not impersonal. As we are individual, the Supreme Personality of Godhead is also individual—but He is the supreme individual. That is the difference between God and the ordinary living entities.

TEXT 17

ज्ञानविज्ञानयोगेन कर्मणामुद्धरन् जटाः ।
हिरण्यकेशः पद्माक्षः पद्ममुद्रापदाम्बुजः ॥१७॥

jñāna-vijñāna-yogena
karmaṇām uddharan jaṭāḥ
hiraṇya-keśaḥ padmākṣaḥ
padma-mudrā-padāmbujaḥ

jñāna—of scriptural knowledge; *vijñāna*—and application; *yogena*—by means of mystic *yoga; karmaṇām*—of material actions; *uddharan*—uprooting; *jaṭāḥ*—the roots; *hiraṇya-keśaḥ*—golden hair; *padma-akṣaḥ*—lotus-eyed; *padma-mudrā*—marked with the sign of the lotus; *pada-ambujaḥ*—having lotus feet.

TRANSLATION

By mystic yoga and the practical application of knowledge from the scriptures, Kapila Muni, who is characterized by His golden hair, His eyes just like lotus petals and His lotus feet, which bear the marks of lotus flowers, will uproot the deep-rooted desire for work in this material world.

PURPORT

In this verse the activities and bodily features of Kapila Muni are very nicely described. The activities of Kapila Muni are forecast herein: He will present the philosophy of Sāṅkhya in such a way that by studying His philosophy people will be able to uproot the deep-rooted desire for *karma*, fruitive activities. Everyone in this material world engages in achieving the fruits of his labor. A man tries to be happy by achieving the fruits of his own honest labor, but actually he becomes more and more entangled. One cannot get out of this entanglement unless he has perfect knowledge, or devotional service.

Those who are trying to get out of the entanglement by speculation are also doing their best, but in the Vedic scriptures we find that if one has taken to the devotional service of the Lord in Kṛṣṇa consciousness, he can very easily uproot the deep-rooted desire for fruitive activities. Sāṅkhya philosophy will be broadcast by Kapila Muni for that purpose. His bodily features are also described herein. *Jñāna* does not refer to ordinary research work. *Jñāna* entails receiving knowledge from the scriptures through the spiritual master by disciplic succession. In the modern age there is a tendency to do research by mental speculation and concoction. But the man who speculates forgets that he himself is subject to the four defects of nature: he is sure to commit mistakes, his senses are imperfect, he is sure to fall into illusion, and he is cheating. Unless one has perfect knowledge from disciplic succession, he simply puts forth some theories of his own creation; therefore he is cheating people. *Jñāna* means knowledge received through disciplic succession from the scriptures, and *vijñāna* means practical application of such knowledge. Kapila Muni's Sāṅkhya system of philosophy is based on *jñāna* and *vijñāna.*

TEXT 18

एष मानवि ते गर्भं प्रविष्टः कैटभार्दनः ।
अविद्यासंशयग्रन्थिं छित्त्वा गां विचरिष्यति ॥१८॥

eṣa mānavi te garbhaṁ
praviṣṭaḥ kaiṭabhārdanaḥ
avidyā-saṁśaya-granthiṁ
chittvā gāṁ vicariṣyati

eṣaḥ—the same Supreme Personality of Godhead; *mānavi*—O daughter of Manu; *te*—your; *garbham*—womb; *praviṣṭaḥ*—has entered; *kaiṭabha-ardanaḥ*—the killer of the demon Kaiṭabha; *avidyā*—of ignorance; *saṁśaya*—and of doubt; *granthim*—the knot; *chittvā*—cutting off; *gām*—the world; *vicariṣyati*—He will travel over.

TRANSLATION

Lord Brahmā then told Devahūti: My dear daughter of Manu, the same Supreme Personality of Godhead who killed the demon Kaiṭabha is now within your womb. He will cut off all the knots of your ignorance and doubt. Then He will travel all over the world.

PURPORT

Here the word *avidyā* is very significant. *Avidyā* means forgetfulness of one's identity. Every one of us is a spirit soul, but we have forgotten. We think, "I am this body." This is called *avidyā. Saṁśaya-granthi* means "doubtfulness." The knot of doubtfulness is tied when the soul identifies with the material world. That knot is also called *ahaṅkāra,* the junction of matter and spirit. By proper knowledge received from the scriptures in disciplic succession and by proper application of that knowledge, one can free himself from this binding combination of matter and spirit. Brahmā assures Devahūti that her son will enlighten her, and after enlightening her He will travel all over the world, distributing the system of Sāṅkhya philosophy.

The word *saṁśaya* means "doubtful knowledge." Speculative and pseudo yogic knowledge is all doubtful. At the present moment the so-called *yoga* system is prosecuted on the understanding that by agitation of the different stations of the bodily construction one can find that he is God. The mental speculators think similarly, but they are all doubtful. Real knowledge is expounded in *Bhagavad-gītā:* "Just become Kṛṣṇa conscious. Just worship Kṛṣṇa and become a devotee of Kṛṣṇa." That is real knowledge, and anyone who follows that system becomes perfect without a doubt.

TEXT 19

अयं सिद्धगणाधीशः साङ्ख्याचार्यैः सुसम्मतः ।
लोके कपिल इत्याख्यां गन्ता ते कीर्तिवर्धनः ॥१९॥

ayaṁ siddha-gaṇādhīśaḥ
sāṅkhyācāryaiḥ susammataḥ
loke kapila ity ākhyāṁ
gantā te kīrti-vardhanaḥ

ayam—this Personality of Godhead; *siddha-gaṇa*—of the perfected sages; *adhīśaḥ*—the head; *sāṅkhya-ācāryaiḥ*—by *ācāryas* expert in Sāṅkhya philosophy; *su-sammataḥ*—approved according to Vedic principles; *loke*—in the world; *kapilaḥ iti*—as Kapila; *ākhyām*—celebrated; *gantā*—He will go about; *te*—your; *kīrti*—fame; *vardhanaḥ*—increasing.

TRANSLATION

Your son will be the head of all the perfected souls. He will be approved by the ācāryas expert in disseminating real knowledge, and among the people He will be celebrated by the name Kapila. As the son of Devahūti, He will increase your fame.

PURPORT

Sāṅkhya philosophy is the philosophical system enunciated by Kapila, the son of Devahūti. The other Kapila, who is not the son of Devahūti, is an imitation. This is the statement of Brahmā, and because we belong to Brahmā's disciplic succession we should accept his statement that the real Kapila is the son of Devahūti and that real Sāṅkhya philosophy is the system of philosophy which He introduced and which will be accepted by the *ācāryas*, the directors of spiritual discipline. The word *susammata* means "accepted by persons who are counted upon to give their good opinion."

TEXT 20

मैत्रेय उवाच
तावाश्वास्य जगत्स्रष्टा कुमारैः सहनारदः ।
हंसो हंसेन यानेन त्रिधामपरमं ययौ ॥२०॥

maitreya uvāca
tāv āśvāsya jagat-sraṣṭā
kumāraiḥ saha-nāradaḥ
haṁso haṁsena yānena
tri-dhāma-paramaṁ yayau

maitreyaḥ uvāca—Maitreya said; *tau*—the couple; *āśvāsya*—having reassured; *jagat-sraṣṭā*—the creator of the universe; *kumāraiḥ*—along with the Kumāras; *saha-nāradaḥ*—with Nārada; *haṁsaḥ*—Lord Brahmā; *haṁsena yānena*—by his swan carrier; *tri-dhāma-paramam*—to the highest planetary system; *yayau*—went.

TRANSLATION

Śrī Maitreya said: After thus speaking to Kardama Muni and his wife Devahūti, Lord Brahmā, the creator of the universe, who is also known as Haṁsa, went back to the highest of the three planetary systems on his swan carrier with the four Kumāras and Nārada.

PURPORT

The words *haṁsena yānena* are very significant here. *Haṁsa-yāna*, the airplane by which Brahmā travels all over outer space, resembles a swan. Brahmā is also known as Haṁsa because he can grasp the essence of everything. His abode is called *tri-dhāma-paramam*. There are three divisions of the universe—the upper planetary system, the middle planetary system and the lower planetary system—but his abode is above even Siddhaloka, the upper planetary system. He returned to his own planet with the four Kumāras and Nārada because they were not going to be married. The other *ṛṣis* who came with him, such as Marīci and Atri, remained there because they were to be married to the daughters of Kardama, but his other sons—Sanat, Sanaka, Sanandana, Sanātana and Nārada—went back with him in his swan-shaped airplane. The four Kumāras and Nārada are *naiṣṭhika-brahmacārīs*. *Naiṣṭhika-brahmacārī* refers to one who never wastes his semen at any time. They were not to attend the marriage ceremony of their other brothers, Marīci and the other sages, and therefore they went back with their father, Haṁsa.

TEXT 21

गते शतधृतौ क्षत्तः कर्दमस्तेन चोदितः ।
यथोदितं स्वदुहितृः प्रादाद्विश्वसृजां ततः ॥२१॥

gate śata-dhṛtau kṣattaḥ
kardamas tena coditaḥ
yathoditaṁ sva-duhitṝḥ
prādād viśva-sṛjāṁ tataḥ

gate—after he departed; *śata-dhṛtau*—Lord Brahmā; *kṣattaḥ*—O Vidura; *kardamaḥ*—Kardama Muni; *tena*—by him; *coditaḥ*—ordered; *yathā-uditam*—as told; *sva-duhitṝḥ*—his own daughters; *prādāt*—handed over; *viśva-sṛjām*—to the creators of the world's population; *tataḥ*—thereafter.

TRANSLATION

O Vidura, after the departure of Brahmā, Kardama Muni, having been ordered by Brahmā, handed over his nine daughters, as instructed, to the nine great sages who created the population of the world.

TEXTS 22–23

मरीचये कलां प्रादादनसूयामथात्रये ।
श्रद्धामङ्गिरसेऽयच्छत्पुलस्त्याय हविर्भुवम् ॥२२॥

पुलहाय गतिं युक्तां क्रतवे च क्रियां सतीम् ।
ख्यातिं च भृगवेऽयच्छद्वसिष्ठायाप्यरुन्धतीम् ॥२३॥

marīcaye kalāṁ prādād
anasūyām athātraye
śraddhām aṅgirase 'yacchat
pulastyāya havirbhuvam

pulahāya gatiṁ yuktāṁ
kratave ca kriyāṁ satīm
khyātiṁ ca bhṛgave 'yacchad
vasiṣṭhāyāpy arundhatīm

marīcaye—unto Marīci; *kalām*—Kalā; *prādāt*—he handed over; *anasūyām*—Anasūyā; *atha*—then; *atraye*—unto Atri; *śraddhām*—Śraddhā; *aṅgirase*—unto Aṅgirā; *ayacchat*—he gave away; *pulastyāya*—unto Pulastya; *havirbhuvam*—Havirbhū; *pulahāya*—unto Pulaha; *gatim*—Gati; *yuktām*—suitable; *kratave*—unto Kratu; *ca*—and; *kriyām*—Kriyā; *satīm*—virtuous; *khyātim*—Khyāti; *ca*—and; *bhṛgave*—unto Bhṛgu; *ayacchat*—he gave away; *vasiṣṭhāya*—unto the sage Vasiṣṭha; *api*—also; *arundhatīm*—Arundhatī.

TRANSLATION

Kardama Muni handed over his daughter Kalā to Marīci, and another daughter, Anasūyā, to Atri. He delivered Śraddhā to Aṅgirā, and Havirbhū to Pulastya. He delivered Gati to Pulaha, the chaste Kriyā to Kratu, Khyāti to Bhṛgu, and Arundhatī to Vasiṣṭha.

TEXT 24

अथर्वणेऽददाच्छान्तिं यया यज्ञो वितन्यते ।
विप्रर्षभान् कृतोद्वाहान् सदारान् समलालयत् ॥२४॥

atharvaṇe 'dadāc chāntiṁ
yayā yajño vitanyate
viprarṣabhān kṛtodvāhān
sadārān samalālayat

atharvaṇe—to Atharvā; *adadāt*—he gave away; *śāntim*—Śānti; *yayā*—by whom; *yajñaḥ*—sacrifice; *vitanyate*—is performed; *vipra-ṛṣabhān*—the foremost *brāhmaṇas; kṛta-udvāhān*—married; *sa-dārān*—with their wives; *samalālayat*—maintained them.

TRANSLATION

He delivered Śānti to Atharvā. Because of Śānti, sacrificial ceremonies are well performed. Thus he got the foremost brāhmaṇas married, and he maintained them along with their wives.

TEXT 25

ततस्त ऋषयः क्षत्तः कृतदारा निमन्त्र्य तम् ।
प्रातिष्ठन्नन्दिमापन्नाः स्वं स्वमाश्रममण्डलम् ॥२५॥

tatas ta ṛṣayaḥ kṣattaḥ
kṛta-dārā nimantrya tam
prātiṣṭhan nandim āpannāḥ
svaṁ svam āśrama-maṇḍalam

tataḥ—then; *te*—they; *ṛṣayaḥ*—the sages; *kṣattaḥ*—O Vidura; *kṛta-dārāḥ*—thus married; *nimantrya*—taking leave of; *tam*—Kardama; *prātiṣṭhan*—they departed; *nandim*—joy; *āpannāḥ*—obtained; *svam svam*—each to his own; *āśrama-maṇḍalam*—hermitage.

TRANSLATION

Thus married, the sages took leave of Kardama and departed full of joy, each for his own hermitage, O Vidura.

TEXT 26

स चावतीर्णं त्रियुगमाज्ञाय विबुधर्षभम् ।
विविक्त उपसङ्गम्य प्रणम्य समभाषत ॥२६॥

sa cāvatīrṇaṁ tri-yugam
ājñāya vibudharṣabham

vivikta upasaṅgamya
praṇamya samabhāṣata

saḥ—the sage Kardama; *ca*—and; *avatīrṇam*—descended; *tri-yugam*—Viṣṇu; *ājñāya*—having understood; *vibudha-ṛṣabham*—the chief of the demigods; *vivikte*—in a secluded place; *upasaṅgamya*—having approached; *praṇamya*—offering obeisances; *samabhāṣata*—he spoke.

TRANSLATION

When Kardama Muni understood that the Supreme Personality of Godhead, the chief of all the demigods, Viṣṇu, had descended, Kardama approached Him in a secluded place, offered obeisances and spoke as follows.

PURPORT

Lord Viṣṇu is called *tri-yuga.* He appears in three *yugas*—Satya, Tretā and Dvāpara—but in Kali-yuga He does not appear. From the prayers of Prahlāda Mahārāja, however, we understand that He appears garbed as a devotee in Kali-yuga. Lord Caitanya is that devotee. Kṛṣṇa appeared in the form of a devotee, but although He never disclosed Himself, Rūpa Gosvāmī could understand His identity, for the Lord cannot hide Himself from a pure devotee. Rūpa Gosvāmī detected Him when he offered his first obeisances to Lord Caitanya. He knew that Lord Caitanya was Kṛṣṇa Himself and therefore offered his obeisances with the following words: "I offer my respects to Kṛṣṇa, who has now appeared as Lord Caitanya." This is also confirmed in the prayers of Prahlāda Mahārāja: in Kali-yuga He does not directly appear, but He appears as a devotee. Viṣṇu, therefore, is known as *tri-yuga.* Another explanation of *tri-yuga* is that He has three pairs of divine attributes, namely power and affluence, piety and renown, and wisdom and dispassion. According to Śrīdhara Svāmī, His three pairs of opulences are complete riches and complete strength, complete fame and complete beauty, and complete wisdom and complete renunciation. There are different interpretations of *tri-yuga,* but it is accepted by all learned scholars that *tri-yuga* means Viṣṇu. When Kardama Muni understood that his son, Kapila, was Viṣṇu Himself, he wanted to offer his obeisances. Therefore, when Kapila was alone he offered his respects and expressed his mind as follows.

TEXT 27

अहो पापच्यमानानां निरये स्वैरमङ्गलैः ।
कालेन भूयसा नूनं प्रसीदन्तीह देवताः ॥२७॥

aho pāpacyamānānāṁ
niraye svair amaṅgalaiḥ
kālena bhūyasā nūnaṁ
prasīdantīha devatāḥ

aho—oh; *pāpacyamānānām*—with those being much afflicted; *niraye*—in the hellish material entanglement; *svaiḥ*—their own; *amaṅgalaiḥ*—by misdeeds; *kālena bhūyasā*—after a long time; *nūnam*—indeed; *prasīdanti*—they are pleased; *iha*—in this world; *devatāḥ*—the demigods.

TRANSLATION

Kardama Muni said: Oh, after a long time the demigods of this universe have become pleased with the suffering souls who are in material entanglement because of their own misdeeds.

PURPORT

This material world is a place for suffering, which is due to the misdeeds of the inhabitants, the conditioned souls themselves. The sufferings are not extraneously imposed upon them; rather, the conditioned souls create their own suffering by their own acts. In the forest, fire takes place automatically. It is not that someone has to go there and set a fire; because of friction among various trees, fire occurs automatically. When there is too much heat from the forest fire of this material world, the demigods, including Brahmā himself, being harassed, approach the Supreme Lord, the Supreme Personality of Godhead, and appeal to Him to alleviate the condition. Then the Supreme Personality of Godhead descends. In other words, when the demigods become distressed by the sufferings of the conditioned souls, they approach the Lord to remedy the suffering, and the Personality of Godhead descends. When the Lord descends, all the demigods become enlivened. Therefore Kardama Muni said, "After many, many years of human suffering, all the demigods are now satisfied because Kapiladeva, the incarnation of Godhead, has appeared."

TEXT 28

बहुजन्मविपक्वेन सम्यग्योगसमाधिना ।
द्रष्टुं यतन्ते यतयः शून्यागारेषु यत्पदम् ॥२८॥

bahu-janma-vipakvena
samyag-yoga-samādhinā
draṣṭuṁ yatante yatayaḥ
śūnyāgāreṣu yat-padam

bahu—many; *janma*—after births; *vipakvena*—which is mature; *samyak*—perfect; *yoga-samādhinā*—by trance in *yoga; draṣṭum*—to see; *yatante*—they endeavor; *yatayaḥ*—the *yogīs; śūnya-agāreṣu*—in secluded places; *yat*—whose; *padam*—feet.

TRANSLATION

After many births, mature yogīs, by complete trance in yoga, endeavor in secluded places to see the lotus feet of the Supreme Personality of Godhead.

PURPORT

Some important things are mentioned here about *yoga.* The word *bahu-janma-vipakvena* means "after many, many births of mature *yoga* practice." And another word, *samyag-yoga-samādhinā,* means "by complete practice of the *yoga* system." Complete practice of *yoga* means *bhakti-yoga;* unless one comes to the point of *bhakti-yoga,* or surrender unto the Supreme Personality of Godhead, one's *yoga* practice is not complete. This same point is corroborated in the *Śrīmad Bhagavad-gītā. Bahūnāṁ janmanām ante:* after many, many births, the *jñānī* who has matured in transcendental knowledge surrenders unto the Supreme Personality of Godhead. Kardama Muni repeats the same statement. After many, many years and many, many births of complete practice of *yoga,* one can see the lotus feet of the Supreme Lord in a secluded place. It is not that after one practices some sitting postures he immediately becomes perfect. One has to perform *yoga* a long time—"many, many births"—to become mature, and a *yogī* has to practice in a secluded place. One cannot practice *yoga* in a city or in a public park and declare that he has become God simply by some exchange of dollars. This is all bogus propaganda. Those who are actually *yogīs* practice in a secluded place, and after many, many births they become successful, provided they surrender unto the Supreme Personality of Godhead. This is the completion of *yoga*.

TEXT 29

स एव भगवानद्य हेलनं नगणय्य नः ।
गृहेषु जातो ग्राम्याणां यः स्वानां पक्षपोषणः ॥२९॥

sa eva bhagavān adya
helanaṁ na gaṇayya naḥ
gṛheṣu jāto grāmyāṇāṁ
yaḥ svānāṁ pakṣa-poṣaṇaḥ

saḥ eva—that very same; *bhagavān*—Supreme Personality of Godhead; *adya*—today; *helanam*—negligence; *na*—not; *gaṇayya*—considering high and low; *naḥ*—our; *gṛheṣu*—in the houses; *jātaḥ*—appeared; *grāmyāṇām*—of ordinary householders; *yaḥ*—He who; *svānām*—of His own devotees; *pakṣa-poṣaṇaḥ*—who supports the party.

TRANSLATION

Not considering the negligence of ordinary householders like us, that very same Supreme Personality of Godhead appears in our homes just to support His devotees.

PURPORT

Devotees are so affectionate toward the Personality of Godhead that although He does not appear before those who practice *yoga* in a secluded place even for many, many births, He agrees to appear in a householder's home where devotees engage in devotional service without material *yoga* practice. In other words, devotional service to the Lord is so easy that even a householder can see the Supreme Personality of Godhead as one of the members of his household, as his son, as Kardama Muni experienced. He was a householder, although a *yogī*, but he had the incarnation of the Supreme Personality of Godhead Kapila Muni as his son.

Devotional service is such a powerful transcendental method that it surpasses all other methods of transcendental realization. The Lord says, therefore, that He lives neither in Vaikuṇṭha nor in the heart of a *yogī*, but He lives where His pure devotees are always chanting and glorifying Him. The Supreme Personality of Godhead is known as *bhakta-vatsala*. He is never described as *jñāni-vatsala* or *yogi-vatsala*. He is always described as *bhakta-vatsala* because He is more inclined toward His devotees than toward other transcendentalists. In *Bhagavad-gītā* it is confirmed that only a devotee can understand Him as He is. *Bhaktyā mām abhijānāti:* "One can understand Me only by devotional service, not otherwise." That understanding alone is real because although *jñānīs*, mental speculators, can realize only the effulgence, or the bodily luster, of the Supreme Personality of Godhead, and *yogīs* can realize only the partial representation of the Supreme Personality of Godhead, a *bhakta* not only realizes Him as He is but also associates with the Personality of Godhead face to face.

TEXT 30

स्वीयं वाक्यमृतं कर्तुमवतीर्णोऽसि मे गृहे ।
चिकीर्षुर्भगवान् ज्ञानं भक्तानां मानवर्धनः ॥३०॥

svīyaṁ vākyam ṛtaṁ kartum
avatīrṇo 'si me gṛhe
cikīrṣur bhagavān jñānaṁ
bhaktānāṁ māna-vardhanaḥ

svīyam—Your own; *vākyam*—words; *ṛtam*—true; *kartum*—to make; *avatīrṇaḥ*—descended; *asi*—You are; *me gṛhe*—in my house; *cikīrṣuḥ*—desirous of disseminating; *bhagavān*—the Personality of Godhead; *jñānam*—knowledge; *bhaktānām*—of the devotees; *māna*—the honor; *vardhanaḥ*—who increases.

TRANSLATION

Kardama Muni said: You, my dear Lord, who are always increasing the honor of Your devotees, have descended in my home just to fulfill Your word and disseminate the process of real knowledge.

PURPORT

When the Lord appeared before Kardama Muni after his mature *yoga* practice, He promised that He would become Kardama's son. He descended as the son of Kardama Muni in order to fulfill that promise. Another purpose of His appearance is *cikīrṣur bhagavān jñānam,* to distribute knowledge. Therefore, He is called *bhaktānāṁ māna-vardhanaḥ,* "He who increases the honor of His devotees." By distributing Sāṅkhya He would increase the honor of the devotees; therefore, Sāṅkhya philosophy is not dry mental speculation. Sāṅkhya philosophy means devotional service. How could the honor of the devotees be increased unless Sāṅkhya were meant for devotional service? Devotees are not interested in speculative knowledge; therefore, the Sāṅkhya enunciated by Kapila Muni is meant to establish one firmly in devotional service. Real knowledge and real liberation is to surrender unto the Supreme Personality of Godhead and engage in devotional service.

TEXT 31

तान्येव तेऽभिरूपाणि रूपाणि भगवंस्तव ।
यानि यानि च रोचन्ते स्वजनानामरूपिणः ॥३१॥

tāny eva te 'bhirūpāṇi
rūpāṇi bhagavaṁs tava
yāni yāni ca rocante
sva-janānām arūpiṇaḥ

tāni—those; *eva*—truly; *te*—Your; *abhirūpāṇi*—suitable; *rūpāṇi*—forms; *bhagavan*—O Lord; *tava*—Your; *yāni yāni*—whichever; *ca*—and; *rocante*—are pleasing; *sva-janānām*—to Your own devotees; *arūpiṇaḥ*—of one with no material form.

TRANSLATION

My dear Lord, although You have no material form, You have Your own innumerable forms. They truly are Your transcendental forms, which are pleasing to Your devotees.

PURPORT

In the *Brahma-saṁhitā* it is stated that the Lord is one Absolute, but He has *ananta*, or innumerable, forms. *Advaitam acyutam anādim ananta-rūpam.* The Lord is the original form, but still He has multiforms. Those multiforms are manifested by Him transcendentally, according to the tastes of His multidevotees. It is understood that once Hanumān, the great devotee of Lord Rāmacandra, said that he knew that Nārāyaṇa, the husband of Lakṣmī, and Rāma, the husband of Sītā, are one and the same, and that there is no difference between Lakṣmī and Sītā, but as for himself, he liked the form of Lord Rāma. In a similar way, some devotees worship the original form of Kṛṣṇa. When we say "Kṛṣṇa" we refer to all forms of the Lord—not only Kṛṣṇa, but Rāma, Nṛsiṁha, Varāha, Nārāyaṇa, etc. The varieties of transcendental forms exist simultaneously. That is also stated in the *Brahma-saṁhitā: rāmādi-mūrtiṣu . . . nānāvatāram.* He already exists in multiforms, but none of the forms are material. Śrīdhara Svāmī has commented that *arūpiṇaḥ*, "without form," means without material form. The Lord has form, otherwise how can it be stated here, *tāny eva te 'bhirūpāṇi rūpāṇi bhagavaṁs tava:* "You have Your forms, but they are not material. Materially You have no form, but spiritually, transcendentally, You have multiforms"? Māyāvādī philosophers cannot understand these transcendental forms of the Lord, and being disappointed, they say that the Supreme Lord is impersonal. But that is not a fact; whenever there is form there is a person. Many times in many Vedic literatures the Lord is described as *puruṣa*, which means "the original form, the original enjoyer." The conclusion is that the Lord has no material form, and yet, according to the liking of different grades of devotees, He simultaneously exists in multiforms, such as Rāma, Nṛsiṁha, Varāha, Nārāyaṇa and Mukunda. There are many thousands and thousands of forms, but they are all *viṣṇu-tattva*, Kṛṣṇa.

TEXT 32

त्वां सूरिभिस्तत्त्वबुभुत्सयाद्धा
सदाभिवादार्हणपादपीठम् ।
ऐश्वर्यवैराग्ययशोऽवबोध-
वीर्यश्रिया पूर्तमहं प्रपद्ये ॥३२॥

tvāṁ sūribhis tattva-bubhutsayāddhā
sadābhivādārhaṇa-pāda-pīṭham
aiśvarya-vairāgya-yaśo-'vabodha-
vīrya-śriyā pūrtam ahaṁ prapadye

tvām—unto You; *sūribhiḥ*—by the great sages; *tattva*—the Absolute Truth; *bubhutsayā*—with a desire to understand; *addhā*—certainly; *sadā*—always; *abhivāda*—of worshipful respects; *arhaṇa*—which are worthy; *pāda*—of Your feet; *pīṭham*—to the seat; *aiśvarya*—opulence; *vairāgya*—renunciation; *yaśaḥ*—fame; *avabodha*—knowledge; *vīrya*—strength; *śriyā*—with beauty; *pūrtam*—who are full; *aham*—I; *prapadye*—surrender.

TRANSLATION

My dear Lord, Your lotus feet are the reservoir that always deserves to receive worshipful homage from all great sages eager to understand the Absolute Truth. You are full in opulence, renunciation, transcendental fame, knowledge, strength and beauty, and therefore I surrender myself unto Your lotus feet.

PURPORT

Actually, those who are searching after the Absolute Truth must take shelter of the lotus feet of the Supreme Personality of Godhead and worship Him. In *Bhagavad-gītā* Lord Kṛṣṇa advised Arjuna many times to surrender unto Him, especially at the end of the Ninth Chapter—*man-manā bhava mad-bhaktaḥ:* "If you want to be perfect, just always think of Me, become My devotee, worship Me and offer your obeisances to Me. In this way you will understand Me, the Personality of Godhead, and ultimately you will come back to Me, back to Godhead, back home." Why is it so? The Lord is always full in six opulences, as mentioned herein: wealth, renunciation, fame, knowledge, strength and beauty. The word *pūrtam* means "in full." No one can claim that all wealth belongs to him, but Kṛṣṇa can claim it, since He has full wealth. Similarly, He is full in knowledge, renunciation, strength and beauty. He is full in everything, and no one can surpass Him. Another one of Kṛṣṇa's names is *asamaurdhva*, which means that no one is equal to or greater than Him.

TEXT 33

परं प्रधानं पुरुषं महान्तं
कालं कविं त्रिवृतं लोकपालम् ।
आत्मानुभूत्यानुगतप्रपञ्चं
स्वच्छन्दशक्तिं कपिलं प्रपद्ये ॥३३॥

paraṁ pradhānaṁ puruṣaṁ mahāntaṁ
kālaṁ kaviṁ tri-vṛtaṁ loka-pālam
ātmānubhūtyānugata-prapañcaṁ
svacchanda-śaktiṁ kapilaṁ prapadye

param—transcendental; *pradhānam*—supreme; *puruṣam*—person; *mahāntam*—who is the origin of the material world; *kālam*—who is time; *kavim*—fully cognizant; *tri-vṛtam*—three modes of material nature; *loka-pālam*—who is the maintainer of all the universes; *ātma*—in Himself; *anubhūtya*—by internal potency; *anugata*—dissolved; *prapañcam*—whose material manifestations; *sva-chanda*—independently; *śaktim*—who is powerful; *kapilam*—to Lord Kapila; *prapadye*—I surrender.

TRANSLATION

I surrender unto the Supreme Personality of Godhead, descended in the form of Kapila, who is independently powerful and transcendental, who is the Supreme Person and the Lord of the sum total of matter and the element of time, who is the fully cognizant maintainer of all the universes under the three modes of

material nature, and who absorbs the material manifestations after their dissolution.

PURPORT

The six opulences—wealth, strength, fame, beauty, knowledge and renunciation—are indicated here by Kardama Muni, who addresses Kapila Muni, his son, as *param.* The word *param* is used in the beginning of *Śrīmad-Bhāgavatam,* in the phrase *paraṁ satyam,* to refer to the *summum bonum,* or the Supreme Personality of Godhead. *Param* is explained further by the next word, *pradhānam,* which means the chief, the origin, the source of everything—*sarva-kāraṇa-kāraṇam*—the cause of all causes. The Supreme Personality of Godhead is not formless; He is *puruṣam,* or the enjoyer, the original person. He is the time element and is all-cognizant. He knows everything—past, present and future—as confirmed in *Bhagavad-gītā.* The Lord says, "I know everything—present, past and future—in every corner of the universe." The material world, which is moving under the spell of the three modes of nature, is also a manifestation of His energy. *Parāsya śaktir vividhaiva śrūyate:* everything that we see is an interaction of His energies (*Śvetāśvatara Up.* 6.8). *Parasya brahmaṇaḥ śaktis tathedam akhilaṁ jagat.* This is the version of the *Viṣṇu Purāṇa.* We can understand that whatever we see is an interaction of the three modes of material nature, but actually it is all an interaction of the Lord's energy. *Loka-pālam:* He is actually the maintainer of all living entities. *Nityo nityānām:* He is the chief of all living entities; He is one, but He maintains many, many living entities. God maintains all other living entities, but no one can maintain God. That is His *svacchanda-śakti;* He is not dependent on others. Someone may call himself independent, but he is still dependent on someone higher. The Personality of Godhead, however, is absolute; there is no one higher than or equal to Him.

Kapila Muni appeared as the son of Kardama Muni, but because Kapila is an incarnation of the Supreme Personality of Godhead, Kardama Muni offered respectful obeisances unto Him with full surrender. Another word in this verse is very important: *ātmānubhūtyānugata-prapañcam.* The Lord descends either as Kapila or Rāma, Nṛsiṁha or Varāha, and whatever forms He assumes in the material world are all manifestations of His own personal internal energy. They are never forms of the material energy. The ordinary living entities who are manifested in this material world have bodies created by the material energy, but when Kṛṣṇa or any one of His expansions or parts of the expansions descends on this material world, although He appears to have a material body, His body is not material. He always has a transcendental body. But fools and rascals, who are called *mūḍhas*, consider Him one of them, and therefore they deride Him. They refuse to accept Kṛṣṇa as the Supreme Personality of Godhead because they cannot understand Him. In *Bhagavad-gītā* Kṛṣṇa says, *avajānanti māṁ mūḍhāḥ:* "Those who are rascals and fools deride Me." When God descends in a form, this does not mean that He assumes His form with the help of the material energy. He manifests His spiritual form as He exists in His spiritual kingdom.

TEXT 34

आ स्माभिपृच्छेऽद्य पतिं प्रजानां
त्वयावतीर्णर्ण उताप्तकामः ।
परिव्रजत्पदवीमास्थितोऽहं
चरिष्ये त्वां हृदि युञ्जन् विशोकः ॥३४॥

ā smābhipṛcche 'dya patiṁ prajānāṁ
tvayāvatīrṇarṇa utāpta-kāmaḥ
parivrajat-padavīm āsthito 'haṁ
carisye tvāṁ hṛdi yuñjan viśokaḥ

ā sma abhipṛcche—I am inquiring; *adya*—now; *patim*—the Lord; *prajānām*—of all created beings; *tvayā*—by You; *avatīrṇa-ṛṇaḥ*—free from debts; *uta*—and; *āpta*—fulfilled; *kāmaḥ*—desires; *parivrajat*—of an itinerant mendicant; *padavīm*—the path; *āsthitaḥ*—accepting; *aham*—I; *cariṣye*—I shall wander; *tvām*—You; *hṛdi*—in my heart; *yuñjan*—keeping; *viśokaḥ*—free from lamentation.

TRANSLATION

Today I have something to ask from You, who are the Lord of all living entities. Since I have now been liberated by You from my

debts to my father, and since all my desires are fulfilled, I wish to accept the order of an itinerant mendicant. Renouncing this family life, I wish to wander about, free from lamentation, thinking always of You in my heart.

PURPORT

Actually, *sannyāsa*, or renunciation of material household life, necessitates complete absorption in Kṛṣṇa consciousness and immersion in the self. One does not take *sannyāsa*, freedom from family responsibility in the renounced order of life, to make another family or to create an embarrassing transcendental fraud in the name of *sannyāsa*. The *sannyāsī's* business is not to become proprietor of so many things and amass money from the innocent public. A *sannyāsī* is proud that he is always thinking of Kṛṣṇa within himself. Of course, there are two kinds of devotees of the Lord. One is called *goṣṭhy-ānandī*, which means those who are preachers and have many followers for preaching the glories of the Lord and who live among those many, many followers just to organize missionary activities. Other devotees are *ātmānandī*, or self-satisfied, and do not take the risk of preaching work. They remain, therefore, alone with God. In this classification was Kardama Muni. He wanted to be free from all anxieties and remain alone within his heart with the Supreme Personality of Godhead. *Parivrāja* means "an itinerant mendicant." A mendicant *sannyāsī* should not live anywhere for more than three days. He must be always moving because his duty is to move from door to door and enlighten people about Kṛṣṇa consciousness.

TEXT 35

श्रीभगवानुवाच
मया प्रोक्तं हि लोकस्य प्रमाणं सत्यलौकिके ।
अथाजनि मया तुभ्यं यदवोचमृतं मुने ॥३५॥

śrī-bhagavān uvāca
mayā proktaṁ hi lokasya
pramāṇaṁ satya-laukike
athājani mayā tubhyaṁ
yad avocam ṛtaṁ mune

śrī-bhagavān uvāca—the Supreme Personality of Godhead said; *mayā*—by Me; *proktam*—spoken; *hi*—in fact; *lokasya*—for the people; *pramāṇam*—authority; *satya*—spoken in scripture; *laukike*—and in ordinary speech; *atha*—therefore; *ajani*—there was birth; *mayā*—by Me; *tubhyam*—to you; *yat*—that which; *avocam*—I said; *ṛtam*—true; *mune*—O sage.

TRANSLATION

The Personality of Godhead Kapila said: Whatever I speak, whether directly or in the scriptures, is authoritative in all respects for the people of the world. O Muni, because I told you before that I would become your son, I have descended to fulfill this truth.

PURPORT

Kardama Muni was to leave his family life to completely engage in the service of the Lord. But since he knew that the Lord Himself, as Kapila, had taken birth in his home as his own son, why was he preparing to leave home to search out self-realization or God realization? God Himself was present in his home—why should he leave home? Such a question may certainly arise. But here it is said that whatever is spoken in the *Vedas* and whatever is practiced in accordance with the injunctions of the *Vedas* is to be accepted as authoritative in society. Vedic authority says that a householder must leave home after his fiftieth year. *Pañcāśordhvaṁ vanaṁ vrajet:* one must leave his family life and enter the forest after the age of fifty. This is an authoritative statement of the *Vedas*, based on the division of social life into four departments of activity—*brahmacarya, gṛhastha, vānaprastha* and *sannyāsa.*

Kardama Muni practiced *yoga* very rigidly as a *brahmacārī* before his marriage, and he became so powerful and attained so much mystic power that his father, Brahmā, ordered him to marry and beget children as a householder. Kardama did that also; he begot nine good daughters and one son, Kapila Muni, and thus his householder duty was also performed nicely, and now his duty was to leave. Even though he had the Supreme Personality of Godhead as his son, he had to respect the authority of the *Vedas.* This is a very important lesson. Even if one has God in his home as his son, one should still follow the Vedic injunctions. It is stated, *mahājano yena gataḥ sa panthāḥ:* one should traverse the path which is followed by great personalities.

Kardama Muni's example is very instructive, for in spite of having the Supreme Personality of Godhead as his son, he left home just to obey the authority of the Vedic injunction. Kardama Muni states here the main purpose of his leaving home: while traveling all over the world as a mendicant, he would always remember the Supreme Personality of Godhead within his heart and thereby be freed from all the anxieties of material existence. In this age of Kali-yuga *sannyāsa* is prohibited because persons in this age are all *śūdras* and cannot follow the rules and regulations of *sannyāsa* life. It is very commonly found that so-called *sannyāsīs* are addicted to nonsense—even to having private relationships with women. This is the abominable situation in this age. Although they dress themselves as *sannyāsīs*, they still cannot free themselves from the four principles of sinful life, namely illicit sex life, meat-eating, intoxication and gambling. Since they are not freed from these four principles, they are cheating the public by posing as *svāmīs.*

In Kali-yuga the injunction is that no one should accept *sannyāsa.* Of course, those who actually follow the rules and regulations must take *sannyāsa.* Generally, however, people are unable to accept *sannyāsa* life, and therefore Caitanya Mahāprabhu stressed, *kalau nāsty eva nāsty eva nāsty eva gatir anyathā.* In this age there is no other alternative, no other alternative, no other alternative than to chant the holy name of the Lord: Hare Kṛṣṇa, Hare Kṛṣṇa, Kṛṣṇa Kṛṣṇa, Hare Hare. The main purpose of *sannyāsa* life is to be in constant companionship with the Supreme Lord, either by thinking of Him within the heart or hearing of Him through aural reception. In this age, hearing is more important than thinking because one's thinking may be disturbed by mental agitation, but if one concentrates on hearing, he will be forced to associate with the sound vibration of Kṛṣṇa. Kṛṣṇa and the sound vibration "Kṛṣṇa" are nondifferent, so if one loudly vibrates Hare Kṛṣṇa, he will be able to think of Kṛṣṇa immediately. This process of chanting is the best process of self-realization in this age; therefore Lord Caitanya preached it so nicely for the benefit of all humanity.

TEXT 36

एतन्मे जन्म लोकेऽस्मिन्मुमुक्षूणां दुराशयात् ।
प्रसंख्यानाय तत्त्वानां सम्मतायात्मदर्शने ॥३६॥

etan me janma loke 'smin
mumukṣūṇāṁ durāśayāt
prasaṅkhyānāya tattvānāṁ
sammatāyātma-darśane

etat—this; *me*—My; *janma*—birth; *loke*—in the world; *asmin*—in this; *mumukṣūṇām*—by those great sages seeking liberation; *durāśayāt*—from unnecessary material desires; *prasaṅkhyānāya*—for explaining; *tattvānām*—of the truths; *sammatāya*—which is highly esteemed; *ātma-darśane*—in self-realization.

TRANSLATION

My appearance in this world is especially to explain the philosophy of Sāṅkhya, which is highly esteemed for self-realization by those desiring freedom from the entanglement of unnecessary material desires.

PURPORT

Here the word *durāśayāt* is very significant. *Dur* refers to trouble or *duḥkha*, miseries. *Āśayāt* means "from the shelter." We conditioned souls have taken shelter of the material body, which is full of troubles and miseries. Foolish people cannot understand the situation, and this is called ignorance, illusion, or the spell of *māyā*. Human society should very seriously understand that the body itself is the source of all miserable life. Modern civilization is supposed to be making advancement in scientific knowledge, but what is this scientific knowledge? It is based on bodily comforts only, without knowledge that however comfortably one maintains his body, the body is destructible. As stated in *Bhagavad-gītā*, *antavanta ime dehāḥ:* these bodies are destined to be destroyed. *Nityasyoktāḥ śarīriṇaḥ* refers to the living soul, or the living spark, within the body. That soul is eternal, but the body is not eternal. For our activity we must have a body; without a body, without sense organs, there is no activity. But people are not inquiring whether it is possible to have an eternal body. Actually they aspire for an eternal body because even though they engage in sense enjoyment, that sense enjoyment is not eternal. They are therefore in want of something which they can enjoy eternally, but they do not understand how to attain that perfection.

Sāṅkhya philosophy, therefore, as stated herein by Kapiladeva, is *tattvānām.* The Sāṅkhya philosophy system is designed to afford understanding of the real truth. What is that real truth? The real truth is knowledge of how to get out of the material body, which is the source of all trouble. Lord Kapila's incarnation, or descent, is especially meant for this purpose. That is clearly stated here.

TEXT 37

एष आत्मपथोऽव्यक्तो नष्टः कालेन भूयसा ।
तं प्रवर्तयितुं देहमिमं विद्धि मया भृतम् ॥३७॥

eṣa ātma-patho 'vyakto
naṣṭaḥ kālena bhūyasā
taṁ pravartayituṁ deham
imaṁ viddhi mayā bhṛtam

eṣaḥ—this; *ātma-pathaḥ*—path of self-realization; *avyaktaḥ*—difficult to be known; *naṣṭaḥ*—lost; *kālena bhūyasā*—in the course of time; *tam*—this; *pravartayitum*—to introduce again; *deham*—body; *imam*—this; *viddhi*—please know; *mayā*—by Me; *bhṛtam*—assumed.

TRANSLATION

This path of self-realization, which is difficult to understand, has now been lost in the course of time. Please know that I have assumed this body of Kapila to introduce and explain this philosophy to human society again.

PURPORT

It is not true that Sāṅkhya philosophy is a new system of philosophy introduced by Kapila as material philosophers introduce new kinds of mental speculative thought to supersede that of another philosopher. On the material platform, everyone, especially the mental speculator, tries to be more prominent than others. The field of activity of the speculators is the mind; there is no limit to the different ways in which one can agitate the mind. The mind can be unlimitedly agitated, and thus one can put forward an unlimited number of theories. Sāṅkhya philosophy is not like that; it is not mental speculation. It is factual, but at the time of Kapila it was lost.

In due course of time, a particular type of knowledge may be lost or may be covered for the time being; that is the nature of this material world. A similar statement was made by Lord Kṛṣṇa in *Bhagavad-gītā*. *Sa kāleneha mahatā yogo naṣṭaḥ:* "In course of time the *yoga* system as stated in *Bhagavad-gītā* was lost." It was coming in *paramparā*, in disciplic succession, but due to the passage of time it was lost. The time factor is so pressing that in the course of time everything within this material world is spoiled or lost. The *yoga* system of *Bhagavad-gītā* was lost before the meeting of Kṛṣṇa and Arjuna. Therefore Kṛṣṇa again enunciated the same ancient *yoga* system to Arjuna, who could actually understand *Bhagavad-gītā*. Similarly, Kapila also said that the system of Sāṅkhya philosophy was not exactly being introduced by Him; it was already current, but in course of time it was mysteriously lost, and therefore He appeared to reintroduce it. That is the purpose of the incarnation of Godhead. *Yadā yadā hi dharmasya glānir bhavati bhārata. Dharma* means the real occupation of the living entity. When there is a discrepancy in the eternal occupation of the living entity, the Lord comes and introduces the real occupation of life. Any so-called religious system that is not in the line of devotional service is called *adharma-saṁsthāpana*. When people forget their eternal relationship with God and engage in something other than devotional service, their engagement is called irreligion. How one can get out of the miserable condition of material life is stated in Sāṅkhya philosophy, and the Lord Himself is explaining this sublime system.

TEXT 38

गच्छ कामं मयापृष्टो मयि संन्यस्तकर्मणा ।
जित्वा सुदुर्जयं मृत्युममृतत्वाय मां भज ॥३८॥

gaccha kāmaṁ mayāpṛṣṭo
mayi sannyasta-karmaṇā

jitvā sudurjayaṁ mṛtyum
amṛtatvāya māṁ bhaja

gaccha—go; *kāmam*—as you wish; *mayā*—by Me; *āpṛṣṭaḥ*—sanctioned; *mayi*—to Me; *sannyasta*—completely surrendered; *karmaṇā*—with your activities; *jitvā*—having conquered; *sudurjayam*—insurmountable; *mṛtyum*—death; *amṛtatvāya*—for eternal life; *mām*—unto Me; *bhaja*—engage in devotional service.

TRANSLATION

Now, being sanctioned by Me, go as you desire, surrendering all your activities to Me. Conquering insurmountable death, worship Me for eternal life.

PURPORT

The purpose of Sāṅkhya philosophy is stated herein. If anyone wants real, eternal life, he has to engage himself in devotional service, or Kṛṣṇa consciousness. To become free from birth and death is not an easy task. Birth and death are natural to this material body. *Sudurjayam* means "very, very difficult to overcome." The modern so-called scientists do not have sufficient means to understand the process of victory over birth and death. Therefore, they set aside the question of birth and death; they do not consider it. They simply engage in the problems of the material body, which is transient and sure to end.

Actually, human life is meant for conquering the insurmountable process of birth and death. That can be done as stated here. *Māṁ bhaja:* one must engage in the devotional service of the Lord. In *Bhagavad-gītā* also the Lord says, *man-manā bhava mad-bhaktaḥ:* "Just become My devotee. Just worship Me." But foolish so-called scholars say that it is not Kṛṣṇa whom we must worship and to whom we must surrender; it is something else. Without Kṛṣṇa's mercy, therefore, no one can understand the Sāṅkhya philosophy or any philosophy which is especially meant for liberation. Vedic knowledge confirms that one becomes entangled in this material life because of ignorance and that one can become free from material embarrassment by becoming situated in factual knowledge. Sāṅkhya means that factual knowledge by which one can get out of the material entanglement.

TEXT 39

मामात्मानं स्वयंज्योतिः सर्वभूतगुहाशयम् ।
आत्मन्येवात्मना वीक्ष्य विशोकोऽभयमृच्छसि ॥३९॥

mām ātmānaṁ svayaṁ-jyotiḥ
sarva-bhūta-guhāśayam
ātmany evātmanā vīkṣya
viśoko 'bhayam ṛcchasi

mām—Me; *ātmānam*—the Supreme Soul, or Paramātmā; *svayam-jyotiḥ*—self-effulgent; *sarva-bhūta*—of all beings; *guhā*—in the hearts; *āśayam*—dwelling; *ātmani*—in your own heart; *eva*—indeed; *ātmanā*—through your intellect; *vīkṣya*—always seeing, always thinking; *viśokaḥ*—free from lamentation; *abhayam*—fearlessness; *ṛcchasi*—you will achieve.

TRANSLATION

In your own heart, through your intellect, you will always see Me, the supreme self-effulgent soul dwelling within the hearts of all living entities. Thus you will achieve the state of eternal life, free from all lamentation and fear.

PURPORT

People are very anxious to understand the Absolute Truth in various ways, especially by experiencing the *brahmajyoti,* or Brahman effulgence, by meditation and by mental speculation. But Kapiladeva uses the word *mām* to emphasize that the Personality of Godhead is the ultimate feature of the Absolute Truth. In *Bhagavad-gītā* the Personality of Godhead always says *mām,* "unto Me," but the rascals misinterpret the clear meaning. *Mām* is the Supreme Personality of Godhead. If one can see the Supreme Personality of Godhead as He appears in different incarnations and understand that He has not assumed a material body but is present in His own eternal, spiritual form, then one can understand the nature of the Personality of Godhead. Since the less intelligent cannot understand this point, it is stressed everywhere again and again. Simply by seeing the form of the Lord as He presents Himself by His own internal potency as Kṛṣṇa or Rāma or Kapila, one can directly see the *brahmajyoti*, because the *brahmajyoti* is no more than the effulgence of His bodily luster. Since the sunshine is the luster of the sun planet, by seeing the sun one automatically sees the sunshine; similarly, by seeing the Supreme Personality of Godhead one simultaneously sees and experiences the Paramātmā feature as well as the impersonal Brahman feature of the Supreme.

The *Bhāgavatam* has already enunciated that the Absolute Truth is present in three features—in the beginning as the impersonal Brahman, in the next stage as the Paramātmā in everyone's heart, and, at last, as the ultimate realization of the Absolute Truth, Bhagavān, the Supreme Personality of Godhead. One who sees the Supreme Person can automatically realize the other features, namely the Paramātmā and Brahman features of the Lord. The words used here are *viśoko 'bhayam ṛcchasi.* Simply by seeing the Personality of Godhead one realizes everything, and the result is that one becomes situated on the platform where there is no lamentation and no fear. This can be attained simply by devotional service to the Personality of Godhead.

TEXT 40

मात्र आध्यात्मिकीं विद्यां शमनीं सर्वकर्मणाम् ।
वितरिष्ये यया चासौ भयं चातितरिष्यति ॥४०॥

mātra ādhyātmikīṁ vidyāṁ
śamanīṁ sarva-karmaṇām
vitariṣye yayā cāsau
bhayaṁ cātitariṣyati

mātre—to My mother; *ādhyātmikīm*—which opens the door of spiritual life; *vidyām*—knowledge; *śamanīm*—ending; *sarva-karmaṇām*—all fruitive activities; *vitariṣye*—I shall give; *yayā*—by which; *ca*—also; *asau*—she; *bhayam*—fear; *ca*—also; *atitariṣyati*—will overcome.

TRANSLATION

I shall also describe this sublime knowledge, which is the door to spiritual life, to My mother, so that she also can attain perfection and self-realization, ending all reactions to fruitive activities. Thus she also will be freed from all material fear.

PURPORT

Kardama Muni was anxious about his good wife, Devahūti, while leaving home, and so the worthy son promised that not only would Kardama Muni be freed from the material entanglement, but Devahūti would also be freed by receiving instruction from her son. A very good example is set here: the husband goes away, taking the *sannyāsa* order for self-realization, but his representative, the son, who is equally educated, remains at home to deliver the mother. A *sannyāsī* is not supposed to take his wife with him. At the *vānaprastha* stage of retired life, or the stage midway between householder life and renounced life, one may keep his wife as an assistant without sex relations, but in the *sannyāsa* order of life one cannot keep his wife with him. Otherwise, a person like Kardama Muni could have kept his wife with him, and there would have been no hindrance to his prosecution of self-realization.

Kardama Muni followed the Vedic injunction that no one in *sannyāsa* life can have any kind of relationship with women. But what is the position of a woman who is left by her husband? She is entrusted to the son, and the son promises that he will deliver his mother from entanglement. A woman is not supposed to take *sannyāsa.* So-called spiritual societies concocted in modern times give *sannyāsa* even to women, although there is no sanction in the Vedic literature for a woman's accepting *sannyāsa.* Otherwise, if it were sanctioned, Kardama Muni could have taken his wife and given her *sannyāsa.* The woman must remain at home. She has only three stages of life: dependency on the father in childhood, dependency on the husband in youth and, in old age, dependency on the grown-up son, such as Kapila. In old age the progress of woman depends on the grown-up son. The ideal son, Kapila Muni, is assuring His father of the deliverance of His mother so that His father may go peacefully without anxiety for his good wife.

TEXT 41

मैत्रेय उवाच
एवं समुदितस्तेन कपिलेन प्रजापतिः ।
दक्षिणीकृत्य तं प्रीतो वनमेव जगाम ह ॥४१॥

maitreya uvāca
evaṁ samuditas tena
kapilena prajāpatiḥ
dakṣiṇī-kṛtya taṁ prīto
vanam eva jagāma ha

maitreyaḥ uvāca—the great sage Maitreya said; *evam*—thus; *samuditaḥ*—addressed; *tena*—by Him; *kapilena*—by Kapila; *prajāpatiḥ*—the progenitor of human society; *dakṣiṇī-kṛtya*—having circumambulated; *tam*—Him; *prītaḥ*—being pacified; *vanam*—to the forest; *eva*—indeed; *jagāma*—he left; *ha*—then.

TRANSLATION

Śrī Maitreya said: Thus when Kardama Muni, the progenitor of human society, was spoken to in fullness by his son, Kapila, he circumambulated Him, and with a good, pacified mind he at once left for the forest.

PURPORT

Going to the forest is compulsory for everyone. It is not a mental excursion upon which one person goes and another does not. Everyone should go to the forest at least as a *vānaprastha.* Forest-going means to take one-hundred-percent shelter of the Supreme Lord, as explained by Prahlāda Mahārāja in his talks with his father. *Sadā samudvigna-dhiyām (Bhāg.* 7.5.5). People who have accepted a temporary, material body are always full of anxieties. One should not, therefore, be very much affected by this material body, but should try to be freed. The preliminary process to become freed is to go to the forest or give up family relationships and exclusively engage in Kṛṣṇa consciousness. That is the purpose of going to the forest. Otherwise, the forest is only a place of monkeys and wild animals. To go to the forest does not mean to become a monkey or a ferocious animal. It means to accept exclusively the shelter of the Supreme Personality of Godhead and engage oneself in full service. One does not actually have to go to the forest. At the present moment this is not at all advisable for a man who has spent his life all along in big cities. As explained by Prahlāda Mahārāja (*hitvātma-pātaṁ gṛham andha-kūpam*), one should not remain always engaged in the responsibilities of family life because family life without Kṛṣṇa consciousness is just like a blind well. Alone in a field, if one falls into a blind well and no one is there to save him, he may cry for years, and no one will see or hear where the crying is coming from. Death is sure. Similarly, those who are forgetful of their eternal relationship with the Supreme Lord are in the blind well of family life; their position is very ominous. Prahlāda Mahārāja advised that one should give up this well somehow or other and take to Kṛṣṇa consciousness and thus be freed from material entanglement, which is full of anxieties.

TEXT 42

व्रतं स आस्थितो मौनमात्मैकशरणो मुनिः ।
निःसङ्गो व्यचरत्क्षोणीमनग्निरनिकेतनः ॥४२॥

vrataṁ sa āsthito maunam
ātmaika-śaraṇo muniḥ
niḥsaṅgo vyacarat kṣoṇīm
anagnir aniketanaḥ

vratam—vow; *saḥ*—he (Kardama); *āsthitaḥ*—accepted; *maunam*—silence; *ātma*—by the Supreme Personality of Godhead; *eka*—exclusively; *śaraṇaḥ*—being sheltered; *muniḥ*—the sage; *niḥsaṅgaḥ*—without association; *vyacarat*—he traveled; *kṣoṇīm*—the earth; *anagniḥ*—without fire; *aniketanaḥ*—without shelter.

TRANSLATION

The sage Kardama accepted silence as a vow in order to think of the Supreme Personality of Godhead and take shelter of Him exclusively. Without association, he traveled over the surface of the globe as a sannyāsī, devoid of any relationship with fire or shelter.

PURPORT

Here the words *anagnir aniketanaḥ* are very significant. A *sannyāsī* should be completely detached from fire and any residential quarters. A *gṛhastha* has a relationship with fire, either for offering sacrifices or for cooking, but a *sannyāsī* is freed from these two responsibilities. He does not have to cook or offer fire for sacrifice because he is always engaged in Kṛṣṇa consciousness; therefore he has already accomplished all ritualistic performances of religion. *Aniketanaḥ* means "without lodging." He should not have his own house, but should depend completely on the Supreme Lord for his food and lodging. He should travel.

Mauna means "silence." Unless one becomes silent, he cannot think completely about the pastimes and activities of the Lord. It is not that because one is a fool and cannot speak nicely he therefore takes the vow of *mauna.* Rather, one becomes silent so that people will not disturb him. It is said by Cāṇakya Paṇḍita that a rascal appears very intelligent as long as he does not speak. But speaking is the test. The so-called silence of a silent impersonalist *svāmī* indicates that he has nothing to say; he simply wants to beg. But the silence adopted by Kardama Muni was not like that. He became silent for relief from nonsensical talk. One is called a *muni* when he remains grave and does not talk nonsense. Mahārāja Ambarīṣa set a very good example; whenever he spoke, he spoke about the pastimes of the Lord. *Mauna* necessitates refraining from nonsensical talking, and engaging the talking facility in the pastimes of the Lord. In that way one can chant and hear about the Lord in order to perfect his life. *Vratam* means that one should take a vow as explained in *Bhagavad-gītā, amānitvam adambhitvam,* without hankering for personal respect and without being proud of one's material position. *Ahiṁsā* means not being violent. There are eighteen processes for attaining knowledge and perfection, and by his vow, Kardama Muni adopted all the principles of self-realization.

TEXT 43

मनो ब्रह्मणि युञ्जानो यत्तत्सदसतः परम् ।
गुणावभासे विगुण एकभक्त्यानुभाविते ॥४३॥

mano brahmaṇi yuñjāno
yat tat sad-asataḥ param

guṇāvabhāse viguṇa
eka-bhaktyānubhāvite

manaḥ—mind; *brahmaṇi*—on the Supreme; *yuñjānaḥ*—fixing; *yat*—which; *tat*—that; *sat-asataḥ*—cause and effect; *param*—beyond; *guṇa-avabhāse*—who manifests the three modes of material nature; *viguṇe*—who is beyond the material modes; *eka-bhaktyā*—by exclusive devotion; *anubhāvite*—who is perceived.

TRANSLATION

He fixed his mind upon the Supreme Personality of Godhead, Parabrahman, who is beyond cause and effect, who manifests the three modes of material nature, who is beyond those three modes, and who is perceived only through unfailing devotional service.

PURPORT

Whenever there is *bhakti*, there must be three things present—the devotee, the devotion and the Lord. Without these three—*bhakta, bhakti* and Bhagavān—there is no meaning to the word *bhakti*. Kardama Muni fixed his mind on the Supreme Brahman and realized Him through *bhakti*, or devotional service. This indicates that he fixed his mind on the personal feature of the Lord because *bhakti* cannot be executed unless one has realization of the personal feature of the Absolute Truth. *Guṇāvabhāse:* He is beyond the three modes of material nature, but it is due to Him that the three modes of material nature are manifested. In other words, although the material energy is an emanation of the Supreme Lord, He is not affected, as we are, by the modes of material nature. We are conditioned souls, but He is not affected, although the material nature has emanated from Him. He is the supreme living entity and is never affected by *māyā*, but we are subordinate, minute living entities, prone to be affected by the limitations of *māyā*. If he is in constant contact with the Supreme Lord by devotional service, the conditioned living entity also becomes freed from the infection of *māyā*. This is confirmed in *Bhagavad-gītā: sa guṇān samatītyaitān*. A person engaged in Kṛṣṇa consciousness is at once liberated from the influence of the three modes of material nature. In other words, once the conditioned soul engages himself in devotional service, he also becomes liberated like the Lord.

TEXT 44

निरहंकृतिर्निर्ममश्च निर्द्वन्द्वः समदृक् स्वदृक् ।
प्रत्यक्प्रशान्तधीर्धीरः प्रशान्तोर्मिरिवोदधिः ॥४४॥

nirahaṅkṛtir nirmamaś ca
nirdvandvaḥ sama-dṛk sva-dṛk
pratyak-praśānta-dhīr dhīraḥ
praśāntormir ivodadhiḥ

nirahaṅkṛtiḥ—without false ego; *nirmamaḥ*—without material affection; *ca*—and; *nirdvandvaḥ*—without duality; *sama-dṛk*—seeing equality; *sva-dṛk*—seeing himself; *pratyak*—turned inward; *praśānta*—perfectly composed; *dhīḥ*—mind; *dhīraḥ*—sober, not disturbed; *praśānta*—calmed; *ūrmiḥ*—whose waves; *iva*—like; *udadhiḥ*—the ocean.

TRANSLATION

Thus he gradually became unaffected by the false ego of material identity and became free from material affection. Undisturbed, equal to everyone and without duality, he could indeed see himself also. His mind was turned inward and was perfectly calm, like an ocean unagitated by waves.

PURPORT

When one's mind is in full Kṛṣṇa consciousness and one fully engages in rendering devotional service to the Lord, he becomes just like an ocean unagitated by waves. This very example is also cited in *Bhagavad-gītā:* one should become like the ocean. The ocean is filled by many thousands of rivers, and millions of tons of its water evaporates into clouds, yet the ocean is the same unagitated ocean. The laws of nature may work, but if one is fixed in devotional service at the lotus feet of the Lord, he is not agitated, for he is introspective. He does not look outside to material nature, but he looks in to the spiritual nature of his existence; with a sober mind, he simply engages in the service of the Lord. Thus he realizes his own self without false identification with matter and without affection for material possessions. Such a great devotee is never in trouble with others because he sees everyone from the platform of spiritual understanding; he sees himself and others in the right perspective.

TEXT 45

वासुदेवे भगवति सर्वज्ञे प्रत्यगात्मनि ।
परेण भक्तिभावेन लब्धात्मा मुक्तबन्धनः ॥४५॥

vāsudeve bhagavati
sarva-jñe pratyag-ātmani
pareṇa bhakti-bhāvena
labdhātmā mukta-bandhanaḥ

vāsudeve—to Vāsudeva; *bhagavati*—the Personality of Godhead; *sarva-jñe*—omniscient; *pratyak-ātmani*—the Supersoul within everyone; *pareṇa*—transcendental; *bhakti-bhāvena*—by devotional service; *labdha-ātmā*—being situated in himself; *mukta-bandhanaḥ*—liberated from material bondage.

TRANSLATION

He thus became liberated from conditioned life and became self-situated in transcendental devotional service to the Personality of Godhead, Vāsudeva, the omniscient Supersoul within everyone.

PURPORT

When one engages in the transcendental devotional service of the Lord one becomes aware that his constitutional position, as an individual soul, is to be eternally a servitor of the Supreme Lord, Vāsudeva. Self-realization does not mean that because the Supreme Soul and the individual soul are both souls they are equal in every respect. The individual soul is prone to be conditioned, and the Supreme Soul is never conditioned. When the conditioned soul realizes that he is subordinate to the Supreme Soul, his position is called *labdhātmā*, self-realization, or *mukta-bandhana*, freedom from material contamination. Material contamination continues as long as one thinks that he is as good as the Supreme Lord or is equal with Him. This condition is the last snare of *māyā*. *Māyā* always influences the conditioned soul. Even after much meditation and speculation, if one continues to think himself one with the Supreme Lord, it is to be understood that he is still in the last snares of the spell of *māyā*.

The word *pareṇa* is very significant. *Para* means "transcendental, untinged by material contamination." Full consciousness that one is an eternal servant of the Lord is called *parā bhakti*. If one has any identification with material things and executes devotional service for attainment of some material gain, that is *viddhā bhakti*, contaminated *bhakti*. One can actually become liberated by execution of *parā bhakti*.

Another word mentioned here is *sarva-jñe*. The Supersoul sitting within the heart is all-cognizant. He knows. I may forget my past activities due to the change of body, but because the Supreme Lord as Paramātmā is sitting within me, He knows everything; therefore the result of my past *karma*, or past activities, is awarded to me. I may forget, but He awards me suffering or enjoyment for the misdeeds or good deeds of my past life. One should not think that he is freed from reaction because he has forgotten the actions of his past life. Reactions will take place, and what kind of reactions there will be is judged by the Supersoul, the witness.

TEXT 46

आत्मानं सर्वभूतेषु भगवन्तमवस्थितम् ।
अपश्यत्सर्वभूतानि भगवत्यपि चात्मनि ॥४६॥

ātmānaṁ sarva-bhūteṣu
bhagavantam avasthitam
apaśyat sarva-bhūtāni
bhagavaty api cātmani

ātmānam—the Supersoul; *sarva-bhūteṣu*—in all living beings; *bhagavantam*—the Supreme Personality of Godhead; *avasthitam*—situated; *apaśyat*—he saw; *sarva-bhūtāni*—all living beings; *bhagavati*—in the Supreme Personality of Godhead; *api*—moreover; *ca*—and; *ātmani*—on the Supersoul.

TRANSLATION

He began to see that the Supreme Personality of Godhead is seated in everyone's heart, and that everyone is existing on Him, because He is the Supersoul of everyone.

PURPORT

That everyone is existing on the Supreme Personality of Godhead does not mean that everyone is also Godhead. This is also explained in *Bhagavad-gītā:* everything is resting on Him, the Supreme Lord, but that does not mean that the Supreme Lord is also everywhere. This mysterious position has to be understood by highly advanced devotees. There are three kinds of devotees—the neophyte devotee, the intermediate devotee and the advanced devotee. The neophyte devotee does not understand the techniques of devotional science, but simply offers devotional service to the Deity in the temple; the intermediate devotee understands who God is, who is a devotee, who is a nondevotee and who is innocent, and he deals with such persons differently. But a person who sees that the Lord is sitting as Paramātmā in everyone's heart and that everything is depending or existing on the transcendental energy of the Supreme Lord is in the highest devotional position.

TEXT 47

इच्छाद्वेषविहीनेन सर्वत्र समचेतसा ।
भगवद्भक्तियुक्तेन प्राप्ता भागवती गतिः ॥४७॥

icchā-dveṣa-vihīnena
sarvatra sama-cetasā
bhagavad-bhakti-yuktena
prāptā bhāgavatī gatiḥ

icchā—desire; *dveṣa*—and hatred; *vihīnena*—freed from; *sarvatra*—everywhere; *sama*—equal; *cetasā*—with the mind; *bhagavat*—unto the Personality of Godhead; *bhakti-yuktena*—by discharging devotional service; *prāptā*—was attained; *bhāgavatī gatiḥ*—the destination of the devotee (going back home, back to Godhead).

TRANSLATION

Freed from all hatred and desire, Kardama Muni, being equal to everyone because of discharging uncontaminated devotional service, ultimately attained the path back to Godhead.

PURPORT

As stated in *Bhagavad-gītā*, only by devotional service can one understand the transcendental nature of the Supreme Lord and, after understanding Him perfectly in His transcendental position, enter into the kingdom of God. The process of entering into the kingdom of God is *tri-pāda-bhūti-gati*, or the path back home, back to Godhead, by which one can attain the ultimate goal of life. Kardama Muni, by his perfect devotional knowledge and service, achieved this ultimate goal, which is known as *bhāgavatī gatiḥ*.

Thus end the Bhaktivedanta purports of the Third Canto, Twenty-fourth Chapter, of the Śrīmad-Bhāgavatam, *entitled "The Renunciation of Kardama Muni."*

CHAPTER TWENTY-FIVE

The Glories of Devotional Service

TEXT 1

शौनक उवाच
कपिलस्तत्त्वसंख्याता भगवानात्ममायया ।
जातः स्वयमजः साक्षादात्मप्रज्ञप्तये नृणाम् ॥ १ ॥

śaunaka uvāca
kapilas tattva-saṅkhyātā
bhagavān ātma-māyayā
jātaḥ svayam ajaḥ sākṣād
ātma-prajñaptaye nṛṇām

śaunakaḥ uvāca—Śrī Śaunaka said; *kapilaḥ*—Lord Kapila; *tattva*—of the truth; *saṅkhyātā*—the expounder; *bhagavān*—the Supreme Personality of Godhead; *ātma-māyayā*—by His internal potency; *jātaḥ*—took birth; *svayam*—Himself; *ajaḥ*—unborn; *sākṣāt*—in person; *ātma-prajñaptaye*—to disseminate transcendental knowledge; *nṛṇām*—for the human race.

TRANSLATION

Śrī Śaunaka said: Although He is unborn, the Supreme Personality of Godhead took birth as Kapila Muni by His internal potency. He descended to disseminate transcendental knowledge for the benefit of the whole human race.

PURPORT

The word *ātma-prajñaptaye* indicates that the Lord descends for the benefit of the human race to give transcendental knowledge. Material necessities are quite sufficiently provided for in the Vedic knowledge, which offers a program for good living conditions and gradual elevation to the platform of goodness. In the mode of goodness one's knowledge expands. On the platform of passion there is no knowledge, for passion is simply an impetus to enjoy material benefits. On the platform of ignorance there is no knowledge and no enjoyment, but simply life almost like that of animals.

The *Vedas* are meant to elevate one from the mode of ignorance to the platform of goodness. When one is situated in the mode of goodness he is able to understand knowledge of the self, or transcendental knowledge. This knowledge cannot be appreciated by any ordinary man. Therefore, since a disciplic succession is required, this knowledge is expounded either by the Supreme Personality of Godhead Himself or by His bona fide devotee. Śaunaka Muni also states here that Kapila, the incarnation of the Supreme Personality of Godhead, took birth, or appeared, simply to appreciate and disseminate transcendental knowledge. Simply to understand that one is not matter but spirit soul (*ahaṁ brahmāsmi:* "I am by nature Brahman") is not sufficient knowledge for understanding the self and his activities. One must be situated in the activities of Brahman. Knowledge of those activities is explained by the Supreme Personality of Godhead Himself. Such transcendental knowledge can be appreciated in human society but not in animal society, as clearly indicated here by the word *nṛṇām,* "for the human beings." Human beings are meant for regulated life. By nature, there is regulation in animal life also, but that is not like the regulative life as described in the scriptures or by the authorities. Human life is regulated life, not animal life. In regulated life only can one understand transcendental knowledge.

TEXT 2

न ह्यस्य वर्ष्मणः पुंसां वरिम्णः सर्वयोगिनाम् ।
विश्रुतौ श्रुतदेवस्य भूरि तृप्यन्ति मेऽसवः ॥ २ ॥

na hy asya varṣmaṇaḥ puṁsāṁ
varimṇaḥ sarva-yoginām
viśrutau śruta-devasya
bhūri tṛpyanti me 'savaḥ

na—not; *hi*—indeed; *asya*—about Him; *varṣmaṇaḥ*—the greatest; *puṁsām*—among men; *varimṇaḥ*—the foremost; *sarva*—all; *yogi-*

nām—of *yogīs; viśrutau*—in hearing; *śruta-devasya*—the master of the *Vedas; bhūri*—repeatedly; *tṛpyanti*—are sated; *me*—my; *asavaḥ*—senses.

TRANSLATION

Śaunaka continued: There is no one who knows more than the Lord Himself. No one is more worshipable or more mature a yogī than He. He is therefore the master of the Vedas, and to hear about Him always is the actual pleasure of the senses.

PURPORT

In *Bhagavad-gītā* it is stated that no one can be equal to or greater than the Supreme Personality of Godhead. This is confirmed in the *Vedas* also: *eko bahūnāṁ yo vidadhāti kāmān.* He is the supreme living entity and is supplying the necessities of all other living entities. Thus all other living entities, both *viṣṇu-tattva* and *jīva-tattva*, are subordinate to the Supreme Personality of Godhead, Kṛṣṇa. The same concept is confirmed here. *Na hy asya varṣmaṇaḥ puṁsām:* amongst the living entities, no one can surpass the Supreme Person because no one is richer, more famous, stronger, more beautiful, wiser or more renounced than He. These qualifications make Him the Supreme Godhead, the cause of all causes. *Yogīs* are very proud of performing wonderful feats, but no one can compare to the Supreme Personality of Godhead.

Anyone who is associated with the Supreme Lord is accepted as a first-class *yogī.* Devotees may not be as powerful as the Supreme Lord, but by constant association with the Lord they become as good as the Lord Himself. Sometimes the devotees act more powerfully than the Lord. Of course, that is the Lord's concession.

Also used here is the word *varimṇaḥ*, meaning "the most worshipful of all *yogīs.*" To hear from Kṛṣṇa is the real pleasure of the senses; therefore He is known as Govinda, for by His words, by His teachings, by His instruction—by everything connected with Him—He enlivens the senses. Whatever He instructs is from the transcendental platform, and His instructions, being absolute, are nondifferent from Him. Hearing from Kṛṣṇa or His expansion or plenary expansion like Kapila is very pleasing to the senses. *Bhagavad-gītā* can be read or heard many times, but because it gives great pleasure, the more one reads *Bhagavad-gītā* the more he gets the appetite to read and understand it, and each time he gets new enlightenment. That is the nature of the transcendental message. Similarly, we find that transcendental happiness in the *Śrīmad-Bhāgavatam.* The more we hear and chant the glories of the Lord, the more we become happy.

TEXT 3

यद्यद्विधत्ते भगवान् स्वच्छन्दात्मात्ममायया ।
तानि मे श्रद्दधानस्य कीर्तन्यान्यनुकीर्तय ॥ ३ ॥

yad yad vidhatte bhagavān
svacchandātmātma-māyayā
tāni me śraddadhānasya
kīrtanyāny anukīrtaya

yat yat—whatever; *vidhatte*—He performs; *bhagavān*—the Personality of Godhead; *sva-chanda-ātmā*—full of self-desire; *ātma-māyayā*—by His internal potency; *tāni*—all of them; *me*—to me; *śraddadhānasya*—faithful; *kīrtanyāni*—worthy of praise; *anukīrtaya*—please describe.

TRANSLATION

Therefore please precisely describe all the activities and pastimes of the Personality of Godhead, who is full of self-desire and who assumes all these activities by His internal potency.

PURPORT

The word *anukīrtaya* is very significant. *Anukīrtaya* means to follow the description—not to create a concocted mental description, but to follow. Śaunaka Ṛṣi requested Sūta Gosvāmī to describe what he had actually heard from his spiritual master, Śukadeva Gosvāmī, about the transcendental pastimes the Lord manifested by His internal energy. Bhagavān, the Supreme Personality of Godhead, has no material body, but He can assume any kind of body by His supreme will. That is made possible by His internal energy.

TEXT 4

सूत उवाच
द्वैपायनसखस्त्वेवं मैत्रेयो भगवांस्तथा ।
प्राहेदं विदुरं प्रीत आन्वीक्षिक्यां प्रचोदितः ॥ ४ ॥

sūta uvāca
dvaipāyana-sakhas tv evaṁ
maitreyo bhagavāṁs tathā
prāhedaṁ viduraṁ prīta
ānvīkṣikyāṁ praceditaḥ

sūtaḥ uvāca—Sūta Gosvāmī said; *dvaipāyana-sakhaḥ*—friend of Vyāsadeva; *tu*—then; *evam*—thus; *maitreyaḥ*—Maitreya; *bhagavān*—worshipful; *tathā*—in that way; *prāha*—spoke; *idam*—this; *viduram*—to Vidura; *prītaḥ*—being pleased; *ānvīkṣikyām*—about transcendental knowledge; *pracoditaḥ*—being asked.

TRANSLATION

Śrī Sūta Gosvāmī said: The most powerful sage Maitreya was a friend of Vyāsadeva. Being encouraged and pleased by Vidura's inquiry about transcendental knowledge, Maitreya spoke as follows.

PURPORT

Questions and answers are very satisfactorily dealt with when the inquirer is bona fide and the speaker is also authorized. Here Maitreya is considered a powerful sage, and therefore he is also described as *bhagavān.* This word can be used not only for the Supreme Personality of Godhead but for anyone who is almost as powerful as the Supreme Lord. Maitreya is addressed as *bhagavān* because he was spiritually far advanced. He was a personal friend of Dvaipāyana Vyāsadeva, a literary incarnation of the Lord. Maitreya was very pleased with the inquiries of Vidura because they were the inquiries of a bona fide, advanced devotee. Thus Maitreya was encouraged to answer. When there are discourses on transcendental topics between devotees of equal mentality, the questions and answers are very fruitful and encouraging.

TEXT 5

मैत्रेय उवाच

पितरि प्रस्थितेऽरण्यं मातुः प्रियचिकीर्षया ।
तस्मिन् बिन्दुसरेऽवात्सीद्भगवान् कपिलः किल ॥५॥

maitreya uvāca
pitari prasthite 'raṇyaṁ
mātuḥ priya-cikīrṣayā
tasmin bindusare 'vātsīd
bhagavān kapilaḥ kila

maitreyaḥ uvāca—Maitreya said; *pitari*—when the father; *prasthite*—left; *araṇyam*—for the forest; *mātuḥ*—His mother; *priya-cikīrṣayā*—with a desire to please; *tasmin*—on that; *bindusare*—Lake Bindu-sarovara; *avātsīt*—He stayed; *bhagavān*—the Lord; *kapilaḥ*—Kapila; *kila*—indeed.

TRANSLATION

Maitreya said: When Kardama left for the forest, Lord Kapila stayed on the strand of the Bindu-sarovara to please His mother, Devahūti.

PURPORT

In the absence of the father it is the duty of the grown son to take charge of his mother and serve her to the best of his ability so that she will not feel separation from her husband, and it is the duty of the husband to leave home as soon as there is a grown son to take chargė of his wife and family affairs. That is the Vedic system of household life. One should not remain continually implicated in household affairs up to the time of death. He must leave. Family affairs and the wife may be taken charge of by a grown son.

TEXT 6

तमासीनमकर्माणं तत्त्वमार्गाग्रदर्शनम् ।
स्वसुतं देवहूत्याह धातुः संस्मरती वचः ॥ ६ ॥

tam āsīnam akarmāṇaṁ
tattva-mārgāgra-darśanam
sva-sutaṁ devahūty āha
dhātuḥ saṁsmaratī vacaḥ

tam—to Him (Kapila); *āsīnam*—seated; *akarmāṇam*—at leisure; *tattva*—of the Absolute Truth; *mārga-agra*—the ultimate goal; *darśanam*—who could show; *sva-sutam*—her son; *devahūtiḥ*—Devahūti; *āha*—said; *dhātuḥ*—of Brahmā; *saṁsmaratī*—remembering; *vacaḥ*—the words.

TRANSLATION

When Kapila, who could show her the ultimate goal of the Absolute Truth, was sitting leisurely before her, Devahūti remembered the words Brahmā had spoken to her, and she therefore began to question Kapila as follows.

TEXT 7

देवहूतिरुवाच
निर्विण्णा नितरां भूमन्नसदिन्द्रियतर्षणात् ।
येन सम्भाव्यमानेन प्रपन्नान्धं तमः प्रभो ॥ ७ ॥

devahūtir uvāca
nirviṇṇā nitarāṁ bhūmann
asad-indriya-tarṣaṇāt
yena sambhāvyamānena
prapannāndhaṁ tamaḥ prabho

devahūtiḥ uvāca—Devahūti said; *nirviṇṇā*—disgusted; *nitarām*—very; *bhūman*—O my Lord; *asat*—impermanent; *indriya*—of the senses; *tarṣaṇāt*—from agitation; *yena*—by which; *sambhāvyamānena*—being prevalent; *prapannā*—I have fallen; *andham tamaḥ*—into the abyss of ignorance; *prabho*—O my Lord.

TRANSLATION

Devahūti said: I am very sick of the disturbance caused by my material senses, for because of this sense disturbance, my Lord, I have fallen into the abyss of ignorance.

PURPORT

Here the word *asad-indriya-tarṣaṇāt* is significant. *Asat* means "impermanent," "temporary," and *indriya* means "senses." Thus *asad-indriya-tarṣaṇāt* means "from being agitated by the temporarily manifest senses of the material body." We are evolving through different statuses of material bodily existence—sometimes in a human body, sometimes in an animal body—and therefore the engagements of our material senses are also changing. Anything which changes is called temporary, or *asat*. We should know that beyond these temporary senses are our permanent senses, which are now covered by the material body. The permanent senses, being contaminated by matter, are not acting properly. Devotional service, therefore, involves freeing the senses from this contamination. When the contamination is completely removed and the senses act in the purity of unalloyed Kṛṣṇa consciousness, we have reached *sad-indriya*, or eternal sensory activities. Eternal sensory activities are called devotional service, whereas temporary sensory activities are called sense gratification. Unless one becomes tired of material sense gratification, there is no opportunity to hear transcendental messages from a person like Kapila. Devahūti expressed that she was tired. Now that her husband had left home, she wanted to get relief by hearing the instructions of Lord Kapila.

TEXT 8

तस्य त्वं तमसोऽन्धस्य दुष्पारस्याद्य पारगम् ।
सच्चक्षुर्जन्मनामन्ते लब्धं मे त्वदनुग्रहात् ॥ ८ ॥

tasya tvaṁ tamaso 'ndhasya
duṣpārasyādya pāragam
sac-cakṣur janmanām ante
labdhaṁ me tvad-anugrahāt

tasya—that; *tvam*—You; *tamasaḥ*—ignorance; *andhasya*—darkness; *duṣpārasya*—difficult to cross; *adya*—now; *pāra-gam*—crossing over; *sat*—transcendental; *cakṣuḥ*—eye; *janmanām*—of births; *ante*—at the end; *labdham*—attained; *me*—my; *tvat-anugrahāt*—by Your mercy.

TRANSLATION

Your Lordship is my only means of getting out of this darkest region of ignorance because You are my transcendental eye, which, by Your mercy only, I have attained after many, many births.

PURPORT

This verse is very instructive, since it indicates the relationship between the spiritual master and the disciple. The disciple or conditioned soul is put into this darkest region of ignorance and therefore is entangled in the material existence of sense gratification. It is very difficult to get out of this entanglement and attain freedom, but if one is fortunate enough to get the association of a spiritual master like Kapila Muni or His representative, then by his grace one can be delivered from the mire of ignorance. The spiritual master is therefore worshiped as one who delivers the disciple from the mire of ignorance with the light of the torch of knowledge. The word *pāragam* is very significant. *Pāragam* refers to one who can take the disciple to the other side. This side is conditioned life; the other side is the life of freedom. The spiritual master takes the disciple to the other side by opening his eyes with knowledge. We are suffering simply because of ignorance. By the instruction of the spiritual master, the darkness of ignorance is removed, and thus the disciple is enabled to go to the side of freedom. It is stated in *Bhagavad-gītā* that after many, many births one surrenders to the Supreme Personality of Godhead. Similarly, if, after many, many births, one is able to find a bona fide spiritual master and surrender to such a bona fide representative of Kṛṣṇa, one can be taken to the side of light.

TEXT 9

य आद्यो भगवान् पुंसामीश्वरो वै भवान् किल ।
लोकस्य तमसान्धस्य चक्षुः सूर्य इवोदितः ॥ ९ ॥

ya ādyo bhagavān puṁsām
īśvaro vai bhavān kila
lokasya tamasāndhasya
cakṣuḥ sūrya ivoditaḥ

yaḥ—He who; *ādyaḥ*—the origin; *bhagavān*—the Supreme Personality of Godhead; *puṁsām*—of all living entities; *īśvaraḥ*—the Lord; *vai*—in fact; *bhavān*—You; *kila*—indeed; *lokasya*—of the universe; *tamasā*—by the darkness of ignorance; *andhasya*—blinded; *cakṣuḥ*—eye; *sūryaḥ*—the sun; *iva*—like; *uditaḥ*—risen.

TRANSLATION

You are the Supreme Personality of Godhead, the origin and Supreme Lord of all living entities. You have arisen to disseminate the rays of the sun in order to dissipate the darkness of the ignorance of the universe.

PURPORT

Kapila Muni is accepted as an incarnation of the Supreme Personality of Godhead, Kṛṣṇa. Here the word *ādyaḥ* means "the origin of all living entities," and *puṁsām īśvaraḥ* means "the Lord (*īśvara*) of the living entities" (*īśvaraḥ paramaḥ kṛṣṇaḥ*). Kapila Muni is the direct expansion of Kṛṣṇa, who is the sun of spiritual knowledge. As the sun dissipates the darkness of the universe, so when the light of the Supreme Personality of Godhead comes down, it at once dissipates the darkness of *māyā*. We have our eyes, but without the light of the sun our eyes are of no value. Similarly, without the light of the Supreme Lord, or without the divine grace of the spiritual master, one cannot see things as they are.

TEXT 10

अथ मे देव सम्मोहमपाक्रष्टुं त्वमर्हसि ।
योऽवग्रहोऽहंममेतीत्येतस्मिन् योजितस्त्वया ॥१०॥

atha me deva sammoham
apākraṣṭuṁ tvam arhasi

yo 'vagraho 'haṁ mametīty
etasmin yojitas tvayā

atha—now; *me*—my; *deva*—O Lord; *sammoham*—delusion; *apākraṣṭum*—to dispel; *tvam*—You; *arhasi*—be pleased; *yaḥ*—which; *avagrahaḥ*—misconception; *aham*—I; *mama*—mine; *iti*—thus; *iti*—thus; *etasmin*—in this; *yojitaḥ*—engaged; *tvayā*—by You.

TRANSLATION

Now be pleased, my Lord, to dispel my great delusion. Due to my feeling of false ego, I have been engaged by Your māyā and have identified myself with the body and consequent bodily relations.

PURPORT

The false ego of identifying one's body as one's self and of claiming things possessed in relationship with this body is called *māyā.* In *Bhagavad-gītā,* Fifteenth Chapter, the Lord says, "I am sitting in everyone's heart, and from Me come everyone's remembrance and forgetfulness." Devahūti has stated that false identification of the body with the self and attachment for possessions in relation to the body are also under the direction of the Lord. Does this mean that the Lord discriminates by engaging one in His devotional service and another in sense gratification? If that were true, it would be an incongruity on the part of the Supreme Lord, but that is not the actual fact. As soon as the living entity forgets his real, constitutional position of eternal servitorship to the Lord and wants instead to enjoy himself by sense gratification, he is captured by *māyā.* This capture by *māyā* is the consciousness of false identification with the body and attachment for the possessions of the body. These are the activities of *māyā,* and since *māyā* is also an agent of the Lord, it is indirectly the action of the Lord. The Lord is merciful; if anyone wants to forget Him and enjoy this material world, He gives him full facility, not directly but through the agency of His material potency. Therefore, since the material potency is the Lord's energy, indirectly it is the Lord who gives the facility to forget Him. Devahūti therefore said, "My engagement in sense gratification was also due to You. Now kindly get me free from this entanglement."

By the grace of the Lord one is allowed to enjoy this material world, but when one is disgusted with material enjoyment and is frustrated, and when one sincerely surrenders unto the lotus feet of the Lord, then the Lord is so kind that He frees one from entanglement. Kṛṣṇa says, therefore, in *Bhagavad-gītā*, "First of all surrender, and then I will take charge of you and free you from all reactions of sinful activities." Sinful activities are those activities performed in forgetfulness of our relationship with the Lord. In this material world, activities for material enjoyment which are considered to be pious are also sinful. For example, one sometimes gives something in charity to a needy person with a view to getting back the money four times increased. Giving with the purpose of gaining something is called charity in the mode of passion. Everything done here is done in the modes of material nature, and therefore all activities but service to the Lord are sinful. Because of sinful activities we become attracted by the illusion of material attachment, and we think, "I am this body." I think of the body as myself and of bodily possessions as "mine." Devahūti requested Lord Kapila to free her from that entanglement of false identification and false possession.

TEXT 11

तं त्वा गताहं शरणं शरण्यं
स्वभृत्यसंसारतरोः कुठारम् ।
जिज्ञासयाहं प्रकृतेः पूरुषस्य
नमामि सद्धर्मविदां वरिष्ठम् ॥११॥

taṁ tvā gatāhaṁ śaraṇaṁ śaraṇyaṁ
sva-bhṛtya-saṁsāra-taroḥ kuṭhāram
jijñāsayāhaṁ prakṛteḥ pūruṣasya
namāmi sad-dharma-vidāṁ variṣṭham

tam—that person; *tvā*—unto You; *gatā*—have gone; *aham*—I; *śaraṇam*—shelter; *śaraṇyam*—worth taking shelter of; *sva-bhṛtya*—for Your dependents; *saṁsāra*—of material existence; *taroḥ*—of the tree; *kuṭhāram*—the ax; *jijñāsayā*—with the desire to know; *aham*—I; *prakṛteḥ*—of matter (woman); *pūruṣasya*—of spirit (man); *namāmi*—I offer obeisances; *sat-dharma*—of the eternal occupation; *vidām*—of the knowers; *variṣṭham*—unto the greatest.

TRANSLATION

Devahūti continued: I have taken shelter of Your lotus feet because You are the only person of whom to take shelter. You are the ax which can cut the tree of material existence. I therefore offer my obeisances unto You, who are the greatest of all transcendentalists, and I inquire from You as to the relationship between man and woman and between spirit and matter.

PURPORT

Sāṅkhya philosophy, as is well known, deals with *prakṛti* and *puruṣa. Puruṣa* is the Supreme Personality of Godhead or anyone who imitates the Supreme Personality of Godhead as an enjoyer, and *prakṛti* means "nature." In this material world, material nature is being exploited by the *puruṣas*, or the living entities. The intricacies in the material world of the relationship of the *prakṛti* and *puruṣa*, or the enjoyed and the enjoyer, is called *saṁsāra*, or material entanglement. Devahūti wanted to cut the tree of material entanglement, and she found the suitable weapon in Kapila Muni. The tree of material existence is explained in the Fifteenth Chapter of *Bhagavad-gītā* as an *aśvattha* tree whose root is upwards and whose branches are downwards. It is recommended there that one has to cut the root of this material existential tree with the ax of detachment. What is the attachment? The attachment involves *prakṛti* and *puruṣa.* The living entities are trying to lord it over material nature. Since the conditioned soul takes material nature to be the object of his enjoyment and he takes the position of the enjoyer, he is therefore called *puruṣa.*

Devahūti questioned Kapila Muni, for she knew that only He could cut her attachment to this material world. The living entities, in the guises of men and women, are trying to enjoy the material energy; therefore in one sense everyone is *puruṣa* because *puruṣa* means "enjoyer" and *prakṛti* means "enjoyed." In this material world both the so-called man and so-called woman are imitating the real *puruṣa;* the Supreme Personality of Godhead is actually the enjoyer in the transcendental sense, whereas all others are *prakṛti.* The living entities are considered *prakṛti.* In *Bhagavad-gītā,* matter is analyzed as *aparā,* or inferior nature, whereas beyond this inferior nature there is another, superior nature—the living entities. Living entities are also *prakṛti,* or enjoyed, but under the spell of *māyā,* the living entities are falsely trying to take the position of enjoyers. That is the cause of *saṁsāra-bandha,* or conditional life. Devahūti wanted to get out of conditional life and place herself in full surrender. The Lord is *śaraṇya,* which means "the only worthy personality to whom one can fully surrender," because He is full of all opulences. If anyone actually wants relief, the best course is to surrender unto the Supreme Personality of Godhead. The Lord is also described here as *sad-dharma-vidāṁ variṣṭham.* This indicates that of all transcendental occupations the best occupation is eternal loving service unto the Supreme Personality of Godhead. *Dharma* is sometimes translated as "religion," but that is not exactly the meaning. *Dharma* actually means "that which one cannot give up," "that which is inseparable from oneself." The warmth of fire is inseparable from fire; therefore warmth is called the *dharma,* or nature, of fire. Similarly, *sad-dharma* means "eternal occupation." That eternal occupation is engagement in the transcendental loving service of the Lord. The purpose of Kapiladeva's Sāṅkhya philosophy is to propagate pure, uncontaminated devotional service, and therefore He is addressed here as the most important personality amongst those who know the transcendental occupation of the living entity.

TEXT 12

मैत्रेय उवाच
इति स्वमातुर्निरवद्यमीप्सितं
निशम्य पुंसामपवर्गवर्धनम् ।
धियाभिनन्द्यात्मवतां सतां गति-
र्बभाष ईषत्स्मितशोभिताननः ॥१२॥

maitreya uvāca
iti sva-mātur niravadyam īpsitaṁ
niśamya puṁsām apavarga-vardhanam

dhiyābhinandyātmavatāṁ satāṁ gatir
babhāṣa īṣat-smita-śobhitānanaḥ

maitreyaḥ uvāca—Maitreya said; *iti*—thus; *sva-mātuḥ*—of His mother; *niravadyam*—uncontaminated; *īpsitam*—desire; *niśamya*—after hearing; *puṁsām*—of people; *apavarga*—cessation of bodily existence; *vardhanam*—increasing; *dhiyā*—mentally; *abhinandya*—having thanked; *ātma-vatām*—interested in self-realization; *satām*—of the transcendentalists; *gatiḥ*—the path; *babhāṣe*—He explained; *īṣat*—slightly; *smita*—smiling; *śobhita*—beautiful; *ānanaḥ*—His face.

TRANSLATION

Maitreya said: After hearing of His mother's uncontaminated desire for transcendental realization, the Lord thanked her within Himself for her questions, and thus, His face smiling, He explained the path of the transcendentalists, who are interested in self-realization.

PURPORT

Devahūti has surrendered her confession of material entanglement and her desire to gain release. Her questions to Lord Kapila are very interesting for persons who are actually trying to get liberation from material entanglement and attain the perfectional stage of human life. Unless one is interested in understanding his spiritual life, or his constitutional position, and unless he also feels inconvenience in material existence, his human form of life is spoiled. One who does not care for these transcendental necessities of life and simply engages like an animal in eating, sleeping, fearing and mating has spoiled his life. Lord Kapila was very much satisfied by His mother's questions because the answers stimulate one's desire for liberation from the conditional life of material existence. Such questions are called *apavarga-vardhanam.* Those who have actual spiritual interest are called *sat,* or devotees. *Satāṁ prasaṅgāt. Sat* means "that which eternally exists," and *asat* means "that which is not eternal." Unless one is situated on the spiritual platform, he is not *sat;* he is *asat.* The *asat* stands on a platform which will not exist, but anyone who stands on the spiritual platform will exist eternally. As spirit soul, everyone exists eternally, but the *asat* has accepted the material world as his shelter, and therefore he is full of anxiety. *Asad-grāhān,* the incompatible situation of the spirit soul who has the false idea of enjoying matter, is the cause of the soul's being *asat.* Actually, the spirit soul is not *asat.* As soon as one is conscious of this fact and takes to Kṛṣṇa consciousness, he becomes *sat. Satāṁ gatiḥ,* the path of the eternal, is very interesting to persons who are after liberation, and His Lordship Kapila began to speak about that path.

TEXT 13

श्रीभगवानुवाच

योग आध्यात्मिकः पुंसां मतो निःश्रेयसाय मे।
अत्यन्तोपरतिर्यत्र दुःखस्य च सुखस्य च ॥१३॥

śrī-bhagavān uvāca
yoga ādhyātmikaḥ puṁsāṁ
mato niḥśreyasāya me
atyantoparatir yatra
duḥkhasya ca sukhasya ca

śrī-bhagavān uvāca—the Personality of Godhead said; *yogaḥ*—the *yoga* system; *ādhyātmikaḥ*—relating to the soul; *puṁsām*—of living entities; *mataḥ*—is approved; *niḥśreyasāya*—for the ultimate benefit; *me*—by Me; *atyanta*—complete; *uparatiḥ*—detachment; *yatra*—where; *duḥkhasya*—from distress; *ca*—and; *sukhasya*—from happiness; *ca*—and.

TRANSLATION

The Personality of Godhead answered: The yoga system which relates to the Lord and the individual soul, which is meant for the ultimate benefit of the living entity, and which causes detachment from all happiness and distress in the material world, is the highest yoga system.

PURPORT

In the material world, everyone is trying to get some material happiness, but as soon as we get some material happiness, there is also material distress. In the material world one cannot have unadulterated happiness. Any kind of happiness one has is contaminated by distress also. For example, if we want to drink milk then we have to bother to maintain a cow and keep her fit to supply milk. Drinking milk is very nice; it is also pleasure. But for the sake of drinking milk one has to accept so much trouble. The *yoga* system, as here stated by the Lord, is meant to end all material happiness and material distress. The best *yoga*, as taught in *Bhagavad-gītā* by Kṛṣṇa, is *bhakti-yoga.* It is also mentioned in the *Gītā* that one should try to be tolerant and not be disturbed by material happiness or distress. Of course, one may say that he is not disturbed by material happiness, but he does not know that just after one enjoys so-called material happiness, material distress will follow. This is the law of the material world. Lord Kapila states that the *yoga* system is the science of the spirit. One practices *yoga* in order to attain perfection on the spiritual platform. There is no question of material happiness or distress. It is transcendental. Lord Kapila will eventually explain how it is transcendental, but the preliminary introduction is given here.

TEXT 14

तमिमं ते प्रवक्ष्यामि यमवोचं पुरानघे ।
ऋषीणां श्रोतुकामानां योगं सर्वाङ्गनैपुणम् ॥१४॥

tam imaṁ te pravakṣyāmi
yam avocaṁ purānaghe
ṛṣīṇāṁ śrotu-kāmānāṁ
yogaṁ sarvāṅga-naipuṇam

tam imam—that very; *te*—to you; *pravakṣyāmi*—I shall explain; *yam*—which; *avocam*—I explained; *purā*—formerly; *anaghe*—O pious mother; *ṛṣīṇām*—to the sages; *śrotu-kāmānām*—eager to hear; *yogam*—*yoga* system; *sarva-aṅga*—in all respects; *naipuṇam*—serviceable and practical.

TRANSLATION

O most pious mother, I shall now explain unto you the ancient yoga system, which I explained formerly to the great sages. It is serviceable and practical in every way.

PURPORT

The Lord does not manufacture a new system of *yoga*. Sometimes it is claimed that someone has become an incarnation of God and is expounding a new theological aspect of the Absolute Truth. But here we find that although Kapila Muni is the Lord Himself and is capable of manufacturing a new doctrine for His mother, He nevertheless says, "I shall just explain the ancient system which I once explained to the great sages because they were also anxious to hear about it." When we have a superexcellent process already present in Vedic scriptures, there is no need to concoct a new system, to mislead the innocent public. At present it has become a fashion to reject the standard system and present something bogus in the name of a newly invented process of *yoga*.

TEXT 15

चेतः खल्वस्य बन्धाय मुक्तये चात्मनो मतम् ।
गुणेषु सक्तं बन्धाय रतं वा पुंसि मुक्तये ॥१५॥

cetaḥ khalv asya bandhāya
muktaye cātmano matam
guṇeṣu saktaṁ bandhāya
rataṁ vā puṁsi muktaye

cetaḥ—consciousness; *khalu*—indeed; *asya*—of him; *bandhāya*—for bondage; *muktaye*—for liberation; *ca*—and; *ātmanaḥ*—of the living entity; *matam*—is considered; *guṇeṣu*—in the three modes of nature; *saktam*—attracted; *bandhāya*—for conditional life; *ratam*—attached; *vā*—or; *puṁsi*—in the Supreme Personality of Godhead; *muktaye*—for liberation.

TRANSLATION

The stage in which the consciousness of the living entity is attracted by the three modes of material nature is called conditional life. But when that same consciousness is attached to the Supreme Personality of Godhead, one is situated in the consciousness of liberation.

PURPORT

There is a distinction here between Kṛṣṇa consciousness and *māyā* consciousness. *Guṇeṣu,* or *māyā* consciousness, involves attachment to the three material modes of nature, under which one works sometimes in goodness and knowledge, sometimes in passion and sometimes in ignorance. These different qualitative activities, with the central attachment for material enjoyment, are the cause of one's conditional life. When the same *cetaḥ,* or consciousness, is transferred to the Supreme Personality of Godhead, Kṛṣṇa, or when one becomes Kṛṣṇa conscious, he is on the path of liberation.

TEXT 16

अहंममाभिमानोत्थैः कामलोभादिभिर्मलैः ।
वीतं यदा मनः शुद्धमदुःखमसुखं समम् ॥१६॥

ahaṁ mamābhimānotthaiḥ
kāma-lobhādibhir malaiḥ
vītaṁ yadā manaḥ śuddham
aduḥkham asukhaṁ samam

aham—I; *mama*—mine; *abhimāna*—from the misconception; *utthaiḥ*—produced; *kāma*—lust; *lobha*—greed; *ādibhiḥ*—and so on; *malaiḥ*—from the impurities; *vītam*—freed; *yadā*—when; *manaḥ*—the mind; *śuddham*—pure; *aduḥkham*—without distress; *asukham*—without happiness; *samam*—equipoised.

TRANSLATION

When one is completely cleansed of the impurities of lust and greed produced from the false identification of the body as "I" and bodily possessions as "mine," one's mind becomes purified. In that pure state he transcends the stage of so-called material happiness and distress.

PURPORT

Kāma and *lobha* are the symptoms of material existence. Everyone always desires to possess something. It is said here that desire and greed are the products of false identification of oneself with the body. When one becomes free from this contamination, then his mind and consciousness also become freed and attain their original state. Mind, consciousness and the living entity exist. Whenever we speak of the living entity, this includes the mind and consciousness. The difference between conditional life and liberated life occurs when we purify the mind and the consciousness. When they are purified, one becomes transcendental to material happiness and distress.

In the beginning Lord Kapila has said that perfect *yoga* enables one to transcend the platform of material distress and happiness. How this can be done is explained here: one has to purify his mind and consciousness. This can be done by the *bhakti-yoga* system. As explained in the *Nārada-pañcarātra*, one's mind and senses should be purified (*tat-paratvena nirmalam*). One's senses must be engaged in devotional service to the Lord. That is the process. The mind must have some engagement. One cannot make the mind vacant. Of course there are some foolish attempts to try to make the mind vacant or void, but that is not possible. The only process that will purify the mind is to engage it in Kṛṣṇa. The mind must be engaged. If we engage our mind in Kṛṣṇa, naturally the consciousness becomes fully purified, and there is no chance of the entrance of material desire and greed.

TEXT 17

तदा पुरुष आत्मानं केवलं प्रकृतेः परम् ।
निरन्तरं स्वयंज्योतिरणिमानमखण्डितम् ॥१७॥

tadā puruṣa ātmānaṁ
kevalaṁ prakṛteḥ param
nirantaraṁ svayaṁ-jyotir
aṇimānam akhaṇḍitam

tadā—then; *puruṣaḥ*—the individual soul; *ātmānam*—himself; *kevalam*—pure; *prakṛteḥ param*—transcendental to material existence; *nirantaram*—nondifferent; *svayam-jyotiḥ*—self-effulgent; *aṇimānam*—infinitesimal; *akhaṇḍitam*—not fragmented.

TRANSLATION

At that time the soul can see himself to be transcendental to material existence and always self-effulgent, never fragmented, although very minute in size.

PURPORT

In the state of pure consciousness, or Kṛṣṇa consciousness, one can see himself as a minute particle nondifferent from the Supreme Lord. As stated in *Bhagavad-gītā*, the *jīva*, or the individual soul, is eternally part and parcel of the Supreme Lord. Just as the sun's rays are minute particles of the brilliant constitution of the sun, so a living entity is a minute particle of the Supreme Spirit. The individual soul and the Supreme Lord are not separated as in material differentiation. The individual soul is a particle from the very beginning. One should not think that because the individual soul is a particle, it is fragmented from the whole spirit. Māyāvāda philosophy enunciates that the whole spirit exists, but a part of it, which is called the *jīva*, is entrapped by illusion. This philosophy, however, is unacceptable because spirit cannot be divided like a fragment of matter. That part, the *jīva*, is eternally a part. As long as the Supreme Spirit exists, His part and parcel also exists. As long as the sun exists, the molecules of the sun's rays also exist.

The *jīva* particle is estimated in the Vedic literature to be one ten-thousandth the size of the upper portion of a hair. It is therefore infinitesimal. The Supreme Spirit is infinite, but the living entity, or the individual soul, is infinitesimal, although it is not different in quality from the Supreme Spirit. Two words in this verse are to be particularly noted. One is *nirantaram*, which means "nondifferent," or "of the same quality." The individual soul is also expressed here as *aṇimānam*. *Aṇimānam* means "infinitesimal." The Supreme Spirit is all-pervading, but the very small spirit is the individual soul. *Akhaṇḍitam* means not exactly "fragmented" but "constitutionally always infinitesimal." No one can separate the molecular parts of the sunshine from the sun, but at the same time the molecular part of the sunshine is not as expansive as the sun itself. Similarly, the living entity, by his constitutional position, is qualitatively the same as the Supreme Spirit, but he is infinitesimal.

TEXT 18

ज्ञानवैराग्ययुक्तेन भक्तियुक्तेन चात्मना ।
परिपश्यत्युदासीनं प्रकृतिं च हतौजसम् ॥१८॥

jñāna-vairāgya-yuktena
bhakti-yuktena cātmanā
paripaśyaty udāsīnaṁ
prakṛtiṁ ca hataujasam

jñāna—knowledge; *vairāgya*—renunciation; *yuktena*—equipped with; *bhakti*—devotional service; *yuktena*—equipped with; *ca*—and; *ātmanā*—by the mind; *paripaśyati*—one sees; *udāsīnam*—indifferent; *prakṛtim*—material existence; *ca*—and; *hata-ojasam*—reduced in strength.

TRANSLATION

In that position of self-realization, by practice of knowledge and renunciation in devotional service, one sees everything in the right perspective; he becomes indifferent to material existence, and the material influence acts less powerfully upon him.

PURPORT

As the contamination of the germs of a particular disease can influence a weaker person, similarly the influence of material nature, or illusory energy, can act on the weaker, or conditioned, soul but not on the liberated soul. Self-realization is the position of the liberated state. One understands his constitutional position by knowledge and *vairāgya*, renunciation. Without knowledge, one cannot have realization. The realization that one is the infinitesimal part and parcel of the Supreme Spirit makes him unattached to material, conditional life. That is the beginning of devotional service. Unless one is liberated from material contamination, one cannot engage himself in the devotional service of the Lord. In this verse, therefore, it is stated, *jñāna-vairāgya-yuktena:* when one is in full knowledge of one's constitutional position and is in the renounced order of life, detached from material attraction, then, by pure devotional service, *bhakti-yuktena*, he can engage himself as a loving servant of the Lord. *Paripaśyati* means that he can see everything in its right perspective. Then the influence of material nature becomes almost nil. This is also confirmed in *Bhagavad-gītā. Brahma-bhūtaḥ prasannātmā:* when one is self-realized he becomes happy and free from the influence of material nature, and at that time he is freed from lamentation and hankering. The Lord states that position as *mad-bhaktiṁ labhate parām*, the real state of beginning devotional service. Similarly, it is confirmed in the *Nārada-pañcarātra* that when the senses are purified they can then be engaged in the devotional service of the Lord. One who is attached to material contamination cannot be a devotee.

TEXT 19

न युज्यमानया भक्त्या भगवत्यखिलात्मनि ।
सदृशोऽस्ति शिवः पन्था योगिनां ब्रह्मसिद्धये ॥१९॥

na yujyamānayā bhaktyā
bhagavaty akhilātmani
sadṛśo 'sti śivaḥ panthā
yoginām̐ brahma-siddhaye

na—not; *yujyamānayā*—being performed; *bhaktyā*—devotional service; *bhagavati*—towards the Supreme Personality of Godhead; *akhila-ātmani*—the Supersoul; *sadṛśaḥ*—like; *asti*—there is; *śivaḥ*—auspicious; *panthāḥ*—path; *yoginām*—of the *yogīs; brahma-siddhaye*—for perfection in self-realization.

TRANSLATION

Perfection in self-realization cannot be attained by any kind of yogī unless he engages in devotional service to the Supreme Personality of Godhead, for that is the only auspicious path.

PURPORT

That knowledge and renunciation are never perfect unless joined by devotional service is explicitly explained here. *Na yujyamānayā* means "without being dovetailed." When there is devotional service, then the question is where to offer that service. Devotional service is to be offered to the Supreme Personality of Godhead, who is the Supersoul of everything, for that is the only reliable path of self-realization, or Brahman realization. The word *brahma-siddhaye* means to understand oneself to be different from matter, to understand oneself to be Brahman. The Vedic words are *ahaṁ brahmāsmi. Brahma-siddhi* means that one should know that he is not matter; he is pure soul. There are different kinds of *yogīs*, but every *yogī* is supposed to engage in self-realization, or Brahman realization. It is clearly stated here that unless one is fully engaged in the devotional service of the Supreme Personality of Godhead one cannot have easy approach to the path of *brahma-siddhi.*

In the beginning of the Second Chapter of *Śrīmad-Bhāgavatam* it is stated that when one engages himself in the devotional service of Vāsudeva, spiritual knowledge and renunciation of the material world automatically become manifest. Thus a devotee does not have to try separately for renunciation or knowledge. Devotional service itself is so powerful that by one's service attitude, everything is revealed. It is stated here, *śivaḥ panthāḥ:* this is the only auspicious path for self-realization. The path of devotional service is the most confidential means for attaining Brahman realization. That perfection in Brahman realization is attained through the auspicious path of devotional service indicates that the so-called Brahman realization, or realization of the *brahmajyoti* effulgence, is not *brahma-siddhi.* Beyond that *brahmajyoti* there is the Supreme Personality of Godhead. In the *Upaniṣads* a devotee prays to the Lord to kindly put aside the effulgence, *brahmajyoti,* so that the devotee may see within the *brahmajyoti* the actual, eternal form of the Lord. Unless one attains realization of the transcendental form of the Lord, there is no question of *bhakti. Bhakti* necessitates the existence of the recipient of devotional service and the devotee who renders devotional service. *Brahma-siddhi* through devotional service is realization of the Supreme Personality of Godhead. The understanding of the effulgent rays of the body of the Supreme Godhead is not the perfect stage of *brahma-siddhi,* or Brahman realization. Nor is the realization of the Paramātmā feature of the Supreme Person perfect, for Bhagavān, the Supreme Personality of Godhead, is *akhilātmā*—He is the Supersoul. One who realizes the Supreme Personality realizes the other features, namely the Paramātmā feature and the Brahman feature, and that total realization is *brahma-siddhi.*

TEXT 20

प्रसङ्गमजरं पाशमात्मनः कवयो विदुः ।
स एव साधुषु कृतो मोक्षद्वारमपावृतम् ॥२०॥

prasaṅgam ajaraṁ pāśam
ātmanaḥ kavayo viduḥ
sa eva sādhuṣu kṛto
mokṣa-dvāram apāvṛtam

prasaṅgam—attachment; *ajaram*—strong; *pāśam*—entanglement; *ātmanaḥ*—of the soul; *kavayaḥ*—learned men; *viduḥ*—know; *saḥ eva*—that same; *sādhuṣu*—to the devotees; *kṛtaḥ*—applied; *mokṣa-dvāram*—the door of liberation; *apāvṛtam*—opened.

TRANSLATION

Every learned man knows very well that attachment for the material is the greatest entanglement of the spirit soul. But that same attachment, when applied to the self-realized devotees, opens the door of liberation.

PURPORT

Here it is clearly stated that attachment for one thing is the cause of bondage in conditioned life, and the same attachment, when applied to something else, opens the door of liberation. Attachment cannot be killed; it has simply to be transferred. Attachment for material things is called material consciousness, and attachment for Kṛṣṇa or His devotee is called Kṛṣṇa consciousness. Consciousness, therefore, is the platform of attachment. It is clearly stated here that when we simply purify the consciousness from material consciousness to Kṛṣṇa consciousness, we attain liberation. Despite the statement that one should give up attachment, desirelessness is not possible for a living entity. A living entity, by constitution, has the propensity to be attached to something. We see that if someone has no object of attachment, if he has no children, then he transfers his attachment to cats and dogs. This indicates that the propensity for attachment cannot be stopped; it must be utilized for the best purpose. Our attachment for material things perpetuates our conditional state, but the same attachment, when transferred to the Supreme Personality of Godhead or His devotee, is the source of liberation.

Here it is recommended that attachment should be transferred to the self-realized devotees, the *sādhus.* And who is a *sādhu*? A *sādhu* is not just an ordinary man with a saffron robe or long beard. A *sādhu* is described in *Bhagavad-gītā* as one who unflinchingly engages in devotional service. Even though one is found not to be following the strict rules and regulations of devotional service, if one simply has unflinching faith in Kṛṣṇa, the Supreme Person, he is understood to be a *sādhu. Sādhur eva sa mantavyaḥ.* A *sādhu* is a strict follower of devotional service. It is recommended here that if one at all wants to realize Brahman, or spiritual perfection, his attachment should be transferred to the *sādhu,* or devotee. Lord Caitanya also confirmed this. *Lava-mātra sādhu-saṅge sarva-siddhi haya:* simply by a moment's association with a *sādhu,* one can attain perfection.

Mahātmā is a synonym of *sādhu.* It is said that service to a *mahātmā,* or elevated devotee of the Lord, is *dvāram āhur vimukteḥ,* the royal road of liberation. *Mahat-sevāṁ dvāram āhur vimuktes tamo-dvāraṁ yoṣitāṁ saṅgi-saṅgam* (*Bhāg.* 5.5.2). Rendering service to the materialists has the opposite effect. If anyone offers service to a gross materialist, or a person engaged only in sense enjoyment, then by association with such a person the door to hell is opened. The same principle is confirmed here. Attachment to a devotee is attachment to the service of the Lord because if one associates with a *sādhu,* the result will be that the *sādhu* will teach him how to become a devotee, a worshiper and a sincere servitor of the Lord. These are the gifts of a *sādhu.* If we want to associate with a *sādhu,* we cannot expect him to give us instructions on how to improve our material condition, but he will give us instructions on how to cut the knot of the contamination of material attraction and how to elevate ourselves in devotional service. That is the result of associating with a *sādhu.* Kapila Muni first of all instructs that the path of liberation begins with such association.

TEXT 21

तितिक्षवः कारुणिकाः सुहृदः सर्वदेहिनाम् ।
अजातशत्रवः शान्ताः साधवः साधुभूषणाः ॥२१॥

titikṣavaḥ kāruṇikāḥ
suhṛdaḥ sarva-dehinām
ajāta-śatravaḥ śāntāḥ
sādhavaḥ sādhu-bhūṣaṇāḥ

titikṣavaḥ—tolerant; *kāruṇikāḥ*—merciful; *suhṛdaḥ*—friendly; *sarva-dehinām*—to all living entities; *ajāta-śatravaḥ*—inimical to none; *śāntāḥ*—peaceful; *sādhavaḥ*—abiding by scriptures; *sādhu-bhūṣaṇāḥ*—adorned with sublime characteristics.

TRANSLATION

The symptoms of a sādhu are that he is tolerant, merciful and friendly to all living entities. He has no enemies, he is peaceful, he abides by the scriptures, and all his characteristics are sublime.

PURPORT

A *sādhu,* as described above, is a devotee of the Lord. His concern, therefore, is to enlighten people in devotional service to the Lord. That is his mercy. He knows that without devotional service to the Lord, human life is spoiled. A devotee travels all over the country, from door to door, preaching, "Be Kṛṣṇa conscious. Be a devotee of Lord Kṛṣṇa. Don't spoil your life in simply fulfilling your animal propensities. Human life is meant for self-realization, or Kṛṣṇa consciousness." These are the preachings of a *sādhu.* He is not satisfied with his own liberation. He always thinks about others. He is the most compassionate personality towards all the fallen souls. One of his qualifications, therefore, is *kāruṇika,* great mercy to the fallen souls. While engaged in preaching work, he has to meet with so many opposing elements, and therefore the *sādhu,* or devotee of the Lord, has to be very tolerant. Someone may ill-treat him because the conditioned souls are not prepared to receive the transcendental knowledge of devotional service. They do not like it; that is their disease. The *sādhu* has the thankless task of impressing upon them the importance of devotional service. Sometimes devotees are personally attacked with violence. Lord Jesus Christ was crucified, Haridāsa Ṭhākura was caned in twenty-two marketplaces, and Lord Caitanya's principal assistant, Nityānanda, was violently attacked by Jagāi and

Mādhāi. But still they were tolerant because their mission was to deliver the fallen souls. One of the qualifications of a *sādhu* is that he is very tolerant and is merciful to all fallen souls. He is merciful because he is the well-wisher of all living entities. He is not only a well-wisher of human society, but a well-wisher of animal society as well. It is said here, *sarva-dehinām*, which indicates all living entities who have accepted material bodies. Not only does the human being have a material body, but other living entities, such as cats and dogs, also have material bodies. The devotee of the Lord is merciful to everyone—the cats, dogs, trees, etc. He treats all living entities in such a way that they can ultimately get salvation from this material entanglement. Śivānanda Sena, one of the disciples of Lord Caitanya, gave liberation to a dog by treating the dog transcendentally. There are many instances where a dog got salvation by association with a *sādhu*, because a *sādhu* engages in the highest philanthropic activities for the benediction of all living entities. Yet although a *sādhu* is not inimical towards anyone, the world is so ungrateful that even a *sādhu* has many enemies.

What is the difference between an enemy and a friend? It is a difference in behavior. A *sādhu* behaves with all conditioned souls for their ultimate relief from material entanglement. Therefore, no one can be more friendly than a *sādhu* in relieving a conditioned soul. A *sādhu* is calm, and he quietly and peacefully follows the principles of scripture. A *sādhu* means one who follows the principles of scripture and at the same time is a devotee of the Lord. One who actually follows the principles of scripture must be a devotee of God because all the *śāstras* instruct us to obey the orders of the Personality of Godhead. *Sādhu*, therefore, means a follower of the scriptural injunctions and a devotee of the Lord. All these characteristics are prominent in a devotee. A devotee develops all the good qualities of the demigods, whereas a nondevotee, even though academically qualified, has no actual good qualifications or good characteristics according to the standard of transcendental realization.

TEXT 22

मय्यनन्येन भावेन भक्तिं कुर्वन्ति ये दृढाम् ।
मत्कृते त्यक्तकर्माणस्त्यक्तस्वजनबान्धवाः ॥२२॥

mayy ananyena bhāvena
bhaktiṁ kurvanti ye dṛḍhām
mat-kṛte tyakta-karmāṇas
tyakta-svajana-bāndhavāḥ

mayi—unto Me; *ananyena bhāvena*—with undeviated mind; *bhaktim*—devotional service; *kurvanti*—perform; *ye*—those who; *dṛḍhām*—staunch; *mat-kṛte*—for My sake; *tyakta*—renounced; *karmāṇaḥ*—activities; *tyakta*—renounced; *sva-jana*—family relationships; *bāndhavāḥ*—friendly acquaintances.

TRANSLATION

Such a sādhu engages in staunch devotional service to the Lord without deviation. For the sake of the Lord he renounces all other connections, such as family relationships and friendly acquaintances within the world.

PURPORT

A person in the renounced order of life, a *sannyāsī,* is also called a *sādhu* because he renounces everything—his home, his comfort, his friends, his relatives, and his duties to friends and to family. He renounces everything for the sake of the Supreme Personality of Godhead. A *sannyāsī* is generally in the renounced order of life, but his renunciation will be successful only when his energy is employed in the service of the Lord with great austerity. It is said here, therefore, *bhaktiṁ kurvanti ye dṛḍhām.* A person who seriously engages in the service of the Lord and is in the renounced order of life is a *sādhu.* A *sādhu* is one who has given up all responsibility to society, family, and worldly humanitarianism, simply for the service of the Lord. As soon as he takes his birth in the world, a person has so many responsibilities and obligations—to the public, to the demigods, to the great sages, to the general living beings, to his parents, to the family forefathers and to many others. When he gives up all such obligations for the sake of the service of the Supreme Lord, he is not punished for such renunciation of obligation. But if for sense gratification a person renounces all such obligations, he is punished by the law of nature.

TEXT 23

मदाश्रयाः कथा मृष्टाः शृण्वन्ति कथयन्ति च ।
तपन्ति विविधास्तापा नैतान्मद्गतचेतसः ॥२३॥

mad-āśrayāḥ kathā mṛṣṭāḥ
śṛṇvanti kathayanti ca
tapanti vividhās tāpā
naitān mad-gata-cetasaḥ

mat-āśrayāḥ—about Me; *kathāḥ*—stories; *mṛṣṭāḥ*—delightful; *śṛṇvanti*—they hear; *kathayanti*—they chant; *ca*—and; *tapanti*—inflict suffering; *vividhāḥ*—various; *tāpāḥ*—the material miseries; *na*—do not; *etān*—unto them; *mat-gata*—fixed on Me; *cetasaḥ*—their thoughts.

TRANSLATION

Engaged constantly in chanting and hearing about Me, the Supreme Personality of Godhead, the sādhus do not suffer from material miseries because they are always filled with thoughts of My pastimes and activities.

PURPORT

There are multifarious miseries in material existence—those pertaining to the body and the mind, those imposed by other living entities and those imposed by natural disturbances. But a *sādhu* is not disturbed by such miserable conditions because his mind is always filled with Kṛṣṇa consciousness, and thus he does not like to talk about anything but the activities of the Lord. Mahārāja Ambarīṣa did not speak of anything but the pastimes of the Lord. *Vacāṁsi vaikuṇṭha-guṇānuvarṇane* (*Bhāg.* 9.4.18). He engaged his words only in glorification of the Supreme Personality of Godhead. *Sādhus* are always interested in hearing about the activities of the Lord or His devotees. Since they are filled with Kṛṣṇa consciousness, they are forgetful of the material miseries. Ordinary conditioned souls, being forgetful of the activities of the Lord, are always full of anxieties and material tribulations. On the other hand, since the devotees always engage in the topics of the Lord, they are forgetful of the miseries of material existence.

TEXT 24

त एते साधवः साध्वि सर्वसङ्गविवर्जिताः ।
सङ्गस्तेष्वथ ते प्रार्थ्यः सङ्गदोषहरा हि ते ॥२४॥

ta ete sādhavaḥ sādhvi
sarva-saṅga-vivarjitāḥ
saṅgas teṣv atha te prārthyaḥ
saṅga-doṣa-harā hi te

te ete—those very; *sādhavaḥ*—devotees; *sādhvi*—virtuous lady; *sarva*—all; *saṅga*—attachments; *vivarjitāḥ*—freed from; *saṅgaḥ*—attachment; *teṣu*—unto them; *atha*—hence; *te*—by you; *prārthyaḥ*—must be sought; *saṅga-doṣa*—the pernicious effects of material attachment; *harāḥ*—counteracters of; *hi*—indeed; *te*—they.

TRANSLATION

O My mother, O virtuous lady, these are the qualities of great devotees who are free from all attachment. You must seek attachment to such holy men, for this counteracts the pernicious effects of material attachment.

PURPORT

Kapila Muni herein advises His mother, Devahūti, that if she wants to be free from material attachment, she should increase her attachment for the *sādhus*, or devotees who are completely freed from all material attachment. In *Bhagavad-gītā*, Fifteenth Chapter, verse 5, it is stated who is qualified to enter into the kingdom of Godhead. It is said there, *nirmāna-mohā jita-saṅga-doṣāḥ.* This refers to one who is completely freed from the puffed-up condition of material possessiveness. A person may be materially very rich, opulent or respectable, but if he at all wants to transfer himself to the spiritual kingdom, back home, back to Godhead, then he has to be freed from the puffed-up condition of material possessiveness, because that is a false position.

The word *moha* used here means the false understanding that one is rich or poor. In this material world, the conception that one is very rich or very poor—or any such consciousness in connection with material existence—is false, because this body itself is false, or temporary. A pure soul who is prepared to be freed from this material entanglement must first of all be free from the association of the three modes of nature. Our consciousness at the present moment is polluted because of association with the three modes of nature; therefore in *Bhagavad-gītā* the same principle is stated. It is advised, *jita-saṅga-doṣāḥ:* one should be freed from the contaminated association of the three modes of material nature. Here also, in the *Śrīmad-Bhāgavatam,* this is confirmed: a pure devotee, who is preparing to transfer himself to the spiritual kingdom, is also freed from the association of the three modes of material nature. We have to seek the association of such devotees. For this reason we have begun the International Society for Krishna Consciousness. There are many mercantile, scientific and other associations in human society to develop a particular type of education or consciousness, but there is no association which helps one to get free from all material association. If anyone has reached the stage where he must become free from this material contamination, then he has to seek the association of devotees, wherein Kṛṣṇa consciousness is exclusively cultured. One can thereby become freed from all material association.

Because a devotee is freed from all contaminated material association, he is not affected by the miseries of material existence. Even though he appears to be in the material world, he is not affected by the miseries of the material world. How is it possible? There is a very good example in the activities of the cat. The cat carries her kittens in her mouth, and when she kills a rat she also carries the booty in her mouth. Thus both are carried in the mouth of the cat, but they are in different conditions. The kitten feels comfort in the mouth of the mother, whereas when the rat is carried in the mouth of the cat, the rat feels the blows of death. Similarly, those who are *sādhavaḥ,* or devotees engaged in Kṛṣṇa consciousness in the transcendental service of the Lord, do not feel the contamination of material miseries, whereas those who are not devotees in Kṛṣṇa consciousness actually feel the miseries of material existence. One should therefore give up the association of materialistic persons and seek the association of persons engaged in Kṛṣṇa consciousness, and by such association he will benefit in spiritual advancement. By their words and instructions, he will be able to cut off his attachment to material existence.

TEXT 25

सतां प्रसङ्गान्मम वीर्यसंविदो
भवन्ति हृत्कर्णरसायनाः कथाः ।
तज्जोषणादाश्वपवर्गवर्त्मनि
श्रद्धा रतिर्भक्तिरनुक्रमिष्यति ॥२५॥

satāṁ prasaṅgān mama vīrya-saṁvido
bhavanti hṛt-karṇa-rasāyanāḥ kathāḥ
taj-joṣaṇād āśv apavarga-vartmani
śraddhā ratir bhaktir anukramiṣyati

satām—of pure devotees; *prasaṅgāt*—through the association; *mama*—My; *vīrya*—wonderful activities; *saṁvidaḥ*—by discussion of; *bhavanti*—become; *hṛt*—to the heart; *karṇa*—to the ear; *rasa-ayanāḥ*—pleasing; *kathāḥ*—the stories; *tat*—of that; *joṣaṇāt*—by cultivation; *āśu*—quickly; *apavarga*—of liberation; *vartmani*—on the path; *śraddhā*—firm faith; *ratiḥ*—attraction; *bhaktiḥ*—devotion; *anu-kramiṣyati*—will follow in order.

TRANSLATION

In the association of pure devotees, discussion of the pastimes and activities of the Supreme Personality of Godhead is very pleasing and satisfying to the ear and the heart. By cultivating such knowledge one gradually becomes advanced on the path of liberation, and thereafter he is freed, and his attraction becomes fixed. Then real devotion and devotional service begin.

PURPORT

The process of advancing in Kṛṣṇa consciousness and devotional service is described here. The first point is that one must seek the association of persons who are Kṛṣṇa conscious and who engage in devotional service. Without such association one cannot make advancement. Simply by theoretical knowledge or study one cannot make any appreciable advancement. One must give up the association of materialistic persons and seek the association of devotees because without the association of devotees one cannot understand the activities of the Lord. Generally, people are convinced of the impersonal feature of the Absolute Truth. Because they do not associate with devotees, they cannot understand that the Absolute Truth can be a person and have personal activities. This is a very difficult subject matter, and unless one has personal understanding of the Absolute Truth, there is no meaning to devotion. Service or devotion cannot be offered to anything impersonal. Service must be offered to a person. Nondevotees cannot appreciate Kṛṣṇa consciousness by reading the *Śrīmad-Bhāgavatam* or any other Vedic literature wherein the activities of the Lord are described; they think that these activities are fictional, manufactured stories because spiritual life is not explained to them in the proper mood. To understand the personal activities of the Lord, one has to seek the association of devotees, and by such association, when one contemplates and tries to understand the transcendental activities of the Lord, the path to liberation is open, and he is freed. One who has firm faith in the Supreme Personality of Godhead becomes fixed, and his attraction for association with the Lord and the devotees increases. Association with devotees means association with the Lord. The devotee who makes this association develops the consciousness for rendering service to the Lord, and then, being situated in the transcendental position of devotional service, he gradually becomes perfect.

TEXT 26

भक्त्या पुमाञ्जातविराग ऐन्द्रियाद्
दृष्टश्रुतान्मद्रचनानुचिन्तया ।
चित्तस्य यत्तो ग्रहणे योगयुक्तो
यतिष्यते ऋजुभिर्योगमार्गैः ॥२६॥

bhaktyā pumāñ jāta-virāga aindriyād
dṛṣṭa-śrutān mad-racanānucintayā
cittasya yatto grahaṇe yoga-yukto
yatiṣyate ṛjubhir yoga-mārgaiḥ

bhaktyā—by devotional service; *pumān*—a person; *jāta-virāgaḥ*—having developed distaste; *aindriyāt*—for sense gratification; *dṛṣṭa*—

seen (in this world); *śrutāt*—heard (in the next world); *mat-racana*—My activities of creation and so on; *anucintayā*—by constantly thinking about; *cittasya*—of the mind; *yattaḥ*—engaged; *grahaṇe*—in the control; *yoga-yuktaḥ*—situated in devotional service; *yatiṣyate*—will endeavor; *ṛjubhiḥ*—easy; *yoga-mārgaiḥ*—by the processes of mystic power.

TRANSLATION

Thus consciously engaged in devotional service in the association of devotees, a person gains distaste for sense gratification, both in this world and in the next, by constantly thinking about the activities of the Lord. This process of Kṛṣṇa consciousness is the easiest process of mystic power; when one is actually situated on that path of devotional service, he is able to control the mind.

PURPORT

In all scriptures people are encouraged to act in a pious way so that they can enjoy sense gratification not only in this life but also in the next. For example, one is promised promotion to the heavenly kingdom of higher planets by pious fruitive activities. But a devotee in the association of devotees prefers to contemplate the activities of the Lord—how He has created this universe, how He is maintaining it, how the creation dissolves, and how in the spiritual kingdom the Lord's pastimes are going on. There are full literatures describing these activities of the Lord, especially *Bhagavad-gītā*, *Brahma-saṁhitā* and *Śrīmad-Bhāgavatam*. The sincere devotee who associates with devotees gets the opportunity to hear and contemplate this subject of the pastimes of the Lord, and the result is that he feels distaste for so-called happiness in this or that world, in heaven or on other planets. The devotees are simply interested in being transferred to the personal association of the Lord; they have no more attraction for temporary so-called happiness. That is the position of one who is *yoga-yukta*. One who is fixed in mystic power is not disturbed by the allurement of this world or that world; he is interested in the matters of spiritual understanding or the spiritual situation. This sublime situation is very easily attained by the easiest process, *bhakti-yoga*. *Ṛjubhir yoga-mārgaiḥ*. A very suitable word used here is *ṛjubhiḥ*, or "very easy." There are different processes of *yoga-mārga*, attaining *yoga* perfection, but this process, devotional service to the Lord, is the easiest. Not only is it the easiest process, but the result is sublime. Everyone, therefore, should try to take this process of Kṛṣṇa consciousness and reach the highest perfection of life.

TEXT 27

असेवयायं प्रकृतेर्गुणानां
ज्ञानेन वैराग्यविजृम्भितेन ।
योगेन मय्यर्पितया च भक्त्या
मां प्रत्यगात्मानमिहावरुन्धे ॥२७॥

asevayāyaṁ prakṛter guṇānāṁ
jñānena vairāgya-vijṛmbhitena
yogena mayy arpitayā ca bhaktyā
māṁ pratyag-ātmānam ihāvarundhe

asevayā—by not engaging in the service; *ayam*—this person; *prakṛteḥ guṇānām*—of the modes of material nature; *jñānena*—by knowledge; *vairāgya*—with renunciation; *vijṛmbhitena*—developed; *yogena*—by practicing *yoga; mayi*—unto Me; *arpitayā*—fixed; *ca*—and; *bhaktyā*—with devotion; *mām*—unto Me; *pratyak-ātmānam*—the Absolute Truth; *iha*—in this very life; *avarundhe*—one attains.

TRANSLATION

Thus by not engaging in the service of the modes of material nature but by developing Kṛṣṇa consciousness, knowledge in renunciation, and by practicing yoga, in which the mind is always fixed in devotional service unto the Supreme Personality of Godhead, one achieves My association in this very life, for I am the Supreme Personality, the Absolute Truth.

PURPORT

When one engages in devotional service to the Lord in the nine different kinds of *bhakti-yoga*, as enunciated in authoritative scriptures, such as hearing (*śravaṇam*), chanting (*kīrtanam*), remembering, offering worship, praying and offering personal service—either in one of them, or two or three or all of them—he naturally has no opportunity to engage in the service of the three modes of material nature. Unless one has good engagements in spiritual service, it is not possible to get out of the attachment to material service. Those who are not devotees, therefore, are interested in so-called humanitarian or philanthropic work, such as opening a hospital or charitable institution. These are undoubtedly good works in the sense that they are pious activities, and their result is that the performer may get some opportunities for sense gratification, either in this life or in the next. Devotional service, however, is beyond the boundary of sense gratification. It is completely spiritual activity. When one engages in the spiritual activities of devotional service, naturally he does not get any opportunity to engage in sense gratificatory activities. Kṛṣṇa conscious activities are performed not blindly but with perfect understanding of knowledge and renunciation. This kind of *yoga* practice, in which the mind is always fixed upon the Supreme Personality of Godhead in devotion, results in liberation in this very life. The person who performs such acts gets in touch with the Supreme Personality of Godhead. Lord Caitanya, therefore, approved the process of hearing from realized devotees about the pastimes of the Lord. It does not matter to what category of this world the audience belongs. If one meekly and submissively hears about the activities of the Lord from a realized soul, he will be able to conquer the Supreme Personality of Godhead, who is unconquerable by any other process. Hearing or associating with devotees is the most important function for self-realization.

TEXT 28

देवहूतिरुवाच

काचित्त्वय्युचिता भक्तिः कीदृशी मम गोचरा ।
यया पदं ते निर्वाणमञ्जसान्वाश्नवा अहम् ॥२८॥

devahūtir uvāca
kācit tvayy ucitā bhaktiḥ
kīdṛśī mama gocarā
yayā padaṁ te nirvāṇam
añjasānvāśnavā aham

devahūtiḥ uvāca—Devahūti said; *kācit*—what; *tvayi*—unto You; *ucitā*—proper; *bhaktiḥ*—devotional service; *kīdṛśī*—what kind; *mama*—by me; *go-carā*—fit to be practiced; *yayā*—by which; *padam*—feet; *te*—Your; *nirvāṇam*—liberation; *añjasā*—immediately; *anvāśnavai*—shall attain; *aham*—I.

TRANSLATION

On hearing this statement of the Lord, Devahūti inquired: What kind of devotional service is worth developing and practicing to help me easily and immediately attain the service of Your lotus feet?

PURPORT

It is stated in *Bhagavad-gītā* that no one is barred from rendering service to the Lord. Whether one is a woman or a laborer or a merchant, if he engages himself in the devotional service of the Lord he is promoted to the highest perfectional state and goes back home, back to Godhead. The devotional service most suitable for different types of devotees is determined and fixed by the mercy of the spiritual master.

TEXT 29

यो योगो भगवद्बाणो निर्वाणात्मंस्त्वयोदितः ।
कीदृशः कति चाङ्गानि यतस्तत्त्वावबोधनम् ॥२९॥

yo yogo bhagavad-bāṇo
nirvāṇātmaṁs tvayoditaḥ
kīdṛśaḥ kati cāṅgāni
yatas tattvāvabodhanam

yaḥ—which; *yogaḥ*—mystic *yoga* process; *bhagavat-bāṇaḥ*—aiming at the Supreme Personality of Godhead; *nirvāṇa-ātman*—O embodiment of *nirvāṇa; tvayā*—by You; *uditaḥ*—explained; *kīdṛśaḥ*—of what nature; *kati*—how many; *ca*—and; *aṅgāni*—branches; *yataḥ*—by which; *tattva*—of the truth; *avabodhanam*—understanding.

TRANSLATION

The mystic yoga system, as You have explained, aims at the Supreme Personality of Godhead and is meant for completely ending material existence. Please let me know the nature of that yoga system. How many ways are there by which one can understand in truth that sublime yoga?

PURPORT

There are different kinds of mystic *yoga* systems aiming for different phases of the Absolute Truth. The *jñāna-yoga* system aims at the impersonal Brahman effulgence, and the *haṭha-yoga* system aims at the localized personal aspect, the Paramātmā feature of the Absolute Truth, whereas *bhakti-yoga*, or devotional service, which is executed in nine different ways, headed by hearing and chanting, aims at complete realization of the Supreme Lord. There are different methods of self-realization. But here Devahūti especially refers to the *bhakti-yoga* system, which has already been primarily explained by the Lord. The different parts of the *bhakti-yoga* system are hearing, chanting, remembering, offering prayers, worshiping the Lord in the temple, accepting service to Him, carrying out His orders, making friendship with Him and ultimately surrendering everything for the service of the Lord. The word *nirvāṇātman* is very significant in this verse. Unless one accepts the process of devotional service, one cannot end the continuation of material existence. As far as *jñānīs* are concerned, they are interested in *jñāna-yoga*, but even if one elevates oneself, after a great performance of austerity, to the Brahman effulgence, there is a chance of falling down again to the material world. Therefore, *jñāna-yoga* does not actually end material existence. Similarly, regarding the *haṭha-yoga* system, which aims at the localized aspect of the Lord, Paramātmā, it has been experienced that many *yogīs*, such as Viśvāmitra, fall down. But *bhakti-yogīs*, once approaching the Supreme Personality of Godhead, never come back to this material world, as it is confirmed in the *Bhagavad-gītā*. *Yad gatvā na nivartante:* upon going, one never comes back. *Tyaktvā dehaṁ punar janma naiti:* after giving up this body, he never comes back again to accept a material body. *Nirvāṇa* does not finish the existence of the soul. The soul is ever existing. Therefore *nirvāṇa* means to end one's material existence, and to end material existence means to go back home, back to Godhead.

Sometimes it is asked how the living entity falls down from the spiritual world to the material world. Here is the answer. Unless one is elevated to the Vaikuṇṭha planets, directly in touch with the Supreme Personality of Godhead, he is prone to fall down, either from the impersonal Brahman realization or from an ecstatic trance of meditation. Another word in this verse, *bhagavad-bāṇaḥ*, is very significant. *Bāṇaḥ* means "arrow." The *bhakti-yoga* system is just like an arrow aiming up to the Supreme Personality of Godhead. The *bhakti-yoga* system never urges one towards the impersonal Brahman effulgence or to the point of Paramātmā realization. This *bāṇaḥ*, or arrow, is so sharp and swift that it goes directly to the Supreme Personality of Godhead, penetrating the regions of impersonal Brahman and localized Paramātmā.

TEXT 30

तदेतन्मे विजानीहि यथाहं मन्दधीर्हरे ।
सुखं बुद्ध्येय दुर्बोधं योषा भवदनुग्रहात् ॥३०॥

tad etan me vijānīhi
yathāhaṁ manda-dhīr hare
sukhaṁ buddhyeya durbodhaṁ
yoṣā bhavad-anugrahāt

tat etat—that same; *me*—to me; *vijānīhi*—please explain; *yathā*—so that; *aham*—I; *manda*—slow; *dhīḥ*—whose intelligence; *hare*—O my Lord; *sukham*—easily; *buddhyeya*—may understand; *durbodham*—very difficult to understand; *yoṣā*—a woman; *bhavat-anugrahāt*—by Your grace.

TRANSLATION

My dear son, Kapila, after all, I am a woman. It is very difficult for me to understand the Absolute Truth because my intelligence is not very great. But if You will kindly explain it to me, even

though I am not very intelligent, I can understand it and thereby feel transcendental happiness.

PURPORT

Knowledge of the Absolute Truth is not very easily understood by ordinary, less intelligent men; but if the spiritual master is kind enough to the disciple, however unintelligent the disciple may be, then by the divine grace of the spiritual master everything is revealed. Viśvanātha Cakravartī Ṭhākura therefore says, *yasya prasādād*, by the mercy of the spiritual master, the mercy of the Supreme Personality of Godhead, *bhagavat-prasādaḥ*, is revealed. Devahūti requested her great son to be merciful towards her because she was a less intelligent woman and also His mother. By the grace of Kapiladeva it was quite possible for her to understand the Absolute Truth, even though the subject matter is very difficult for ordinary persons, especially women.

TEXT 31

मैत्रेय उवाच
विदित्वार्थं कपिलो मातुरित्थं
जातस्नेहो यत्र तन्वाभिजातः ।
तत्त्वाम्नायं यत्प्रवदन्ति सांख्यं
प्रोवाच वै भक्तिवितानयोगम् ॥३१॥

maitreya uvāca
viditvārthaṁ kapilo mātur itthaṁ
jāta-sneho yatra tanvābhijātaḥ
tattvāmnāyaṁ yat pravadanti sāṅkhyaṁ
provāca vai bhakti-vitāna-yogam

maitreyaḥ uvāca—Maitreya said; *viditvā*—having known; *artham*—purpose; *kapilaḥ*—Lord Kapila; *mātuḥ*—of His mother; *ittham*—thus; *jāta-snehaḥ*—became compassionate; *yatra*—upon her; *tanvā*—from her body; *abhijātaḥ*—born; *tattva-āmnāyam*—truths received by disciplic succession; *yat*—which; *pravadanti*—they call; *sāṅkhyam*—

Sāṅkhya philosophy; *provāca*—He described; *vai*—in fact; *bhakti*—devotional service; *vitāna*—spreading; *yogam*—mystic *yoga.*

TRANSLATION

Śrī Maitreya said: After hearing the statement of His mother, Kapila could understand her purpose, and He became compassionate towards her because of being born of her body. He described the Sāṅkhya system of philosophy, which is a combination of devotional service and mystic realization, as received by disciplic succession.

TEXT 32

श्रीभगवानुवाच
देवानां गुणलिङ्गानामानुश्रविककर्मणाम् ।
सत्त्व एवैकमनसो वृत्तिः स्वाभाविकी तु या ।
अनिमित्ता भागवती भक्तिः सिद्धेर्गरीयसी ॥३२॥

śrī-bhagavān uvāca
devānāṁ guṇa-liṅgānām
ānuśravika-karmaṇām
sattva evaika-manaso
vṛttiḥ svābhāvikī tu yā
animittā bhāgavatī
bhaktiḥ siddher garīyasī

śrī-bhagavān uvāca—the Supreme Personality of Godhead said; *devānām*—of the senses or of the presiding deities of the senses; *guṇa-liṅgānām*—which detect sense objects; *ānuśravika*—according to scripture; *karmaṇām*—which work; *sattve*—unto the mind or unto the Lord; *eva*—only; *eka-manasaḥ*—of a man of undivided mind; *vṛttiḥ*—inclination; *svābhāvikī*—natural; *tu*—in fact; *yā*—which; *animittā*—without motive; *bhāgavatī*—to the Personality of Godhead; *bhaktiḥ*—devotional service; *siddheḥ*—than salvation; *garīyasī*—better.

TRANSLATION

Lord Kapila said: The senses are symbolic representations of the demigods, and their natural inclination is to work under the direction of the Vedic injunctions. As the senses are representatives of the demigods, so the mind is the representative of the Supreme Personality of Godhead. The mind's natural duty is to serve. When that service spirit is engaged in devotional service to the Personality of Godhead, without any motive, that is far better even than salvation.

PURPORT

The senses of the living entity are always engaged in some occupation, either in activities prescribed in the injunctions of the *Vedas* or in material activities. The natural inclination of the senses is to work for something, and the mind is the center of the senses. The mind is actually the leader of the senses; therefore it is called *sattva.* Similarly, the leader of all the demigods who are engaged in the activities of this material world—the sun-god, moon-god, Indra and others—is the Supreme Personality of Godhead.

It is stated in the Vedic literature that the demigods are different limbs of the universal body of the Supreme Personality of Godhead. Our senses are also controlled by different demigods; our senses are representations of various demigods, and the mind is the representation of the Supreme Personality of Godhead. The senses, led by the mind, act under the influence of the demigods. When the service is ultimately aimed at the Supreme Personality of Godhead, the senses are in their natural position. The Lord is called Hṛṣīkeśa, for He is actually the proprietor and ultimate master of the senses. The senses and the mind are naturally inclined to work, but when they are materially contaminated they work for some material benefit or for the service of the demigods, although actually they are meant to serve the Supreme Personality of Godhead. The senses are called *hṛṣīka,* and the Supreme Personality of Godhead is called Hṛṣīkeśa. Indirectly, all the senses are naturally inclined to serve the Supreme Lord. That is called *bhakti.*

Kapiladeva said that when the senses, without desire for material profit or other selfish motives, are engaged in the service of the Supreme

Personality of Godhead, one is situated in devotional service. That spirit of service is far better than *siddhi,* salvation. *Bhakti,* the inclination to serve the Supreme Personality of Godhead, is in a transcendental position far better than *mukti,* or liberation. Thus *bhakti* is the stage after liberation. Unless one is liberated one cannot engage the senses in the service of the Lord. When the senses are engaged either in material activities of sense gratification or in the activities of the Vedic injunctions, there is some motive, but when the same senses are engaged in the service of the Lord and there is no motive, that is called *animittā* and is the natural inclination of the mind. The conclusion is that when the mind, without being deviated either by Vedic injunctions or by material activities, is fully engaged in Kṛṣṇa consciousness, or devotional service to the Supreme Personality of Godhead, it is far better than the most aspired-for liberation from material entanglement.

TEXT 33

जरयत्याशु या कोशं निगीर्णमनलो यथा ॥३३॥

jarayaty āśu yā kośaṁ
nigīrṇam analo yathā

jarayati—dissolves; *āśu*—quickly; *yā*—which; *kośam*—the subtle body; *nigīrṇam*—things eaten; *analaḥ*—fire; *yathā*—as.

TRANSLATION

Bhakti, devotional service, dissolves the subtle body of the living entity without separate effort, just as fire in the stomach digests all that we eat.

PURPORT

Bhakti is in a far higher position than *mukti* because a person's endeavor to get liberation from the material encagement is automatically served in devotional service. The example is given here that the fire in the stomach can digest whatever we eat. If the digestive power is sufficient, then whatever we can eat will be digested by the fire in the stomach. Similarly, a devotee does not have to try separately to attain liberation. That very service to the Supreme Personality of Godhead is the process of his liberation because to engage oneself in the service of the Lord is to liberate oneself from material entanglement. Śrī Bilvamaṅgala Ṭhākura explained this position very nicely. He said, "If I have unflinching devotion unto the lotus feet of the Supreme Lord, then *mukti*, or liberation, serves me as my maidservant. *Mukti*, the maidservant, is always ready to do whatever I ask."

For a devotee, liberation is no problem at all. Liberation takes place without separate endeavor. *Bhakti*, therefore, is far better then *mukti* or the impersonalist position. The impersonalists undergo severe penances and austerities to attain *mukti*, but the *bhakta*, simply by engaging himself in the *bhakti* process, especially in chanting Hare Kṛṣṇa, Hare Kṛṣṇa, Kṛṣṇa Kṛṣṇa, Hare Hare/ Hare Rāma, Hare Rāma, Rāma Rāma, Hare Hare, immediately develops control over the tongue by engaging it in chanting, and accepting the remnants of foodstuff offered to the Personality of Godhead. As soon as the tongue is controlled, naturally all other senses are controlled automatically. Sense control is the perfection of the *yoga* principle, and one's liberation begins immediately as soon as he engages himself in the service of the Lord. It is confirmed by Kapiladeva that *bhakti*, or devotional service, is *garīyasī*, more glorious than *siddhi*, liberation.

TEXT 34

नैकात्मतां मे स्पृहयन्ति केचिन्
मत्पादसेवाभिरता मदीहाः ।
येऽन्योन्यतो भागवताः प्रसज्य
सभाजयन्ते मम पौरुषाणि ॥३४॥

naikātmatāṁ me spṛhayanti kecin
mat-pāda-sevābhiratā mad-īhāḥ
ye 'nyonyato bhāgavatāḥ prasajya
sabhājayante mama pauruṣāṇi

na—never; *eka-ātmatām*—merging into oneness; *me*—My; *spṛhayanti*—they desire; *kecit*—any; *mat-pāda-sevā*—the service of My lotus feet; *abhiratāḥ*—engaged in; *mat-īhāḥ*—endeavoring to attain Me;

ye—those who; *anyonyataḥ*—mutually; *bhāgavatāḥ*—pure devotees; *prasajya*—assembling; *sabhājayante*—glorify; *mama*—My; *pauruṣāṇi*—glorious activities.

TRANSLATION

A pure devotee, who is attached to the activities of devotional service and who always engages in the service of My lotus feet, never desires to become one with Me. Such a devotee, who is unflinchingly engaged, always glorifies My pastimes and activities.

PURPORT

There are five kinds of liberation stated in the scriptures. One is to become one with the Supreme Personality of Godhead, or to forsake one's individuality and merge into the Supreme Spirit. This is called *ekātmatām.* A devotee never accepts this kind of liberation. The other four liberations are: to be promoted to the same planet as God (Vaikuṇṭha), to associate personally with the Supreme Lord, to achieve the same opulence as the Lord and to attain the same bodily features as the Supreme Lord. A pure devotee, as will be explained by Kapila Muni, does not aspire for any of the five liberations. He especially despises as hellish the idea of becoming one with the Supreme Personality of Godhead. Śrī Prabodhānanda Sarasvatī, a great devotee of Lord Caitanya, said, *kaivalyaṁ narakāyate:* "The happiness of becoming one with the Supreme Lord, which is aspired for by the Māyāvādīs, is considered hellish." That oneness is not for pure devotees.

There are many so-called devotees who think that in the conditioned state we may worship the Personality of Godhead but that ultimately there is no personality; they say that since the Absolute Truth is impersonal, one can imagine a personal form of the impersonal Absolute Truth for the time being, but as soon as one becomes liberated the worship stops. That is the theory put forward by the Māyāvāda philosophy. Actually the impersonalists do not merge into the existence of the Supreme Person but into His personal bodily luster, which is called the *brahmajyoti.* Although that *brahmajyoti* is not different from His personal body, that sort of oneness (merging into the bodily luster of the Personality of Godhead) is not accepted by a pure devotee because the devotees engage in greater pleasure than the so-called pleasure of merging into His existence. The greatest pleasure is to serve the Lord. Devotees are always thinking about how to serve Him; they are always designing ways and means to serve the Supreme Lord, even in the midst of the greatest obstacles of material existence.

The Māyāvādīs accept the description of the pastimes of the Lord as stories, but actually they are not stories; they are historical facts. Pure devotees accept the narrations of the pastimes of the Lord not as stories but as Absolute Truth. The words *mama pauruṣāṇi* are significant. Devotees are very much attached to glorifying the activities of the Lord, whereas the Māyāvādīs cannot even think of these activities. According to them the Absolute Truth is impersonal. Without personal existence, how can there be activity? The impersonalists take the activities mentioned in the *Śrīmad-Bhāgavatam*, *Bhagavad-gītā* and other Vedic literatures as fictitious stories, and therefore they interpret them most mischievously. The have no idea of the Personality of Godhead. They unnecessarily poke their noses into the scripture and interpret it in a deceptive way in order to mislead the innocent public. The activities of Māyāvāda philosophy are very dangerous to the public, and therefore Lord Caitanya warned us never to hear from any Māyāvādī about any scripture. They will spoil the entire process, and the person hearing them will never be able to come to the path of devotional service to attain the highest perfection, or will be able to do so only after a very long time.

It is clearly stated by Kapila Muni that *bhakti* activities, or activities in devotional service, are transcendental to *mukti*. This is called *pañcama-puruṣārtha*. Generally, people engage in the activities of religion, economic development and sense gratification, and ultimately they work with an idea that they are going to become one with the Supreme Lord (*mukti*). But *bhakti* is transcendental to all these activities. The *Śrīmad-Bhāgavatam*, therefore, begins by stating that all kinds of pretentious religiosity is completely eradicated from the *Bhāgavatam*. Ritualistic activities for economic development and sense gratification and, after frustration in sense gratification, the desire to become one with the Supreme Lord, are all completely rejected in the *Bhāgavatam*. The *Bhāgavatam* is especially meant for the pure devotees, who always engage in Kṛṣṇa consciousness, in the activities of the Lord, and always glorify these transcendental activities. Pure devotees worship the transcendental activities of the Lord in Vṛndāvana, Dvārakā and Mathurā as they are narrated in the *Śrīmad-Bhāgavatam* and other *Purāṇas.* The Māyāvādī philosophers completely reject them as stories, but actually they are great and worshipable subject matters and thus are relishable only for devotees. That is the difference between a Māyāvādī and a pure devotee.

TEXT 35

पश्यन्ति ते मे रुचिराण्यम्ब सन्तः
प्रसन्नवक्त्रारुणलोचनानि ।
रूपाणि दिव्यानि वरप्रदानि
साकं वाचं स्पृहणीयां वदन्ति ॥३५॥

paśyanti te me rucirāṇy amba santaḥ
prasanna-vaktrāruṇa-locanāni
rūpāṇi divyāni vara-pradāni
sākaṁ vācaṁ spṛhaṇīyāṁ vadanti

paśyanti—see; *te*—they; *me*—My; *rucirāṇi*—beautiful; *amba*—O mother; *santaḥ*—devotees; *prasanna*—smiling; *vaktra*—face; *aruṇa*—like the morning sun; *locanāni*—eyes; *rūpāṇi*—forms; *divyāni*—transcendental; *vara-pradāni*—benevolent; *sākam*—with Me; *vācam*—words; *spṛhaṇīyām*—favorable; *vadanti*—they speak.

TRANSLATION

O My mother, My devotees always see the smiling face of My form, with eyes like the rising morning sun. They like to see My various transcendental forms, which are all benevolent, and they also talk favorably with Me.

PURPORT

Māyāvādīs and atheists accept the forms of the Deities in the temple of the Lord as idols, but devotees do not worship idols. They directly worship the Personality of Godhead in His *arcā* incarnation. *Arcā* refers to the form which we can worship in our present condition. Actually, in our present state it is not possible to see God in His spiritual form because our material eyes and senses cannot conceive of a spiritual form. We cannot even see the spiritual form of the individual soul. When a man dies we cannot see how the spiritual form leaves the body. That is the defect of our material senses. In order to be seen by our material senses, the Supreme Personality of Godhead accepts a favorable form which is called *arcā-vigraha.* This *arcā-vigraha,* sometimes called the *arcā* incarnation, is not different from Him. Just as the Supreme Personality of Godhead accepts various incarnations, He takes on forms made out of matter—clay, wood, metal and jewels.

There are many śāstric injunctions which give instructions for carving forms of the Lord. These forms are not material. If God is all-pervading, then He is also in the material elements. There is no doubt about it. But the atheists think otherwise. Although they preach that everything is God, when they go to the temple and see the form of the Lord, they deny that He is God. According to their own theory, everything is God. Then why is the Deity not God? Actually, they have no conception of God. The devotees' vision, however, is different; their vision is smeared with love of God. As soon as they see the Lord in His different forms, the devotees become saturated with love, for they do not find any difference between the Lord and His form in the temple, as do the atheists. The smiling face of the Deity in the temple is beheld by the devotees as transcendental and spiritual, and the decoration of the body of the Lord is very much appreciated by the devotees. It is the duty of the spiritual master to teach how to decorate the Deity in the temple, how to cleanse the temple and how to worship the Deity. There are different procedures and rules and regulations which are followed in temples of Viṣṇu, and devotees go there and see the Diety, the *vigraha,* and spiritually enjoy the form because all of the Deities are benevolent. The devotees express their minds before the Deity, and in many instances the Deity also gives answers. But one must be a very elevated devotee in order to be able to speak with the Supreme Lord. Sometimes the Lord informs the devotee through dreams. These exchanges of feelings between the Deity and the devotee are not understandable by atheists, but actually the devotee enjoys them. Kapila Muni is explaining how the devotees see the decorated body and face of the Deity and how they speak with Him in devotional service.

TEXT 36

तैर्दर्शनीयावयवैरुदार-
विलासहासेक्षितवामसूक्तैः ।
हृतात्मनो हृतप्राणांश्च भक्ति-
रनिच्छतो मे गतिमण्वीं प्रयुङ्क्ते ॥३६॥

tair darśanīyāvayavair udāra-
vilāsa-hāsekṣita-vāma-sūktaiḥ
hṛtātmano hṛta-prāṇāṁś ca bhaktir
anicchato me gatim aṇvīṁ prayuṅkte

taiḥ—by those forms; *darśanīya*—charming; *avayavaiḥ*—whose limbs; *udāra*—exalted; *vilāsa*—pastimes; *hāsa*—smiling; *īkṣita*—glances; *vāma*—pleasing; *sūktaiḥ*—whose delightful words; *hṛta*—captivated; *ātmanaḥ*—their minds; *hṛta*—captivated; *prāṇān*—their senses; *ca*—and; *bhaktiḥ*—devotional service; *anicchataḥ*—unwilling; *me*—My; *gatim*—abode; *aṇvīm*—subtle; *prayuṅkte*—secures.

TRANSLATION

Upon seeing the charming forms of the Lord, smiling and attractive, and hearing His very pleasing words, the pure devotee almost loses all other consciousness. His senses are freed from all other engagements, and he becomes absorbed in devotional service. Thus in spite of his unwillingness, he attains liberation without separate endeavor.

PURPORT

There are three divisions of devotees—first-class, second-class and third-class. Even the third-class devotees are liberated souls. It is explained in this verse that although they do not have knowledge, simply by seeing the beautiful decoration of the Deity in the temple, the devotee is absorbed in thought of Him and loses all other consciousness. Simply by fixing oneself in Kṛṣṇa consciousness, engaging the senses in the service of the Lord, one is imperceptibly liberated. This is also confirmed in *Bhagavad-gītā.* Simply by discharging uncontaminated devotional service as prescribed in the scriptures, one becomes equal to Brahman. In *Bhagavad-gītā* it is said, *brahma-bhūyāya kalpate.* This means that the living entity in his original state is Brahman because he is part and parcel of the Supreme Brahman. But simply because of his forgetfulness of his real nature as an eternal servitor of the Lord, he is overwhelmed and captured by *māyā.* His forgetfulness of his real constitutional position is *māyā.* Otherwise he is eternally Brahman.

When one is trained to become conscious of his position, he understands that he is the servitor of the Lord. "Brahman" refers to a state of self-realization. Even the third-class devotee—who is not advanced in knowledge of the Absolute Truth but simply offers obeisances with great devotion, thinks of the Lord, sees the Lord in the temple and brings forth flowers and fruits to offer to the Deity—becomes imperceptibly liberated. *Śraddhayānvitāḥ:* with great devotion the devotees offer worshipful respects and paraphernalia to the Deity. The Deities of Rādhā and Kṛṣṇa, Lakṣmī and Nārāyaṇa, and Rāma and Sītā are very attractive to devotees, so much so that when they see the statue decorated in the temple of the Lord they become fully absorbed in thought of the Lord. That is the state of liberation. In other words, it is confirmed herewith that even a third-class devotee is in the transcendental position, above those who are trying for liberation by speculation or by other methods. Even great impersonalists like Śukadeva Gosvāmī and the four Kumāras were attracted by the beauty of the Deities in the temple, by the decorations and by the aroma of *tulasī* offered to the Lord, and they became devotees. Even though they were in the liberated state, instead of remaining impersonalists they were attracted by the beauty of the Lord and became devotees.

Here the word *vilāsa* is very important. *Vilāsa* refers to the activities or pastimes of the Lord. It is a prescribed duty in temple worship that not only should one visit the temple to see the Deity nicely decorated, but at the same time he should hear the recitation of *Śrīmad-Bhāgavatam, Bhagavad-gītā* or some similar literature, which is regularly recited in the temple. It is the system in Vṛndāvana that in every temple there is recitation of the *śāstras.* Even third-class devotees who have no literary knowledge or no time to read *Śrīmad-Bhāgavatam* or *Bhagavad-gītā* get the opportunity to hear about the pastimes of the Lord. In this way their minds may remain always absorbed in the thought of the Lord—His form, His activities and His transcendental nature. This state of Kṛṣṇa consciousness is a liberated stage. Lord Caitanya, therefore, recommended five important processes in the discharge of devotional service: (1) to chant the holy names of the Lord, Hare Kṛṣṇa, Hare Kṛṣṇa, Kṛṣṇa Kṛṣṇa, Hare Hare/ Hare Rāma, Hare Rāma, Rāma Rāma, Hare Hare, (2) to associate with devotees and serve them as far as possible, (3) to hear *Śrīmad-Bhāgavatam,* (4) to see the decorated temple and the Deity and, if possible, (5) to live in a place like Vṛndāvana or Mathurā. These five items alone can help a devotee achieve the highest perfectional stage. This is confirmed in *Bhagavad-gītā* and here in the *Śrīmad-Bhāgavatam.* That third-class devotees can also imperceptibly achieve liberation is accepted in all Vedic literatures.

TEXT 37

अथो विभूतिं मम मायाविनस्ता-
मैश्वर्यमष्टाङ्गमनुप्रवृत्तम् ।
श्रियं भागवतीं वास्पृहयन्ति भद्रां
परस्य मे तेऽश्नुवते तु लोके ॥३७॥

atho vibhūtiṁ mama māyāvinas tām
aiśvaryam aṣṭāṅgam anupravṛttam
śriyaṁ bhāgavatīṁ vāspṛhayanti bhadrāṁ
parasya me te 'śnuvate tu loke

atho—then; *vibhūtim*—opulence; *mama*—of Me; *māyāvinaḥ*—of the Lord of *māyā; tām*—that; *aiśvaryam*—mystic perfection; *aṣṭa-aṅgam*—consisting of eight parts; *anupravṛttam*—following; *śriyam*—splendor; *bhāgavatīm*—of the kingdom of God; *vā*—or; *aspṛhayanti*—they do not desire; *bhadrām*—blissful; *parasya*—of the Supreme Lord; *me*—of Me; *te*—those devotees; *aśnuvate*—enjoy; *tu*—but; *loke*—in this life.

TRANSLATION

Thus because he is completely absorbed in thought of Me, the devotee does not desire even the highest benediction obtainable in

the upper planetary systems, including Satyaloka. He does not desire the eight material perfections obtained from mystic yoga, nor does he desire to be elevated to the kingdom of God. Yet even without desiring them, the devotee enjoys, even in this life, all the offered benedictions.

PURPORT

The *vibhūti*, or opulences, offered by *māyā* are of many varieties. We have experience of different varieties of material enjoyment even on this planet, but if one is able to promote himself to higher planets like Candraloka, the sun or, still higher, Maharloka, Janaloka and Tapoloka, or even ultimately the highest planet, which is inhabited by Brahmā and is called Satyaloka, there are immense possibilities for material enjoyment. For example, the duration of life on higher planets is far, far greater than on this planet. It is said that on the moon the duration of life is such that our six months are equal to one day. We cannot even imagine the duration of life on the highest planet. It is stated in *Bhagavad-gītā* that Brahmā's twelve hours are inconceivable even to our mathematicians. These are all descriptions of the external energy of the Lord, or *māyā.* Besides these, there are other opulences which the *yogīs* can achieve by their mystic power. They are also material. A devotee does not aspire for all these material pleasures, although they are available to him simply by wishing. By the grace of the Lord, a devotee can achieve wonderful success simply by willing, but a real devotee does not like that. Lord Caitanya Mahāprabhu has taught that one should not desire material opulence or material reputation, nor should one try to enjoy material beauty; one should simply aspire to be absorbed in the devotional service of the Lord, even if one does not get liberation but has to continue the process of birth and death unlimitedly. Actually, however, to one who engages in Kṛṣṇa consciousness, liberation is already guaranteed. Devotees enjoy all the benefits of the higher planets and the Vaikuṇṭha planets also. It is especially mentioned here, *bhāgavatīṁ bhadrām.* In the Vaikuṇṭha planets everything is eternally peaceful, yet a pure devotee does not even aspire to be promoted there. But still he gets that advantage; he enjoys all the facilities of the material and spiritual worlds, even during the present life-span.

TEXT 38

न कर्हिचिन्मत्पराः शान्तरूपे
नङ्क्ष्यन्ति नो मेऽनिमिषो लेढि हेतिः ।
येषामहं प्रिय आत्मा सुतश्च
सखा गुरुः सुहृदो दैवमिष्टम् ॥३८॥

na karhicin mat-parāḥ śānta-rūpe
naṅkṣyanti no me 'nimiṣo leḍhi hetiḥ
yeṣām ahaṁ priya ātmā sutaś ca
sakhā guruḥ suhṛdo daivam iṣṭam

na—not; *karhicit*—ever; *mat-parāḥ*—My devotees; *śānta-rūpe*—O mother; *naṅkṣyanti*—will lose; *no*—not; *me*—My; *animiṣaḥ*—time; *leḍhi*—destroys; *hetiḥ*—weapon; *yeṣām*—of whom; *aham*—I; *priyaḥ*—dear; *ātmā*—self; *sutaḥ*—son; *ca*—and; *sakhā*—friend; *guruḥ*—preceptor; *suhṛdaḥ*—benefactor; *daivam*—Deity; *iṣṭam*—chosen.

TRANSLATION

The Lord continued: My dear mother, devotees who receive such transcendental opulences are never bereft of them; neither weapons nor the change of time can destroy such opulences. Because the devotees accept Me as their friend, their relative, their son, preceptor, benefactor and Supreme Deity, they cannot be deprived of their possessions at any time.

PURPORT

It is stated in *Bhagavad-gītā* that one may elevate himself to the higher planetary systems, even up to Brahmaloka, by dint of pious activities, but when the effects of such pious activities are finished, one again comes back to this earth to begin a new life of activities. Thus even though one is promoted to the higher planetary system for enjoyment and a long duration of life, still that is not a permanent settlement. But as far as the devotees are concerned, their assets—the achievement of devotional service and the consequent opulence of Vaikuṇṭha, even on this planet—are never destroyed. In this verse Kapiladeva addresses His mother as *śānta-rūpā*, indicating that the opulences of devotees are fixed because devotees are eternally fixed in the Vaikuṇṭha atmosphere, which is called *śānta-rūpa* because it is in the mode of pure goodness, undisturbed by the modes of passion and ignorance. Once one is fixed in the devotional service of the Lord, his position of transcendental service cannot be destroyed, and the pleasure and service simply increase unlimitedly. For the devotees engaged in Kṛṣṇa consciousness, in the Vaikuṇṭha atmosphere, there is no influence of time. In the material world the influence of time destroys everything, but in the Vaikuṇṭha atmosphere there is no influence of time or of the demigods because there are no demigods in the Vaikuṇṭha planets. Here our activities are controlled by different demigods; even if we move our hand and leg, the action is controlled by the demigods. But in the Vaikuṇṭha atmosphere there is no influence of the demigods or of time; therefore there is no question of destruction. When the time element is present, there is the certainty of destruction, but when there is no time element—past, present or future—then everything is eternal. Therefore this verse uses the words *na naṅkṣyanti*, indicating that the transcendental opulences will never be destroyed.

The reason for freedom from destruction is also described. The devotees accept the Supreme Lord as the most dear personality and reciprocate with Him in different relationships. They accept the Supreme Personality of Godhead as the dearmost friend, the dearmost relative, the dearmost son, the dearmost preceptor, the dearmost well-wisher or the dearmost Deity. The Lord is eternal; therefore any relationship in which we accept Him is also eternal. It is clearly confirmed herein that the relationships cannot be destroyed, and therefore the opulences of those relationships are never destroyed. Every living entity has the propensity to love someone. We can see that if someone has no object of love, he generally directs his love to a pet animal like a cat or a dog. Thus the eternal propensity for love in all living entities is always searching for a place to reside. From this verse we can learn that we can love the Supreme Personality of Godhead as our dearmost object—as a friend, as a son, as a preceptor or as a well-wisher—and there will be no cheating and no end to such love. We shall eternally enjoy the relationship with the Supreme Lord in different aspects. A special feature of this verse is the acceptance of the Supreme Lord as the supreme preceptor. *Bhagavad-gītā* was spoken directly by the Supreme Lord, and Arjuna accepted Kṛṣṇa as *guru,* or spiritual master. Similarly, we should accept only Kṛṣṇa as the supreme spiritual master.

Kṛṣṇa, of course, means Kṛṣṇa and His confidential devotees; Kṛṣṇa is not alone. When we speak of Kṛṣṇa, "Kṛṣṇa" means Kṛṣṇa in His name, in His form, in His qualities, in His abode and in His associates. Kṛṣṇa is never alone, for the devotees of Kṛṣṇa are not impersonalists. For example, a king is always associated with his secretary, his commander, his servant and so much paraphernalia. As soon as we accept Kṛṣṇa and His associates as our preceptors, no ill effects can destroy our knowledge. In the material world the knowledge which we acquire may change because of the influence of time, but nevertheless the conclusions received from *Bhagavad-gītā,* directly from the speeches of the Supreme Lord, Kṛṣṇa, can never change. There is no use interpreting *Bhagavad-gītā;* it is eternal.

Kṛṣṇa, the Supreme Lord, should be accepted as one's best friend. He will never cheat. He will always give His friendly advice and friendly protection to the devotee. If Kṛṣṇa is accepted as a son, He will never die. Here we have a very loving son or child, but the father and mother, or those who are affectionate towards him, always hope, "May my son not die." But Kṛṣṇa actually never will die. Therefore those who accept Kṛṣṇa, or the Supreme Lord, as their son will never be bereft of their son. In many instances devotees have accepted the Deity as a son. In Bengal there are many such instances, and even after the death of the devotee, the Deity performs the *śrāddha* ceremony for the father. The relationship is never destroyed. People are accustomed to worship different forms of demigods, but in *Bhagavad-gītā* such a mentality is condemned; therefore one should be intelligent enough to worship only the Supreme Personality of Godhead in His different forms such as Lakṣmī-Nārāyaṇa, Sītā-Rāma and Rādhā-Kṛṣṇa. Thus one will never be cheated. By worshiping the demigods one may elevate himself to the higher planets, but during the dissolution of the material world, the deity and the abode of the deity will be destroyed. But one who worships the Supreme Personality of Godhead is promoted to the Vaikuṇṭha planets, where there is no influence of time, destruction or annihilation. The conclusion is that the time influence cannot act upon devotees who have accepted the Supreme Personality of Godhead as everything.

TEXTS 39–40

इमं लोकं तथैवामुमात्मानमुभयायिनम् ।
आत्मानमनु ये चेह ये रायः पशवो गृहाः ॥३९॥
विसृज्य सर्वानन्यांश्च मामेवं विश्वतोमुखम् ।
भजन्त्यनन्यया भक्त्या तान्मृत्योरतिपारये ॥४०॥

imaṁ lokaṁ tathaivāmum
ātmānam ubhayāyinam
ātmānam anu ye ceha
ye rāyaḥ paśavo gṛhāḥ

visṛjya sarvān anyāṁś ca
mām evaṁ viśvato-mukham
bhajanty ananyayā bhaktyā
tān mṛtyor atipāraye

imam—this; *lokam*—world; *tathā*—accordingly; *eva*—certainly; *amum*—that world; *ātmānam*—the subtle body; *ubhaya*—in both; *ayinam*—traveling; *ātmānam*—the body; *anu*—in relationship with; *ye*—those who; *ca*—also; *iha*—in this world; *ye*—that which; *rāyaḥ*—wealth; *paśavaḥ*—cattle; *gṛhāḥ*—houses; *visṛjya*—having given up; *sarvān*—all; *anyān*—other; *ca*—and; *mām*—Me; *evam*—thus; *viśvataḥ-mukham*—the all-pervading Lord of the universe; *bhajanti*—they worship; *ananyayā*—unflinching; *bhaktyā*—by devotional service; *tān*—them; *mṛtyoḥ*—of death; *atipāraye*—I take to the other side.

TRANSLATION

Thus the devotee who worships Me, the all-pervading Lord of the universe, in unflinching devotional service, gives up all aspirations to be promoted to heavenly planets or to become happy in

this world with wealth, children, cattle, home or anything in relationship with the body. I take him to the other side of birth and death.

PURPORT

Unflinching devotional service, as described in these two verses, means engaging oneself in full Kṛṣṇa consciousness, or devotional service, accepting the Supreme Lord as all in all. Since the Supreme Lord is all-inclusive, if anyone worships Him with unflinching faith, he has automatically achieved all other opulences and performed all other duties. The Lord promises herein that He takes His devotee to the other side of birth and death. Lord Caitanya, therefore, recommended that one who aspires to go beyond birth and death should have no material possessions. This means that one should not try to be happy in this world or to be promoted to the heavenly world, nor should he try for material wealth, children, houses or cattle.

How liberation is imperceptibly achieved by a pure devotee and what the symptoms are have been explained. For the conditioned soul there are two statuses of living. One status is in this present life, and the other is our preparation for the next life. If I am in the mode of goodness then I may be preparing for promotion to the higher planets, if I am in the mode of passion then I shall remain here in a society where activity is very prominent, and if I am in the mode of ignorance I may be degraded to animal life or a lower grade of human life. But for a devotee there is no concern for this life or the next life because in any life he does not desire elevation in material prosperity or a high-grade or low-grade life. He prays to the Lord, "My dear Lord, it does not matter where I am born, but let me be born, even as an ant, in the house of a devotee." A pure devotee does not pray to the Lord for liberation from this material bondage. Actually, the pure devotee never thinks that he is fit for liberation. Considering his past life and his mischievous activities, he thinks that he is fit to be sent to the lowest region of hell. If in this life I am trying to become a devotee, this does not mean that in my many past lives I was one-hundred-percent pious. That is not possible. A devotee, therefore, is always conscious of his real position. Only by his full surrender to the Lord, by the Lord's grace, are his sufferings made shorter. As stated in

Bhagavad-gītā, "Surrender unto Me, and I will give you protection from all kinds of sinful reaction." That is His mercy. But this does not mean that one who has surrendered to the lotus feet of the Lord has committed no misdeeds in his past life. A devotee always prays, "For my misdeeds, may I be born again and again, but my only prayer is that I may not forget Your service." The devotee has that much mental strength, and he prays to the Lord: "May I be born again and again, but let me be born in the home of Your pure devotee so that I may again get a chance to develop myself."

A pure devotee is not anxious to elevate himself in his next birth. He has already given up that sort of hope. In any life in which one is born, as a householder, or even as an animal, one must have some children, some resources or some possessions, but a devotee is not anxious to possess anything. He is satisfied with whatever is obtainable by God's grace. He is not at all attached to improving his social status or improving the status of education of his children. He is not neglectful—he is dutiful—but he does not spend too much time on the upliftment of temporary household or social life. He fully engages in the service of the Lord, and for other affairs he simply spares as much time as absolutely necessary (*yathārham upayuñjataḥ*). Such a pure devotee does not care for what is going to happen in the next life or in this life; he does not care even for family, children or society. He fully engages in the service of the Lord in Kṛṣṇa consciousness. It is stated in *Bhagavad-gītā* that without the knowledge of the devotee, the Lord arranges for His devotee to be immediately transferred to His transcendental abode just after leaving his body. After quitting his body he does not go into the womb of another mother. The ordinary common living entity, after death, is transferred to the womb of another mother, according to his *karma*, or activities, to take another type of body. But as far as the devotee is concerned, he is at once transferred to the spiritual world in the association of the Lord. That is the Lord's special mercy. How it is possible is explained in the following verses. Because He is all-powerful, the Lord can do anything and everything. He can excuse all sinful reactions. He can immediately transfer a person to Vaikuṇṭhaloka. That is the inconceivable power of the Supreme Personality of Godhead, who is favorably disposed to the pure devotees.

TEXT 41

नान्यत्र मद्भगवतः प्रधानपुरुषेश्वरात् ।
आत्मनः सर्वभूतानां भयं तीव्रं निवर्तते ॥४१॥

nānyatra mad bhagavataḥ
pradhāna-puruṣeśvarāt
ātmanaḥ sarva-bhūtānāṁ
bhayaṁ tīvraṁ nivartate

na—not; *anyatra*—otherwise; *mat*—than Myself; *bhagavataḥ*—the Supreme Personality of Godhead; *pradhāna-puruṣa-īśvarāt*—the Lord of both *prakṛti* and *puruṣa; ātmanaḥ*—the soul; *sarva-bhūtānām*—of all living beings; *bhayam*—fear; *tīvram*—terrible; *nivartate*—is forsaken.

TRANSLATION

The terrible fear of birth and death can never be forsaken by anyone who resorts to any shelter other than Myself, for I am the almighty Lord, the Supreme Personality of Godhead, the original source of all creation, and also the Supreme Soul of all souls.

PURPORT

It is indicated herein that the cycle of birth and death cannot be stopped unless one is a pure devotee of the Supreme Lord. It is said, *hariṁ vinā na sṛtiṁ taranti.* One cannot surpass the cycle of birth and death unless one is favored by the Supreme Personality of Godhead. The same concept is confirmed herewith: one may take to the system of understanding the Absolute Truth by one's own imperfect sensory speculation, or one may try to realize the self by the mystic *yoga* process; but whatever one may do, unless he comes to the point of surrendering to the Supreme Personality of Godhead, no process can give him liberation. One may ask if this means that those who are undergoing so much penance and austerity by strictly following the rules and regulations are endeavoring in vain. The answer is given by *Śrīmad-Bhāgavatam* (10.2.32): *ye 'nye 'ravindākṣa vimukta-māninaḥ.* Lord Brahmā and other demigods prayed to the Lord when Kṛṣṇa was in the womb of

Devakī: "My dear lotus-eyed Lord, there are persons who are puffed up with the thought that they have become liberated or one with God or have become God, but in spite of thinking in such a puffed-up way, their intelligence is not laudable. They are less intelligent." It is stated that their intelligence, whether high or low, is not even purified. In purified intelligence a living entity cannot think otherwise than to surrender. *Bhagavad-gītā,* therefore, confirms that purified intelligence arises in the person of a very wise man. *Bahūnāṁ janmanām ante jñānavān māṁ prapadyate.* After many, many births, one who is actually advanced in intelligence surrenders unto the Supreme Lord.

Without the surrendering process, one cannot achieve liberation. The *Bhāgavatam* says, "Those who are simply puffed up, thinking themselves liberated by some nondevotional process, are not polished or clear in intelligence, for they have not yet surrendered unto You. In spite of executing all kinds of austerities and penances or even arriving at the brink of spiritual realization in Brahman realization, they think that they are in the effulgence of Brahman, but actually, because they have no transcendental activities, they fall down to material activities." One should not be satisfied simply with knowing that one is Brahman. He must engage himself in the service of the Supreme Brahman; that is *bhakti.* The engagement of Brahman should be the service of Parabrahman. It is said that unless one becomes Brahman one cannot serve Brahman. The Supreme Brahman is the Supreme Personality of Godhead, and the living entity is also Brahman. Without realization that he is Brahman, spirit soul, an eternal servitor of the Lord, if one simply thinks that he is Brahman, his realization is only theoretical. He has to realize and at the same time engage himself in the devotional service of the Lord; then he can exist in the Brahman status. Otherwise he falls down.

The *Bhāgavatam* says that because nondevotees neglect the transcendental loving service of the lotus feet of the Personality of Godhead, their intelligence is not sufficient, and therefore these persons fall down. The living entity must have some activity. If he does not engage in the activity of transcendental service, he must fall down to material activity. As soon as one falls down to material activity, there is no rescue from the cycle of birth and death. It is stated here by Lord Kapila, "Without My mercy" (*nānyatra mad bhagavataḥ*). The Lord is stated here to be Bhagavān, the Supreme Personality of Godhead, indicating that He is full of all opulences and is therefore perfectly competent to deliver one from the cycle of birth and death. He is also called *pradhāna* because He is the Supreme. He is equal to everyone, but to one who surrenders to Him He is especially favorable. It is also confirmed in *Bhagavad-gītā* that the Lord is equal to everyone; no one is His enemy and no one is His friend. But to one who surrenders unto Him, He is especially inclined. By the grace of the Lord, simply by surrendering unto Him one can get out of this cycle of birth and death. Otherwise, one may go on in many, many lives and may many times attempt other processes for liberation.

TEXT 42

मद्भयाद्वाति वातोऽयं सूर्यस्तपति मद्भयात् ।
वर्षतीन्द्रो दहत्यग्निर्मृत्युश्चरति मद्भयात् ॥४२॥

mad-bhayād vāti vāto 'yaṁ
sūryas tapati mad-bhayāt
varṣatīndro dahaty agnir
mṛtyuś carati mad-bhayāt

mat-bhayāt—out of fear of Me; *vāti*—blows; *vātaḥ*—wind; *ayam*—this; *sūryaḥ*—the sun; *tapati*—shines; *mat-bhayāt*—out of fear of Me; *varṣati*—showers rain; *indraḥ*—Indra; *dahati*—burns; *agniḥ*—fire; *mṛtyuḥ*—death; *carati*—goes; *mat-bhayāt*—out of fear of Me.

TRANSLATION

It is because of My supremacy that the wind blows, out of fear of Me; the sun shines out of fear of Me, and the lord of the clouds, Indra, sends forth showers out of fear of Me. Fire burns out of fear of Me, and death goes about taking its toll out of fear of Me.

PURPORT

The Supreme Personality of Godhead, Kṛṣṇa, says in *Bhagavad-gītā* that the natural laws being enacted are correct in all activities because of His superintendence. No one should think that nature is working automatically, without superintendence. The Vedic literature says that the clouds are controlled by the demigod Indra, heat is distributed by the sun-god, the soothing moonlight is distributed by Candra, and the air is blowing under the arrangement of the demigod Vāyu. But above all these demigods, the Supreme Personality of Godhead is the chief living entity. *Nityo nityānāṁ cetanaś cetanānām.* The demigods are also ordinary living entities, but due to their faithfulness—their devotional service attitude—they have been promoted to such posts. These different demigods, or directors, such as Candra, Varuṇa and Vāyu, are called *adhikāri-devatā.* The demigods are departmental heads. The government of the Supreme Lord consists not only of one planet or two or three; there are millions of planets and millions of universes. The Supreme Personality of Godhead has a huge government, and He requires assistants. The demigods are considered His bodily limbs. These are the descriptions of Vedic literature. Under these circumstances, the sun-god, the moon-god, the fire-god and the air-god are working under the direction of the Supreme Lord. It is confirmed in the *Bhagavad-gītā, mayādhyakṣeṇa prakṛtiḥ sūyate sa-carācaram.* The natural laws are being conducted under His superintendence. Because He is in the background, everything is being performed punctually and regularly.

One who has taken shelter of the Supreme Personality of Godhead is completely protected from all other influences. He no longer serves or is obliged to anyone else. Of course he is not disobedient to anyone, but his full power of thought is absorbed in the service of the Lord. The statements by the Supreme Personality of Godhead Kapila that under His direction the air is blowing, the fire is burning and the sun is giving heat are not sentimental. The impersonalist may say that the *Bhāgavatam* devotees create and imagine someone as the Supreme Personality of Godhead and assign qualifications to Him; but actually it is neither imagination nor an imposition of artificial power in the name of Godhead. In the *Vedas* it is said, *bhīṣāsmād vātaḥ pavate/ bhīṣodeti sūryaḥ:* "By fear of the Supreme Lord the wind-god and the sun-god are acting." *Bhīṣāsmād agniś cendraś ca/ mṛtyur dhāvati pañcamaḥ:* "Agni, Indra and Mṛtyu are also acting under His direction." These are the statements of the *Vedas.*

TEXT 43

ज्ञानवैराग्ययुक्तेन भक्तियोगेन योगिनः ।
क्षेमाय पादमूलं मे प्रविशन्त्यकुतोभयम् ॥४३॥

jñāna-vairāgya-yuktena
bhakti-yogena yoginaḥ
kṣemāya pāda-mūlaṁ me
praviśanty akuto-bhayam

jñāna—with knowledge; *vairāgya*—and renunciation; *yuktena*—equipped; *bhakti-yogena*—by devotional service; *yoginaḥ*—the *yogīs;* *kṣemāya*—for eternal benefit; *pāda-mūlam*—feet; *me*—My; *praviśanti*—take shelter of; *akutaḥ-bhayam*—without fear.

TRANSLATION

The yogīs, equipped with transcendental knowledge and renunciation and engaged in devotional service for their eternal benefit, take shelter of My lotus feet, and since I am the Lord, they are thus eligible to enter into the kingdom of Godhead without fear.

PURPORT

One who actually wants to be liberated from the entanglement of this material world and go back home, back to Godhead, is actually a mystic *yogī.* The words explicitly used here are *yuktena bhakti-yogena.* Those *yogīs,* or mystics, who engage in devotional service are the first-class *yogīs.* The first-class *yogīs,* as described in *Bhagavad-gītā,* are those who are constantly thinking of the Lord, the Supreme Personality of Godhead, Kṛṣṇa. These *yogīs* are not without knowledge and renunciation. To become a *bhakti-yogī* means to automatically attain knowledge and renunciation. That is the consequent result of *bhakti-yoga.* In the *Bhāgavatam,* First Canto, Second Chapter, it is also confirmed that one who engages in the devotional service of Vāsudeva, Kṛṣṇa, has complete transcendental knowledge and renunciation, and there is no explanation for these attainments. *Ahaitukī*—without reason, they come. Even if a person is completely illiterate, the transcendental knowledge of the scriptures is revealed unto him simply because of his engagement in devotional service. That is also stated in the Vedic literature. To anyone who has full faith in the Supreme Personality of Godhead and the spiritual master, all the import of the Vedic literatures is revealed. He does not have to seek separately; the *yogīs* who engage in devotional service are full in knowledge and renunciation. If there is a lack of knowledge and renunciation, it is to be understood that one is not in full devotional service. The conclusion is that one cannot be sure of entrance into the spiritual realm—in either the impersonal *brahmajyoti* effulgence of the Lord or the Vaikuṇṭha planets within that Brahman effulgence—unless he is surrendered unto the lotus feet of the Supreme Lord. The surrendered souls are called *akuto-bhaya.* They are doubtless and fearless, and their entrance into the spiritual kingdom is guaranteed.

TEXT 44

एतावानेव लोकेऽस्मिन् पुंसां निःश्रेयसोदयः ।
तीव्रेण भक्तियोगेन मनो मय्यर्पितं स्थिरम् ॥४४॥

etāvān eva loke 'smin
puṁsāṁ niḥśreyasodayaḥ
tīvreṇa bhakti-yogena
mano mayy arpitaṁ sthiram

etāvān eva—only so far; *loke asmin*—in this world; *puṁsām*—of men; *niḥśreyasa*—final perfection of life; *udayaḥ*—the attainment of; *tīvreṇa*—intense; *bhakti-yogena*—by practice of devotional service; *manaḥ*—mind; *mayi*—in Me; *arpitam*—fixed; *sthiram*—steady.

TRANSLATION

Therefore persons whose minds are fixed on the Lord engage in the intensive practice of devotional service. That is the only means for attainment of the final perfection of life.

PURPORT

Here the words *mano mayy arpitam,* which mean "the mind being fixed on Me," are significant. One should fix his mind on the lotus feet of Kṛṣṇa or His incarnation. To be fixed steadily in that freedom is the way of liberation. Ambarīṣa Mahārāja is an example. He fixed his mind on the lotus feet of the Lord, he spoke only on the pastimes of the Lord, he smelled only the flowers and *tulasī* offered to the Lord, he walked only to the temple of the Lord, he engaged his hands in cleansing the temple, he engaged his tongue in tasting the foodstuff offered to the Lord, and he engaged his ears for hearing the great pastimes of the Lord. In that way all his senses were engaged. First of all, the mind should be engaged at the lotus feet of the Lord, very steadily and naturally. Because the mind is the master of the senses, when the mind is engaged, all the senses become engaged. That is *bhakti-yoga. Yoga* means controlling the senses. The senses cannot be controlled in the proper sense of the term; they are always agitated. This is true also with a child—how long can he be forced to sit down silently? It is not possible. Even Arjuna said, *cañcalaṁ hi manaḥ kṛṣṇa:* "The mind is always agitated." The best course is to fix the mind on the lotus feet of the Lord. *Mano mayy arpitaṁ sthiram.* If one seriously engages in Kṛṣṇa consciousness, that is the highest perfectional stage. All Kṛṣṇa conscious activities are on the highest perfectional level of human life.

Thus end the Bhaktivedanta purports of the Third Canto, Twenty-fifth Chapter, of the Śrīmad-Bhāgavatam, *entitled "The Glories of Devotional Service."*

CHAPTER TWENTY-SIX

Fundamental Principles of Material Nature

TEXT 1

श्रीभगवानुवाच
अथ ते सम्प्रवक्ष्यामि तत्त्वानां लक्षणं पृथक् ।
यद्विदित्वा विमुच्येत पुरुषः प्राकृतैर्गुणैः ॥ १ ॥

śrī-bhagavān uvāca
atha te sampravakṣyāmi
tattvānāṁ lakṣaṇaṁ pṛthak
yad viditvā vimucyeta
puruṣaḥ prākṛtair guṇaiḥ

śrī-bhagavān uvāca—the Personality of Godhead said; *atha*—now; *te*—to you; *sampravakṣyāmi*—I shall describe; *tattvānām*—of the categories of the Absolute Truth; *lakṣaṇam*—the distinctive features; *pṛthak*—one by one; *yat*—which; *viditvā*—knowing; *vimucyeta*—one can be released; *puruṣaḥ*—any person; *prākṛtaiḥ*—of the material nature; *guṇaiḥ*—from the modes.

TRANSLATION

The Personality of Godhead, Kapila, continued: My dear mother, now I shall describe unto you the different categories of the Absolute Truth, knowing which any person can be released from the influence of the modes of material nature.

PURPORT

As stated in *Bhagavad-gītā,* one can understand the Supreme Personality of Godhead, the Absolute Truth, only through devotional service (*bhaktyā mām abhijānāti*). As stated in the *Bhāgavatam,* the object of devotional service is *mām*, Kṛṣṇa. And, as explained in the *Caitanya-caritāmṛta*, to understand Kṛṣṇa means to understand Kṛṣṇa in His personal form with His internal energy, His external energy, His expansions and His incarnations. There are many diverse departments of knowledge in understanding Kṛṣṇa. Sāṅkhya philosophy is especially meant for persons who are conditioned by this material world. It is generally understood by the *paramparā* system, or by disciplic succession, to be the science of devotional service. Preliminary studies of devotional service have already been explained. Now the analytical study of devotional service will be explained by the Lord, who says that by such an analytical study, one becomes freed from the modes of material nature. The same assertion is confirmed in *Bhagavad-gītā. Tato māṁ tattvato jñātvā:* by understanding the Lord according to various categories, one can become eligible to enter into the kingdom of God. This is also explained here. By understanding the science of devotional service in Sāṅkhya philosophy, one can become free from the modes of material nature. The eternal self, after becoming freed from the spell of material nature, becomes eligible to enter into the kingdom of God. As long as one has even a slight desire to enjoy or lord it over material nature, there is no chance of his being freed from the influence of nature's material modes. Therefore, one has to understand the Supreme Personality of Godhead analytically, as explained in the Sāṅkhya system of philosophy by Lord Kapiladeva.

TEXT 2

ज्ञानं निःश्रेयसार्थाय पुरुषस्यात्मदर्शनम् ।
यदाहुर्वर्णये तत्ते हृदयग्रन्थिभेदनम् ॥ २ ॥

jñānaṁ niḥśreyasārthāya
puruṣasyātma-darśanam
yad āhur varṇaye tat te
hṛdaya-granthi-bhedanam

jñānam—knowledge; *niḥśreyasa-arthāya*—for the ultimate perfection; *puruṣasya*—of a man; *ātma-darśanam*—self-realization; *yat*—which; *āhuḥ*—they said; *varṇaye*—I shall explain; *tat*—that; *te*—to you; *hṛdaya*—in the heart; *granthi*—the knots; *bhedanam*—cuts.

TRANSLATION

Knowledge is the ultimate perfection of self-realization. I shall explain that knowledge unto you by which the knots of attachment to the material world are cut.

PURPORT

It is said that by proper understanding of the pure self, or by self-realization, one can be freed from material attachment. Knowledge leads one to attain the ultimate perfection of life and to see oneself as he is. The *Śvetāśvatara Upaniṣad* (3.8) also confirms this. *Tam eva viditvāti-mṛtyum eti:* simply by understanding one's spiritual position, or by seeing oneself as he is, one can be freed from material entanglement. In various ways, the seeing of oneself is described in the Vedic literatures, and it is confirmed in the *Bhāgavatam* (*puruṣasya ātma-darśanam*) that one has to see oneself and know what he is. As Kapiladeva explains to His mother, this "seeing" can be done by hearing from the proper authoritative source. Kapiladeva is the greatest authority because He is the Personality of Godhead, and if someone accepts whatever is explained *as it is,* without interpretation, then he can see himself.

Lord Caitanya explained to Sanātana Gosvāmī the real constitutional position of the individual. He said directly that each and every individual soul is eternally a servitor of Kṛṣṇa. *Jīvera 'svarūpa' haya—kṛṣṇera 'nitya-dāsa':* every individual soul is eternally a servitor. When one is fixed in the understanding that he is part and parcel of the Supreme Soul and that his eternal position is to serve in association with the Supreme Lord, he becomes self-realized. This position of rightly understanding oneself cuts the knot of material attraction (*hṛdaya-granthi-bhedanam*). Due to false ego, or false identification of oneself with the body and the material world, one is entrapped by *māyā,* but as soon as one understands that he is qualitatively the same substance as the Supreme Lord because he belongs to the same category of spirit soul, and that his perpetual position is to serve, one attains *ātma-darśanam* and *hṛdaya-granthi-bhedanam,* self-realization. When one can cut the knot of attachment to the material world, his understanding is called knowledge. *Ātma-darśanam* means to see oneself by knowledge; therefore, when one is freed from the false ego by the cultivation of real knowledge, he sees himself, and that is the ultimate necessity of human life. The soul is thus isolated from the entanglement of the twenty-four categories of material nature. Pursuit of the systematic philosophic process called Sāṅkhya is called knowledge and self-revelation.

TEXT 3

अनादिरात्मा पुरुषो निर्गुणः प्रकृतेः परः ।
प्रत्यग्धामा स्वयंज्योतिर्विश्वं येन समन्वितम् ॥ ३ ॥

anādir ātmā puruṣo
nirguṇaḥ prakṛteḥ paraḥ
pratyag-dhāmā svayaṁ-jyotir
viśvaṁ yena samanvitam

anādiḥ—without a beginning; *ātmā*—the Supreme Soul; *puruṣaḥ*—the Personality of Godhead; *nirguṇaḥ*—transcendental to the material modes of nature; *prakṛteḥ paraḥ*—beyond this material world; *pratyak-dhāmā*—perceivable everywhere; *svayam-jyotiḥ*—self-effulgent; *viśvam*—the entire creation; *yena*—by whom; *samanvitam*—is maintained.

TRANSLATION

The Supreme Personality of Godhead is the Supreme Soul, and He has no beginning. He is transcendental to the material modes of nature and beyond the existence of this material world. He is perceivable everywhere because He is self-effulgent, and by His self-effulgent luster the entire creation is maintained.

PURPORT

The Supreme Personality of Godhead is described as being without beginning. He is *puruṣa*, the Supreme Spirit. *Puruṣa* means "person." When we think of a person in our present experience, that person has a beginning. This means that he has taken birth and that there is a history from the beginning of his life. But the Lord is particularly mentioned here as *anādi*, beginningless. If we examine all persons, we will find that everyone has a beginning, but when we approach a person who has no beginning, He is the Supreme Person. That is the definition given in the *Brahma-saṁhitā. Īśvaraḥ paramaḥ kṛṣṇaḥ:* the Supreme Personality of Godhead is Kṛṣṇa, the supreme controller; He is without beginning, and He is the beginning of everyone. This definition is found in all Vedic literatures.

The Lord is described as the soul, or spirit. What is the definition of spirit? Spirit is perceivable everywhere. Brahman means "great." His greatness is perceived everywhere. And what is that greatness? Consciousness. We have personal experience of consciousness, for it is spread all over the body; in every hair follicle of our body we can feel consciousness. This is individual consciousness. Similarly, there is superconsciousness. The example can be given of a small light and the sunlight. The sunlight is perceived everywhere, even within the room or in the sky, but the small light is experienced within a specific limit. Similarly, our consciousness is perceived within the limit of our particular body, but the superconsciousness, or the existence of God, is perceived everywhere. He is present everywhere by His energy. It is stated in the *Viṣṇu Purāṇa* that whatever we find, anywhere and everywhere, is the distribution of the energy of the Supreme Lord. In *Bhagavad-gītā* also it is confirmed that the Lord is all-pervading and exists everywhere by His two kinds of energy, one spiritual and the other material. Both the spiritual and material energies are spread everywhere, and that is the proof of the existence of the Supreme Personality of Godhead.

The existence of consciousness everywhere is not temporary. It is without beginning, and because it is without beginning, it is also without end. The theory that consciousness develops at a certain stage of material combination is not accepted herein, for the consciousness which exists everywhere is said to be without beginning. The materialistic or atheistic theory stating that there is no soul, that there is no God and that consciousness is the result of a combination of matter is not acceptable. Matter is not beginningless; it has a beginning. As this material body has a beginning, the universal body does also. And as our material body has begun on the basis of our soul, the entire gigantic universal body has begun on the basis of the Supreme Soul. The *Vedānta-sūtra* says, *janmādy asya.* This entire material exhibition—its creation, its growth, its maintenance and its dissolution—is an emanation from the Supreme

Person. In *Bhagavad-gītā* also, the Lord says, "I am the beginning, the source of birth of everything."

The Supreme Personality of Godhead is described here. He is not a temporary person, nor does He have a beginning. He is without a cause, and He is the cause of all causes. *Paraḥ* means "transcendental," "beyond the creative energy." The Lord is the creator of the creative energy. We can see that there is a creative energy in the material world, but He is not under this energy. He is *prakṛti-paraḥ*, beyond this energy. He is not subjected to the threefold miseries created by the material energy because He is beyond it. The modes of material nature do not touch Him. It is explained here, *svayaṁ-jyotiḥ:* He is light Himself. We have experience in the material world of one light's being a reflection of another, just as moonlight is a reflection of the sunlight. Sunlight is also the reflection of the *brahmajyoti.* Similarly, *brahmajyoti,* the spiritual effulgence, is a reflection of the body of the Supreme Lord. This is confirmed in the *Brahma-saṁhitā: yasya prabhā prabhavataḥ.* The *brahmajyoti,* or Brahman effulgence, is due to His bodily luster. Therefore it is said here, *svayaṁ-jyotiḥ:* He Himself is light. His light is distributed in different ways, as the *brahmajyoti,* as sunlight and as moonlight. *Bhagavad-gītā* confirms that in the spiritual world there is no need of sunlight, moonlight or electricity. The *Upaniṣads* also confirm this; because the bodily luster of the Supreme Personality of Godhead is sufficient to illuminate the spiritual world, there is no need of sunlight, moonlight or any other light or electricity. This self-illumination also contradicts the theory that the spirit soul, or the spiritual consciousness, develops at a certain point in material combination. The term *svayaṁ-jyotiḥ* indicates that there is no tinge of anything material or any material reaction. It is confirmed here that the concept of the Lord's all-pervasiveness is due to His illumination everywhere. We have experience that the sun is situated in one place, but the sunlight is diffused all around for millions and millions of miles. That is our practical experience. Similarly, although the supreme light is situated in His personal abode, Vaikuṇṭha or Vṛndāvana, His light is diffused not only in the spiritual world but beyond that. In the material world also, that light is reflected by the sun globe, and the sunlight is reflected by the moon globe. Thus although He is situated in His own abode, His light is distributed all over the spiritual and material worlds. The *Brahma-saṁhitā*

(5.37) confirms this. *Goloka eva nivasaty akhilātma-bhūtaḥ:* He is living in Goloka, but still He is present all over the creation. He is the Supersoul of everything, the Supreme Personality of Godhead, and He has innumerable transcendental qualities. It is also concluded that although He is undoubtedly a person, He is not a *puruṣa* of this material world. Māyāvādī philosophers cannot understand that beyond this material world there can be a person; therefore they are impersonalists. But it is explained very nicely here that the Personality of Godhead is beyond material existence.

TEXT 4

स एष प्रकृतिं सूक्ष्मां दैवीं गुणमयीं विभुः ।
यदृच्छयैवोपगतामभ्यपद्यत लीलया ॥ ४ ॥

sa eṣa prakṛtiṁ sūkṣmāṁ
daivīṁ guṇamayīṁ vibhuḥ
yadṛcchayaivopagatām
abhyapadyata līlayā

saḥ eṣaḥ—that same Supreme Personality of Godhead; *prakṛtim*—material energy; *sūkṣmām*—subtle; *daivīm*—related to Viṣṇu; *guṇamayīm*—invested with the three modes of material nature; *vibhuḥ*—the greatest of the great; *yadṛcchayā*—of His own will; *iva*—quite; *upagatām*—obtained; *abhyapadyata*—He accepted; *līlayā*—as His pastime.

TRANSLATION

As His pastime, that Supreme Personality of Godhead, the greatest of the great, accepted the subtle material energy, which is invested with three material modes of nature and which is related with Viṣṇu.

PURPORT

In this verse the word *guṇamayīm* is very significant. *Daivīm* means "the energy of the Supreme Personality of Godhead," and *guṇamayīm* means "invested with the three modes of material nature." When the material energy of the Supreme Personality of Godhead appears, this *guṇamayīm* energy acts as a manifestation of the energies of the three modes; it acts as a covering. The energy emanated from the Supreme Personality of Godhead manifests in two ways—as an emanation from the Supreme Lord and as a covering of the Lord's face. In *Bhagavad-gītā* it is said that because the whole world is illusioned by the three modes of material nature, the common conditioned soul, being covered by such energy, cannot see the Supreme Personality of Godhead. The example of a cloud is very nicely given. All of a sudden there may appear a big cloud in the sky. This cloud is perceived in two ways. To the sun the cloud is a creation of its energy, but to the ordinary common man in the conditioned state, it is a covering to the eyes; because of the cloud, the sun cannot be seen. It is not that the sun is actually covered by the cloud; only the vision of the ordinary being is covered. Similarly, although *māyā* cannot cover the Supreme Lord, who is beyond *māyā*, the material energy covers the ordinary living entities. Those conditioned souls who are covered are individual living entities, and He from whose energy *māyā* is created is the Supreme Personality of Godhead.

In another place in the *Śrīmad-Bhāgavatam*, in the First Canto, Seventh Chapter, it is stated that Vyāsadeva, by his spiritual vision, saw the Supreme Lord and the material energy standing behind Him. This indicates that material energy cannot cover the Lord, just as darkness cannot cover the sun. Darkness can cover a jurisdiction which is very insignificant in comparison to that of the sun. Darkness can cover a small cave, but not the open sky. Similarly, the covering capacity of the material energy is limited and cannot act on the Supreme Personality of Godhead, who is therefore called *vibhu.* As the appearance of a cloud is accepted by the sun, so the appearance of the material energy at a certain interval is accepted by the Lord. Although His material energy is utilized to create the material world, this does not mean that He is covered by that energy. Those who are covered by the material energy are called conditioned souls. The Lord accepts the material energy for His material pastimes in creation, maintenance and dissolution. But the conditioned soul is covered; he cannot understand that beyond this material energy there is the Supreme Personality of Godhead, who is the cause of all causes, just as a less intelligent person cannot understand that beyond the covering of the clouds there is bright sunshine.

TEXT 5

गुणैर्विचित्राः सृजतीं सरूपाः प्रकृतिं प्रजाः ।
विलोक्य मुमुहे सद्यः स इह ज्ञानगूहया ॥ ५ ॥

guṇair vicitrāḥ sṛjatīṁ
sa-rūpāḥ prakṛtiṁ prajāḥ
vilokya mumuhe sadyaḥ
sa iha jñāna-gūhayā

guṇaiḥ—by the threefold modes; *vicitrāḥ*—variegated; *sṛjatīm*—creating; *sa-rūpāḥ*—with forms; *prakṛtim*—material nature; *prajāḥ*—living entities; *vilokya*—having seen; *mumuhe*—was illusioned; *sadyaḥ*—at once; *saḥ*—the living entity; *iha*—in this world; *jñāna-gūhayā*—by the knowledge-covering feature.

TRANSLATION

Divided into varieties by her threefold modes, material nature creates the forms of the living entities, and the living entities, seeing this, are illusioned by the knowledge-covering feature of the illusory energy.

PURPORT

Material energy has the power to cover knowledge, but this covering cannot be applied to the Supreme Personality of Godhead. It is applicable only to the *prajāḥ,* or those who are born with material bodies, the conditioned souls. The different kinds of living entities vary according to the modes of material nature, as explained in *Bhagavad-gītā* and other Vedic literature. In *Bhagavad-gītā* (7.12) it is very nicely explained that although the modes of goodness, passion and ignorance are born of the Supreme Personality of Godhead, He is not subject to them. In other words, the energy emanating from the Supreme Personality of Godhead cannot act on Him; it acts on the conditioned souls, who are covered by the material energy. The Lord is the father of all living entities because He impregnates material energy with the conditioned souls. Therefore, the conditioned souls get bodies created by the material energy, whereas the father of the living entities is aloof from the three modes.

It is stated in the previous verse that the material energy was accepted by the Supreme Personality of Godhead in order that He might exhibit pastimes for the living entities who wanted to enjoy and lord it over the material energy. This world was created through the material energy of the Lord for the so-called enjoyment of such living entities. Why this material world was created for the sufferings of the conditioned souls is a very intricate question. There is a hint in the previous verse in the word *līlayā*, which means "for the pastimes of the Lord." The Lord wants to rectify the enjoying temperament of the conditioned souls. It is stated in *Bhagavad-gītā* that no one is the enjoyer but the Supreme Personality of Godhead. This material energy is created, therefore, for anyone who pretends to enjoy. An example can be cited here that there is no necessity for the government's creation of a separate police department, but because it is a fact that some of the citizens will not accept the state laws, a department to deal with criminals is necessary. There is no necessity, but at the same time there is a necessity. Similarly, there was no necessity to create this material world for the sufferings of the conditioned souls, but at the same time there are certain living entities, known as *nitya-baddha*, who are eternally conditioned. We say that they have been conditioned from time immemorial because no one can trace out when the living entity, the part and parcel of the Supreme Lord, became rebellious against the supremacy of the Lord.

It is a fact that there are two classes of men—those who are obedient to the laws of the Supreme Lord and those who are atheists or agnostics, who do not accept the existence of God and who want to create their own laws. They want to establish that everyone can create his own laws or his own religious path. Without tracing out the beginning of the existence of these two classes, we can take it for granted that some of the living entities revolted against the laws of the Lord. Such entities are called conditioned souls, for they are conditioned by the three modes of material nature. Therefore the words *guṇair vicitrāḥ* are used here.

In this material world there are 8,400,000 species of life. As spirit souls, they are all transcendental to this material world. Why, then, do they exhibit themselves in different stages of life? The answer is given here: they are under the spell of the three modes of material nature. Because they were created by the material energy, their bodies are made of the material elements. Covered by the material body, the spiritual identity is lost, and therefore the word *mumuhe* is used here, indicating that they have forgotten their own spiritual identity. This forgetfulness of spiritual identity is present in the *jīvas*, or souls, who are conditioned, being subject to be covered by the energy of material nature. *Jñāna-gūhayā* is another word used. *Gūhā* means "covering." Because the knowledge of the minute conditioned souls is covered, they are exhibited in so many species of life. It is said in the *Śrīmad-Bhāgavatam*, Seventh Chapter, First Canto, "The living entities are illusioned by the material energy." In the *Vedas* also it is stated that the eternal living entities are covered by different modes and that they are called tricolored—red, white and blue—living entities. Red is the representation of the mode of passion, white is the representation of the mode of goodness, and blue is the representation of the mode of ignorance. These modes of material nature belong to the material energy, and therefore the living entities under these different modes of material nature have different kinds of material bodies. Because they are forgetful of their spiritual identities, they think the material bodies to be themselves. To the conditioned soul, "me" means the material body. This is called *moha*, or bewilderment.

It is repeatedly said in the *Kaṭha Upaniṣad* that the Supreme Personality of Godhead is never affected by the influence of material nature. It is, rather, the conditioned souls, or the minute infinitesimal parts and parcels of the Supreme, who are affected by the influence of material nature and who appear in different bodies under the material modes.

TEXT 6

एवं पराभिध्यानेन कर्तृत्वं प्रकृतेः पुमान् ।
कर्मसु क्रियमाणेषु गुणैरात्मनि मन्यते ॥ ६ ॥

evaṁ parābhidhyānena
kartṛtvaṁ prakṛteḥ pumān
karmasu kriyamāṇeṣu
guṇair ātmani manyate

evam—in this way; *para*—other; *abhidhyānena*—by identification; *kartṛtvam*—the performance of activities; *prakṛteḥ*—of the material nature; *pumān*—the living entity; *karmasu kriyamāṇeṣu*—while the activities are being performed; *guṇaiḥ*—by the three modes; *ātmani*—to himself; *manyate*—he considers.

TRANSLATION

Because of his forgetfulness, the transcendental living entity accepts the influence of material energy as his field of activities, and thus actuated, he wrongly applies the activities to himself.

PURPORT

The forgetful living entity can be compared to a man who is under the influence of disease and has become mad or to a man haunted by ghosts, who acts without control and yet thinks himself to be in control. Under the influence of material nature, the conditioned soul becomes absorbed in material consciousness. In this consciousness, whatever is done under the influence of the material energy is accepted by the conditioned soul as self-actuated. Actually, the soul in his pure state of existence should be in Kṛṣṇa consciousness. When a person is not acting in Kṛṣṇa consciousness, he is understood to be acting in material consciousness. Consciousness cannot be killed, for the symptom of the living entity is consciousness. The material consciousness simply has to be purified. One becomes liberated by accepting Kṛṣṇa, or the Supreme Lord, as master and by changing the mode of consciousness from material consciousness to Kṛṣṇa consciousness.

TEXT 7

तदस्य संसृतिर्बन्धः पारतन्त्र्यं च तत्कृतम् ।
भवत्यकर्तुरीशस्य साक्षिणो निर्वृतात्मनः ॥ ७ ॥

tad asya saṁsṛtir bandhaḥ
pāra-tantryaṁ ca tat-kṛtam
bhavaty akartur īśasya
sākṣiṇo nirvṛtātmanaḥ

tat—from the misconception; *asya*—of the conditioned soul; *saṁsṛtiḥ*—conditioned life; *bandhaḥ*—bondage; *pāra-tantryam*—dependence; *ca*—and; *tat-kṛtam*—made by that; *bhavati*—is; *akartuḥ*—of the nondoer; *īśasya*—independent; *sākṣiṇaḥ*—the witness; *nirvṛta-ātmanaḥ*—joyful by nature.

TRANSLATION

Material consciousness is the cause of one's conditional life, in which conditions are enforced upon the living entity by the material energy. Although the spirit soul does not do anything and is transcendental to such activities, he is thus affected by conditional life.

PURPORT

The Māyāvādī philosopher, who does not differentiate between the Supreme Spirit and the individual spirit, says that the conditional existence of the living entity is his *līlā*, or pastime. But the word "pastime" implies employment in the activities of the Lord. The Māyāvādīs misuse the word and say that even if the living entity has become a stool-eating hog, he is also enjoying his pastimes. This is a most dangerous interpretation. Actually the Supreme Lord is the leader and maintainer of all living entities. His pastimes are transcendental to any material activity. Such pastimes of the Lord cannot be dragged to the level of the conditional activities of the living entities. In conditional life the living entity actually remains as if a captive in the hands of material energy. Whatever the material energy dictates, the conditioned soul does. He has no responsibility; he is simply the witness of the action, but he is forced to act in that way due to his offense in his eternal relationship with Kṛṣṇa. Lord Kṛṣṇa therefore says in *Bhagavad-gītā* that *māyā*, His material energy, is so forceful that it is insurmountable. But if a living entity simply understands that his constitutional position is to serve Kṛṣṇa and he tries to act on this principle, then however conditioned he may be, the influence of *māyā* immediately vanishes. This is clearly stated in *Bhagavad-gītā*, Seventh Chapter: Kṛṣṇa takes charge of anyone who surrenders to Him in helplessness, and thus the influence of *māyā*, or conditional life, is removed.

The spirit soul is actually *sac-cid-ānanda*—eternal, full of bliss and full of knowledge. Under the clutches of *māyā*, however, he suffers from continued birth, death, disease and old age. One has to be serious to cure this condition of material existence and transfer himself to Kṛṣṇa consciousness, for thus his long suffering may be mitigated without difficulty. In summary, the suffering of the conditioned soul is due to his attachment to material nature. This attachment should thus be transferred from matter to Kṛṣṇa.

TEXT 8

कार्यकारणकर्तृत्वे कारणं प्रकृतिं विदुः ।
भोक्तृत्वे सुखदुःखानां पुरुषं प्रकृतेः परम् ॥ ८ ॥

kārya-kāraṇa-kartṛtve
kāraṇaṁ prakṛtiṁ viduḥ
bhoktṛtve sukha-duḥkhānāṁ
puruṣaṁ prakṛteḥ param

kārya—the body; *kāraṇa*—the senses; *kartṛtve*—regarding the demigods; *kāraṇam*—the cause; *prakṛtim*—material nature; *viduḥ*—the learned understand; *bhoktṛtve*—regarding the perception; *sukha*—of happiness; *duḥkhānām*—and of distress; *puruṣam*—the spirit soul; *prakṛteḥ*—to material nature; *param*—transcendental.

TRANSLATION

The cause of the conditioned soul's material body and senses, and the senses' presiding deities, the demigods, is the material nature. This is understood by learned men. The feelings of happiness and distress of the soul, who is transcendental by nature, are caused by the spirit soul himself.

PURPORT

In *Bhagavad-gītā* it is said that when the Lord descends to this material world, He comes as a person by His own energy, *ātma-māyā*. He is not forced by any superior energy. He comes by His own will, and this can be called His pastime, or *līlā*. But here it is clearly stated that the conditioned soul is forced to take a certain type of body and senses under the three modes of material nature. That body is not received according to his own choice. In other words, a conditioned soul has no free choice;

he has to accept a certain type of body according to his *karma.* But when there are bodily reactions as felt in happiness and distress, it is to be understood that the cause is the spirit soul himself. If he so desires, the spirit soul can change this conditional life of dualities by choosing to serve Kṛṣṇa. The living entity is the cause of his own suffering, but he can also be the cause of his eternal happiness. When he wants to engage in Kṛṣṇa consciousness, a suitable body is offered to him by the internal potency, the spiritual energy of the Lord, and when he wants to satisfy his senses, a material body is offered. Thus it is his free choice to accept a spiritual body or a material body, but once the body is accepted he has to enjoy or suffer the consequences. The Māyāvādī philosopher's presentation is that the living entity enjoys his pastimes by accepting the body of a hog. This theory is not acceptable, however, because the word "pastime" implies voluntary acceptance for enjoyment. Therefore this interpretation is most misleading. When there is enforced acceptance for suffering, it is not a pastime. The Lord's pastimes and the conditioned living entity's acceptance of karmic reaction are not on the same level.

TEXT 9

देवहूतिरुवाच
प्रकृतेः पुरुषस्यापि लक्षणं पुरुषोत्तम ।
ब्रूहि कारणयोरस्य सदसच्च यदात्मकम् ॥ ९ ॥

devahūtir uvāca
prakṛteḥ puruṣasyāpi
lakṣaṇaṁ puruṣottama
brūhi kāraṇayor asya
sad-asac ca yad-ātmakam

devahūtiḥ uvāca—Devahūti said; *prakṛteḥ*—of His energies; *puruṣasya*—of the Supreme Person; *api*—also; *lakṣaṇam*—characteristics; *puruṣa-uttama*—O Supreme Personality of Godhead; *brūhi*—kindly explain; *kāraṇayoḥ*—causes; *asya*—of this creation; *sat-asat*—manifest and unmanifest; *ca*—and; *yat-ātmakam*—consisting of which.

TRANSLATION

Devahūti said: O Supreme Personality of Godhead, kindly explain the characteristics of the Supreme Person and His energies, for both of these are the causes of this manifest and unmanifest creation.

PURPORT

Prakṛti, or material nature, is connected with both the Supreme Lord and the living entities, just as a woman is connected with her husband as a wife and with her children as a mother. In *Bhagavad-gītā* the Lord says that He impregnates mother nature with children, living entities, and thereafter all species of living entities become manifest. The relationship of all living entities with material nature has been explained. Now an understanding of the relationship between material nature and the Supreme Lord is sought by Devahūti. The product of that relationship is stated to be the manifest and unmanifest material world. The unmanifest material world is the subtle *mahat-tattva*, and from that *mahat-tattva* the material manifestation has emerged.

In the Vedic literatures it is said that by the glance of the Supreme Lord the total material energy is impregnated, and then everything is born of material nature. It is also confirmed in the Ninth Chapter of *Bhagavad-gītā* that under His glance, *adhyakṣeṇa*—under His direction and by His will—nature is working. It is not that nature works blindly. After understanding the position of the conditioned souls in relation to material nature, Devahūti wanted to know how nature works under the direction of the Lord and what the relationship is between the material nature and the Lord. In other words, she wanted to learn the characteristics of the Supreme Lord in relation to the material nature.

The relationship of the living entities with matter and that of the Supreme Lord with matter are certainly not on the same level, although the Māyāvādīs may interpret it in that way. When it is said that the living entities are bewildered, the Māyāvādī philosophers ascribe this bewilderment to the Supreme Lord. But that is not applicable. The Lord is never bewildered. That is the difference between personalists and impersonalists. Devahūti is not unintelligent. She has enough intelligence to understand that the living entities are not on the level of the Supreme Lord. Because the living entities are infinitesimal, they become bewildered or conditioned by material nature, but this does not mean that the Supreme Lord is also conditioned or bewildered. The difference between the conditioned soul and the Lord is that the Lord is the Lord, the master of material nature, and He is therefore not subject to its control. He is controlled neither by spiritual nature nor by material nature. He is the supreme controller Himself, and He cannot be compared to the ordinary living entities, who are controlled by the laws of material nature.

Two words used in this verse are *sat* and *asat.* The cosmic manifestation is *asat*—it does not exist—but the material energy of the Supreme Lord is *sat*, or ever existing. Material nature is ever existing in its subtle form as the energy of the Lord, but it sometimes manifests this nonexistent or temporarily existent nature, the cosmos. An analogy may be made with the father and mother: the mother and the father exist, but sometimes the mother begets children. Similarly, this cosmic manifestation, which comes from the unmanifest material nature of the Supreme Lord, sometimes appears and again disappears. But the material nature is ever existing, and the Lord is the supreme cause for both the subtle and gross manifestations of this material world.

TEXT 10

श्रीभगवानुवाच
यत्तत्त्रिगुणमव्यक्तं नित्यं सदसदात्मकम् ।
प्रधानं प्रकृतिं प्राहुरविशेषं विशेषवत् ॥१०॥

śrī-bhagavān uvāca
yat tat tri-guṇam avyaktaṁ
nityaṁ sad-asad-ātmakam
pradhānaṁ prakṛtiṁ prāhur
aviśeṣaṁ viśeṣavat

śrī-bhagavān uvāca—the Supreme Personality of Godhead said; *yat*—now further; *tat*—that; *tri-guṇam*—combination of the three modes; *avyaktam*—unmanifested; *nityam*—eternal; *sat-asat-ātmakam*—consisting of cause and effect; *pradhānam*—the *pradhāna; prakṛtim*—*prakṛti; prāhuḥ*—they call; *aviśeṣam*—undifferentiated; *viśeṣa-vat*—possessing differentiation.

TRANSLATION

The Supreme Personality of Godhead said: The unmanifested eternal combination of the three modes is the cause of the manifest state and is called pradhāna. It is called prakṛti when in the manifested stage of existence.

PURPORT

The Lord points out material nature in its subtle stage, which is called *pradhāna*, and He analyzes this *pradhāna*. The explanation of *pradhāna* and *prakṛti* is that *pradhāna* is the subtle, undifferentiated sum total of all material elements. Although they are undifferentiated, one can understand that the total material elements are contained therein. When the total material elements are manifested by the interaction of the three modes of material nature, the manifestation is called *prakṛti*. Impersonalists say that Brahman is without variegatedness and without differentiation. One may say that *pradhāna* is the Brahman stage, but actually the Brahman stage is not *pradhāna*. *Pradhāna* is distinct from Brahman because in Brahman there is no existence of the material modes of nature. One may argue that the *mahat-tattva* is also different from *pradhāna* because in the *mahat-tattva* there are manifestations. The actual explanation of *pradhāna*, however, is given here: when the cause and effect are not clearly manifested (*avyakta*), the reaction of the total elements does not take place, and that stage of material nature is called *pradhāna*. *Pradhāna* is not the time element because in the time element there are actions and reactions, creation and annihilation. Nor is it the *jīva*, or marginal potency of living entities, or designated, conditioned living entities, because the designations of the living entities are not eternal. One adjective used in this connection is *nitya*, which indicates eternality. Therefore the condition of material nature immediately previous to its manifestation is called *pradhāna*.

TEXT 11

पञ्चभिः पञ्चभिर्ब्रह्म चतुर्भिर्दशभिस्तथा ।
एतच्चतुर्विंशतिकं गणं प्राधानिकं विदुः ॥११॥

pañcabhiḥ pañcabhir brahma
caturbhir daśabhis tathā
etac catur-viṁśatikaṁ
gaṇaṁ prādhānikaṁ viduḥ

pañcabhiḥ—with the five (gross elements); *pañcabhiḥ*—the five (subtle elements); *brahma*—Brahman; *caturbhiḥ*—the four (internal senses); *daśabhiḥ*—the ten (five senses for gathering knowledge and five organs of action); *tathā*—in that way; *etat*—this; *catuḥ-viṁśatikam*—consisting of twenty-four elements; *gaṇam*—aggregate; *prādhānikam*—comprising the *pradhāna; viduḥ*—they know.

TRANSLATION

The aggregate elements, namely the five gross elements, the five subtle elements, the four internal senses, the five senses for gathering knowledge and the five outward organs of action, are known as the pradhāna.

PURPORT

According to *Bhagavad-gītā,* the sum total of the twenty-four elements described herein is called the *yonir mahad-brahma.* The sum total of the living entities is impregnated into this *yonir mahad-brahma,* and they are born in different forms, beginning from Brahmā down to the insignificant ant. In the *Śrīmad-Bhāgavatam* and other Vedic literatures, the sum total of the twenty-four elements, *pradhāna,* is also described as *yonir mahad-brahma;* it is the source of the birth and subsistence of all living entities.

TEXT 12

महाभूतानि पञ्चैव भूरापोऽग्निर्मरुन्नभः ।
तन्मात्राणि च तावन्ति गन्धादीनि मतानि मे ॥१२॥

mahā-bhūtāni pañcaiva
bhūr āpo 'gnir marun nabhaḥ
tan-mātrāṇi ca tāvanti
gandhādīni matāni me

mahā-bhūtāni—the gross elements; *pañca*—five; *eva*—exactly; *bhūḥ*—earth; *āpaḥ*—water; *agniḥ*—fire; *marut*—air; *nabhaḥ*—ether; *tat-mātrāṇi*—the subtle elements; *ca*—also; *tāvanti*—so many; *gandha-ādīni*—smell and so on (taste, color, touch and sound); *matāni*—considered; *me*—by Me.

TRANSLATION

There are five gross elements, namely earth, water, fire, air and ether. There are also five subtle elements: smell, taste, color, touch and sound.

TEXT 13

इन्द्रियाणि दश श्रोत्रं त्वग्दृग्रसननासिकाः ।
वाक्करौ चरणौ मेढ्रं पायुर्दशम उच्यते ॥१३॥

indriyāṇi daśa śrotraṁ
tvag dṛg rasana-nāsikāḥ
vāk karau caraṇau meḍhraṁ
pāyur daśama ucyate

indriyāṇi—the senses; *daśa*—ten; *śrotram*—the sense of hearing; *tvak*—the sense of touch; *dṛk*—the sense of sight; *rasana*—the sense of taste; *nāsikāḥ*—the sense of smell; *vāk*—the organ of speech; *karau*—two hands; *caraṇau*—the organs for traveling (legs); *meḍhram*—the generative organ; *pāyuḥ*—the evacuating organ; *daśamaḥ*—the tenth; *ucyate*—is called.

TRANSLATION

The senses for acquiring knowledge and the organs for action number ten, namely the auditory sense, the sense of taste, the tactile sense, the sense of sight, the sense of smell, the active organ for speaking, the active organs for working, and those for traveling, generating and evacuating.

TEXT 14

मनो बुद्धिरहङ्कारश्चित्तमित्यन्तरात्मकम् ।
चतुर्धा लक्ष्यते भेदो वृत्त्या लक्षणरूपया ॥१४॥

mano buddhir ahaṅkāraś
cittam ity antar-ātmakam
caturdhā lakṣyate bhedo
vṛttyā lakṣaṇa-rūpayā

manaḥ—the mind; *buddhiḥ*—intelligence; *ahaṅkāraḥ*—ego; *cittam*—consciousness; *iti*—thus; *antaḥ-ātmakam*—the internal, subtle senses; *catuḥ-dhā*—having four aspects; *lakṣyate*—is observed; *bhedaḥ*—the distinction; *vṛttyā*—by their functions; *lakṣaṇa-rūpayā*—representing different characteristics.

TRANSLATION

The internal, subtle senses are experienced as having four aspects, in the shape of mind, intelligence, ego and contaminated consciousness. Distinctions between them can be made only by different functions, since they represent different characteristics.

PURPORT

The four internal senses, or subtle senses, described herein are defined by different characteristics. When pure consciousness is polluted by material contamination and when identification with the body becomes prominent, one is said to be situated under false ego. Consciousness is the function of the soul, and therefore behind consciousness there is soul. Consciousness polluted by material contamination is called *ahaṅkāra.*

TEXT 15

एतावानेव सङ्ख्यातो ब्रह्मणः सगुणस्य ह ।
सन्निवेशो मया प्रोक्तो यः कालः पञ्चविंशकः ॥१५॥

etāvān eva saṅkhyāto
brahmaṇaḥ sa-guṇasya ha
sanniveśo mayā prokto
yaḥ kālaḥ pañca-viṁśakaḥ

etāvān—so much; *eva*—just; *saṅkhyātaḥ*—enumerated; *brahmaṇaḥ*—of Brahman; *sa-guṇasya*—with material qualities; *ha*—indeed;

sanniveśaḥ—arrangement; *mayā*—by Me; *proktaḥ*—spoken; *yaḥ*—which; *kālaḥ*—time; *pañca-viṁśakaḥ*—the twenty-fifth.

TRANSLATION

All these are considered the qualified Brahman. The mixing element, which is known as time, is counted as the twenty-fifth element.

PURPORT

According to the Vedic version there is no existence beyond Brahman. *Sarvaṁ khalv idaṁ brahma* (*Chāndogya Upaniṣad* 3.14.1). It is stated also in the *Viṣṇu Purāṇa* that whatever we see is *parasya brahmaṇaḥ śaktiḥ;* everything is an expansion of the energy of the Supreme Absolute Truth, Brahman. When Brahman is mixed with the three qualities goodness, passion and ignorance, there results the material expansion, which is sometimes called *saguṇa* Brahman and which consists of these twenty-five elements. In the *nirguṇa* Brahman, where there is no material contamination, or in the spiritual world, the three modes—goodness, passion and ignorance—are not present. Where *nirguṇa* Brahman is found, simple unalloyed goodness prevails. *Saguṇa* Brahman is described by the Sāṅkhya system of philosophy as consisting of twenty-five elements, including the time factor (past, present and future).

TEXT 16

प्रभावं पौरुषं प्राहुः कालमेके यतो भयम् ।
अहङ्कारविमूढस्य कर्तुः प्रकृतिमीयुषः ॥१६॥

prabhāvaṁ pauruṣaṁ prāhuḥ
kālam eke yato bhayam
ahaṅkāra-vimūḍhasya
kartuḥ prakṛtim īyuṣaḥ

prabhāvam—the influence; *pauruṣam*—of the Supreme Personality of Godhead; *prāhuḥ*—they have said; *kālam*—the time factor;

eke—some; *yataḥ*—from which; *bhayam*—fear; *ahaṅkāra-vimūḍhasya*—deluded by false ego; *kartuḥ*—of the individual soul; *prakṛtim*—material nature; *īyuṣaḥ*—having contacted.

TRANSLATION

The influence of the Supreme Personality of Godhead is felt in the time factor, which causes fear of death due to the false ego of the deluded soul who has contacted material nature.

PURPORT

The living entity's fear of death is due to his false ego of identifying with the body. Everyone is afraid of death. Actually there is no death for the spirit soul, but due to our absorption in the identification of body as self, the fear of death develops. It is also stated in the *Śrīmad-Bhāgavatam* (11.2.37), *bhayaṁ dvitīyābhiniveśataḥ syāt. Dvitīya* refers to matter, which is beyond spirit. Matter is the secondary manifestation of spirit, for matter is produced from spirit. Just as the material elements described are caused by the Supreme Lord, or the Supreme Spirit, the body is also a product of the spirit soul. Therefore, the material body is called *dvitīya,* or "the second." One who is absorbed in this second element or second exhibition of the spirit is afraid of death. When one is fully convinced that he is not his body, there is no question of fearing death, since the spirit soul does not die.

If the spirit soul engages in the spiritual activities of devotional service, he is completely freed from the platform of birth and death. His next position is complete spiritual freedom from a material body. The fear of death is the action of the *kāla,* or the time factor, which represents the influence of the Supreme Personality of Godhead. In other words, time is destructive. Whatever is created is subject to destruction and dissolution, which is the action of time. Time is a representation of the Lord, and it reminds us also that we must surrender unto the Lord. The Lord speaks to every conditioned soul as time. He says in *Bhagavad-gītā* that if someone surrenders unto Him, then there is no longer any problem of birth and death. We should therefore accept the time factor as the Supreme Personality of Godhead standing before us. This is further explained in the following verse.

TEXT 17

प्रकृतेर्गुणसाम्यस्य निर्विशेषस्य मानवि ।
चेष्टा यतः स भगवान् काल इत्युपलक्षितः ॥१७॥

prakṛter guṇa-sāmyasya
nirviśeṣasya mānavi
ceṣṭā yataḥ sa bhagavān
kāla ity upalakṣitaḥ

prakṛteḥ—of material nature; *guṇa-sāmyasya*—without interaction of the three modes; *nirviśeṣasya*—without specific qualities; *mānavi*—O daughter of Manu; *ceṣṭā*—movement; *yataḥ*—from whom; *saḥ*—He; *bhagavān*—the Supreme Personality of Godhead; *kālaḥ*—time; *iti*—thus; *upalakṣitaḥ*—is designated.

TRANSLATION

My dear mother, O daughter of Svāyambhuva Manu, the time factor, as I have explained, is the Supreme Personality of Godhead, from whom the creation begins as a result of the agitation of the neutral, unmanifested nature.

PURPORT

The unmanifested state of material nature, *pradhāna*, is being explained. The Lord says that when the unmanifested material nature is agitated by the glance of the Supreme Personality of Godhead, it begins to manifest itself in different ways. Before this agitation, it remains in the neutral state, without interaction by the three modes of material nature. In other words, material nature cannot produce any variety of manifestations without the contact of the Supreme Personality of Godhead. This is very nicely explained in *Bhagavad-gītā.* The Supreme Personality of Godhead is the cause of the products of material nature. Without His contact, material nature cannot produce anything.

In the *Caitanya-caritāmṛta* also, a very suitable example is given in this connection. Although the nipples on a goat's neck appear to be breast nipples, they do not give milk. Similarly, material nature appears to the material scientist to act and react in a wonderful manner, but in reality it cannot act without the agitator, time, who is the representation of the Supreme Personality of Godhead. When time agitates the neutral state of material nature, material nature begins to produce varieties of manifestations. Ultimately it is said that the Supreme Personality of Godhead is the cause of creation. As a woman cannot produce children unless impregnated by a man, material nature cannot produce or manifest anything unless it is impregnated by the Supreme Personality of Godhead in the form of the time factor.

TEXT 18

अन्तः पुरुषरूपेण कालरूपेण यो बहिः ।
समन्वेत्येष सत्त्वानां भगवानात्ममायया ॥१८॥

antaḥ puruṣa-rūpeṇa
kāla-rūpeṇa yo bahiḥ
samanvety eṣa sattvānāṁ
bhagavān ātma-māyayā

antaḥ—within; *puruṣa-rūpeṇa*—in the form of Supersoul; *kāla-rūpeṇa*—in the form of time; *yaḥ*—He who; *bahiḥ*—without; *samanveti*—exists; *eṣaḥ*—He; *sattvānām*—of all living entities; *bhagavān*—the Supreme Personality of Godhead; *ātma-māyayā*—by His potencies.

TRANSLATION

By exhibiting His potencies, the Supreme Personality of Godhead adjusts all these different elements, keeping Himself within as the Supersoul and without as time.

PURPORT

Here it is stated that within the heart the Supreme Personality of Godhead resides as the Supersoul. This situation is also explained in *Bhagavad-gītā:* the Supersoul rests beside the individual soul and acts as a witness. This is also confirmed elsewhere in the Vedic literature: two birds are sitting on the same tree of the body; one is witnessing, and the other is eating the fruits of the tree. This *puruṣa*, or Paramātmā, who resides within the body of the individual soul, is described in *Bhagavad-gītā* (13.23) as the *upadraṣṭā*, witness, and the *anumantā*, sanctioning authority. The conditioned soul engages in the happiness and distress of the particular body given him by the arrangement of the external energy of the Supreme Lord. But the supreme living being, or the Paramātmā, is different from the conditioned soul. He is described in *Bhagavad-gītā* as *maheśvara*, or the Supreme Lord. He is Paramātmā, not *jīvātmā*. Paramātmā means the Supersoul, who is sitting by the side of the conditioned soul just to sanction his activities. The conditioned soul comes to this material world in order to lord it over material nature. Since one cannot do anything without the sanction of the Supreme Lord, He lives with the *jīva* soul as witness and sanction-giver. He is also *bhoktā*; He gives maintenance and sustenance to the conditioned soul.

Since the living entity is constitutionally part and parcel of the Supreme Personality of Godhead, the Lord is very affectionate to the living entities. Unfortunately, when the living entity is bewildered or illusioned by the external energy, he becomes forgetful of his eternal relationship with the Lord, but as soon as he becomes aware of his constitutional position, he is liberated. The minute independence of the conditioned soul is exhibited by his marginal position. If he likes, he can forget the Supreme Personality of Godhead and come into the material existence with a false ego to lord it over material nature, but if he likes he can turn his face to the service of the Lord. The individual living entity is given that independence. His conditional life is ended and his life becomes successful as soon as he turns his face to the Lord, but by misusing his independence he enters into material existence. Yet the Lord is so kind that, as Supersoul, He always remains with the conditioned soul. The concern of the Lord is neither to enjoy nor to suffer from the material body. He remains with the *jīva* simply as sanction-giver and witness so that the living entity can receive the results of his activities, good or bad.

Outside the body of the conditioned soul, the Supreme Personality of Godhead remains as the time factor. According to the Sāṅkhya system of philosophy, there are twenty-five elements. The twenty-four elements already described plus the time factor make twenty-five. According to some learned philosophers, the Supersoul is included to make a total of twenty-six elements.

TEXT 19

दैवात्क्षुभितधर्मिण्यां स्वस्यां योनौ परः पुमान् ।
आधत्त वीर्यं सासूत महत्तत्त्वं हिरण्मयम् ॥१९॥

daivāt kṣubhita-dharmiṇyāṁ
svasyāṁ yonau paraḥ pumān
ādhatta vīryaṁ sāsūta
mahat-tattvaṁ hiraṇmayam

daivāt—by the destiny of the conditioned souls; *kṣubhita*—agitated; *dharmiṇyām*—whose equilibrium of the modes; *svasyām*—His own; *yonau*—in the womb (material nature); *paraḥ pumān*—the Supreme Personality of Godhead; *ādhatta*—impregnated; *vīryam*—semen (His internal potency); *sā*—she (material nature); *asūta*—delivered; *mahat-tattvam*—the sum total of cosmic intelligence; *hiraṇmayam*—known as Hiraṇmaya.

TRANSLATION

After the Supreme Personality of Godhead impregnates material nature with His internal potency, material nature delivers the sum total of the cosmic intelligence, which is known as Hiraṇmaya. This takes place in material nature when she is agitated by the destinations of the conditioned souls.

PURPORT

This impregnation of material nature is described in *Bhagavad-gītā*, Fourteenth Chapter, verse 3. Material nature's primal factor is the *mahat-tattva*, or breeding source of all varieties. This part of material nature, which is called *pradhāna* as well as Brahman, is impregnated by the Supreme Personality of Godhead and delivers varieties of living entities. Material nature in this connection is called Brahman because it is a perverted reflection of the spiritual nature.

It is described in the *Viṣṇu Purāṇa* that the living entities belong to the spiritual nature. The potency of the Supreme Lord is spiritual, and the living entities, although they are called marginal potency, are also spiritual. If the living entities were not spiritual, this description of impregnation by the Supreme Lord would not be applicable. The Supreme Lord does not put His semen into that which is not spiritual, but it is stated here that the Supreme Person puts His semen into material nature. This means that the living entities are spiritual by nature. After impregnation, material nature delivers all kinds of living entities, beginning from the greatest living creature, Lord Brahmā, down to the insignificant ant, in all varieties of form. In *Bhagavad-gītā* (14.4) material nature is clearly mentioned as *sarva-yoniṣu.* This means that of all varieties of species—demigods, human beings, animals, birds and beasts (whatever is manifested)—material nature is the mother, and the Supreme Personality of Godhead is the seed-giving father. Generally it is experienced that the father gives life to the child but the mother gives its body; although the seed of life is given by the father, the body develops within the womb of the mother. Similarly, the spiritual living entities are impregnated into the womb of material nature, but the body, being supplied by material nature, takes on many different species and forms of life. The theory that the symptoms of life are manifest by the interaction of the twenty-four material elements is not supported here. The living force comes directly from the Supreme Personality of Godhead and is completely spiritual. Therefore, no material scientific advancement can produce life. The living force comes from the spiritual world and has nothing to do with the interaction of the material elements.

TEXT 20

विश्वमात्मगतं व्यञ्जन् कूटस्थो जगदङ्कुरः ।
स्वतेजसापिबत्तीव्रमात्मप्रस्वापनं तमः ॥२०॥

viśvam ātma-gataṁ vyañjan
kūṭa-stho jagad-aṅkuraḥ
sva-tejasāpibat tīvram
ātma-prasvāpanaṁ tamaḥ

viśvam—the universe; *ātma-gatam*—contained within itself; *vyañjan*—manifesting; *kūṭa-sthaḥ*—unchangeable; *jagat-aṅkuraḥ*—the root of all cosmic manifestations; *sva-tejasā*—by its own effulgence; *apibat*—

swallowed; *tīvram*—dense; *ātma-prasvāpanam*—which had covered the *mahat-tattva; tamaḥ*—darkness.

TRANSLATION

Thus, after manifesting variegatedness, the effulgent mahat-tattva, which contains all the universes within itself, which is the root of all cosmic manifestations and which is not destroyed at the time of annihilation, swallows the darkness that covered the effulgence at the time of dissolution.

PURPORT

Since the Supreme Personality of Godhead is ever existing, all-blissful and full of knowledge, His different energies are also ever existing in the dormant stage. Thus when the *mahat-tattva* was created, it manifested the material ego and swallowed up the darkness which covered the cosmic manifestation at the time of dissolution. This idea can be further explained. A person at night remains inactive, covered by the darkness of night, but when he is awakened in the morning, the covering of night, or the forgetfulness of the sleeping state, disappears. Similarly, when the *mahat-tattva* appears after the night of dissolution, the effulgence is manifested to exhibit the variegatedness of this material world.

TEXT 21

यत्तत्सत्त्वगुणं स्वच्छं शान्तं भगवतः पदम् ।
यदाहुर्वासुदेवाख्यं चित्तं तन्महदात्मकम् ॥२१॥

yat tat sattva-guṇaṁ svacchaṁ
śāntaṁ bhagavataḥ padam
yad āhur vāsudevākhyaṁ
cittaṁ tan mahad-ātmakam

yat—which; *tat*—that; *sattva-guṇam*—the mode of goodness; *svaccham*—clear; *śāntam*—sober; *bhagavataḥ*—of the Personality of Godhead; *padam*—the status of understanding; *yat*—which; *āhuḥ*—is called; *vāsudeva-ākhyam*—by the name *vāsudeva; cittam*—consciousness; *tat*—that; *mahat-ātmakam*—manifest in the *mahat-tattva.*

TRANSLATION

The mode of goodness, which is the clear, sober status of understanding the Personality of Godhead and which is generally called vāsudeva, or consciousness, becomes manifest in the mahat-tattva.

PURPORT

The *vāsudeva* manifestation, or the status of understanding the Supreme Personality of Godhead, is called pure goodness, or *śuddha-sattva.* In the *śuddha-sattva* status there is no infringement of the other qualities, namely passion and ignorance. In the Vedic literature there is mention of the Lord's expansion as the four Personalities of Godhead—Vāsudeva, Saṅkarṣaṇa, Pradyumna and Aniruddha. Here in the reappearance of the *mahat-tattva* the four expansions of Godhead occur. He who is seated within as Supersoul expands first as Vāsudeva.

The *vāsudeva* stage is free from infringement by material desires and is the status in which one can understand the Supreme Personality of Godhead, or the objective which is described in the *Bhagavad-gītā* as *adbhuta.* This is another feature of the *mahat-tattva.* The *vāsudeva* expansion is also called Kṛṣṇa consciousness, for it is free from all tinges of material passion and ignorance. This clear state of understanding helps one to know the Supreme Personality of Godhead. The *vāsudeva* status is also explained in *Bhagavad-gītā* as *kṣetra-jña,* which refers to the knower of the field of activities as well as the Superknower. The living being who has occupied a particular type of body knows that body, but the Superknower, Vāsudeva, knows not only a particular type of body but also the field of activities in all the different varieties of bodies. In order to be situated in clear consciousness, or Kṛṣṇa consciousness, one must worship Vāsudeva. Vāsudeva is Kṛṣṇa alone. When Kṛṣṇa, or Viṣṇu, is alone, without the accompaniment of His internal energy, He is Vāsudeva. When He is accompanied by His internal potency, He is called Dvārakādhīśa. To have clear consciousness, or Kṛṣṇa consciousness, one has to worship Vāsudeva. It is also explained in *Bhagavad-gītā* that after many, many births one surrenders to Vāsudeva. Such a great soul is very rare.

In order to get release from the false ego, one has to worship Saṅkarṣaṇa. Saṅkarṣaṇa is also worshiped through Lord Śiva; the snakes which cover the body of Lord Śiva are representations of Saṅkarṣaṇa, and Lord Śiva is always absorbed in meditation upon Saṅkarṣaṇa. One who is actually a worshiper of Lord Śiva as a devotee of Saṅkarṣaṇa can be released from false, material ego. If one wants to get free from mental disturbances, one has to worship Aniruddha. For this purpose, worship of the moon planet is also recommended in the Vedic literature. Similarly, to be fixed in one's intelligence one has to worship Pradyumna, who is reached through the worship of Brahmā. These matters are explained in Vedic literature.

TEXT 22

स्वच्छत्वमविकारित्वं शान्तत्वमिति चेतसः ।
वृत्तिभिर्लक्षणं प्रोक्तं यथापां प्रकृतिः परा ॥२२॥

svacchatvam avikāritvaṁ
śāntatvam iti cetasaḥ
vṛttibhir lakṣaṇaṁ proktaṁ
yathāpāṁ prakṛtiḥ parā

svacchatvam—clarity; *avikāritvam*—freedom from all distraction; *śāntatvam*—serenity; *iti*—thus; *cetasaḥ*—of consciousness; *vṛttibhiḥ*—by characteristics; *lakṣaṇam*—traits; *proktam*—called; *yathā*—as; *apām*—of water; *prakṛtiḥ*—natural state; *parā*—pure.

TRANSLATION

After the manifestation of the mahat-tattva, these features appear simultaneously. As water in its natural state, before coming in contact with earth, is clear, sweet and unruffled, so the characteristic traits of pure consciousness are complete serenity, clarity, and freedom from distraction.

PURPORT

The pure status of consciousness, or Kṛṣṇa consciousness, exists in the beginning; just after creation, consciousness is not polluted. The more one becomes materially contaminated, however, the more consciousness becomes obscured. In pure consciousness one can perceive a slight reflection of the Supreme Personality of Godhead. As in clear, unagitated water, free from impurities, one can see everything clearly, so in pure consciousness, or Kṛṣṇa consciousness, one can see things as they are. One can see the reflection of the Supreme Personality of Godhead, and one can see his own existence as well. This state of consciousness is very pleasing, transparent and sober. In the beginning, consciousness is pure.

TEXTS 23–24

महत्तत्त्वाद्विकुर्वाणाद्भगवद्वीर्यसम्भवात् ।
क्रियाशक्तिरहङ्कारस्त्रिविधः समपद्यत ॥२३॥
वैकारिकस्तैजसश्च तामसश्च यतो भवः ।
मनसश्चेन्द्रियाणां च भूतानां महतामपि ॥२४॥

mahat-tattvād vikurvāṇād
bhagavad-vīrya-sambhavāt
kriyā-śaktir ahaṅkāras
tri-vidhaḥ samapadyata

vaikārikas taijasaś ca
tāmasaś ca yato bhavaḥ
manasaś cendriyāṇāṁ ca
bhūtānāṁ mahatām api

mahat-tattvāt—from the *mahat-tattva; vikurvāṇāt*—undergoing a change; *bhagavat-vīrya-sambhavāt*—evolved from the Lord's own energy; *kriyā-śaktiḥ*—endowed with active power; *ahaṅkāraḥ*—the material ego; *tri-vidhaḥ*—of the three kinds; *samapadyata*—sprang up; *vaikārikaḥ*—material ego in transformed goodness; *taijasaḥ*—material ego in passion; *ca*—and; *tāmasaḥ*—material ego in ignorance; *ca*—also; *yataḥ*—from which; *bhavaḥ*—the origin; *manasaḥ*—of the mind; *ca*—

and; *indriyāṇām*—of the senses for perception and action; *ca*—and; *bhūtānām mahatām*—of the five gross elements; *api*—also.

TRANSLATION

The material ego springs up from the mahat-tattva, which evolved from the Lord's own energy. The material ego is endowed predominantly with active power of three kinds—good, passionate and ignorant. It is from these three types of material ego that the mind, the senses of perception, the organs of action, and the gross elements evolve.

PURPORT

In the beginning, from clear consciousness, or the pure state of Kṛṣṇa consciousness, the first contamination sprang up. This is called false ego, or identification of the body as self. The living entity exists in the natural state of Kṛṣṇa consciousness, but he has marginal independence, and this allows him to forget Kṛṣṇa. Originally, pure Kṛṣṇa consciousness exists, but because of misuse of marginal independence there is a chance of forgetting Kṛṣṇa. This is exhibited in actual life; there are many instances in which someone acting in Kṛṣṇa consciousness suddenly changes. In the *Upaniṣads* it is stated, therefore, that the path of spiritual realization is just like the sharp edge of a razor. The example is very appropriate. One shaves his cheeks with a sharp razor very nicely, but as soon as his attention is diverted from the activity, he immediately cuts his cheek because he mishandles the razor.

Not only must one come to the stage of pure Kṛṣṇa consciousness, but one must also be very careful. Any inattentiveness or carelessness may cause falldown. This falldown is due to false ego. From the status of pure consciousness, the false ego is born because of misuse of independence. We cannot argue about why false ego arises from pure consciousness. Factually, there is always the chance that this will happen, and therefore one has to be very careful. False ego is the basic principle for all material activities, which are executed in the modes of material nature. As soon as one deviates from pure Kṛṣṇa consciousness, he increases his entanglement in material reaction. The entanglement of materialism is the material mind, and from this material mind, the senses and material organs become manifest.

TEXT 25

सहस्रशिरसं साक्षाद्यमनन्तं प्रचक्षते ।
सङ्कर्षणाख्यं पुरुषं भूतेन्द्रियमनोमयम् ॥२५॥

sahasra-śirasaṁ sākṣād
yam anantaṁ pracakṣate
saṅkarṣaṇākhyaṁ puruṣaṁ
bhūtendriya-manomayam

sahasra-śirasam—with a thousand heads; *sākṣāt*—directly; *yam*—whom; *anantam*—Ananta; *pracakṣate*—they call; *saṅkarṣaṇa-ākhyam*—Saṅkarṣaṇa by name; *puruṣam*—the Supreme Personality of Godhead; *bhūta*—the gross elements; *indriya*—the senses; *manaḥ-mayam*—consisting of the mind.

TRANSLATION

The threefold ahaṅkāra, the source of the gross elements, the senses and the mind, is identical with them because it is their cause. It is known by the name of Saṅkarṣaṇa, who is directly Lord Ananta with a thousand heads.

TEXT 26

कर्तृत्वं करणत्वं च कार्यत्वं चेति लक्षणम् ।
शान्तघोरविमूढत्वमिति वा स्यादहंकृतेः ॥२६॥

kartṛtvaṁ karaṇatvaṁ ca
kāryatvaṁ ceti lakṣaṇam
śānta-ghora-vimūḍhatvam
iti vā syād ahaṅkṛteḥ

kartṛtvam—being the doer; *karaṇatvam*—being the instrument; *ca*—and; *kāryatvam*—being the effect; *ca*—also; *iti*—thus; *lakṣaṇam*—characteristic; *śānta*—serene; *ghora*—active; *vimūḍhatvam*—being dull; *iti*—thus; *vā*—or; *syāt*—may be; *ahaṅkṛteḥ*—of the false ego.

TRANSLATION

This false ego is characterized as the doer, as an instrument and as an effect. It is further characterized as serene, active or dull according to how it is influenced by the modes of goodness, passion and ignorance.

PURPORT

Ahaṅkāra, or false ego, is transformed into the demigods, the controlling directors of material affairs. As an instrument, the false ego is represented as different senses and sense organs, and as the result of the combination of the demigods and the senses, material objects are produced. In the material world we are producing so many things, and this is called advancement of civilization, but factually the advancement of civilization is a manifestation of the false ego. By false ego all material things are produced as objects of enjoyment. One has to cease increasing artificial necessities in the form of material objects. One great *ācārya*, Narottama dāsa Ṭhākura, has lamented that when one deviates from pure consciousness of Vāsudeva, or Kṛṣṇa consciousness, he becomes entangled in material activities. The exact words he uses are, *sat-saṅga chāḍi' kainu asate vilāsa/ te-kāraṇe lāgila ye karma-bandha-phāṅsa:* "I have given up the pure status of consciousness because I wanted to enjoy in the temporary, material manifestation; therefore I have been entangled in the network of actions and reactions."

TEXT 27

वैकारिकाद्विकुर्वाणान्मनस्तत्त्वमजायत ।
यत्सङ्कल्पविकल्पाभ्यां वर्तते कामसम्भवः ॥२७॥

vaikārikād vikurvāṇān
manas-tattvam ajāyata
yat-saṅkalpa-vikalpābhyāṁ
vartate kāma-sambhavaḥ

vaikārikāt—from the false ego of goodness; *vikurvāṇāt*—undergoing transformation; *manaḥ*—the mind; *tattvam*—principle; *ajāyata*—

evolved; *yat*—whose; *saṅkalpa*—thoughts; *vikalpābhyām*—and by reflections; *vartate*—happens; *kāma-sambhavaḥ*—the rise of desire.

TRANSLATION

From the false ego of goodness, another transformation takes place. From this evolves the mind, whose thoughts and reflections give rise to desire.

PURPORT

The symptoms of the mind are determination and rejection, which are due to different kinds of desires. We desire that which is favorable to our sense gratification, and we reject that which is not favorable to sense gratification. The material mind is not fixed, but the very same mind can be fixed when engaged in the activities of Kṛṣṇa consciousness. Otherwise, as long as the mind is on the material platform, it is hovering, and all this rejection and acceptance is *asat*, temporary. It is stated that he whose mind is not fixed in Kṛṣṇa consciousness must hover between acceptance and rejection. However advanced a man is in academic qualifications, as long as he is not fixed in Kṛṣṇa consciousness he will simply accept and reject and will never be able to fix his mind on a particular subject matter.

TEXT 28

यद्विदुर्ह्यनिरुद्धाख्यं हृषीकाणामधीश्वरम् ।
शारदेन्दीवरश्यामं संराध्यं योगिभिः शनैः ॥२८॥

yad vidur hy aniruddhākhyaṁ
hṛṣīkāṇām adhīśvaram
śāradendīvara-śyāmaṁ
saṁrādhyaṁ yogibhiḥ śanaiḥ

yat—which mind; *viduḥ*—is known; *hi*—indeed; *aniruddha-ākhyam*—by the name Aniruddha; *hṛṣīkāṇām*—of the senses; *adhīśvaram*—the supreme ruler; *śārada*—autumnal; *indīvara*—like a blue lotus; *śyāmam*—bluish; *saṁrādhyam*—who is found; *yogibhiḥ*—by the *yogīs*; *śanaiḥ*—gradually.

TRANSLATION

The mind of the living entity is known by the name of Lord Aniruddha, the supreme ruler of the senses. He possesses a bluish-black form resembling a lotus flower growing in the autumn. He is found slowly by the yogīs.

PURPORT

The system of *yoga* entails controlling the mind, and the Lord of the mind is Aniruddha. It is stated that Aniruddha is four-handed, with Sudarśana *cakra,* conchshell, club and lotus flower. There are twenty-four forms of Viṣṇu, each differently named. Among these twenty-four forms, Saṅkarṣaṇa, Aniruddha, Pradyumna and Vāsudeva are depicted very nicely in the *Caitanya-caritāmṛta,* where it is stated that Aniruddha is worshiped by the *yogīs.* Meditation upon voidness is a modern invention of the fertile brain of some speculator. Actually the process of *yoga* meditation, as prescribed in this verse, should be fixed upon the form of Aniruddha. By meditating on Aniruddha one can become free from the agitation of acceptance and rejection. When one's mind is fixed upon Aniruddha, one gradually becomes God-realized; he approaches the pure status of Kṛṣṇa consciousness, which is the ultimate goal of *yoga.*

TEXT 29

तैजसात्तु विकुर्वाणाद् बुद्धितत्त्वमभूत्सति ।
द्रव्यस्फुरणविज्ञानमिन्द्रियाणामनुग्रहः ॥२९॥

taijasāt tu vikurvāṇād
buddhi-tattvam abhūt sati
dravya-sphuraṇa-vijñānam
indriyāṇām anugrahaḥ

taijasāt—from the false ego in passion; *tu*—then; *vikurvāṇāt*—undergoing transformation; *buddhi*—intelligence; *tattvam*—principle; *abhūt*—took birth; *sati*—O virtuous lady; *dravya*—objects; *sphuraṇa*—coming into view; *vijñānam*—ascertaining; *indriyāṇām*—to the senses; *anugrahaḥ*—giving assistance.

TRANSLATION

By transformation of the false ego in passion, intelligence takes birth, O virtuous lady. The functions of intelligence are to help in ascertaining the nature of objects when they come into view, and to help the senses.

PURPORT

Intelligence is the discriminating power to understand an object, and it helps the senses make choices. Therefore intelligence is supposed to be the master of the senses. The perfection of intelligence is attained when one becomes fixed in the activities of Kṛṣṇa consciousness. By the proper use of intelligence one's consciousness is expanded, and the ultimate expansion of consciousness is Kṛṣṇa consciousness.

TEXT 30

संशयोऽथ विपर्यासो निश्चयः स्मृतिरेव च ।
स्वाप इत्युच्यते बुद्धेर्लक्षणं वृत्तितः पृथक् ॥३०॥

saṁśayo 'tha viparyāso
niścayaḥ smṛtir eva ca
svāpa ity ucyate buddher
lakṣaṇaṁ vṛttitaḥ pṛthak

saṁśayaḥ—doubt; *atha*—then; *viparyāsaḥ*—misapprehension; *niścayaḥ*—correct apprehension; *smṛtiḥ*—memory; *eva*—also; *ca*—and; *svāpaḥ*—sleep; *iti*—thus; *ucyate*—are said; *buddheḥ*—of intelligence; *lakṣaṇam*—characteristics; *vṛttitaḥ*—by their functions; *pṛthak*—different.

TRANSLATION

Doubt, misapprehension, correct apprehension, memory and sleep, as determined by their different functions, are said to be the distinct characteristics of intelligence.

PURPORT

Doubt is one of the important functions of intelligence; blind acceptance of something does not give evidence of intelligence. Therefore the word *saṁśaya* is very important; in order to cultivate intelligence, one should be doubtful in the beginning. But doubting is not very favorable when information is received from the proper source. In *Bhagavad-gītā* the Lord says that doubting the words of the authority is the cause of destruction.

As described in the Patañjali *yoga* system, *pramāṇa-viparyaya-vikalpa-nidra-smṛtyaḥ*. By intelligence only one can understand things as they are. By intelligence only can one understand whether or not he is the body. The study to determine whether one's identity is spiritual or material begins in doubt. When one is able to analyze his actual position, the false identification with the body is detected. This is *viparyāsa*. When false identification is detected, then real identification can be understood. Real understanding is described here as *niścayaḥ*, or proved experimental knowledge. This experimental knowledge can be achieved when one has understood the false knowledge. By experimental or proved knowledge, one can understand that he is not the body but spirit soul.

Smṛti means "memory," and *svāpa* means "sleep." Sleep is also necessary to keep the intelligence in working order. If there is no sleep, the brain cannot work nicely. In *Bhagavad-gītā* it is especially mentioned that persons who regulate eating, sleeping and other necessities of the body in the proper proportion become very successful in the *yoga* process. These are some of the aspects of the analytical study of intelligence as described in both the Patañjali *yoga* system and the Sāṅkhya philosophy system of Kapiladeva in *Śrīmad-Bhāgavatam*.

TEXT 31

तैजसानीन्द्रियाण्येव क्रियाज्ञानविभागशः ।
प्राणस्य हि क्रियाशक्तिर्बुद्धेर्विज्ञानशक्तिता ॥३१॥

taijasānīndriyāṇy eva
kriyā-jñāna-vibhāgaśaḥ
prāṇasya hi kriyā-śaktir
buddher vijñāna-śaktitā

taijasāni—produced from egoism in the mode of passion; *indriyāṇi*—the senses; *eva*—certainly; *kriyā*—action; *jñāna*—knowledge;

vibhāgaśaḥ—according to; *prāṇasya*—of the vital energy; *hi*—indeed; *kriyā-śaktiḥ*—the senses of action; *buddheḥ*—of the intelligence; *vijñāna-śaktitā*—the senses for acquiring knowledge.

TRANSLATION

Egoism in the mode of passion produces two kinds of senses—the senses for acquiring knowledge and the senses of action. The senses of action depend on the vital energy, and the senses for acquiring knowledge depend on intelligence.

PURPORT

It has been explained in the previous verses that mind is the product of ego in goodness and that the function of the mind is acceptance and rejection according to desire. But here intelligence is said to be the product of ego in passion. That is the distinction between mind and intelligence; mind is a product of egoism in goodness, and intelligence is a product of egoism in passion. The desire to accept something and reject something is a very important factor of the mind. Since mind is a product of the mode of goodness, if it is fixed upon the Lord of the mind, Aniruddha, then the mind can be changed to Kṛṣṇa consciousness. It is stated by Narottama dāsa Ṭhākura that we always have desires. Desire cannot be stopped. But if we transfer our desires to please the Supreme Personality of Godhead, that is the perfection of life. As soon as the desire is transferred to lording it over material nature, it becomes contaminated by matter. Desire has to be purified. In the beginning, this purification process has to be carried out by the order of the spiritual master, since the spiritual master knows how the disciple's desires can be transformed into Kṛṣṇa consciousness. As far as intelligence is concerned, it is clearly stated here that it is a product of egoism in passion. By practice one comes to the point of the mode of goodness, and by surrendering or fixing the mind upon the Supreme Personality of Godhead, one becomes a very great personality, or *mahātmā*. In *Bhagavad-gītā* it is clearly said, *sa mahātmā sudurlabhaḥ:* "Such a great soul is very rare."

In this verse it is clear that both kinds of senses, the senses for acquiring knowledge and the senses for action, are products of egoism in the mode of passion. And because the sense organs for activity and for acquiring knowledge require energy, the vital energy, or life energy, is also produced by egoism in the mode of passion. We can actually see, therefore, that those who are very passionate can improve in material acquisition very quickly. It is recommended in the Vedic scriptures that if one wants to encourage a person in acquiring material possessions, one should also encourage him in sex life. We naturally find that those who are addicted to sex life are also materially advanced because sex life or passionate life is the impetus for the material advancement of civilization. For those who want to make spiritual advancement, there is almost no existence of the mode of passion. Only the mode of goodness is prominent. We find that those who engage in Kṛṣṇa consciousness are materially poor, but one who has eyes can see who is the greater. Although he appears to be materially poor, a person in Kṛṣṇa consciousness is not actually a poor man, but the person who has no taste for Kṛṣṇa consciousness and appears to be very happy with material possessions is actually poor. Persons infatuated by material consciousness are very intelligent in discovering things for material comforts, but they have no access to understanding the spirit soul and spiritual life. Therefore, if anyone wants to advance in spiritual life, he has to come back to the platform of purified desire, the purified desire for devotional service. As stated in the *Nārada-pañcarātra*, engagement in the service of the Lord when the senses are purified in Kṛṣṇa consciousness is called pure devotion.

TEXT 32

तामसाच्च विकुर्वाणाद्भगवद्वीर्यचोदितात् ।
शब्दमात्रमभूत्तस्मान्नभः श्रोत्रं तु शब्दगम् ॥३२॥

tāmasāc ca vikurvāṇād
bhagavad-vīrya-coditāt
śabda-mātram abhūt tasmān
nabhaḥ śrotraṁ tu śabdagam

tāmasāt—from egoism in ignorance; *ca*—and; *vikurvāṇāt*—undergoing transformation; *bhagavat-vīrya*—by the energy of the Supreme Personality of Godhead; *coditāt*—impelled; *śabda-mātram*—the subtle element sound; *abhūt*—was manifested; *tasmāt*—from that; *nabhaḥ*—

ether; *śrotram*—the sense of hearing; *tu*—then; *śabda-gam*—which catches sound.

TRANSLATION

When egoism in ignorance is agitated by the sex energy of the Supreme Personality of Godhead, the subtle element sound is manifested, and from sound come the ethereal sky and the sense of hearing.

PURPORT

It appears from this verse that all the objects of our sense gratification are the products of egoism in ignorance. It is understood from this verse that by agitation of the element of egoism in ignorance, the first thing produced was sound, which is the subtle form of ether. It is stated also in the *Vedānta-sūtra* that sound is the origin of all objects of material possession and that by sound one can also dissolve this material existence. *Anāvṛttiḥ śabdāt* means "liberation by sound." The entire material manifestation began from sound, and sound can also end material entanglement, if it has a particular potency. The particular sound capable of doing this is the transcendental vibration Hare Kṛṣṇa. Our entanglement in material affairs has begun from material sound. Now we must purify that sound in spiritual understanding. There is sound in the spiritual world also. If we approach that sound, then our spiritual life begins, and the other requirements for spiritual advancement can be supplied. We have to understand very clearly that sound is the beginning of the creation of all material objects for our sense gratification. Similarly, if sound is purified, our spiritual necessities also are produced from sound.

Here it is said that from sound the ether became manifested and that the air became manifested from ether. How the ethereal sky comes from sound, how the air comes from sky and how fire comes from air will be explained later on. Sound is the cause of the sky, and sky is the cause of *śrotram*, the ear. The ear is the first sense for receiving knowledge. One must give aural reception to any knowledge one wants to receive, either material or spiritual. Therefore *śrotram* is very important. The Vedic knowledge is called *śruti;* knowledge has to be received by hearing. By hearing only can we have access to either material or spiritual enjoyment.

In the material world, we manufacture many things for our material comfort simply by hearing. They are already there, but just by hearing, one can transform them. If we want to build a very high skyscraper, this does not mean that we have to create it. The materials for the skyscraper—wood, metal, earth, etc.—are already there, but we make our intimate relationship with those already created material elements by hearing how to utilize them. Modern economic advancement for creation is also a product of hearing, and similarly one can create a favorable field of spiritual activities by hearing from the right source. Arjuna was a gross materialist in the bodily conception of life and was suffering from the bodily concept very acutely. But simply by hearing, Arjuna became a spiritualized, Kṛṣṇa conscious person. Hearing is very important, and that hearing is produced from the sky. By hearing only can we make proper use of that which already exists. The principle of hearing to properly utilize preconceived materials is applicable to spiritual paraphernalia as well. We must hear from the proper spiritual source.

TEXT 33

अर्थाश्रयत्वं शब्दस्य द्रष्टुर्लिङ्गत्वमेव च ।
तन्मात्रत्वं च नभसो लक्षणं कवयो विदुः ॥३३॥

arthāśrayatvaṁ śabdasya
draṣṭur liṅgatvam eva ca
tan-mātratvaṁ ca nabhaso
lakṣaṇaṁ kavayo viduḥ

artha-āśrayatvam—that which conveys the meaning of an object; *śabdasya*—of sound; *draṣṭuḥ*—of the speaker; *liṅgatvam*—that which indicates the presence; *eva*—also; *ca*—and; *tat-mātratvam*—the subtle element; *ca*—and; *nabhasaḥ*—of ether; *lakṣaṇam*—definition; *kavayaḥ*—learned persons; *viduḥ*—know.

TRANSLATION

Persons who are learned and who have true knowledge define sound as that which conveys the idea of an object, indicates the

presence of a speaker screened from our view and constitutes the subtle form of ether.

PURPORT

It is very clear herein that as soon as we speak of hearing, there must be a speaker; without a speaker there is no question of hearing. Therefore the Vedic knowledge, which is known as *śruti,* or that which is received by hearing, is also called *apauruṣa. Apauruṣa* means "not spoken by any person materially created." It is stated in the beginning of *Śrīmad-Bhāgavatam, tene brahma hṛdā.* The sound of Brahman, or *Veda,* was first impregnated into the heart of Brahmā, the original learned man (*ādi-kavaye*). How did he become learned? Whenever there is learning, there must be a speaker and the process of hearing. But Brahmā was the first created being. Who spoke to him? Since no one was there, who was the spiritual master to give knowledge? He was the only living creature; therefore the Vedic knowledge was imparted within his heart by the Supreme Personality of Godhead, who is seated within everyone as Paramātmā. Vedic knowledge is understood to be spoken by the Supreme Lord, and therefore it is free from the defects of material understanding. Material understanding is defective. If we hear something from a conditioned soul, it is full of defects. All material and mundane information is tainted by illusion, error, cheating and imperfection of the senses. Because Vedic knowledge was imparted by the Supreme Lord, who is transcendental to material creation, it is perfect. If we receive that Vedic knowledge from Brahmā in disciplic succession, then we receive perfect knowledge.

Every word we hear has a meaning behind it. As soon as we hear the word "water," there is a substance—water—behind the word. Similarly, as soon as we hear the word "God," there is a meaning to it. If we receive that meaning and explanation of "God" from God Himself, then it is perfect. But if we speculate about the meaning of "God," it is imperfect. *Bhagavad-gītā,* which is the science of God, is spoken by the Personality of Godhead Himself. This is perfect knowledge. Mental speculators or so-called philosophers who are researching what is actually God will never understand the nature of God. The science of God has to be understood in disciplic succession from Brahmā, who was first instructed about knowledge of God by God Himself. We can understand the knowledge of God by hearing *Bhagavad-gītā* from a person authorized in the disciplic succession.

When we speak of seeing, there must be form. By our sense perception, the beginning experience is the sky. Sky is the beginning of form. And from the sky, other forms emanate. The objects of knowledge and sense perception begin, therefore, from the sky.

TEXT 34

भूतानां छिद्रदातृत्वं बहिरन्तरमेव च ।
प्राणेन्द्रियात्मधिष्ण्यत्वं नभसो वृत्तिलक्षणम् ॥३४॥

bhūtānāṁ chidra-dātṛtvaṁ
bahir antaram eva ca
prāṇendriyātma-dhiṣṇyatvaṁ
nabhaso vṛtti-lakṣaṇam

bhūtānām—of all living entities; *chidra-dātṛtvam*—the accommodation of room; *bahiḥ*—external; *antaram*—internal; *eva*—also; *ca*—and; *prāṇa*—of the vital air; *indriya*—the senses; *ātma*—and the mind; *dhiṣṇyatvam*—being the field of activities; *nabhasaḥ*—of the ethereal element; *vṛtti*—activities; *lakṣaṇam*—characteristics.

TRANSLATION

The activities and characteristics of the ethereal element can be observed as accommodation for the room for the external and internal existences of all living entities, namely the field of activities of the vital air, the senses and the mind.

PURPORT

The mind, the senses and the vital force, or living entity, have forms, although they are not visible to the naked eye. Form rests in subtle existence in the sky, and internally it is perceived as the veins within the body and the circulation of the vital air. Externally there are invisible forms of sense objects. The production of the invisible sense objects is the external activity of the ethereal element, and the circulation of vital air and blood is its internal activity. That subtle forms exist in the ether has been proven by modern science by transmission of television, by which forms or photographs of one place are transmitted to another place by the action of the ethereal element. That is very nicely explained here. This verse is the potential basis of great scientific research work, for it explains how subtle forms are generated from the ethereal element, what their characteristics and actions are, and how the tangible elements, namely air, fire, water and earth, are manifested from the subtle form. Mental activities, or psychological actions of thinking, feeling and willing, are also activities on the platform of ethereal existence. The statement in *Bhagavad-gītā* that the mental situation at the time of death is the basis of the next birth is also corroborated in this verse. Mental existence transforms into tangible form as soon as there is an opportunity due to contamination or development of the gross elements from subtle form.

TEXT 35

नभसः शब्दतन्मात्रात्कालगत्या विकुर्वतः ।
स्पर्शोऽभवत्ततो वायुस्त्वक् स्पर्शस्य च संग्रहः ॥३५॥

nabhasaḥ śabda-tanmātrāt
kāla-gatyā vikurvataḥ
sparśo 'bhavat tato vāyus
tvak sparśasya ca saṅgrahaḥ

nabhasaḥ—from ether; *śabda-tanmātrāt*—which evolves from the subtle element sound; *kāla-gatyā*—under the impulse of time; *vikurvataḥ*—undergoing transformation; *sparśaḥ*—the subtle element touch; *abhavat*—evolved; *tataḥ*—thence; *vāyuḥ*—air; *tvak*—the sense of touch; *sparśasya*—of touch; *ca*—and; *saṅgrahaḥ*—perception.

TRANSLATION

From ethereal existence, which evolves from sound, the next transformation takes place under the impulse of time, and thus the subtle element touch and thence the air and sense of touch become prominent.

PURPORT

In the course of time, when the subtle forms are transformed into gross forms, they become the objects of touch. The objects of touch and the tactile sense also develop after this evolution in time. Sound is the first sense object to exhibit material existence, and from the perception of sound, touch perception evolves and from touch perception the perception of sight. That is the way of the gradual evolution of our perceptive objects.

TEXT 36

मृदुत्वं कठिनत्वं च शैत्यमुष्णत्वमेव च ।
एतत्स्पर्शस्य स्पर्शत्वं तन्मात्रत्वं नभस्वतः ॥३६॥

mṛdutvaṁ kaṭhinatvaṁ ca
śaityam uṣṇatvam eva ca
etat sparśasya sparśatvaṁ
tan-mātratvaṁ nabhasvataḥ

mṛdutvam—softness; *kaṭhinatvam*—hardness; *ca*—and; *śaityam*—cold; *uṣṇatvam*—heat; *eva*—also; *ca*—and; *etat*—this; *sparśasya*—of the subtle element touch; *sparśatvam*—the distinguishing attributes; *tat-mātratvam*—the subtle form; *nabhasvataḥ*—of air.

TRANSLATION

Softness and hardness and cold and heat are the distinguishing attributes of touch, which is characterized as the subtle form of air.

PURPORT

Tangibility is the proof of form. In actuality, objects are perceived in two different ways. They are either soft or hard, cold or hot, etc. This tangible action of the tactile sense is the result of the evolution of air, which is produced from the sky.

TEXT 37

चालनं व्यूहनं प्राप्तिर्नेतृत्वं द्रव्यशब्दयोः ।
सर्वेन्द्रियाणामात्मत्वं वायोः कर्माभिलक्षणम् ॥३७॥

cālanaṁ vyūhanaṁ prāptir
netṛtvaṁ dravya-śabdayoḥ
sarvendriyāṇām ātmatvaṁ
vāyoḥ karmābhilakṣaṇam

cālanam—moving; *vyūhanam*—mixing; *prāptiḥ*—allowing approach; *netṛtvam*—carrying; *dravya-śabdayoḥ*—particles of substances and sound; *sarva-indriyāṇām*—of all the senses; *ātmatvam*—providing for the proper functioning; *vāyoḥ*—of air; *karma*—by actions; *abhilakṣaṇam*—the distinct characteristics.

TRANSLATION

The action of the air is exhibited in movements, mixing, allowing approach to the objects of sound and other sense perceptions, and providing for the proper functioning of all other senses.

PURPORT

We can perceive the action of the air when the branches of a tree move or when dry leaves on the ground collect together. Similarly, it is only by the action of the air that a body moves, and when the air circulation is impeded, many diseases result. Paralysis, nervous breakdowns, madness and many other diseases are actually due to an insufficient circulation of air. In the Āyur-vedic system these diseases are treated on the basis of air circulation. If from the beginning one takes care of the process of air circulation, such diseases cannot take place. From the *Āyur-veda* as well as from the *Śrīmad-Bhāgavatam* it is clear that so many activities are going on internally and externally because of air alone, and as soon as there is some deficiency in the air circulation, these activities cannot take place. Here it is clearly stated, *netṛtvaṁ dravya-śabdayoḥ.* Our sense of proprietorship over action is also due to the activity of the air. If the air circulation is stifled, we cannot approach a place after hearing. If someone calls us, we hear the sound because of the air circulation, and we approach that sound or the place from which the sound comes. It is clearly said in this verse that these are all movements of the air. The ability to detect odors is also due to the action of the air.

TEXT 38

वायोश्च स्पर्शतन्मात्राद्रूपं दैवेरितादभूत् ।
समुत्थितं ततस्तेजश्चक्षू रूपोपलम्भनम् ॥३८॥

vāyoś ca sparśa-tanmātrād
rūpaṁ daiveritād abhūt
samutthitaṁ tatas tejaś
cakṣū rūpopalambhanam

vāyoḥ—from air; *ca*—and; *sparśa-tanmātrāt*—which evolves from the subtle element touch; *rūpam*—form; *daiva-īritāt*—according to destiny; *abhūt*—evolved; *samutthitam*—arose; *tataḥ*—from that; *tejaḥ*—fire; *cakṣuḥ*—sense of sight; *rūpa*—color and form; *upalambhanam*—perceiving.

TRANSLATION

By interactions of the air and the sensations of touch, one receives different forms according to destiny. By evolution of such forms, there is fire, and the eye sees different forms in color.

PURPORT

Because of destiny, the touch sensation, the interactions of air, and the situation of the mind, which is produced of the ethereal element, one receives a body according to his previous activities. Needless to say, a living entity transmigrates from one form to another. His form changes according to destiny and by the arrangement of a superior authority which controls the interaction of air and the mental situation. Form is the combination of different types of sense perception. Predestined activities are the plans of the mental situation and the interaction of air.

TEXT 39

द्रव्याकृतित्वं गुणता व्यक्तिसंस्थात्वमेव च ।
तेजस्त्वं तेजसः साध्वि रूपमात्रस्य वृत्तयः ॥३९॥

dravyākṛtitvaṁ guṇatā
vyakti-saṁsthātvam eva ca
tejastvaṁ tejasaḥ sādhvi
rūpa-mātrasya vṛttayaḥ

dravya—of an object; *ākṛtitvam*—dimension; *guṇatā*—quality; *vyakti-saṁsthātvam*—individuality; *eva*—also; *ca*—and; *tejastvam*—effulgence; *tejasaḥ*—of fire; *sādhvi*—O virtuous lady; *rūpa-mātrasya*—of the subtle element form; *vṛttayaḥ*—the characteristics.

TRANSLATION

My dear mother, the characteristics of form are understood by dimension, quality and individuality. The form of fire is appreciated by its effulgence.

PURPORT

Every form that we appreciate has its particular dimensions and characteristics. The quality of a particular object is appreciated by its utility. But the form of sound is independent. Forms which are invisible can be understood only by touch; that is the independent appreciation of invisible form. Visible forms are understood by analytical study of their constitution. The constitution of a certain object is appreciated by its internal action. For example, the form of salt is appreciated by the interaction of salty tastes, and the form of sugar is appreciated by the interaction of sweet tastes. Tastes and qualitative constitution are the basic principles in understanding the form of an object.

TEXT 40

द्योतनं पचनं पानमदनं हिममर्दनम् ।
तेजसो वृत्तयस्त्वेताः शोषणं क्षुत्तृडेव च ॥४०॥

dyotanaṁ pacanaṁ pānam
adanaṁ hima-mardanam
tejaso vṛttayas tv etāḥ
śoṣaṇaṁ kṣut tṛḍ eva ca

dyotanam—illumination; *pacanam*—cooking, digesting; *pānam*—drinking; *adanam*—eating; *hima-mardanam*—destroying cold; *tejasaḥ*—of fire; *vṛttayaḥ*—functions; *tu*—indeed; *etāḥ*—these; *śoṣaṇam*—evaporating; *kṣut*—hunger; *tṛṭ*—thirst; *eva*—also; *ca*—and.

TRANSLATION

Fire is appreciated by its light and by its ability to cook, to digest, to destroy cold, to evaporate, and to give rise to hunger, thirst, eating and drinking.

PURPORT

The first symptoms of fire are distribution of light and heat, and the existence of fire is also perceived in the stomach. Without fire we cannot digest what we eat. Without digestion there is no hunger and thirst or power to eat and drink. When there is insufficient hunger and thirst, it is understood that there is a shortage of fire within the stomach, and the Āyur-vedic treatment is performed in connection with the fire element, *agni-māndyam.* Since fire is increased by the secretion of bile, the treatment is to increase bile secretion. The Āyur-vedic treatment thus corroborates the statements in *Śrīmad-Bhāgavatam.* The characteristic of fire in subduing the influence of cold is known to everyone. Severe cold can always be counteracted by fire.

TEXT 41

रूपमात्राद्विकुर्वाणात्तेजसो दैवचोदितात् ।
रसमात्रमभूत्तस्मादम्भो जिह्वा रसग्रहः ॥४१॥

rūpa-mātrād vikurvāṇāt
tejaso daiva-coditāt
rasa-mātram abhūt tasmād
ambho jihvā rasa-grahaḥ

rūpa-mātrāt—which evolves from the subtle element form; *vikurvāṇāt*—undergoing transformation; *tejasaḥ*—from fire; *daiva-coditāt*—under a superior arrangement; *rasa-mātram*—the subtle element taste; *abhūt*—became manifested; *tasmāt*—from that; *ambhaḥ*—water; *jihvā*—the sense of taste; *rasa-grahaḥ*—which perceives taste.

TRANSLATION

By the interaction of fire and the visual sensation, the subtle element taste evolves under a superior arrangement. From taste, water is produced, and the tongue, which perceives taste, is also manifested.

PURPORT

The tongue is described here as the instrument for acquiring knowledge of taste. Because taste is a product of water, there is always saliva on the tongue.

TEXT 42

कषायो मधुरस्तिक्तः कट्वम्ल इति नैकधा ।
भौतिकानां विकारेण रस एको विभिद्यते ॥४२॥

kaṣāyo madhuras tiktaḥ
kaṭv amla iti naikadhā
bhautikānāṁ vikāreṇa
rasa eko vibhidyate

kaṣāyaḥ—astringent; *madhuraḥ*—sweet; *tiktaḥ*—bitter; *kaṭu*—pungent; *amlaḥ*—sour; *iti*—thus; *na-ekadhā*—manifoldly; *bhautikānām*—of other substances; *vikāreṇa*—by transformation; *rasaḥ*—the subtle element taste; *ekaḥ*—originally one; *vibhidyate*—is divided.

TRANSLATION

Although originally one, taste becomes manifold as astringent, sweet, bitter, pungent, sour and salty due to contact with other substances.

TEXT 43

क्लेदनं पिण्डनं तृप्तिः प्राणनाप्यायनोन्दनम् ।
तापापनोदो भूयस्त्वमम्भसो वृत्तयस्त्विमाः ॥४३॥

kledanaṁ piṇḍanaṁ tṛptiḥ
prāṇanāpyāyanondanam
tāpāpanodo bhūyastvam
ambhaso vṛttayas tv imāḥ

kledanam—moistening; *piṇḍanam*—coagulating; *tṛptiḥ*—causing satisfaction; *prāṇana*—maintaining life; *āpyāyana*—refreshing; *undanam*—softening; *tāpa*—heat; *apanodaḥ*—driving away; *bhūyastvam*—being in abundance; *ambhasaḥ*—of water; *vṛttayaḥ*—the characteristic functions; *tu*—in fact; *imāḥ*—these.

TRANSLATION

The characteristics of water are exhibited by its moistening other substances, coagulating various mixtures, causing satisfaction, maintaining life, softening things, driving away heat, incessantly supplying itself to reservoirs of water, and refreshing by slaking thirst.

PURPORT

Starvation can be mitigated by drinking water. It is sometimes found that if a person who has taken a vow to fast takes a little water at intervals, the exhaustion of fasting is at once mitigated. In the *Vedas* it is also stated, *āpomayaḥ prāṇaḥ:* "Life depends on water." With water, anything can be moistened or dampened. Flour dough can be prepared with a mixture of water. Mud is made by mixing earth with water. As stated in the beginning of *Śrīmad-Bhāgavatam,* water is the cementing ingredient of different material elements. If we build a house, water is actually the constituent in making the bricks. Fire, water and air are the exchanging elements for the entire material manifestation, but water is most prominent. Also, excessive heat can be reduced simply by pouring water on the heated field.

TEXT 44

रसमात्राद्विकुर्वाणादम्भसो दैवचोदितात् ।
गन्धमात्रमभूत्तस्मात्पृथ्वी घ्राणस्तु गन्धगः ॥४४॥

rasa-mātrād vikurvāṇād
ambhaso daiva-coditāt
gandha-mātram abhūt tasmāt
pṛthvī ghrāṇas tu gandhagaḥ

rasa-mātrāt—which evolves from the subtle element taste; *vikurvāṇāt*—undergoing transformation; *ambhasaḥ*—from water; *daiva-coditāt*—by a superior arrangement; *gandha-mātram*—the subtle element odor; *abhūt*—became manifest; *tasmāt*—from that; *pṛthvī*—earth; *ghrāṇaḥ*—the olfactory sense; *tu*—in fact; *gandha-gaḥ*—which perceives aromas.

TRANSLATION

Due to the interaction of water with the taste perception, the subtle element odor evolves under superior arrangement. Thence the earth and the olfactory sense, by which we can variously experience the aroma of the earth, become manifest.

TEXT 45

करम्भपूतिसौरभ्यशान्तोग्राम्लादिभिः पृथक् ।
द्रव्यावयववैषम्याद्गन्ध एको विभिद्यते ॥४५॥

karambha-pūti-saurabhya-
śāntogrāmlādibhiḥ pṛthak
dravyāvayava-vaiṣamyād
gandha eko vibhidyate

karambha—mixed; *pūti*—offensive; *saurabhya*—fragrant; *śānta*—mild; *ugra*—strong, pungent; *amla*—acid; *ādibhiḥ*—and so on; *pṛthak*—separately; *dravya*—of substance; *avayava*—of portions; *vaiṣamyāt*—according to diversity; *gandhaḥ*—odor; *ekaḥ*—one; *vibhidyate*—is divided.

TRANSLATION

Odor, although one, becomes many—as mixed, offensive, fragrant, mild, strong, acidic and so on—according to the proportions of associated substances.

PURPORT

Mixed smell is sometimes perceived in foodstuffs prepared from various ingredients, such as vegetables mixed with different kinds of spices and asafetida. Bad odors are perceived in filthy places, good smells are perceived from camphor, menthol and similar other products, pungent smells are perceived from garlic and onions, and acidic smells are perceived from turmeric and similar sour substances. The original aroma is the odor emanating from the earth, and when it is mixed with different substances, this odor appears in different ways.

TEXT 46

भावनं ब्रह्मणः स्थानं धारणं सद्विशेषणम् ।
सर्वसत्त्वगुणोद्भेदः पृथिवीवृत्तिलक्षणम् ॥४६॥

bhāvanaṁ brahmaṇaḥ sthānaṁ
dhāraṇaṁ sad-viśeṣaṇam
sarva-sattva-guṇodbhedaḥ
pṛthivī-vṛtti-lakṣaṇam

bhāvanam—modeling forms; *brahmaṇaḥ*—of the Supreme Brahman; *sthānam*—constructing places of residence; *dhāraṇam*—containing substances; *sat-viśeṣaṇam*—distinguishing the open space; *sarva*—all; *sattva*—of existence; *guṇa*—qualities; *udbhedaḥ*—the place for manifestation; *pṛthivī*—of earth; *vṛtti*—of the functions; *lakṣaṇam*—the characteristics.

TRANSLATION

The characteristics of the functions of earth can be perceived by modeling forms of the Supreme Brahman, by constructing places of residence, by preparing pots to contain water, etc. In other words, the earth is the place of sustenance for all elements.

PURPORT

Different elements, such as sound, sky, air, fire and water, can be perceived in the earth. Another feature of the earth especially mentioned here is that earth can manifest different forms of the Supreme Personality of Godhead. By this statement of Kapila's it is confirmed that the

Supreme Personality of Godhead, Brahman, has innumerable forms, which are described in the scriptures. By manipulation of earth and its products, such as stone, wood and jewels, these forms of the Supreme Lord can be present before our eyes. When a form of Lord Kṛṣṇa or Lord Viṣṇu is manifested by presentation of a statue made of earth, it is not imaginary. The earth gives shape to the Lord's forms as described in the scriptures.

In the *Brahma-saṁhitā* there is description of Lord Kṛṣṇa's lands, the variegatedness of the spiritual abode, and the forms of the Lord playing a flute with His spiritual body. All these forms are described in the scriptures, and when they are thus presented they become worshipable. They are not imaginary as the Māyāvāda philosophy says. Sometimes the word *bhāvana* is misinterpreted as "imagination." But *bhāvana* does not mean "imagination"; it means giving actual shape to the description of Vedic literature. Earth is the ultimate transformation of all living entities and their respective modes of material nature.

TEXT 47

नभोगुणविशेषोऽर्थो यस्य तच्छ्रोत्रमुच्यते ।
वायोर्गुणविशेषोऽर्थो यस्य तत्स्पर्शनं विदुः ॥४७॥

nabho-guṇa-viśeṣo 'rtho
yasya tac chrotram ucyate
vāyor guṇa-viśeṣo 'rtho
yasya tat sparśanaṁ viduḥ

nabhaḥ-guṇa-viśeṣaḥ—the distinctive characteristic of sky (sound); *arthaḥ*—object of perception; *yasya*—whose; *tat*—that; *śrotram*—the auditory sense; *ucyate*—is called; *vāyoḥ guṇa-viśeṣaḥ*—the distinctive characteristic of air (touch); *arthaḥ*—object of perception; *yasya*—whose; *tat*—that; *sparśanam*—the tactile sense; *viduḥ*—they know.

TRANSLATION

The sense whose object of perception is sound is called the auditory sense, and that whose object of perception is touch is called the tactile sense.

PURPORT

Sound is one of the qualifications of the sky and is the subject matter for hearing. Similarly, touch is the qualification of the air and is the subject of the touch sensation.

TEXT 48

तेजोगुणविशेषोऽर्थो यस्य तच्चक्षुरुच्यते ।
अम्भोगुणविशेषोऽर्थो यस्य तद्रसनं विदुः ।
भूमेर्गुणविशेषोऽर्थो यस्य स घ्राण उच्यते ॥४८॥

tejo-guṇa-viśeṣo 'rtho
yasya tac cakṣur ucyate
ambho-guṇa-viśeṣo 'rtho
yasya tad rasanaṁ viduḥ
bhūmer guṇa-viśeṣo 'rtho
yasya sa ghrāṇa ucyate

tejaḥ-guṇa-viśeṣaḥ—the distinctive characteristic of fire (form); *arthaḥ*—object of perception; *yasya*—whose; *tat*—that; *cakṣuḥ*—the sense of sight; *ucyate*—is called; *ambhaḥ-guṇa-viśeṣaḥ*—the distinctive characteristic of water (taste); *arthaḥ*—object of perception; *yasya*—whose; *tat*—that; *rasanam*—the sense of taste; *viduḥ*—they know; *bhūmeḥ guṇa-viśeṣaḥ*—the distinctive characteristic of earth (odor); *arthaḥ*—object of perception; *yasya*—whose; *saḥ*—that; *ghrāṇaḥ*—the sense of smell; *ucyate*—is called.

TRANSLATION

The sense whose object of perception is form, the distinctive characteristic of fire, is the sense of sight. The sense whose object of perception is taste, the distinctive characteristic of water, is known as the sense of taste. Finally, the sense whose object of perception is odor, the distinctive characteristic of earth, is called the sense of smell.

TEXT 49

परस्य दृश्यते धर्मो ह्यपरस्मिन् समन्वयात् ।
अतो विशेषो भावानां भूमावेवोपलक्ष्यते ॥४९॥

parasya dṛśyate dharmo
hy aparasmin samanvayāt
ato viśeṣo bhāvānāṁ
bhūmāv evopalakṣyate

parasya—of the cause; *dṛśyate*—is observed; *dharmaḥ*—the characteristics; *hi*—indeed; *aparasmin*—in the effect; *samanvayāt*—in order; *ataḥ*—hence; *viśeṣaḥ*—the distinctive characteristic; *bhāvānām*—of all the elements; *bhūmau*—in earth; *eva*—alone; *upalakṣyate*—is observed.

TRANSLATION

Since the cause exists in its effect as well, the characteristics of the former are observed in the latter. That is why the peculiarities of all the elements exist in the earth alone.

PURPORT

Sound is the cause of the sky, sky is the cause of the air, air is the cause of fire, fire is the cause of water, and water is the cause of earth. In the sky there is only sound; in the air there are sound and touch; in the fire there are sound, touch and form; in water there are sound, touch, form and taste; and in the earth there are sound, touch, form, taste and smell. Therefore earth is the reservoir of all the qualities of the other elements. Earth is the sum total of all other elements. The earth has all five qualities of the elements, water has four qualities, fire has three, air has two, and the sky has only one quality, sound.

TEXT 50

एतान्यसंहत्य यदा महदादीनि सप्त वै ।
कालकर्मगुणोपेतो जगदादिरुपाविशत् ॥५०॥

etāny asaṁhatya yadā
mahad-ādīni sapta vai
kāla-karma-guṇopeto
jagad-ādir upāviśat

etāni—these; *asaṁhatya*—being unmixed; *yadā*—when; *mahat-ādīni*—the *mahat-tattva*, false ego and five gross elements; *sapta*—all together seven; *vai*—in fact; *kāla*—time; *karma*—work; *guṇa*—and the three modes of material nature; *upetaḥ*—accompanied by; *jagat-ādiḥ*—the origin of creation; *upāviśat*—entered.

TRANSLATION

When all these elements were unmixed, the Supreme Personality of Godhead, the origin of creation, along with time, work, and the qualities of the modes of material nature, entered into the universe with the total material energy in seven divisions.

PURPORT

After stating the generation of the causes, Kapiladeva speaks about the generation of the effects. At that time when the causes were unmixed, the Supreme Personality of Godhead, in His feature of Garbhodakaśāyī Viṣṇu, entered within each universe. Accompanying Him were all of the seven primary elements—the five material elements, the total energy (*mahat-tattva*) and the false ego. This entrance of the Supreme Personality of Godhead involves His entering even the atoms of the material world. This is confirmed in the *Brahma-saṁhitā* (5.35): *aṇḍāntara-stha-paramāṇu-cayāntara-stham.* He is not only within the universe, but within the atoms also. He is within the heart of every living entity. Garbhodakaśāyī Viṣṇu, the Supreme Personality of Godhead, entered into everything.

TEXT 51

ततस्तेनानुविद्धेभ्यो युक्तेभ्योऽण्डमचेतनम् ।
उत्थितं पुरुषो यस्मादुदतिष्ठदसौ विराट् ॥५१॥

tatas tenānuviddhebhyo
yuktebhyo 'ṇḍam acetanam
utthitaṁ puruṣo yasmād
udatiṣṭhad asau virāṭ

tataḥ—then; *tena*—by the Lord; *anuviddhebhyaḥ*—from these seven principles, roused into activity; *yuktebhyaḥ*—united; *aṇḍam*—an egg; *acetanam*—unintelligent; *utthitam*—arose; *puruṣaḥ*—Cosmic Being; *yasmāt*—from which; *udatiṣṭhat*—appeared; *asau*—that; *virāṭ*—celebrated.

TRANSLATION

From these seven principles, roused into activity and united by the presence of the Lord, an unintelligent egg arose, from which appeared the celebrated Cosmic Being.

PURPORT

In sex life, the combination of matter from the parents, which involves emulsification and secretion, creates the situation whereby a soul is received within matter, and the combination of matter gradually develops into a complete body. The same principle exists in the universal creation: the ingredients were present, but only when the Lord entered into the material elements was matter actually agitated. That is the cause of creation. We can see this in our ordinary experience. Although we may have clay, water and fire, the elements take the shape of a brick only when we labor to combine them. Without the living energy, there is no possibility that matter can take shape. Similarly, this material world does not develop unless agitated by the Supreme Lord as the *virāṭ-puruṣa. Yasmād udatiṣṭhad asau virāṭ:* by His agitation, space was created, and the universal form of the Lord also manifested therein.

TEXT 52

एतदण्डं विशेषाख्यं क्रमवृद्धैर्दशोत्तरैः ।
तोयादिभिः परिवृतं प्रधानेनावृतैर्बहिः ।
यत्र लोकवितानोऽयं रूपं भगवतो हरेः ॥५२॥

etad aṇḍaṁ viśeṣākhyaṁ
krama-vṛddhair daśottaraiḥ
toyādibhiḥ parivṛtaṁ
pradhānenāvṛtair bahiḥ

yatra loka-vitāno 'yaṁ
rūpaṁ bhagavato hareḥ

etat—this; *aṇḍam*—egg; *viśeṣa-ākhyam*—called *viśeṣa; krama*—one after another; *vṛddhaiḥ*—increased; *daśa*—ten times; *uttaraiḥ*—greater; *toya-ādibhiḥ*—by water and so on; *parivṛtam*—enveloped; *pradhānena*—by *pradhāna; āvṛtaiḥ*—covered; *bahiḥ*—on the outside; *yatra*—where; *loka-vitānaḥ*—the extension of the planetary systems; *ayam*—this; *rūpam*—form; *bhagavataḥ*—of the Supreme Personality of Godhead; *hareḥ*—of Lord Hari.

TRANSLATION

This universal egg, or the universe in the shape of an egg, is called the manifestation of material energy. Its layers of water, air, fire, sky, ego and mahat-tattva increase in thickness one after another. Each layer is ten times bigger than the previous one, and the final outside layer is covered by pradhāna. Within this egg is the universal form of Lord Hari, of whose body the fourteen planetary systems are parts.

PURPORT

This universe, or the universal sky which we can visualize with its innumerable planets, is shaped just like an egg. As an egg is covered by a shell, the universe is also covered by various layers. The first layer is water, the next is fire, then air, then sky, and the ultimate holding crust is *pradhāna.* Within this egglike universe is the universal form of the Lord as the *virāṭ-puruṣa.* All the different planetary situations are parts of His body. This is already explained in the beginning of *Śrīmad-Bhāgavatam,* Second Canto. The planetary systems are considered to form different bodily parts of that universal form of the Lord. Persons who cannot directly engage in the worship of the transcendental form of the Lord are advised to think of and worship this universal form. The lowest planetary system, Pātāla, is considered to be the sole of the Supreme Lord, and the earth is considered to be the belly of the Lord. Brahmaloka, or the highest planetary system, where Brahmā lives, is considered to be the head of the Lord.

This *virāṭ-puruṣa* is considered an incarnation of the Lord. The original form of the Lord is Kṛṣṇa, as confirmed in *Brahma-saṁhitā: ādi-puruṣa.* The *virāṭ-puruṣa* is also *puruṣa,* but He is not *ādi-puruṣa.* The *ādi-puruṣa* is Kṛṣṇa. *Īśvaraḥ paramaḥ kṛṣṇaḥ sac-cid-ānanda-vigrahaḥ/ anādir ādir govindaḥ.* In *Bhagavad-gītā* Kṛṣṇa is also accepted as the *ādi-puruṣa,* the original. Kṛṣṇa says, "No one is greater than I." There are innumerable expansions of the Lord, and all of them are *puruṣas,* or enjoyers, but neither the *virāṭ-puruṣa* nor the *puruṣa-avatāras*—Kāraṇodakaśāyī Viṣṇu, Garbhodakaśāyī Viṣṇu and Kṣīrodakaśāyī Viṣṇu—nor any of the many other expansions, is the original. In each universe there are Garbhodakaśāyī Viṣṇu, the *virāṭ-puruṣa* and Kṣīrodakaśāyī Viṣṇu. The active manifestation of the *virāṭ-puruṣa* is described here. Persons who are in the lower grade of understanding regarding the Supreme Personality of Godhead may think of the universal form of the Lord, for that is advised in the *Bhāgavatam.*

The dimensions of the universe are estimated here. The outer covering is made of layers of water, air, fire, sky, ego and *mahat-tattva,* and each layer is ten times greater than the one previous. The space within the hollow of the universe cannot be measured by any human scientist or anyone else, and beyond the hollow there are seven coverings, each one ten times greater than the one preceding it. The layer of water is ten times greater than the diameter of the universe, and the layer of fire is ten times greater than that of water. Similarly, the layer of air is ten times greater than that of fire. These dimensions are all inconceivable to the tiny brain of a human being.

It is also stated that this description is of only one egglike universe. There are innumerable universes besides this one, and some of them are many, many times greater. It is considered, in fact, that this universe is the smallest; therefore the predominating superintendent, or Brahmā, has only four heads for management. In other universes, which are far greater than this one, Brahmā has more heads. In the *Caitanya-caritāmṛta* it is stated that all these Brahmās were called one day by Lord Kṛṣṇa on the inquiry of the small Brahmā, who, after seeing all the larger Brahmās, was thunderstruck. That is the inconceivable potency of the Lord. No one can measure the length and breadth of God by speculation or by false identification with God. These attempts are symptoms of lunacy.

TEXT 53

हिरण्मयादण्डकोशादुत्थाय सलिलेशयात् ।
तमाविश्य महादेवो बहुधा निर्बिभेद खम् ॥५३॥

hiraṇmayād aṇḍa-kośād
utthāya salile śayāt
tam āviśya mahā-devo
bahudhā nirbibheda kham

hiraṇmayāt—golden; *aṇḍa-kośāt*—from the egg; *utthāya*—arising; *salile*—on the water; *śayāt*—lying; *tam*—in it; *āviśya*—having entered; *mahā-devaḥ*—the Supreme Personality of Godhead; *bahudhā*—in many ways; *nirbibheda*—divided; *kham*—apertures.

TRANSLATION

The Supreme Personality of Godhead, the virāṭ-puruṣa, situated Himself in that golden egg, which was lying on the water, and He divided it into many departments.

TEXT 54

निरभिद्यतास्य प्रथमं मुखं वाणी ततोऽभवत् ।
वाण्या वह्निरथो नासे प्राणोतो घ्राण एतयोः ॥५४॥

nirabhidyatāsya prathamaṁ
mukhaṁ vāṇī tato 'bhavat
vāṇyā vahnir atho nāse
prāṇoto ghrāṇa etayoḥ

nirabhidyata—appeared; *asya*—of Him; *prathamam*—first of all; *mukham*—a mouth; *vāṇī*—the organ of speech; *tataḥ*—then; *abhavat*—came forth; *vāṇyā*—with the organ of speech; *vahniḥ*—the god of fire; *athaḥ*—then; *nāse*—the two nostrils; *prāṇa*—the vital air; *utaḥ*—joined; *ghrāṇaḥ*—the olfactory sense; *etayoḥ*—in them.

TRANSLATION

First of all a mouth appeared in Him, and then came forth the organ of speech, and with it the god of fire, the deity who presides over that organ. Then a pair of nostrils appeared, and in them appeared the olfactory sense, as well as prāṇa, the vital air.

PURPORT

With the manifestation of speech, fire also became manifested, and with the manifestation of nostrils the vital air, the breathing process and the sense of smell also became manifested.

TEXT 55

घ्राणाद्वायुरभिद्येतामक्षिणी चक्षुरेतयोः ।
तस्मात्सूर्यो न्यभिद्येतां कर्णौ श्रोत्रं ततो दिशः ॥५५॥

ghrāṇād vāyur abhidyetām
akṣiṇī cakṣur etayoḥ
tasmāt sūryo nyabhidyetāṁ
karṇau śrotraṁ tato diśaḥ

ghrāṇāt—from the olfactory sense; *vāyuḥ*—the wind-god; *abhidyetām*—appeared; *akṣiṇī*—the two eyes; *cakṣuḥ*—the sense of sight; *etayoḥ*—in them; *tasmāt*—from that; *sūryaḥ*—the sun-god; *nyabhidyetām*—appeared; *karṇau*—the two ears; *śrotram*—the auditory sense; *tataḥ*—from that; *diśaḥ*—the deities presiding over the directions.

TRANSLATION

In the wake of the olfactory sense came the wind-god, who presides over that sense. Thereafter a pair of eyes appeared in the universal form, and in them the sense of sight. In the wake of this sense came the sun-god, who presides over it. Next there appeared in Him a pair of ears, and in them the auditory sense and in its wake the Dig-devatās, or the deities who preside over the directions.

PURPORT

The appearance of different bodily parts of the Lord's universal form and the appearance of the presiding deities of those bodily parts is being described. As in the womb of a mother a child gradually grows different bodily parts, so in the universal womb the universal form of the Lord gives rise to the creation of various paraphernalia. The senses appear, and over each of them there is a presiding deity. It is corroborated by this statement of *Śrīmad-Bhāgavatam*, and also by *Brahma-saṁhitā*, that the sun appeared after the appearance of the eyes of the universal form of the Lord. The sun is dependent on the eyes of the universal form. The *Brahma-saṁhitā* also says that the sun is the eye of the Supreme Personality of Godhead, Kṛṣṇa. *Yac-cakṣur eṣa savitā. Savitā* means "the sun." The sun is the eye of the Supreme Personality of Godhead. Actually, everything is created by the universal body of the Supreme Godhead. Material nature is simply the supplier of materials. The creation is actually done by the Supreme Lord, as confirmed in *Bhagavad-gītā* (9.10). *Mayādhyakṣeṇa prakṛtiḥ sūyate sa-carācaram:* "Under My direction does material nature create all moving and nonmoving objects in the cosmic creation."

TEXT 56

निर्बिभेद विराजस्त्वग्रोमश्मश्र्वादयस्ततः ।
तत ओषधयश्चासन् शिश्नं निर्बिभिदे ततः ॥५६॥

nirbibheda virājas tvag-
roma-śmaśrv-ādayas tataḥ
tata oṣadhayaś cāsan
śiśnaṁ nirbibhide tataḥ

nirbibheda—appeared; *virājaḥ*—of the universal form; *tvak*—skin; *roma*—hair; *śmaśru*—beard, mustache; *ādayaḥ*—and so on; *tataḥ*—then; *tataḥ*—thereupon; *oṣadhayaḥ*—the herbs and drugs; *ca*—and; *āsan*—appeared; *śiśnam*—genitals; *nirbibhide*—appeared; *tataḥ*—after this.

TRANSLATION

Then the universal form of the Lord, the virāṭ-puruṣa, manifested His skin, and thereupon the hair, mustache and beard appeared. After this all the herbs and drugs became manifested, and then His genitals also appeared.

PURPORT

The skin is the site of the touch sensation. The demigods who control the production of herbs and medicinal drugs are the deities presiding over the tactile sense.

TEXT 57

रेतस्तस्मादाप आसन्निरभिद्यत वै गुदम् ।
गुदादपानोऽपानाच्च मृत्युर्लोकभयङ्करः ॥५७॥

retas tasmād āpa āsan
nirabhidyata vai gudam
gudād apāno 'pānāc ca
mṛtyur loka-bhayaṅkaraḥ

retaḥ—semen; *tasmāt*—from that; *āpaḥ*—the god who presides over the waters; *āsan*—appeared; *nirabhidyata*—was manifested; *vai*—indeed; *gudam*—an anus; *gudāt*—from the anus; *apānaḥ*—the organ of defecation; *apānāt*—from the organ of defecation; *ca*—and; *mṛtyuḥ*—death; *loka-bhayam-karaḥ*—causing fear throughout the universe.

TRANSLATION

After this, semen (the faculty of procreation) and the god who presides over the waters appeared. Next appeared an anus and then the organs of defecation and thereupon the god of death, who is feared throughout the universe.

PURPORT

It is understood herewith that the faculty to discharge semen is the cause of death. Therefore, *yogīs* and transcendentalists who want to live for greater spans of life voluntarily restrain themselves from discharging semen. The more one can restrain the discharge of semen, the more one can be aloof from the problem of death. There are many *yogīs* living up to three hundred or seven hundred years by this process, and in the *Bhāgavatam* it is clearly stated that discharging semen is the cause of horrible death. The more one is addicted to sexual enjoyment, the more susceptible he is to a quick death.

TEXT 58

हस्तौ च निरभिद्येतां बलं ताभ्यां ततः स्वराट् ।
पादौ च निरभिद्येतां गतिस्ताभ्यां ततो हरिः ॥५८॥

hastau ca nirabhidyetāṁ
balaṁ tābhyāṁ tataḥ svarāṭ
pādau ca nirabhidyetāṁ
gatis tābhyāṁ tato hariḥ

hastau—the two hands; *ca*—and; *nirabhidyetām*—were manifested; *balam*—power; *tābhyām*—from them; *tataḥ*—thereafter; *svarāṭ*—Lord Indra; *pādau*—the two feet; *ca*—and; *nirabhidyetām*—became manifested; *gatiḥ*—the process of movement; *tābhyām*—from them; *tataḥ*—then; *hariḥ*—Lord Viṣṇu.

TRANSLATION

Thereafter the two hands of the universal form of the Lord became manifested, and with them the power of grasping and dropping things, and after that Lord Indra appeared. Next the legs became manifested, and with them the process of movement, and after that Lord Viṣṇu appeared.

PURPORT

The deity presiding over the hands is Indra, and the presiding deity of movement is the Supreme Personality of Godhead, Viṣṇu. Viṣṇu appeared on the appearance of the legs of the *virāṭ-puruṣa*.

TEXT 59

नाड्योऽस्य निरभिद्यन्त ताभ्यो लोहितमाभृतम् ।
नद्यस्ततः समभवन्नुदरं निरभिद्यत ॥५९॥

nāḍyo 'sya nirabhidyanta
tābhyo lohitam ābhṛtam
nadyas tataḥ samabhavann
udaraṁ nirabhidyata

nāḍyaḥ—the veins; *asya*—of the universal form; *nirabhidyanta*—became manifested; *tābhyaḥ*—from them; *lohitam*—blood; *ābhṛtam*—was produced; *nadyaḥ*—the rivers; *tataḥ*—from that; *samabhavan*—appeared; *udaram*—the stomach; *nirabhidyata*—became manifested.

TRANSLATION

The veins of the universal body became manifested and thereafter the red corpuscles, or blood. In their wake came the rivers (the deities presiding over the veins), and then appeared an abdomen.

PURPORT

Blood veins are compared to rivers; when the veins were manifested in the universal form, the rivers in the various planets were also manifested. The controlling deity of the rivers is also the controlling deity of the nervous system. In Āyur-vedic treatment, those who are suffering from the disease of nervous instability are recommended to take a bath by dipping into a flowing river.

TEXT 60

क्षुत्पिपासे ततः स्यातां समुद्रस्त्वेतयोरभूत् ।
अथास्य हृदयं भिन्नं हृदयान्मन उत्थितम् ॥६०॥

kṣut-pipāse tataḥ syātāṁ
samudras tv etayor abhūt
athāsya hṛdayaṁ bhinnaṁ
hṛdayān mana utthitam

kṣut-pipāse—hunger and thirst; *tataḥ*—then; *syātām*—appeared; *samudraḥ*—the ocean; *tu*—then; *etayoḥ*—in their wake; *abhūt*—appeared; *atha*—then; *asya*—of the universal form; *hṛdayam*—a heart; *bhinnam*—appeared; *hṛdayāt*—from the heart; *manaḥ*—the mind; *utthitam*—appeared.

TRANSLATION

Next grew feelings of hunger and thirst, and in their wake came the manifestation of the oceans. Then a heart became manifest, and in the wake of the heart the mind appeared.

PURPORT

The ocean is considered to be the presiding deity of the abdomen, where the feelings of hunger and thirst originate. When there is an irregularity in hunger and thirst, one is advised, according to Āyur-vedic treatment, to take a bath in the ocean.

TEXT 61

मनसश्चन्द्रमा जातो बुद्धिर्बुद्धेर्गिरां पतिः ।
अहङ्कारस्ततो रुद्रश्चित्तं चैत्यस्ततोऽभवत् ॥६१॥

manasaś candramā jāto
buddhir buddher girāṁ patiḥ
ahaṅkāras tato rudraś
cittaṁ caityas tato 'bhavat

manasaḥ—from the mind; *candramāḥ*—the moon; *jātaḥ*—appeared; *buddhiḥ*—intelligence; *buddheḥ*—from intelligence; *girām patiḥ*—the lord of speech (Brahmā); *ahaṅkāraḥ*—false ego; *tataḥ*—then; *rudraḥ*—Lord Śiva; *cittam*—consciousness; *caityaḥ*—the deity presiding over consciousness; *tataḥ*—then; *abhavat*—appeared.

TRANSLATION

After the mind, the moon appeared. Intelligence appeared next, and after intelligence, Lord Brahmā appeared. Then the false

ego appeared and then Lord Śiva, and after the appearance of Lord Śiva came consciousness and the deity presiding over consciousness.

PURPORT

The moon appeared after the appearance of mind, and this indicates that the moon is the presiding deity of mind. Similarly, Lord Brahmā, appearing after intelligence, is the presiding deity of intelligence, and Lord Śiva, who appears after false ego, is the presiding deity of false ego. In other words, it is indicated that the moon-god is in the mode of goodness, whereas Lord Brahmā is in the mode of passion and Lord Śiva is in the mode of ignorance. The appearance of consciousness after the appearance of false ego indicates that, from the beginning, material consciousness is under the mode of ignorance and that one therefore has to purify himself by purifying his consciousness. This purificatory process is called Kṛṣṇa consciousness. As soon as the consciousness is purified, the false ego disappears. Identification of the body with the self is called false identification, or false ego. Lord Caitanya confirms this in His *Śikṣāṣṭaka.* He states that the first result of chanting the *mahā-mantra,* Hare Kṛṣṇa, is that dirt is cleared from the consciousness, or the mirror of the mind, and then at once the blazing fire of material existence is over. The blazing fire of material existence is due to false ego, but as soon as the false ego is removed, one can understand his real identity. At that point he is actually liberated from the clutches of *māyā.* As soon as one is freed from the clutches of false ego, his intelligence also becomes purified, and then his mind is always engaged upon the lotus feet of the Supreme Personality of Godhead.

The Supreme Personality of Godhead appeared on the full-moon day as Gauracandra, or the spotless transcendental moon. The material moon has spots on it, but on the transcendental moon, Gauracandra, there are no spots. In order to fix the purified mind in the service of the Supreme Lord, one has to worship the spotless moon, Gauracandra. Those who are materially passionate or those who want to exhibit their intelligence for material advancement in life are generally worshipers of Lord Brahmā, and persons who are in the gross ignorance of identifying with the body worship Lord Śiva. Materialists like Hiraṇyakaśipu and Rāvaṇa are worshipers of Lord Brahmā or Lord Śiva, but Prahlāda and other devotees in the service of Kṛṣṇa consciousness worship the Supreme Lord, the Personality of Godhead.

TEXT 62

एते ह्यभ्युत्थिता देवा नैवास्योत्थापनेऽशकन् ।
पुनराविविशुः खानि तमुत्थापयितुं क्रमात् ॥६२॥

ete hy abhyutthitā devā
naivāsyotthāpane 'śakan
punar āviviśuḥ khāni
tam utthāpayituṁ kramāt

ete—these; *hi*—indeed; *abhyutthitāḥ*—manifested; *devāḥ*—demigods; *na*—not; *eva*—at all; *asya*—of the *virāṭ-puruṣa; utthāpane*—in waking; *aśakan*—were able; *punaḥ*—again; *āviviśuḥ*—they entered; *khāni*—the apertures of the body; *tam*—Him; *utthāpayitum*—to awaken; *kramāt*—one after another.

TRANSLATION

When the demigods and presiding deities of the various senses were thus manifested, they wanted to wake their origin of appearance. But upon failing to do so, they reentered the body of the virāṭ-puruṣa one after another in order to wake Him.

PURPORT

In order to wake the sleeping Deity-controller within, one has to rechannel the sense activities from concentration on the outside to concentration inside. In the following verses, the sense activities which are required to wake the *virāṭ-puruṣa* will be explained very nicely.

TEXT 63

वह्निर्वाचा मुखं भेजे नोदतिष्ठत्तदा विराट् ।
घ्राणेन नासिके वायुर्नोदतिष्ठत्तदा विराट् ॥६३॥

vahnir vācā mukhaṁ bheje
nodatiṣṭhat tadā virāṭ
ghrāṇena nāsike vāyur
nodatiṣṭhat tadā virāṭ

vahniḥ—the god of fire; *vācā*—with the organ of speech; *mukham*—the mouth; *bheje*—entered; *na*—not; *udatiṣṭhat*—did arise; *tadā*—then; *virāṭ*—the *virāṭ-puruṣa; ghrāṇena*—with the olfactory sense; *nāsike*—into His two nostrils; *vāyuḥ*—the god of the winds; *na*—not; *udatiṣṭhat*—did arise; *tadā*—then; *virāṭ*—the *virāṭ-puruṣa.*

TRANSLATION

The god of fire entered His mouth with the organ of speech, but the virāṭ-puruṣa could not be aroused. Then the god of wind entered His nostrils with the sense of smell, but still the virāṭ-puruṣa refused to be awakened.

TEXT 64

अक्षिणी चक्षुषादित्यो नोदतिष्ठत्तदा विराट् ।
श्रोत्रेण कर्णौ च दिशो नोदतिष्ठत्तदा विराट् ॥६४॥

akṣiṇī cakṣuṣādityo
nodatiṣṭhat tadā virāṭ
śrotreṇa karṇau ca diśo
nodatiṣṭhat tadā virāṭ

akṣiṇī—His two eyes; *cakṣuṣā*—with the sense of sight; *ādityaḥ*—the sun-god; *na*—not; *udatiṣṭhat*—did arise; *tadā*—then; *virāṭ*—the *virāṭ-puruṣa; śrotreṇa*—with the sense of hearing; *karṇau*—His two ears; *ca*—and; *diśaḥ*—the deities presiding over the directions; *na*—not; *udatiṣṭhat*—did arise; *tadā*—then; *virāṭ*—the *virāṭ-puruṣa.*

TRANSLATION

The sun-god entered the eyes of the virāṭ-puruṣa with the sense of sight, but still the virāṭ-puruṣa did not get up. Similarly, the predominatlng deities uf the directions cntered through His ears with the sense of hearing, but still He did not get up.

TEXT 65

त्वचं रोमभिरोषध्यो नोदतिष्ठत्तदा विराट् ।
रेतसा शिश्नमापस्तु नोदतिष्ठत्तदा विराट् ॥६५॥

tvacaṁ romabhir oṣadhyo
nodatiṣṭhat tadā virāṭ
retasā śiśnam āpas tu
nodatiṣṭhat tadā virāṭ

tvacam—the skin of the *virāṭ-puruṣa; romabhiḥ*—with the hair on the body; *oṣadhyaḥ*—the deities presiding over the herbs and plants; *na*—not; *udatiṣṭhat*—did arise; *tadā*—then; *virāṭ*—the *virāṭ-puruṣa; retasā*—with the faculty of procreation; *śiśnam*—the organ of generation; *āpaḥ*—the water-god; *tu*—then; *na*—not; *udatiṣṭhat*—did arise; *tadā*—then; *virāṭ*—the *virāṭ-puruṣa.*

TRANSLATION

The predominating deities of the skin, herbs and seasoning plants entered the skin of the virāṭ-puruṣa with the hair of the body, but the Cosmic Being refused to get up even then. The god predominating over water entered His organ of generation with the faculty of procreation, but the virāṭ-puruṣa still would not rise.

TEXT 66

गुदं मृत्युरपानेन नोदतिष्ठत्तदा विराट् ।
हस्ताविन्द्रो बलेनैव नोदतिष्ठत्तदा विराट् ॥६६॥

gudaṁ mṛtyur apānena
nodatiṣṭhat tadā virāṭ
hastāv indro balenaiva
nodatiṣṭhat tadā virāṭ

gudam—His anus; *mṛtyuḥ*—the god of death; *apānena*—with the organ of defecation; *na*—not; *udatiṣṭhat*—did arise; *tadā*—even then; *virāṭ*—the *virāṭ-puruṣa; hastau*—the two hands; *indraḥ*—Lord Indra;

balena—with their power to grasp and drop things; *eva*—indeed; *na*—not; *udatiṣṭhat*—did arise; *tadā*—even then; *virāṭ*—the *virāṭ-puruṣa.*

TRANSLATION

The god of death entered His anus with the organ of defecation, but the virāṭ-puruṣa could not be spurred to activity. The god Indra entered the hands with their power of grasping and dropping things, but the virāṭ-puruṣa would not get up even then.

TEXT 67

विष्णुर्गत्यैव चरणौ नोदतिष्ठत्तदा विराट् ।
नाडीर्नद्यो लोहितेन नोदतिष्ठत्तदा विराट् ॥६७॥

viṣṇur gatyaiva caraṇau
nodatiṣṭhat tadā virāṭ
nāḍīr nadyo lohitena
nodatiṣṭhat tadā virāṭ

viṣṇuḥ—Lord Viṣṇu; *gatyā*—with the faculty of locomotion; *eva*—indeed; *caraṇau*—His two feet; *na*—not; *udatiṣṭhat*—did arise; *tadā*—even then; *virāṭ*—the *virāṭ-puruṣa; nāḍīḥ*—His blood vessels; *nadyaḥ*—the rivers or river-gods; *lohitena*—with the blood, with the power of circulation; *na*—not; *udatiṣṭhat*—did stir; *tadā*—even then; *virāṭ*—the *virāṭ-puruṣa.*

TRANSLATION

Lord Viṣṇu entered His feet with the faculty of locomotion, but the virāṭ-puruṣa refused to stand up even then. The rivers entered His blood vessels with the blood and the power of circulation, but still the Cosmic Being could not be made to stir.

TEXT 68

क्षुत्तृड्भ्यामुदरं सिन्धुर्नोदतिष्ठत्तदा विराट् ।
हृदयं मनसा चन्द्रो नोदतिष्ठत्तदा विराट् ॥६८॥

kṣut-tṛḍbhyām udaraṁ sindhur
nodatiṣṭhat tadā virāṭ
hṛdayaṁ manasā candro
nodatiṣṭhat tadā virāṭ

kṣut-tṛḍbhyām—with hunger and thirst; *udaram*—His abdomen; *sindhuḥ*—the ocean or ocean-god; *na*—not; *udatiṣṭhat*—did arise; *tadā*—even then; *virāṭ*—the *virāṭ-puruṣa; hṛdayam*—His heart; *manasā*—with the mind; *candraḥ*—the moon-god; *na*—not; *udatiṣṭhat*—did arise; *tadā*—even then; *virāṭ*—the *virāṭ-puruṣa.*

TRANSLATION

The ocean entered His abdomen with hunger and thirst, but the Cosmic Being refused to rise even then. The moon-god entered His heart with the mind, but the Cosmic Being would not be roused.

TEXT 69

बुद्ध्या ब्रह्मापि हृदयं नोदतिष्ठत्तदा विराट् ।
रुद्रोऽभिमत्या हृदयं नोदतिष्ठत्तदा विराट् ॥६९॥

buddhyā brahmāpi hṛdayaṁ
nodatiṣṭhat tadā virāṭ
rudro 'bhimatyā hṛdayaṁ
nodatiṣṭhat tadā virāṭ

buddhyā—with intelligence; *brahmā*—Lord Brahmā; *api*—also; *hṛdayam*—His heart; *na*—not; *udatiṣṭhat*—did arise; *tadā*—even then; *virāṭ*—the *virāṭ-puruṣa; rudraḥ*—Lord Śiva; *abhimatyā*—with the ego; *hṛdayam*—His heart; *na*—not; *udatiṣṭhat*—did arise; *tadā*—even then; *virāṭ*—the *virāṭ-puruṣa.*

TRANSLATION

Brahmā also entered His heart with intelligence, but even then the Cosmic Being could not be prevailed upon to get up. Lord Rudra also entered His heart with the ego, but even then the Cosmic Being did not stir.

TEXT 70

चित्तेन हृदयं चैत्यः क्षेत्रज्ञः प्राविशद्यदा ।
विराट् तदैव पुरुषः सलिलादुदतिष्ठत ॥७०॥

cittena hṛdayaṁ caityaḥ
kṣetra-jñaḥ prāviśad yadā
virāṭ tadaiva puruṣaḥ
salilād udatiṣṭhata

cittena—along with reason, consciousness; *hṛdayam*—the heart; *caityaḥ*—the deity presiding over consciousness; *kṣetra-jñaḥ*—the knower of the field; *prāviśat*—entered; *yadā*—when; *virāṭ*—the *virāṭ-puruṣa; tadā*—then; *eva*—just; *puruṣaḥ*—the Cosmic Being; *salilāt*—from the water; *udatiṣṭhata*—arose.

TRANSLATION

However, when the inner controller, the deity presiding over consciousness, entered the heart with reason, at that very moment the Cosmic Being arose from the causal waters.

TEXT 71

यथा प्रसुप्तं पुरुषं प्राणेन्द्रियमनोधियः ।
प्रभवन्ति विना येन नोत्थापयितुमोजसा ॥७१॥

yathā prasuptaṁ puruṣaṁ
prāṇendriya-mano-dhiyaḥ
prabhavanti vinā yena
notthāpayitum ojasā

yathā—just as; *prasuptam*—sleeping; *puruṣam*—a man; *prāṇa*—the vital air; *indriya*—the senses for working and recording knowledge; *manaḥ*—the mind; *dhiyaḥ*—the intelligence; *prabhavanti*—are able; *vinā*—without; *yena*—whom (the Supersoul); *na*—not; *utthāpayitum*—to arouse; *ojasā*—by their own power.

TRANSLATION

When a man is sleeping, all his material assets—namely the vital energy, the senses for recording knowledge, the senses for working, the mind and the intelligence—cannot arouse him. He can be aroused only when the Supersoul helps him.

PURPORT

The explanation of Sāṅkhya philosophy is described here in detail in the sense that the *virāṭ-puruṣa,* or the universal form of the Supreme Personality of Godhead, is the original source of all the various sense organs and their presiding deities. The relationship between the *virāṭ-puruṣa* and the presiding deities or the living entities is so intricate that simply by exercising the sense organs, which are related to their presiding deities, the *virāṭ-puruṣa* cannot be aroused. It is not possible to arouse the *virāṭ-puruṣa* or to link with the Supreme Absolute Personality of Godhead by material activities. Only by devotional service and detachment can one perform the process of linking with the Absolute.

TEXT 72

तमस्मिन् प्रत्यगात्मानं धिया योगप्रवृत्तया ।
भक्त्या विरक्त्या ज्ञानेन विविच्यात्मनि चिन्तयेत् ॥ ७२॥

tam asmin pratyag-ātmānaṁ
dhiyā yoga-pravṛttayā
bhaktyā viraktyā jñānena
vivicyātmani cintayet

tam—upon Him; *asmin*—in this; *pratyak-ātmānam*—the Supersoul; *dhiyā*—with the mind; *yoga-pravṛttayā*—engaged in devotional service; *bhaktyā*—through devotion; *viraktyā*—through detachment; *jñānena*—through spiritual knowledge; *vivicya*—considering carefully; *ātmani*—in the body; *cintayet*—one should contemplate.

TRANSLATION

Therefore, through devotion, detachment and advancement in spiritual knowledge acquired through concentrated devotional

service, one should contemplate that Supersoul as present in this very body although simultaneously apart from it.

PURPORT

One can realize the Supersoul within oneself. He is within one's body but apart from the body, or transcendental to the body. Although sitting in the same body as the individual soul, the Supersoul has no affection for the body, whereas the individual soul does. One has to detach himself, therefore, from this material body, by discharging devotional service. It is clearly mentioned here (*bhaktyā*) that one has to execute devotional service to the Supreme. As it is stated in the First Canto, Second Chapter, of *Śrīmad-Bhāgavatam* (1.2.7), *vāsudeve bhagavati bhakti-yogaḥ prayojitaḥ.* When Vāsudeva, the all-pervading Viṣṇu, the Supreme Personality of Godhead, is served in completely pure devotion, detachment from the material world immediately begins. The purpose of Sāṅkhya is to detach oneself from material contamination. This can be achieved simply by devotional service to the Supreme Personality of Godhead.

When one is detached from the attraction of material prosperity, one can actually concentrate his mind upon the Supersoul. As long as the mind is distracted towards the material, there is no possibility of concentrating one's mind and intelligence upon the Supreme Personality of Godhead or His partial representation, Supersoul. In other words, one cannot concentrate one's mind and energy upon the Supreme unless one is detached from the material world. Following detachment from the material world, one can actually attain transcendental knowledge of the Absolute Truth. As long as one is entangled in sense enjoyment, or material enjoyment, it is not possible to understand the Absolute Truth. This is also confirmed in *Bhagavad-gītā* (18.54). One who is freed from material contamination is joyful and can enter into devotional service, and by devotional service he can be liberated.

In the *Śrīmad-Bhāgavatam,* First Canto, it is stated that one becomes joyful by discharging devotional service. In that joyful attitude, one can understand the science of God, or Kṛṣṇa consciousness; otherwise it is not possible. The analytical study of the elements of material nature and the concentration of the mind upon the Supersoul are the sum and substance of the Sāṅkhya philosophical system. The perfection of this *sāṅkhya-yoga* culminates in devotional service unto the Absolute Truth.

Thus end the Bhaktivedanta purports of the Third Canto, Twenty-sixth Chapter, of the Śrīmad-Bhāgavatam, *entitled "Fundamental Principles of Material Nature."*

CHAPTER TWENTY-SEVEN

Understanding Material Nature

TEXT 1

श्रीभगवानुवाच
प्रकृतिस्थोऽपि पुरुषो नाज्यते प्राकृतैर्गुणैः ।
अविकारादकर्तृत्वान्निर्गुणत्वाज्जलार्कवत् ॥ १ ॥

śrī-bhagavān uvāca
prakṛti-stho 'pi puruṣo
nājyate prākṛtair guṇaiḥ
avikārād akartṛtvān
nirguṇatvāj jalārkavat

śrī-bhagavān uvāca—the Personality of Godhead said; *prakṛti-sthaḥ*—residing in the material body; *api*—although; *puruṣaḥ*—the living entity; *na*—not; *ajyate*—is affected; *prākṛtaiḥ*—of material nature; *guṇaiḥ*—by the modes; *avikārāt*—from being without change; *akartṛtvāt*—by freedom from proprietorship; *nirguṇatvāt*—from being unaffected by the qualities of material nature; *jala*—on water; *arka-vat*—like the sun.

TRANSLATION

The Personality of Godhead Kapila continued: When the living entity is thus unaffected by the modes of material nature, because he is unchanging and does not claim proprietorship, he remains apart from the reactions of the modes, although abiding in a material body, just as the sun remains aloof from its reflection on water.

PURPORT

In the previous chapter Lord Kapiladeva has concluded that simply by beginning the discharge of devotional service one can attain detachment and transcendental knowledge for understanding the science of God. Here the same principle is confirmed. A person who is detached from the modes of material nature remains just like the sun reflected on water. When the sun is reflected on water, the movement of the water or the coolness or unsteadiness of the water cannot affect the sun. Similarly, *vāsudeve bhagavati bhakti-yogaḥ prayojitaḥ* (*Bhāg.* 1.2.7): when one engages fully in the activities of devotional service, *bhakti-yoga*, he becomes just like the sun reflected on water. Although a devotee appears to be in the material world, actually he is in the transcendental world. As the reflection of the sun appears to be on the water but is many millions of miles away from the water, so one engaged in the *bhakti-yoga* process is *nirguṇa*, or unaffected by the qualities of material nature.

Avikāra means "without change." It is confirmed in *Bhagavad-gītā* that each and every living entity is part and parcel of the Supreme Lord, and thus his eternal position is to cooperate or to dovetail his energy with the Supreme Lord. That is his unchanging position. As soon as he employs his energy and activities for sense gratification, this change of position is called *vikāra*. Similarly, even in this material body, when he practices devotional service under the direction of the spiritual master, he comes to the position which is without change because that is his natural duty. As stated in the *Śrīmad-Bhāgavatam*, liberation means reinstatement in one's original position. The original position is one of rendering service to the Lord (*bhakti-yogena, bhaktyā*). When one becomes detached from material attraction and engages fully in devotional service, that is changlessness. *Akartṛtvāt* means not doing anything for sense gratification. When one does something at his own risk, there is a sense of proprietorship and therefore a reaction, but when one does everything for Kṛṣṇa, there is no proprietorship over the activities. By changlessness and by not claiming the proprietorship of activities, one can immediately situate himself in the transcendental position in which one is not touched by the modes of material nature, just as the reflection of the sun is unaffected by the water.

TEXT 2

स एष यर्हि प्रकृतेर्गुणेष्वभिविषज्जते ।
अहंक्रियाविमूढात्मा कर्तास्मीत्यभिमन्यते ॥ २ ॥

sa eṣa yarhi prakṛter
guṇeṣv abhiviṣajjate
ahaṅkriyā-vimūḍhātmā
kartāsmīty abhimanyate

saḥ—that very living entity; *eṣaḥ*—this; *yarhi*—when; *prakṛteḥ*—of material nature; *guṇeṣu*—in the modes; *abhiviṣajjate*—is absorbed; *ahaṅkriyā*—by false ego; *vimūḍha*—bewildered; *ātmā*—the individual soul; *kartā*—the doer; *asmi*—I am; *iti*—thus; *abhimanyate*—he thinks.

TRANSLATION

When the soul is under the spell of material nature and false ego, identifying his body as the self, he becomes absorbed in material activities, and by the influence of false ego he thinks that he is the proprietor of everything.

PURPORT

Actually the conditioned soul is forced to act under the pressure of the modes of material nature. The living entity has no independence. When he is under the direction of the Supreme Personality of Godhead he is free, but when, under the impression that he is satisfying his senses, he engages in sense gratificatory activities, he is actually under the spell of material nature. In *Bhagavad-gītā* it is said, *prakṛteḥ kriyamāṇāni:* one acts according to the particular modes of nature he has acquired. *Guṇa* refers to the qualities of nature. He is under the qualities of nature, but he falsely thinks that he is the proprietor. This false sense of proprietorship can be avoided simply by engaging oneself in devotional service under the direction of the Supreme Lord or His bona fide representative. Arjuna, in *Bhagavad-gītā*, was trying to accept for himself the responsibility for killing his grandfather and teacher in the fight, but he became freed from that proprietorship of action when he acted under the direction of Kṛṣṇa. He fought, but he was actually freed from the reactions of fighting, although in the beginning, when he was nonviolent, unwilling to fight, the entire responsibility was upon him. That is the difference between liberation and conditioning. A conditioned soul may be very good and act in the mode of goodness, but still he is conditioned under the spell of material nature. A devotee, however, acts completely under the direction of the Supreme Lord. Thus his actions may not appear to be of a very high quality to the common man, but the devotee has no responsibility.

TEXT 3

तेन संसारपदवीमवशोऽभ्येत्यनिर्वृतः ।
प्रासङ्गिकैः कर्मदोषैः सदसन्मिश्रयोनिषु ॥ ३ ॥

tena saṁsāra-padavīm
avaśo 'bhyety anirvṛtaḥ
prāsaṅgikaiḥ karma-doṣaiḥ
sad-asan-miśra-yoniṣu

tena—by this; *saṁsāra*—of repeated birth and death; *padavīm*—the path; *avaśaḥ*—helplessly; *abhyeti*—he undergoes; *anirvṛtaḥ*—discontented; *prāsaṅgikaiḥ*—resulting from association with material nature; *karma-doṣaiḥ*—by faulty actions; *sat*—good; *asat*—bad; *miśra*—mixed; *yoniṣu*—in different species of life.

TRANSLATION

The conditioned soul therefore transmigrates into different species of life, higher and lower, because of his association with the modes of material nature. Unless he is relieved of material activities, he has to accept this position because of his faulty work.

PURPORT

Here the word *karma-doṣaiḥ* means "by faulty actions." This refers to any activity, good or bad, performed in this material world—they are all contaminated, faulty actions because of material association. The foolish conditioned soul may think that he is offering charity by opening hospitals for material benefit or by opening an educational institution for material education, but he does not know that all such work is also faulty because it will not give him relief from the process of transmigration from one body to another. It is clearly stated here, *sad-asan-miśra-yoniṣu.* This means that one may take birth in a very high family or he may take his birth in higher planets, among the demigods, for his so-called pious activities in the material world. But this work is also faulty because it does not give liberation. To take birth in a nice place or a high family does not mean that one avoids undergoing the material tribulations, the pangs of birth, death, old age and disease. A conditioned soul under the spell of material nature cannot understand that any action he performs for sense gratification is faulty and that only his activities in devotional service to the Lord can give him release from the reaction of faulty activities. Because he does not cease such faulty activities, he has to change to different bodies, some high and some low. That is called *saṁsāra-padavīm*, which means this material world, from which there is no release. One who desires material liberation has to turn his activities to devotional service. There is no alternative.

TEXT 4

अर्थे ह्यविद्यमानेऽपि संसृतिर्न निवर्तते ।
ध्यायतो विषयानस्य स्वप्नेऽनर्थागमो यथा ॥ ४ ॥

arthe hy avidyamāne 'pi
saṁsṛtir na nivartate
dhyāyato viṣayān asya
svapne 'narthāgamo yathā

arthe—real cause; *hi*—certainly; *avidyamāne*—not existing; *api*—although; *saṁsṛtiḥ*—the material existential condition; *na*—not; *nivartate*—does cease; *dhyāyataḥ*—contemplating; *viṣayān*—objects of the senses; *asya*—of the living entity; *svapne*—in a dream; *anartha*—of disadvantages; *āgamaḥ*—arrival; *yathā*—like.

TRANSLATION

Actually a living entity is transcendental to material existence, but because of his mentality of lording it over material nature, his material existential condition does not cease, and just as in a dream, he is affected by all sorts of disadvantages.

PURPORT

The example of a dream is very appropriate. Due to different mental conditions, in dreams we are put into advantageous and disadvantageous positions. Similarly, the spirit soul has nothing to do with this material nature, but because of his mentality of lording it over, he is put into the position of conditional existence.

Conditional existence is described here as *dhyāyato viṣayān asya. Viṣaya* means "an object of enjoyment." As long as one continues to think that he can enjoy material advantages, he is in conditioned life, but as soon as he comes to his senses, he develops the knowledge that he is not the enjoyer, for the only enjoyer is the Supreme Personality of Godhead. As confirmed in *Bhagavad-gītā* (5.29), He is the beneficiary for all the results of sacrifices and penances (*bhoktāraṁ yajña-tapasām*), and He is the proprietor of all the three worlds (*sarva-loka-maheśvaram*). He is the actual friend of all living entities. But instead of leaving proprietorship, enjoyment and the actual position as the friend of all living entities to the Supreme Personality of Godhead, we claim that we are the proprietors, the enjoyers and the friends. We perform philanthropic work, thinking that we are the friends of human society. Someone may proclaim himself to be a very good national worker, the best friend of the people and of the country, but actually he cannot be the greatest friend of everyone. The only friend is Kṛṣṇa. One should try to raise the consciousness of the conditioned soul to the platform of understanding that Kṛṣṇa is his actual friend. If one makes friendship with Kṛṣṇa, one will never be cheated, and he will get all help needed. Arousing this consciousness of the conditioned soul is the greatest service, not posing oneself as a great friend of another living entity. The power of friendship is limited. Although one claims to be a friend, he cannot be a friend unlimitedly. There are an unlimited number of living entities, and our resources are limited; therefore we cannot be of any real benefit to the people in general. The best service to the people in general is to awaken them to Kṛṣṇa consciousness so that they may know that the supreme enjoyer, the supreme proprietor and the supreme friend is Kṛṣṇa. Then this illusory dream of lording it over material nature will vanish.

TEXT 5

अत एव शनैश्चित्तं प्रसक्तमसतां पथि ।
भक्तियोगेन तीव्रेण विरक्त्या च नयेद्वशम् ॥ ५ ॥

ata eva śanaiś cittaṁ
prasaktam asatāṁ pathi
bhakti-yogena tīvreṇa
viraktyā ca nayed vaśam

ataḥ eva—therefore; *śanaiḥ*—gradually; *cittam*—mind, consciousness; *prasaktam*—attached; *asatām*—of material enjoyments; *pathi*—on the path; *bhakti-yogena*—by devotional service; *tīvreṇa*—very serious; *viraktyā*—without attachment; *ca*—and; *nayet*—he must bring; *vaśam*—under control.

TRANSLATION

It is the duty of every conditioned soul to engage his polluted consciousness, which is now attached to material enjoyment, in very serious devotional service with detachment. Thus his mind and consciousness will be under full control.

PURPORT

The process of liberation is very nicely explained in this verse. The cause of one's becoming conditioned by material nature is his thinking himself the enjoyer, the proprietor or the friend of all living entities. This false thinking is a result of contemplation on sense enjoyment. When one thinks that he is the best friend to his countrymen, to society or to humanity and he engages in various nationalistic, philanthropic and altruistic activities, all that is just so much concentration on sense gratification. The so-called national leader or humanist does not serve everyone; he serves his senses only. That is a fact. But the conditioned soul cannot understand this because he is bewildered by the spell of material nature. It is therefore recommended in this verse that one engage very seriously in the devotional service of the Lord. This means that one should not think that he is the proprietor, benefactor, friend or enjoyer. He should always be cognizant that the real enjoyer is Kṛṣṇa, the Supreme Personality of Godhead; that is the basic principle of *bhakti-yoga.* One must be firmly convinced of these three principles: one should always think that Kṛṣṇa is the proprietor, Kṛṣṇa is the enjoyer and Kṛṣṇa is the friend. Not only should he understand these principles himself, but he should try to convince others and propagate Kṛṣṇa consciousness.

As soon as one engages in such serious devotional service of the Lord, naturally the propensity to falsely claim lordship over material nature disappears. That detachment is called *vairāgya.* Instead of being absorbed in so-called material lordship, one engages in Kṛṣṇa consciousness; that is control of consciousness. The *yoga* process necessitates controlling the senses. *Yoga indriya-saṁyamaḥ.* Since the senses are always active, their activities should be engaged in devotional service—one cannot stop their activities. If one wants to artificially stop the activities of the senses, his attempt will be a failure. Even the great *yogī* Viśvāmitra, who was trying to control his senses by the *yoga* process, fell victim to the beauty of Menakā. There are many such instances. Unless one's mind and consciousness are fully engaged in devotional service, there is always the opportunity for the mind to become occupied with desires for sense gratification.

One particular point mentioned in this verse is very significant. It is said here, *prasaktam asatāṁ pathi:* the mind is always attracted by *asat,* the temporary, material existence. Because we have been associated with material nature since time immemorial, we have become accustomed to our attachment to this temporary material nature. The mind has to be fixed at the eternal lotus feet of the Supreme Lord. *Sa vai manaḥ kṛṣṇa-padāravindayoḥ.* One has to fix the mind at the lotus feet of Kṛṣṇa; then everything will be very nice. Thus the seriousness of *bhakti-yoga* is stressed in this verse.

TEXT 6

यमादिभिर्योगपथैरभ्यसञ् श्रद्धयान्वितः ।
मयि भावेन सत्येन मत्कथाश्रवणेन च ॥ ६ ॥

yamādibhir yoga-pathair
abhyasañ śraddhayānvitaḥ
mayi bhāvena satyena
mat-kathā-śravaṇena ca

yama-ādibhiḥ—beginning with *yama; yoga-pathaiḥ*—by the *yoga* system; *abhyasan*—practicing; *śraddhayā anvitaḥ*—with great faith;

mayi—unto Me; *bhāvena*—with devotion; *satyena*—unalloyed; *mat-kathā*—stories about Me; *śravaṇena*—by hearing; *ca*—and.

TRANSLATION

One has to become faithful by practicing the controlling process of the yoga system and must elevate himself to the platform of unalloyed devotional service by chanting and hearing about Me.

PURPORT

Yoga is practiced in eight different stages: *yama, niyama, āsana, prāṇāyāma, pratyāhāra, dhāraṇā, dhyāna* and *samādhi. Yama* and *niyama* mean practicing the controlling process by following strict regulations, and *āsana* refers to the sitting postures. These help raise one to the standard of faithfulness in devotional service. The practice of *yoga* by physical exercise is not the ultimate goal; the real end is to concentrate and to control the mind and train oneself to be situated in faithful devotional service.

Bhāvena, or *bhāva*, is a very important factor in the practice of *yoga* or in any spiritual process. *Bhāva* is explained in *Bhagavad-gītā* (10.8). *Budhā bhāva-samanvitāḥ:* one should be absorbed in the thought of love of Kṛṣṇa. When one knows that Kṛṣṇa, the Supreme Personality of Godhead, is the source of everything and that everything emanates from Him (*ahaṁ sarvasya prabhavaḥ*), then one understands the *Vedānta* aphorism *janmādy asya yataḥ* ("the original source of everything"), and then he can become absorbed in *bhāva*, or the preliminary stage of love of Godhead.

Rūpa Gosvāmī explains very nicely in *Bhakti-rasāmṛta-sindhu* how this *bhāva*, or preliminary stage of love of God, is achieved. He states that one first of all has to become faithful (*śraddhayānvitaḥ*). Faith is attained by controlling the senses, either by *yoga* practice, following the rules and regulations and practicing the sitting postures, or by engaging directly in *bhakti-yoga*, as recommended in the previous verse. Of the nine different items of *bhakti-yoga*, the first and foremost is to chant and hear about the Lord. That is also mentioned here. *Mat-kathā-śravaṇena ca.* One may come to the standard of faithfulness by following the rules and regulations of the *yoga* system, and the same goal can be achieved simply by chanting and hearing about the transcendental activities of the Lord. The word *ca* is significant. *Bhakti-yoga* is direct, and the other process is indirect. But even if the indirect process is taken, there is no success unless one comes fully to the direct process of hearing and chanting the glories of the Lord. Therefore the word *satyena* is used here. In this connection Svāmī Śrīdhara comments that *satyena* means *niṣkapaṭena*, "without duplicity." The impersonalists are full of duplicity. Sometimes they pretend to execute devotional service, but their ultimate idea is to become one with the Supreme. This is duplicity, *kapaṭa*. The *Bhāgavatam* does not allow this duplicity. In the beginning of *Śrīmad-Bhāgavatam* it is clearly stated, *paramo nirmatsarāṇām:* "This treatise *Śrīmad-Bhāgavatam* is meant for those who are completely free from envy." The same point is again stressed here. Unless one is completely faithful to the Supreme Personality of Godhead and engages himself in the process of hearing and chanting the glories of the Lord, there is no possibility for liberation.

TEXT 7

सर्वभूतसमत्वेन निर्वैरेणाप्रसङ्गतः ।
ब्रह्मचर्येण मौनेन स्वधर्मेण बलीयसा ॥ ७ ॥

sarva-bhūta-samatvena
nirvaireṇāprasaṅgataḥ
brahmacaryeṇa maunena
sva-dharmeṇa balīyasā

sarva—all; *bhūta*—living entities; *samatvena*—by seeing equally; *nirvaireṇa*—without enmity; *aprasaṅgataḥ*—without intimate connections; *brahma-caryeṇa*—by celibacy; *maunena*—by silence; *sva-dharmeṇa*—by one's occupation; *balīyasā*—by offering the result.

TRANSLATION

In executing devotional service, one has to see every living entity equally, without enmity towards anyone yet without intimate connections with anyone. One has to observe celibacy, be grave

and execute his eternal activities, offering the results to the Supreme Personality of Godhead.

PURPORT

A devotee of the Supreme Personality of Godhead who seriously engages in devotional service is equal to all living entities. There are various species of living entities, but a devotee does not see the outward covering; he sees the inner soul inhabiting the body. Because each and every soul is part and parcel of the Supreme Personality of Godhead, he does not see any difference. That is the vision of a learned devotee. As explained in *Bhagavad-gītā*, a devotee or a learned sage does not see any difference between a learned *brāhmaṇa*, a dog, an elephant or a cow because he knows that the body is the outer covering only and that the soul is actually part and parcel of the Supreme Lord. A devotee has no enmity towards any living entity, but that does not mean that he mixes with everyone. That is prohibited. *Aprasaṅgataḥ* means "not to be in intimate touch with everyone." A devotee is concerned with his execution of devotional service, and he should therefore mix with devotees only, in order to advance his objective. He has no business mixing with others, for although he does not see anyone as his enemy, his dealings are only with persons who engage in devotional service.

A devotee should observe the vow of celibacy. Celibacy does not necessitate that one be absolutely free from sex life; satisfaction with one's wife is permitted also under the vow of celibacy. The best policy is to avoid sex life altogether. That is preferable. Otherwise, a devotee can get married under religious principles and live peacefully with a wife.

A devotee should not speak needlessly. A serious devotee has no time to speak of nonsense. He is always busy in Kṛṣṇa consciousness. Whenever he speaks, he speaks about Kṛṣṇa. *Mauna* means "silence." Silence does not mean that one should not speak at all, but that he should not speak of nonsense. He should be very enthusiastic in speaking about Kṛṣṇa. Another important item described here is *sva-dharmeṇa*, or being exclusively occupied in one's eternal occupation, which is to act as the eternal servitor of the Lord, or to act in Kṛṣṇa consciousness. The next word, *balīyasā*, means "offering the results of all activities to the Supreme Personality of Godhead." A devotee does not act on his personal account for sense gratification. Whatever he earns, whatever he eats and whatever he does, he offers for the satisfaction of the Supreme Personality of Godhead.

TEXT 8

यदृच्छयोपलब्धेन सन्तुष्टो मितभुङ् मुनिः ।
विविक्तशरणः शान्तो मैत्रः करुण आत्मवान् ॥ ८ ॥

yadṛcchayopalabdhena
santuṣṭo mita-bhuṅ muniḥ
vivikta-śaraṇaḥ śānto
maitraḥ karuṇa ātmavān

yadṛcchayā—without difficulty; *upalabdhena*—with what is obtained; *santuṣṭaḥ*—satisfied; *mita*—little; *bhuk*—eating; *muniḥ*—thoughtful; *vivikta-śaraṇaḥ*—living in a secluded place; *śāntaḥ*—peaceful; *maitraḥ*—friendly; *karuṇaḥ*—compassionate; *ātma-vān*—self-possessed, self-realized.

TRANSLATION

For his income a devotee should be satisfied with what he earns without great difficulty. He should not eat more than what is necessary. He should live in a secluded place and always be thoughtful, peaceful, friendly, compassionate and self-realized.

PURPORT

Everyone who has accepted a material body must maintain the necessities of the body by acting or earning some livelihood. A devotee should only work for such income as is absolutely necessary. He should be satisfied always with such income and should not endeavor to earn more and more simply to accumulate the unnecessary. A person in the conditioned state who has no money is always found working very hard to earn some with the object of lording it over material nature. Kapiladeva instructs that we should not endeavor hard for things which may come automatically, without extraneous labor. The exact word used in this connection, *yadṛcchayā*, means that every living entity has a predestined happiness and distress in his present body; this is called the law of *karma*. It is not possible that simply by endeavors to accumulate more money a person will be able to do so, otherwise almost everyone would be on the same level of wealth. In reality everyone is earning and acquiring according to his predestined *karma.* According to the *Bhāgavatam* conclusion, we are sometimes faced with dangerous or miserable conditions without endeavoring for them, and similarly we may have prosperous conditions without endeavoring for them. We are advised to let these things come as predestined. We should engage our valuable time in prosecuting Kṛṣṇa consciousness. In other words, one should be satisfied by his natural condition. If by predestination one is put into a certain condition of life which is not very prosperous in comparison to another's position, one should not be disturbed. He should simply try to utilize his valuable time to advance in Kṛṣṇa consciousness. Advancement in Kṛṣṇa consciousness does not depend on any materially prosperous or distressed condition; it is free from the conditions imposed by material life. A very poor man can execute Kṛṣṇa consciousness as effectively as a very rich man. One should therefore be very satisfied with his position as offered by the Lord.

Another word here is *mita-bhuk.* This means that one should eat only as much as necessary to maintain the body and soul together. One should not be gluttonous to satisfy the tongue. Grains, fruits, milk and similar foods are allotted for human consumption. One should not be excessively eager to satisfy the tongue and eat that which is not meant for humanity. Particularly, a devotee should eat only *prasāda,* or food which is offered to the Personality of Godhead. His position is to accept the remnants of those foodstuffs. Innocent foods like grains, vegetables, fruits, flowers and milk preparations are offered to the Lord, and therefore there is no scope for offering foods which are in the modes of passion and ignorance. A devotee should not be greedy. It is also recommended that the devotee should be *muni,* or thoughtful; he should always think of Kṛṣṇa and how to render better service to the Supreme Personality of Godhead. That should be his only anxiety. As a materialist is always thoughtful about improving his material condition, a devotee's thoughts should always be engaged in improving his condition in Kṛṣṇa consciousness; therefore he should be a *muni.*

The next item recommended is that a devotee should live in a secluded place. Generally a common man is interested in pounds, shillings and pence, or materialistic advancement in life, which is unnecessary for a devotee. A devotee should select a place of residence where everyone is interested in devotional service. Generally, therefore, a devotee goes to a sacred place of pilgrimage where devotees live. It is recommended that he live in a place where there is no large number of ordinary men. It is very important to live in a secluded place (*vivikta-śaraṇa*). The next item is *śānta*, or peacefulness. The devotee should not be agitated. He should be satisfied with his natural income, eat only as much as he needs to keep his health, live in a secluded place and always remain peaceful. Peace of mind is necessary for prosecuting Kṛṣṇa consciousness.

The next item is *maitra*, friendliness. A devotee should be friendly to everyone, but his intimate friendship should be with devotees only. With others he should be official. He may say, "Yes, sir, what you say is all right," but he is not intimate with them. A devotee should, however, have compassion for persons who are innocent, who are neither atheistic nor very much advanced in spiritual realization. A devotee should be compassionate towards them and instruct them as far as possible in making advancement in Kṛṣṇa consciousness. A devotee should always remain *ātmavān*, or situated in his spiritual position. He should not forget that his main concern is to make advancement in spiritual consciousness, or Kṛṣṇa consciousness, and he should not ignorantly identify himself with the body or the mind. *Ātmā* means the body or the mind, but here the word *ātmavān* especially means that one should be self-possessed. He should always remain in the pure consciousness that he is spirit soul and not the material body or the mind. That will make him progress confidently in Kṛṣṇa consciousness.

TEXT 9

सानुबन्धे च देहेऽस्मिन्नकुर्वन्नसदाग्रहम् ।
ज्ञानेन दृष्टतत्त्वेन प्रकृतेः पुरुषस्य च ॥ ९ ॥

sānubandhe ca dehe 'sminn
akurvann asad-āgraham
jñānena dṛṣṭa-tattvena
prakṛteḥ puruṣasya ca

sa-anubandhe—with bodily relationships; *ca*—and; *dehe*—towards the body; *asmin*—this; *akurvan*—not doing; *asat-āgraham*—bodily concept of life; *jñānena*—through knowledge; *dṛṣṭa*—having seen; *tat-tvena*—the reality; *prakṛteḥ*—of matter; *puruṣasya*—of spirit; *ca*—and.

TRANSLATION

One's seeing power should be increased through knowledge of spirit and matter, and one should not unnecessarily identify himself with the body and thus become attracted by bodily relationships.

PURPORT

The conditioned souls are eager to identify with the body and consider that the body is "myself" and that anything in relationship with the body or possessions of the body is "mine." In Sanskrit this is called *ahaṁ mamatā*, and it is the root cause of all conditional life. A person should see things as the combination of matter and spirit. He should distinguish between the nature of matter and the nature of spirit, and his real identification should be with spirit, not with matter. By this knowledge, one should avoid the false, bodily concept of life.

TEXT 10

निवृत्तबुद्ध्यवस्थानो दूरीभूतान्यदर्शनः ।
उपलभ्यात्मनात्मानं चक्षुषेवार्कमात्मदृक् ॥१०॥

nivṛtta-buddhy-avasthāno
dūrī-bhūtānya-darśanaḥ
upalabhyātmanātmānaṁ
cakṣuṣevārkam ātma-dṛk

nivṛtta—transcended; *buddhi-avasthānaḥ*—the stages of material consciousness; *dūrī-bhūta*—far off; *anya*—other; *darśanaḥ*—conceptions of life; *upalabhya*—having realized; *ātmanā*—by his purified intellect; *ātmānam*—his own self; *cakṣuṣā*—with his eyes; *iva*—as; *arkam*—the sun; *ātma-dṛk*—the self-realized.

TRANSLATION

One should be situated in the transcendental position, beyond the stages of material consciousness, and should be aloof from all

other conceptions of life. Thus realizing freedom from false ego, one should see his own self just as he sees the sun in the sky.

PURPORT

Consciousness acts in three stages under the material conception of life. When we are awake, consciousness acts in a particular way, when we are asleep it acts in a different way, and when we are in deep sleep, consciousness acts in still another way. To become Kṛṣṇa conscious, one has to become transcendental to these three stages of consciousness. Our present consciousness should be freed from all perceptions of life other than consciousness of Kṛṣṇa, the Supreme Personality of Godhead. This is called *dūrī-bhūtānya-darśanaḥ*, which means that when one attains perfect Kṛṣṇa consciousness he does not see anything but Kṛṣṇa. In the *Caitanya-caritāmṛta* it is said that the perfect devotee may see many movable and immovable objects, but in everything he sees that the energy of Kṛṣṇa is acting. As soon as he remembers the energy of Kṛṣṇa, he immediately remembers Kṛṣṇa in His personal form. Therefore in all his observations he sees Kṛṣṇa only. In the *Brahma-saṁhitā* (5.38) it is stated that when one's eyes are smeared with love of Kṛṣṇa (*premāñjana-cchurita*), he always sees Kṛṣṇa, outside and inside. This is confirmed here; one should be freed from all other vision, and in that way he is freed from the false egoistic identification and sees himself as the eternal servitor of the Lord. *Cakṣuṣevārkam:* as we can see the sun without a doubt, one who is fully developed in Kṛṣṇa consciousness sees Kṛṣṇa and His energy. By this vision one becomes *ātma-dṛk*, or self-realized. When the false ego of identifying the body with the self is removed, actual vision of life is perceivable. The senses, therefore, also become purified. Real service of the Lord begins when the senses are purified. One does not have to stop the activities of the senses, but the false ego of identifying with the body has to be removed. Then the senses automatically become purified, and with purified senses one can actually discharge devotional service.

TEXT 11

मुक्तलिङ्गं सदाभासमसति प्रतिपद्यते ।
सतो बन्धुमसच्चक्षुः सर्वानुस्यूतमद्वयम् ॥११॥

mukta-liṅgaṁ sad-ābhāsam
asati pratipadyate
sato bandhum asac-cakṣuḥ
sarvānusyūtam advayam

mukta-liṅgam—transcendental; *sat-ābhāsam*—manifest as a reflection; *asati*—in the false ego; *pratipadyate*—he realizes; *sataḥ bandhum*—the support of the material cause; *asat-cakṣuḥ*—the eye (revealer) of the illusory energy; *sarva-anusyūtam*—entered into everything; *advayam*—without a second.

TRANSLATION

A liberated soul realizes the Absolute Personality of Godhead, who is transcendental and who is manifest as a reflection even in the false ego. He is the support of the material cause and He enters into everything. He is absolute, one without a second, and He is the eyes of the illusory energy.

PURPORT

A pure devotee can see the presence of the Supreme Personality of Godhead in everything materially manifested. He is present there only as a reflection, but a pure devotee can realize that in the darkness of material illusion the only light is the Supreme Lord, who is its support. It is confirmed in *Bhagavad-gītā* that the background of the material manifestation is Lord Kṛṣṇa. And, as confirmed in the *Brahma-saṁhitā*, Kṛṣṇa is the cause of all causes. In the *Brahma-saṁhitā* it is stated that the Supreme Lord, by His partial or plenary expansion, is present not only within this universe and each and every universe, but in every atom, although He is one without a second. The word *advayam*, "without a second," which is used in this verse, indicates that although the Supreme Personality of Godhead is represented in everything, including the atoms, He is not divided. His presence in everything is explained in the next verse.

TEXT 12

यथा जलस्थ आभासः स्थलस्थेनावदृश्यते ।
स्वाभासेन तथा सूर्यो जलस्थेन दिवि स्थितः ॥१२॥

yathā jala-stha ābhāsaḥ
sthala-sthenāvadṛśyate
svābhāsena tathā sūryo
jala-sthena divi sthitaḥ

yathā—as; *jala-sthaḥ*—situated on water; *ābhāsaḥ*—a reflection; *sthala-sthena*—situated on the wall; *avadṛśyate*—is perceived; *sva-ābhāsena*—by its reflection; *tathā*—in that way; *sūryaḥ*—the sun; *jala-sthena*—situated on the water; *divi*—in the sky; *sthitaḥ*—situated.

TRANSLATION

The presence of the Supreme Lord can be realized just as the sun is realized first as a reflection on water, and again as a second reflection on the wall of a room, although the sun itself is situated in the sky.

PURPORT

The example given herewith is perfect. The sun is situated in the sky, far, far away from the surface of the earth, but its reflection can be seen in a pot of water in the corner of a room. The room is dark, and the sun is far away in the sky, but the sun's reflection on the water illuminates the darkness of the room. A pure devotee can realize the presence of the Supreme Personality of Godhead in everything by the reflection of His energy. In the *Viṣṇu Purāṇa* it is stated that as the presence of fire is understood by heat and light, so the Supreme Personality of Godhead, although one without a second, is perceived everywhere by the diffusion of His different energies. It is confirmed in the *Īśopaniṣad* that the presence of the Lord is perceived everywhere by the liberated soul, just as the sunshine and the reflection can be perceived everywhere although the sun is situated far away from the surface of the globe.

TEXT 13

एवं त्रिवृदहङ्कारो भूतेन्द्रियमनोमयैः ।
स्वाभासैर्लक्षितोऽनेन सदाभासेन सत्यदृक् ॥१३॥

evaṁ trivṛd-ahaṅkāro
bhūtendriya-manomayaiḥ

svābhāsair lakṣito 'nena
sad-ābhāsena satya-dṛk

evam—thus; *tri-vṛt*—the threefold; *ahaṅkāraḥ*—false ego; *bhūta-indriya-manaḥ-mayaiḥ*—consisting of body, senses and mind; *sva-ābhāsaiḥ*—by its own reflections; *lakṣitaḥ*—is revealed; *anena*—by this; *sat-ābhāsena*—by a reflection of Brahman; *satya-dṛk*—the self-realized soul.

TRANSLATION

The self-realized soul is thus reflected first in the threefold ego and then in the body, senses and mind.

PURPORT

The conditioned soul thinks, "I am this body," but a liberated soul thinks, "I am not this body. I am spirit soul." This "I am" is called ego, or identification of the self. "I am this body" or "Everything in relationship to the body is mine" is called false ego, but when one is self-realized and thinks that he is an eternal servitor of the Supreme Lord, that identification is real ego. One conception is in the darkness of the threefold qualities of material nature—goodness, passion and ignorance—and the other is in the pure state of goodness, called *śuddha-sattva* or *vāsudeva.* When we say that we give up our ego, this means that we give up our false ego, but real ego is always present. When one is reflected through the material contamination of the body and mind in false identification, he is in the conditional state, but when he is reflected in the pure stage he is called liberated. The identification of oneself with one's material possessions in the conditional stage must be purified, and one must identify himself in relationship with the Supreme Lord. In the conditioned state one accepts everything as an object of sense gratification, and in the liberated state one accepts everything for the service of the Supreme Lord. Kṛṣṇa consciousness, devotional service, is the actual liberated stage of a living entity. Otherwise, both accepting and rejecting on the material platform or in voidness or impersonalism are imperfect conditions for the pure soul.

By the understanding of the pure soul, called *satya-dṛk,* one can see everything as a reflection of the Supreme Personality of Godhead. A concrete example can be given in this connection. A conditioned soul sees a very beautiful rose, and he thinks that the nice aromatic flower should be used for his own sense gratification. This is one kind of vision. A liberated soul, however, sees the same flower as a reflection of the Supreme Lord. He thinks, "This beautiful flower is made possible by the superior energy of the Supreme Lord; therefore it belongs to the Supreme Lord and should be utilized in His service." These are two kinds of vision. The conditioned soul sees the flower for his own enjoyment, and the devotee sees the flower as an object to be used in the service of the Lord. In the same way, one can see the reflection of the Supreme Lord in one's own senses, mind and body—in everything. With that correct vision, one can engage everything in the service of the Lord. It is stated in the *Bhakti-rasāmṛta-sindhu* that one who has engaged everything—his vital energy, his wealth, his intelligence and his words—in the service of the Lord, or who desires to engage all these in the service of the Lord, no matter how he is situated, is to be considered a liberated soul, or *satya-dṛk.* Such a man has understood things as they are.

TEXT 14

भूतसूक्ष्मेन्द्रियमनोबुद्ध्यादिष्विह निद्रया ।
लीनेष्वसति यस्तत्र विनिद्रो निरहंक्रियः ॥१४॥

bhūta-sūkṣmendriya-mano-
buddhy-ādiṣv iha nidrayā
līneṣv asati yas tatra
vinidro nirahaṅkriyaḥ

bhūta—the material elements; *sūkṣma*—the objects of enjoyment; *indriya*—the material senses; *manaḥ*—mind; *buddhi*—intelligence; *ādiṣu*—and so on; *iha*—here; *nidrayā*—by sleep; *līneṣu*—merged; *asati*—in the unmanifest; *yaḥ*—who; *tatra*—there; *vinidraḥ*—awake; *nirahaṅkriyaḥ*—freed from false ego.

TRANSLATION

Although a devotee appears to be merged in the five material elements, the objects of material enjoyment, the material senses

and material mind and intelligence, he is understood to be awake and to be freed from the false ego.

PURPORT

The explanation by Rūpa Gosvāmī in the *Bhakti-rasāmṛta-sindhu* of how a person can be liberated even in this body is more elaborately explained in this verse. The living entity who has become *satya-dṛk,* who realizes his position in relationship with the Supreme Personality of Godhead, may remain apparently merged in the five elements of matter, the five material sense objects, the ten senses and the mind and intelligence, but still he is considered to be awake and to be freed from the reaction of false ego. Here the word *līna* is very significant. The Māyāvādī philosophers recommend merging in the impersonal effulgence of Brahman; that is their ultimate goal, or destination. That merging is also mentioned here. But in spite of merging, one can keep his individuality. The example given by Jīva Gosvāmī is that a green bird that enters a green tree appears to merge in the color of greenness, but actually the bird does not lose its individuality. Similarly, a living entity merged either in the material nature or in the spiritual nature does not give up his individuality. Real individuality is to understand oneself to be the eternal servitor of the Supreme Lord. This information is received from the mouth of Lord Caitanya. He said clearly, upon the inquiry of Sanātana Gosvāmī, that *a living entity is the servitor of Kṛṣṇa eternally.* Kṛṣṇa also confirms in *Bhagavad-gītā* that the living entity is eternally His part and parcel. The part and parcel is meant to serve the whole. This is individuality. It is so even in this material existence, when the living entity apparently merges in matter. His gross body is made up of five elements, his subtle body is made of mind, intelligence, false ego and contaminated consciousness, and he has five active senses and five knowledge-acquiring senses. In this way he merges in matter. But even while merged in the twenty-four elements of matter, he can keep his individuality as the eternal servitor of the Lord. Either in the spiritual nature or in the material nature, such a servitor is to be considered a liberated soul. That is the explanation of the authorities, and it is confirmed in this verse.

TEXT 15

मन्यमानस्तदात्मानमनष्टो नष्टवन्मृषा ।
नष्टेऽहङ्करणे द्रष्टा नष्टवित्त इवातुरः ॥१५॥

manyamānas tadātmānam
anaṣṭo naṣṭavan mṛṣā
naṣṭe 'haṅkaraṇe draṣṭā
naṣṭa-vitta ivāturaḥ

manyamānaḥ—thinking; *tadā*—then; *ātmānam*—himself; *anaṣṭaḥ*—although not lost; *naṣṭa-vat*—as lost; *mṛṣā*—falsely; *naṣṭe ahaṅkaraṇe*—because of the disappearance of the ego; *draṣṭā*—the seer; *naṣṭa-vittaḥ*—one who has lost his fortune; *iva*—like; *āturaḥ*—distressed.

TRANSLATION

The living entity can vividly feel his existence as the seer, but because of the disappearance of the ego during the state of deep sleep, he falsely takes himself to be lost, like a man who has lost his fortune and feels distressed, thinking himself to be lost.

PURPORT

Only in ignorance does a living entity think that he is lost. If by attainment of knowledge he comes to the real position of his eternal existence, he knows that he is not lost. An appropriate example is mentioned herein: *naṣṭa-vitta ivāturaḥ.* A person who has lost a great sum of money may think that he is lost, but actually he is not lost—only his money is lost. But due to his absorption in the money or identification with the money, he thinks that he is lost. Similarly, when we falsely identify with matter as our field of activities, we think that we are lost, although actually we are not. As soon as a person is awakened to the pure knowledge of understanding that he is an eternal servitor of the Lord, his own real position is revived. A living entity can never be lost. When one forgets his identity in deep sleep, he becomes absorbed in dreams, and he may think himself a different person or may think himself lost. But actually his identity is intact. This concept of being lost is due to false ego, and it continues as long as one is not awakened to the sense of his existence as an eternal servitor of the Lord. The Māyāvādī philosophers' concept of becoming one with the Supreme Lord is another symptom of being lost in false ego. One may falsely claim that he is the Supreme Lord, but actually he is not. This is the last snare of *māyā*'s influence upon the living entity. To think oneself equal with the Supreme Lord or to think oneself to be the Supreme Lord Himself is also due to false ego.

TEXT 16

एवं प्रत्यवमृश्यासावात्मानं प्रतिपद्यते ।
साहङ्कारस्य द्रव्यस्य योऽवस्थानमनुग्रहः ॥१६॥

evaṁ pratyavamṛśyāsāv
ātmānaṁ pratipadyate
sāhaṅkārasya dravyasya
yo 'vasthānam anugrahaḥ

evam—thus; *pratyavamṛśya*—after understanding; *asau*—that person; *ātmānam*—his self; *pratipadyate*—realizes; *sa-ahaṅkārasya*—accepted under false ego; *dravyasya*—of the situation; *yaḥ*—who; *avasthānam*—resting place; *anugrahaḥ*—the manifester.

TRANSLATION

When, by mature understanding, one can realize his individuality, then the situation he accepts under false ego becomes manifest to him.

PURPORT

The Māyāvādī philosophers' position is that at the ultimate issue the individual is lost, everything becomes one, and there is no distinction between the knower, the knowable and knowledge. But by minute analysis we can see that this is not correct. Individuality is never lost, even when one thinks that the three different principles, namely the knower, the knowable and knowledge, are amalgamated or merged into one. The very concept that the three merge into one is another form of knowledge, and since the perceiver of the knowledge still exists, how can one say that the knower, knowledge and knowable have become one? The individual soul who is perceiving this knowledge still remains an individual. Both in material existence and in spiritual existence the individuality continues; the only difference is in the quality of the identity. In the material identity, the false ego acts, and because of false identification, one takes things to be different from what they actually are. That is the basic principle of conditional life. Similarly, when the false ego is purified, one takes everything in the right perspective. That is the state of liberation.

It is stated in the *Īśopaniṣad* that everything belongs to the Lord. *Īśāvāsyam idaṁ sarvam.* Everything exists on the energy of the Supreme Lord. This is also confirmed in *Bhagavad-gītā.* Because everything is produced of His energy and exists on His energy, the energy is not different from Him—but still the Lord declares, "I am not there." When one clearly understands one's constitutional position, everything becomes manifest. False egoistic acceptance of things conditions one, whereas acceptance of things as they are makes one liberated. The example given in the previous verse is applicable here: due to absorption of one's identity in his money, when the money is lost he thinks that he is also lost. But actually he is not identical with the money, nor does the money belong to him. When the actual situation is revealed, we understand that the money does not belong to any individual person or living entity, nor is it produced by man. Ultimately the money is the property of the Supreme Lord, and there is no question of its being lost. But as long as one falsely thinks, "I am the enjoyer," or "I am the Lord," this concept of life continues, and one remains conditioned. As soon as this false ego is eliminated, one is liberated. As confirmed in the *Bhāgavatam,* situation in one's real constitutional position is called *mukti,* or liberation.

TEXT 17

देवहूतिरुवाच
पुरुषं प्रकृतिर्ब्रह्मन्न विमुञ्चति कर्हिचित् ।
अन्योन्यापाश्रयत्वाच्च नित्यत्वादनयोः प्रभो ॥१७॥

devahūtir uvāca
puruṣaṁ prakṛtir brahman

na vimuñcati karhicit
anyonyāpāśrayatvāc ca
nityatvād anayoḥ prabho

devahūtiḥ uvāca—Devahūti said; *puruṣam*—the spirit soul; *prakṛtiḥ*—material nature; *brahman*—O *brāhmaṇa; na*—not; *vimuñcati*—does release; *karhicit*—at any time; *anyonya*—to one another; *apāśrayatvāt*—from attraction; *ca*—and; *nityatvāt*—from eternality; *anayoḥ*—of them both; *prabho*—O my Lord.

TRANSLATION

Śrī Devahūti inquired: My dear brāhmaṇa, does material nature ever give release to the spirit soul? Since one is attracted to the other eternally, how is their separation possible?

PURPORT

Devahūti, the mother of Kapiladeva, here makes her first inquiry. Although one may understand that spirit soul and matter are different, their actual separation is not possible, either by philosophical speculation or by proper understanding. The spirit soul is the marginal potency of the Supreme Lord, and matter is the external potency of the Lord. The two eternal potencies have somehow or other been combined, and since it is so difficult to separate one from the other, how is it possible for the individual soul to become liberated? By practical experience one can see that when the soul is separated from the body, the body has no real existence, and when the body is separated from the soul one cannot perceive the existence of the soul. As long as the soul and the body are combined, we can understand that there is life. But when they are separated, there is no manifested existence of the body or the soul. This question asked by Devahūti of Kapiladeva is more or less impelled by the philosophy of voidism. The voidists say that consciousness is a product of a combination of matter and that as soon as the consciousness is gone, the material combination dissolves, and therefore there is ultimately nothing but voidness. This absence of consciousness is called *nirvāṇa* in Māyāvāda philosophy.

TEXT 18

यथा गन्धस्य भूमेश्च न भावो व्यतिरेकतः ।
अपां रसस्य च यथा तथा बुद्धेः परस्य च ॥१८॥

yathā gandhasya bhūmeś ca
na bhāvo vyatirekataḥ
apāṁ rasasya ca yathā
tathā buddheḥ parasya ca

yathā—as; *gandhasya*—of aroma; *bhūmeḥ*—of earth; *ca*—and; *na*—no; *bhāvaḥ*—existence; *vyatirekataḥ*—separate; *apām*—of water; *rasasya*—of taste; *ca*—and; *yathā*—as; *tathā*—so; *buddheḥ*—of intelligence; *parasya*—of consciousness, spirit; *ca*—and.

TRANSLATION

As there is no separate existence of the earth and its aroma or of water and its taste, there cannot be any separate existence of intelligence and consciousness.

PURPORT

The example is given here that anything material has an aroma. The flower, the earth—everything—has an aroma. If the aroma is separated from the matter, the matter cannot be identified. If there is no taste to water, the water has no meaning; if there is no heat in the fire, the fire has no meaning. Similarly, when there is want of intelligence, spirit has no meaning.

TEXT 19

अकर्तुः कर्मबन्धोऽयं पुरुषस्य यदाश्रयः ।
गुणेषु सत्सु प्रकृतेः कैवल्यं तेष्वतः कथम् ॥१९॥

akartuḥ karma-bandho 'yaṁ
puruṣasya yad-āśrayaḥ
guṇeṣu satsu prakṛteḥ
kaivalyaṁ teṣv ataḥ katham

akartuḥ—of the passive performer, the nondoer; *karma-bandhaḥ*—bondage to fruitive activities; *ayam*—this; *puruṣasya*—of the soul; *yat-āśrayaḥ*—caused by attachment to the modes; *guṇeṣu*—while the modes; *satsu*—are existing; *prakṛteḥ*—of material nature; *kaivalyam*—freedom; *teṣu*—those; *ataḥ*—hence; *katham*—how.

TRANSLATION

Hence even though he is the passive performer of all activities, how can there be freedom for the soul as long as material nature acts on him and binds him?

PURPORT

Although the living entity desires freedom from the contamination of matter, he is not given release. Actually, as soon as a living entity puts himself under the control of the modes of material nature, his acts are influenced by the qualities of material nature, and he becomes passive. It is confirmed in *Bhagavad-gītā, prakṛteḥ kriyamāṇāni guṇaiḥ:* the living entity acts according to the qualities or modes of material nature. He falsely thinks that he is acting, but unfortunately he is passive. In other words, he has no opportunity to get out of the control of material nature because it has already conditioned him. In *Bhagavad-gītā* it is also stated that it is very difficult to get out of the clutches of material nature. One may try in different ways to think that everything is void in the ultimate issue, that there is no God and that even if the background of everything is spirit, it is impersonal. This speculation may go on, but actually it is very difficult to get out of the clutches of material nature. Devahūti poses the question that although one may speculate in many ways, where is liberation as long as one is under the spell of material nature? The answer is also found in *Bhagavad-gītā* (7.14): only one who has surrendered himself unto the lotus feet of the Supreme Lord Kṛṣṇa (*mām eva ye prapadyante*) can be freed from the clutches of *māyā.*

Since Devahūti is gradually coming to the point of surrender, her questions are very intelligent. How can one be liberated? How can one be in a pure state of spiritual existence as long as he is strongly held by the modes of material nature? This is also an indication to the false meditator. There are many so-called meditators who think, "I am the Supreme Spirit Soul. I am conducting the activities of material nature. Under my direction the sun is moving and the moon is rising." They think that by such contemplation or meditation they can become free, but it is seen that just three minutes after finishing such nonsensical meditation, they are immediately captured by the modes of material nature. Immediately after his high-sounding meditation, a "meditator" becomes thirsty and wants to smoke or drink. He is under the strong grip of material nature, yet he thinks that he is already free from the clutches of *māyā.* This question of Devahūti's is for such a person who falsely claims that he is everything, that ultimately everything is void, and that there are no sinful or pious activities. These are all atheistic inventions. Actually, unless a living entity surrenders unto the Supreme Personality of Godhead as instructed in *Bhagavad-gītā,* there is no liberation or freedom from the clutches of *māyā.*

TEXT 20

क्वचित् तत्त्वावमर्शेन निवृत्तं भयमुल्बणम् ।
अनिवृत्तनिमित्तत्वात्पुनः प्रत्यवतिष्ठते ॥२०॥

kvacit tattvāvamarśena
nivṛttaṁ bhayam ulbaṇam
anivṛtta-nimittatvāt
punaḥ pratyavatiṣṭhate

kvacit—in a certain case; *tattva*—the fundamental principles; *avamarśena*—by reflecting upon; *nivṛttam*—avoided; *bhayam*—fear; *ulbaṇam*—great; *anivṛtta*—not ceased; *nimittatvāt*—since the cause; *punaḥ*—again; *pratyavatiṣṭhate*—it appears.

TRANSLATION

Even if the great fear of bondage is avoided by mental speculation and inquiry into the fundamental principles, it may still appear again, since its cause has not ceased.

PURPORT

Material bondage is caused by putting oneself under the control of matter because of the false ego of lording it over material nature. *Bhagavad-gītā* (7.27) states, *icchā-dveṣa-samutthena.* Two kinds of propensities arise in the living entity. One propensity is *icchā*, which means desire to lord it over material nature or to be as great as the Supreme Lord. Everyone desires to be the greatest personality in this material world. *Dveṣa* means "envy." When one becomes envious of Kṛṣṇa, or the Supreme Personality of Godhead, one thinks, "Why should Kṛṣṇa be the all and all? I'm as good as Kṛṣṇa." These two items, desire to be the Lord and envy of the Lord, are the beginning cause of material bondage. As long as a philosopher, salvationist or voidist has some desire to be supreme, to be everything, or to deny the existence of God, the cause remains, and there is no question of his liberation.

Devahūti very intelligently says, "One may theoretically analyze and say that by knowledge he has become freed, but actually, as long as the cause exists, he is not free." *Bhagavad-gītā* confirms that after performing such speculative activities for many, many births, when one actually comes to his real consciousness and surrenders unto the Supreme Lord, Kṛṣṇa, then the fulfillment of his research in knowledge is actually achieved. There is a gulf of difference between theoretical freedom and actual freedom from material bondage. The *Bhāgavatam* (10.14.4) says that if one gives up the auspicious path of devotional service and simply tries to know things by speculation, one wastes his valuable time (*kliśyanti ye kevala-bodha-labdhaye*). The result of such a labor of love is simply labor; there is no other result. The labor of speculation is ended only by exhaustion. The example is given that there is no benefit in husking the skin of an empty paddy; the rice is already gone. Similarly, simply by the speculative process one cannot be freed from material bondage, for the cause still exists. One has to nullify the cause, and then the effect will be nullified. This is explained by the Supreme Personality of Godhead in the following verses.

TEXT 21

श्रीभगवानुवाच
अनिमित्तनिमित्तेन स्वधर्मेणामलात्मना ।
तीव्रया मयि भक्त्या च श्रुतसम्भृतया चिरम् ॥२१॥

śrī-bhagavān uvāca
animitta-nimittena
sva-dharmeṇāmalātmanā

tīvrayā mayi bhaktyā ca
śruta-sambhṛtayā ciram

śrī-bhagavān uvāca—the Supreme Personality of Godhead said; *animitta-nimittena*—without desiring the fruits of activities; *sva-dharmeṇa*—by executing one's prescribed duties; *amala-ātmanā*—with a pure mind; *tīvrayā*—serious; *mayi*—unto Me; *bhaktyā*—by devotional service; *ca*—and; *śruta*—hearing; *sambhṛtayā*—endowed with; *ciram*—for a long time.

TRANSLATION

The Supreme Personality of Godhead said: One can get liberation by seriously discharging devotional service unto Me and thereby hearing for a long time about Me or from Me. By thus executing one's prescribed duties, there will be no reaction, and one will be freed from the contamination of matter.

PURPORT

Śrīdhara Svāmī comments in this connection that by association with material nature alone one does not become conditioned. Conditional life begins only after one is infected by the modes of material nature. If someone is in contact with the police department, that does not mean that he is a criminal. As long as one does not commit criminal acts, even though there is a police department, he is not punished. Similarly, the liberated soul is not affected, although he is in the material nature. Even the Supreme Personality of Godhead is supposed to be in association with material nature when He descends, but He is not affected. One has to act in such a way that in spite of being in the material nature he is not affected by contamination. Although the lotus flower is in association with water, it does not mix with the water. That is how one has to live, as described here by the Personality of Godhead Kapiladeva (*animitta-nimittena sva-dharmeṇāmalātmanā*).

One can be liberated from all adverse circumstances simply by seriously engaging in devotional service. How this devotional service develops and becomes mature is explained here. In the beginning one has to perform his prescribed duties with a clean mind. Clean consciousness means Kṛṣṇa consciousness. One has to perform his prescribed duties in Kṛṣṇa consciousness. There is no necessity of changing one's prescribed duties; one simply has to act in Kṛṣṇa consciousness. In discharging Kṛṣṇa conscious duties, one should determine whether, by his professional or occupational duties, Kṛṣṇa, the Supreme Personality of Godhead, is satisfied. In another place in the *Bhāgavatam* it is said, *svanuṣṭhitasya dharmasya saṁsiddhir hari-toṣaṇam:* everyone has some prescribed duties to perform, but the perfection of such duties will be reached only if the Supreme Personality of Godhead, Hari, is satisfied by such actions. For example, Arjuna's prescribed duty was to fight, and the perfection of his fighting was tested by the satisfaction of Kṛṣṇa. Kṛṣṇa wanted him to fight, and when he fought for the satisfaction of the Lord, that was the perfection of his professional devotional duty. On the other hand, when, contrary to the wish of Kṛṣṇa, he was not willing to fight, that was imperfect.

If one wants to perfect his life, he should discharge his prescribed duties for the satisfaction of Kṛṣṇa. One must act in Kṛṣṇa consciousness, for such action will never produce any reaction (*animitta-nimittena*). This is also confirmed in *Bhagavad-gītā. Yajñārthāt karmaṇo 'nyatra:* all activities should be performed simply for Yajña, or the satisfaction of Viṣṇu. Anything done otherwise, without the satisfaction of Viṣṇu, or Yajña, produces bondage, so here it is also prescribed by Kapila Muni that one can transcend material entanglement by acting in Kṛṣṇa consciousness, which means seriously engaging in devotional service. This serious devotional service can develop by hearing for long periods of time. Chanting and hearing is the beginning of the process of devotional service. One should associate with devotees and hear from them about the Lord's transcendental appearance, activities, disappearance, instructions, etc.

There are two kinds of *śruti*, or scripture. One is spoken by the Lord, and the other is spoken about the Lord and His devotees. *Bhagavad-gītā* is the former and *Śrīmad-Bhāgavatam* the latter. One must hear these scriptures repeatedly from reliable sources in order to become fixed in serious devotional service. Through engagement in such devotional service, one becomes freed from the contamination of *māyā*. It is stated in the *Śrīmad-Bhāgavatam* that hearing about the Supreme Personality of Godhead cleanses the heart of all contamination caused by the influence of the three modes of material nature. By continuous, regular hearing, the effects of the contamination of lust and greed to enjoy or lord it over material nature diminish, and when lust and greed diminish, one then becomes situated in the mode of goodness. This is the stage of Brahman realization, or spiritual realization. In this way one becomes fixed on the transcendental platform. Remaining fixed on the transcendental platform is liberation from material entanglement.

TEXT 22

ज्ञानेन दृष्टतत्त्वेन वैराग्येण बलीयसा ।
तपोयुक्तेन योगेन तीव्रेणात्मसमाधिना ॥२२॥

jñānena dṛṣṭa-tattvena
vairāgyeṇa balīyasā
tapo-yuktena yogena
tīvreṇātma-samādhinā

jñānena—in knowledge; *dṛṣṭa-tattvena*—with vision of the Absolute Truth; *vairāgyeṇa*—with renunciation; *balīyasā*—very strong; *tapaḥ-yuktena*—by engagement in austerity; *yogena*—by mystic *yoga;* *tīvreṇa*—firmly fixed; *ātma-samādhinā*—by self-absorption.

TRANSLATION

This devotional service has to be performed strongly in perfect knowledge and with transcendental vision. One must be strongly renounced and must engage in austerity and perform mystic yoga in order to be firmly fixed in self-absorption.

PURPORT

Devotional service in Kṛṣṇa consciousness cannot be performed blindly due to material emotion or mental concoction. It is specifically mentioned here that one has to perform devotional service in full knowledge by visualizing the Absolute Truth. We can understand about the Absolute Truth by evolving transcendental knowledge, and the result of such transcendental knowledge will be manifested by renunciation. That renunciation is not temporary or artificial, but is very strong. It is said that development of Kṛṣṇa consciousness is exhibited by proportionate material detachment, or *vairāgya.* If one does not separate himself from material enjoyment, it is to be understood that he is not advancing in Kṛṣṇa consciousness. Renunciation in Kṛṣṇa consciousness is so strong that it cannot be deviated by any attractive illusion. One has to perform devotional service in full *tapasya,* austerity. One should fast on the two Ekādaśī days, which fall on the eleventh day of the waxing and waning moon, and on the birthdays of Lord Kṛṣṇa, Lord Rāma and Caitanya Mahāprabhu. There are many such fasting days. *Yogena* means "by controlling the senses and mind." *Yoga indriya-saṁyamaḥ. Yogena* implies that one is seriously absorbed in the self and is able, by development of knowledge, to understand his constitutional position in relationship with the Superself. In this way one becomes fixed in devotional service, and his faith cannot be shaken by any material allurement.

TEXT 23

प्रकृतिः पुरुषस्येह दह्यमाना त्वहर्निशम् ।
तिरोभवित्री शनकैरग्नेर्योनिरिवारणिः ॥२३॥

prakṛtiḥ puruṣasyeha
dahyamānā tv ahar-niśam
tiro-bhavitrī śanakair
agner yonir ivāraṇiḥ

prakṛtiḥ—the influence of material nature; *puruṣasya*—of the living entity; *iha*—here; *dahyamānā*—being consumed; *tu*—but; *ahaḥ-niśam*—day and night; *tiraḥ-bhavitrī*—disappearing; *śanakaiḥ*—gradually; *agneḥ*—of fire; *yoniḥ*—the cause of appearance; *iva*—as; *araṇiḥ*—wooden sticks.

TRANSLATION

The influence of material nature has covered the living entity, and thus it is as if the living entity were always in a blazing fire.

But by the process of seriously discharging devotional service, this influence can be removed, just as wooden sticks which cause a fire are themselves consumed by it.

PURPORT

Fire is conserved in wooden sticks, and when circumstances are favorable, the fire is ignited. But the wooden sticks which are the cause of the fire are also consumed by the fire if it is properly dealt with. Similarly, the living entity's conditional life of material existence is due to his desire to lord it over material nature and due to his envy of the Supreme Lord. Thus his main diseases are that he wants to be one with the Supreme Lord or he wants to become the lord of material nature. The *karmīs* try to utilize the resources of material nature and thus become its lord and enjoy sense gratification, and the *jñānīs*, the salvationists, who have become frustrated in enjoying the material resources, want to become one with the Supreme Personality of Godhead or merge into the impersonal effulgence. These two diseases are due to material contamination. Material contamination can be consumed by devotional service because in devotional service these two diseases, namely the desire to lord it over material nature and the desire to become one with the Supreme Lord, are absent. Therefore the cause of material existence is at once consumed by the careful discharge of devotional service in Kṛṣṇa consciousness.

A devotee in full Kṛṣṇa consciousness appears superficially to be a great *karmī*, always working, but the inner significance of the devotee's activities is that they are meant for the satisfaction of the Supreme Lord. This is called *bhakti*, or devotional service. Arjuna was apparently a fighter, but when by his fighting he satisfied the senses of Lord Kṛṣṇa, he became a devotee. Since a devotee also engages in philosophical research to understand the Supreme Person as He is, his activities may thus appear to be like those of a mental speculator, but actually he is trying to understand the spiritual nature and transcendental activities. Thus although the tendency for philosophical speculation exists, the material effects of fruitive activities and empiric speculation do not, because this activity is meant for the Supreme Personality of Godhead.

TEXT 24

भुक्तभोगा परित्यक्ता दृष्टदोषा च नित्यशः ।
नेश्वरस्याशुभं धत्ते स्वे महिम्नि स्थितस्य च ॥२४॥

bhukta-bhogā parityaktā
dṛṣṭa-doṣā ca nityaśaḥ
neśvarasyāśubhaṁ dhatte
sve mahimni sthitasya ca

bhukta—enjoyed; *bhogā*—enjoyment; *parityaktā*—given up; *dṛṣṭa*—discovered; *doṣā*—faultiness; *ca*—and; *nityaśaḥ*—always; *na*—not; *īśvarasya*—of the independent; *aśubham*—harm; *dhatte*—she inflicts; *sve mahimni*—in his own glory; *sthitasya*—situated; *ca*—and.

TRANSLATION

By discovering the faultiness of his desiring to lord it over material nature and by therefore giving it up, the living entity becomes independent and stands in his own glory.

PURPORT

Because the living entity is not actually the enjoyer of the material resources, his attempt to lord it over material nature is, at the ultimate issue, frustrated. As a result of frustration, he desires more power than the ordinary living entity and thus wants to merge into the existence of the supreme enjoyer. In this way he develops a plan for greater enjoyment.

When one is actually situated in devotional service, that is his independent position. Less intelligent men cannot understand the position of the eternal servant of the Lord. Because the word "servant" is used, they become confused; they cannot understand that this servitude is not the servitude of this material world. To be the servant of the Lord is the greatest position. If one can understand this and can thus revive one's original nature of eternal servitorship of the Lord, one stands fully independent. A living entity's independence is lost by material contact. In the spiritual field he has full independence, and therefore there is no question of becoming dependent upon the three modes of material nature. This position is attained by a devotee, and therefore he gives up the tendency for material enjoyment after seeing its faultiness.

The difference between a devotee and an impersonalist is that an impersonalist tries to become one with the Supreme so that he can enjoy without impediment, whereas a devotee gives up the entire mentality of enjoying and engages in the transcendental loving service of the Lord. That is his constitutional glorified position. At that time he is *īśvara*, fully independent. The real *īśvara* or *īśvaraḥ paramaḥ*, the supreme *īśvara*, or supreme independent, is Kṛṣṇa. The living entity is *īśvara* only when engaged in the service of the Lord. In other words, transcendental pleasure derived from loving service to the Lord is actual independence.

TEXT 25

यथा ह्यप्रतिबुद्धस्य प्रस्वापो बह्वनर्थभृत् ।
स एव प्रतिबुद्धस्य न वै मोहाय कल्पते ॥२५॥

yathā hy apratibuddhasya
prasvāpo bahv-anartha-bhṛt
sa eva pratibuddhasya
na vai mohāya kalpate

yathā—as; *hi*—indeed; *apratibuddhasya*—of one who is sleeping; *prasvāpaḥ*—the dream; *bahu-anartha-bhṛt*—bearing many inauspicious things; *saḥ eva*—that very dream; *pratibuddhasya*—of one who is awake; *na*—not; *vai*—certainly; *mohāya*—for bewildering; *kalpate*—is capable.

TRANSLATION

In the dreaming state one's consciousness is almost covered, and one sees many inauspicious things, but when he is awakened and fully conscious, such inauspicious things cannot bewilder him.

PURPORT

In the condition of dreaming, when one's consciousness is almost covered, one may see many unfavorable things which cause disturbance or anxiety, but upon awakening, although he remembers what happened in the dream, he is not disturbed. Similarly the position of self-realization, or understanding of one's real relationship with the Supreme Lord, makes one completely satisfied, and the three modes of material nature, which are the cause of all disturbances, cannot affect him. In contaminated consciousness one sees everything to be for his own enjoyment, but in pure consciousness, or Kṛṣṇa consciousness, he sees that everything exists for the enjoyment of the supreme enjoyer. That is the difference between the dream state and wakefulness. The state of contaminated consciousness is compared to dream consciousness, and Kṛṣṇa consciousness is compared to the awakened stage of life. Actually, as stated in *Bhagavad-gītā*, the only absolute enjoyer is Kṛṣṇa. One who can understand that Kṛṣṇa is the proprietor of all the three worlds and that He is the friend of everyone is peaceful and independent. As long as a conditioned soul does not have this knowledge, he wants to be the enjoyer of everything; he wants to become a humanitarian or philanthropist and open hospitals and schools for his fellow human beings. This is all illusion, for one cannot benefit anyone by such material activities. If one wishes to benefit his fellow brother, he must awaken his dormant Kṛṣṇa consciousness. The Kṛṣṇa conscious position is that of *pratibuddha*, which means "pure consciousness."

TEXT 26

एवं विदिततत्त्वस्य प्रकृतिर्मयि मानसम् ।
युञ्जतो नापकुरुत आत्मारामस्य कर्हिचित् ॥२६॥

evaṁ vidita-tattvasya
prakṛtir mayi mānasam
yuñjato nāpakuruta
ātmārāmasya karhicit

evam—thus; *vidita-tattvasya*—to one who knows the Absolute Truth; *prakṛtiḥ*—material nature; *mayi*—on Me; *mānasam*—the mind; *yuñjataḥ*—fixing; *na*—not; *apakurute*—can do harm; *ātma-ārāmasya*—to one who rejoices in the self; *karhicit*—at any time.

TRANSLATION

The influence of material nature cannot harm an enlightened soul, even though he engages in material activities, because he knows the truth of the Absolute, and his mind is fixed on the Supreme Personality of Godhead.

PURPORT

Lord Kapila says that *mayi mānasam*, a devotee whose mind is always fixed upon the lotus feet of the Supreme Personality of Godhead, is called *ātmārāma* or *vidita-tattva. Ātmārāma* means "one who rejoices in the self," or "one who enjoys in the spiritual atmosphere." *Ātmā*, in the material sense, means the body or the mind, but when referring to one whose mind is fixed on the lotus feet of the Supreme Lord, *ātmārāma* means "one who is fixed in spiritual activities in relationship with the Supreme Soul." The Supreme Soul is the Personality of Godhead, and the individual soul is the living entity. When they engage in reciprocation of service and benediction, the living entity is said to be in the *ātmārāma* position. This *ātmārāma* position can be attained by one who knows the truth as it is. The truth is that the Supreme Personality of Godhead is the enjoyer and that the living entities are meant for His service and enjoyment. One who knows this truth, and who tries to engage all resources in the service of the Lord, escapes all material reactions and influences of the modes of material nature.

An example may be cited in this connection. Just as a materialist engages in constructing a big skyscraper, a devotee engages in constructing a big temple for Viṣṇu. Superficially, the skyscraper constructor and temple constructor are on the same level, for both are collecting wood, stone, iron and other building materials. But the person who constructs a skyscraper is a materialist, and the person who constructs a temple of Viṣṇu is *ātmārāma.* The materialist tries to satisfy himself in relation to his body by constructing a skyscraper, but the devotee tries to satisfy the Superself, the Supreme Personality of Godhead, by constructing the temple. Although both are engaged in the association of material activities, the devotee is liberated, and the materialist is conditioned. This is because the devotee, who is constructing the temple, has fixed his mind upon the Supreme Personality of Godhead, but the nondevotee, who is constructing the skyscraper, has his mind fixed in sense gratification. If, while performing any activity, even in material existence, one's mind is fixed upon the lotus feet of the Personality of Godhead, one will not be entangled or conditioned. The worker in devotional service, in full Kṛṣṇa consciousness, is always independent of the influence of material nature.

TEXT 27

यदैवमध्यात्मरतः कालेन बहुजन्मना ।
सर्वत्र जातवैराग्य आब्रह्मभुवनान्मुनिः ॥२७॥

yadaivam adhyātma-rataḥ
kālena bahu-janmanā
sarvatra jāta-vairāgya
ābrahma-bhuvanān muniḥ

yadā—when; *evam*—thus; *adhyātma-rataḥ*—engaged in self-realization; *kālena*—for many years; *bahu-janmanā*—for many births; *sarvatra*—everywhere; *jāta-vairāgyaḥ*—detachment is born; *ā-brahma-bhuvanāt*—up to Brahmaloka; *muniḥ*—a thoughtful person.

TRANSLATION

When a person thus engages in devotional service and self-realization for many, many years and births, he becomes completely reluctant to enjoy any one of the material planets, even up to the highest planet, which is known as Brahmaloka; he becomes fully developed in consciousness.

PURPORT

Anyone engaged in devotional service to the Supreme Personality of Godhead is known as a devotee, but there is a distinction between pure devotees and mixed devotees. A mixed devotee engages in devotional service for the spiritual benefit of being eternally engaged in the transcendental abode of the Lord in full bliss and knowledge. In material existence, when a devotee is not completely purified, he expects material benefit from the Lord in the form of relief from material miseries, or he wants material gain, advancement in knowledge of the relationship between the Supreme Personality of Godhead and the living entity, or knowledge as to the real nature of the Supreme Lord. When a person is transcendental to these conditions, he is called a pure devotee. He does not engage himself in the service of the Lord for any material benefit or for understanding of the Supreme Lord. His one interest is that he loves the Supreme Personality of Godhead, and he spontaneously engages in satisfying Him.

The highest example of pure devotional service is that of the *gopīs* in Vṛndāvana. They are not interested in understanding Kṛṣṇa, but only in loving Him. That platform of love is the pure state of devotional service. Unless one is advanced to this pure state of devotional service, there is a tendency to desire elevation to a higher material position. A mixed devotee may desire to enjoy a comfortable life on another planet with a greater span of life, such as on Brahmaloka. These are material desires, but because a mixed devotee engages in the service of the Lord, ultimately, after many, many lives of material enjoyment, he undoubtedly develops Kṛṣṇa consciousness, and the symptom of this Kṛṣṇa consciousness is that he is no longer interested in any sort of materially elevated life. He does not even aspire to become a personality like Lord Brahmā.

TEXTS 28–29

मद्भक्तः प्रतिबुद्धार्थो मत्प्रसादेन भूयसा ।
निःश्रेयसं स्वसंस्थानं कैवल्याख्यं मदाश्रयम् ॥२८॥
प्राप्नोतीहाञ्जसा धीरः स्वदृशाच्छिन्नसंशयः ।
यद्गत्वा न निवर्तेत योगी लिङ्गाद्विनिर्गमे ॥२९॥

mad-bhaktaḥ pratibuddhārtho
mat-prasādena bhūyasā
niḥśreyasaṁ sva-saṁsthānaṁ
kaivalyākhyaṁ mad-āśrayam

prāpnotīhāñjasā dhīraḥ
sva-dṛśā cchina-saṁśayaḥ

yad gatvā na nivarteta
yogī liṅgād vinirgame

mat-bhaktaḥ—My devotee; *pratibuddha-arthaḥ*—self-realized; *mat-prasādena*—by My causeless mercy; *bhūyasā*—unlimited; *niḥśreya-sam*—the ultimate perfectional goal; *sva-saṁsthānam*—his abode; *kaivalya-ākhyam*—called *kaivalya; mat-āśrayam*—under My protection; *prāpnoti*—attains; *iha*—in this life; *añjasā*—truly; *dhīraḥ*—steady; *sva-dṛśā*—by knowledge of the self; *chinna-saṁśayaḥ*—freed from doubts; *yat*—to that abode; *gatvā*—having gone; *na*—never; *nivarteta*—comes back; *yogī*—the mystic devotee; *liṅgāt*—from the subtle and gross material bodies; *vinirgame*—after departing.

TRANSLATION

My devotee actually becomes self-realized by My unlimited causeless mercy, and thus, when freed from all doubts, he steadily progresses towards his destined abode, which is directly under the protection of My spiritual energy of unadulterated bliss. That is the ultimate perfectional goal of the living entity. After giving up the present material body, the mystic devotee goes to that transcendental abode and never comes back.

PURPORT

Actual self-realization means becoming a pure devotee of the Lord. The existence of a devotee implies the function of devotion and the object of devotion. Self-realization ultimately means to understand the Personality of Godhead and the living entities; to know the individual self and the reciprocal exchanges of loving service between the Supreme Personality of Godhead and the living entity is real self-realization. This cannot be attained by the impersonalists or other transcendentalists; they cannot understand the science of devotional service. Devotional service is revealed to the pure devotee by the unlimited causeless mercy of the Lord. This is especially spoken of here by the Lord—*mat-prasādena*, "by My special grace." This is also confirmed in *Bhagavad-gītā.* Only those who engage in devotional service with love and faith receive the necessary intelligence from the Supreme Personality of Godhead so that gradually and progressively they can advance to the abode of the Personality of Godhead.

Niḥśreyasa means "the ultimate destination." *Sva-saṁsthāna* indicates that the impersonalists have no particular place to stay. The impersonalists sacrifice their individuality so that the living spark can merge into the impersonal effulgence emanating from the transcendental body of the Lord, but the devotee has a specific abode. The planets rest in the sunshine, but the sunshine itself has no particular resting place. When one reaches a particular planet, then he has a resting place. The spiritual sky, which is known as *kaivalya*, is simply blissful light on all sides, and it is under the protection of the Supreme Personality of Godhead. As stated in *Bhagavad-gītā* (14.27), *brāhmaṇo hi pratiṣṭhāham:* the impersonal Brahman effulgence rests on the body of the Supreme Personality of Godhead. In other words, the bodily effulgence of the Supreme Personality of Godhead is *kaivalya*, or impersonal Brahman. In that impersonal effulgence there are spiritual planets, which are known as Vaikuṇṭhas, chief of which is Kṛṣṇaloka. Some devotees are elevated to the Vaikuṇṭha planets, and some are elevated to the planet Kṛṣṇaloka. According to the desire of the particular devotee, he is offered a particular abode, which is known as *sva-saṁsthāna*, his desired destination. By the grace of the Lord, the self-realized devotee engaged in devotional service understands his destination even while in the material body. He therefore performs his devotional activities steadily, without doubting, and after quitting his material body he at once reaches the destination for which he has prepared himself. After reaching that abode, he never comes back to this material world.

The words *liṅgād vinirgame*, which are used here, mean "after being freed from the two kinds of material bodies, subtle and gross." The subtle body is made of mind, intelligence, false ego and contaminated consciousness, and the gross body is made of five elements—earth, water, fire, air and ether. When one is transferred to the spiritual world, he gives up both the subtle and gross bodies of this material world. He enters the spiritual sky in his pure, spiritual body and is stationed in one of the spiritual planets. Although the impersonalists also reach that spiritual sky after giving up the subtle and gross material bodies, they are not placed in the spiritual planets; as they desire, they are allowed to merge in the spiritual effulgence emanating from the transcendental body of the Lord. The word *sva-saṁsthānam* is also very significant. As a living entity prepares himself, so he attains his abode. The impersonal Brahman effulgence is offered to the impersonalists, but those who want to associate with the Supreme Personality of Godhead in His transcendental form as Nārāyaṇa in the Vaikuṇṭhas, or with Kṛṣṇa in Kṛṣṇaloka, go to those abodes, wherefrom they never return.

TEXT 30

यदा न योगोपचितासु चेतो
मायासु सिद्धस्य विषज्जतेऽङ्ग ।
अनन्यहेतुष्वथ मे गतिः स्याद्
आत्यन्तिकी यत्र न मृत्युहासः ॥३०॥

yadā na yogopacitāsu ceto
māyāsu siddhasya viṣajjate 'ṅga
ananya-hetuṣv atha me gatiḥ syād
ātyantikī yatra na mṛtyu-hāsaḥ

yadā—when; *na*—not; *yoga-upacitāsu*—to powers developed by *yoga; cetaḥ*—the attention; *māyāsu*—manifestations of *māyā; siddhasya*—of a perfect *yogī; viṣajjate*—is attracted; *aṅga*—My dear mother; *ananya-hetuṣu*—having no other cause; *atha*—then; *me*—to Me; *gatiḥ*—his progress; *syāt*—becomes; *ātyantikī*—unlimited; *yatra*—where; *na*—not; *mṛtyu-hāsaḥ*—power of death.

TRANSLATION

When a perfect yogī's attention is no longer attracted to the by-products of mystic powers, which are manifestations of the external energy, his progress towards Me becomes unlimited, and thus the power of death cannot overcome him.

PURPORT

Yogīs are generally attracted to the by-products of mystic yogic power, for they can become smaller than the smallest or greater than the greatest, achieve anything they desire, have power even to create a planet, or bring anyone they like under their subjection. *Yogīs* who have incomplete information of the result of devotional service are attracted by these powers, but these powers are material; they have nothing to do with spiritual progress. As other material powers are created by the material energy, mystic yogic powers are also material. A perfect *yogī*'s mind is not attracted by any material power, but is simply attracted by unalloyed service to the Supreme Lord. For a devotee, the process of merging into the Brahman effulgence is considered to be hellish, and yogic power or the preliminary perfection of yogic power, to be able to control the senses, is automatically achieved. As for elevation to higher planets, a devotee considers this to be simply hallucinatory. A devotee's attention is concentrated only upon the eternal loving service of the Lord, and therefore the power of death has no influence over him. In such a devotional state, a perfect *yogī* can attain the status of immortal knowledge and bliss.

Thus end the Bhaktivedanta purports of the Third Canto, Twenty-seventh Chapter, of the Śrīmad-Bhāgavatam, *entitled "Understanding Material Nature."*

CHAPTER TWENTY-EIGHT

Kapila's Instructions on the Execution of Devotional Service

TEXT 1

श्रीभगवानुवाच

योगस्य लक्षणं वक्ष्ये सबीजस्य नृपात्मजे ।
मनो येनैव विधिना प्रसन्नं याति सत्पथम् ॥ १ ॥

śrī-bhagavān uvāca
yogasya lakṣaṇaṁ vakṣye
sabījasya nṛpātmaje
mano yenaiva vidhinā
prasannaṁ yāti sat-patham

śrī-bhagavān uvāca—the Personality of Godhead said; *yogasya*—of the *yoga* system; *lakṣaṇam*—description; *vakṣye*—I shall explain; *sa-bījasya*—authorized; *nṛpa-ātma-je*—O daughter of the King; *manaḥ*—the mind; *yena*—by which; *eva*—certainly; *vidhinā*—by practice; *prasannam*—joyful; *yāti*—attains; *sat-patham*—the path of the Absolute Truth.

TRANSLATION

The Personality of Godhead said: My dear mother, O daughter of the King, now I shall explain to you the system of yoga, the object of which is to concentrate the mind. By practicing this system one can become joyful and progressively advance towards the path of the Absolute Truth.

PURPORT

The *yoga* process explained by Lord Kapiladeva in this chapter is authorized and standard, and therefore these instructions should be followed very carefully. To begin, the Lord says that by *yoga* practice one can make progress towards understanding the Absolute Truth, the Supreme Personality of Godhead. In the previous chapter it has been clearly stated that the desired result of *yoga* is not to achieve some wonderful mystic power. One should not be at all attracted by such mystic power, but should attain progressive realization on the path of understanding the Supreme Personality of Godhead. This is also confirmed in *Bhagavad-gītā*, which states in the last verse of the Sixth Chapter that the greatest *yogī* is he who constantly thinks of Kṛṣṇa within himself, or he who is Kṛṣṇa conscious.

It is stated here that by following the system of *yoga* one can become joyful. Lord Kapila, the Personality of Godhead, who is the highest authority on *yoga*, here explains the *yoga* system known as *aṣṭāṅga-yoga*, which comprises eight different practices, namely *yama*, *niyama*, *āsana*, *prāṇāyāma*, *pratyāhāra*, *dhāraṇā*, *dhyāna* and *samādhi*. By all these stages of practice one must realize Lord Viṣṇu, who is the target of all *yoga*. There are so-called *yoga* practices in which one concentrates the mind on voidness or on the impersonal, but this is not approved by the authorized *yoga* system as explained by Kapiladeva. Even Patañjali explains that the target of all *yoga* is Viṣṇu. *Aṣṭāṅga-yoga* is therefore part of Vaiṣṇava practice because its ultimate goal is realization of Viṣṇu. The achievement of success in *yoga* is not acquisition of mystic power, which is condemned in the previous chapter, but, rather, freedom from all material designations and situation in one's constitutional position. That is the ultimate achievement in *yoga* practice.

TEXT 2

स्वधर्माचरणं शक्त्या विधर्माच्च निवर्तनम् ।
दैवाल्लब्धेन सन्तोष आत्मविच्चरणार्चनम् ॥ २ ॥

sva-dharmācaraṇaṁ śaktyā
vidharmāc ca nivartanam
daivāl labdhena santoṣa
ātmavic-caraṇārcanam

sva-dharma-ācaraṇam—executing one's prescribed duties; *śaktyā*—to the best of one's ability; *vidharmāt*—unauthorized duties; *ca*—and;

nivartanam—avoiding; *daivāt*—by the grace of the Lord; *labdhena*—with what is achieved; *santoṣaḥ*—satisfied; *ātma-vit*—of the self-realized soul; *caraṇa*—the feet; *arcanam*—worshiping.

TRANSLATION

One should execute his prescribed duties to the best of his ability and avoid performing duties not allotted to him. One should be satisfied with as much gain as he achieves by the grace of the Lord, and one should worship the lotus feet of a spiritual master.

PURPORT

In this verse there are many important words which could be very elaborately explained, but we shall briefly discuss the important aspects of each. The final statement is *ātmavic-caraṇārcanam. Ātma-vit* means a self-realized soul or bona fide spiritual master. Unless one is self-realized and knows what his relationship with the Supersoul is, he cannot be a bona fide spiritual master. Here it is recommended that one should seek out a bona fide spiritual master and surrender unto him (*arcanam*), for by inquiring from and worshiping him one can learn spiritual activities.

The first recommendation is *sva-dharmācaraṇam.* As long as we have this material body there are various duties prescribed for us. Such duties are divided by a system of four social orders: *brāhmaṇa, kṣatriya, vaiśya* and *śūdra.* These particular duties are mentioned in the *śāstra*, and particularly in *Bhagavad-gītā. Sva-dharmācaraṇam* means that one must discharge the prescribed duties of his particular division of society faithfully and to the best of his ability. One should not accept another's duty. If one is born in a particular society or community, he should perform the prescribed duties for that particular division. If, however, one is fortunate enough to transcend the designation of birth in a particular society or community by being elevated to the standard of spiritual identity, then his *sva-dharma*, or duty, is solely that of serving the Supreme Personality of Godhead. The actual duty of one who is advanced in Kṛṣṇa consciousness is to serve the Lord. As long as one remains in the bodily concept of life, he may act according to the duties of social convention, but if one is elevated to the spiritual platform, he must simply serve the Supreme Lord; that is the real execution of *sva-dharma.*

TEXT 3

ग्राम्यधर्मनिवृत्तिश्च मोक्षधर्मरतिस्तथा ।
मितमेध्यादनं शश्वद्विविक्तक्षेमसेवनम् ॥ ३ ॥

grāmya-dharma-nivṛttiś ca
mokṣa-dharma-ratis tathā
mita-medhyādanaṁ śaśvad
vivikta-kṣema-sevanam

grāmya—conventional; *dharma*—religious practice; *nivṛttiḥ*—ceasing; *ca*—and; *mokṣa*—for salvation; *dharma*—religious practice; *ratiḥ*—being attracted to; *tathā*—in that way; *mita*—little; *medhya*—pure; *adanam*—eating; *śaśvat*—always; *vivikta*—secluded; *kṣema*—peaceful; *sevanam*—dwelling.

TRANSLATION

One should cease performing conventional religious practices and should be attracted to those which lead to salvation. One should eat very frugally and should always remain secluded so that he can achieve the highest perfection of life.

PURPORT

It is recommended herein that religious practice for economic development or the satisfaction of sense desires should be avoided. Religious practices should be executed only to gain freedom from the clutches of material nature. It is stated in the beginning of *Śrīmad-Bhāgavatam* that the topmost religious practice is that by which one can attain to the transcendental devotional service of the Lord, without reason or cause. Such religious practice is never hampered by any impediments, and by its performance one actually becomes satisfied. Here this is recommended as *mokṣa-dharma*, religious practice for salvation, or transcendence of the clutches of material contamination. Generally people execute religious practices for economic development or sense gratification, but that is not recommended for one who wants to advance in *yoga*.

The next important phrase is *mita-medhyādanam*, which means that one should eat very frugally. It is recommended in the Vedic literatures that a *yogī* eat only half what he desires according to his hunger. If one is so hungry that he could devour one pound of foodstuffs, then instead of eating one pound, he should consume only half a pound and supplement this with four ounces of water; one fourth of the stomach should be left empty for passage of air in the stomach. If one eats in this manner, he will avoid indigestion and disease. The *yogī* should eat in this way, as recommended in the *Śrīmad-Bhāgavatam* and all other standard scriptures. The *yogī* should live in a secluded place, where his *yoga* practice will not be disturbed.

TEXT 4

अहिंसा सत्यमस्तेयं यावदर्थपरिग्रहः ।
ब्रह्मचर्यं तपः शौचं स्वाध्यायः पुरुषार्चनम् ॥ ४ ॥

ahiṁsā satyam asteyaṁ
yāvad-artha-parigrahaḥ
brahmacaryaṁ tapaḥ śaucaṁ
svādhyāyaḥ puruṣārcanam

ahiṁsā—nonviolence; *satyam*—truthfulness; *asteyam*—refraining from theft; *yāvat-artha*—as much as necessary; *parigrahaḥ*—possessing; *brahmacaryam*—celibacy; *tapaḥ*—austerity; *śaucam*—cleanliness; *sva-adhyāyaḥ*—study of the *Vedas; puruṣa-arcanam*—worship of the Supreme Personality of Godhead.

TRANSLATION

One should practice nonviolence and truthfulness, should avoid thieving and be satisfied with possessing as much as he needs for his maintenance. He should abstain from sex life, perform austerity, be clean, study the Vedas and worship the supreme form of the Supreme Personality of Godhead.

PURPORT

The word *puruṣārcanam* in this verse means worshiping the Supreme Personality of Godhead, especially the form of Lord Kṛṣṇa. In *Bhagavad-gītā* it is confirmed by Arjuna that Kṛṣṇa is the original *puruṣa*, or Personality of Godhead, *puruṣaṁ śāśvatam.* Therefore in *yoga* practice one not only must concentrate his mind on the person of Kṛṣṇa, but must also worship the form or Deity of Kṛṣṇa daily.

A *brahmacārī* practices celibacy, controlling his sex life. One cannot enjoy unrestricted sex life and practice *yoga;* this is rascaldom. So-called *yogīs* advertise that one can go on enjoying as one likes and simultaneously become a *yogī,* but this is totally unauthorized. It is very clearly explained here that one must observe celibacy. *Brahmacaryam* means that one leads his life simply in relationship with Brahman, or in full Kṛṣṇa consciousness. Those who are too addicted to sex life cannot observe the regulations which will lead them to Kṛṣṇa consciousness. Sex life should be restricted to persons who are married. A person whose sex life is restricted in marriage is also called a *brahmacārī.*

The word *asteyam* is also very important for a *yogī. Asteyam* means "to refrain from theft." In the broader sense, everyone who accumulates more than he needs is a thief. According to spiritual communism, one cannot possess more than he needs for his personal maintenance. That is the law of nature. Anyone who accumulates more money or more possessions than he needs is called a thief, and one who simply accumulates wealth without spending for sacrifice or for worship of the Personality of Godhead is a great thief.

Svādhyāyaḥ means "reading the authorized Vedic scriptures." Even if one is not Kṛṣṇa conscious and is practicing the *yoga* system, he must read standard Vedic literatures in order to understand. Performance of *yoga* alone is not sufficient. Narottama dāsa Ṭhākura, a great devotee and *ācārya* in the Gauḍīya Vaiṣṇava-sampradāya, says that all spiritual activities should be understood from three sources, namely saintly persons, standard scriptures and the spiritual master. These three guides are very important for progress in spiritual life. The spiritual master prescribes standard literature for the prosecution of the *yoga* of devotional service, and he himself speaks only from scriptural reference. Therefore reading standard scriptures is necessary for executing *yoga.* Practicing *yoga* without reading the standard literatures is simply a waste of time.

TEXT 5

मौनं सदासनजयः स्थैर्यं प्राणजयः शनैः ।
प्रत्याहारश्चेन्द्रियाणां विषयान्मनसा हृदि ॥ ५ ॥

maunaṁ sad-āsana-jayaḥ
sthairyaṁ prāṇa-jayaḥ śanaiḥ
pratyāhāraś cendriyāṇāṁ
viṣayān manasā hṛdi

maunam—silence; *sat*—good; *āsana*—yogic postures; *jayaḥ*—controlling; *sthairyam*—steadiness; *prāṇa-jayaḥ*—controlling the vital air; *śanaiḥ*—gradually; *pratyāhāraḥ*—withdrawal; *ca*—and; *indriyāṇām*—of the senses; *viṣayāt*—from the sense objects; *manasā*—with the mind; *hṛdi*—on the heart.

TRANSLATION

One must observe silence, acquire steadiness by practicing different yogic postures, control the breathing of the vital air, withdraw the senses from sense objects and thus concentrate the mind on the heart.

PURPORT

The yogic practices in general and *haṭha-yoga* in particular are not ends in themselves; they are means to the end of attaining steadiness. First one must be able to sit properly, and then the mind and attention will become steady enough for practicing *yoga*. Gradually, one must control the circulation of vital air, and with such control he will be able to withdraw the senses from sense objects. In the previous verse it is stated that one must observe celibacy. The most important aspect of sense control is controlling sex life. That is called *brahmacarya*. By practicing the different sitting postures and controlling the vital air, one can control and restrain the senses from unrestricted sense enjoyment.

TEXT 6

स्वधिष्ण्यानामेकदेशे मनसा प्राणधारणम् ।
वैकुण्ठलीलाभिध्यानं समाधानं तथात्मनः ॥ ६ ॥

sva-dhiṣṇyānām eka-deśe
manasā prāṇa-dhāraṇam
vaikuṇṭha-līlābhidhyānaṁ
samādhānaṁ tathātmanaḥ

sva-dhiṣṇyānām—within the vital air circles; *eka-deśe*—in one spot; *manasā*—with the mind; *prāṇa*—the vital air; *dhāraṇam*—fixing; *vaikuṇṭha-līlā*—on the pastimes of the Supreme Personality of Godhead; *abhidhyānam*—concentration; *samādhānam*—*samādhi; tathā*—thus; *ātmanaḥ*—of the mind.

TRANSLATION

Fixing the vital air and the mind in one of the six circles of vital air circulation within the body, thus concentrating one's mind on the transcendental pastimes of the Supreme Personality of Godhead, is called samādhi, or samādhāna, of the mind.

PURPORT

There are six circles of vital air circulation within the body. The first circle is within the belly, the second circle is in the area of the heart, the third is in the area of the lungs, the fourth is on the palate, the fifth is between the eyebrows, and the highest, the sixth circle, is above the brain. One has to fix his mind and the circulation of the vital air and thus think of the transcendental pastimes of the Supreme Lord. It is never mentioned that one should concentrate on the impersonal or void. It is clearly stated, *vaikuṇṭha-līlā. Līlā* means "pastimes." Unless the Absolute Truth, the Personality of Godhead, has transcendental activities, where is the scope for thinking of these pastimes? It is through the processes of devotional service, chanting and hearing of the pastimes of the Supreme Personality of Godhead, that one can achieve this concentration. As described in the *Śrīmad-Bhāgavatam*, the Lord appears and disappears according to His relationships with different devotees. The Vedic literatures contain many narrations of the Lord's pastimes, including the Battle of Kurukṣetra and historical facts relating to the life and precepts of devotees like Prahlāda Mahārāja, Dhruva Mahārāja and Ambarīṣa Mahārāja. One need only concentrate his mind on one such narration and become always absorbed in its thought. Then he will be in *samādhi. Samādhi* is not an artificial bodily state; it is the state achieved when the mind is virtually absorbed in thoughts of the Supreme Personality of Godhead.

TEXT 7

एतैरन्यैश्च पथिभिर्मनो दुष्टमसत्पथम् ।
बुद्धया युञ्जीत शनकैर्जितप्राणो ह्यतन्द्रितः ॥ ७ ॥

etair anyaiś ca pathibhir
mano duṣṭam asat-patham
buddhyā yuñjīta śanakair
jita-prāṇo hy atandritaḥ

etaiḥ—by these; *anyaiḥ*—by other; *ca*—and; *pathibhiḥ*—processes; *manaḥ*—the mind; *duṣṭam*—contaminated; *asat-patham*—on the path of material enjoyment; *buddhyā*—by the intelligence; *yuñjīta*—one must control; *śanakaiḥ*—gradually; *jita-prāṇaḥ*—the life air being fixed; *hi*—indeed; *atandritaḥ*—alert.

TRANSLATION

By these processes, or any other true process, one must control the contaminated, unbridled mind, which is always attracted by material enjoyment, and thus fix himself in thought of the Supreme Personality of Godhead.

PURPORT

Etair anyaiś ca. The general *yoga* process entails observing the rules and regulations, practicing the different sitting postures, concentrating the mind on the vital circulation of the air and then thinking of the Supreme Personality of Godhead in His Vaikuṇṭha pastimes. This is the general process of *yoga.* This same concentration can be achieved by other recommended processes, and therefore *anyaiś ca,* other methods, also can be applied. The essential point is that the mind, which is contaminated by material attraction, has to be bridled and concentrated on the Supreme Personality of Godhead. It cannot be fixed on something void or impersonal. For this reason, so-called *yoga* practices of voidism and impersonalism are not recommended in any standard *yoga-śāstra.* The real *yogī* is the devotee because his mind is always concentrated on the pastimes of Lord Kṛṣṇa. Therefore Kṛṣṇa consciousness is the topmost *yoga* system.

TEXT 8

शुचौ देशे प्रतिष्ठाप्य विजितासन आसनम् ।
तस्मिन् स्वस्ति समासीन ऋजुकायः समभ्यसेत् ॥८॥

śucau deśe pratiṣṭhāpya
vijitāsana āsanam
tasmin svasti samāsīna
ṛju-kāyaḥ samabhyaset

śucau deśe—in a sanctified place; *pratiṣṭhāpya*—after placing; *vijita-āsanaḥ*—controlling the sitting postures; *āsanam*—a seat; *tasmin*—in that place; *svasti samāsīnaḥ*—sitting in an easy posture; *ṛju-kāyaḥ*—keeping the body erect; *samabhyaset*—one should practice.

TRANSLATION

After controlling one's mind and sitting postures, one should spread a seat in a secluded and sanctified place, sit there in an easy posture, keeping the body erect, and practice breath control.

PURPORT

Sitting in an easy posture is called *svasti samāsīnaḥ*. It is recommended in the *yoga* scripture that one should put the soles of the feet between the two thighs and ankles and sit straight; that posture will help one to concentrate his mind on the Supreme Personality of Godhead. This very process is also recommended in *Bhagavad-gītā*, Sixth Chapter. It is further suggested that one sit in a secluded, sanctified spot. The seat should consist of deerskin and *kuśa* grass, topped with cotton.

TEXT 9

प्राणस्य शोधयेन्मार्गं पूरकुम्भकरेचकैः ।
प्रतिकूलेन वा चित्तं यथा स्थिरमचञ्चलम् ॥९॥

prāṇasya śodhayen mārgaṁ
pūra-kumbhaka-recakaiḥ
pratikūlena vā cittaṁ
yathā sthiram acañcalam

prāṇasya—of vital air; *śodhayet*—one should clear; *mārgam*—the passage; *pūra-kumbhaka-recakaiḥ*—by inhaling, retaining and exhaling; *pratikūlena*—by reversing; *vā*—or; *cittam*—the mind; *yathā*—so that; *sthiram*—steady; *acañcalam*—free from disturbances.

TRANSLATION

The yogī should clear the passage of vital air by breathing in the following manner: first he should inhale very deeply, then hold the breath in, and finally exhale. Or, reversing the process, the yogī can first exhale, then hold the breath outside, and finally inhale. This is done so that the mind may become steady and free from external disturbances.

PURPORT

These breathing exercises are performed to control the mind and fix it on the Supreme Personality of Godhead. *Sa vai manaḥ kṛṣṇa-padāravindayoḥ:* the devotee Ambarīṣa Mahārāja fixed his mind on the lotus feet of Kṛṣṇa twenty-four hours a day. The process of Kṛṣṇa consciousness is to chant Hare Kṛṣṇa and to hear the sound attentively so that the mind is fixed upon the transcendental vibration of Kṛṣṇa's name, which is nondifferent from Kṛṣṇa the personality. The real purpose of controlling the mind by the prescribed method of clearing the passage of the life air is achieved immediately if one fixes his mind directly on the lotus feet of Kṛṣṇa. The *haṭha-yoga* system, or breathing system, is especially recommended for those who are very absorbed in the concept of bodily existence, but one who can perform the simple process of chanting Hare Kṛṣṇa can fix the mind more easily.

Three different activities are recommended for clearing the passage of breath: *pūraka*, *kumbhaka* and *recaka.* Inhaling the breath is called *pūraka*, sustaining it within is called *kumbhaka*, and finally exhaling it is called *recaka.* These recommended processes can also be performed in the reverse order. After exhaling, one can keep the air outside for some time and then inhale. The nerves through which inhalation and exhalation are conducted are technically called *iḍā* and *piṅgalā*. The ultimate purpose of clearing the *iḍā* and *piṅgalā* passages is to divert the mind from material enjoyment. As stated in *Bhagavad-gītā*, one's mind is his enemy, and one's mind is also his friend; its position varies according to the different dealings of the living entity. If we divert our mind to thoughts of material enjoyment, then our mind becomes an enemy, and if we concentrate our mind on the lotus feet of Kṛṣṇa, then our mind is a friend. By the *yoga* system of *pūraka*, *kumbhaka* and *recaka* or by directly fixing the mind on the sound vibration of Kṛṣṇa or on the form of Kṛṣṇa, the same purpose is achieved. In *Bhagavad-gītā* (8.8) it is said that one must practice the breathing exercise (*abhyāsa-yoga-yuktena*). By virtue of these processes of control, the mind cannot wander to external thoughts (*cetasā nānya-gāminā*). Thus one can fix his mind constantly on the Supreme Personality of Godhead and can attain (*yāti*) Him.

Practicing the *yoga* system of exercise and breath control is very difficult for a person in this age, and therefore Lord Caitanya recommended, *kīrtanīyaḥ sadā hariḥ:* one should always chant the holy name of the Supreme Lord, Kṛṣṇa, because Kṛṣṇa is the most suitable name of the Supreme Personality of Godhead. The name Kṛṣṇa and the Supreme Person Kṛṣṇa are nondifferent. Therefore, if one concentrates his mind on hearing and chanting Hare Kṛṣṇa, the same result is achieved.

TEXT 10

मनोऽचिरात्स्याद्विरजं जितश्वासस्य योगिनः ।
वाय्वग्निभ्यां यथा लोहं ध्मातं त्यजति वै मलम् ॥१०॥

mano 'cirāt syād virajaṁ
jita-śvāsasya yoginaḥ
vāyv-agnibhyāṁ yathā lohaṁ
dhmātaṁ tyajati vai malam

manaḥ—the mind; *acirāt*—soon; *syāt*—can be; *virajam*—free from disturbances; *jita-śvāsasya*—whose breathing is controlled; *yoginaḥ*—of the *yogī; vāyu-agnibhyām*—by air and fire; *yathā*—just as; *loham*—gold; *dhmātam*—fanned; *tyajati*—becomes freed from; *vai*—certainly; *malam*—impurity.

TRANSLATION

The yogīs who practice such breathing exercises are very soon freed from all mental disturbances, just as gold, when put into fire and fanned with air, becomes free from all impurities.

PURPORT

This process of purifying the mind is also recommended by Lord Caitanya; He says that one should chant Hare Kṛṣṇa. He says further, *paraṁ vijayate:* "All glories to Śrī Kṛṣṇa *saṅkīrtana*!" All glories are given to the chanting of the holy names of Kṛṣṇa because as soon as one begins this process of chanting, the mind becomes purified. *Ceto-darpaṇa-mārjanam:* by chanting the holy name of Kṛṣṇa one is cleansed of the dirt that accumulates in the mind. One can purify the mind either by the breathing process or by the chanting process, just as one can purify gold by putting it in a fire and fanning it with a bellows.

TEXT 11

प्राणायामैर्दहेद्दोषान्धारणाभिश्च किल्बिषान् ।
प्रत्याहारेण संसर्गान्ध्यानेनानीश्वरान् गुणान् ॥ ११ ॥

prāṇāyāmair dahed doṣān
dhāraṇābhiś ca kilbiṣān
pratyāhāreṇa saṁsargān
dhyānenānīśvarān guṇān

prāṇāyāmaiḥ—by practice of *prāṇāyāma; dahet*—one can eradicate; *doṣān*—contaminations; *dhāraṇābhiḥ*—by concentrating the mind; *ca*—and; *kilbiṣān*—sinful activities; *pratyāhāreṇa*—by restraining the senses; *saṁsargān*—material association; *dhyānena*—by meditating; *anīśvarān guṇān*—the modes of material nature.

TRANSLATION

By practicing the process of prāṇāyāma, one can eradicate the contamination of his physiological condition, and by concentrating the mind one can become free from all sinful activities. By restraining the senses one can free himself from material association, and by meditating on the Supreme Personality of Godhead one can become free from the three modes of material attachment.

PURPORT

According to Āyur-vedic medical science the three items *kapha, pitta* and *vāyu* (phlegm, bile and air) maintain the physiological condition of the body. Modern medical science does not accept this physiological analysis as valid, but the ancient Āyur-vedic process of treatment is based upon these items. Āyur-vedic treatment concerns itself with the cause of these three elements, which are mentioned in many places in the *Bhāgavatam* as the basic conditions of the body. Here it is recommended that by practicing the breathing process of *prāṇāyāma* one can be released from contamination created by the principal physiological elements, by concentrating the mind one can become free from sinful activities, and by withdrawing the senses one can free himself from material association.

Ultimately, one has to meditate on the Supreme Personality of Godhead in order to be elevated to the transcendental position where he is no longer affected by the three modes of material nature. It is also confirmed in *Bhagavad-gītā* that one who engages himself in unalloyed devotional service at once becomes transcendental to the three modes of material nature and immediately realizes his identification with Brahman. *Sa guṇān samatītyaitān brahma-bhūyāya kalpate.* For every item in the *yoga* system there is a parallel activity in *bhakti-yoga*, but the practice of *bhakti-yoga* is easier for this age. What was introduced by Lord Caitanya is not a new interpretation. *Bhakti-yoga* is a feasible process that begins with chanting and hearing. *Bhakti-yoga* and other *yogas* have as their ultimate goal the same Personality of Godhead, but one is practical, and the others are difficult. One has to purify his physiological condition by concentration and by restraint of the senses; then he can fix his mind upon the Supreme Personality of Godhead. That is called *samādhi*.

TEXT 12

यदा मनः स्वं विरजं योगेन सुसमाहितम् ।
काष्ठां भगवतो ध्यायेत्स्वनासाग्रावलोकनः ॥१२॥

yadā manaḥ svaṁ virajaṁ
yogena susamāhitam
kāṣṭhāṁ bhagavato dhyāyet
sva-nāsāgrāvalokanaḥ

yadā—when; *manaḥ*—the mind; *svam*—own; *virajam*—purified; *yogena*—by *yoga* practice; *su-samāhitam*—controlled; *kāṣṭhām*—the plenary expansion; *bhagavataḥ*—of the Supreme Personality of Godhead; *dhyāyet*—one should meditate upon; *sva-nāsā-agra*—the tip of one's nose; *avalokanaḥ*—looking at.

TRANSLATION

When the mind is perfectly purified by this practice of yoga, one should concentrate on the tip of the nose with half-closed eyes and see the form of the Supreme Personality of Godhead.

PURPORT

It is clearly mentioned here that one has to meditate upon the expansion of Viṣṇu. The word *kāṣṭhām* refers to Paramātmā, the expansion of the expansion of Viṣṇu. *Bhagavataḥ* refers to Lord Viṣṇu, the Supreme Personality of Godhead. The Supreme Godhead is Kṛṣṇa; from Him comes the first expansion, Baladeva, and from Baladeva come Saṅkarṣaṇa, Aniruddha and many other forms, followed by the *puruṣa-avatāras*. As mentioned in the previous verses (*puruṣārcanam*), this *puruṣa* is represented as the Paramātmā, or Supersoul. A description of the Supersoul, upon whom one must meditate, will be given in the following verses. In this verse it is clearly stated that one must meditate by fixing the vision on the tip of the nose and concentrating one's mind on the *kalā*, or the plenary expansion, of Viṣṇu.

TEXT 13

प्रसन्नवदनाम्भोजं पद्मगर्भारुणेक्षणम् ।
नीलोत्पलदलश्यामं शङ्खचक्रगदाधरम् ॥१३॥

prasanna-vadanāmbhojaṁ
padma-garbhāruṇekṣaṇam
nīlotpala-dala-śyāmaṁ
śaṅkha-cakra-gadā-dharam

prasanna—cheerful; *vadana*—countenance; *ambhojam*—lotuslike; *padma-garbha*—the interior of a lotus; *aruṇa*—ruddy; *īkṣaṇam*—with eyes; *nīla-utpala*—blue lotus; *dala*—petals; *śyāmam*—swarthy; *śaṅkha*—conch; *cakra*—discus; *gadā*—club; *dharam*—bearing.

TRANSLATION

The Supreme Personality of Godhead has a cheerful, lotuslike countenance with ruddy eyes like the interior of a lotus and a swarthy body like the petals of a blue lotus. He bears a conch, discus and mace in three of His hands.

PURPORT

It is definitely recommended herein that one concentrate his mind upon the form of Viṣṇu. There are twelve different forms of Viṣṇu, which are described in *Teachings of Lord Caitanya.* One cannot concentrate his mind on anything void or impersonal; the mind should be fixed on the personal form of the Lord, whose attitude is cheerful, as described in this verse. *Bhagavad-gītā* states that meditation on the impersonal or void features is very troublesome to the meditator. Those who are attached to the impersonal or void features of meditation have to undergo a difficult process because we are not accustomed to concentrating our minds upon anything impersonal. Actually such concentration is not even possible. *Bhagavad-gītā* also confirms that one should concentrate his mind on the Personality of Godhead.

The color of the Personality of Godhead, Kṛṣṇa, is described here as *nīlotpala-dala,* meaning that it is likc that of a lotus flower with petals tinted blue and white. People always ask why Kṛṣṇa is blue. The color of the Lord has not been imagined by an artist. It is described in authoritative scripture. In the *Brahma-saṁhitā* also, the color of Kṛṣṇa's body is compared to that of a bluish cloud. The color of the Lord is not poetical imagination. There are authoritative descriptions in the *Brahma-saṁhitā, Śrīmad-Bhāgavatam, Bhagavad-gītā* and many of the *Purāṇas* of the Lord's body, His weapons and all other paraphernalia. The Lord's appearance is described here as *padma-garbhāruṇekṣaṇam.* His eyes resemble the inside of a lotus flower, and in His four hands He holds the four symbols: conchshell, discus, mace and lotus.

TEXT 14

लसत्पङ्कजकिञ्जल्कपीतकौशेयवाससम् ।
श्रीवत्सवक्षसं भ्राजत्कौस्तुभामुक्तकन्धरम् ॥१४॥

lasat-paṅkaja-kiñjalka-
pīta-kauśeya-vāsasam
śrīvatsa-vakṣasaṁ bhrājat
kaustubhāmukta-kandharam

lasat—shining; *paṅkaja*—of a lotus; *kiñjalka*—filaments; *pīta*—yellow; *kauśeya*—silk cloth; *vāsasam*—whose garment; *śrīvatsa*—bearing the mark of Śrīvatsa; *vakṣasam*—breast; *bhrājat*—brilliant; *kaustubha*—Kaustubha gem; *āmukta*—put on; *kandharam*—His neck.

TRANSLATION

His loins are covered by a shining cloth, yellowish like the filaments of a lotus. On His breast He bears the mark of Śrīvatsa, a curl of white hair. The brilliant Kaustubha gem is suspended from His neck.

PURPORT

The exact color of the garment of the Supreme Lord is described as saffron-yellow, just like the pollen of a lotus flower. The Kaustubha gem hanging on His chest is also described. His neck is beautifully decorated with jewels and pearls. The Lord is full in six opulences, one of which is wealth. He is very richly dressed with valuable jewels which are not visible within this material world.

TEXT 15

मत्तद्विरेफकलया परीतं वनमालया ।
परार्ध्यहारवलयकिरीटाङ्गदनूपुरम् ॥१५॥

matta-dvirepha-kalayā
parītaṁ vana-mālayā
parārdhya-hāra-valaya-
kirīṭāṅgada-nūpuram

matta—intoxicated; *dvi-repha*—with bees; *kalayā*—humming; *parītam*—garlanded; *vana-mālayā*—with a garland of forest flowers; *parārdhya*—priceless; *hāra*—pearl necklace; *valaya*—bracelets; *kirīṭa*—a crown; *aṅgada*—armlets; *nūpuram*—anklets.

TRANSLATION

He also wears around His neck a garland of attractive sylvan flowers, and a swarm of bees, intoxicated by its delicious fragrance, hums about the garland. He is further superbly adorned with a pearl necklace, a crown and pairs of armlets, bracelets and anklets.

PURPORT

From this description it appears that the flower garland of the Supreme Personality of Godhead is fresh. Actually, in Vaikuṇṭha, or the spiritual sky, there is nothing but freshness. Even the flowers picked from the trees and plants remain fresh, for everything in the spiritual sky retains its originality and does not fade. The fragrance of the flowers picked from the trees and made into garlands does not fade, for both the trees and the flowers are spiritual. When the flower is taken from the tree, it remains the same; it does not lose its aroma. The bees are equally attracted to the flowers whether they are on the garland or on the trees. The significance of spirituality is that everything is eternal and inexhaustible. Everything taken from everything remains everything, or, as has been stated, in the spiritual world one minus one equals one, and one plus one equals one. The bees hum around the fresh flowers, and their sweet sound is enjoyed by the Lord. The Lord's bangles, necklace, crown and anklets are all bedecked with invaluable jewels. Since the jewels and pearls are spiritual, there is no material calculation of their value.

TEXT 16

काञ्चीगुणोल्लसच्छ्रोणिं हृदयाम्भोजविष्टरम् ।
दर्शनीयतमं शान्तं मनोनयनवर्धनम् ॥१६॥

kāñcī-guṇollasac-chroṇiṁ
hṛdayāmbhoja-viṣṭaram
darśanīyatamaṁ śāntaṁ
mano-nayana-vardhanam

kāñcī—girdle; *guṇa*—quality; *ullasat*—brilliant; *śroṇim*—His loins and hips; *hṛdaya*—heart; *ambhoja*—lotus; *viṣṭaram*—whose seat; *darśanīya-tamam*—most charming to look at; *śāntam*—serene; *manaḥ*—minds, hearts; *nayana*—eyes; *vardhanam*—gladdening.

TRANSLATION

His loins and hips encircled by a girdle, He stands on the lotus of His devotee's heart. He is most charming to look at, and His serene aspect gladdens the eyes and souls of the devotees who behold Him.

PURPORT

The word *darśanīyatamam*, which is used in this verse, means that the Lord is so beautiful that the devotee-*yogī* does not wish to see anything else. His desire to see beautiful objects is completely satisfied by the sight of the Lord. In the material world we want to see beauty, but the desire is never satisfied. Because of material contamination, all the propensities we feel in the material world are ever unsatisfied. But when our desires to see, hear, touch, etc., are dovetailed for the satisfaction of the Supreme Personality of Godhead, they are on the level of the topmost perfection.

Although the Supreme Personality of Godhead in His eternal form is so beautiful and pleasing to the heart of the devotee, He does not attract the impersonalists, who want to meditate on His impersonal aspect. Such impersonal meditation is simply fruitless labor. The actual *yogīs,* with half-closed eyes, fix on the form of the Supreme Personality of Godhead, not upon anything void or impersonal.

TEXT 17

अपीच्यदर्शनं शश्वत्सर्वलोकनमस्कृतम् ।
सन्तं वयसि कैशोरे भृत्यानुग्रहकातरम् ॥१७॥

apīcya-darśanaṁ śaśvat
sarva-loka-namaskṛtam
santaṁ vayasi kaiśore
bhṛtyānugraha-kātaram

apīcya-darśanam—very beautiful to see; *śaśvat*—eternal; *sarva-loka*—by all the inhabitants of every planet; *namaḥ-kṛtam*—worshipable; *santam*—situated; *vayasi*—in youth; *kaiśore*—in boyhood; *bhṛtya*—upon His devotee; *anugraha*—to bestow blessings; *kātaram*—eager.

TRANSLATION

The Lord is eternally very beautiful, and He is worshipable by all the inhabitants of every planet. He is ever youthful and always eager to bestow His blessing upon His devotees.

PURPORT

The word *sarva-loka-namaskṛtam* means that He is worshipable by everyone on every planet. There are innumerable planets in the material world and innumerable planets in the spiritual world as well. On each planet there are innumerable inhabitants who worship the Lord, for the Lord is worshipable by all but the impersonalists. The Supreme Lord is very beautiful. The word *śaśvat* is significant. It is not that He appears beautiful to the devotees but is ultimately impersonal. *Śaśvat* means "ever existing." That beauty is not temporary. It is ever existing—He is always youthful. In the *Brahma-saṁhitā* (5.33) it is also stated: *advaitam acyutam anādim ananta-rūpam ādyaṁ purāṇa-puruṣaṁ nava-yauvanaṁ ca.* The original person is one without a second, yet He never appears old; He always appears as ever fresh as a blooming youth.

The Lord's facial expression always indicates that He is ready to show favor and benediction to the devotees; for the nondevotees, however, He is silent. As stated in *Bhagavad-gītā*, although He acts equally to everyone because He is the Supreme Personality of Godhead and because all living entities are His sons, He is especially inclined to those engaged in devotional service. The same fact is confirmed here: He is always anxious to show favor to the devotees. Just as the devotees are always eager to render service unto the Supreme Personality of Godhead, the Lord is also very eager to bestow benediction upon the pure devotees.

TEXT 18

कीर्तन्यतीर्थयशसं पुण्यश्लोकयशस्करम् ।
ध्यायेद्देवं समग्राङ्गं यावन्न च्यवते मनः ॥१८॥

kīrtanya-tīrtha-yaśasaṁ
puṇya-śloka-yaśaskaram
dhyāyed devaṁ samagrāṅgaṁ
yāvan na cyavate manaḥ

kīrtanya—worth singing; *tīrtha-yaśasam*—the glories of the Lord; *puṇya-śloka*—of the devotees; *yaśaḥ-karam*—enhancing the glory; *dhyāyet*—one should meditate; *devam*—upon the Lord; *samagra-aṅgam*—all the limbs; *yāvat*—as much as; *na*—not; *cyavate*—deviates; *manaḥ*—the mind.

TRANSLATION

The glory of the Lord is always worth singing, for His glories enhance the glories of His devotees. One should therefore meditate upon the Supreme Personality of Godhead and upon His devotees. One should meditate on the eternal form of the Lord until the mind becomes fixed.

PURPORT

One has to fix his mind on the Supreme Personality of Godhead constantly. When one is accustomed to thinking of one of the innumerable forms of the Lord—Kṛṣṇa, Viṣṇu, Rāma, Nārāyaṇa, etc.—he has reached the perfection of *yoga.* This is confirmed in the *Brahma-saṁhitā:* a person who has developed pure love for the Lord, and whose eyes are smeared with the ointment of transcendental loving exchange, always sees within his heart the Supreme Personality of Godhead. The devotees especially see the Lord in the beautiful blackish form of Śyāmasundara. That is the perfection of *yoga.* This *yoga* system should be continued until the mind does not vacillate for a moment. *Oṁ tad viṣṇoḥ paramaṁ padaṁ sadā paśyanti sūrayaḥ:* the form of Viṣṇu is the highest individuality and is always visible to sages and saintly persons.

The same purpose is served when a devotee worships the form of the Lord in the temple. There is no difference between devotional service in the temple and meditation on the form of the Lord, since the form of the Lord is the same whether He appears within the mind or in some concrete element. There are eight kinds of forms recommended for the devotees to see. The forms may be made out of sand, clay, wood or stone, they may be contemplated within the mind or made of jewels, metal or painted colors, but all the forms are of the same value. It is not that one who meditates on the form within the mind sees differently from one who worships the form in the temple. The Supreme Personality of Godhead is absolute, and there is therefore no difference between the two. The impersonalists, who desire to disregard the eternal form of the Lord, imagine some round figure. They especially prefer the *oṁkāra,* which also has form. In *Bhagavad-gītā* it is stated that *oṁkāra* is the letter form of the Lord. Similarly, there are statue forms and painting forms of the Lord.

Another significant word in this verse is *puṇya-śloka-yaśaskaram.* The devotee is called *puṇya-śloka.* As one becomes purified by chanting the holy name of the Lord, so one can become purified simply by chanting the name of a holy devotee. The pure devotee of the Lord and the Lord Himself are nondifferent. It is sometimes feasible to chant the name of a holy devotee. This is a very sanctified process. Lord Caitanya was once chanting the holy names of the *gopīs* when His students criticized Him: "Why are You chanting the names of the *gopīs*? Why not 'Kṛṣṇa'?" Lord Caitanya was irritated by the criticism, and so there was some misunderstanding between Him and His students. He wanted to chastise them for desiring to instruct Him on the transcendental process of chanting.

The beauty of the Lord is that the devotees who are connected with His activities are also glorified. Arjuna, Prahlāda, Janaka Mahārāja, Bali Mahārāja and many other devotees were not even in the renounced order of life, but were householders. Some of them, such as Prahlāda Mahārāja and Bali Mahārāja, were born of demoniac families. Prahlāda Mahārāja's father was a demon, and Bali Mahārāja was the grandson of Prahlāda Mahārāja, but still they have become famous because of their association with the Lord. Anyone who is eternally associated with the Lord is glorified with the Lord. The conclusion is that a perfect *yogī* should always be accustomed to seeing the form of the Lord, and unless the mind is fixed in that way, he should continue practicing *yoga*.

TEXT 19

स्थितं व्रजन्तमासीनं शयानं वा गुहाशयम् ।
प्रेक्षणीयेहितं ध्यायेच्छुद्धभावेन चेतसा ॥१९॥

sthitaṁ vrajantam āsīnaṁ
śayānaṁ vā guhāśayam
prekṣaṇīyehitaṁ dhyāyec
chuddha-bhāvena cetasā

sthitam—standing; *vrajantam*—moving; *āsīnam*—sitting; *śayānam*—lying down; *vā*—or; *guhā-āśayam*—the Lord dwelling in the heart; *prekṣaṇīya*—beautiful; *īhitam*—pastimes; *dhyāyet*—he should visualize; *śuddha-bhāvena*—pure; *cetasā*—by the mind.

TRANSLATION

Thus always merged in devotional service, the yogī visualizes the Lord standing, moving, lying down or sitting within him, for the pastimes of the Supreme Lord are always beautiful and attractive.

PURPORT

The process of meditating on the form of the Supreme Personality of Godhead within oneself and the process of chanting the glories and pastimes of the Lord are the same. The only difference is that hearing and fixing the mind on the pastimes of the Lord is easier than visualizing the form of the Lord within one's heart because as soon as one begins to think of the Lord, especially in this age, the mind becomes disturbed, and due to so much agitation, the process of seeing the Lord within the mind is interrupted. When there is sound vibrated praising the transcendental pastimes of the Lord, however, one is forced to hear. That hearing process enters into the mind, and the practice of *yoga* is automatically performed. For example, even a child can hear and derive the benefit of meditating on the pastimes of the Lord simply by listening to a reading from the *Bhāgavatam* that describes the Lord as He is going to the pasturing ground with His cows and friends. Hearing includes applying the mind. In this age of Kali-yuga, Lord Caitanya has recommended that one should always engage in chanting and hearing *Bhagavad-gītā.* The Lord also says that the *mahātmās*, or great souls, always engage in the process of chanting the glories of the Lord, and just by hearing, others derive the same benefit. *Yoga* necessitates meditation on the transcendental pastimes of the Lord, whether He is standing, moving, lying down, etc.

TEXT 20

तस्मिँल्लब्धपदं चित्तं सर्वावयवसंस्थितम् ।
विलक्ष्यैकत्र संयुज्यादङ्गे भगवतो मुनिः ॥२०॥

tasmil̐ labdha-padaṁ cittaṁ
sarvāvayava-saṁsthitam
vilakṣyaikatra saṁyujyād
aṅge bhagavato muniḥ

tasmin—on the form of the Lord; *labdha-padam*—fixed; *cittam*—the mind; *sarva*—all; *avayava*—limbs; *saṁsthitam*—fixed upon; *vilakṣya*—having distinguished; *ekatra*—in one place; *saṁyujyāt*—should fix the mind; *aṅge*—on each limb; *bhagavataḥ*—of the Lord; *muniḥ*—the sage.

TRANSLATION

In fixing his mind on the eternal form of the Lord, the yogī should not take a collective view of all His limbs, but should fix the mind on each individual limb of the Lord.

PURPORT

The word *muni* is very significant. *Muni* means one who is very expert in mental speculation or in thinking, feeling and willing. He is not mentioned here as a devotee or *yogī*. Those who try to meditate on the form of the Lord are called *munis*, or less intelligent, whereas those who render actual service to the Lord are called *bhakti-yogīs*. The thought process described below is for the education of the *muni*. In order to convince the *yogī* that the Absolute Truth, or Supreme Personality of Godhead, is never impersonal at any time, the following verses prescribe observing the Lord in His personal form, limb after limb. To think of the Lord as a whole may sometimes be impersonal; therefore, it is recommended here that one first think of His lotus feet, then His ankles, then the thighs, then the waist, then the chest, then the neck, then the face and so on. One should begin from the lotus feet and gradually rise to the upper limbs of the transcendental body of the Lord.

TEXT 21

सञ्चिन्तयेद्भगवतश्चरणारविन्दं
वज्राङ्कुशध्वजसरोरुहलाञ्छनाढ्यम् ।
उत्तुङ्गरक्तविलसन्नखचक्रवाल-
ज्योत्स्नाभिराहतमहद्धृदयान्धकारम् ॥२१॥

sañcintayed bhagavataś caraṇāravindaṁ
vajrāṅkuśa-dhvaja-saroruha-lāñchanāḍhyam
uttuṅga-rakta-vilasan-nakha-cakravāla-
jyotsnābhir āhata-mahad-dhṛdayāndhakāram

sañcintayet—he should concentrate; *bhagavataḥ*—of the Lord; *caraṇa-aravindam*—on the lotus feet; *vajra*—thunderbolt; *aṅkuśa*—goad (rod for driving elephants); *dhvaja*—banner; *saroruha*—lotus; *lāñchana*—marks; *āḍhyam*—adorned with; *uttuṅga*—prominent; *rakta*—red; *vilasat*—brilliant; *nakha*—nails; *cakravāla*—the circle of the moon; *jyotsnābhiḥ*—with splendor; *āhata*—dispelled; *mahat*—thick; *hṛdaya*—of the heart; *andhakāram*—darkness.

TRANSLATION

The devotee should first concentrate his mind on the Lord's lotus feet, which are adorned with the marks of a thunderbolt, a goad, a banner and a lotus. The splendor of their beautiful ruby nails resembles the orbit of the moon and dispels the thick gloom of one's heart.

PURPORT

The Māyāvādī says that because one is unable to fix his mind on the impersonal existence of the Absolute Truth, one can imagine any form he likes and fix his mind on that imaginary form; but such a process is not recommended here. Imagination is always imagination and results only in further imagination.

A concrete description of the eternal form of the Lord is given here. The Lord's sole is depicted with distinctive lines resembling a thunderbolt, a flag, a lotus flower and a goad. The luster of His toenails, which are brilliantly prominent, resembles the light of the moon. If a *yogī* looks upon the marks of the Lord's sole and on the blazing brilliance of His nails, then he can be freed from the darkness of ignorance in material existence. This liberation is not achieved by mental speculation, but by seeing the light emanating from the lustrous toenails of the Lord. In other words, one has to fix his mind first on the lotus feet of the Lord if he wants to be freed from the darkness of ignorance in material existence.

TEXT 22

यच्छौचनिःसृतसरित्प्रवरोदकेन
तीर्थेन मूर्ध्न्यधिकृतेन शिवः शिवोऽभूत्।
ध्यातुर्मनःशमलशैलनिसृष्टवज्रं
ध्यायेच्चिरं भगवतश्चरणारविन्दम् ॥२२॥

yac-chauca-niḥsṛta-sarit-pravarodakena
tīrthena mūrdhny adhikṛtena śivaḥ śivo 'bhūt
dhyātur manaḥ-śamala-śaila-nisṛṣṭa-vajraṁ
dhyāyec ciraṁ bhagavataś caraṇāravindam

yat—the Lord's lotus feet; *śauca*—washing; *niḥsṛta*—gone forth; *sarit-pravara*—of the Ganges; *udakena*—by the water; *tīrthena*—holy; *mūrdhni*—on his head; *adhikṛtena*—borne; *śivaḥ*—Lord Śiva; *śivaḥ*—auspicious; *abhūt*—became; *dhyātuḥ*—of the meditator; *manaḥ*—in the mind; *śamala-śaila*—the mountain of sin; *nisṛṣṭa*—hurled; *vajram*—thunderbolt; *dhyāyet*—one should meditate; *ciram*—for a long time; *bhagavataḥ*—of the Lord; *caraṇa-aravindam*—on the lotus feet.

TRANSLATION

The blessed Lord Śiva becomes all the more blessed by bearing on his head the holy waters of the Ganges, which has its source in the water that washed the Lord's lotus feet. The Lord's feet act like thunderbolts hurled to shatter the mountain of sin stored in the mind of the meditating devotee. One should therefore meditate on the lotus feet of the Lord for a long time.

PURPORT

In this verse the position of Lord Śiva is specifically mentioned. The impersonalist suggests that the Absolute Truth has no form and that one can therefore equally imagine the form of Viṣṇu or Lord Śiva or the goddess Durgā or their son Gaṇeśa. But actually the Supreme Personality of Godhead is the supreme master of everyone. In the *Caitanya-caritāmṛta* (*Ādi* 5.142) it is said, *ekale īśvara kṛṣṇa, āra saba bhṛtya:* the Supreme Lord is Kṛṣṇa, and everyone else, including Lord Śiva and Lord Brahmā—not to mention other demigods—is a servant of Kṛṣṇa. The same principle is described here. Lord Śiva is important because he is holding on his head the holy Ganges water, which has its origin in the footwash of Lord Viṣṇu. In the *Hari-bhakti-vilāsa,* by Sanātana Gosvāmī, it is said that anyone who puts the Supreme Lord and the demigods, including Lord Śiva and Lord Brahmā, on the same level, at once becomes a *pāṣaṇḍī,* or atheist. We should never consider that the Supreme Lord Viṣṇu and the demigods are on an equal footing.

Another significant point of this verse is that the mind of the conditioned soul, on account of its association with the material energy from time immemorial, contains heaps of dirt in the form of desires to lord it over material nature. This dirt is like a mountain, but a mountain can be shattered when hit by a thunderbolt. Meditating on the lotus feet of the Lord acts like a thunderbolt on the mountain of dirt in the mind of the *yogī.* If a *yogī* wants to shatter the mountain of dirt in his mind, he should concentrate on the lotus feet of the Lord and not imagine something void or impersonal. Because the dirt has accumulated like a solid mountain, one must meditate on the lotus feet of the Lord for quite a long time. For one who is accustomed to thinking of the lotus feet of the Lord constantly, however, it is a different matter. The devotees are so fixed on the lotus feet of the Lord that they do not think of anything else. Those who practice the *yoga* system must meditate on the lotus feet of the Lord for a long time after following the regulative principles and thereby controlling the senses.

It is specifically mentioned here, *bhagavataś caraṇāravindam:* one has to think of the lotus feet of the Lord. The Māyāvādīs imagine that one can think of the lotus feet of Lord Śiva or Lord Brahmā or the goddess Durgā to achieve liberation, but this is not so. *Bhagavataḥ* is specifically mentioned. *Bhagavataḥ* means "of the Supreme Personality of Godhead, Viṣṇu," and no one else. Another significant phrase in this verse is *śivaḥ śivo 'bhūt.* By his constitutional position, Lord Śiva is always great and auspicious, but since he has accepted on his head the Ganges water, which emanated from the lotus feet of the Lord, he has become even more auspicious and important. The stress is on the lotus feet of the Lord. A relationship with the lotus feet of the Lord can even enhance the importance of Lord Śiva, what to speak of other, ordinary living entities.

TEXT 23

जानुद्वयं जलजलोचनया जनन्या
लक्ष्म्याखिलस्य सुरवन्दितया विधातुः।
ऊर्वोर्निधाय करपल्लवरोचिषा यत्
संलालितं हृदि विभोरभवस्य कुर्यात् ॥२३॥

jānu-dvayaṁ jalaja-locanayā jananyā
lakṣmyākhilasya sura-vanditayā vidhātuḥ
ūrvor nidhāya kara-pallava-rociṣā yat
saṁlālitaṁ hṛdi vibhor abhavasya kuryāt

jānu-dvayam—up to the knees; *jalaja-locanayā*—lotus-eyed; *jananyā*—mother; *lakṣmyā*—by Lakṣmī; *akhilasya*—of the entire universe; *sura-vanditayā*—worshiped by the demigods; *vidhātuḥ*—of Brahmā; *ūrvoḥ*—at the thighs; *nidhāya*—having placed; *kara-pallava-rociṣā*—with her lustrous fingers; *yat*—which; *saṁlālitam*—massaged; *hṛdi*—in the heart; *vibhoḥ*—of the Lord; *abhavasya*—transcendental to material existence; *kuryāt*—one should meditate.

TRANSLATION

The yogī should fix in his heart the activities of Lakṣmī, the goddess of fortune, who is worshiped by all demigods and is the mother of the supreme person, Brahmā. She can always be found massaging the legs and thighs of the transcendental Lord, very carefully serving Him in this way.

PURPORT

Brahmā is the appointed lord of the universe. Because his father is Garbhodakaśāyī Viṣṇu, Lakṣmī, the goddess of fortune, is automatically his mother. Lakṣmījī is worshiped by all demigods and by the inhabitants of other planets as well. Human beings are also eager to receive favor from the goddess of fortune. Lakṣmī is always engaged in massaging the legs and thighs of the Supreme Personality of Godhead Nārāyaṇa, who is lying on the ocean of Garbha within the universe. Brahmā is described here as the son of the goddess of fortune, but actually he was not born of her womb. Brahmā takes his birth from the abdomen of the Lord Himself. A lotus flower grows from the abdomen of Garbhodakaśāyī Viṣṇu, and Brahmā is born there. Therefore Lakṣmījī's massaging of the thighs of the Lord should not be taken as the behavior of an ordinary wife. The Lord is transcendental to the behavior of the ordinary male and female. The word *abhavasya* is very significant, for it indicates that He could produce Brahmā without the assistance of the goddess of fortune.

Since transcendental behavior is different from mundane behavior, it should not be taken that the Lord receives service from His wife just as a demigod or human being might receive service from his wife. It is advised here that the *yogī* always keep this picture in his heart. The devotee always thinks of this relationship between Lakṣmī and Nārāyaṇa;

therefore he does not meditate on the mental plane as impersonalists and voidists do.

Bhava means "one who accepts a material body," and *abhava* means "one who does not accept a material body but descends in the original, spiritual body." Lord Nārāyaṇa is not born of anything material. Matter is generated from matter, but He is not born of matter. Brahmā is born after the creation, but since the Lord existed before the creation, the Lord has no material body.

TEXT 24

ऊरू सुपर्णभुजयोरधिशोभमाना-
वोजोनिधी अतसिकाकुसुमावभासौ ।
व्यालम्बिपीतवरवाससि वर्तमान-
काञ्चीकलापपरिरम्भि नितम्बबिम्बम्॥२४॥

ūrū suparṇa-bhujayor adhi śobhamānāv
ojo-nidhī atasikā-kusumāvabhāsau
vyālambi-pīta-vara-vāsasi vartamāna-
kāñcī-kalāpa-parirambhi nitamba-bimbam

ūrū—the two thighs; *suparṇa*—of Garuḍa; *bhujayoḥ*—the two shoulders; *adhi*—on; *śobhamānau*—beautiful; *ojaḥ-nidhī*—the storehouse of all energy; *atasikā-kusuma*—of the linseed flower; *avabhāsau*—like the luster; *vyālambi*—extending down; *pīta*—yellow; *vara*—exquisite; *vāsasi*—on the cloth; *vartamāna*—being; *kāñcī-kalāpa*—by a girdle; *parirambhi*—encircled; *nitamba-bimbam*—His rounded hips.

TRANSLATION

Next, the yogī should fix his mind in meditation on the Personality of Godhead's thighs, the storehouse of all energy. The Lord's thighs are whitish blue, like the luster of the linseed flower, and appear most graceful when the Lord is carried on the shoulders of Garuḍa. Also the yogī should contemplate His rounded hips, which are encircled by a girdle that rests on the exquisite yellow silk cloth that extends down to His ankles.

PURPORT

The Personality of Godhead is the reservoir of all strength, and His strength rests on the thighs of His transcendental body. His whole body is full of opulences: all riches, all strength, all fame, all beauty, all knowledge and all renunciation. The *yogī* is advised to meditate upon the transcendental form of the Lord, beginning from the soles of the feet and then gradually rising to the knees, to the thighs, and finally arriving at the face. The system of meditating on the Supreme Personality of Godhead begins from His feet.

The description of the transcendental form of the Lord is exactly represented in the *arcā-vigraha*, the statue in the temples. Generally, the lower part of the body of the statue of the Lord is covered with yellow silk. That is the Vaikuṇṭha dress, or the dress the Lord wears in the spiritual sky. This cloth extends down to the Lord's ankles. Thus, since the *yogī* has so many transcendental objectives on which to meditate, there is no reason for his meditating on something imaginary, as is the practice of the so-called *yogīs* whose objective is impersonal.

TEXT 25

नाभिह्रदं भुवनकोशगुहोदरस्थं
यत्रात्मयोनिधिषणाखिललोकपद्मम् ।
व्यूढं हरिन्मणिवृषस्तनयोरमुष्य
ध्यायेद् द्वयं विशदहारमयूखगौरम् ॥२५॥

nābhi-hradaṁ bhuvana-kośa-guhodara-sthaṁ
yatrātma-yoni-dhiṣaṇākhila-loka-padmam
vyūḍhaṁ harin-maṇi-vṛṣa-stanayor amuṣya
dhyāyed dvayaṁ viśada-hāra-mayūkha-gauram

nābhi-hradam—the navel lake; *bhuvana-kośa*—of all the worlds; *guhā*—the foundation; *udara*—on the abdomen; *stham*—situated; *yatra*—where; *ātma-yoni*—of Brahmā; *dhiṣaṇa*—residence; *akhila-loka*—containing all planetary systems; *padmam*—lotus; *vyūḍham*—sprang up; *harit-maṇi*—like emeralds; *vṛṣa*—most exquisite; *stanayoḥ*—of nipples; *amuṣya*—of the Lord; *dhyāyet*—he should meditate on; *dvayam*—the pair; *viśada*—white; *hāra*—of pearl necklaces; *mayūkha*—from the light; *gauram*—whitish.

TRANSLATION

The yogī should then meditate on His moonlike navel in the center of His abdomen. From His navel, which is the foundation of the entire universe, sprang the lotus stem containing all the different planetary systems. The lotus is the residence of Brahmā, the first created being. In the same way, the yogī should concentrate his mind on the Lord's nipples, which resemble a pair of most exquisite emeralds and which appear whitish because of the rays of the milk-white pearl necklaces adorning His chest.

PURPORT

The *yogī* is advised next to meditate upon the navel of the Lord, which is the foundation of all material creation. Just as a child is connected to his mother by the umbilical cord, so the first-born living creature, Brahmā, by the supreme will of the Lord, is connected to the Lord by a lotus stem. In the previous verse it was stated that the goddess of fortune, Lakṣmī, who engages in massaging the legs, ankles and thighs of the Lord, is called the mother of Brahmā, but actually Brahmā is born from the abdomen of the Lord, not from the abdomen of his mother. These are inconceivable conceptions of the Lord, and one should not think materially, "How can the father give birth to a child?"

It is explained in the *Brahma-saṁhitā* that each limb of the Lord has the potency of every other limb; because everything is spiritual, His parts are not conditioned. The Lord can see with His ears. The material ear can hear but cannot see, but we understand from the *Brahma-saṁhitā* that the Lord can also see with His ears and hear with His eyes. Any organ of His transcendental body can function as any other organ. His abdomen is the foundation of all the planetary systems. Brahmā holds the post of the creator of all planetary systems, but his engineering energy is generated from the abdomen of the Lord. Any creative function in the universe always has a direct connecting link with the Lord. The necklace of pearls which decorates the upper portion of the Lord's body is also spiritual, and therefore the *yogī* is advised to gaze at the whitish luster of the pearls decorating His chest.

TEXT 26

वक्षोऽधिवासमृषभस्य महाविभूतेः
पुंसां मनोनयननिर्वृतिमादधानम् ।
कण्ठं च कौस्तुभमणेरधिभूषणार्थं
कुर्यान्मनस्यखिललोकनमस्कृतस्य ॥२६॥

vakṣo 'dhivāsam ṛṣabhasya mahā-vibhūteḥ
puṁsāṁ mano-nayana-nirvṛtim ādadhānam
kaṇṭhaṁ ca kaustubha-maṇer adhibhūṣaṇārthaṁ
kuryān manasy akhila-loka-namaskṛtasya

vakṣaḥ—the chest; *adhivāsam*—the abode; *ṛṣabhasya*—of the Supreme Personality of Godhead; *mahā-vibhūteḥ*—of Mahā-Lakṣmī; *puṁsām*—of persons; *manaḥ*—to the mind; *nayana*—to the eyes; *nirvṛtim*—transcendental pleasure; *ādadhānam*—bestowing; *kaṇṭham*—the neck; *ca*—also; *kaustubha-maṇeḥ*—of the Kaustubha gem; *adhibhūṣaṇa-artham*—which enhances the beauty; *kuryāt*—he should meditate on; *manasi*—in the mind; *akhila-loka*—by the entire universe; *namaskṛtasya*—who is adored.

TRANSLATION

The yogī should then meditate on the chest of the Supreme Personality of Godhead, the abode of goddess Mahā-Lakṣmī. The Lord's chest is the source of all transcendental pleasure for the mind and full satisfaction for the eyes. The yogī should then imprint on his mind the neck of the Personality of Godhead, who is adored by the entire universe. The neck of the Lord serves to enhance the beauty of the Kaustubha gem, which hangs on His chest.

PURPORT

In the *Upaniṣads* it is said that the various energies of the Lord are working to create, destroy and maintain. These inconceivable varieties of energy are stored in the bosom of the Lord. As people generally say, God is all-powerful. That prowess is represented by Mahā-Lakṣmī, the reservoir of all energies, who is situated on the bosom of the transcendental form of the Lord. The *yogī* who can meditate perfectly on that spot on the transcendental form of the Lord can derive many material powers, which comprise the eight perfections of the *yoga* system.

It is stated herein that the beauty of the neck of the Lord enhances the beauty of the Kaustubha gem rather than vice versa. The gem itself becomes more beautiful because it is situated on the neck of the Lord. A *yogī* is therefore recommended to meditate upon the Lord's neck. The Lord's transcendental form can either be meditated upon in the mind or placed in a temple in the form of a statue and decorated in such a way that everyone can contemplate it. Temple worship, therefore, is meant for persons who are not so advanced that they can meditate upon the form of the Lord. There is no difference between constantly visiting the temple and directly seeing the transcendental form of the Lord; they are of equal value. The advantageous position of the *yogī* is that he can sit anywhere in a solitary place and meditate upon the form of the Lord. A less advanced person, however, has to go to the temple, and as long as he does not go to the temple he is unable to see the form of the Lord. Either by hearing, seeing or meditating, the objective is the transcendental form of the Lord; there is no question of voidness or impersonalism. The Lord can bestow the blessings of transcendental pleasure upon either the visitor of the temple, the meditator-*yogī* or one who hears about the Lord's transcendental form from scriptures like the *Śrīmad-Bhāgavatam* or *Bhagavad-gītā.* There are nine processes for executing devotional service, of which *smaraṇam*, or meditation, is one. *Yogīs* take advantage of the process of *smaraṇam*, whereas *bhakti-yogīs* take special advantage of the process of hearing and chanting.

TEXT 27

बाहूंश्च मन्दरगिरेः परिवर्तनेन
निर्णिक्तबाहुवलयानधिलोकपालान् ।
सञ्चिन्तयेद्दशशतारमसह्यतेजः
शङ्खं च तत्करसरोरुहराजहंसम् ॥२७॥

bāhūṁś ca mandara-gireḥ parivartanena
nirṇikta-bāhu-valayān adhiloka-pālān
sañcintayed daśa-śatāram asahya-tejaḥ
śaṅkhaṁ ca tat-kara-saroruha-rāja-haṁsam

bāhūn—the arms; *ca*—and; *mandara-gireḥ*—of Mount Mandara; *parivartanena*—by the revolving; *nirṇikta*—polished; *bāhu-valayān*—the arm ornaments; *adhiloka-pālān*—the source of the controllers of the universe; *sañcintayet*—one should meditate on; *daśa-śata-aram*—the Sudarśana disc (ten hundred spokes); *asahya-tejaḥ*—dazzling luster; *śaṅkham*—the conch; *ca*—also; *tat-kara*—in the hand of the Lord; *saroruha*—lotuslike; *rāja-haṁsam*—like a swan.

TRANSLATION

The yogī should further meditate upon the Lord's four arms, which are the source of all the powers of the demigods who control the various functions of material nature. Then the yogī should concentrate on the polished ornaments, which were burnished by Mount Mandara as it revolved. He should also duly contemplate the Lord's discus, the Sudarśana cakra, which contains one thousand spokes and a dazzling luster, as well as the conch, which looks like a swan in His lotuslike palm.

PURPORT

All departments of law and order emanate from the arms of the Supreme Personality of Godhead. The law and order of the universe is directed by different demigods, and it is here said to emanate from the Lord's arms. Mandara Hill is mentioned here because when the ocean was churned by the demons on one side and the demigods on the other, Mandara Hill was taken as the churning rod. The Lord in His tortoise incarnation became the pivot for the churning rod, and thus His ornaments were polished by the turning of Mandara Hill. In other words, the ornaments on the arms of the Lord are as brilliant and lustrous as if they had been polished very recently. The wheel in the hand of the Lord, called the Sudarśana *cakra,* has one thousand spokes. The *yogī* is advised to meditate upon each of the spokes. He should meditate upon each and every one of the component parts of the transcendental form of the Lord.

TEXT 28

कौमोदकीं भगवतो दयितां स्मरेत
दिग्धामरातिभटशोणितकर्दमेन ।
मालां मधुव्रतवरूथगिरोपघुष्टां
चैत्यस्य तत्त्वममलं मणिमस्य कण्ठे ॥२८॥

kaumodakīṁ bhagavato dayitāṁ smareta
digdhām arāti-bhaṭa-śoṇita-kardamena
mālāṁ madhuvrata-varūtha-giropaghuṣṭāṁ
caityasya tattvam amalaṁ maṇim asya kaṇṭhe

kaumodakīm—the club named Kaumodakī; *bhagavataḥ*—of the Personality of Godhead; *dayitām*—very dear; *smareta*—one should remember; *digdhām*—smeared; *arāti*—of the enemies; *bhaṭa*—soldiers; *śoṇita-kardamena*—with the bloodstains; *mālām*—the garland; *madhuvrata*—of bumblebees; *varūtha*—of a swarm; *girā*—with the sound; *upaghuṣṭām*—surrounded; *caityasya*—of the living entity; *tattvam*—principle, truth; *amalam*—pure; *maṇim*—the pearl necklace; *asya*—of the Lord; *kaṇṭhe*—on the neck.

TRANSLATION

The yogī should meditate upon His club, which is named Kaumodakī and is very dear to Him. This club smashes the demons, who are always inimical soldiers, and is smeared with their blood. One should also concentrate on the nice garland on the neck of the Lord, which is always surrounded by bumblebees, with their nice buzzing sound, and one should meditate upon the pearl necklace on the Lord's neck, which is considered to represent the pure living entities who are always engaged in His service.

PURPORT

The *yogī* must contemplate the different parts of the transcendental body of the Lord. Here it is stated that the constitutional position of the living entities should be understood. There are two kinds of living entities mentioned here. One is called the *arāti.* They are averse to understanding the pastimes of the Supreme Personality of Godhead. For them, the Lord appears with His hand clutching the terrible mace, which is always smeared with bloodstains from His killing of demons. Demons are also sons of the Supreme Personality of Godhead. As stated in *Bhagavad-gītā*, all the different species of living entities are sons of the Supreme Personality of Godhead. There are, however, two classes of living entities, who act in two different ways. The Supreme Lord keeps on His neck those living entities who are pure, as one protects the jewels and pearls on the bosom and neck of one's body. Those living entities in pure Kṛṣṇa consciousness are symbolized by the pearls on His neck. Those who are demons and are inimical towards the pastimes of the Supreme Personality of Godhead are punished by His mace, which is always smeared with the blood of such fallen living entities. The club of the Lord is very dear to Him because He uses this instrument to smash the bodies of the demons and mix their blood. As mud is kneaded with water and earth, so the earthly bodies of the enemies of the Lord, or the atheists, are smashed by the club of the Lord, which becomes muddied with the blood of such demons.

TEXT 29

भृत्यानुकम्पितधियेह गृहीतमूर्तेः
सञ्चिन्तयेद्भगवतो वदनारविन्दम् ।
यद्विस्फुरन्मकरकुण्डलवल्गितेन
विद्योतितामलकपोलमुदारनासम् ॥२९॥

bhṛtyānukampita-dhiyeha gṛhīta-mūrteḥ
sañcintayed bhagavato vadanāravindam
yad visphuran-makara-kuṇḍala-valgitena
vidyotitāmala-kapolam udāra-nāsam

bhṛtya—for the devotees; *anukampita-dhiyā*—out of compassion; *iha*—in this world; *gṛhīta-mūrteḥ*—who presents different forms; *sañcintayet*—one should meditate on; *bhagavataḥ*—of the Personality of Godhead; *vadana*—countenance; *aravindam*—lotuslike; *yat*—which; *visphuran*—glittering; *makara*—alligator-shaped; *kuṇḍala*—of

His earrings; *valgitena*—by the oscillation; *vidyotita*—illuminated; *amala*—crystal clear; *kapolam*—His cheeks; *udāra*—prominent; *nāsam*—His nose.

TRANSLATION

The yogī should then meditate on the lotuslike countenance of the Lord, who presents His different forms in this world out of compassion for the anxious devotees. His nose is prominent, and His crystal-clear cheeks are illuminated by the oscillation of His glittering alligator-shaped earrings.

PURPORT

The Lord descends to the material world out of His deep compassion for His devotees. There are two reasons for the Lord's appearance or incarnation in the material world. Whenever there is a discrepancy in the discharge of religious principles and there is prominence of irreligion, the Lord descends for the protection of the devotees and the destruction of the nondevotees. When He appears, His main purpose is to give solace to His devotees. He does not have to come Himself to destroy the demons, for He has many agents; even the external energy, *māyā*, has sufficient strength to kill them. But when He comes to show compassion to His devotees, He kills the nondevotees as a matter of course.

The Lord appears in the particular form loved by a particular type of devotee. There are millions of forms of the Lord, but they are one Absolute. As stated in the *Brahma-saṁhitā, advaitam acyutam anādim ananta-rūpam:* all the different forms of the Lord are one, but some devotees want to see Him in the form of Rādhā and Kṛṣṇa, others prefer Him as Sītā and Rāmacandra, others would see Him as Lakṣmī-Nārāyaṇa, and others want to see Him as four-handed Nārāyaṇa, Vāsudeva. The Lord has innumerable forms, and He appears in a particular form as preferred by a particular type of devotee. A *yogī* is advised to meditate upon the forms that are approved by devotees. A *yogī* cannot imagine a form for meditation. Those so-called *yogīs* who manufacture a circle or target are engaged in nonsense. Actually, a *yogī* must meditate upon the form of the Supreme Personality of Godhead that has been experienced by the Lord's pure devotees. *Yogī* means devotee. *Yogīs* who are not actually pure devotees should follow in the footsteps of devotees. It is especially mentioned here that the *yogī* should meditate upon the form which is thus approved; he cannot manufacture a form of the Lord.

TEXT 30

यच्छ्रीनिकेतमलिभिः परिसेव्यमानं
भूत्या स्वया कुटिलकुन्तलवृन्दजुष्टम् ।
मीनद्वयाश्रयमधिक्षिपदब्जनेत्रं
ध्यायेन्मनोमयमतन्द्रित उल्लसद्भ्रु ॥३०॥

yac chrī-niketam alibhiḥ parisevyamānaṁ
bhūtyā svayā kuṭila-kuntala-vṛnda-juṣṭam
mīna-dvayāśrayam adhikṣipad abja-netraṁ
dhyāyen manomayam atandrita ullasad-bhru

yat—which face of the Lord; *śrī-niketam*—a lotus; *alibhiḥ*—by bees; *parisevyamānam*—surrounded; *bhūtyā*—by elegance; *svayā*—its; *kuṭila*—curly; *kuntala*—of hair; *vṛnda*—by a multitude; *juṣṭam*—adorned; *mīna*—of fish; *dvaya*—a pair; *āśrayam*—dwelling; *adhikṣipat*—putting to shame; *abja*—a lotus; *netram*—having eyes; *dhyāyet*—one should meditate on; *manaḥ-mayam*—formed in the mind; *atandritaḥ*—attentive; *ullasat*—dancing; *bhru*—having eyebrows.

TRANSLATION

The yogī then meditates upon the beautiful face of the Lord, which is adorned with curly hair and decorated by lotuslike eyes and dancing eyebrows. A lotus surrounded by swarming bees and a pair of swimming fish would be put to shame by its elegance.

PURPORT

One important statement here is *dhyāyen manomayam. Manomayam* is not imagination. Impersonalists think that the *yogī* can imagine any form he likes, but, as stated here, the *yogī* must meditate upon the form of the Lord which is experienced by devotees. Devotees never imagine a form of the Lord. They are not satisfied by something imaginary. The Lord has different eternal forms; each devotee likes a particular form and thus engages himself in the service of the Lord by worshiping that form. The Lord's form is depicted in different ways according to scriptures. As already discussed, there are eight kinds of representations of the original form of the Lord. These representations can be produced by the use of clay, stone, wood, paint, sand, etc., depending upon the resources of the devotee.

Manomayam is a carving of the form of the Lord within the mind. This is included as one of the eight different carvings of the form of the Lord. It is not imagination. Meditation on the actual form of the Lord may be manifested in different manners, but one should not conclude that one has to imagine a form. There are two comparisons in this verse: first, the Lord's face is compared to a lotus, and then His black hair is compared to humming bees swarming around the lotus, and His two eyes are compared to two fish swimming about. A lotus flower on the water is very beautiful when surrounded by humming bees and fish. The Lord's face is self-sufficient and complete. His beauty defies the natural beauty of a lotus.

TEXT 31

तस्यावलोकमधिकं कृपयातिघोर-
तापत्रयोपशमनाय निसृष्टमक्ष्णोः ।
स्निग्धस्मितानुगुणितं विपुलप्रसादं
ध्यायेच्चिरं विपुलभावनया गुहायाम् ॥३१॥

tasyāvalokam adhikaṁ kṛpayātighora-
tāpa-trayopaśamanāya nisṛṣṭam akṣṇoḥ
snigdha-smitānuguṇitaṁ vipula-prasādaṁ
dhyāyec ciraṁ vipula-bhāvanayā guhāyām

tasya—of the Personality of Godhead; *avalokam*—glances; *adhikam*—frequent; *kṛpayā*—with compassion; *atighora*—most fearful; *tāpa-traya*—threefold agonies; *upaśamanāya*—soothing; *nisṛṣṭam*—cast; *akṣṇoḥ*—from His eyes; *snigdha*—loving; *smita*—smiles; *anuguṇitam*—accompanied by; *vipula*—abundant; *prasādam*—full of grace; *dhyāyet*—he should contemplate; *ciram*—for a long time; *vipula*—full; *bhāvanayā*—with devotion; *guhāyām*—in the heart.

TRANSLATION

The yogīs should contemplate with full devotion the compassionate glances frequently cast by the Lord's eyes, for they soothe the most fearful threefold agonies of His devotees. His glances, accompanied by loving smiles, are full of abundant grace.

PURPORT

As long as one is in conditional life, in the material body, it is natural that he will suffer from anxieties and agonies. One cannot avoid the influence of material energy, even when one is on the transcendental plane. Sometimes disturbances come, but the agonies and anxieties of the devotees are at once mitigated when they think of the Supreme Personality of Godhead in His beautiful form or the smiling face of the Lord. The Lord bestows innumerable favors upon His devotee, and the greatest manifestation of His grace is His smiling face, which is full of compassion for His pure devotees.

TEXT 32

हासं हरेरवनताखिललोकतीव्र-
शोकाश्रुसागरविशोषणमत्युदारम् ।
सम्मोहनाय रचितं निजमाययास्य
भ्रूमण्डलं मुनिकृते मकरध्वजस्य ॥३२॥

hāsaṁ harer avanatākhila-loka-tīvra-
śokāśru-sāgara-viśoṣaṇam atyudāram
sammohanāya racitaṁ nija-māyayāsya
bhrū-maṇḍalaṁ muni-kṛte makara-dhvajasya

hāsam—the smile; *hareḥ*—of Lord Śrī Hari; *avanata*—bowed; *akhila*—all; *loka*—for persons; *tīvra-śoka*—caused by intense grief; *aśru-sāgara*—the ocean of tears; *viśoṣaṇam*—drying up; *ati-udāram*—most benevolent; *sammohanāya*—for charming; *racitam*—manifested; *nija-māyayā*—by His internal potency; *asya*—His; *bhrū-maṇḍalam*—

arched eyebrows; *muni-kṛte*—for the good of the sages; *makara-dhvajasya*—of the sex-god.

TRANSLATION

A yogī should similarly meditate on the most benevolent smile of Lord Śrī Hari, a smile which, for all those who bow to Him, dries away the ocean of tears caused by intense grief. The yogī should also meditate on the Lord's arched eyebrows, which are manifested by His internal potency in order to charm the sex-god for the good of the sages.

PURPORT

The entire universe is full of miseries, and therefore the inhabitants of this material universe are always shedding tears out of intense grief. There is a great ocean of water made from such tears, but for one who surrenders unto the Supreme Personality of Godhead, the ocean of tears is at once dried up. One need only see the charming smile of the Supreme Lord. In other words, the bereavement of material existence immediately subsides when one sees the charming smile of the Lord.

It is stated in this verse that the charming eyebrows of the Lord are so fascinating that they cause one to forget the charms of sense attraction. The conditioned souls are shackled to material existence because they are captivated by the charms of sense gratification, especially sex life. The sex-god is called Makara-dhvaja. The charming brows of the Supreme Personality of Godhead protect the sages and devotees from being charmed by material lust and sex attraction. Yāmunācārya, a great *ācārya*, said that ever since he had seen the charming pastimes of the Lord, the charms of sex life had become abominable for him, and the mere thought of sex enjoyment would cause him to spit and turn his face. Thus if anyone wants to be aloof from sex attraction, he must see the charming smile and fascinating eyebrows of the Supreme Personality of Godhead.

TEXT 33

ध्यानायनं प्रहसितं बहुलाधरोष्ठ-
भासारुणायिततनुद्विजकुन्दपङ्क्ति ।
ध्यायेत्स्वदेहकुहरेऽवसितस्य विष्णो-
र्भक्त्यार्द्रयार्पितमना न पृथग्दिदृक्षेत् ॥३३॥

dhyānāyanaṁ prahasitaṁ bahulādharoṣṭha-
bhāsāruṇāyita-tanu-dvija-kunda-paṅkti
dhyāyet svadeha-kuhare 'vasitasya viṣṇor
bhaktyārdrayārpita-manā na pṛthag didṛkṣet

dhyāna-ayanam—easily meditated upon; *prahasitam*—the laughter; *bahula*—abundant; *adhara-oṣṭha*—of His lips; *bhāsa*—by the splendor; *aruṇāyita*—rendered rosy; *tanu*—small; *dvija*—teeth; *kunda-paṅkti*—like a row of jasmine buds; *dhyāyet*—he should meditate upon; *sva-deha-kuhare*—in the core of his heart; *avasitasya*—who resides; *viṣṇoḥ*—of Viṣṇu; *bhaktyā*—with devotion; *ārdrayā*—steeped in love; *arpita-manāḥ*—his mind being fixed; *na*—not; *pṛthak*—anything else; *didṛkṣet*—he should desire to see.

TRANSLATION

With devotion steeped in love and affection, the yogī should meditate within the core of his heart upon the laughter of Lord Viṣṇu. The laughter of Viṣṇu is so captivating that it can be easily meditated upon. When the Supreme Lord is laughing, one can see His small teeth, which resemble jasmine buds rendered rosy by the splendor of His lips. Once devoting his mind to this, the yogī should no longer desire to see anything else.

PURPORT

It is recommended that the *yogī* visualize the laughter of the Lord after studying His smile very carefully. These particular descriptions of meditation on the smile, laughter, face, lips and teeth all indicate conclusively that God is not impersonal. It is described herein that one should meditate on the laughter or smiling of Viṣṇu. There is no other activity that can completely cleanse the heart of the devotee. The exceptional beauty of the laughter of Lord Viṣṇu is that when He smiles His small teeth, which resemble the buds of jasmine flowers, at once become reddish, reflecting His rosy lips. If the *yogī* is able to place the beautiful face of the Lord in the core of his heart, he will be completely satisfied. In other words, when one is absorbed in seeing the beauty of the Lord within himself, the material attraction can no longer disturb him.

TEXT 34

एवं हरौ भगवति प्रतिलब्धभावो
भक्त्या द्रवद्धृदय उत्पुलकः प्रमोदात्।
औत्कण्ठ्यबाष्पकलया मुहुरर्द्यमान-
स्तच्चापि चित्तबडिशं शनकैर्वियुङ्क्ते ॥३४॥

evaṁ harau bhagavati pratilabdha-bhāvo
bhaktyā dravad-dhṛdaya utpulakaḥ pramodāt
autkaṇṭhya-bāṣpa-kalayā muhur ardyamānas
tac cāpi citta-baḍiśaṁ śanakair viyuṅkte

evam—thus; *harau*—towards Lord Hari; *bhagavati*—the Personality of Godhead; *pratilabdha*—developed; *bhāvaḥ*—pure love; *bhaktyā*—by devotional service; *dravat*—melting; *hṛdayaḥ*—his heart; *utpulakaḥ*—experiencing standing of the hairs of the body; *pramodāt*—from excessive joy; *autkaṇṭhya*—occasioned by intense love; *bāṣpa-kalayā*—by a stream of tears; *muhuḥ*—constantly; *ardyamānaḥ*—being afflicted; *tat*—that; *ca*—and; *api*—even; *citta*—the mind; *baḍiśam*—hook; *śanakaiḥ*—gradually; *viyuṅkte*—withdraws.

TRANSLATION

By following this course, the yogī gradually develops pure love for the Supreme Personality of Godhead, Hari. In the course of his progress in devotional service, the hairs on his body stand erect through excessive joy, and he is constantly bathed in a stream of tears occasioned by intense love. Gradually, even the mind, which he used as a means to attract the Lord, as one attracts a fish to a hook, withdraws from material activity.

PURPORT

Here it is clearly mentioned that meditation, which is an action of the mind, is not the perfect stage of *samādhi*, or absorption. In the beginning the mind is employed in attracting the form of the Supreme Personality of Godhead, but in the higher stages there is no question of using the mind. A devotee becomes accustomed to serving the Supreme Lord by purification of his senses. In other words, the *yoga* principles of meditation are required as long as one is not situated in pure devotional service. The mind is used to purify the senses, but when the senses are purified by meditation, there is no need to sit in a particular place and try to meditate upon the form of the Lord. One becomes so habituated that he automatically engages in the personal service of the Lord. When the mind forcibly is engaged upon the form of the Lord, this is called *nirbīja-yoga*, or lifeless *yoga*, for the *yogī* does not automatically engage in the personal service of the Lord. But when he is constantly thinking of the Lord, that is called *sabīja-yoga*, or living *yoga*. One has to be promoted to the platform of living *yoga*.

One should engage in the service of the Lord twenty-four hours a day, as confirmed in the *Brahma-saṁhitā*. The stage of *premāñjana-cchurita* can be attained by developing complete love. When one's love for the Supreme Personality of Godhead in devotional service is fully developed, one always sees the Lord, even without artificially meditating on His form. His vision is divine because he has no other engagement. At this stage of spiritual realization it is not necessary to engage the mind artificially. Since the meditation recommended in the lower stages is a means to come to the platform of devotional service, those already engaged in the transcendental loving service of the Lord are above such meditation. This stage of perfection is called Kṛṣṇa consciousness.

TEXT 35

मुक्ताश्रयं यर्हि निर्विषयं विरक्तं
निर्वाणमृच्छति मनः सहसा यथार्चिः ।
आत्मानमत्र पुरुषोऽव्यवधानमेक-
मन्वीक्षते प्रतिनिवृत्तगुणप्रवाहः ॥३५॥

muktāśrayaṁ yarhi nirviṣayaṁ viraktaṁ
nirvāṇam ṛcchati manaḥ sahasā yathārciḥ
ātmānam atra puruṣo 'vyavadhānam ekam
anvīkṣate pratinivṛtta-guṇa-pravāhaḥ

mukta-āśrayam—situated in liberation; *yarhi*—at which time; *nir-viṣayam*—detached from sense objects; *viraktam*—indifferent; *nir-vāṇam*—extinction; *ṛcchati*—obtains; *manaḥ*—the mind; *sahasā*—immediately; *yathā*—like; *arciḥ*—the flame; *ātmānam*—the mind; *atra*—at this time; *puruṣaḥ*—a person; *avyavadhānam*—without separation; *ekam*—one; *anvīkṣate*—experiences; *pratinivṛtta*—freed; *guṇa-pravāhaḥ*—from the flow of material qualities.

TRANSLATION

When the mind is thus completely freed from all material contamination and detached from material objectives, it is just like the flame of a lamp. At that time the mind is actually dovetailed with that of the Supreme Lord and is experienced as one with Him because it is freed from the interactive flow of the material qualities.

PURPORT

In the material world the activities of the mind are acceptance and rejection. As long as the mind is in material consciousness, it must be forcibly trained to accept meditation on the Supreme Personality of Godhead, but when one is actually elevated to loving the Supreme Lord, the mind is automatically absorbed in thought of the Lord. In such a position a *yogī* has no other thought than to serve the Lord. This dovetailing of the mind with the desires of the Supreme Personality of Godhead is called *nirvāṇa*, or making the mind one with the Supreme Lord.

The best example of *nirvāṇa* is cited in *Bhagavad-gītā*. In the beginning the mind of Arjuna deviated from Kṛṣṇa's. Kṛṣṇa wanted Arjuna to fight, but Arjuna did not want to, so there was disagreement. But after hearing *Bhagavad-gītā* from the Supreme Personality of Godhead, Arjuna dovetailed his mind with Kṛṣṇa's desire. This is called oneness. This oneness, however, did not cause Arjuna and Kṛṣṇa to lose their individualities. The Māyāvādī philosophers cannot understand this. They think that oneness necessitates loss of individuality. Actually, however, we find in *Bhagavad-gītā* that individuality is not lost. When the mind is completely purified in love of Godhead, the mind becomes the mind of the Supreme Personality of Godhead. The mind at that time does not act separately, nor does it act without inspiration to fulfill the desire of the Lord. The individual liberated soul has no other activity. *Pratinivṛtta-*

guṇa-pravāhaḥ. In the conditioned state the mind is always engaged in activity impelled by the three modes of the material world, but in the transcendental stage, the material modes cannot disturb the mind of the devotee. The devotee has no other concern than to satisfy the desires of the Lord. That is the highest stage of perfection, called *nirvāṇa* or *nirvāṇa-mukti.* At this stage the mind becomes completely free from material desire.

Yathārciḥ. Arciḥ means "flame." When a lamp is broken or the oil is finished, we see that the flame of the lamp goes out. But according to scientific understanding, the flame is not extinguished; it is conserved. This is conservation of energy. Similarly, when the mind stops functioning on the material platform, it is conserved in the activities of the Supreme Lord. The Māyāvādī philosophers' conception of cessation of the functions of the mind is explained here: cessation of the mental functions means cessation of activities conducted under the influence of the three modes of material nature.

TEXT 36

सोऽप्येतया चरमया मनसो निवृत्त्या
तस्मिन्महिम्न्यवसितः सुखदुःखबाह्ये ।
हेतुत्वमप्यसति कर्तरि दुःखयोर्यत्
स्वात्मन् विधत्त उपलब्धपरात्मकाष्ठः ॥३६॥

so 'py etayā caramayā manaso nivṛttyā
tasmin mahimny avasitaḥ sukha-duḥkha-bāhye
hetutvam apy asati kartari duḥkhayor yat
svātman vidhatta upalabdha-parātma-kāṣṭhaḥ

saḥ—the *yogī; api*—moreover; *etayā*—by this; *caramayā*—ultimate; *manasaḥ*—of the mind; *nivṛttyā*—by cessation of material reaction; *tasmin*—in his; *mahimni*—ultimate glory; *avasitaḥ*—situated; *sukha-duḥkha-bāhye*—outside of happiness and distress; *hetutvam*—the cause; *api*—indeed; *asati*—a product of ignorance; *kartari*—in the false ego; *duḥkhayoḥ*—of pleasure and pain; *yat*—which; *sva-ātman*—to his own self; *vidhatte*—he attributes; *upalabdha*—realized; *para-ātma*—of the Personality of Godhead; *kāṣṭhaḥ*—the highest truth.

TRANSLATION

Thus situated in the highest transcendental stage, the mind ceases from all material reaction and becomes situated in its own glory, transcendental to all material conceptions of happiness and distress. At that time the yogī realizes the truth of his relationship with the Supreme Personality of Godhead. He discovers that pleasure and pain as well as their interactions, which he attributed to his own self, are actually due to the false ego, which is a product of ignorance.

PURPORT

Forgetfulness of one's relationship with the Supreme Personality of Godhead is a product of ignorance. By *yoga* practice one can eradicate this ignorance of thinking oneself independent of the Supreme Lord. One's actual relationship is eternally that of love. The living entity is meant to render transcendental loving service to the Lord. Forgetfulness of that sweet relationship is called ignorance, and in ignorance one is impelled by the three material modes of nature to think himself the enjoyer. When the devotee's mind is purified and he understands that his mind has to be dovetailed with the desires of the Supreme Personality of Godhead, he has attained the perfectional, transcendental stage, which is beyond the perception of material distress and happiness.

As long as one acts on his own account, he is subject to all the material perceptions of so-called happiness and distress. Actually there is no happiness. Just as there is no happiness in any of the activities of a madman, so in material activities the mental concoctions of happiness and distress are false. Actually everything is distress.

When the mind is dovetailed to act according to the desire of the Lord, one has attained the transcendental stage. The desire to lord it over material nature is the cause of ignorance, and when that desire is completely extinguished and the desires are dovetailed with those of the Supreme Lord, one has reached the perfectional stage. *Upalabdha-parātma-kāṣṭhaḥ. Upalabdha* means "realization." Realization necessarily indicates individuality. In the perfectional, liberated stage, there is actual realization. *Nivṛttyā* means that the living entity keeps his individuality; oneness means that he realizes happiness in the happiness of the Supreme Lord. In the Supreme Lord there is nothing but happiness.

Ānandamayo 'bhyāsāt: the Lord is by nature full of transcendental happiness. In the liberated stage, oneness with the Supreme Lord means that one has no realization other than happiness. But the individual still exists, otherwise this word *upalabdha*, indicating individual realization of transcendental happiness, would not have been used.

TEXT 37

देहं च तं न चरमः स्थितमुत्थितं वा
सिद्धो विपश्यति यतोऽध्यगमत्स्वरूपम् ।
दैवादुपेतमथ दैववशादपेतं
वासो यथा परिकृतं मदिरामदान्धः ॥३७॥

deham ca tam na caramaḥ sthitam utthitam vā
siddho vipaśyati yato 'dhyagamat svarūpam
daivād upetam atha daiva-vaśād apetam
vāso yathā parikṛtam madirā-madāndhaḥ

deham—material body; *ca*—and; *tam*—that; *na*—not; *caramaḥ*—last; *sthitam*—sitting; *utthitam*—rising; *vā*—or; *siddhaḥ*—the realized soul; *vipaśyati*—can conceive; *yataḥ*—because; *adhyagamat*—he has achieved; *sva-rūpam*—his real identity; *daivāt*—according to destiny; *upetam*—arrived; *atha*—moreover; *daiva-vaśāt*—according to destiny; *apetam*—departed; *vāsaḥ*—clothing; *yathā*—as; *parikṛtam*—put on; *madirā-mada-andhaḥ*—one who is blinded by intoxication.

TRANSLATION

Because he has achieved his real identity, the perfectly realized soul has no conception of how the material body is moving or acting, just as an intoxicated person cannot understand whether or not he has clothing on his body.

PURPORT

This stage of life is explained by Rūpa Gosvāmī in his *Bhakti-rasāmṛta-sindhu.* A person whose mind is completely dovetailed with the desire of the Supreme Personality of Godhead, and who engages one hundred percent in the service of the Lord, forgets his material bodily demands.

TEXT 38

देहोऽपि दैववशगः खलु कर्म यावत्
स्वारम्भकं प्रतिसमीक्षत एव सासुः ।
तं सप्रपञ्चमधिरूढसमाधियोगः
स्वाप्नं पुनर्न भजते प्रतिबुद्धवस्तुः ॥३८॥

deho 'pi daiva-vaśagaḥ khalu karma yāvat
svārambhakaṁ pratisamīkṣata eva sāsuḥ
taṁ sa-prapañcam adhirūḍha-samādhi-yogaḥ
svāpnaṁ punar na bhajate pratibuddha-vastuḥ

dehaḥ—the body; *api*—moreover; *daiva-vaśa-gaḥ*—under the control of the Personality of Godhead; *khalu*—indeed; *karma*—activities; *yāvat*—as much as; *sva-ārambhakam*—begun by himself; *pratisamīkṣate*—continues to function; *eva*—certainly; *sa-asuḥ*—along with the senses; *tam*—the body; *sa-prapañcam*—with its expansions; *adhirūḍha-samādhi-yogaḥ*—being situated in *samādhi* by *yoga* practice; *svāpnam*—born in a dream; *punaḥ*—again; *na*—not; *bhajate*—he does accept as his own; *pratibuddha*—awake; *vastuḥ*—to his constitutional position.

TRANSLATION

The body of such a liberated yogī, along with the senses, is taken charge of by the Supreme Personality of Godhead, and it functions until its destined activities are finished. The liberated devotee, being awake to his constitutional position and thus situated in samādhi, the highest perfectional stage of yoga, does not accept the by-products of the material body as his own. Thus he considers his bodily activities to be like the activities of a body in a dream.

PURPORT

The following questions may be posed. As long as the liberated soul is in contact with the body, why don't the bodily activities affect him?

Doesn't he actually become contaminated by the action and reaction of material activities? In answer to such questions, this verse explains that the material body of a liberated soul is taken charge of by the Supreme Personality of Godhead. It is not acting due to the living force of the living entity; it is simply acting as a reaction to past activities. Even after being switched off, an electric fan moves for some time. That movement is not due to the electric current, but is a continuation of the last movement; similarly, although a liberated soul appears to be acting just like an ordinary man, his actions are to be accepted as the continuation of past activities. In a dream one may see himself expanded through many bodies, but when awake he can understand that those bodies were all false. Similarly, although a liberated soul has the by-products of the body—children, wife, house, etc.—he does not identify himself with those bodily expansions. He knows that they are all products of the material dream. The gross body is made of the gross elements of matter, and the subtle body is made of mind, intelligence, ego and contaminated consciousness. If one can accept the subtle body of a dream as false and not identify oneself with that body, then certainly an awake person need not identify with the gross body. As one who is awake has no connection with the activities of the body in a dream, an awakened, liberated soul has no connection with the activities of the present body. In other words, because he is acquainted with his constitutional position, he never accepts the bodily concept of life.

TEXT 39

यथा पुत्राच्च वित्ताच्च पृथङ्मर्त्यः प्रतीयते ।
अप्यात्मत्वेनाभिमताद्देहादेः पुरुषस्तथा ॥३९॥

yathā putrāc ca vittāc ca
pṛthaṅ martyaḥ pratīyate
apy ātmatvenābhimatād
dehādeḥ puruṣas tathā

yathā—as; *putrāt*—from a son; *ca*—and; *vittāt*—from wealth; *ca*—also; *pṛthak*—differently; *martyaḥ*—a mortal man; *pratīyate*—is understood; *api*—even; *ātmatvena*—by nature; *abhimatāt*—for which one has affection; *deha-ādeḥ*—from his material body, senses and mind; *puruṣaḥ*—the liberated soul; *tathā*—similarly.

TRANSLATION

Because of great affection for family and wealth, one accepts a son and some money as his own, and due to affection for the material body, one thinks that it is his. But actually, as one can understand that his family and wealth are different from him, the liberated soul can understand that he and his body are not the same.

PURPORT

The status of real knowledge is explained in this verse. There are many children, but we accept some children as our sons and daughters because of our affection for them, although we know very well that these children are different from us. Similarly, because of great affection for money, we accept some amount of wealth in the bank as ours. In the same way, we claim that the body is ours because of affection for it. I say that it is "my" body. I then extend that possessive concept and say, "It is my hand, my leg," and further, "It is my bank balance, my son, my daughter." But actually I know that the son and the money are separate from me. It is the same with the body; I am separate from my body. It is a question of understanding, and the proper understanding is called *pratibuddha.* By obtaining knowledge in devotional service, or Kṛṣṇa consciousness, one can become a liberated soul.

TEXT 40

यथोल्मुकाद्विस्फुलिङ्गाद्धूमाद्वापि स्वसम्भवात् ।
अप्यात्मत्वेनाभिमताद्यथाग्निः पृथगुल्मुकात् ॥४०॥

yatholmukād visphuliṅgād
dhūmād vāpi sva-sambhavāt
apy ātmatvenābhimatād
yathāgniḥ pṛthag ulmukāt

yathā—as; *ulmukāt*—from the flames; *visphuliṅgāt*—from the sparks; *dhūmāt*—from the smoke; *vā*—or; *api*—even; *sva-sambha-*

vāt—produced from itself; *api*—although; *ātmatvena*—by nature; *abhimatāt*—intimately connected; *yathā*—as; *agniḥ*—the fire; *pṛthak*—different; *ulmukāt*—from the flames.

TRANSLATION

The blazing fire is different from the flames, from the sparks and from the smoke, although all are intimately connected because they are born from the same blazing wood.

PURPORT

Although the blazing firewood, the sparks, the smoke and the flame cannot stay apart because each of them is part and parcel of the fire, still they are different from one another. A less intelligent person accepts the smoke as fire, although fire and smoke are completely different. The heat and light of the fire are separate, although one cannot differentiate fire from heat and light.

TEXT 41

भूतेन्द्रियान्तःकरणात्प्रधानाज्जीवसंज्ञितात् ।
आत्मा तथा पृथग्द्रष्टा भगवान् ब्रह्मसंज्ञितः ॥४१॥

bhūtendriyāntaḥ-karaṇāt
pradhānāj jīva-saṁjñitāt
ātmā tathā pṛthag draṣṭā
bhagavān brahma-saṁjñitaḥ

bhūta—the five elements; *indriya*—the senses; *antaḥ-karaṇāt*—from the mind; *pradhānāt*—from the *pradhāna; jīva-saṁjñitāt*—from the *jīva* soul; *ātmā*—the Paramātmā; *tathā*—so; *pṛthak*—different; *draṣṭā*—the seer; *bhagavān*—the Personality of Godhead; *brahma-saṁjñitaḥ*—called Brahman.

TRANSLATION

The Supreme Personality of Godhead, who is known as paraṁ brahma, is the seer. He is different from the jīva soul, or individual living entity, who is combined with the senses, the five elements and consciousness.

PURPORT

A clear conception of the complete whole is given herewith. The living entity is different from the material elements, and the supreme living entity, the Personality of Godhead, who is the creator of the material elements, is also different from the individual living entity. This philosophy is propounded by Lord Caitanya as *acintya-bhedābheda-tattva.* Everything is simultaneously one with and different from everything else. The cosmic manifestation created by the Supreme Lord by His material energy is also simultaneously different and nondifferent from Him. The material energy is nondifferent from the Supreme Lord, but at the same time, because that energy is acting in a different way, it is different from Him. Similarly, the individual living entity is one with and different from the Supreme Lord. This "simultaneously one and different" philosophy is the perfect conclusion of the *Bhāgavata* school, as confirmed here by Kapiladeva.

Living entities are compared to the sparks of a fire. As stated in the previous verse, fire, flame, smoke and firewood are combined together. Here the living entity, the material elements and the Supreme Personality of Godhead are combined together. The exact position of the living entities is just like that of the sparks of a fire; they are part and parcel. The material energy is compared to the smoke. The fire is also part and parcel of the Supreme Lord. In the *Viṣṇu Purāṇa* it is said that whatever we can see or experience, either in the material or spiritual world, is an expansion of the different energies of the Supreme Lord. As fire distributes its light and heat from one place, the Supreme Personality of Godhead distributes His different energies all over His creation.

The four principles of the Vaiṣṇava philosophic doctrine are *śuddha-advaita* (purified oneness), *dvaita-advaita* (simultaneous oneness and difference), *viśiṣṭa-advaita* and *dvaita.* All four principles of Vaiṣṇava philosophy are based on the thesis of *Śrīmad-Bhāgavatam* explained in these two verses.

TEXT 42

सर्वभूतेषु चात्मानं सर्वभूतानि चात्मनि ।
ईक्षेतानन्यभावेन भूतेष्विव तदात्मताम् ॥४२॥

sarva-bhūteṣu cātmānaṁ
sarva-bhūtāni cātmani
īkṣetānanya-bhāvena
bhūteṣv iva tad-ātmatām

sarva-bhūteṣu—in all manifestations; *ca*—and; *ātmānam*—the soul; *sarva-bhūtāni*—all manifestations; *ca*—also; *ātmani*—in the Supreme Spirit; *īkṣeta*—he should see; *ananya-bhāvena*—with equal vision; *bhūteṣu*—in all manifestations; *iva*—as; *tat-ātmatām*—the nature of itself.

TRANSLATION

A yogī should see the same soul in all manifestations, for all that exists is a manifestation of different energies of the Supreme. In this way the devotee should see all living entities without distinction. That is realization of the Supreme Soul.

PURPORT

As stated in the *Brahma-saṁhitā,* not only does the Supreme Soul enter each and every universe, but He enters even the atoms. The Supreme Soul is present everywhere in the dormant stage, and when one can see the presence of the Supreme Soul everywhere, one is liberated from material designations.

The word *sarva-bhūteṣu* is to be understood as follows. There are four different divisions of species—living entities which sprout from the earth, living entities born of fermentation or germination, living entities which come from eggs and living entities which come from the embryo. These four divisions of living entities are expanded in 8,400,000 species of life. A person who is freed from material designations can see the same quality of spirit present everywhere or in every manifested living entity. Less intelligent men think that plants and grass grow out of the earth automatically, but one who is actually intelligent and has realized the self can see that this growth is not automatic; the cause is the soul, and the forms come out in material bodies under different conditions. By fermentation in the laboratory many germs are born, but this is due to the presence of the soul. The material scientist thinks that eggs are lifeless, but that is not a fact. From Vedic scripture we can understand that living entities in different forms are generated under different conditions. Birds evolve from eggs, and beasts and human beings are born from the embryo. The perfect vision of the *yogī* or devotee is that he sees the presence of the living entity everywhere.

TEXT 43

स्वयोनिषु यथा ज्योतिरेकं नाना प्रतीयते ।
योनीनां गुणवैषम्यात्तथात्मा प्रकृतौ स्थितः ॥४३॥

sva-yoniṣu yathā jyotir
ekaṁ nānā pratīyate
yonīnāṁ guṇa-vaiṣamyāt
tathātmā prakṛtau sthitaḥ

sva-yoniṣu—in forms of wood; *yathā*—as; *jyotiḥ*—fire; *ekam*—one; *nānā*—differently; *pratīyate*—is exhibited; *yonīnām*—of different wombs; *guṇa-vaiṣamyāt*—from the different conditions of the modes; *tathā*—so; *ātmā*—the spirit soul; *prakṛtau*—in the material nature; *sthitaḥ*—situated.

TRANSLATION

As fire is exhibited in different forms of wood, so, under different conditions of the modes of material nature, the pure spirit soul manifests itself in different bodies.

PURPORT

It is to be understood that the body is designated. *Prakṛti* is an interaction by the three modes of material nature, and according to these modes, someone has a small body, and someone has a very large body. For example, the fire in a big piece of wood appears very big, and in a stick the fire appears small. Actually, the quality of fire is the same everywhere, but the manifestation of material nature is such that according to the fuel, the fire appears bigger and smaller. Similarly, the soul in the universal body, although of the same quality, is different from the soul in the smaller body.

The small particles of soul are just like sparks of the larger soul. The greatest soul is the Supersoul, but the Supersoul is quantitatively different from the small soul. The Supersoul is described in the Vedic literature as the supplier of all necessities of the smaller soul (*nityo nityānām*). One who understands this distinction between the Supersoul and the individual soul is above lamentation and is in a peaceful position. When the smaller soul thinks himself quantitatively as big as the larger soul, he is under the spell of *māyā*, for that is not his constitutional position. No one can become the greater soul simply by mental speculation.

The smallness or greatness of different souls is described in the *Varāha Purāṇa* as *svāṁśa-vibhinnāṁśa*. The *svāṁśa* soul is the Supreme Personality of Godhead, and the *vibhinnāṁśa* souls, or small particles, are eternally small particles, as confirmed in *Bhagavad-gītā* (*mamaivāṁśo jīva-loke jīva-bhūtaḥ sanātanaḥ*). The small living entities are eternally part and parcel, and therefore it is not possible for them to be quantitatively as great as the Supersoul.

TEXT 44

तस्मादिमां स्वां प्रकृतिं दैवीं सदसदात्मिकाम् ।
दुर्विभाव्यां पराभाव्य स्वरूपेणावतिष्ठते ॥४४॥

tasmād imāṁ svāṁ prakṛtiṁ
daivīṁ sad-asad-ātmikām
durvibhāvyāṁ parābhāvya
svarūpeṇāvatiṣṭhate

tasmāt—thus; *imām*—this; *svām*—own; *prakṛtim*—material energy; *daivīm*—divine; *sat-asat-ātmikām*—consisting of cause and effect; *durvibhāvyām*—difficult to understand; *parābhāvya*—after conquering; *sva-rūpeṇa*—in the self-realized position; *avatiṣṭhate*—he remains.

TRANSLATION

Thus the yogī can be in the self-realized position after conquering the insurmountable spell of māyā, who presents herself as both the cause and effect of this material manifestation and is therefore very difficult to understand.

PURPORT

It is stated in *Bhagavad-gītā* that the spell of *māyā*, which covers the knowledge of the living entity, is insurmountable. However, one who surrenders unto Kṛṣṇa, the Supreme Personality of Godhead, can conquer this seemingly insurmountable spell of *māyā*. Here also it is stated that the *daivī prakṛti*, or the external energy of the Supreme Lord, is *durvibhāvyā*, very difficult to understand and very difficult to conquer. One must, however, conquer this insurmountable spell of *māyā*, and this is possible, by the grace of the Lord, when God reveals Himself to the surrendered soul. It is also stated here, *svarūpeṇāvatiṣṭhate. Svarūpa* means that one has to know that he is not the Supreme Soul, but rather, part and parcel of the Supreme Soul; that is self-realization. To think falsely that one is the Supreme Soul and that one is all-pervading is not *svarūpa*. This is not realization of his actual position. The real position is that one is part and parcel. It is recommended here that one remain in that position of actual self-realization. In *Bhagavad-gītā* this understanding is defined as Brahman realization.

After Brahman realization, one can engage in the activities of Brahman. As long as one is not self-realized, he engages in activities based on false identification with the body. When one is situated in his real self, then the activities of Brahman realization begin. The Māyāvādī philosophers say that after Brahman realization, all activities stop, but that is not actually so. If the soul is so active in its abnormal condition, existing under the covering of matter, how can one deny its activity when free? An example may be cited here. If a man in a diseased condition is very active, how can one imagine that when he is free from the disease he will be inactive? Naturally the conclusion is that when one is free from all disease his activities are pure. It may be said that the activities of Brahman realization are different from those of conditional life, but that does not stop activity. This is indicated in *Bhagavad-gītā* (18.54): after one realizes oneself to be Brahman, devotional service begins. *Mad-bhaktiṁ labhate parām:* after Brahman realization, one can engage in the devotional service of the Lord. Therefore devotional service of the Lord is activity in Brahman realization.

For those who engage in devotional service there is no spell of *māyā*, and their situation is all-perfect. The duty of the living entity, as a part and parcel of the whole, is to render devotional service to the whole. That is the ultimate perfection of life.

Thus end the Bhaktivedanta purports of the Third Canto, Twenty-eighth Chapter, of the Śrīmad-Bhāgavatam, *entitled "Lord Kapila's Instructions on the Execution of Devotional Service."*

CHAPTER TWENTY-NINE

Explanation of Devotional Service by Lord Kapila

TEXTS 1–2

देवहूतिरुवाच
लक्षणं महदादीनां प्रकृतेः पुरुषस्य च ।
स्वरूपं लक्ष्यतेऽमीषां येन तत्पारमार्थिकम् ॥ १ ॥
यथा सांख्येषु कथितं यन्मूलं तत्प्रचक्षते ।
भक्तियोगस्य मे मार्गं ब्रूहि विस्तरशः प्रभो ॥ २ ॥

devahūtir uvāca
lakṣaṇaṁ mahad-ādīnāṁ
prakṛteḥ puruṣasya ca
svarūpaṁ lakṣyate 'mīṣāṁ
yena tat-pāramārthikam

yathā sāṅkhyeṣu kathitaṁ
yan-mūlaṁ tat pracakṣate
bhakti-yogasya me mārgaṁ
brūhi vistaraśaḥ prabho

devahūtiḥ uvāca—Devahūti said; *lakṣaṇam*—symptoms; *mahat-ādīnām*—of the *mahat-tattva* and so on; *prakṛteḥ*—of material nature; *puruṣasya*—of the spirit; *ca*—and; *svarūpam*—the nature; *lakṣyate*—is described; *amīṣām*—of those; *yena*—by which; *tat-pārama-arthikam*—the true nature of them; *yathā*—as; *sāṅkhyeṣu*—in Sāṅkhya philosophy; *kathitam*—is explained; *yat*—of which; *mūlam*—ultimate end; *tat*—that; *pracakṣate*—they call; *bhakti-yogasya*—of devotional service; *me*—to me; *mārgam*—the path; *brūhi*—please explain; *vistara-śaḥ*—at length; *prabho*—my dear Lord Kapila.

TRANSLATION

Devahūti inquired: My dear Lord, You have already very scientifically described the symptoms of the total material nature and the characteristics of the spirit according to the Sāṅkhya system of philosophy. Now I shall request You to explain the path of devotional service, which is the ultimate end of all philosophical systems.

PURPORT

In this Twenty-ninth Chapter, the glories of devotional service are elaborately explained, and the influence of time on the conditioned soul is also described. The purpose of elaborately describing the influence of time is to detach the conditioned soul from his material activities, which are considered to be simply a waste of time. In the previous chapter, material nature, the spirit and the Supreme Lord, or Supersoul, are analytically studied, and in this chapter the principles of *bhakti-yoga*, or devotional service—the execution of activities in the eternal relationship between the living entities and the Personality of Godhead—are explained.

Bhakti-yoga, devotional service, is the basic principle of all systems of philosophy; all philosophy which does not aim for devotional service to the Lord is considered merely mental speculation. But of course *bhakti-yoga* with no philosophical basis is more or less sentiment. There are two classes of men. Some consider themselves intellectually advanced and simply speculate and meditate, and others are sentimental and have no philosophical basis for their propositions. Neither of these can achieve the highest goal of life—or, if they do, it will take them many, many years. Vedic literature therefore suggests that there are three elements—namely the Supreme Lord, the living entity and their eternal relationship—and the goal of life is to follow the principles of *bhakti*, or devotional service, and ultimately attain to the planet of the Supreme Lord in full devotion and love as an eternal servitor of the Lord.

Sāṅkhya philosophy is the analytical study of all existence. One has to understand everything by examining its nature and characteristics. This is called acquirement of knowledge. But one should not simply acquire knowledge without reaching the goal of life or the basic principle for acquiring knowledge—*bhakti-yoga.* If we give up *bhakti-yoga* and simply busy ourselves in the analytical study of the nature of things as they are, then the result will be practically nil. It is stated in the *Bhāgavatam* that such engagement is something like husking a paddy. There is no use beating the husk if the grain has already been removed. By the scientific study of material nature, the living entity and the Supersoul, one has to understand the basic principle of devotional service to the Lord.

TEXT 3

विरागो येन पुरुषो भगवन् सर्वतो भवेत् ।
आचक्ष्व जीवलोकस्य विविधा मम संसृतीः ॥ ३ ॥

virāgo yena puruṣo
bhagavan sarvato bhavet
ācakṣva jīva-lokasya
vividhā mama saṁsṛtīḥ

virāgaḥ—detached; *yena*—by which; *puruṣaḥ*—a person; *bhagavan*—my dear Lord; *sarvataḥ*—completely; *bhavet*—may become; *ācakṣva*—please describe; *jīva-lokasya*—for the people in general; *vividhāḥ*—manifold; *mama*—for myself; *saṁsṛtīḥ*—repetition of birth and death.

TRANSLATION

Devahūti continued: My dear Lord, please also describe in detail, both for me and for people in general, the continual process of birth and death, for by hearing of such calamities we may become detached from the activities of this material world.

PURPORT

In this verse the word *saṁsṛtīḥ* is very important. *Śreyaḥ-sṛti* means the prosperous path of advancement towards the Supreme Personality of Godhead, and *saṁsṛti* means the continued journey on the path of birth and death towards the darkest region of material existence. People who have no knowledge of this material world, God and their actual intimate relationship with Him are actually going to the darkest region of material existence in the name of progress in the material advancement of civilization. To enter the darkest region of material existence means to enter into a species of life other than the human species. Ignorant men do not know that after this life they are completely under the grip of material nature and will be offered a life which may not be very congenial. How a living entity gets different kinds of bodies will be explained in the next chapter. This continual change of bodies in birth and death is called *saṁsāra*. Devahūti requests her glorious son, Kapila Muni, to explain about this continued journey to impress upon the conditioned souls that they are undergoing a path of degradation by not understanding the path of *bhakti-yoga*, devotional service.

TEXT 4

कालस्येश्वररूपस्य परेषां च परस्य ते ।
स्वरूपं बत कुर्वन्ति यद्धेतोः कुशलं जनाः ॥ ४ ॥

kālasyeśvara-rūpasya
pareṣāṁ ca parasya te
svarūpaṁ bata kurvanti
yad-dhetoḥ kuśalaṁ janāḥ

kālasya—of time; *īśvara-rūpasya*—a representation of the Lord; *pareṣām*—of all others; *ca*—and; *parasya*—the chief; *te*—of You; *svarūpam*—the nature; *bata*—oh; *kurvanti*—perform; *yat-hetoḥ*—by whose influence; *kuśalam*—pious activities; *janāḥ*—people in general.

TRANSLATION

Please also describe eternal time, which is a representation of Your form and by whose influence people in general engage in the performance of pious activities.

PURPORT

However ignorant one may be regarding the path of good fortune and the path down to the darkest region of ignorance, everyone is aware of the influence of eternal time, which devours all the effects of our material activities. The body is born at a certain time, and immediately the influence of time acts upon it. From the date of the birth of the body, the influence of death is also acting; the advancement of age entails the influence of time on the body. If a man is thirty or fifty years old, then the influence of time has already devoured thirty or fifty years of the duration of his life.

Everyone is conscious of the last stage of life, when he will meet the cruel hands of death, but some consider their age and circumstances, concern themselves with the influence of time and thus engage in pious activities so that in the future they will not be put into a low family or an animal species. Generally, people are attached to sense enjoyment and so aspire for life on the heavenly planets. Therefore, they engage themselves in charitable or other pious activities, but actually, as stated in *Bhagavad-gītā*, one cannot get relief from the chain of birth and death even if he goes to the highest planet, Brahmaloka, because the influence of time is present everywhere within this material world. In the spiritual world, however, the time factor has no influence.

TEXT 5

लोकस्य मिथ्याभिमतेरचक्षुष-
श्चिरं प्रसुप्तस्य तमस्यनाश्रये ।
श्रान्तस्य कर्मस्वनुविद्धया धिया
त्वमाविरासीः किल योगभास्करः ॥ ५ ॥

lokasya mithyābhimater acakṣuṣaś
ciraṁ prasuptasya tamasy anāśraye
śrāntasya karmasv anuviddhayā dhiyā
tvam āvirāsīḥ kila yoga-bhāskaraḥ

lokasya—of the living entities; *mithyā-abhimateḥ*—deluded by false ego; *acakṣuṣaḥ*—blind; *ciram*—for a very long time; *prasuptasya*—sleeping; *tamasi*—in darkness; *anāśraye*—without shelter; *śrāntasya*—fatigued; *karmasu*—to material activities; *anuviddhayā*—attached;

dhiyā—with the intelligence; *tvam*—You; *āvirāsīḥ*—have appeared; *kila*—indeed; *yoga*—of the *yoga* system; *bhāskaraḥ*—the sun.

TRANSLATION

My dear Lord, You are just like the sun, for You illuminate the darkness of the conditional life of the living entities. Because their eyes of knowledge are not open, they are sleeping eternally in that darkness without Your shelter, and therefore they are falsely engaged by the actions and reactions of their material activities, and they appear to be very fatigued.

PURPORT

It appears that Śrīmatī Devahūti, the glorious mother of Lord Kapiladeva, is very compassionate for the regrettable condition of people in general, who, not knowing the goal of life, are sleeping in the darkness of illusion. It is the general feeling of the Vaiṣṇava, or devotee of the Lord, that he should awaken them. Similarly, Devahūti is requesting her glorious son to illuminate the lives of the conditioned souls so that their most regrettable conditional life may be ended. The Lord is described herein as *yoga-bhāskara*, the sun of the system of all *yoga*. Devahūti has already requested her glorious son to describe *bhakti-yoga*, and the Lord has described *bhakti-yoga* as the ultimate *yoga* system.

Bhakti-yoga is the sunlike illumination for delivering the conditioned souls, whose general condition is described here. They have no eyes to see their own interests. They do not know that the goal of life is not to increase the material necessities of existence, because the body will not exist more than a few years. The living beings are eternal, and they have their eternal need. If one engages only in caring for the necessities of the body, not caring for the eternal necessities of life, then he is part of a civilization whose advancement puts the living entities in the darkest region of ignorance. Sleeping in that darkest region, one does not get any refreshment, but, rather, gradually becomes fatigued. He invents many processes to adjust this fatigued condition, but he fails and thus remains confused. The only path for mitigating his fatigue in the struggle for existence is the path of devotional service, or the path of Kṛṣṇa consciousness.

TEXT 6

मैत्रेय उवाच

इति मातुर्वचः श्लक्ष्णं प्रतिनन्द्य महामुनिः ।
आबभाषे कुरुश्रेष्ठ प्रीतस्तां करुणार्दितः ॥ ६ ॥

maitreya uvāca
iti mātur vacaḥ ślakṣṇaṁ
pratinandya mahā-muniḥ
ābabhāṣe kuru-śreṣṭha
prītas tāṁ karuṇārditaḥ

maitreyaḥ uvāca—Maitreya said; *iti*—thus; *mātuḥ*—of His mother; *vacaḥ*—the words; *ślakṣṇam*—gentle; *pratinandya*—welcoming; *mahā-muniḥ*—the great sage Kapila; *ābabhāṣe*—spoke; *kuru-śreṣṭha*—O best among the Kurus, Vidura; *prītaḥ*—pleased; *tām*—to her; *karuṇā*—with compassion; *arditaḥ*—moved.

TRANSLATION

Śrī Maitreya said: O best amongst the Kurus, the great sage Kapila, moved by great compassion and pleased by the words of His glorious mother, spoke as follows.

PURPORT

Lord Kapila was very satisfied by the request of His glorious mother because she was thinking not only in terms of her personal salvation but in terms of all the fallen conditioned souls. The Lord is always compassionate towards the fallen souls of this material world, and therefore He comes Himself or sends His confidential servants to deliver them. Since He is perpetually compassionate towards them, if some of His devotees also become compassionate towards them, He is very pleased with the devotees. In *Bhagavad-gītā* it is clearly stated that persons who are trying to elevate the condition of the fallen souls by preaching the conclusion of *Bhagavad-gītā*—namely, full surrender unto the Personality of Godhead—are very dear to Him. Thus when the Lord saw that His beloved mother was very compassionate towards the fallen souls, He was pleased, and He also became compassionate towards her.

TEXT 7

श्रीभगवानुवाच
भक्तियोगो बहुविधो मार्गैर्भामिनि भाव्यते ।
स्वभावगुणमार्गेण पुंसां भावो विभिद्यते ॥ ७ ॥

śrī-bhagavān uvāca
bhakti-yogo bahu-vidho
mārgair bhāmini bhāvyate
svabhāva-guṇa-mārgeṇa
puṁsāṁ bhāvo vibhidyate

śrī-bhagavān uvāca—the Personality of Godhead replied; *bhakti-yogaḥ*—devotional service; *bahu-vidhaḥ*—multifarious; *mārgaiḥ*—with paths; *bhāmini*—O noble lady; *bhāvyate*—is manifest; *sva-bhāva*—nature; *guṇa*—qualities; *mārgeṇa*—in terms of behavior; *puṁsām*—of the executors; *bhāvaḥ*—the appearance; *vibhidyate*—is divided.

TRANSLATION

Lord Kapila, the Personality of Godhead, replied: O noble lady, there are multifarious paths of devotional service in terms of the different qualities of the executor.

PURPORT

Pure devotional service in Kṛṣṇa consciousness is one because in pure devotional service there is no demand from the devotee to be fulfilled by the Lord. But generally people take to devotional service with a purpose. As stated in *Bhagavad-gītā*, people who are not purified take to devotional service with four purposes. A person who is distressed because of material conditions becomes a devotee of the Lord and approaches the Lord for mitigation of his distress. A person in need of money approaches the Lord to ask for some improvement in his monetary condition. Others, who are not in distress or in need of monetary assistance but are seeking knowledge in order to understand the Absolute Truth, also take to devotional service, and they inquire into the nature of the Supreme Lord. This is very nicely described in *Bhagavad-gītā* (7.16). Actually the path of devotional service is one without a second, but according to the devotees' condition, devotional service appears in multifarious varieties, as will be nicely explained in the following verses.

TEXT 8

अभिसन्धाय यो हिंसां दम्भं मात्सर्यमेव वा ।
संरम्भी भिन्नदृग्भावं मयि कुर्यात्स तामसः ॥ ८ ॥

abhisandhāya yo hiṁsāṁ
dambhaṁ mātsaryam eva vā
saṁrambhī bhinna-dṛg bhāvaṁ
mayi kuryāt sa tāmasaḥ

abhisandhāya—having in view; *yaḥ*—he who; *hiṁsām*—violence; *dambham*—pride; *mātsaryam*—envy; *eva*—indeed; *vā*—or; *saṁrambhī*—angry; *bhinna*—separate; *dṛk*—whose vision; *bhāvam*—devotional service; *mayi*—to Me; *kuryāt*—may do; *saḥ*—he; *tāmasaḥ*—in the mode of ignorance.

TRANSLATION

Devotional service executed by a person who is envious, proud, violent and angry, and who is a separatist, is considered to be in the mode of darkness.

PURPORT

It has already been stated in the *Śrīmad-Bhāgavatam*, First Canto, Second Chapter, that the highest, most glorious religion is the attainment of causeless, unmotivated devotional service. In pure devotional service, the only motive should be to please the Supreme Personality of Godhead. That is not actually a motive; that is the pure condition of the living entity. In the conditioned stage, when one engages in devotional service, he should follow the instruction of the bona fide spiritual master in full surrender. The spiritual master is the manifested representation of the Supreme Lord because he receives and presents the instructions of the Lord, as they are, by disciplic succession. It is described in *Bhagavad-gītā* that the teachings therein should be received by disciplic succession, otherwise there is adulteration. To act under the direction of a bona fide spiritual master with a motive to satisfy the Supreme Personality of Godhead is pure devotional service. But if one has a motive for personal sense gratification, his devotional service is manifested differently. Such a man may be violent, proud, envious and angry, and his interests are separate from the Lord's.

One who approaches the Supreme Lord to render devotional service, but who is proud of his personality, envious of others or vengeful, is in the mode of anger. He thinks that he is the best devotee. Devotional service executed in this way is not pure; it is mixed and is of the lowest grade, *tāmasaḥ.* Śrīla Viśvanātha Cakravartī Ṭhākura advises that a Vaiṣṇava who is not of good character should be avoided. A Vaiṣṇava is one who has taken the Supreme Personality of Godhead as the ultimate goal of life, but if one is not pure and still has motives, then he is not a Vaiṣṇava of the first order of good character. One may offer his respects to such a Vaiṣṇava because he has accepted the Supreme Lord as the ultimate goal of life, but one should not keep company with a Vaiṣṇava who is in the mode of ignorance.

TEXT 9

विषयानभिसन्धाय यश ऐश्वर्यमेव वा ।
अर्चादावर्चयेद्यो मां पृथग्भावः स राजसः ॥ ९ ॥

viṣayān abhisandhāya
yaśa aiśvaryam eva vā
arcādāv arcayed yo māṁ
pṛthag-bhāvaḥ sa rājasaḥ

viṣayān—sense objects; *abhisandhāya*—aiming at; *yaśaḥ*—fame; *aiśvaryam*—opulence; *eva*—indeed; *vā*—or; *arcā-ādau*—in worship of the Deity and so on; *arcayet*—may worship; *yaḥ*—he who; *mām*—Me; *pṛthak-bhāvaḥ*—a separatist; *saḥ*—he; *rājasaḥ*—in the mode of passion.

TRANSLATION

The worship of Deities in the temple by a separatist, with a motive for material enjoyment, fame and opulence, is devotion in the mode of passion.

PURPORT

The word "separatist" must be understood carefully. The Sanskrit words in this connection are *bhinna-dṛk* and *pṛthag-bhāvaḥ.* A separatist is one who sees his interest as separate from that of the Supreme Lord. Mixed devotees, or devotees in the modes of passion and ignorance, think that the interest of the Supreme Lord is supplying the orders of the devotee; the interest of such devotees is to draw from the Lord as much as possible for their sense gratification. This is the separatist mentality. Actually, pure devotion is explained in the previous chapter: the mind of the Supreme Lord and the mind of the devotee should be dovetailed. A devotee should not wish anything but to execute the desire of the Supreme. That is oneness. When the devotee has an interest or will different from the interest of the Supreme Lord, his mentality is that of a separatist. When the so-called devotee desires material enjoyment, without reference to the interest of the Supreme Lord, or he wants to become famous or opulent by utilizing the mercy or grace of the Supreme Lord, he is in the mode of passion.

Māyāvādīs, however, interpret this word "separatist" in a different way. They say that while worshiping the Lord, one should think himself one with the Supreme Lord. This is another adulterated form of devotion within the modes of material nature. The conception that the living entity is one with the Supreme is in the mode of ignorance. Oneness is actually based on oneness of interest. A pure devotee has no interest but to act on behalf of the Supreme Lord. When one has even a tinge of personal interest, his devotion is mixed with the three modes of material nature.

TEXT 10

कर्मनिर्हारमुद्दिश्य परस्मिन् वा तदर्पणम् ।
यजेद्यष्टव्यमिति वा पृथग्भावः स सात्त्विकः ॥१०॥

karma-nirhāram uddiśya
parasmin vā tad-arpaṇam
yajed yaṣṭavyam iti vā
pṛthag-bhāvaḥ sa sāttvikaḥ

karma—fruitive activities; *nirhāram*—freeing himself from; *uddiśya*—with the purpose of; *parasmin*—to the Supreme Personality of Godhead; *vā*—or; *tat-arpaṇam*—offering the result of activities; *yajet*—may worship; *yaṣṭavyam*—to be worshiped; *iti*—thus; *vā*—or; *pṛthak-bhāvaḥ*—separatist; *saḥ*—he; *sāttvikaḥ*—in the mode of goodness.

TRANSLATION

When a devotee worships the Supreme Personality of Godhead and offers the results of his activities in order to free himself from the inebrieties of fruitive activities, his devotion is in the mode of goodness.

PURPORT

The *brāhmaṇas, kṣatriyas, vaiśyas* and *śūdras,* along with the *brahmacārīs, gṛhasthas, vānaprasthas* and *sannyāsīs,* are the members of the eight divisions of *varṇas* and *āśramas,* and they have their respective duties to perform for the satisfaction of the Supreme Personality of Godhead. When such activities are performed and the results are offered to the Supreme Lord, they are called *karmārpaṇam,* duties performed for the satisfaction of the Lord. If there is any inebriety or fault, it is atoned for by this offering process. But if this offering process is in the mode of goodness rather than in pure devotion, then the interest is different. The four *āśramas* and the four *varṇas* act for some benefit in accordance with their personal interests. Therefore such activities are in the mode of goodness; they cannot be counted in the category of pure devotion. Pure devotional service as described by Rūpa Gosvāmī is free from all material desires. *Anyābhilāṣitā-śūnyam.* There can be no excuse for personal or material interest. Devotional activities should be transcendental to fruitive activities and empiric philosophical speculation. Pure devotional service is transcendental to all material qualities.

Devotional service in the modes of ignorance, passion and goodness can be divided into eighty-one categories. There are different devotional activities, such as hearing, chanting, remembering, worshiping, offering prayer, rendering service and surrendering everything, and each of them can be divided into three qualitative categories. There is hearing in the mode of passion, in the mode of ignorance and in the mode of goodness. Similarly, there is chanting in the mode of ignorance, passion and goodness, etc. Three multiplied by nine equals twenty-seven, and when again multiplied by three it becomes eighty-one. One has to transcend all such mixed materialistic devotional service in order to reach the standard of pure devotional service, as explained in the next verses.

TEXTS 11–12

मद्गुणश्रुतिमात्रेण मयि सर्वगुहाशये ।
मनोगतिरविच्छिन्ना यथा गङ्गाम्भसोऽम्बुधौ ॥११॥
लक्षणं भक्तियोगस्य निर्गुणस्य ह्युदाहृतम् ।
अहैतुक्यव्यवहिता या भक्तिः पुरुषोत्तमे ॥१२॥

mad-guṇa-śruti-mātreṇa
mayi sarva-guhāśaye
mano-gatir avicchinnā
yathā gaṅgāmbhaso 'mbudhau

lakṣaṇaṁ bhakti-yogasya
nirguṇasya hy udāhṛtam
ahaituky avyavahitā
yā bhaktiḥ puruṣottame

mat—of Me; *guṇa*—qualities; *śruti*—by hearing; *mātreṇa*—just; *mayi*—towards Me; *sarva-guhā-āśaye*—residing in everyone's heart; *manaḥ-gatiḥ*—the heart's course; *avicchinnā*—continuous; *yathā*—as; *gaṅgā*—of the Ganges; *ambhasaḥ*—of the water; *ambudhau*—towards the ocean; *lakṣaṇam*—the manifestation; *bhakti-yogasya*—of devotional service; *nirguṇasya*—unadulterated; *hi*—indeed; *udāhṛtam*—exhibited; *ahaituki*—causeless; *avyavahitā*—not separated; *yā*—which;

bhaktiḥ—devotional service; *puruṣa-uttame*—towards the Supreme Personality of Godhead.

TRANSLATION

The manifestation of unadulterated devotional service is exhibited when one's mind is at once attracted to hearing the transcendental name and qualities of the Supreme Personality of Godhead, who is residing in everyone's heart. Just as the water of the Ganges flows naturally down towards the ocean, such devotional ecstasy, uninterrupted by any material condition, flows towards the Supreme Lord.

PURPORT

The basic principle of this unadulterated, pure devotional service is love of Godhead. *Mad-guṇa-śruti-mātreṇa* means "just after hearing about the transcendental qualities of the Supreme Personality of Godhead." These qualities are called *nirguṇa.* The Supreme Lord is uncontaminated by the modes of material nature; therefore He is attractive to the pure devotee. There is no need to practice meditation to attain such attraction; the pure devotee is already in the transcendental stage, and the affinity between him and the Supreme Personality of Godhead is natural and is compared to the Ganges water flowing towards the sea. The flow of the Ganges water cannot be stopped by any condition; similarly, a pure devotee's attraction for the transcendental name, form and pastimes of the Supreme Godhead cannot be stopped by any material condition. The word *avicchinnā,* "without interruptions," is very important in this connection. No material condition can stop the flow of the devotional service of a pure devotee.

The word *ahaitukī* means "without reason." A pure devotee does not render loving service to the Personality of Godhead for any cause or for any benefit, material or spiritual. This is the first symptom of unalloyed devotion. *Anyābhilāṣitā-śūnyam:* he has no desire to fulfill by rendering devotional service. Such devotional service is meant for the *puruṣottama,* the Supreme Personality, and not for anyone else. Sometimes pseudodevotees show devotion to many demigods, thinking the forms of the demigods to be the same as the Supreme Personality of Godhead's form.

It is specifically mentioned herein, however, that *bhakti*, devotional service, is meant only for the Supreme Personality of Godhead, Nārāyaṇa, Viṣṇu, or Kṛṣṇa, not for anyone else.

Avyavahitā means "without cessation." A pure devotee must engage in the service of the Lord twenty-four hours a day, without cessation; his life is so molded that at every minute and every second he engages in some sort of devotional service to the Supreme Personality of Godhead. Another meaning of the word *avyavahitā* is that the interest of the devotee and the interest of the Supreme Lord are on the same level. The devotee has no interest but to fulfill the transcendental desire of the Supreme Lord. Such spontaneous service unto the Supreme Lord is transcendental and is never contaminated by the material modes of nature. These are the symptoms of pure devotional service, which is free from all contamination of material nature.

TEXT 13

सालोक्यसार्ष्टिसामीप्यसारूप्यैकत्वमप्युत ।
दीयमानं न गृह्णन्ति विना मत्सेवनं जनाः ॥१३॥

sālokya-sārṣṭi-sāmīpya-
sārūpyaikatvam apy uta
dīyamānaṁ na gṛhṇanti
vinā mat-sevanaṁ janāḥ

sālokya—living on the same planet; *sārṣṭi*—having the same opulence; *sāmīpya*—to be a personal associate; *sārūpya*—having the same bodily features; *ekatvam*—oneness; *api*—also; *uta*—even; *dīyamānam*—being offered; *na*—not; *gṛhṇanti*—do accept; *vinā*—without; *mat*—My; *sevanam*—devotional service; *janāḥ*—pure devotees.

TRANSLATION

A pure devotee does not accept any kind of liberation—sālokya, sārṣṭi, sāmīpya, sārūpya or ekatva—even though they are offered by the Supreme Personality of Godhead.

PURPORT

Lord Caitanya teaches us how to execute pure devotional service out of spontaneous love for the Supreme Personality of Godhead. In the *Śikṣāṣṭaka*, He prays to the Lord: "O Lord, I do not wish to gain from You any wealth, nor do I wish to have a beautiful wife, nor do I wish to have many followers. All I want from You is that in life after life I may remain a pure devotee at Your lotus feet." There is a similarity between the prayers of Lord Caitanya and the statements of *Śrīmad-Bhāgavatam*. Lord Caitanya prays, "in life after life," indicating that a devotee does not even desire the cessation of birth and death. The *yogīs* and empiric philosophers desire cessation of the process of birth and death, but a devotee is satisfied to remain even in this material world and execute devotional service.

It is clearly stated herein that a pure devotee does not desire *ekatva*, oneness with the Supreme Lord, as desired by the impersonalists, the mental speculators and the meditators. To become one with the Supreme Lord is beyond the dream of a pure devotee. Sometimes he may accept promotion to the Vaikuṇṭha planets to serve the Lord there, but he will never accept merging into the Brahman effulgence, which he considers worse than hellish. Such *ekatva*, or merging into the effulgence of the Supreme Lord, is called *kaivalya*, but the happiness derived from *kaivalya* is considered by the pure devotee to be hellish. The devotee is so fond of rendering service to the Supreme Lord that the five kinds of liberation are not important to him. If one is engaged in pure transcendental loving service to the Lord, it is understood that he has already achieved the five kinds of liberation.

When a devotee is promoted to the spiritual world, Vaikuṇṭha, he receives four kinds of facilities. One of these is *sālokya*, living on the same planet as the Supreme Personality. The Supreme Person, in His different plenary expansions, lives on innumerable Vaikuṇṭha planets, and the chief planet is Kṛṣṇaloka. Just as within the material universe the chief planet is the sun, in the spiritual world the chief planet is Kṛṣṇaloka. From Kṛṣṇaloka, the bodily effulgence of Lord Kṛṣṇa is distributed not only to the spiritual world but to the material world as well; it is covered by matter, however, in the material world. In the spiritual world there are innumerable Vaikuṇṭha planets, and on each one the Lord is the predominating Deity. A devotee can be promoted to one such

Vaikuṇṭha planet to live with the Supreme Personality of Godhead.

In *sārṣṭi* liberation the opulence of the devotee is equal to the opulence of the Supreme Lord. *Sāmīpya* means to be a personal associate of the Supreme Lord. In *sārūpya* liberation the bodily features of the devotee are exactly like those of the Supreme Person but for two or three symptoms found exclusively on the transcendental body of the Lord. Śrīvatsa, for example, the hair on the chest of the Lord, particularly distinguishes Him from His devotees.

A pure devotee does not accept these five kinds of spiritual existence, even if they are offered, and he certainly does not hanker after material benefits, which are all insignificant in comparison with spiritual benefits. When Prahlāda Mahārāja was offered some material benefit, he stated: "My Lord, I have seen that my father achieved all kinds of material benefits, and even the demigods were afraid of his opulence, but still, in a second, You have finished his life and all his material prosperity." For a devotee there is no question of desiring any material or spiritual prosperity. He simply aspires to serve the Lord. That is his highest happiness.

TEXT 14

स एव भक्तियोगाख्य आत्यन्तिक उदाहृतः ।
येनातिव्रज्य त्रिगुणं मद्भावायोपपद्यते ॥१४॥

sa eva bhakti-yogākhya
ātyantika udāhṛtaḥ
yenātivrajya tri-guṇaṁ
mad-bhāvāyopapadyate

saḥ—this; *eva*—indeed; *bhakti-yoga*—devotional service; *ākhyaḥ*—called; *ātyantikaḥ*—the highest platform; *udāhṛtaḥ*—explained; *yena*—by which; *ativrajya*—overcoming; *tri-guṇam*—the three modes of material nature; *mat-bhāvāya*—to My transcendental stage; *upapadyate*—one attains.

TRANSLATION

By attaining the highest platform of devotional service, as I have explained, one can overcome the influence of the three modes of

material nature and be situated in the transcendental stage, as is the Lord.

PURPORT

Śrīpāda Śaṅkarācārya, who is supposed to be the leader of the impersonalist school of philosophers, has admitted in the beginning of his comments on *Bhagavad-gītā* that Nārāyaṇa, the Supreme Personality of Godhead, is beyond the material creation; except for Him, everything is within the material creation. It is also confirmed in the Vedic literature that before the creation there was only Nārāyaṇa; neither Lord Brahmā nor Lord Śiva existed. Only Nārāyaṇa, or the Supreme Personality of Godhead, Viṣṇu, or Kṛṣṇa, is always in the transcendental position, beyond the influence of material creation.

The material qualities of goodness, passion and ignorance cannot affect the position of the Supreme Personality of Godhead; therefore He is called *nirguṇa* (free from all tinges of material qualities). Here the same fact is confirmed by Lord Kapila: one who is situated in pure devotional service is transcendentally situated, as is the Lord. Just as the Lord is unaffected by the influence of the material modes, so too are His pure devotees. One who is not affected by the three modes of material nature is called a liberated soul, or *brahma-bhūta* soul. *Brahma-bhūtaḥ prasannātmā* is the stage of liberation. *Ahaṁ brahmāsmi:* "I am not this body." This is applicable only to the person who constantly engages in the devotional service of Kṛṣṇa and is thus in the transcendental stage; he is above the influence of the three modes of material nature.

It is the misconception of the impersonalists that one can worship any imaginary form of the Lord, or Brahman, and at the end merge in the Brahman effulgence. Of course, to merge into the bodily effulgence (Brahman) of the Supreme Lord is also liberation, as explained in the previous verse. *Ekatva* is also liberation, but that sort of liberation is never accepted by any devotee, for qualitative oneness is immediately attained as soon as one is situated in devotional service. For a devotee, that qualitative equality, which is the result of impersonal liberation, is already attained; he does not have to try for it separately. It is clearly stated here that simply by pure devotional service one becomes qualitatively as good as the Lord Himself.

TEXT 15

निषेवितेनानिमित्तेन स्वधर्मेण महीयसा ।
क्रियायोगेन शस्तेन नातिहिंस्रेण नित्यशः ॥१५॥

niṣevitenānimittena
sva-dharmeṇa mahīyasā
kriyā-yogena śastena
nātihiṁsreṇa nityaśaḥ

niṣevitena—executed; *animittena*—without attachment to the result; *sva-dharmeṇa*—by one's prescribed duties; *mahīyasā*—glorious; *kriyā-yogena*—by devotional activities; *śastena*—auspicious; *na*—without; *atihiṁsreṇa*—excessive violence; *nityaśaḥ*—regularly.

TRANSLATION

A devotee must execute his prescribed duties, which are glorious, without material profit. Without excessive violence, one should regularly perform one's devotional activities.

PURPORT

One has to execute his prescribed duties according to his social position as a *brāhmaṇa*, *kṣatriya*, *vaiśya* or *śūdra*. The prescribed duties of the four classes of men in human society are also described in *Bhagavad-gītā*. The activities of *brāhmaṇas* are to control the senses and to become simple, clean, learned devotees. The *kṣatriyas* have the spirit for ruling, they are not afraid on the battlefield, and they are charitable. The *vaiśyas*, or the mercantile class of men, trade in commodities, protect cows and develop agricultural produce. The *śūdras*, or laborer class, serve the higher classes because they themselves are not very intelligent.

From every position, as confirmed in *Bhagavad-gītā*, *sva-karmaṇā tam abhyarcya:* one can serve the Supreme Lord by performing one's prescribed duty. It is not that only the *brāhmaṇas* can serve the Supreme Lord and not the *śūdras*. Anyone can serve the Supreme Lord by performing his prescribed duties under the direction of a spiritual master, or representative of the Supreme Personality of Godhead. No one should think that his prescribed duties are inferior. A *brāhmaṇa* can serve the Lord by using his intelligence, and the *kṣatriya* can serve the Supreme Lord by using his military arts, just as Arjuna served Kṛṣṇa. Arjuna was a warrior; he had no time to study *Vedānta* or other highly intellectual books. The damsels in Vrajadhāma were girls born of the *vaiśya* class, and they engaged in protecting cows and producing agriculture. Kṛṣṇa's foster father, Nanda Mahārāja, and his associates were all *vaiśyas.* They were not at all educated, but they could serve Kṛṣṇa by loving Him and by offering everything to Him. Similarly, there are many instances in which *caṇḍālas,* or those lower than *śūdras,* have served Kṛṣṇa. Also, the sage Vidura was considered a *śūdra* because his mother happened to be *śūdra.* There are no distinctions, for it is declared by the Lord in *Bhagavad-gītā* that anyone engaged specifically in devotional service is elevated to the transcendental position without a doubt. Everyone's prescribed duty is glorious if it is performed in devotional service of the Lord, without desire for profit. Such loving service must be performed without reason, without impediment, and spontaneously. Kṛṣṇa is lovable, and one has to serve Him in whatever capacity one can. That is pure devotional service.

Another significant phrase in this verse is *nātihiṁsreṇa* ("with minimum violence or sacrifice of life"). Even if a devotee has to commit violence, it should not be done beyond what is necessary. Sometimes the question is put before us: "You ask us not to eat meat, but you are eating vegetables. Do you think that is not violence?" The answer is that eating vegetables is violence, and vegetarians are also committing violence against other living entities because vegetables also have life. Nondevotees are killing cows, goats and so many other animals for eating purposes, and a devotee, who is vegetarian, is also killing. But here, significantly, it is stated that every living entity has to live by killing another entity; that is the law of nature. *Jīvo jīvasya jīvanam:* one living entity is the life for another living entity. But for a human being, that violence should be committed only as much as necessary.

A human being is not to eat anything which is not offered to the Supreme Personality of Godhead. *Yajña-śiṣṭāśinaḥ santaḥ:* one becomes freed from all sinful reactions by eating foodstuffs which are offered to Yajña, the Supreme Personality of Godhead. A devotee therefore eats only *prasāda,* or foodstuffs offered to the Supreme Lord, and Kṛṣṇa says that when a devotee offers Him foodstuffs from the vegetable kingdom, with devotion, He eats that. A devotee is to offer to Kṛṣṇa foodstuffs prepared from vegetables. If the Supreme Lord wanted foodstuffs prepared from animal food, the devotee could offer this, but He does not order to do that.

We have to commit violence; that is a natural law. We should not, however, commit violence extravagantly, but only as much as ordered by the Lord. Arjuna engaged in the art of killing, and although killing is, of course, violence, he killed the enemy simply on Kṛṣṇa's order. In the same way, if we commit violence as it is necessary, by the order of the Lord, that is called *nātihiṁsā.* We cannot avoid violence, for we are put into a conditional life in which we have to commit violence, but we should not commit more violence than necessary or than ordered by the Supreme Personality of Godhead.

TEXT 16

मद्धिष्ण्यदर्शनस्पर्शपूजास्तुत्यभिवन्दनैः ।
भूतेषु मद्भावनया सत्त्वेनासङ्गमेन च ॥१६॥

mad-dhiṣṇya-darśana-sparśa-
pūjā-stuty-abhivandanaiḥ
bhūteṣu mad-bhāvanayā
sattvenāsaṅgamena ca

mat—My; *dhiṣṇya*—statue; *darśana*—seeing; *sparśa*—touching; *pūjā*—worshiping; *stuti*—praying to; *abhivandanaiḥ*—by offering obeisances; *bhūteṣu*—in all living entities; *mat*—of Me; *bhāvanayā*—with thought; *sattvena*—by the mode of goodness; *asaṅgamena*—with detachment; *ca*—and.

TRANSLATION

The devotee should regularly see My statues in the temple, touch My lotus feet and offer worshipable paraphernalia and prayer. He should see in the spirit of renunciation, from the mode of goodness, and see every living entity as spiritual.

PURPORT

Temple worship is one of the duties of a devotee. It is especially recommended for neophytes, but those who are advanced should not refrain from temple worship. There is a distinction in the manner a neophyte and an advanced devotee appreciate the Lord's presence in the temple. A neophyte considers the *arcā-vigraha* (the statue of the Lord) to be different from the original Personality of Godhead; he considers it a representation of the Supreme Lord in the form of a Deity. But an advanced devotee accepts the Deity in the temple as the Supreme Personality of Godhead. He does not see any difference between the original form of the Lord and the statue, or *arcā* form of the Lord, in the temple. This is the vision of a devotee whose devotional service is in the highest stage of *bhāva*, or love of Godhead, whereas a neophyte's worship in the temple is a matter of routine duty.

Temple Deity worship is one of the functions of a devotee. He goes regularly to see the Deity nicely decorated, and with veneration and respect he touches the lotus feet of the Lord and presents offerings of worship, such as fruits, flowers and prayers. At the same time, to advance in devotional service, a devotee should see other living entities as spiritual sparks, parts and parcels of the Supreme Lord. A devotee is to offer respect to every entity that has a relationship with the Lord. Because every living entity originally has a relationship with the Lord as part and parcel, a devotee should try to see all living entities on the same equal level of spiritual existence. As stated in *Bhagavad-gītā*, a *paṇḍita*, one who is learned, sees equally a very learned *brāhmaṇa*, a *śūdra*, a hog, a dog and a cow. He does not see the body, which is only an outward dress. He does not see the dress of a *brāhmaṇa*, or that of a cow or of a hog. He sees the spiritual spark, part and parcel of the Supreme Lord. If a devotee does not see every living entity as part and parcel of the Supreme Lord, he is considered *prākṛta-bhakta*, a materialistic devotee. He is not completely situated on the spiritual platform; rather, he is in the lowest stage of devotion. He does, however, show all respect to the Deity.

Although a devotee sees all living entities on the level of spiritual existence, he is not interested in associating with everyone. Simply because a tiger is part and parcel of the Supreme Lord does not mean that we embrace him because of his spiritual relationship with the Supreme

Lord. We must associate only with persons who have developed Kṛṣṇa consciousness.

We should befriend and offer special respect to persons who are developed in Kṛṣṇa consciousness. Other living entities are undoubtedly part and parcel of the Supreme Lord, but because their consciousness is still covered and not developed in Kṛṣṇa consciousness, we should renounce their association. It is said by Viśvanātha Cakravartī Ṭhākura that even if one is a Vaiṣṇava, if he is not of good character his company should be avoided, although he may be offered the respect of a Vaiṣṇava. Anyone who accepts Viṣṇu as the Supreme Personality of Godhead is accepted as a Vaiṣṇava, but a Vaiṣṇava is expected to develop all the good qualities of the demigods.

The exact meaning of the word *sattvena* is given by Śrīdhara Svāmī as being synonymous with *dhairyeṇa,* or patience. One must perform devotional service with great patience. One should not give up the execution of devotional service because one or two attempts have not been successful. One must continue. Śrī Rūpa Gosvāmī also confirms that one should be very enthusiastic and execute devotional service with patience and confidence. Patience is necessary for developing the confidence that "Kṛṣṇa will certainly accept me because I am engaging in devotional service." One has only to execute service according to the rules and regulations to insure success.

TEXT 17

महतां बहुमानेन दीनानामनुकम्पया ।
मैत्र्या चैवात्मतुल्येषु यमेन नियमेन च ॥१७॥

mahatāṁ bahu-mānena
dīnānām anukampayā
maitryā caivātma-tulyeṣu
yamena niyamena ca

mahatām—to the great souls; *bahu-mānena*—with great respect; *dīnānām*—to the poor; *anukampayā*—with compassion; *maitryā*—with friendship; *ca*—also; *eva*—certainly; *ātma-tulyeṣu*—to persons who are equals; *yamena*—with control of the senses; *niyamena*—with regulation; *ca*—and.

TRANSLATION

The pure devotee should execute devotional service by giving the greatest respect to the spiritual master and the ācāryas. He should be compassionate to the poor and make friendship with persons who are his equals, but all his activities should be executed under regulation and with control of the senses.

PURPORT

In *Bhagavad-gītā*, Thirteenth Chapter, it is clearly stated that one should execute devotional service and advance on the path of spiritual knowledge by accepting the *ācārya. Ācāryopāsanam:* one should worship an *ācārya*, a spiritual master who knows things as they are. The spiritual master must be in the disciplic succession from Kṛṣṇa. The predecessors of the spiritual master are his spiritual master, his grand spiritual master, his great-grand spiritual master and so on, who form the disciplic succession of *ācāryas.*

It is recommended herewith that all the *ācāryas* be given the highest respect. It is stated, *guruṣu nara-matiḥ. Guruṣu* means "unto the *ācāryas*," and *nara-matiḥ* means "thinking like a common man." To think of the Vaiṣṇavas, the devotees, as belonging to a particular caste or community, to think of the *ācāryas* as ordinary men or to think of the Deity in the temple as being made of stone, wood or metal, is condemned. *Niyamena:* one should offer the greatest respect to the *ācāryas* according to the standard regulations. A devotee should also be compassionate to the poor. This does not refer to those who are poverty-stricken materially. According to devotional vision, a man is poor if he is not in Kṛṣṇa consciousness. A man may be very rich materially, but if he is not Kṛṣṇa conscious, he is considered poor. On the other hand, many *ācāryas*, such as Rūpa Gosvāmī and Sanātana Gosvāmī, used to live beneath trees every night. Superficially it appeared that they were poverty-stricken, but from their writings we can understand that in spiritual life they were the richest personalities.

A devotee shows compassion to those poor souls who are wanting in spiritual knowledge by enlightening them in order to elevate them to Kṛṣṇa consciousness. That is one of the duties of a devotee. He should also make friendship with persons who are on an equal level with himself or who have the same understanding that he does. For a devotee, there is no point in making friendships with ordinary persons; he should make friendship with other devotees so that by discussing among themselves, they may elevate one another on the path of spiritual understanding. This is called *iṣṭa-goṣṭhī.*

In *Bhagavad-gītā* there is reference to *bodhayantaḥ parasparam,* "discussing among themselves." Generally pure devotees utilize their valuable time in chanting and discussing various activities of Lord Kṛṣṇa or Lord Caitanya amongst themselves. There are innumerable books, such as the *Purāṇas, Mahābhārata, Bhāgavatam, Bhagavad-gītā* and *Upaniṣads,* which contain countless subjects for discussion among two devotees or more. Friendship should be cemented between persons with mutual interests and understanding. Such persons are said to be *sva-jāti,* "of the same caste." The devotee should avoid a person whose character is not fixed in the standard understanding; even though he may be a Vaiṣṇava, or a devotee of Kṛṣṇa, if his character is not correctly representative, then he should be avoided. One should steadily control the senses and the mind and strictly follow the rules and regulations, and he should make friendship with persons of the same standard.

TEXT 18

आध्यात्मिकानुश्रवणान्नामसङ्कीर्तनाच्च मे ।
आर्जवेनार्यसङ्गेन निरहङ्क्रियया तथा ॥१८॥

ādhyātmikānuśravaṇān
nāma-saṅkīrtanāc ca me
ārjavenārya-saṅgena
nirahaṅkriyayā tathā

ādhyātmika—spiritual matters; *anuśravaṇāt*—from hearing; *nāma-saṅkīrtanāt*—from chanting the holy name; *ca*—and; *me*—My; *ārjavena*—with straightforward behavior; *ārya-saṅgena*—with association of saintly persons; *nirahaṅkriyayā*—without false ego; *tathā*—thus.

TRANSLATION

A devotee should always try to hear about spiritual matters and should always utilize his time in chanting the holy name of the

Lord. His behavior should always be straightforward and simple, and although he is not envious but friendly to everyone, he should avoid the company of persons who are not spiritually advanced.

PURPORT

In order to advance in spiritual understanding, one has to hear from authentic sources about spiritual knowledge. One can understand the reality of spiritual life by following strict regulative principles and by controlling the senses. To have control it is necessary that one be nonviolent and truthful, refrain from stealing, abstain from sex life and possess only that which is absolutely necessary for keeping the body and soul together. One should not eat more than necessary, he should not collect more paraphernalia than necessary, he should not talk unnecessarily with common men, and he should not follow the rules and regulations without purpose. He should follow the rules and regulations so that he may actually make advancement.

There are eighteen qualifications mentioned in *Bhagavad-gītā*, among which is simplicity. One should be without pride; one should not demand unnecessary respect from others, and one should be nonviolent. *Amānitvam adambhitvam ahiṁsā.* One should be very tolerant and simple, one should accept the spiritual master, and one should control the senses. These are mentioned here and in *Bhagavad-gītā* as well. One should hear from authentic sources how to advance in spiritual life; such instructions should be taken from the *ācārya* and should be assimilated.

It is especially mentioned here, *nāma-saṅkīrtanāc ca:* one should chant the holy names of the Lord—Hare Kṛṣṇa, Hare Kṛṣṇa, Kṛṣṇa Kṛṣṇa, Hare Hare/ Hare Rāma, Hare Rāma, Rāma Rāma, Hare Hare—either individually or with others. Lord Caitanya has given special stress to chanting of these holy names of the Lord as the basic principle of spiritual advancement. Another word used here is *ārjavena*, meaning "without diplomacy." A devotee should not make plans out of self-interest. Of course, preachers sometimes have to make some plan to execute the mission of the Lord under proper guidance, but regarding personal self-interest, a devotee should always be without diplomacy, and he should avoid the company of persons who are not advancing in spiritual life. Another word is *ārya.* Āryans are persons who are advancing in knowledge of Kṛṣṇa consciousness as well as in material prosperity. The difference between the Āryan and non-Āryan, the *sura* and *asura*, is in their standards of spiritual advancement. Association with persons who are not spiritually advanced is forbidden. Lord Caitanya advised, *asat-saṅga-tyāga:* one should avoid persons who are attached to the temporary. *Asat* is one who is too materially attached, who is not a devotee of the Lord and who is too attached to women or enjoyable material things. Such a person, according to Vaiṣṇava philosophy, is a persona non grata.

A devotee should not be proud of his acquisitions. The symptoms of a devotee are meekness and humility. Although spiritually very advanced, he will always remain meek and humble, as Kavirāja Gosvāmī and all the other Vaiṣṇavas have taught us by personal example. Caitanya Mahāprabhu taught that one should be humbler than the grass on the street and more tolerant than the tree. One should not be proud or falsely puffed up. In this way one will surely advance in spiritual life.

TEXT 19

मद्धर्मणो गुणैरेतैः परिसंशुद्ध आशयः ।
पुरुषस्याञ्जसाभ्येति श्रुतमात्रगुणं हि माम् ॥१९॥

mad-dharmaṇo guṇair etaiḥ
parisaṁśuddha āśayaḥ
puruṣasyāñjasābhyeti
śruta-mātra-guṇaṁ hi mām

mat-dharmaṇaḥ—of My devotee; *guṇaiḥ*—with the attributes; *etaiḥ*—these; *parisaṁśuddhaḥ*—completely purified; *āśayaḥ*—consciousness; *puruṣasya*—of a person; *añjasā*—instantly; *abhyeti*—approaches; *śruta*—by hearing; *mātra*—simply; *guṇam*—quality; *hi*—certainly; *mām*—Me.

TRANSLATION

When one is fully qualified with all these transcendental attributes and his consciousness is thus completely purified, he is immediately attracted simply by hearing My name or hearing of My transcendental quality.

PURPORT

In the beginning of this instruction, the Lord explained to His mother that *mad-guṇa-śruti-mātreṇa*, simply by hearing of the name, quality, form, etc., of the Supreme Personality of Godhead, one is immediately attracted. A person becomes fully qualified with all transcendental qualities by following the rules and regulations, as recommended in different scriptures. We have developed certain unnecessary qualities by material association, and by following the above process we become free from that contamination. To develop transcendental qualities, as explained in the previous verse, one must become free from these contaminated qualities.

TEXT 20

यथा वातरथो घ्राणमावृङ्क्ते गन्ध आशयात् ।
एवं योगरतं चेत आत्मानमविकारि यत् ॥२०॥

yathā vāta-ratho ghrāṇam
āvṛṅkte gandha āśayāt
evaṁ yoga-rataṁ ceta
ātmānam avikāri yat

yathā—as; *vāta*—of air; *rathaḥ*—the chariot; *ghrāṇam*—sense of smell; *āvṛṅkte*—catches; *gandhaḥ*—aroma; *āśayāt*—from the source; *evam*—similarly; *yoga-ratam*—engaged in devotional service; *cetaḥ*—consciousness; *ātmānam*—the Supreme Soul; *avikāri*—unchanging; *yat*—which.

TRANSLATION

As the chariot of air carries an aroma from its source and immediately catches the sense of smell, similarly, one who constantly engages in devotional service, in Kṛṣṇa consciousness, can catch the Supreme Soul, who is equally present everywhere.

PURPORT

As a breeze carrying a pleasant fragrance from a garden of flowers at once captures the organ of smell, so one's consciousness, saturated with devotion, can at once capture the transcendental existence of the Supreme Personality of Godhead, who, in His Paramātmā feature, is present everywhere, even in the heart of every living being. It is stated in *Bhagavad-gītā* that the Supreme Personality of Godhead is *kṣetra-jña*, present within this body, but He is also simultaneously present in every other body. Since the individual soul is present only in a particular body, he is altered when another individual soul does not cooperate with him. The Supersoul, however, is equally present everywhere. Individual souls may disagree, but the Supersoul, being equally present in every body, is called unchanging, or *avikāri*. The individual soul, when fully saturated with Kṛṣṇa consciousness, can understand the presence of the Supersoul. It is confirmed in *Bhagavad-gītā* that (*bhaktyā mām abhijānāti*) a person saturated with devotional service in full Kṛṣṇa consciousness can understand the Supreme Personality of Godhead, either as Supersoul or as the Supreme Person.

TEXT 21

अहं सर्वेषु भूतेषु भूतात्मावस्थितः सदा ।
तमवज्ञाय मां मर्त्यः कुरुतेऽर्चाविडम्बनम् ॥२१॥

ahaṁ sarveṣu bhūteṣu
bhūtātmāvasthitaḥ sadā
tam avajñāya māṁ martyaḥ
kurute 'rcā-viḍambanam

aham—I; *sarveṣu*—in all; *bhūteṣu*—living entities; *bhūta-ātmā*—the Supersoul in all beings; *avasthitaḥ*—situated; *sadā*—always; *tam*—that Supersoul; *avajñāya*—disregarding; *mām*—Me; *martyaḥ*—a mortal man; *kurute*—performs; *arcā*—of worship of the Deity; *viḍambanam*—imitation.

TRANSLATION

I am present in every living entity as the Supersoul. If someone neglects or disregards that Supersoul everywhere and engages himself in the worship of the Deity in the temple, that is simply imitation.

PURPORT

In purified consciousness, or Kṛṣṇa consciousness, one sees the presence of Kṛṣṇa everywhere. If, therefore, one only engages in Deity worship in the temple and does not consider other living entities, then he is in the lowest grade of devotional service. One who worships the Deity in the temple and does not show respect to others is a devotee on the material platform, in the lowest stage of devotional service. A devotee should try to understand everything in relationship with Kṛṣṇa and try to serve everything in that spirit. To serve everything means to engage everything in the service of Kṛṣṇa. If a person is innocent and does not know his relationship with Kṛṣṇa, an advanced devotee should try to engage him in the service of Kṛṣṇa. One who is advanced in Kṛṣṇa consciousness can engage not only the living being but everything in the service of Kṛṣṇa.

TEXT 22

यो मां सर्वेषु भूतेषु सन्तमात्मानमीश्वरम् ।
हित्वार्चां भजते मौढ्याद्भस्मन्येव जुहोति सः ॥२२॥

yo māṁ sarveṣu bhūteṣu
santam ātmānam īśvaram
hitvārcāṁ bhajate mauḍhyād
bhasmany eva juhoti saḥ

yaḥ—one who; *mām*—Me; *sarveṣu*—in all; *bhūteṣu*—living entities; *santam*—being present; *ātmānam*—the Paramātmā; *īśvaram*—the Supreme Lord; *hitvā*—disregarding; *arcām*—the Deity; *bhajate*—worships; *mauḍhyāt*—because of ignorance; *bhasmani*—into ashes; *eva*—only; *juhoti*—offers oblations; *saḥ*—he.

TRANSLATION

One who worships the Deity of Godhead in the temples but does not know that the Supreme Lord, as Paramātmā, is situated in every living entity's heart, must be in ignorance and is compared to one who offers oblations into ashes.

PURPORT

It is stated clearly herein that the Supreme Personality of Godhead, in His plenary expansion of Supersoul, is present in all living entities. The living entities have 8,400,000 different kinds of bodies, and the Supreme Personality of Godhead is living in every body both as the individual soul and as the Supersoul. Since the individual soul is part and parcel of the Supreme Lord, in that sense the Lord is living in every body, and, as Supersoul, the Lord is also present as a witness. In both cases the presence of God in every living entity is essential. Therefore persons who profess to belong to some religious sect but who do not feel the presence of the Supreme Personality of Godhead in every living entity, and everywhere else, are in the mode of ignorance.

If, without this preliminary knowledge of the Lord's omnipresence, one simply attaches himself to the rituals in a temple, church or mosque, it is as if he were offering butter into ashes rather than into the fire. One offers sacrifices by pouring clarified butter into a fire and chanting Vedic *mantras*, but even if there are Vedic *mantras* and all conditions are favorable, if the clarified butter is poured on ashes, then such a sacrifice will be useless. In other words, a devotee should not ignore any living entity. The devotee must know that in every living entity, however insignificant he may be, even in an ant, God is present, and therefore every living entity should be kindly treated and should not be subjected to any violence. In modern civilized society, slaughterhouses are regularly maintained and supported by a certain type of religious principle. But without knowledge of the presence of God in every living entity, any so-called advancement of human civilization, either spiritual or material, is to be understood as being in the mode of ignorance.

TEXT 23

द्विषतः परकाये मां मानिनो भिन्नदर्शिनः ।
भूतेषु बद्धवैरस्य न मनः शान्तिमृच्छति ॥२३॥

dviṣataḥ para-kāye māṁ
mānino bhinna-darśinaḥ
bhūteṣu baddha-vairasya
na manaḥ śāntim ṛcchati

dviṣataḥ—of one who is envious; *para-kāye*—towards the body of another; *mām*—unto Me; *māninaḥ*—offering respect; *bhinna-darśinaḥ*—of a separatist; *bhūteṣu*—towards living entities; *baddha-vairasya*—of one who is inimical; *na*—not; *manaḥ*—the mind; *śāntim*—peace; *ṛcchati*—attains.

TRANSLATION

One who offers Me respect but is envious of the bodies of others and is therefore a separatist never attains peace of mind, because of his inimical behavior towards other living entities.

PURPORT

In this verse, two phrases, *bhūteṣu baddha-vairasya* ("inimical towards others") and *dviṣataḥ para-kāye* ("envious of another's body"), are significant. One who is envious of or inimical towards others never experiences any happiness. A devotee's vision, therefore, must be perfect. He should ignore bodily distinctions and should see only the presence of the part and parcel of the Supreme Lord, and the Lord Himself in His plenary expansion as Supersoul. That is the vision of a pure devotee. The bodily expression of a particular type of living entity is always ignored by the devotee.

It is expressed herein that the Lord is always eager to deliver the conditioned souls, who have been encaged within material bodies. Devotees are expected to carry the message or desire of the Lord to such conditioned souls and enlighten them with Kṛṣṇa consciousness. Thus they may be elevated to transcendental, spiritual life, and the mission of their lives will be successful. Of course this is not possible for living entities who are lower than human beings, but in human society it is feasible that all living entities can be enlightened with Kṛṣṇa consciousness. Even living entities who are lower than human can be raised to Kṛṣṇa consciousness by other methods. For example, Śivānanda Sena, a great devotee of Lord Caitanya, delivered a dog by feeding him *prasāda.* Distribution of *prasāda,* or remnants of foodstuffs offered to the Lord, even to the ignorant masses of people and to animals, gives such living entities the chance for elevation to Kṛṣṇa consciousness. Factually it happened that the same dog, when met by Lord Caitanya at Purī, was liberated from the material condition.

It is especially mentioned here that a devotee must be free from all violence (*jīvāhiṁsā*). Lord Caitanya has recommended that a devotee not commit violence to any living entity. Sometimes the question is raised that since vegetables also have life and devotees take vegetable foodstuffs, isn't that violence? Firstly, however, taking some leaves, twigs or fruit from a tree or plant does not kill the plant. Besides that, *jīvāhiṁsā* means that since every living entity has to pass through a particular type of body according to his past *karma*, although every living entity is eternal, he should not be disturbed in his gradual evolution. A devotee has to execute the principles of devotional service exactly as they are, and he must know that however insignificant a living entity may be, the Lord is present within him. A devotee must realize this universal presence of the Lord.

TEXT 24

अहमुच्चावचैर्द्रव्यैः क्रिययोत्पन्नयानघे ।
नैव तुष्येऽर्चितोऽर्चायां भूतग्रामावमानिनः ॥२४॥

aham uccāvacair dravyaiḥ
kriyayotpannayānaghe
naiva tuṣye 'rcito 'rcāyāṁ
bhūta-grāmāvamāninaḥ

aham—I; *ucca-avacaiḥ*—with various; *dravyaiḥ*—paraphernalia; *kriyayā*—by religious rituals; *utpannayā*—accomplished; *anaghe*—O sinless mother; *na*—not; *eva*—certainly; *tuṣye*—am pleased; *arcitaḥ*—worshiped; *arcāyām*—in the Deity form; *bhūta-grāma*—to other living entities; *avamāninaḥ*—with those who are disrespectful.

TRANSLATION

My dear Mother, even if he worships with proper rituals and paraphernalia, a person who is ignorant of My presence in all living entities never pleases Me by the worship of My Deities in the temple.

PURPORT

There are sixty-four different prescriptions for worship of the Deity in the temple. There are many items offered to the Deity, some valuable and some less valuable. It is prescribed in *Bhagavad-gītā:* "If a devotee offers Me a small flower, a leaf, some water or a little fruit, I will accept it." The real purpose is to exhibit one's loving devotion to the Lord; the offerings themselves are secondary. If one has not developed loving devotion to the Lord and simply offers many kinds of foodstuffs, fruits and flowers without real devotion, the offering will not be accepted by the Lord. We cannot bribe the Personality of Godhead. He is so great that our bribery has no value. Nor has He any scarcity; since He is full in Himself, what can we offer Him? Everything is produced by Him. We simply offer to show our love and gratitude to the Lord.

This gratitude and love for God is exhibited by a pure devotee, who knows that the Lord lives in every living entity. As such, temple worship necessarily includes distribution of *prasāda.* It is not that one should create a temple in his private apartment or private room, offer something to the Lord, and then eat. Of course, that is better than simply cooking foodstuffs and eating without understanding one's relationship with the Supreme Lord; people who act in this manner are just like animals. But the devotee who wants to elevate himself to the higher level of understanding must know that the Lord is present in every living entity, and, as stated in the previous verse, one should be compassionate to other living entities. A devotee should worship the Supreme Lord, be friendly to persons who are on the same level and be compassionate to the ignorant. One should exhibit his compassion for ignorant living entities by distributing *prasāda.* Distribution of *prasāda* to the ignorant masses of people is essential for persons who make offerings to the Personality of Godhead.

Real love and devotion is accepted by the Lord. Many valuable foodstuffs may be presented to a person, but if the person is not hungry, all such offerings are useless for him. Similarly, we may offer many valuable items to the Deity, but if we have no real sense of devotion and no real sense of the Lord's presence everywhere, then we are lacking in devotional service; in such a state of ignorance, we cannot offer anything acceptable to the Lord.

TEXT 25

अर्चादावर्चयेत्तावदीश्वरं मां स्वकर्मकृत् ।
यावन्न वेद स्वहृदि सर्वभूतेष्ववस्थितम् ॥२५॥

arcādāv arcayet tāvad
īśvaraṁ māṁ sva-karma-kṛt
yāvan na veda sva-hṛdi
sarva-bhūteṣv avasthitam

arcā-ādau—beginning with worship of the Deity; *arcayet*—one should worship; *tāvat*—so long; *īśvaram*—the Supreme Personality of Godhead; *mām*—Me; *sva*—his own; *karma*—prescribed duties; *kṛt*—performing; *yāvat*—as long as; *na*—not; *veda*—he realizes; *sva-hṛdi*—in his own heart; *sarva-bhūteṣu*—in all living entities; *avasthitam*—situated.

TRANSLATION

Performing his prescribed duties, one should worship the Deity of the Supreme Personality of Godhead until one realizes My presence in his own heart and in the hearts of other living entities as well.

PURPORT

Worship of the Deity of the Supreme Personality of Godhead is prescribed herewith even for persons who are simply discharging their prescribed duties. There are prescribed duties for the different social classes of men—the *brāhmaṇas*, the *vaiśyas*, the *kṣatriyas* and the *śūdras*—and for the different *āśramas*—*brahmacarya*, *gṛhastha*, *vānaprastha* and *sannyāsa*. One should worship the Deity of the Lord until one appreciates the presence of the Lord in every living entity. In other words, one should not be satisfied simply by discharging his duties properly; he must realize his relationship and the relationship of all other living entities with the Supreme Personality of Godhead. If he does not understand this, then even though he discharges his prescribed duties properly, it is to be understood that he is simply laboring without profit.

The word *sva-karma-kṛt* in this verse is very significant. *Sva-karma-kṛt* is one who engages in discharging his prescribed duties. It is not that one who has become a devotee of the Lord or who engages in devotional service should give up his prescribed duties. No one should be lazy under the plea of devotional service. One has to execute devotional service according to his prescribed duties. *Sva-karma-kṛt* means that one should discharge the duties prescribed for him without neglect.

TEXT 26

आत्मनश्च परस्यापि यः करोत्यन्तरोदरम् ।
तस्य भिन्नदृशो मृत्युर्विदधे भयमुल्बणम् ॥२६॥

ātmanaś ca parasyāpi
yaḥ karoty antarodaram
tasya bhinna-dṛśo mṛtyur
vidadhe bhayam ulbaṇam

ātmanaḥ—of himself; *ca*—and; *parasya*—of another; *api*—also; *yaḥ*—one who; *karoti*—discriminates; *antarā*—between; *udaram*—the body; *tasya*—of him; *bhinna-dṛśaḥ*—having a differential outlook; *mṛtyuḥ*—as death; *vidadhe*—I cause; *bhayam*—fear; *ulbaṇam*—great.

TRANSLATION

As the blazing fire of death, I cause great fear to whoever makes the least discrimination between himself and other living entities because of a differential outlook.

PURPORT

There are bodily differentiations among all varieties of living entities, but a devotee should not distinguish between one living entity and another on such a basis; a devotee's outlook should be that both the soul and Supersoul are equally present in all varieties of living entities.

TEXT 27

अथ मां सर्वभूतेषु भूतात्मानं कृतालयम् ।
अर्हयेद्दानमानाभ्यां मैत्र्याभिन्नेन चक्षुषा ॥२७॥

atha māṁ sarva-bhūteṣu
bhūtātmānaṁ kṛtālayam

arhayed dāna-mānābhyāṁ
maitryābhinnena cakṣuṣā

atha—therefore; *mām*—Me; *sarva-bhūteṣu*—in all creatures; *bhūta-ātmānam*—the Self in all beings; *kṛta-ālayam*—abiding; *arhayet*—one should propitiate; *dāna-mānābhyām*—through charity and respect; *maitryā*—through friendship; *abhinnena*—equal; *cakṣuṣā*—by viewing.

TRANSLATION

Therefore, through charitable gifts and attention, as well as through friendly behavior and by viewing all to be alike, one should propitiate Me, who abide in all creatures as their very Self.

PURPORT

It should not be misunderstood that because the Supersoul is dwelling within the heart of a living entity, the individual soul has become equal to Him. The equality of the Supersoul and the individual soul is misconceived by the impersonalist. Here it is distinctly mentioned that the individual soul should be recognized in relationship with the Supreme Personality of Godhead. The method of worshiping the individual soul is described here as either giving charitable gifts or behaving in a friendly manner, free from any separatist outlook. The impersonalist sometimes accepts a poor individual soul as being *daridra-nārāyaṇa*, meaning that Nārāyaṇa, the Supreme Personality of Godhead, has become poor. This is a contradiction. The Supreme Personality of Godhead is full in all opulences. He can agree to live with a poor soul or even with an animal, but this does not make Him poor.

There are two Sanskrit words used here, *māna* and *dāna*. *Māna* indicates a superior, and *dāna* indicates one who gives charitable gifts or is compassionate towards an inferior. We cannot treat the Supreme Personality of Godhead as an inferior who is dependent on our charitable gifts. When we give charity, it is to a person who is inferior in his material or economic condition. Charity is not given to a rich man. Similarly, it is explicitly stated here that *māna*, respect, is offered to a superior, and charity is offered to an inferior. The living entities, according to different results of fruitive activities, may become rich or poor, but the Supreme Personality of Godhead is unchangeable; He is always full in six opulences. Treating a living entity equally does not mean treating him as one would treat the Supreme Personality of Godhead. Compassion and friendliness do not necessitate falsely elevating someone to the exalted position of the Supreme Personality of Godhead. We should not, at the same time, misunderstand that the Supersoul situated in the heart of an animal like a hog and the Supersoul situated in the heart of a learned *brāhmaṇa* are different. The Supersoul in all living entities is the same Supreme Personality of Godhead. By His omnipotency, He can live anywhere, and He can create His Vaikuṇṭha situation everywhere. That is His inconceivable potency. Therefore, when Nārāyaṇa is living in the heart of a hog, He does not become a hog-Nārāyaṇa. He is always Nārāyaṇa and is unaffected by the body of the hog.

TEXT 28

जीवाःश्रेष्ठा ह्यजीवानां ततः प्राणभृतः शुभे ।
ततः सचित्ताः प्रवरास्ततश्चेन्द्रियवृत्तयः ॥२८॥

jīvāḥ śreṣṭhā hy ajīvānāṁ
tataḥ prāṇa-bhṛtaḥ śubhe
tataḥ sa-cittāḥ pravarās
tataś cendriya-vṛttayaḥ

jīvāḥ—living entities; *śreṣṭhāḥ*—better; *hi*—indeed; *ajīvānām*—than inanimate objects; *tataḥ*—than them; *prāṇa-bhṛtaḥ*—entities with life symptoms; *śubhe*—O blessed mother; *tataḥ*—than them; *sa-cittāḥ*—entities with developed consciousness; *pravarāḥ*—better; *tataḥ*—than them; *ca*—and; *indriya-vṛttayaḥ*—those with sense perception.

TRANSLATION

Living entities are superior to inanimate objects, O blessed mother, and among them, living entities who display life symptoms are better. Animals with developed consciousness are

better than them, and better still are those who have developed sense perception.

PURPORT

In the previous verse it was explained that living entities should be honored by charitable gifts and friendly behavior, and in this verse and in the following verses, the description of different grades of living entities is given so that one can know when to behave friendly and when to give charity. For example, a tiger is a living entity, part and parcel of the Supreme Personality of Godhead, and the Supreme Lord is living in the heart of the tiger as Supersoul. But does this mean that we have to treat the tiger in a friendly manner? Certainly not. We have to treat him differently, giving him charity in the form of *prasāda.* The many saintly persons in the jungles do not treat the tigers in a friendly way, but they supply *prasāda* foodstuffs to them. The tigers come, take the food and go away, just as a dog does. According to the Vedic system, a dog is not allowed to enter the house. Because of their uncleanliness, cats and dogs are not allowed within the apartment of a gentleman, but are so trained that they stand outside. The compassionate householder will supply *prasāda* to the dogs and cats, who eat outside and then go away. We must treat the lower living entities compassionately, but this does not mean that we have to treat them in the same way we treat other human beings. The feeling of equality must be there, but the treatment should be discriminating. Just how discrimination should be maintained is given in the following six verses concerning the different grades of living conditions.

The first division is made between dead, stonelike matter and the living organism. A living organism is sometimes manifested even in stone. Experience shows that some hills and mountains grow. This is due to the presence of the soul within that stone. Above that, the next manifestation of the living condition is development of consciousness, and the next manifestation is the development of sense perception. In the *Mokṣa-dharma* section of the *Mahābhārata* it is stated that trees have developed sense perception; they can see and smell. We know by experience that trees can see. Sometimes in its growth a large tree changes its course of development to avoid some hindrances. This means that a tree can see, and according to *Mahābhārata*, a tree can also smell. This indicates the development of sense perception.

TEXT 29

तत्रापि स्पर्शवेदिभ्यः प्रवरा रसवेदिनः ।
तेभ्यो गन्धविदः श्रेष्ठास्ततः शब्दविदो वराः ॥२९॥

tatrāpi sparśa-vedibhyaḥ
pravarā rasa-vedinaḥ
tebhyo gandha-vidaḥ śreṣṭhās
tataḥ śabda-vido varāḥ

tatra—among them; *api*—moreover; *sparśa-vedibhyaḥ*—than those perceiving touch; *pravarāḥ*—better; *rasa-vedinaḥ*—those perceiving taste; *tebhyaḥ*—than them; *gandha-vidaḥ*—those perceiving smell; *śreṣṭhāḥ*—better; *tataḥ*—than them; *śabda-vidaḥ*—those perceiving sound; *varāḥ*—better.

TRANSLATION

Among the living entities who have developed sense perception, those who have developed the sense of taste are better than those who have developed only the sense of touch. Better than them are those who have developed the sense of smell, and better still are those who have developed the sense of hearing.

PURPORT

Although Westerners accept that Darwin first expounded the doctrine of evolution, the science of anthropology is not new. The development of the evolutionary process was known long before from the *Bhāgavatam*, which was written five thousand years ago. There are records of the statements of Kapila Muni, who was present almost in the beginning of the creation. This knowledge has existed since the Vedic time, and all these sequences are disclosed in Vedic literature; the theory of gradual evolution or anthropology is not new to the *Vedas*.

It is said here that amongst the trees there are also evolutionary processes; the different kinds of trees have touch perception. It is said that better than the trees are the fish because fish have developed the sense of taste. Better than the fish are the bees, who have developed the sense of smell, and better than them are the serpents because serpents have developed the sense of hearing. In the darkness of night a snake can find its eatables simply by hearing the frog's very pleasant cry. The snake can understand, "There is the frog," and he captures the frog simply because of its sound vibration. This example is sometimes given for persons who vibrate sounds simply for death. One may have a very nice tongue that can vibrate sound like the frogs, but that kind of vibration is simply calling death. The best use of the tongue and of sound vibration is to chant Hare Kṛṣṇa, Hare Kṛṣṇa, Kṛṣṇa Kṛṣṇa, Hare Hare/ Hare Rāma, Hare Rāma, Rāma Rāma, Hare Hare. That will protect one from the hands of cruel death.

TEXT 30

रूपभेदविदस्तत्र ततश्चोभयतोदतः ।
तेषां बहुपदाः श्रेष्ठाश्चतुष्पादस्ततो द्विपात् ॥३०॥

rūpa-bheda-vidas tatra
tataś cobhayato-dataḥ
teṣāṁ bahu-padāḥ śreṣṭhāś
catuṣ-pādas tato dvi-pāt

rūpa-bheda—distinctions of form; *vidaḥ*—those who perceive; *tatra*—than them; *tataḥ*—than them; *ca*—and; *ubhayataḥ*—in both jaws; *dataḥ*—those with teeth; *teṣām*—of them; *bahu-padāḥ*—those who have many legs; *śreṣṭhāḥ*—better; *catuḥ-pādaḥ*—four-legged; *tataḥ*—than them; *dvi-pāt*—two-legged.

TRANSLATION

Better than those living entities who can perceive sound are those who can distinguish between one form and another. Better than them are those who have developed upper and lower sets of teeth, and better still are those who have many legs. Better than them are the quadrupeds, and better still are the human beings.

PURPORT

It is said that certain birds, such as crows, can distinguish one form from another. Living entities that have many legs, like the wasp, are better than plants and grasses, which have no legs. Four-legged animals are better than many-legged living entities, and better than the animals is the human being, who has only two legs.

TEXT 31

ततो वर्णाश्च चत्वारस्तेषां ब्राह्मण उत्तमः ।
ब्राह्मणेष्वपि वेदज्ञो ह्यर्थज्ञोऽभ्यधिकस्ततः ॥३१॥

tato varṇāś ca catvāras
teṣāṁ brāhmaṇa uttamaḥ
brāhmaṇeṣv api veda-jño
hy artha-jño 'bhyadhikas tataḥ

tataḥ—among them; *varṇāḥ*—classes; *ca*—and; *catvāraḥ*—four; *teṣām*—of them; *brāhmaṇaḥ*—a *brāhmaṇa; uttamaḥ*—best; *brāhmaṇeṣu*—among the *brāhmaṇas; api*—moreover; *veda*—the *Vedas; jñaḥ*—one who knows; *hi*—certainly; *artha*—the purpose; *jñaḥ*—one who knows; *abhyadhikaḥ*—better; *tataḥ*—than him.

TRANSLATION

Among human beings, the society which is divided according to quality and work is best, and in that society, the intelligent men, who are designated as brāhmaṇas, are best. Among the brāhmaṇas, one who has studied the Vedas is the best, and among the brāhmaṇas who have studied the Vedas, one who knows the actual purport of Veda is the best.

PURPORT

The system of four classifications in human society according to quality and work is very scientific. This system of *brāhmaṇas, kṣatriyas, vaiśyas* and *śūdras* has now become vitiated as the present caste system in India, but it appears that this system has been current a very long time, since it is mentioned in *Śrīmad-Bhāgavatam* and *Bhagavad-gītā*. Unless there is such a division of the social orders in human society, including the intelligent class, the martial class, the mercantile class and the laborer class, there is always confusion as to who is to work for what purpose. A person trained to the stage of understanding the Absolute Truth is a *brāhmaṇa*, and when such a *brāhmaṇa* is *veda-jña*, he understands the purpose of *Veda*. The purpose of *Veda* is to understand the Absolute. One who understands the Absolute Truth in three phases, namely Brahman, Paramātmā and Bhagavān, and who understands the term *Bhagavān* to mean the Supreme Personality of Godhead, is considered to be the best of the *brāhmaṇas*, or a Vaiṣṇava.

TEXT 32

अर्थज्ञात्संशयच्छेत्ता ततः श्रेयान् स्वकर्मकृत् ।
मुक्तसङ्गस्ततो भूयानदोग्धा धर्ममात्मनः ॥३२॥

artha-jñāt saṁśaya-cchettā
tataḥ śreyān sva-karma-kṛt
mukta-saṅgas tato bhūyān
adogdhā dharmam ātmanaḥ

artha-jñāt—than one who knows the purpose of the *Vedas; saṁśaya*—doubts; *chettā*—one who cuts off; *tataḥ*—than him; *śreyān*—better; *sva-karma*—his prescribed duties; *kṛt*—one who executes; *mukta-saṅgaḥ*—liberated from material association; *tataḥ*—than him; *bhūyān*—better; *adogdhā*—not executing; *dharmam*—devotional service; *ātmanaḥ*—for himself.

TRANSLATION

Better than the brāhmaṇa who knows the purpose of the Vedas is he who can dissipate all doubts, and better than him is one who strictly follows the brahminical principles. Better than him is one who is liberated from all material contamination, and better than him is a pure devotee, who executes devotional service without expectation of reward.

PURPORT

Artha-jña brāhmaṇa refers to one who has made a thorough analytical study of the Absolute Truth and who knows that the Absolute Truth is realized in three different phases, namely Brahman, Paramātmā and Bhagavān. If someone not only has this knowledge but is able to clear all doubts if questioned about the Absolute Truth, he is considered better. Further, there may be a learned *brāhmaṇa*-Vaiṣṇava who can explain clearly and eradicate all doubts, but if he does not follow the Vaiṣṇava principles, then he is not situated on a higher level. One must be able to clear all doubts and simultaneously be situated in the brahminical characteristics. Such a person, who knows the purpose of the Vedic injunctions, who can employ the principles laid down in the Vedic literatures and who teaches his disciples in that way, is called an *ācārya.* The position of an *ācārya* is that he executes devotional service with no desire for elevation to a higher position of life.

The highest perfectional *brāhmaṇa* is the Vaiṣṇava. A Vaiṣṇava who knows the science of the Absolute Truth but is not able to preach such knowledge to others is described as being in the lower stage, one who not only understands the principles of the science of God but can also preach is in the second stage, and one who not only can preach but who also sees everything in the Absolute Truth and the Absolute Truth in everything is in the highest class of Vaiṣṇavas. It is mentioned here that a Vaiṣṇava is already a *brāhmaṇa;* in fact, the highest stage of brahminical perfection is reached when one becomes a Vaiṣṇava.

TEXT 33

तस्मान्मय्यर्पिताशेषक्रियार्थात्मा निरन्तरः ।
मय्यर्पितात्मनः पुंसो मयि संन्यस्तकर्मणः ।
न पश्यामि परं भूतमकर्तुः समदर्शनात् ॥३३॥

tasmān mayy arpitāśeṣa-
kriyārthātmā nirantaraḥ
mayy arpitātmanaḥ puṁso
mayi sannyasta-karmaṇaḥ

na paśyāmi paraṁ bhūtam
akartuḥ sama-darśanāt

tasmāt—than him; *mayi*—unto Me; *arpita*—offered; *aśeṣa*—all; *kriyā*—actions; *artha*—wealth; *ātmā*—life, soul; *nirantaraḥ*—without cessation; *mayi*—unto Me; *arpita*—offered; *ātmanaḥ*—whose mind; *puṁsaḥ*—than a person; *mayi*—unto Me; *sannyasta*—dedicated; *karmaṇaḥ*—whose activities; *na*—not; *paśyāmi*—I see; *param*—greater; *bhūtam*—living entity; *akartuḥ*—without proprietorship; *sama*—same; *darśanāt*—whose vision.

TRANSLATION

Therefore I do not find a greater person than he who has no interest outside of Mine and who therefore engages and dedicates all his activities and all his life—everything—unto Me without cessation.

PURPORT

In this verse the word *sama-darśanāt* means that he no longer has any separate interest; the devotee's interest and the Supreme Personality of Godhead's interest are one. For example, Lord Caitanya, in the role of a devotee, also preached the same philosophy. He preached that Kṛṣṇa is the worshipful Lord, the Supreme Personality of Godhead, and that the interest of His pure devotees is the same as His own.

Sometimes Māyāvādī philosophers, due to a poor fund of knowledge, define the word *sama-darśanāt* to mean that a devotee should see himself as one with the Supreme Personality of Godhead. This is foolishness. When one thinks himself one with the Supreme Personality of Godhead, there is no question of serving Him. When there is service, there must be a master. Three things must be present for there to be service: the master, the servant and the service. Here it is clearly stated that he who has dedicated his life, all his activities, his mind and his soul—everything—for the satisfaction of the Supreme Lord, is considered to be the greatest person.

The word *akartuḥ* means "without any sense of proprietorship." Everyone wants to act as the proprietor of his actions so that he can enjoy the result. A devotee, however, has no such desire; he acts because the Personality of Godhead wants him to act in a particular way. He has no personal motive. When Lord Caitanya preached Kṛṣṇa consciousness, it was not with the purpose that people would call Him Kṛṣṇa, the Supreme Personality of Godhead; rather, He preached that Kṛṣṇa is the Supreme Personality of Godhead and should be worshiped as such. A devotee who is a most confidential servant of the Lord never does anything for his personal account, but does everything for the satisfaction of the Supreme Lord. It is clearly stated, therefore, *mayi sannyasta-karmaṇaḥ:* the devotee works, but he works for the Supreme. It is also stated, *mayy arpitātmanaḥ:* "He gives his mind unto Me." These are the qualifications of a devotee, who, according to this verse, is accepted as the highest of all human beings.

TEXT 34

मनसैतानि भूतानि प्रणमेद्बहु मानयन् ।
ईश्वरो जीवकलया प्रविष्टो भगवानिति ॥३४॥

manasaitāni bhūtāni
praṇamed bahu mānayan
īśvaro jīva-kalayā
praviṣṭo bhagavān iti

manasā—with the mind; *etāni*—to these; *bhūtāni*—living entities; *praṇamet*—he offers respects; *bahu mānayan*—showing regard; *īśvaraḥ*—the controller; *jīva*—of the living entities; *kalayā*—by His expansion as the Supersoul; *praviṣṭaḥ*—has entered; *bhagavān*—the Supreme Personality of Godhead; *iti*—thus.

TRANSLATION

Such a perfect devotee offers respects to every living entity because he is under the firm conviction that the Supreme Personality of Godhead has entered the body of every living entity as the Supersoul, or controller.

PURPORT

A perfect devotee, as described above, does not make the mistake of thinking that because the Supreme Personality of Godhead as Paramātmā has entered into the body of every living entity, every living entity has become the Supreme Personality of Godhead. This is foolishness. Suppose a person enters into a room; that does not mean that the room has become that person. Similarly, that the Supreme Lord has entered into each of the 8,400,000 particular types of material bodies does not mean that each of these bodies has become the Supreme Lord. Because the Supreme Lord is present, however, a pure devotee accepts each body as the temple of the Lord, and since the devotee offers respect to such temples in full knowledge, he gives respect to every living entity in relationship with the Lord. Māyāvādī philosophers wrongly think that because the Supreme Person has entered the body of a poor man, the Supreme Lord has become *daridra-nārāyaṇa*, or poor Nārāyaṇa. These are all blasphemous statements of atheists and nondevotees.

TEXT 35

भक्तियोगश्च योगश्च मया मानव्युदीरितः ।
ययोरेकतरेणैव पुरुषः पुरुषं व्रजेत् ॥३५॥

bhakti-yogaś ca yogaś ca
mayā mānavy udīritaḥ
yayor ekatareṇaiva
puruṣaḥ puruṣaṁ vrajet

bhakti-yogaḥ—devotional service; *ca*—and; *yogaḥ*—mystic *yoga; ca*—also; *mayā*—by Me; *mānavi*—O daughter of Manu; *udīritaḥ*—described; *yayoḥ*—of which two; *ekatareṇa*—by either one; *eva*—alone; *puruṣaḥ*—a person; *puruṣam*—the Supreme Person; *vrajet*—can achieve.

TRANSLATION

My dear mother, O daughter of Manu, a devotee who applies the science of devotional service and mystic yoga in this way can

achieve the abode of the Supreme Person simply by that devotional service.

PURPORT

Herein the Supreme Personality of Godhead Kapiladeva perfectly explains that the mystic *yoga* system, consisting of eight different kinds of *yoga* activities, has to be performed with the aim of coming to the perfectional stage of *bhakti-yoga.* It is not acceptable for one to be satisfied simply by practicing the sitting postures and thinking himself complete. By meditation one must attain the stage of devotional service. As previously described, a *yogī* is advised to meditate on the form of Lord Viṣṇu from point to point, from the ankles to the legs to the knees to the thighs to the chest to the neck, and in this way gradually up to the face and then to the ornaments. There is no question of impersonal meditation.

When, by meditation on the Supreme Personality of Godhead in all detail, one comes to the point of love of God, that is the point of *bhakti-yoga,* and at that point he must actually render service to the Lord out of transcendental love. Anyone who practices *yoga* and comes to the point of devotional service can attain the Supreme Personality of Godhead in His transcendental abode. Here it is clearly stated, *puruṣaḥ puruṣaṁ vrajet:* the *puruṣa,* the living entity, goes to the Supreme Person. The Supreme Personality of Godhead and the living entity are qualitatively one; both are defined as *puruṣa.* The quality of *puruṣa* exists both in the Supreme Godhead and in the living entity. *Puruṣa* means "enjoyer," and the spirit of enjoyment is present both in the living entity and in the Supreme Lord. The difference is that the quantity of enjoyment is not equal. The living entity cannot experience the same quantity of enjoyment as the Supreme Personality of Godhead. An analogy may be made with a rich man and a poor man: the propensity for enjoyment is present in both, but the poor man cannot enjoy in the same quantity as the rich man. When the poor man dovetails his desires with those of the rich man, however, and when there is cooperation between the poor man and the rich man, or between the big and the small man, then the enjoyment is shared equally. That is like *bhakti-yoga. Puruṣaḥ puruṣaṁ vrajet:* when the living entity enters into the kingdom of God and cooperates with the Supreme Lord by giving Him enjoyment, he enjoys the same facility or the same amount of pleasure as the Supreme Personality of Godhead.

On the other hand, when the living entity wants to enjoy by imitating the Supreme Personality of Godhead, his desire is called *māyā*, and it puts him in the material atmosphere. A living entity who wants to enjoy on his personal account and not cooperate with the Supreme Lord is engaged in materialistic life. As soon as he dovetails his enjoyment with the Supreme Personality of Godhead, he is engaged in spiritual life. An example may be cited here: The different limbs of the body cannot enjoy life independently; they must cooperate with the whole body and supply food to the stomach. In so doing, all the different parts of the body enjoy equally in cooperation with the whole body. That is the philosophy of *acintya-bhedābheda*, simultaneous oneness and difference. The living entity cannot enjoy life in opposition to the Supreme Lord; he has to dovetail his activities with the Lord by practicing *bhakti-yoga*.

It is said herein that one can approach the Supreme Personality of Godhead by either the *yoga* process or the *bhakti-yoga* process. This indicates that factually there is no difference between *yoga* and *bhakti-yoga* because the target of both is Viṣṇu. In the modern age, however, a *yoga* process has been manufactured which aims at something void and impersonal. Actually, *yoga* means meditation on the form of Lord Viṣṇu. If the *yoga* practice is actually performed according to the standard direction, there is no difference between *yoga* and *bhakti-yoga*.

TEXT 36

एतद्भगवतो रूपं ब्रह्मणः परमात्मनः ।
परं प्रधानं पुरुषं दैवं कर्मविचेष्टितम् ॥३६॥

etad bhagavato rūpaṁ
brahmaṇaḥ paramātmanaḥ
paraṁ pradhānaṁ puruṣaṁ
daivaṁ karma-viceṣṭitam

etat—this; *bhagavataḥ*—of the Supreme Personality of Godhead; *rūpam*—form; *brahmaṇaḥ*—of Brahman; *parama-ātmanaḥ*—of Paramātmā; *param*—transcendental; *pradhānam*—chief; *puruṣam*—personality; *daivam*—spiritual; *karma-viceṣṭitam*—whose activities.

TRANSLATION

This puruṣa whom the individual soul must approach is the eternal form of the Supreme Personality of Godhead, who is known as Brahman and Paramātmā. He is the transcendental chief personality, and His activities are all spiritual.

PURPORT

In order to distinguish the personality whom the individual soul must approach, it is described herein that this *puruṣa,* the Supreme Personality of Godhead, is the chief amongst all living entities and is the ultimate form of the impersonal Brahman effulgence and Paramātmā manifestation. Since He is the origin of the Brahman effulgence and Paramātmā manifestation, He is described herewith as the chief personality. It is confirmed in the *Kaṭha Upaniṣad, nityo nityānām:* there are many eternal living entities, but He is the chief maintainer. This is confirmed in *Bhagavad-gītā* also, where Lord Kṛṣṇa says, *ahaṁ sarvasya prabhavaḥ:* "I am the origin of everything, including the Brahman effulgence and Paramātmā manifestation." His activities are transcendental, as confirmed in *Bhagavad-gītā. Janma karma ca me divyam:* the activities and the appearance and disappearance of the Supreme Personality of Godhead are transcendental; they are not to be considered material. Anyone who knows this fact—that the appearance, disappearance and activities of the Lord are beyond material activities or material conception—is liberated. *Yo vetti tattvataḥ/ tyaktvā dehaṁ punar janma:* such a person, after quitting his body, does not come back again to this material world, but goes to the Supreme Person. It is confirmed here, *puruṣaḥ puruṣaṁ vrajet:* the living entity goes to the Supreme Personality simply by understanding His transcendental nature and activities.

TEXT 37

रूपभेदास्पदं दिव्यं काल इत्यभिधीयते ।
भूतानां महदादीनां यतो भिन्नदृशां भयम् ॥३७॥

rūpa-bhedāspadaṁ divyaṁ
kāla ity abhidhīyate

bhūtānāṁ mahad-ādīnāṁ
yato bhinna-dṛśāṁ bhayam

rūpa-bheda—of the transformation of forms; *āspadam*—the cause; *divyam*—divine; *kālaḥ*—time; *iti*—thus; *abhidhīyate*—is known; *bhūtānām*—of living entities; *mahat-ādīnām*—beginning with Lord Brahmā; *yataḥ*—because of which; *bhinna-dṛśām*—with separate vision; *bhayam*—fear.

TRANSLATION

The time factor, who causes the transformation of the various material manifestations, is another feature of the Supreme Personality of Godhead. Anyone who does not know that time is the same Supreme Personality is afraid of the time factor.

PURPORT

Everyone is afraid of the activities of time, but a devotee who knows that the time factor is another representation or manifestation of the Supreme Personality of Godhead has nothing to fear from the influence of time. The phrase *rūpa-bhedāspadam* is very significant. By the influence of time, so many forms are changing. For example, when a child is born his form is small, but in the course of time that form changes into a larger form, the body of a boy, and then the body of a young man. Similarly, everything is changed and transformed by the time factor, or by the indirect control of the Supreme Personality of Godhead. Usually, we do not see any difference between the body of a child and the body of a boy or young man because we know that these changes are due to the action of the time factor. There is cause for fear for a person who does not know how time acts.

TEXT 38

योऽन्तः प्रविश्य भूतानि भूतैरत्त्यखिलाश्रयः ।
स विष्ण्वाख्योऽधियज्ञोऽसौ कालः कलयतां प्रभुः ॥३८॥

yo 'ntaḥ praviśya bhūtāni
bhūtair atty akhilāśrayaḥ

sa viṣṇv-ākhyo 'dhiyajño 'sau
kālaḥ kalayatāṁ prabhuḥ

yaḥ—He who; *antaḥ*—within; *praviśya*—entering; *bhūtāni*—living entities; *bhūtaiḥ*—by living entities; *atti*—annihilates; *akhila*—of everyone; *āśrayaḥ*—the support; *saḥ*—He; *viṣṇu*—Viṣṇu; *ākhyaḥ*—named; *adhiyajñaḥ*—the enjoyer of all sacrifices; *asau*—that; *kālaḥ*—time factor; *kalayatām*—of all masters; *prabhuḥ*—the master.

TRANSLATION

Lord Viṣṇu, the Supreme Personality of Godhead, who is the enjoyer of all sacrifices, is the time factor and the master of all masters. He enters everyone's heart, He is the support of everyone, and He causes every being to be annihilated by another.

PURPORT

Lord Viṣṇu, the Supreme Personality of Godhead, is clearly described in this passage. He is the supreme enjoyer, and all others are working as His servants. As stated in the *Caitanya-caritāmṛta* (*Ādi* 5.14), *ekale īśvara kṛṣṇa:* the only Supreme Lord is Viṣṇu. *Āra saba bhṛtya:* all others are His servants. Lord Brahmā, Lord Śiva and other demigods are all servants. The same Viṣṇu enters everyone's heart as Paramātmā, and He causes the annihilation of every being through another being.

TEXT 39

न चास्य कश्चिद्दयितो न द्वेष्यो न च बान्धवः ।
आविशत्यप्रमत्तोऽसौ प्रमत्तं जनमन्तकृत् ॥३९॥

na cāsya kaścid dayito
na dveṣyo na ca bāndhavaḥ
āviśaty apramatto 'sau
pramattaṁ janam anta-kṛt

na—not; *ca*—and; *asya*—of the Supreme Personality of Godhead; *kaścit*—anyone; *dayitaḥ*—dear; *na*—not; *dveṣyaḥ*—enemy; *na*—not; *ca*—and; *bāndhavaḥ*—friend; *āviśati*—approaches; *apramattaḥ*—attentive; *asau*—He; *pramattam*—inattentive; *janam*—persons; *anta-kṛt*—the destroyer.

TRANSLATION

No one is dear to the Supreme Personality of Godhead, nor is anyone His enemy or friend. But He gives inspiration to those who have not forgotten Him and destroys those who have.

PURPORT

Forgetfulness of one's relationship with Lord Viṣṇu, the Supreme Personality of Godhead, is the cause of one's repeated birth and death. A living entity is as eternal as the Supreme Lord, but due to his forgetfulness he is put into this material nature and transmigrates from one body to another, and when the body is destroyed, he thinks that he is also destroyed. Actually, this forgetfulness of his relationship with Lord Viṣṇu is the cause of his destruction. Anyone who revives his consciousness of the original relationship receives inspiration from the Lord. This does not mean that the Lord is someone's enemy and someone else's friend. He helps everyone; one who is not bewildered by the influence of material energy is saved, and one who is bewildered is destroyed. It is said, therefore, *hariṁ vinā na sṛtiṁ taranti:* no one can be saved from the repetition of birth and death without the help of the Supreme Lord. It is therefore the duty of all living entities to take shelter of the lotus feet of Viṣṇu and thus save themselves from the cycle of birth and death.

TEXT 40

यद्भयाद्वाति वातोऽयं सूर्यस्तपति यद्भयात् ।
यद्भयाद्वर्षते देवो भगणो भाति यद्भयात् ॥४०॥

yad-bhayād vāti vāto 'yaṁ
sūryas tapati yad-bhayāt
yad-bhayād varṣate devo
bha-gaṇo bhāti yad-bhayāt

yat—of whom (the Supreme Personality of Godhead); *bhayāt*—out of fear; *vāti*—blows; *vātaḥ*—the wind; *ayam*—this; *sūryaḥ*—sun; *tapati*—shines; *yat*—of whom; *bhayāt*—out of fear; *yat*—of whom;

bhayāt—out of fear; *varṣate*—sends rains; *devaḥ*—the god of rain; *bha-gaṇaḥ*—the host of heavenly bodies; *bhāti*—shine; *yat*—of whom; *bhayāt*—out of fear.

TRANSLATION

Out of fear of the Supreme Personality of Godhead the wind blows, out of fear of Him the sun shines, out of fear of Him the rain pours forth showers, and out of fear of Him the host of heavenly bodies shed their luster.

PURPORT

The Lord states in *Bhagavad-gītā, mayādhyakṣeṇa prakṛtiḥ sūyate:* "Nature is working under My direction." The foolish person thinks that nature is working automatically, but such an atheistic theory is not supported in the Vedic literature. Nature is working under the superintendence of the Supreme Personality of Godhead. That is confirmed in *Bhagavad-gītā,* and we also find here that the sun shines under the direction of the Lord, and the cloud pours forth showers of rain under the direction of the Lord. All natural phenomena are under superintendence of the Supreme Personality of Godhead, Viṣṇu.

TEXT 41

यद्वनस्पतयो भीता लताश्चौषधिभिः सह ।
स्वे स्वे कालेऽभिगृह्णन्ति पुष्पाणि च फलानि च ॥४१॥

yad vanaspatayo bhītā
latāś cauṣadhibhiḥ saha
sve sve kāle 'bhigṛhṇanti
puṣpāṇi ca phalāni ca

yat—because of whom; *vanaḥ-patayaḥ*—the trees; *bhītāḥ*—fearful; *latāḥ*—creepers; *ca*—and; *oṣadhibhiḥ*—herbs; *saha*—with; *sve sve kāle*—each in its own season; *abhigṛhṇanti*—bear; *puṣpāṇi*—flowers; *ca*—and; *phalāni*—fruits; *ca*—also.

TRANSLATION

Out of fear of the Supreme Personality of Godhead the trees, creepers, herbs and seasonal plants and flowers blossom and fructify, each in its own season.

PURPORT

As the sun rises and sets and the seasonal changes ensue at their appointed times by the superintendence of the Supreme Personality of Godhead, so the seasonal plants, flowers, herbs and trees all grow under the direction of the Supreme Lord. It is not that plants grow automatically, without any cause, as the atheistic philosophers say. Rather, they grow in pursuance of the supreme order of the Supreme Personality of Godhead. It is confirmed in the Vedic literature that the Lord's diverse energies are working so nicely that it appears that everything is being done automatically.

TEXT 42

स्रवन्ति सरितो भीता नोत्सर्पत्युदधिर्यतः ।
अग्निरिन्धे सगिरिभिर्भूर्न मज्जति यद्भयात् ॥४२॥

sravanti sarito bhītā
notsarpaty udadhir yataḥ
agnir indhe sa-giribhir
bhūr na majjati yad-bhayāt

sravanti—flow; *saritaḥ*—rivers; *bhītāḥ*—fearful; *na*—not; *utsarpati*—overflows; *uda-dhiḥ*—the ocean; *yataḥ*—because of whom; *agniḥ*—fire; *indhe*—burns; *sa-giribhiḥ*—with its mountains; *bhūḥ*—the earth; *na*—not; *majjati*—sinks; *yat*—of whom; *bhayāt*—out of fear.

TRANSLATION

Out of fear of the Supreme Personality of Godhead the rivers flow, and the ocean never overflows. Out of fear of Him only does fire burn and does the earth, with its mountains, not sink in the water of the universe.

PURPORT

We can understand from the Vedic literature that this universe is half filled with water, on which Garbhodakaśāyī Viṣṇu is lying. From His abdomen a lotus flower has grown, and within the stem of that lotus flower all the different planets exist. The material scientist explains that all these different planets are floating because of the law of gravity or some other law; but the actual lawmaker is the Supreme Personality of Godhead. When we speak of law, we must understand that there must be a lawmaker. The material scientists can discover laws of nature, but they are unable to recognize the lawmaker. From *Śrīmad-Bhāgavatam* and *Bhagavad-gītā* we can know who the lawmaker is: the lawmaker is the Supreme Personality of Godhead.

It is said here that the planets do not sink. Since they are floating under the order or energy of the Supreme Godhead, they do not fall down into the water which covers half the universe. All the planets are heavy, with their various mountains, seas, oceans, cities, palaces and buildings, and yet they are floating. It is understood from this passage that all the other planets that are floating in the air have oceans and mountains similar to those on this planet.

TEXT 43

नभो ददाति श्वसतां पदं यन्नियमाददः ।
लोकं स्वदेहं तनुते महान् सप्तभिरावृतम् ॥४३॥

nabho dadāti śvasatāṁ
padaṁ yan-niyamād adaḥ
lokaṁ sva-dehaṁ tanute
mahān saptabhir āvṛtam

nabhaḥ—the sky; *dadāti*—gives; *śvasatām*—to the living entities; *padam*—abode; *yat*—of whom (the Supreme Personality of Godhead); *niyamāt*—under the control; *adaḥ*—that; *lokam*—the universe; *sva-deham*—own body; *tanute*—expands; *mahān*—the *mahat-tattva; saptabhiḥ*—with the seven (layers); *āvṛtam*—covered.

TRANSLATION

Subject to the control of the Supreme Personality of Godhead, the sky allows outer space to accommodate all the various planets, which hold innumerable living entities. The total universal body expands with its seven coverings under His supreme control.

PURPORT

It is understood from this verse that all the planets in outer space are floating, and they all hold living entities. The word *śvasatām* means "those who breathe," or the living entities. In order to accommodate them, there are innumerable planets. Every planet is a residence for innumerable living entities, and the necessary space is provided in the sky by the supreme order of the Lord. It is also stated here that the total universal body is increasing. It is covered by seven layers, and as there are five elements within the universe, so the total elements, in layers, cover the outside of the universal body. The first layer is of earth, and it is ten times greater in size than the space within the universe; the second layer is water, and that is ten times greater than the earthly layer; the third covering is fire, which is ten times greater than the water covering. In this way each layer is ten times greater than the previous one.

TEXT 44

गुणाभिमानिनो देवाः सर्गादिष्वस्य यद्भयात् ।
वर्तन्तेऽनुयुगं येषां वश एतच्चराचरम् ॥४४॥

guṇābhimānino devāḥ
sargādiṣv asya yad-bhayāt
vartante 'nuyugaṁ yeṣāṁ
vaśa etac carācaram

guṇa—the modes of material nature; *abhimāninaḥ*—in charge of; *devāḥ*—the demigods; *sarga-ādiṣu*—in the matter of creation and so on; *asya*—of this world; *yat-bhayāt*—out of fear of whom; *vartante*—carry out functions; *anuyugam*—according to the *yugas; yeṣām*—of whom;

vaśe—under the control; *etat*—this; *cara-acaram*—everything animate and inanimate.

TRANSLATION

Out of fear of the Supreme Personality of Godhead, the directing demigods in charge of the modes of material nature carry out the functions of creation, maintenance and destruction; everything animate and inanimate within this material world is under their control.

PURPORT

The three modes of material nature, namely goodness, passion and ignorance, are under the control of three deities—Brahmā, Viṣṇu and Lord Śiva. Lord Viṣṇu is in charge of the mode of goodness, Lord Brahmā is in charge of the mode of passion, and Lord Śiva is in charge of the mode of ignorance. Similarly, there are many other demigods in charge of the air department, the water department, the cloud department, etc. Just as the government has many different departments, so, within this material world, the government of the Supreme Lord has many departments, and all these departments function in proper order out of fear of the Supreme Personality of Godhead. Demigods are undoubtedly controlling all matter, animate and inanimate, within the universe, but above them the supreme controller is the Personality of Godhead. Therefore in the *Brahma-saṁhitā* it is said, *īśvaraḥ paramaḥ kṛṣṇaḥ.* Undoubtedly there are many controllers in the departmental management of this universe, but the supreme controller is Kṛṣṇa.

There are two kinds of dissolutions. One kind of dissolution takes place when Brahmā goes to sleep during his night, and the final dissolution takes place when Brahmā dies. As long as Brahmā does not die, creation, maintenance and destruction are actuated by different demigods under the superintendence of the Supreme Lord.

TEXT 45

सोऽनन्तोऽन्तकरः कालोऽनादिरादिकृदव्ययः ।
जनं जनेन जनयन्मारयन्मृत्युनान्तकम् ॥४५॥

so 'nanto 'nta-karaḥ kālo
'nādir ādi-kṛd avyayaḥ
janaṁ janena janayan
mārayan mṛtyunāntakam

saḥ—that; *anantaḥ*—endless; *anta-karaḥ*—destroyer; *kālaḥ*—time; *anādiḥ*—without beginning; *ādi-kṛt*—the creator; *avyayaḥ*—not liable to change; *janam*—persons; *janena*—by persons; *janayan*—creating; *mārayan*—destroying; *mṛtyunā*—by death; *antakam*—the lord of death.

TRANSLATION

The eternal time factor has no beginning and no end. It is the representative of the Supreme Personality of Godhead, the maker of the criminal world. It brings about the end of the phenomenal world, it carries on the work of creation by bringing one individual into existence from another, and likewise it dissolves the universe by destroying even the lord of death, Yamarāja.

PURPORT

By the influence of eternal time, which is a representative of the Supreme Personality of Godhead, the father begets a son, and the father dies by the influence of cruel death. But by time's influence, even the lord of cruel death is killed. In other words, all the demigods within the material world are temporary, like ourselves. Our lives last for one hundred years at the most, and similarly, although their lives may last for millions and billions of years, the demigods are not eternal. No one can live within this material world eternally. The phenomenal world is created, maintained and destroyed by the finger signal of the Supreme Personality of Godhead. Therefore a devotee does not desire anything in this material world. A devotee desires only to serve the Supreme Personality of Godhead. This servitude exists eternally; the Lord exists eternally, His servitor exists eternally, and the service exists eternally.

Thus end the Bhaktivedanta purports of the Third Canto, Twenty-ninth Chapter, of the Śrīmad-Bhāgavatam, *entitled "Explanation of Devotional Service by Lord Kapila."*

CHAPTER THIRTY

Description by Lord Kapila of Adverse Fruitive Activities

TEXT 1

कपिल उवाच

तस्यैतस्य जनो नूनं नायं वेदोरुविक्रमम् ।
काल्यमानोऽपि बलिनो वायोरिव घनावलिः ॥ १ ॥

kapila uvāca
tasyaitasya jano nūnaṁ
nāyaṁ vedoru-vikramam
kālyamāno 'pi balino
vāyor iva ghanāvaliḥ

kapilaḥ uvāca—Lord Kapila said; *tasya etasya*—of this very time factor; *janaḥ*—person; *nūnam*—certainly; *na*—not; *ayam*—this; *veda*—knows; *uru-vikramam*—the great strength; *kālyamānaḥ*—being carried off; *api*—although; *balinaḥ*—powerful; *vāyoḥ*—of the wind; *iva*—like; *ghana*—of clouds; *āvaliḥ*—a mass.

TRANSLATION

The Personality of Godhead said: As a mass of clouds does not know the powerful influence of the wind, a person engaged in material consciousness does not know the powerful strength of the time factor, by which he is being carried.

PURPORT

The great politician-*paṇḍita* named Cāṇakya said that even one moment of time cannot be returned even if one is prepared to pay millions of dollars. One cannot calculate the amount of loss there is in wasting valuable time. Either materially or spiritually, one should be very alert in utilizing the time which he has at his disposal. A conditioned soul lives in a particular body for a fixed measurement of time, and it is recommended in the scriptures that within that small measurement of time one has to finish Kṛṣṇa consciousness and thus gain release from the influence of the time factor. But, unfortunately, those who are not in Kṛṣṇa consciousness are carried away by the strong power of time without their knowledge, as clouds are carried by the wind.

TEXT 2

यं यमर्थमुपादत्ते दुःखेन सुखहेतवे ।
तं तं धुनोति भगवान् पुमाञ्छोचति यत्कृते ॥ २ ॥

yaṁ yam artham upādatte
duḥkhena sukha-hetave
taṁ taṁ dhunoti bhagavān
pumāñ chocati yat-kṛte

yam yam—whatever; *artham*—object; *upādatte*—one acquires; *duḥkhena*—with difficulty; *sukha-hetave*—for happiness; *tam tam*—that; *dhunoti*—destroys; *bhagavān*—the Supreme Personality of Godhead; *pumān*—the person; *śocati*—laments; *yat-kṛte*—for which reason.

TRANSLATION

Whatever is produced by the materialist with great pain and labor for so-called happiness, the Supreme Personality, as the time factor, destroys, and for this reason the conditioned soul laments.

PURPORT

The main function of the time factor, which is a representative of the Supreme Personality of Godhead, is to destroy everything. The materialists, in material consciousness, are engaged in producing so many things in the name of economic development. They think that by advancing in satisfying the material needs of man they will be happy, but they forget that everything they have produced will be destroyed in due course of time. From history we can see that there were many powerful empires on the surface of the globe that were constructed with great pain and great perseverance, but in due course of time they have all been destroyed. Still the foolish materialists cannot understand that they are simply wasting time in producing material necessities, which are destined to be vanquished in due course of time. This waste of energy is due to the ignorance of the mass of people, who do not know that they are eternal and that they have an eternal engagement also. They do not know that this span of life in a particular type of body is but a flash in the eternal journey. Not knowing this fact, they take the small flash of life to be everything, and they waste time in improving economic conditions.

TEXT 3

यदध्रुवस्य देहस्य सानुबन्धस्य दुर्मतिः ।
ध्रुवाणि मन्यते मोहाद् गृहक्षेत्रवसूनि च ॥ ३ ॥

yad adhruvasya dehasya
sānubandhasya durmatiḥ
dhruvāṇi manyate mohād
gṛha-kṣetra-vasūni ca

yat—because; *adhruvasya*—temporary; *dehasya*—of the body; *sa-anubandhasya*—with that which is related; *durmatiḥ*—a misguided person; *dhruvāṇi*—permanent; *manyate*—thinks; *mohāt*—because of ignorance; *gṛha*—home; *kṣetra*—land; *vasūni*—wealth; *ca*—and.

TRANSLATION

The misguided materialist does not know that his very body is impermanent and that the attractions of home, land and wealth, which are in relationship to that body, are also temporary. Out of ignorance only, he thinks that everything is permanent.

PURPORT

The materialist thinks that persons engaged in Kṛṣṇa consciousness are crazy fellows wasting time by chanting Hare Kṛṣṇa, but actually he does not know that he himself is in the darkest region of craziness because of accepting his body as permanent. And, in relation to his body, he accepts his home, his country, his society and all other paraphernalia as permanent. This materialistic acceptance of the permanency of home, land, etc., is called the illusion of *māyā.* This is clearly mentioned here. *Mohād gṛha-kṣetra-vasūni:* out of illusion only does the materialist accept his home, his land and his money as permanent. Out of this illusion, the family life, national life and economic development, which are very important factors in modern civilization, have grown. A Kṛṣṇa conscious person knows that this economic development of human society is but temporary illusion.

In another part of *Śrīmad-Bhāgavatam*, the acceptance of the body as oneself, the acceptance of others as kinsmen in relationship to this body and the acceptance of the land of one's birth as worshipable are declared to be the products of an animal civilization. When, however, one is enlightened in Kṛṣṇa consciousness, he can use these for the service of the Lord. That is a very suitable proposition. Everything has a relationship with Kṛṣṇa. When all economic development and material advancement are utilized to advance the cause of Kṛṣṇa consciousness, a new phase of progressive life arises.

TEXT 4

जन्तुर्वै भव एतस्मिन् यां यां योनिमनुव्रजेत् ।
तस्यां तस्यां स लभते निर्वृतिं न विरज्यते ॥ ४ ॥

jantur vai bhava etasmin
yāṁ yāṁ yonim anuvrajet
tasyāṁ tasyāṁ sa labhate
nirvṛtiṁ na virajyate

jantuḥ—the living entity; *vai*—certainly; *bhave*—in worldly existence; *etasmin*—this; *yām yām*—whatever; *yonim*—species; *anuvrajet*—he may obtain; *tasyām tasyām*—in that; *saḥ*—he; *labhate*—achieves; *nirvṛtim*—satisfaction; *na*—not; *virajyate*—is averse.

TRANSLATION

The living entity, in whatever species of life he appears, finds a particular typc of satisfaction in that species, and he is never averse to being situated in such a condition.

PURPORT

The satisfaction of the living entity in a particular type of body, even if it is most abominable, is called illusion. A man in a higher position may feel dissatisfaction with the standard of life of a lower-grade man, but the lower-grade man is satisfied in that position because of the spell of *māyā*, the external energy. *Māyā* has two phases of activities. One is called *prakṣepātmikā*, and the other is called *āvaraṇātmikā*. *Āvaraṇātmikā* means "covering," and *prakṣepātmikā* means "pulling down." In any condition of life, the materialistic person or animal will be satisfied because his knowledge is covered by the influence of *māyā*. In the lower grade or lower species of life, the development of consciousness is so poor that one cannot understand whether he is happy or distressed. This is called *āvaraṇātmikā*. Even a hog, who lives by eating stool, finds himself happy, although a person in a higher mode of life sees that the hog is eating stool. How abominable that life is!

TEXT 5

नरकस्थोऽपि देहं वै न पुमांस्त्यक्तुमिच्छति ।
नारक्यां निर्वृतौ सत्यां देवमायाविमोहितः ॥ ५ ॥

naraka-stho 'pi dehaṁ vai
na pumāṁs tyaktum icchati
nārakyāṁ nirvṛtau satyāṁ
deva-māyā-vimohitaḥ

naraka—in hell; *sthaḥ*—situated; *api*—even; *deham*—body; *vai*—indeed; *na*—not; *pumān*—person; *tyaktum*—to leave; *icchati*—wishes; *nārakyām*—hellish; *nirvṛtau*—enjoyment; *satyām*—when existing; *deva-māyā*—by the illusory energy of Viṣṇu; *vimohitaḥ*—deluded.

TRANSLATION

The conditioned living entity is satisfied in his own particular species of life; while deluded by the covering influence of the illusory energy, he feels little inclined to cast off his body, even when in hell, for he takes delight in hellish enjoyment.

PURPORT

It is said that once Indra, the King of heaven, was cursed by his spiritual master, Bṛhaspati, on account of his misbehavior, and he became a hog on this planet. After many days, when Brahmā wanted to recall him to his heavenly kingdom, Indra, in the form of a hog, forgot everything of his royal position in the heavenly kingdom, and he refused to go back. This is the spell of *māyā*. Even Indra forgets his heavenly standard of life and is satisfied with the standard of a hog's life. By the influence of *māyā* the conditioned soul becomes so affectionate towards his particular type of body that if he is offered, "Give up this body, and immediately you will have a king's body," he will not agree. This attachment strongly affects all conditioned living entities. Lord Kṛṣṇa is personally canvassing, "Give up everything in this material world. Come to Me, and I shall give you all protection," but we are not agreeable. We think, "We are quite all right. Why should we surrender unto Kṛṣṇa and go back to His kingdom?" This is called illusion, or *māyā*. Everyone is satisfied with his standard of living, however abominable it may be.

TEXT 6

आत्मजायासुतागारपशुद्रविणबन्धुषु ।
निरूढमूलहृदय आत्मानं बहु मन्यते ॥ ६ ॥

ātma-jāyā-sutāgāra-
paśu-draviṇa-bandhuṣu
nirūḍha-mūla-hṛdaya
ātmānaṁ bahu manyate

ātma—body; *jāyā*—wife; *suta*—children; *agāra*—home; *paśu*—animals; *draviṇa*—wealth; *bandhuṣu*—in friends; *nirūḍha-mūla*—deep-rooted; *hṛdayaḥ*—his heart; *ātmānam*—himself; *bahu*—highly; *manyate*—he thinks.

TRANSLATION

Such satisfaction with one's standard of living is due to deep-rooted attraction for body, wife, home, children, animals, wealth and friends. In such association, the conditioned soul thinks himself quite perfect.

PURPORT

This so-called perfection of human life is a concoction. Therefore, it is said that the materialist, however materially qualified he may be, is worthless because he is hovering on the mental plane, which will drag him again to the material existence of temporary life. One who acts on the mental plane cannot get promotion to the spiritual. Such a person is always sure to glide down again to material life. In the association of so-called society, friendship and love, the conditioned soul appears completely satisfied.

TEXT 7

सन्दह्यमानसर्वाङ्ग एषामुद्वहनाधिना ।
करोत्यविरतं मूढो दुरितानि दुराशयः ॥ ७ ॥

sandahyamāna-sarvāṅga
eṣām udvahanādhinā
karoty aviratam̐ mūḍho
duritāni durāśayaḥ

sandahyamāna—burning; *sarva*—all; *aṅgaḥ*—his limbs; *eṣām*—these family members; *udvahana*—for maintaining; *ādhinā*—with anxiety; *karoti*—he performs; *aviratam*—always; *mūḍhaḥ*—the fool; *duritāni*—sinful activities; *durāśayaḥ*—evil-minded.

TRANSLATION

Although he is always burning with anxiety, such a fool always performs all kinds of mischievous activities, with a hope which is never to be fulfilled, in order to maintain his so-called family and society.

PURPORT

It is said that it is easier to maintain a great empire than to maintain a small family, especially in these days, when the influence of Kali-yuga is so strong that everyone is harassed and full of anxieties because of accepting the false presentation of *māyā*'s family. The family we maintain is created by *māyā;* it is the perverted reflection of the family in Kṛṣṇaloka. In Kṛṣṇaloka there are also family, friends, society, father and mother; everything is there, but they are eternal. Here, as we change bodies, our family relationships also change. Sometimes we are in a family of human beings, sometimes in a family of demigods, sometimes a family of cats, or sometimes a family of dogs. Family, society and friendship are flickering, and so they are called *asat.* It is said that as long as we are attached to this *asat,* temporary, nonexisting society and family, we are always full of anxieties. The materialists do not know that the family, society and friendship here in this material world are only shadows, and thus they become attached. Naturally their hearts are always burning, but in spite of all inconvenience, they still work to maintain such false families because they have no information of the real family association with Kṛṣṇa.

TEXT 8

आक्षिप्तात्मेन्द्रियः स्त्रीणामसतीनां च मायया ।
रहोरचितयालापैः शिशूनां कलभाषिणाम् ॥ ८ ॥

ākṣiptātmendriyaḥ strīṇām
asatīnāṁ ca māyayā
raho racitayālāpaiḥ
śiśūnāṁ kala-bhāṣiṇām

ākṣipta—charmed; *ātma*—heart; *indriyaḥ*—his senses; *strīṇām*—of women; *asatīnām*—false; *ca*—and; *māyayā*—by *māyā; rahaḥ*—in a solitary place; *racitayā*—displayed; *ālāpaiḥ*—by the talking; *śiśūnām*—of the children; *kala-bhāṣiṇām*—with sweet words.

TRANSLATION

He gives heart and senses to a woman, who falsely charms him with māyā. He enjoys solitary embraces and talking with her, and he is enchanted by the sweet words of the small children.

PURPORT

Family life within the kingdom of illusory energy, *māyā,* is just like a prison for the eternal living entity. In prison a prisoner is shackled by iron chains and iron bars. Similarly, a conditioned soul is shackled by the charming beauty of a woman, by her solitary embraces and talks of so-called love, and by the sweet words of his small children. Thus he forgets his real identity.

In this verse the words *strīṇām asatīnām* indicate that womanly love is just to agitate the mind of man. Actually, in the material world there is no love. Both the woman and the man are interested in their sense gratification. For sense gratification a woman creates an illusory love, and the man becomes enchanted by such false love and forgets his real duty. When there are children as the result of such a combination, the next attraction is to the sweet words of the children. The love of the woman at home and the talk of the children make one a secure prisoner, and thus he cannot leave his home. Such a person is termed, in Vedic language, a *gṛhamedhī*, which means "one whose center of attraction is home." *Gṛhastha* refers to one who lives with family, wife and children, but whose real purpose of living is to develop Kṛṣṇa consciousness. One is therefore advised to become a *gṛhastha* and not a *gṛhamedhī*. The *gṛhastha*'s concern is to get out of the family life created by illusion and enter into real family life with Kṛṣṇa, whereas the *gṛhamedhī*'s business is to repeatedly chain himself to so-called family life, in one life after another, and perpetually remain in the darkness of *māyā*.

TEXT 9

गृहेषु कूटधर्मेषु दुःखतन्त्रेष्वतन्द्रितः ।
कुर्वन्दुःखप्रतीकारं सुखवन्मन्यते गृही ॥ ९ ॥

gṛheṣu kūṭa-dharmeṣu
duḥkha-tantreṣv atandritaḥ
kurvan duḥkha-pratīkāraṁ
sukhavan manyate gṛhī

gṛheṣu—in family life; *kūṭa-dharmeṣu*—involving the practice of falsehood; *duḥkha-tantreṣu*—spreading miseries; *atandritaḥ*—attentive; *kurvan*—doing; *duḥkha-pratīkāram*—counteraction of miseries; *sukha-vat*—as happiness; *manyate*—thinks; *gṛhī*—the householder.

TRANSLATION

The attached householder remains in his family life, which is full of diplomacy and politics. Always spreading miseries and controlled by acts of sense gratification, he acts just to counteract the reactions of all his miseries, and if he can successfully counteract such miseries, he thinks that he is happy.

PURPORT

In *Bhagavad-gītā* the Personality of Godhead Himself certifies the material world as an impermanent place that is full of miseries. There is no question of happiness in this material world, either individually or in terms of family, society or country. If something is going on in the name of happiness, that is also illusion. Here in this material world, happiness means successful counteraction to the effects of distress. The material world is so made that unless one becomes a clever diplomat, his life will be a failure. Not to speak of human society, even the society of lower animals, the birds and bees, cleverly manages its bodily demands of eating, sleeping and mating. Human society competes nationally or individually, and in the attempt to be successful the entire human society becomes full of diplomacy. We should always remember that in spite of all diplomacy and all intelligence in the struggle for our existence, everything will end in a second by the supreme will. Therefore, all our attempts to become happy in this material world are simply a delusion offered by *māyā*.

TEXT 10

अर्थैरापादितैर्गुर्व्या हिंसयेतस्ततश्च तान् ।
पुष्णाति येषां पोषेण शेषभुग्यात्यधः स्वयम् ॥१०॥

arthair āpāditair gurvyā
hiṁsayetas-tataś ca tān
puṣṇāti yeṣāṁ poṣeṇa
śeṣa-bhug yāty adhaḥ svayam

arthaiḥ—by wealth; *āpāditaiḥ*—secured; *gurvyā*—great; *hiṁsayā*—by violence; *itaḥ-tataḥ*—here and there; *ca*—and; *tān*—them (family members); *puṣṇāti*—he maintains; *yeṣām*—of whom; *poṣeṇa*—because of the maintenance; *śeṣa*—remnants; *bhuk*—eating; *yāti*—he goes; *adhaḥ*—downwards; *svayam*—himself.

TRANSLATION

He secures money by committing violence here and there, and although he employs it in the service of his family, he himself eats only a little portion of the food thus purchased, and he goes to hell for those for whom he earned the money in such an irregular way.

PURPORT

There is a Bengali proverb, "The person for whom I have stolen accuses me of being a thief." The family members, for whom an attached person acts in so many criminal ways, are never satisfied. In illusion an attached person serves such family members, and by serving them he is destined to enter into a hellish condition of life. For example, a thief steals something to maintain his family, and he is caught and imprisoned. This is the sum and substance of material existence and attachment to material society, friendship and love. Although an attached family man is always engaged in getting money by hook or by crook for the maintenance of his family, he cannot enjoy more than what he could consume even without such criminal activities. A man who eats eight ounces of foodstuffs may have to maintain a big family and earn money by any means to support that family, but he himself is not offered more than what he can eat, and sometimes he eats the remnants that are left after his family members are fed. Even by earning money by unfair means, he cannot enjoy life for himself. That is called the covering illusion of *māyā*.

The process of illusory service to society, country and community is exactly the same everywhere; the same principle is applicable even to big national leaders. A national leader who is very great in serving his country is sometimes killed by his countrymen because of irregular service. In other words, one cannot satisfy his dependents by this illusory service, although one cannot get out of the service because servant is his constitutional position. A living entity is constitutionally part and parcel of the Supreme Being, but he forgets that he has to render service to the

Supreme Being and diverts his attention to serving others; this is called *māyā*. By serving others he falsely thinks that he is master. The head of a family thinks of himself as the master of the family, or the leader of a nation thinks of himself as the master of the nation, whereas actually he is serving, and by serving *māyā* he is gradually going to hell. Therefore, a sane man should come to the point of Kṛṣṇa consciousness and engage in the service of the Supreme Lord, applying his whole life, all of his wealth, his entire intelligence and his full power of speaking.

TEXT 11

वार्तायां लुप्यमानायामारब्धायां पुनः पुनः ।
लोभाभिभूतो निःसत्त्वः परार्थे कुरुते स्पृहाम् ॥११॥

vārtāyāṁ lupyamānāyām
ārabdhāyāṁ punaḥ punaḥ
lobhābhibhūto niḥsattvaḥ
parārthe kurute spṛhām

vārtāyām—when his occupation; *lupyamānāyām*—is hampered; *ārabdhāyām*—undertaken; *punaḥ punaḥ*—again and again; *lobha*—by greed; *abhibhūtaḥ*—overwhelmed; *niḥsattvaḥ*—ruined; *para-arthe*—for the wealth of others; *kurute spṛhām*—he longs.

TRANSLATION

When he suffers reverses in his occupation, he tries again and again to improve himself, but when he is baffled in all attempts and is ruined, he accepts money from others because of excessive greed.

TEXT 12

कुटुम्बभरणाकल्पो मन्दभाग्यो वृथोद्यमः ।
श्रिया विहीनः कृपणो ध्यायञ्छ्वसिति मूढधीः ॥१२॥

kuṭumba-bharaṇākalpo
manda-bhāgyo vṛthodyamaḥ

śriyā vihīnaḥ kṛpaṇo
dhyāyañ chvasiti mūḍha-dhīḥ

kuṭumba—his family; *bharaṇa*—in maintaining; *akalpaḥ*—unable; *manda-bhāgyaḥ*—the unfortunate man; *vṛthā*—in vain; *udyamaḥ*—whose effort; *śriyā*—beauty, wealth; *vihīnaḥ*—bereft of; *kṛpaṇaḥ*—wretched; *dhyāyan*—grieving; *śvasiti*—he sighs; *mūḍha*—bewildered; *dhīḥ*—his intelligence.

TRANSLATION

Thus the unfortunate man, unsuccessful in maintaining his family members, is bereft of all beauty. He always thinks of his failure, grieving very deeply.

TEXT 13

एवं स्वभरणाकल्पं तत्कलत्रादयस्तथा ।
नाद्रियन्ते यथापूर्वं कीनाशा इव गोजरम् ॥१३॥

evaṁ sva-bharaṇākalpaṁ
tat-kalatrādayas tathā
nādriyante yathā pūrvaṁ
kīnāśā iva go-jaram

evam—thus; *sva-bharaṇa*—to maintain them; *akalpam*—unable; *tat*—his; *kalatra*—wife; *ādayaḥ*—and so on; *tathā*—so; *na*—not; *ādriyante*—do respect; *yathā*—as; *pūrvam*—before; *kīnāśāḥ*—farmers; *iva*—like; *go-jaram*—an old ox.

TRANSLATION

Seeing him unable to support them, his wife and others do not treat him with the same respect as before, even as miserly farmers do not accord the same treatment to their old and worn-out oxen.

PURPORT

Not only in the present age but from time immemorial, no one has liked an old man who is unable to earn in the family. Even in the modern age, in some communities or states, the old men are given poison so that they will die as soon as possible. In some cannibalistic communities, the old grandfather is sportingly killed, and a feast is held in which his body is eaten. The example is given that a farmer does not like an old bull who has ceased to work. Similarly, when an attached person in family life becomes old and is unable to earn, he is no longer liked by his wife, sons, daughters and other kinsmen, and he is consequently neglected, what to speak of not being given respect. It is judicious, therefore, to give up family attachment before one attains old age and take shelter of the Supreme Personality of Godhead. One should employ himself in the Lord's service so that the Supreme Lord can take charge of him, and he will not be neglected by his so-called kinsmen.

TEXT 14

तत्राप्यजातनिर्वेदो भ्रियमाणः स्वयम्भृतैः ।
जरयोपात्तवैरूप्यो मरणाभिमुखो गृहे ॥१४॥

tatrāpy ajāta-nirvedo
bhriyamāṇaḥ svayam bhṛtaiḥ
jarayopātta-vairūpyo
maraṇābhimukho gṛhe

tatra—there; *api*—although; *ajāta*—not arisen; *nirvedaḥ*—aversion; *bhriyamāṇaḥ*—being maintained; *svayam*—by himself; *bhṛtaiḥ*—by those who were maintained; *jarayā*—by old age; *upātta*—obtained; *vairūpyaḥ*—deformation; *maraṇa*—death; *abhimukhaḥ*—approaching; *gṛhe*—at home.

TRANSLATION

The foolish family man does not become averse to family life although he is maintained by those whom he once maintained. Deformed by the influence of old age, he prepares himself to meet ultimate death.

PURPORT

Family attraction is so strong that even if one is neglected by family members in his old age, he cannot give up family affection, and he remains at home just like a dog. In the Vedic way of life one has to give up family life when he is strong enough. It is advised that before getting too weak and being baffled in material activities, and before becoming diseased, one should give up family life and engage oneself completely in the service of the Lord for the remaining days of his life. It is enjoined, therefore, in the Vedic scriptures, that as soon as one passes fifty years of age, he must give up family life and live alone in the forest. After preparing himself fully, he should become a *sannyāsī* to distribute the knowledge of spiritual life to each and every home.

TEXT 15

आस्तेऽवमत्योपन्यस्तं गृहपाल इवाहरन् ।
आमयाव्यप्रदीप्ताग्निरल्पाहारोऽल्पचेष्टितः ॥१५॥

āste 'vamatyopanyastaṁ
gṛha-pāla ivāharan
āmayāvy apradīptāgnir
alpāhāro 'lpa-ceṣṭitaḥ

āste—he remains; *avamatyā*—negligently; *upanyastam*—what is placed; *gṛha-pālaḥ*—a dog; *iva*—like; *āharan*—eating; *āmayāvī*—diseased; *apradīpta-agniḥ*—having dyspepsia; *alpa*—little; *āhāraḥ*—eating; *alpa*—little; *ceṣṭitaḥ*—his activity.

TRANSLATION

Thus he remains at home just like a pet dog and eats whatever is so negligently given to him. Afflicted with many illnesses, such as dyspepsia and loss of appetite, he eats only very small morsels of food, and he becomes an invalid, who cannot work any more.

PURPORT

Before meeting death one is sure to become a diseased invalid, and when he is neglected by his family members, his life becomes less than a dog's because he is put into so many miserable conditions. Vedic literatures enjoin, therefore, that before the arrival of such miserable conditions, one should leave home and die without the knowledge of his family members. If a man leaves home and dies without his family's knowing, that is considered to be a glorious death. But an attached family man wants his family members to carry him in a great procession even after his death, and although he will not be able to see how the procession goes, he still desires that his body be taken gorgeously in procession. Thus he is happy without even knowing where he has to go when he leaves his body for the next life.

TEXT 16

वायुनोत्क्रमतोत्तारः कफसंरुद्धनाडिकः ।
कासश्वासकृतायासः कण्ठे घुरघुरायते ॥१६॥

vāyunotkramatottāraḥ
kapha-saṁruddha-nāḍikaḥ
kāsa-śvāsa-kṛtāyāsaḥ
kaṇṭhe ghura-ghurāyate

vāyunā—by air; *utkramatā*—bulging out; *uttāraḥ*—his eyes; *kapha*—with mucus; *saṁruddha*—congested; *nāḍikaḥ*—his windpipe; *kāsa*—coughing; *śvāsa*—breathing; *kṛta*—done; *āyāsaḥ*—difficulty; *kaṇṭhe*—in the throat; *ghura-ghurāyate*—he produces a sound like "*ghura-ghura.*"

TRANSLATION

In that diseased condition, one's eyes bulge due to the pressure of air from within, and his glands become congested with mucus. He has difficulty breathing, and upon exhaling and inhaling he produces a sound like "ghura-ghura," a rattling within the throat.

TEXT 17

शयानः परिशोचद्भिः परिवीतः स्वबन्धुभिः ।
वाच्यमानोऽपि न ब्रूते कालपाशवशं गतः ॥१७॥

śayānaḥ pariśocadbhiḥ
parivītaḥ sva-bandhubhiḥ
vācyamāno 'pi na brūte
kāla-pāśa-vaśaṁ gataḥ

śayānaḥ—lying down; *pariśocadbhiḥ*—lamenting; *parivītaḥ*—surrounded; *sva-bandhubhiḥ*—by his relatives and friends; *vācyamānaḥ*—being urged to speak; *api*—although; *na*—not; *brūte*—he speaks; *kāla*—of time; *pāśa*—the noose; *vaśam*—under the control of; *gataḥ*—gone.

TRANSLATION

In this way he comes under the clutches of death and lies down, surrounded by lamenting friends and relatives, and although he wants to speak with them, he no longer can because he is under the control of time.

PURPORT

For formality's sake, when a man is lying on his deathbed, his relatives come to him, and sometimes they cry very loudly, addressing the dying man: "Oh, my father!" "Oh, my friend!" or "Oh, my husband!" In that pitiable condition the dying man wants to speak with them and instruct them of his desires, but because he is fully under the control of the time factor, death, he cannot express himself, and that causes him inconceivable pain. He is already in a painful condition because of disease, and his glands and throat are choked up with mucus. He is already in a very difficult position, and when he is addressed by his relatives in that way, his grief increases.

TEXT 18

एवं कुटुम्बभरणे व्यापृतात्माजितेन्द्रियः ।
म्रियते रुदतां स्वानामुरुवेदनयास्तधीः ॥१८॥

evaṁ kuṭumba-bharaṇe
vyāpṛtātmājitendriyaḥ
mriyate rudatāṁ svānām
uru-vedanayāsta-dhīḥ

evam—thus; *kuṭumba-bharaṇe*—in maintaining a family; *vyāpṛta*—engrossed; *ātmā*—his mind; *ajita*—uncontrolled; *indriyaḥ*—his senses; *mriyate*—he dies; *rudatām*—while crying; *svānām*—his relatives; *uru*—great; *vedanayā*—with pain; *asta*—bereft of; *dhīḥ*—consciousness.

TRANSLATION

Thus the man, who engaged with uncontrolled senses in maintaining a family, dies in great grief, seeing his relatives crying. He dies most pathetically, in great pain and without consciousness.

PURPORT

In *Bhagavad-gītā* it is said that at the time of death one will be absorbed in the thoughts which he cultivated during his lifetime. A person who had no other idea than to properly maintain his family members must have family affairs in his last thoughts. That is the natural sequence for a common man. The common man does not know the destiny of his life; he is simply busy in his flash of life, maintaining his family. At the last stage, no one is satisfied with how he has improved the family economic condition; everyone thinks that he could not provide sufficiently. Because of his deep family affection, he forgets his main duty of controlling the senses and improving his spiritual consciousness. Sometimes a dying man entrusts the family affairs to either his son or some relative, saying, "I am going. Please look after the family." He does not know where he is going, but even at the time of death he is anxious about how his family will be maintained. Sometimes it is seen that a dying man requests the physician to increase his life at least for a few years so that the family maintenance plan which he has begun can be completed. These are the material diseases of the conditioned soul. He completely forgets his real engagement—to become Kṛṣṇa conscious—and is always serious about planning to maintain his family, although he changes families one after another.

TEXT 19

यमदूतौ तदा प्राप्तौ भीमौ सरभसेक्षणौ ।
स दृष्ट्वा त्रस्तहृदयः शकृन्मूत्रं विमुञ्चति ॥१९॥

yama-dūtau tadā prāptau
bhīmau sarabhasekṣaṇau
sa dṛṣṭvā trasta-hṛdayaḥ
śakṛn-mūtraṁ vimuñcati

yama-dūtau—two messengers of Yamarāja; *tadā*—at that time; *prāptau*—arrived; *bhīmau*—terrible; *sa-rabhasa*—full of wrath; *īkṣaṇau*—their eyes; *saḥ*—he; *dṛṣṭvā*—seeing; *trasta*—frightened; *hṛdayaḥ*—his heart; *śakṛt*—stool; *mūtram*—urine; *vimuñcati*—he passes.

TRANSLATION

At death, he sees the messengers of the lord of death come before him, their eyes full of wrath, and in great fear he passes stool and urine.

PURPORT

There are two kinds of transmigration of a living entity after passing away from the present body. One kind of transmigration is to go to the controller of sinful activities, who is known as Yamarāja, and the other is to go to the higher planets, up to Vaikuṇṭha. Here Lord Kapila describes how persons engaged in activities of sense gratification to maintain a family are treated by the messengers of Yamarāja, called Yamadūtas. At the time of death the Yamadūtas become the custodians of those persons who have strongly gratified their senses. They take charge of the dying man and take him to the planet where Yamarāja resides. The conditions there are described in the following verses.

TEXT 20

यातनादेह आवृत्य पाशैर्बद्ध्वा गले बलात् ।
नयतो दीर्घमध्वानं दण्ड्यं राजभटा यथा ॥२०॥

yātanā-deha āvṛtya
pāśair baddhvā gale balāt
nayato dīrgham adhvānaṁ
daṇḍyaṁ rāja-bhaṭā yathā

yātanā—for punishment; *dehe*—his body; *āvṛtya*—covering; *pāśaiḥ*—with ropes; *baddhvā*—binding; *gale*—by the neck; *balāt*—by force; *nayataḥ*—they lead; *dīrgham*—long; *adhvānam*—distance; *daṇḍyam*—a criminal; *rāja-bhaṭāḥ*—the king's soldiers; *yathā*—as.

TRANSLATION

As a criminal is arrested for punishment by the constables of the state, a person engaged in criminal sense gratification is similarly arrested by the Yamadūtas, who bind him by the neck with strong rope and cover his subtle body so that he may undergo severe punishment.

PURPORT

Every living entity is covered by a subtle and gross body. The subtle body is the covering of mind, ego, intelligence and consciousness. It is said in the scriptures that the constables of Yamarāja cover the subtle body of the culprit and take him to the abode of Yamarāja to be punished in a way that he is able to tolerate. He does not die from this punishment because if he died, then who would suffer the punishment? It is not the business of the constables of Yamarāja to put one to death. In fact, it is not possible to kill a living entity because factually he is eternal; he simply has to suffer the consequences of his activities of sense gratification.

The process of punishment is explained in the *Caitanya-caritāmṛta.* Formerly the king's men would take a criminal in a boat in the middle of the river. They would dunk him by grasping a bunch of his hair and thrusting him completely underwater, and when he was almost suffocated, the king's constables would take him out of the water and allow him to breathe for some time, and then they would again dunk him in the water to suffocate. This sort of punishment is inflicted upon the forgotten soul by Yamarāja, as will be described in the following verses.

TEXT 21

तयोर्निर्भिन्नहृदयस्तर्जनैर्जातवेपथुः ।
पथि श्वभिर्भक्ष्यमाण आर्तोऽघं स्वमनुस्मरन् ॥२१॥

tayor nirbhinna-hṛdayas
tarjanair jāta-vepathuḥ
pathi śvabhir bhakṣyamāṇa
ārto 'ghaṁ svam anusmaran

tayoḥ—of the Yamadūtas; *nirbhinna*—broken; *hṛdayaḥ*—his heart; *tarjanaiḥ*—by the threatening; *jāta*—arisen; *vepathuḥ*—trembling; *pathi*—on the road; *śvabhiḥ*—by dogs; *bhakṣyamāṇaḥ*—being bitten; *ārtaḥ*—distressed; *agham*—sins; *svam*—his; *anusmaran*—remembering.

TRANSLATION

While carried by the constables of Yamarāja, he is overwhelmed and trembles in their hands. While passing on the road he is bitten by dogs, and he can remember the sinful activities of his life. He is thus terribly distressed.

PURPORT

It appears from this verse that while passing from this planet to the planet of Yamarāja, the culprit arrested by Yamarāja's constables meets many dogs, which bark and bite just to remind him of his criminal activities of sense gratification. It is said in *Bhagavad-gītā* that one becomes almost blind and is bereft of all sense when he is infuriated by the desire for sense gratification. He forgets everything. *Kāmais tais tair hṛta-jñānāḥ.* One is bereft of all intelligence when he is too attracted by sense gratification, and he forgets that he has to suffer the consequences also. Here the chance for recounting his activities of sense gratification is given by the dogs engaged by Yamarāja. While we live in the gross body, such activities of sense gratification are encouraged even by modern government regulations. In every state all over the world, such activities are encouraged by the government in the form of birth control. Women are supplied pills, and they are allowed to go to a clinical laboratory to get assistance for abortions. This is going on as a result of sense gratification. Actually sex life is meant for begetting a good child, but because people have no control over the senses and there is no institution to train them to control the senses, the poor fellows fall victim to the criminal offenses of sense gratification, and they are punished after death as described in these pages of *Śrīmad-Bhāgavatam.*

TEXT 22

क्षुत्तृट्परीतोऽर्कदवानलानिलैः
सन्तप्यमानः पथि तप्तवालुके ।

कृच्छ्रेण पृष्ठे कशया च ताडित-
श्चलत्यशक्तोऽपि निराश्रमोदके ॥२२॥

kṣut-tṛṭ-parīto 'rka-davānalānilaiḥ
santapyamānaḥ pathi tapta-vāluke
kṛcchreṇa pṛṣṭhe kaśayā ca tāḍitaś
calaty aśakto 'pi nirāśramodake

kṣut-tṛṭ—by hunger and thirst; *parītaḥ*—afflicted; *arka*—sun; *dava-anala*—forest fires; *anilaiḥ*—by winds; *santapyamānaḥ*—being scorched; *pathi*—on a road; *tapta-vāluke*—of hot sand; *kṛcchreṇa*—painfully; *pṛṣṭhe*—on the back; *kaśayā*—with a whip; *ca*—and; *tāḍitaḥ*—beaten; *calati*—he moves; *aśaktaḥ*—unable; *api*—although; *nirāśrama-udake*—without shelter or water.

TRANSLATION

Under the scorching sun, the criminal has to pass through roads of hot sand with forest fires on both sides. He is whipped on the back by the constables because of his inability to walk, and he is afflicted by hunger and thirst, but unfortunately there is no drinking water, no shelter and no place for rest on the road.

TEXT 23

तत्र तत्र पतञ्छ्रान्तो मूर्च्छितः पुनरुत्थितः ।
पथा पापीयसा नीतस्तरसा यमसादनम् ॥२३॥

tatra tatra patañ chrānto
mūrcchitaḥ punar utthitaḥ
pathā pāpīyasā nītas
tarasā yama-sādanam

tatra tatra—here and there; *patan*—falling; *śrāntaḥ*—fatigued; *mūrcchitaḥ*—unconscious; *punaḥ*—again; *utthitaḥ*—risen; *pathā*—by the road; *pāpīyasā*—very inauspicious; *nītaḥ*—brought; *tarasā*—quickly; *yama-sādanam*—to the presence of Yamarāja.

TRANSLATION

While passing on that road to the abode of Yamarāja, he falls down in fatigue, and sometimes he becomes unconscious, but he is forced to rise again. In this way he is very quickly brought to the presence of Yamarāja.

TEXT 24

योजनानां सहस्राणि नवतिं नव चाध्वनः ।
त्रिभिर्मुहूर्तैर्द्वाभ्यां वा नीतः प्राप्नोति यातनाः ॥२४॥

yojanānāṁ sahasrāṇi
navatiṁ nava cādhvanaḥ
tribhir muhūrtair dvābhyāṁ vā
nītaḥ prāpnoti yātanāḥ

yojanānām—of *yojanas; sahasrāṇi*—thousands; *navatim*—ninety; *nava*—nine; *ca*—and; *adhvanaḥ*—from a distance; *tribhiḥ*—three; *muhūrtaiḥ*—within moments; *dvābhyām*—two; *vā*—or; *nītaḥ*—brought; *prāpnoti*—he receives; *yātanāḥ*—punishments.

TRANSLATION

Thus he has to pass ninety-nine thousand yojanas within two or three moments, and then he is at once engaged in the torturous punishment which he is destined to suffer.

PURPORT

One *yojana* is calculated to be eight miles, and he has to pass along a road which is therefore as much as 792,000 miles. Such a long distance is passed over within a few moments only. The subtle body is covered by the constables so that the living entity can pass such a long distance quickly and at the same time tolerate the suffering. This covering, although material, is of such fine elements that material scientists cannot discover what the coverings are made of. To pass 792,000 miles within a few moments seems wonderful to the modern space travelers. They have so far traveled at a speed of 18,000 miles per hour, but here we see that a criminal passes 792,000 miles within a few seconds only, although the process is not spiritual but material.

TEXT 25

आदीपनं स्वगात्राणां वेष्टयित्वोल्मुकादिभिः ।
आत्ममांसादनं क्वापि स्वकृत्तं परतोऽपि वा ॥२५॥

ādīpanaṁ sva-gātrāṇāṁ
veṣṭayitvolmukādibhiḥ
ātma-māṁsādanaṁ kvāpi
sva-kṛttaṁ parato 'pi vā

ādīpanam—setting on fire; *sva-gātrāṇām*—of his own limbs; *veṣṭayitvā*—having been surrounded; *ulmuka-ādibhiḥ*—by pieces of burning wood and so on; *ātma-māṁsa*—of his own flesh; *adanam*—eating; *kva api*—sometimes; *sva-kṛttam*—done by himself; *parataḥ*—by others; *api*—else; *vā*—or.

TRANSLATION

He is placed in the midst of burning pieces of wood, and his limbs are set on fire. In some cases he is made to eat his own flesh or have it eaten by others.

PURPORT

From this verse through the next three verses the description of punishment will be narrated. The first description is that the criminal has to eat his own flesh, burning with fire, or allow others like himself who are present there to eat. In the last great war, people in concentration camps sometimes ate their own stool, so there is no wonder that in the Yamasādana, the abode of Yamarāja, one who had a very enjoyable life eating others' flesh has to eat his own flesh.

TEXT 26

जीवतश्चान्त्राभ्युद्धारः श्वगृध्रैर्यमसादने ।
सर्पवृश्चिकदंशाद्यैर्दशद्भिश्चात्मवैशसम् ॥२६॥

jīvataś cāntrābhyuddhāraḥ
śva-gṛdhrair yama-sādane
sarpa-vṛścika-daṁśādyair
daśadbhiś cātma-vaiśasam

jīvataḥ—alive; *ca*—and; *antra*—of his entrails; *abhyuddhāraḥ*—pulling out; *śva-gṛdhraiḥ*—by dogs and vultures; *yama-sādane*—in the abode of Yamarāja; *sarpa*—by serpents; *vṛścika*—scorpions; *daṁśa*—gnats; *ādyaiḥ*—and so on; *daśadbhiḥ*—biting; *ca*—and; *ātma-vaiśasam*—torment of himself.

TRANSLATION

His entrails are pulled out by the hounds and vultures of hell, even though he is still alive to see it, and he is subjected to torment by serpents, scorpions, gnats and other creatures that bite him.

TEXT 27

कृन्तनं चावयवशो गजादिभ्यो भिदापनम् ।
पातनं गिरिशृङ्गेभ्यो रोधनं चाम्बुगर्तयोः ॥२७॥

kṛntanaṁ cāvayavaśo
gajādibhyo bhidāpanam
pātanaṁ giri-śṛṅgebhyo
rodhanaṁ cāmbu-gartayoḥ

kṛntanam—cutting off; *ca*—and; *avayavaśaḥ*—limb by limb; *gaja-ādibhyaḥ*—by elephants and so on; *bhidāpanam*—tearing; *pātanam*—hurling down; *giri*—of hills; *śṛṅgebhyaḥ*—from the tops; *rodhanam*—enclosing; *ca*—and; *ambu-gartayoḥ*—in water or in a cave.

TRANSLATION

Next his limbs are lopped off and torn asunder by elephants. He is hurled down from hilltops, and he is also held captive either in water or in a cave.

TEXT 28

यास्तामिस्रान्धतामिस्रा रौरवाद्याश्च यातनाः ।
भुङ्क्ते नरो वा नारी वा मिथः सङ्गेन निर्मिताः ॥२८॥

yās tāmisrāndha-tāmisrā
rauravādyāś ca yātanāḥ

bhuṅkte naro vā nārī vā
mithaḥ saṅgena nirmitāḥ

yāḥ—which; *tāmisra*—the name of a hell; *andha-tāmisrāḥ*—the name of a hell; *raurava*—the name of a hell; *ādyāḥ*—and so on; *ca*—and; *yātanāḥ*—punishments; *bhuṅkte*—undergoes; *naraḥ*—man; *vā*—or; *nārī*—woman; *vā*—or; *mithaḥ*—mutual; *saṅgena*—by association; *nirmitāḥ*—caused.

TRANSLATION

Men and women whose lives were built upon indulgence in illicit sex life are put into many kinds of miserable conditions in the hells known as Tāmisra, Andha-tāmisra and Raurava.

PURPORT

Materialistic life is based on sex life. The existence of all the materialistic people, who are undergoing severe tribulation in the struggle for existence, is based on sex. Therefore, in the Vedic civilization sex life is allowed only in a restricted way; it is for the married couple and only for begetting children. But when sex life is indulged in for sense gratification illegally and illicitly, both the man and the woman await severe punishment in this world or after death. In this world also they are punished by virulent diseases like syphilis and gonorrhea, and in the next life, as we see in this passage of *Śrīmad-Bhāgavatam*, they are put into different kinds of hellish conditions to suffer. In *Bhagavad-gītā*, First Chapter, illicit sex life is also very much condemned, and it is said that one who produces children by illicit sex life is sent to hell. It is confirmed here in the *Bhāgavatam* that such offenders are put into hellish conditions of life in Tāmisra, Andha-tāmisra and Raurava.

TEXT 29

अत्रैव नरकः स्वर्ग इति मातः प्रचक्षते ।
या यातना वै नारक्यस्ता इहाप्युपलक्षिताः ॥२९॥

atraiva narakaḥ svarga
iti mātaḥ pracakṣate

yā yātanā vai nārakyas
tā ihāpy upalakṣitāḥ

atra—in this world; *eva*—even; *narakaḥ*—hell; *svargaḥ*—heaven; *iti*—thus; *mātaḥ*—O mother; *pracakṣate*—they say; *yāḥ*—which; *yātanāḥ*—punishments; *vai*—certainly; *nārakyaḥ*—hellish; *tāḥ*—they; *iha*—here; *api*—also; *upalakṣitāḥ*—visible.

TRANSLATION

Lord Kapila continued: My dear mother, it is sometimes said that we experience hell or heaven on this planet, for hellish punishments are sometimes visible on this planet also.

PURPORT

Sometimes unbelievers do not accept these statements of scripture regarding hell. They disregard such authorized descriptions. Lord Kapila therefore confirms them by saying that these hellish conditions are also visible on this planet. It is not that they are only on the planet where Yamarāja lives. On the planet of Yamarāja, the sinful man is given the chance to practice living in the hellish conditions which he will have to endure in the next life, and then he is given a chance to take birth on another planet to continue his hellish life. For example, if a man is to be punished to remain in hell and eat stool and urine, then first of all he practices such habits on the planet of Yamarāja, and then he is given a particular type of body, that of a hog, so that he can eat stool and think that he is enjoying life. It is stated previously that in any hellish condition, the conditioned soul thinks he is happy. Otherwise, it would not be possible for him to suffer hellish life.

TEXT 30

एवं कुटुम्बं बिभ्राण उदरम्भर एव वा ।
विसृज्येहोभयं प्रेत्य भुङ्क्ते तत्फलमीदृशम् ॥३०॥

evaṁ kuṭumbaṁ bibhrāṇa
udaram bhara eva vā

visṛjyehobhayaṁ pretya
bhuṅkte tat-phalam īdṛśam

evam—in this way; *kuṭumbam*—family; *bibhrāṇaḥ*—he who maintained; *udaram*—stomach; *bharaḥ*—he who maintained; *eva*—only; *vā*—or; *visṛjya*—after giving up; *iha*—here; *ubhayam*—both of them; *pretya*—after death; *bhuṅkte*—he undergoes; *tat*—of that; *phalam*—result; *īdṛśam*—such.

TRANSLATION

After leaving this body, the man who maintained himself and his family members by sinful activities suffers a hellish life, and his relatives suffer also.

PURPORT

The mistake of modern civilization is that man does not believe in the next life. But whether he believes or not, the next life is there, and one has to suffer if one does not lead a responsible life in terms of the injunctions of authoritative scriptures like the *Vedas* and *Purāṇas*. Species lower than human beings are not responsible for their actions because they are made to act in a certain way, but in the developed life of human consciousness, if one is not responsible for his activities, then he is sure to get a hellish life, as described herein.

TEXT 31

एकः प्रपद्यते ध्वान्तं हित्वेदं स्वकलेवरम् ।
कुशलेतरपाथेयो भूतद्रोहेण यद् भृतम् ॥३१॥

ekaḥ prapadyate dhvāntaṁ
hitvedaṁ sva-kalevaram
kuśaletara-pātheyo
bhūta-droheṇa yad bhṛtam

ekaḥ—alone; *prapadyate*—he enters; *dhvāntam*—darkness; *hitvā*—after quitting; *idam*—this; *sva*—his; *kalevaram*—body; *kuśala-itara*—sin; *pātheyaḥ*—his passage money; *bhūta*—to other living entities; *droheṇa*—by injury; *yat*—which body; *bhṛtam*—was maintained.

TRANSLATION

He goes alone to the darkest regions of hell after quitting the present body, and the money he acquired by envying other living entities is the passage money with which he leaves this world.

PURPORT

When a man earns money by unfair means and maintains his family and himself with that money, the money is enjoyed by many members of the family, but he alone goes to hell. A person who enjoys life by earning money or by envying another's life, and who enjoys with family and friends, will have to enjoy alone the resultant sinful reactions accrued from such violent and illicit life. For example, if a man secures some money by killing someone and with that money maintains his family, those who enjoy the black money earned by him are also partially responsible and are also sent to hell, but he who is the leader is especially punished. The result of material enjoyment is that one takes with him the sinful reaction only, and not the money. The money he earned is left in this world, and he takes only the reaction.

In this world also, if a person acquires some money by murdering someone, the family is not hanged, although its members are sinfully contaminated. But the man who commits the murder and maintains his family is himself hanged as a murderer. The direct offender is more responsible for sinful activities than the indirect enjoyer. The great learned scholar Cāṇakya Paṇḍita says, therefore, that whatever one has in his possession had better be spent for the cause of *sat*, or the Supreme Personality of Godhead, because one cannot take his possessions with him. They remain here, and they will be lost. Either we leave the money or the money leaves us, but we will be separated. The best use of money as long as it is within our possession is to spend it to acquire Kṛṣṇa consciousness.

TEXT 32

दैवेनासादितं तस्य शमलं निरये पुमान् ।
भुङ्क्ते कुटुम्बपोषस्य हृतवित्त इवातुरः ॥३२॥

daivenāsāditaṁ tasya
śamalaṁ niraye pumān
bhuṅkte kuṭumba-poṣasya
hṛta-vitta ivāturaḥ

daivena—by the arrangement of the Supreme Personality of Godhead; *āsāditam*—obtained; *tasya*—his; *śamalam*—sinful reaction; *niraye*—in a hellish condition; *pumān*—the man; *bhuṅkte*—undergoes; *kuṭumba-poṣasya*—of maintaining a family; *hṛta-vittaḥ*—one whose wealth is lost; *iva*—like; *āturaḥ*—suffering.

TRANSLATION

Thus, by the arrangement of the Supreme Personality of Godhead, the maintainer of kinsmen is put into a hellish condition to suffer for his sinful activities, like a man who has lost his wealth.

PURPORT

The example set herein is that the sinful person suffers just like a man who has lost his wealth. The human form of body is achieved by the conditioned soul after many, many births and is a very valuable asset. Instead of utilizing this life to get liberation, if one uses it simply for the purpose of maintaining his so-called family and therefore performs foolish and unauthorized action, he is compared to a man who has lost his wealth and who, upon losing it, laments. When wealth is lost, there is no use lamenting, but as long as there is wealth, one has to utilize it properly and thereby gain eternal profit. It may be argued that when a man leaves his money earned by sinful activities, he also leaves his sinful activities here with his money. But it is especially mentioned herein that by superior arrangement (*daivenāsāditam*), although the man leaves behind him his sinfully earned money, he carries the effect of it. When a man steals some money, if he is caught and agrees to return it, he is not freed from the criminal punishment. By the law of the state, even though he returns the money, he has to undergo the punishment. Similarly, the money earned by a criminal process may be left by the man when dying, but by superior arrangement he carries with him the effect, and therefore he has to suffer hellish life.

TEXT 33

केवलेन ह्यधर्मेण कुटुम्बभरणोत्सुकः ।
याति जीवोऽन्धतामिस्रं चरमं तमसः पदम् ॥३३॥

kevalena hy adharmeṇa
kuṭumba-bharaṇotsukaḥ
yāti jīvo 'ndha-tāmisraṁ
caramaṁ tamasaḥ padam

kevalena—simply; *hi*—certainly; *adharmeṇa*—by irreligious activities; *kuṭumba*—family; *bharaṇa*—to maintain; *utsukaḥ*—eager; *yāti*—goes; *jīvaḥ*—a person; *andha-tāmisram*—to Andha-tāmisra; *caramam*—ultimate; *tamasaḥ*—of darkness; *padam*—region.

TRANSLATION

Therefore a person who is very eager to maintain his family and kinsmen simply by black methods certainly goes to the darkest region of hell, which is known as Andha-tāmisra.

PURPORT

Three words in this verse are very significant. *Kevalena* means "only by black methods," *adharmeṇa* means "unrighteous" or "irreligious," and *kuṭumba-bharaṇa* means "family maintenance." Maintaining one's family is certainly the duty of a householder, but one should be eager to earn his livelihood by the prescribed method, as stated in the scriptures. In *Bhagavad-gītā* it is described that the Lord has divided the social system into four classifications of castes, or *varṇas*, according to quality and work. Apart from *Bhagavad-gītā*, in every society a man is known according to his quality and work. For example, when a man is constructing wooden furniture, he is called a carpenter, and a man who works with an anvil and iron is called a blacksmith. Similarly, a man who is engaged in the medical or engineering fields has a particular duty and designation. All these human activities have been divided by the Supreme Lord into four *varṇas*, namely *brāhmaṇa*, *kṣatriya*, *vaiśya* and *śūdra*. In *Bhagavad-gītā* and in other Vedic literatures, the specific duties of the *brāhmaṇa, kṣatriya, vaiśya* and *śūdra* are mentioned.

One should work honestly according to his qualification. He should not earn his livelihood unfairly, by means for which he is not qualified. If a *brāhmaṇa* who works as a priest so that he may enlighten his followers with the spiritual way of life is not qualified as a priest, then he is cheating the public. One should not earn by such unfair means. The same is applicable to a *kṣatriya* or to a *vaiśya.* It is especially mentioned that the means of livelihood of those who are trying to advance in Kṛṣṇa consciousness must be very fair and uncomplicated. Here it is mentioned that he who earns his livelihood by unfair means (*kevalena*) is sent to the darkest hellish region. Otherwise, if one maintains his family by prescribed methods and honest means, there is no objection to one's being a family man.

TEXT 34

अधस्तान्नरलोकस्य यावतीर्यातनादयः ।
क्रमशः समनुक्रम्य पुनरत्राव्रजेच्छुचिः ॥३४॥

adhastān nara-lokasya
yāvatīr yātanādayaḥ
kramaśaḥ samanukramya
punar atrāvrajec chuciḥ

adhastāt—from below; *nara-lokasya*—human birth; *yāvatīḥ*—as many; *yātanā*—punishments; *ādayaḥ*—and so on; *kramaśaḥ*—in a regular order; *samanukramya*—having gone through; *punaḥ*—again; *atra*—here, on this earth; *āvrajet*—he may return; *śuciḥ*—pure.

TRANSLATION

Having gone through all the miserable, hellish conditions and having passed in a regular order through the lowest forms of animal life prior to human birth, and having thus been purged of his sins, one is reborn again as a human being on this earth.

PURPORT

Just as a prisoner, who has undergone troublesome prison life, is set free again, the person who has always engaged in impious and mischievous activities is put into hellish conditions, and when he has undergone different hellish lives, namely those of lower animals like cats, dogs and hogs, by the gradual process of evolution he again comes back as a human being. In *Bhagavad-gītā* it is stated that even though a person engaged in the practice of the *yoga* system may not finish perfectly and may fall down for some reason or other, his next life as a human being is guaranteed. It is stated that such a person, who has fallen from the path of *yoga* practice, is given a chance in his next life to take birth in a very rich family or in a very pious family. It is interpreted that "rich family" refers to a big mercantile family because generally people who engage in trades and mercantile business are very rich. One who engaged in the process of self-realization, or connecting with the Supreme Absolute Truth, but fell short is allowed to take birth in such a rich family, or he is allowed to take birth in the family of pious *brāhmaṇas;* either way, he is guaranteed to appear in human society in his next life. It can be concluded that if someone is not willing to enter into hellish life, as in Tāmisra or Andha-tāmisra, then he must take to the process of Kṛṣṇa consciousness, which is the first-class *yoga* system, because even if one is unable to attain complete Kṛṣṇa consciousness in this life, he is guaranteed at least to take his next birth in a human family. He cannot be sent into a hellish condition. Kṛṣṇa consciousness is the purest life, and it protects all human beings from gliding down to hell to take birth in a family of dogs or hogs.

Thus end the Bhaktivedanta purports of the Third Canto, Thirtieth Chapter, of the Śrīmad-Bhāgavatam, *entitled "Description by Lord Kapila of Adverse Fruitive Activities."*

CHAPTER THIRTY-ONE

Lord Kapila's Instructions on the Movements of the Living Entities

TEXT 1

श्रीभगवानुवाच

कर्मणा दैवनेत्रेण जन्तुर्देहोपपत्तये ।
स्त्रियाः प्रविष्ट उदरं पुंसो रेतःकणाश्रयः ॥ १ ॥

śrī-bhagavān uvāca
karmaṇā daiva-netreṇa
jantur dehopapattaye
striyāḥ praviṣṭa udaraṁ
puṁso retaḥ-kaṇāśrayaḥ

śrī-bhagavān uvāca—the Supreme Personality of Godhead said; *karmaṇā*—by the result of work; *daiva-netreṇa*—under the supervision of the Lord; *jantuḥ*—the living entity; *deha*—a body; *upapattaye*—for obtaining; *striyāḥ*—of a woman; *praviṣṭaḥ*—enters; *udaram*—the womb; *puṁsaḥ*—of a man; *retaḥ*—of semen; *kaṇa*—a particle; *āśrayaḥ*—dwelling in.

TRANSLATION

The Personality of Godhead said: Under the supervision of the Supreme Lord and according to the result of his work, the living entity, the soul, is made to enter into the womb of a woman through the particle of male semen to assume a particular type of body.

PURPORT

As stated in the last chapter, after suffering different kinds of hellish conditions, a man comes again to the human form of body. The same topic is continued in this chapter. In order to give a particular type of human form to a person who has already suffered hellish life, the soul is transferred to the semen of a man who is just suitable to become his father. During sexual intercourse, the soul is transferred through the semen of the father into the mother's womb in order to produce a particular type of body. This process is applicable to all embodied living entities, but it is especially mentioned for the man who was transferred to the Andha-tāmisra hell. After suffering there, when he who has had many types of hellish bodies, like those of dogs and hogs, is to come again to the human form, he is given the chance to take his birth in the same type of body from which he degraded himself to hell.

Everything is done by the supervision of the Supreme Personality of Godhead. Material nature supplies the body, but it does so under the direction of the Supersoul. It is said in *Bhagavad-gītā* that a living entity is wandering in this material world on a chariot made by material nature. The Supreme Lord, as Supersoul, is always present with the individual soul. He directs material nature to supply a particular type of body to the individual soul according to the result of his work, and the material nature supplies it. Here one word, *retaḥ-kaṇāśrayaḥ*, is very significant because it indicates that it is not the semen of the man that creates life within the womb of a woman; rather, the living entity, the soul, takes shelter in a particle of semen and is then pushed into the womb of a woman. Then the body develops. There is no possibility of creating a living entity without the presence of the soul simply by sexual intercourse. The materialistic theory that there is no soul and that a child is born simply by material combination of the sperm and ovum is not very feasible. It is unacceptable.

TEXT 2

कललं त्वेकरात्रेण पञ्चरात्रेण बुद्बुदम् ।
दशाहेन तु कर्कन्धूः पेश्यण्डं वा ततः परम् ॥ २ ॥

kalalaṁ tv eka-rātreṇa
pañca-rātreṇa budbudam
daśāhena tu karkandhūḥ
peśy aṇḍaṁ vā tataḥ param

kalalam—mixing of the sperm and ovum; *tu*—then; *eka-rātreṇa*—on the first night; *pañca-rātreṇa*—by the fifth night; *budbudam*—a bubble; *daśa-ahena*—in ten days; *tu*—then; *karkandhūḥ*—like a plum; *peśī*—a lump of flesh; *aṇḍam*—an egg; *vā*—or; *tataḥ*—thence; *param*—afterwards.

TRANSLATION

On the first night, the sperm and ovum mix, and on the fifth night the mixture ferments into a bubble. On the tenth night it develops into a form like a plum, and after that, it gradually turns into a lump of flesh or an egg, as the case may be.

PURPORT

The body of the soul develops in four different ways according to its different sources. One kind of body, that of the trees and plants, sprouts from the earth; the second kind of body grows from perspiration, as with flies, germs and bugs; the third kind of body develops from eggs; and the fourth develops from an embryo. This verse indicates that after emulsification of the ovum and sperm, the body gradually develops either into a lump of flesh or into an egg, as the case may be. In the case of birds it develops into an egg, and in the case of animals and human beings it develops into a lump of flesh.

TEXT 3

मासेन तु शिरो द्वाभ्यां बाह्वङ्घ्र्याद्यङ्गविग्रहः ।
नखलोमास्थिचर्माणि लिङ्गच्छिद्रोद्भवस्त्रिभिः ॥ ३ ॥

māsena tu śiro dvābhyāṁ
bāhv-aṅghry-ādy-aṅga-vigrahaḥ
nakha-lomāsthi-carmāṇi
liṅga-cchidrodbhavas tribhiḥ

māsena—within a month; *tu*—then; *śiraḥ*—a head; *dvābhyām*—in two months; *bāhu*—arms; *aṅghri*—feet; *ādi*—and so on; *aṅga*—limbs; *vigrahaḥ*—form; *nakha*—nails; *loma*—body hair; *asthi*—bones; *carmāṇi*—and skin; *liṅga*—organ of generation; *chidra*—apertures; *udbhavaḥ*—appearance; *tribhiḥ*—within three months.

TRANSLATION

In the course of a month, a head is formed, and at the end of two months the hands, feet and other limbs take shape. By the end of three months, the nails, fingers, toes, body hair, bones and skin appear, as do the organ of generation and the other apertures in the body, namely the eyes, nostrils, ears, mouth and anus.

TEXT 4

चतुर्भिर्धातवः सप्त पञ्चभिः क्षुत्तृडुद्भवः ।
षड्भिर्जरायुणा वीतः कुक्षौ भ्राम्यति दक्षिणे ॥ ४ ॥

caturbhir dhātavaḥ sapta
pañcabhiḥ kṣut-tṛḍ-udbhavaḥ
ṣaḍbhir jarāyuṇā vītaḥ
kukṣau bhrāmyati dakṣiṇe

caturbhiḥ—within four months; *dhātavaḥ*—ingredients; *sapta*—seven; *pañcabhiḥ*—within five months; *kṣut-tṛṭ*—of hunger and thirst; *udbhavaḥ*—appearance; *ṣaḍbhiḥ*—within six months; *jarāyuṇā*—by the amnion; *vītaḥ*—enclosed; *kukṣau*—in the abdomen; *bhrāmyati*—moves; *dakṣiṇe*—on the right side.

TRANSLATION

Within four months from the date of conception, the seven essential ingredients of the body, namely chyle, blood, flesh, fat, bone, marrow and semen, come into existence. At the end of five months, hunger and thirst make themselves felt, and at the end of six months, the fetus, enclosed by the amnion, begins to move on the right side of the abdomen.

PURPORT

When the body of the child is completely formed at the end of six months, the child, if he is male, begins to move on the right side, and if female, she tries to move on the left side.

TEXT 5

मातुर्जग्धान्नपानाद्यैरेधद्धातुरसम्मते ।
शेते विण्मूत्रयोर्गर्ते स जन्तुर्जन्तुसम्भवे ॥ ५ ॥

mātur jagdhānna-pānādyair
edhad-dhātur asammate
śete viṇ-mūtrayor garte
sa jantur jantu-sambhave

mātuḥ—of the mother; *jagdha*—taken; *anna-pāna*—by the food and drink; *ādyaiḥ*—and so on; *edhat*—increasing; *dhātuḥ*—the ingredients of his body; *asammate*—abominable; *śete*—remains; *viṭ-mūtrayoḥ*—of stools and urine; *garte*—in a hollow; *saḥ*—that; *jantuḥ*—fetus; *jantu*—of worms; *sambhave*—the breeding place.

TRANSLATION

Deriving its nutrition from the food and drink taken by the mother, the fetus grows and remains in that abominable residence of stools and urine, which is the breeding place of all kinds of worms.

PURPORT

In the *Mārkaṇḍeya Purāṇa* it is said that in the intestine of the mother the umbilical cord, which is known as *āpyāyanī*, joins the mother to the abdomen of the child, and through this passage the child within the womb accepts the mother's assimilated foodstuff. In this way the child is fed by the mother's intestine within the womb and grows from day to day. The statement of the *Mārkaṇḍeya Purāṇa* about the child's situation within the womb is exactly corroborated by modern medical science, and thus the authority of the *Purāṇas* cannot be disproved, as is sometimes attempted by the Māyāvādī philosophers.

Since the child depends completely on the assimilated foodstuff of the mother, during pregnancy there are restrictions on the food taken by the mother. Too much salt, chili, onion and similar food is forbidden for the pregnant mother because the child's body is too delicate and new for him to tolerate such pungent food. Restrictions and precautions to be taken by the pregnant mother, as enunciated in the *smṛti* scriptures of Vedic literature, are very useful. We can understand from the Vedic literature how much care is taken to beget a nice child in society. The *garbhādhāna* ceremony before sexual intercourse was compulsory for persons in the higher grades of society, and it is very scientific. Other processes recommended in the Vedic literature during pregnancy are also very important. To take care of the child is the primary duty of the parents because if such care is taken, society will be filled with good population to maintain the peace and prosperity of the society, country and human race.

TEXT 6

कृमिभिः क्षतसर्वाङ्गः सौकुमार्यात्प्रतिक्षणम् ।
मूर्च्छामाप्नोत्युरुक्लेशस्तत्रत्यैः क्षुधितैर्मुहुः ॥ ६ ॥

kṛmibhiḥ kṣata-sarvāṅgaḥ
saukumāryāt pratikṣaṇam
mūrcchām āpnoty uru-kleśas
tatratyaiḥ kṣudhitair muhuḥ

kṛmibhiḥ—by worms; *kṣata*—bitten; *sarva-aṅgaḥ*—all over the body; *saukumāryāt*—because of tenderness; *prati-kṣaṇam*—moment after moment; *mūrcchām*—unconsciousness; *āpnoti*—he obtains; *uru-kleśaḥ*—whose suffering is great; *tatratyaiḥ*—being there (in the abdomen); *kṣudhitaiḥ*—hungry; *muhuḥ*—again and again.

TRANSLATION

Bitten again and again all over the body by the hungry worms in the abdomen itself, the child suffers terrible agony because of his tenderness. He thus becomes unconscious moment after moment because of the terrible condition.

PURPORT

The miserable condition of material existence is not only felt when we come out of the womb of the mother, but is also present within the womb. Miserable life begins from the moment the living entity begins to contact his material body. Unfortunately, we forget this experience and do not take the miseries of birth very seriously. In *Bhagavad-gītā*, therefore, it is specifically mentioned that one should be very alert to understand the specific difficulties of birth and death. Just as during the formation of this body we have to pass through so many difficulties within the womb of the mother, at the time of death there are also many difficulties. As described in the previous chapter, one has to transmigrate from one body to another, and the transmigration into the bodies of dogs and hogs is especially miserable. But despite such miserable conditions, due to the spell of *māyā* we forget everything and become enamored by the present so-called happiness, which is described as actually no more than a counteraction to distress.

TEXT 7

कटुतीक्ष्णोष्णलवणरूक्षाम्लादिभिरुल्बणैः ।
मातृभुक्तैरुपस्पृष्टः सर्वाङ्गोत्थितवेदनः ॥ ७ ॥

kaṭu-tīkṣṇoṣṇa-lavaṇa-
rūkṣāmlādibhir ulbaṇaiḥ
mātṛ-bhuktair upaspṛṣṭaḥ
sarvāṅgotthita-vedanaḥ

kaṭu—bitter; *tīkṣṇa*—pungent; *uṣṇa*—hot; *lavaṇa*—salty; *rūkṣa*—dry; *amla*—sour; *ādibhiḥ*—and so on; *ulbaṇaiḥ*—excessive; *mātṛ-bhuktaiḥ*—by foods eaten by the mother; *upaspṛṣṭaḥ*—affected; *sarva-aṅga*—all over the body; *utthita*—arisen; *vedanaḥ*—pain.

TRANSLATION

Owing to the mother's eating bitter, pungent foodstuffs, or food which is too salty or too sour, the body of the child incessantly suffers pains which are almost intolerable.

PURPORT

All descriptions of the child's bodily situation in the womb of the mother are beyond our conception. It is very difficult to remain in such a position, but still the child has to remain. Because his consciousness is not very developed, the child can tolerate it, otherwise he would die.

That is the benediction of *māyā*, who endows the suffering body with the qualifications for tolerating such terrible tortures.

TEXT 8

उल्बेन संवृतस्तस्मिन्नन्त्रैश्च बहिरावृतः ।
आस्ते कृत्वा शिरः कुक्षौ भुग्नपृष्ठशिरोधरः ॥ ८ ॥

ulbena saṁvṛtas tasminn
antraiś ca bahir āvṛtaḥ
āste kṛtvā śiraḥ kukṣau
bhugna-pṛṣṭha-śirodharaḥ

ulbena—by the amnion; *saṁvṛtaḥ*—enclosed; *tasmin*—in that place; *antraiḥ*—by the intestines; *ca*—and; *bahiḥ*—outside; *āvṛtaḥ*—covered; *āste*—he lies; *kṛtvā*—having put; *śiraḥ*—the head; *kukṣau*—towards the belly; *bhugna*—bent; *pṛṣṭha*—back; *śiraḥ-dharaḥ*—neck.

TRANSLATION

Placed within the amnion and covered outside by the intestines, the child remains lying on one side of the abdomen, his head turned towards his belly and his back and neck arched like a bow.

PURPORT

If a grown man were put into such a condition as the child within the abdomen, completely entangled in all respects, it would be impossible for him to live even for a few seconds. Unfortunately, we forget all these sufferings and try to be happy in this life, not caring for the liberation of the soul from the entanglement of birth and death. It is an unfortunate civilization in which these matters are not plainly discussed to make people understand the precarious condition of material existence.

TEXT 9

अकल्पः स्वाङ्गचेष्टायां शकुन्त इव पञ्जरे ।
तत्र लब्धस्मृतिर्दैवात्कर्म जन्मशतोद्भवम् ।
स्मरन्दीर्घमनुच्छ्वासं शर्म किं नाम विन्दते ॥ ९ ॥

akalpaḥ svāṅga-ceṣṭāyāṁ
śakunta iva pañjare
tatra labdha-smṛtir daivāt
karma janma-śatodbhavam
smaran dīrgham anucchvāsaṁ
śarma kiṁ nāma vindate

akalpaḥ—unable; *sva-aṅga*—his limbs; *ceṣṭāyām*—to move; *śakuntaḥ*—a bird; *iva*—like; *pañjare*—in a cage; *tatra*—there; *labdha-smṛtiḥ*—having gained his memory; *daivāt*—by fortune; *karma*—activities; *janma-śata-udbhavam*—occurring during the last hundred births; *smaran*—remembering; *dīrgham*—for a long time; *anucchvāsam*—sighing; *śarma*—peace of mind; *kim*—what; *nāma*—then; *vindate*—can he achieve.

TRANSLATION

The child thus remains just like a bird in a cage, without freedom of movement. At that time, if the child is fortunate, he can remember all the troubles of his past one hundred births, and he grieves wretchedly. What is the possibility of peace of mind in that condition?

PURPORT

After birth the child may forget about the difficulties of his past lives, but when we are grown-up we can at least understand the grievous tortures undergone at birth and death by reading the authorized scriptures like *Śrīmad-Bhāgavatam.* If we do not believe in the scriptures, that is a different question, but if we have faith in the authority of such descriptions, then we must prepare for our freedom in the next life; that is possible in this human form of life. One who does not take heed of these indications of suffering in human existence is said to be undoubtedly committing suicide. It is said that this human form of life is the only means for crossing over the nescience of *māyā*, or material existence. We have a very efficient boat in this human form of body, and there is a very expert captain, the spiritual master; the scriptural injunctions are like favorable winds. If we do not cross over the ocean of the nescience of material existence in spite of all these facilities, then certainly we are all intentionally committing suicide.

TEXT 10

आरभ्य सप्तमान्मासाल्लब्धबोधोऽपि वेपितः ।
नैकत्रास्ते सूतिवातैर्विष्ठाभूरिव सोदरः ॥१०॥

ārabhya saptamān māsāl
labdha-bodho 'pi vepitaḥ
naikatrāste sūti-vātair
viṣṭhā-bhūr iva sodaraḥ

ārabhya—beginning; *saptamāt māsāt*—from the seventh month; *labdha-bodhaḥ*—endowed with consciousness; *api*—although; *vepitaḥ*—tossed; *na*—not; *ekatra*—in one place; *āste*—he remains; *sūti-vātaiḥ*—by the winds for childbirth; *viṣṭhā-bhūḥ*—the worm; *iva*—like; *sa-udaraḥ*—born of the same womb.

TRANSLATION

Thus endowed with the development of consciousness from the seventh month after his conception, the child is tossed downward by the airs that press the embryo during the weeks preceding delivery. Like the worms born of the same filthy abdominal cavity, he cannot remain in one place.

PURPORT

At the end of the seventh month the child is moved by the bodily air and does not remain in the same place, for the entire uterine system becomes slackened before delivery. The worms have been described here as *sodara. Sodara* means "born of the same mother." Since the child is born from the womb of the mother and the worms are also born of fermentation within the womb of the same mother, under the circumstances the child and the worms are actually brothers. We are very anxious to establish universal brotherhood among human beings, but we should take into consideration that even the worms are our brothers, what to speak of other living entities. Therefore, we should be concerned about all living entities.

TEXT 11

नाथमान ऋषिर्भीतः सप्तवध्रिः कृताञ्जलिः ।
स्तुवीत तं विक्लवया वाचा येनोदरेऽर्पितः ॥११॥

nāthamāna ṛṣir bhītaḥ
sapta-vadhriḥ kṛtāñjaliḥ
stuvīta taṁ viklavayā
vācā yenodare 'rpitaḥ

nāthamānaḥ—appealing; *ṛṣiḥ*—the living entity; *bhītaḥ*—frightened; *sapta-vadhriḥ*—bound by the seven layers; *kṛta-añjaliḥ*—with folded hands; *stuvīta*—prays; *tam*—to the Lord; *viklavayā*—faltering; *vācā*—with words; *yena*—by whom; *udare*—in the womb; *arpitaḥ*—he was placed.

TRANSLATION

The living entity in this frightful condition of life, bound by seven layers of material ingredients, prays with folded hands, appealing to the Lord, who has put him in that condition.

PURPORT

It is said that when a woman is having labor pains she promises that she will never again become pregnant and suffer from such a severely painful condition. Similarly, when one is undergoing some surgical operation he promises that he will never again act in such a way as to become diseased and have to undergo medical surgery, or when one falls into danger, he promises that he will never again make the same mistake. Similarly, the living entity, when put into a hellish condition of life, prays to the Lord that he will never again commit sinful activities and have to be put into the womb for repeated birth and death. In the hellish condition within the womb the living entity is very much afraid of being born again, but when he is out of the womb, when he is in full life and good health, he forgets everything and commits again and again the same sins for which he was put into that horrible condition of existence.

TEXT 12

जन्तुरुवाच
तस्योपसन्नमवितुं जगदिच्छयात्त-
नानातनोर्भुवि चलच्चरणारविन्दम् ।
सोऽहं व्रजामि शरणं ह्यकुतोभयं मे
येनेदृशी गतिरदर्श्यसतोऽनुरूपा ॥१२॥

jantur uvāca
tasyopasannam avituṁ jagad icchayātta-
nānā-tanor bhuvi calac-caraṇāravindam
so 'haṁ vrajāmi śaraṇaṁ hy akuto-bhayaṁ me
yenedṛśī gatir adarśy asato 'nurūpā

jantuḥ uvāca—the human soul says; *tasya*—of the Supreme Personality of Godhead; *upasannam*—having approached for protection; *avitum*—to protect; *jagat*—the universe; *icchayā*—by His own will; *ātta-nānā-tanoḥ*—who accepts various forms; *bhuvi*—on the earth; *calat*—walking; *caraṇa-aravindam*—the lotus feet; *saḥ aham*—I myself; *vrajāmi*—go; *śaraṇam*—unto the shelter; *hi*—indeed; *akutaḥ-bhayam*—giving relief from all fear; *me*—for me; *yena*—by whom; *īdṛśī*—such; *gatiḥ*—condition of life; *adarśi*—was considered; *asataḥ*—impious; *anurūpā*—befitting.

TRANSLATION

The human soul says: I take shelter of the lotus feet of the Supreme Personality of Godhead, who appears in His various eternal forms and walks on the surface of the world. I take shelter of Him only, because He can give me relief from all fear and from Him I have received this condition of life, which is just befitting my impious activities.

PURPORT

The word *calac-caraṇāravindam* refers to the Supreme Personality of Godhead, who actually walks or travels upon the surface of the world.

For example, Lord Rāmacandra actually walked on the surface of the world, and Lord Kṛṣṇa also walked just like an ordinary man. The prayer is therefore offered to the Supreme Personality of Godhead, who descends to the surface of this earth, or any part of this universe, for the protection of the pious and the destruction of the impious. It is confirmed in *Bhagavad-gītā* that when there is an increase of irreligion and discrepancies arise in the real religious activities, the Supreme Lord comes to protect the pious and kill the impious. This verse indicates Lord Kṛṣṇa.

Another significant point in this verse is that the Lord comes, *icchayā*, by His own will. As Kṛṣṇa confirms in *Bhagavad-gītā*, *sambhavāmy ātma-māyayā:* "I appear at My will, by My internal potential power." He is not forced to come by the laws of material nature. It is stated here, *icchayā:* He does not *assume* any form, as the impersonalists think, because He comes at His own will, and the form in which He descends is His eternal form. As the Supreme Lord puts the living entity into the condition of horrible existence, He can also deliver him, and therefore one should seek shelter at the lotus feet of Kṛṣṇa. Kṛṣṇa demands, "Give up everything and surrender unto Me." And it is also said in *Bhagavad-gītā* that anyone who approaches Him does not come back again to accept a form in material existence, but goes back to Godhead, back home, never to return.

TEXT 13

यस्त्वत्र बद्ध इव कर्मभिरावृतात्मा
भूतेन्द्रियाशयमयीमवलम्ब्य मायाम् ।
आस्ते विशुद्धमविकारमखण्डबोध-
मातप्यमानहृदयेऽवसितं नमामि ॥१३॥

yas tv atra baddha iva karmabhir āvṛtātmā
bhūtendriyāśayamayīm avalambya māyām
āste viśuddham avikāram akhaṇḍa-bodham
ātapyamāna-hṛdaye 'vasitaṁ namāmi

yaḥ—who; *tu*—also; *atra*—here; *baddhaḥ*—bound; *iva*—as if; *karmabhiḥ*—by activities; *āvṛta*—covered; *ātmā*—the pure soul; *bhūta*—

the gross elements; *indriya*—the senses; *āśaya*—the mind; *mayīm*—consisting of; *avalambya*—having fallen; *māyām*—into *māyā; āste*—remains; *viśuddham*—completely pure; *avikāram*—without change; *akhaṇḍa-bodham*—possessed of unlimited knowledge; *ātapyamāna*—repentant; *hṛdaye*—in the heart; *avasitam*—residing; *namāmi*—I offer my respectful obeisances.

TRANSLATION

I, the pure soul, appearing now bound by my activities, am lying in the womb of my mother by the arrangement of māyā. I offer my respectful obeisances unto Him who is also here with me but who is unaffected and changeless. He is unlimited, but He is perceived in the repentant heart. To Him I offer my respectful obeisances.

PURPORT

As stated in the previous verse, the *jīva* soul says, "I take shelter of the Supreme Lord." Therefore, constitutionally, the *jīva* soul is the subordinate servitor of the Supreme Soul, the Personality of Godhead. Both the Supreme Soul and the *jīva* soul are sitting in the same body, as confirmed in the *Upaniṣads.* They are sitting as friends, but one is suffering, and the other is aloof from suffering.

In this verse it is said, *viśuddham avikāram akhaṇḍa-bodham:* the Supersoul is always sitting apart from all contamination. The living entity is contaminated and suffering because he has a material body, but that does not mean that because the Lord is also with him, He also has a material body. He is *avikāram,* changeless. He is always the same Supreme, but unfortunately the Māyāvādī philosophers, because of their impure hearts, cannot understand that the Supreme Soul, the Supersoul, is different from the individual soul. It is said here, *ātapyamāna-hṛdaye 'vasitam:* He is in the heart of every living entity, but He can be realized only by a soul who is repentant. The individual soul becomes repentant that he forgot his constitutional position, wanted to become one with the Supreme Soul and tried his best to lord it over material nature. He has been baffled, and therefore he is repentant. At that time, Supersoul, or the relationship between the Supersoul and the individual soul, is realized. As it is confirmed in *Bhagavad-gītā,* after many, many births the knowledge comes to the conditioned soul that Vāsudeva is great, *He* is master, and *He* is Lord. The individual soul is the servant, and therefore he surrenders unto Him. At that time he becomes a *mahātmā*, a great soul. Therefore, a fortunate living being who comes to this understanding, even within the womb of his mother, has his liberation assured.

TEXT 14

यः पञ्चभूतरचिते रहितः शरीरे
च्छन्नोऽयथेन्द्रियगुणार्थचिदात्मकोऽहम् ।
तेनाविकुण्ठमहिमानमृषिं तमेनं
वन्दे परं प्रकृतिपूरुषयोः पुमांसम् ॥१४॥

yaḥ pañca-bhūta-racite rahitaḥ śarīre
cchanno 'yathendriya-guṇārtha-cid-ātmako 'ham
tenāvikuṇṭha-mahimānam ṛṣim tam enaṁ
vande paraṁ prakṛti-pūruṣayoḥ pumāṁsam

yaḥ—who; *pañca-bhūta*—five gross elements; *racite*—made of; *rahitaḥ*—separated; *śarīre*—in the material body; *channaḥ*—covered; *ayathā*—unfitly; *indriya*—senses; *guṇa*—qualities; *artha*—objects of senses; *cit*—ego; *ātmakaḥ*—consisting of; *aham*—I; *tena*—by a material body; *avikuṇṭha-mahimānam*—whose glories are unobscured; *ṛṣim*—all-knowing; *tam*—that; *enam*—unto Him; *vande*—I offer obeisances; *param*—transcendental; *prakṛti*—to material nature; *pūruṣayoḥ*—to the living entities; *pumāṁsam*—unto the Supreme Personality of Godhead.

TRANSLATION

I am separated from the Supreme Lord because of my being in this material body, which is made of five elements, and therefore my qualities and senses are being misused, although I am essentially spiritual. Because the Supreme Personality of Godhead is transcendental to material nature and the living entities, because He is devoid of such a material body, and because He is always glorious in His spiritual qualities, I offer my obeisances unto Him.

PURPORT

The difference between the living entity and the Supreme Personality of Godhead is that the living entity is prone to be subjected to material nature, whereas the Supreme Godhead is always transcendental to material nature as well as to the living entities. When the living entity is put into material nature, then his senses and qualities are polluted, or designated. There is no possibility for the Supreme Lord to become embodied by material qualities or material senses, for He is above the influence of material nature and cannot possibly be put in the darkness of ignorance like the living entities. Because of His full knowledge, He is never subjected to the influence of material nature. Material nature is always under His control, and it is therefore not possible that material nature can control the Supreme Personality of Godhead.

Since the identity of the living entity is very minute, he is prone to be subjected to material nature, but when he is freed from this material body, which is false, he attains the same, spiritual nature as the Supreme Lord. At that time there is no qualitative difference between him and the Supreme Lord, but because he is not so quantitatively powerful as to never be put under the influence of material nature, he is quantitatively different from the Lord.

The entire process of devotional service is to purify oneself of this contamination of material nature and put oneself on the spiritual platform, where he is qualitatively one with the Supreme Personality of Godhead. In the *Vedas* it is said that the living entity is always free. *Asaṅgo hy ayaṁ puruṣaḥ.* The living entity is liberated. His material contamination is temporary, and his actual position is that he is liberated. This liberation is achieved by Kṛṣṇa consciousness, which begins from the point of surrender. Therefore it is said here, "I offer my respectful obeisances unto the Supreme Person."

TEXT 15

यन्माययोरुगुणकर्मनिबन्धनेऽस्मिन्
सांसारिके पथि चरंस्तदभिश्रमेण ।
नष्टस्मृतिः पुनरयं प्रवृणीत लोकं
युक्त्या कया महदनुग्रहमन्तरेण ॥१५॥

yan-māyayoru-guṇa-karma-nibandhane 'smin
sāṁsārike pathi caraṁs tad-abhiśrameṇa
naṣṭa-smṛtiḥ punar ayaṁ pravṛṇīta lokaṁ
yuktyā kayā mahad-anugraham antareṇa

yat—of the Lord; *māyayā*—by the *māyā; uru-guṇa*—arising from the great modes; *karma*—activities; *nibandhane*—with bonds; *asmin*—this; *sāṁsārike*—of repeated birth and death; *pathi*—on the path; *caran*—wandering; *tat*—of him; *abhiśrameṇa*—with great pains; *naṣṭa*—lost; *smṛtiḥ*—memory; *punaḥ*—again; *ayam*—this living entity; *pravṛṇīta*—may realize; *lokam*—his true nature; *yuktyā kayā*—by what means; *mahat-anugraham*—the mercy of the Lord; *antareṇa*—without.

TRANSLATION

The human soul further prays: The living entity is put under the influence of material nature and continues a hard struggle for existence on the path of repeated birth and death. This conditional life is due to his forgetfulness of his relationship with the Supreme Personality of Godhead. Therefore, without the Lord's mercy, how can he again engage in the transcendental loving service of the Lord?

PURPORT

The Māyāvādī philosophers say that simply by cultivation of knowledge by mental speculation, one can be liberated from the condition of material bondage. But here it is said one is liberated not by knowledge but by the mercy of the Supreme Lord. The knowledge the conditioned soul gains by mental speculation, however powerful it may be, is always too imperfect to approach the Absolute Truth. It is said that without the mercy of the Supreme Personality of Godhead one cannot understand Him or His actual form, quality and name. Those who are not in devotional service go on speculating for many, many thousands of years, but they are still unable to understand the nature of the Absolute Truth.

One can be liberated in the knowledge of the Absolute Truth simply by the mercy of the Supreme Personality of Godhead. It is clearly said herein that our memory is lost because we are now covered by His material energy. Arguments may be put forward as to why we have been put under the influence of this material energy by the supreme will of the Lord. This is explained in *Bhagavad-gītā*, where the Lord says, "I am sitting in everyone's heart, and due to Me one is forgetful or one is alive in knowledge." The forgetfulness of the conditioned soul is also due to the direction of the Supreme Lord. A living entity misuses his little independence when he wants to lord it over material nature. This misuse of independence, which is called *māyā*, is always available, otherwise there would be no independence. Independence implies that one can use it properly or improperly. It is not static; it is dynamic. Therefore, misuse of independence is the cause of being influenced by *māyā.*

Māyā is so strong that the Lord says that it is very difficult to surmount her influence. But one can do so very easily "if he surrenders unto Me." *Mām eva ye prapadyante:* anyone who surrenders unto Him can overcome the influence of the stringent laws of material nature. It is clearly said here that a living entity is put under the influence of *māyā* by His will, and if anyone wants to get out of this entanglement, this can be made possible simply by His mercy.

The activities of the conditioned souls under the influence of material nature are explained here. Every conditioned soul is engaged in different types of work under the influence of material nature. We can see in the material world that the conditioned soul acts so powerfully that he is playing wonderfully in creating the so-called advancements of material civilization for sense gratification. But actually his position is to know that he is an eternal servant of the Supreme Lord. When he is actually in perfect knowledge, he knows that the Lord is the supreme worshipful object and that the living entity is His eternal servant. Without this knowledge, he engages in material activities; that is called ignorance.

TEXT 16

ज्ञानं यदेतददधात्कतमः स देव-
त्रैकालिकं स्थिरचरेष्वनुवर्तितांशः ।
तं जीवकर्मपदवीमनुवर्तमाना-
स्तापत्रयोपशमनाय वयं भजेम ॥१६॥

jñānaṁ yad etad adadhāt katamaḥ sa devas
trai-kālikaṁ sthira-careṣv anuvartitāṁśaḥ

taṁ jīva-karma-padavīm anuvartamānās
tāpa-trayopaśamanāya vayaṁ bhajema

jñānam—knowledge; *yat*—which; *etat*—this; *adadhāt*—gave; *katamaḥ*—who other than; *saḥ*—that; *devaḥ*—the Personality of Godhead; *trai-kālikam*—of the three phases of time; *sthira-careṣu*—in the inanimate and animate objects; *anuvartita*—dwelling; *aṁśaḥ*—His partial representation; *tam*—unto Him; *jīva*—of the *jīva* souls; *karma-padavīm*—the path of fruitive activities; *anuvartamānāḥ*—who are pursuing; *tāpa-traya*—from the threefold miseries; *upaśamanāya*—for getting free; *vayam*—we; *bhajema*—must surrender.

TRANSLATION

No one other than the Supreme Personality of Godhead, as the localized Paramātmā, the partial representation of the Lord, is directing all inanimate and animate objects. He is present in the three phases of time—past, present and future. Therefore, the conditioned soul is engaged in different activities by His direction, and in order to get free from the threefold miseries of this conditional life, we have to surrender unto Him only.

PURPORT

When a conditioned soul is seriously anxious to get out of the influence of the material clutches, the Supreme Personality of Godhead, who is situated within him as Paramātmā, gives him this knowledge: "Surrender unto Me." As the Lord says in *Bhagavad-gītā*, "Give up all other engagements. Just surrender unto Me." It is to be accepted that the source of knowledge is the Supreme Person. This is also confirmed in *Bhagavad-gītā. Mattaḥ smṛtir jñānam apohanaṁ ca.* The Lord says, "Through Me one gets real knowledge and memory, and one also forgets through Me." To one who wants to be materially satisfied or who wants to lord it over material nature, the Lord gives the opportunity to forget His service and engage in the so-called happiness of material activities. Similarly, when one is frustrated in lording it over material nature and is very serious about getting out of this material entanglement, the Lord, from within, gives him the knowledge that he has to surrender unto Him; then there is liberation.

This knowledge cannot be imparted by anyone other than the Supreme Lord or His representative. In the *Caitanya-caritāmṛta* Lord Caitanya instructs Rūpa Gosvāmī that the living entities wander in life after life, undergoing the miserable conditions of material existence. But when one is very anxious to get free from the material entanglement, he gets enlightenment through a spiritual master and Kṛṣṇa. This means that Kṛṣṇa as the Supersoul is seated within the heart of the living entity, and when the living entity is serious, the Lord directs him to take shelter of His representative, a bona fide spiritual master. Directed from within and guided externally by the spiritual master, one attains the path of Kṛṣṇa consciousness, which is the way out of the material clutches.

Therefore there is no possibility of one's being situated in his own position unless he is blessed by the Supreme Personality of Godhead. Unless he is enlightened with the supreme knowledge, one has to undergo the severe penalties of the hard struggle for existence in the material nature. The spiritual master is therefore the mercy manifestation of the Supreme Person. The conditioned soul has to take direct instruction from the spiritual master, and thus he gradually becomes enlightened to the path of Kṛṣṇa consciousness. The seed of Kṛṣṇa consciousness is sown within the heart of the conditioned soul, and when one hears instruction from the spiritual master, the seed fructifies, and one's life is blessed.

TEXT 17

देह्यन्यदेहविवरे जठराग्निनासृग्-
विण्मूत्रकूपपतितो भृशतप्तदेहः ।
इच्छन्नितो विवसितुं गणयन् स्वमासान्
निर्वास्यते कृपणधीर्भगवन् कदा नु ॥१७॥

dehy anya-deha-vivare jaṭharāgnināsṛg-
viṇ-mūtra-kūpa-patito bhṛśa-tapta-dehaḥ
icchann ito vivasituṁ gaṇayan sva-māsān
nirvāsyate kṛpaṇa-dhīr bhagavan kadā nu

dehī—the embodied soul; *anya-deha*—of another body; *vivare*—in the abdomen; *jaṭhara*—of the stomach; *agninā*—by the fire; *asṛk*—of blood; *viṭ*—stool; *mūtra*—and urine; *kūpa*—in a pool; *patitaḥ*—fallen; *bhṛśa*—strongly; *tapta*—scorched; *dehaḥ*—his body; *icchan*—desiring; *itaḥ*—from that place; *vivasitum*—to get out; *gaṇayan*—counting; *sva-māsān*—his months; *nirvāsyate*—will be released; *kṛpaṇa-dhīḥ*—person of miserly intelligence; *bhagavan*—O Lord; *kadā*—when; *nu*—indeed.

TRANSLATION

Fallen into a pool of blood, stool and urine within the abdomen of his mother, his own body scorched by the mother's gastric fire, the embodied soul, anxious to get out, counts his months and prays, "O my Lord, when shall I, a wretched soul, be released from this confinement?"

PURPORT

The precarious condition of the living entity within the womb of his mother is described here. On one side of where the child is floating is the heat of gastric fire, and on the other side are urine, stool, blood and discharges. After seven months the child, who has regained his consciousness, feels the horrible condition of his existence and prays to the Lord. Counting the months until his release, he becomes greatly anxious to get out of the confinement. The so-called civilized man does not take account of this horrible condition of life, and sometimes, for the purpose of sense gratification, he tries to kill the child by methods of contraception or abortion. Unserious about the horrible condition in the womb, such persons continue in materialism, grossly misusing the chance of the human form of life.

The word *kṛpaṇa-dhīḥ* is significant in this verse. *Dhī* means "intelligence," and *kṛpaṇa* means "miserly." Conditional life is for persons who are of miserly intelligence or who do not properly utilize their intelligence. In the human form of life the intelligence is developed, and one has to utilize that developed intelligence to get out of the cycle of birth and death. One who does not do so is a miser, just like a person who has immense wealth but does not utilize it, keeping it simply to see. A person who does not actually utilize his human intelligence to get out of the clutches of *māyā*, the cycle of birth and death, is accepted as miserly.

The exact opposite of miserly is *udāra,* "very magnanimous." A *brāhmaṇa* is called *udāra* because he utilizes his human intelligence for spiritual realization. He uses that intelligence to preach Kṛṣṇa consciousness for the benefit of the public, and therefore he is magnanimous.

TEXT 18

येनेदृशीं गतिमसौ दशमास्य ईश
संग्राहितः पुरुदयेन भवादृशेन ।
स्वेनैव तुष्यतु कृतेन स दीननाथः
को नाम तत्प्रति विनाञ्जलिमस्य कुर्यात् ॥१८॥

yenedṛśīṁ gatim asau daśa-māsya īśa
saṅgrāhitaḥ puru-dayena bhavādṛśena
svenaiva tuṣyatu kṛtena sa dīna-nāthaḥ
ko nāma tat-prati vināñjalim asya kuryāt

yena—by whom (the Lord); *īdṛśīm*—such; *gatim*—a condition; *asau*—that person (myself); *daśa-māsyaḥ*—ten months old; *īśa*—O Lord; *saṅgrāhitaḥ*—was made to accept; *puru-dayena*—very merciful; *bhavādṛśena*—incomparable; *svena*—own; *eva*—alone; *tuṣyatu*—may He be pleased; *kṛtena*—with His act; *saḥ*—that; *dīna-nāthaḥ*—refuge of the fallen souls; *kaḥ*—who; *nāma*—indeed; *tat*—that mercy; *prati*—in return; *vinā*—except with; *añjalim*—folded hands; *asya*—of the Lord; *kuryāt*—can repay.

TRANSLATION

My dear Lord, by Your causeless mercy I am awakened to consciousness, although I am only ten months old. For this causeless mercy of the Supreme Personality of Godhead, the friend of all fallen souls, there is no way to express my gratitude but to pray with folded hands.

PURPORT

As stated in *Bhagavad-gītā,* intelligence and forgetfulness are both supplied by the Supersoul sitting with the individual soul within the body. When He sees that a conditioned soul is very serious about getting out of the clutches of the material influence, the Supreme Lord gives intelligence internally as Supersoul and externally as the spiritual master, or, as an incarnation of the Personality of Godhead Himself, He helps by speaking instructions such as *Bhagavad-gītā.* The Lord is always seeking the opportunity to reclaim the fallen souls to His abode, the kingdom of God. We should always feel very much obliged to the Personality of Godhead, for He is always anxious to bring us into the happy condition of eternal life. There is no sufficient means to repay the Personality of Godhead for His act of benediction; therefore, we can simply feel gratitude and pray to the Lord with folded hands. This prayer of the child in the womb may be questioned by some atheistic people. How can a child pray in such a nice way in the womb of his mother? Everything is possible by the grace of the Lord. The child is put into such a precarious condition externally, but internally he is the same, and the Lord is there. By the transcendental energy of the Lord, everything is possible.

TEXT 19

पश्यत्ययं धिषणया ननु सप्तवध्रिः
शारीरके दमशरीर्यपरः स्वदेहे ।
यत्सृष्टयासं तमहं पुरुषं पुराणं
पश्ये बहिर्हृदि च चैत्यमिव प्रतीतम् ॥१९॥

paśyaty ayaṁ dhiṣaṇayā nanu sapta-vadhriḥ
śārīrake dama-śarīry aparaḥ sva-dehe
yat-sṛṣṭayāsaṁ tam ahaṁ puruṣaṁ purāṇaṁ
paśye bahir hṛdi ca caityam iva pratītam

paśyati—sees; *ayam*—this living entity; *dhiṣaṇayā*—with intelligence; *nanu*—only; *sapta-vadhriḥ*—bound by the seven layers of material coverings; *śārīrake*—agreeable and disagreeable sense perceptions; *dama-śarīrī*—having a body for self-control; *aparaḥ*—another; *sva-dehe*—in his body; *yat*—by the Supreme Lord; *sṛṣṭayā*—endowed; *āsam*—was; *tam*—Him; *aham*—I; *puruṣam*—person; *purāṇam*—oldest; *paśye*—see; *bahiḥ*—outside; *hṛdi*—in the heart; *ca*—and; *caityam*—the source of the ego; *iva*—indeed; *pratītam*—recognized.

TRANSLATION

The living entity in another type of body sees only by instinct; he knows only the agreeable and disagreeable sense perceptions of that particular body. But I have a body in which I can control my senses and can understand my destination; therefore, I offer my respectful obeisances to the Supreme Personality of Godhead, by whom I have been blessed with this body and by whose grace I can see Him within and without.

PURPORT

The evolutionary process of different types of bodies is something like that of a fructifying flower. Just as there are different stages in the growth of a flower—the bud stage, the blooming stage and the full-fledged, fully grown stage of aroma and beauty—there are 8,400,000 species of bodies in gradual evolution, and there is systematic progress from the lower species of life to the higher. The human form of life is supposed to be the highest, for it offers consciousness for getting out of the clutches of birth and death. The fortunate child in the womb of his mother realizes his superior position and is thereby distinguished from other bodies. Animals in bodies lower than that of the human being are conscious only as far as their bodily distress and happiness are concerned; they cannot think of more than their bodily necessities of life—eating, sleeping, mating and defending. But in the human form of life, by the grace of God, the consciousness is so developed that a man can evaluate his exceptional position and thus realize the self and the Supreme Lord.

The word *dama-śarīrī* means that we have a body in which we can control the senses and the mind. The complication of materialistic life is due to an uncontrolled mind and uncontrolled senses. One should feel grateful to the Supreme Personality of Godhead for having obtained such a nice human form of body, and one should properly utilize it. The distinction between an animal and a man is that the animal cannot control himself and has no sense of decency, whereas the human being has the sense of decency and can control himself. If this controlling power is not exhibited by the human being, then he is no better than an animal. By controlling the senses, or by the process of *yoga* regulation, one can understand the position of his self, the Supersoul, the world and their interrelation; everything is possible by controlling the senses. Otherwise, we are no better than animals.

Real self-realization by means of controlling the senses is explained herein. One should try to see the Supreme Personality of Godhead and one's own self also. To think oneself the same as the Supreme is not self-realization. Here it is clearly explained that the Supreme Lord is *anādi*, or *purāṇa*, and He has no other cause. The living entity is born of the Supreme Godhead as part and parcel. It is confirmed in the *Brahma-saṁhitā, anādir ādir govindaḥ:* Govinda, the Supreme Person, has no cause. He is unborn. But the living entity is born of Him. As confirmed in *Bhagavad-gītā, mamaivāṁśaḥ:* both the living entity and the Supreme Lord are unborn, but it has to be understood that the supreme cause of the part and parcel is the Supreme Personality of Godhead. *Brahma-saṁhitā* therefore says that everything has come from the Supreme Personality of Godhead (*sarva-kāraṇa-kāraṇam*). The *Vedānta-sūtra* confirms this also. *Janmādy asya yataḥ:* the Absolute Truth is the original source of everyone's birth. Kṛṣṇa also says in *Bhagavad-gītā, ahaṁ sarvasya prabhavaḥ:* "I am the source of birth of everything, including Brahmā and Lord Śiva and the living entities." This is self-realization. One should know that he is under the control of the Supreme Lord and not think that he is fully independent. Otherwise, why should he be put into conditional life?

TEXT 20

सोऽहं वसन्नपि विभो बहुदुःखवासं
गर्भान्न निर्जिगमिषे बहिरन्धकूपे ।
यत्रोपयातमुपसर्पति देवमाया
मिथ्यामतिर्यदनु संसृतिचक्रमेतत् ॥२०॥

so 'haṁ vasann api vibho bahu-duḥkha-vāsaṁ
garbhān na nirjigamiṣe bahir andha-kūpe
yatropayātam upasarpati deva-māyā
mithyā matir yad-anu saṁsṛti-cakram etat

saḥ aham—I myself; *vasan*—living; *api*—although; *vibho*—O Lord; *bahu-duḥkha*—with many miseries; *vāsam*—in a condition; *garbhāt*—from the abdomen; *na*—not; *nirjigamiṣe*—I wish to depart; *bahiḥ*—outside; *andha-kūpe*—in the blind well; *yatra*—where; *upayātam*—one who goes there; *upasarpati*—she captures; *deva-māyā*—the external energy of the Lord; *mithyā*—false; *matiḥ*—identification; *yat*—which *māyā; anu*—according to; *saṁsṛti*—of continual birth and death; *cakram*—cycle; *etat*—this.

TRANSLATION

Therefore, my Lord, although I am living in a terrible condition, I do not wish to depart from my mother's abdomen to fall again into the blind well of materialistic life. Your external energy, called deva-māyā, at once captures the newly born child, and immediately false identification, which is the beginning of the cycle of continual birth and death, begins.

PURPORT

As long as the child is within the womb of his mother, he is in a very precarious and horrible condition of life, but the benefit is that he revives pure consciousness of his relationship with the Supreme Lord and prays for deliverance. But once he is outside the abdomen, when a child is born, *māyā*, or the illusory energy, is so strong that he is immediately overpowered into considering his body to be his self. *Māyā* means "illusion," or that which is actually not. In the material world, everyone is identifying with his body. This false egoistic consciousness of "I am this body" at once develops after the child comes out of the womb. The mother and other relatives are awaiting the child, and as soon as he is born, the mother feeds him, and everyone takes care of him. The living entity soon forgets his position and becomes entangled in bodily relationships. The entire material existence is entanglement in this bodily conception of life. Real knowledge means to develop the consciousness of "I am not this body. I am spirit soul, an eternal part and parcel of the Supreme Lord." Real knowledge entails renunciation, or nonacceptance of this body as the self.

By the influence of *māyā*, the external energy, one forgets everything just after birth. Therefore the child is praying that he prefers to remain within the womb rather than come out. It is said that Śukadeva Gosvāmī, on this consideration, remained for sixteen years within the womb of his mother; he did not want to be entangled in false bodily identification. After cultivating such knowledge within the womb of his mother, he came out at the end of sixteen years and immediately left home so that he might not be captured by the influence of *māyā.* The influence of *māyā* is also explained in *Bhagavad-gītā* as insurmountable. But insurmountable *māyā* can be overcome simply by Kṛṣṇa consciousness. That is also confirmed in *Bhagavad-gītā* (7.14): *mām eva ye prapadyante māyām etāṁ taranti te.* Whoever surrenders unto the lotus feet of Kṛṣṇa can get out of this false conception of life. By the influence of *māyā* only, one forgets his eternal relationship with Kṛṣṇa and identifies himself with his body and the by-products of the body—namely wife, children, society, friendship and love. Thus he becomes a victim of the influence of *māyā,* and his materialistic life of continued birth and death becomes still more stringent.

TEXT 21

तस्मादहं विगतविक्लव उद्धरिष्य
आत्मानमाशु तमसः सुहृदात्मनैव ।
भूयो यथा व्यसनमेतदनेकरन्ध्रं
मा मे भविष्यदुपसादितविष्णुपादः ॥२१॥

tasmād ahaṁ vigata-viklava uddhariṣya
ātmānam āśu tamasaḥ suhṛdātmanaiva
bhūyo yathā vyasanam etad aneka-randhraṁ
mā me bhaviṣyad upasādita-viṣṇu-pādaḥ

tasmāt—therefore; *aham*—I; *vigata*—ceased; *viklavaḥ*—agitation; *uddhariṣye*—shall deliver; *ātmānam*—myself; *āśu*—quickly; *tamasaḥ*—from the darkness; *suhṛdā ātmanā*—with friendly intelligence; *eva*—indeed; *bhūyaḥ*—again; *yathā*—so that; *vyasanam*—plight; *etat*—this; *aneka-randhram*—entering many wombs; *mā*—not; *me*—my; *bhaviṣyat*—may occur; *upasādita*—placed (in my mind); *viṣṇu-pādaḥ*—the lotus feet of Lord Viṣṇu.

TRANSLATION

Therefore, without being agitated any more, I shall deliver myself from the darkness of nescience with the help of my friend, clear consciousness. Simply by keeping the lotus feet of Lord Viṣṇu in my mind, I shall be saved from entering into the wombs of many mothers for repeated birth and death.

PURPORT

The miseries of material existence begin from the very day when the spirit soul takes shelter in the ovum and sperm of the mother and father, they continue after he is born from the womb, and then they are further prolonged. We do not know where the suffering ends. It does not end, however, by one's changing his body. The change of body is taking place at every moment, but that does not mean that we are improving from the fetal condition of life to a more comfortable condition. The best thing is, therefore, to develop Kṛṣṇa consciousness. Here it is stated, *upasādita-viṣṇu-pādaḥ.* This means realization of Kṛṣṇa consciousness. One who is intelligent, by the grace of the Lord, and develops Kṛṣṇa consciousness, is successful in his life because simply by keeping himself in Kṛṣṇa consciousness, he will be saved from the repetition of birth and death.

The child prays that it is better to remain within the womb of darkness and be constantly absorbed in Kṛṣṇa consciousness than to get out and again fall a victim to the illusory energy. The illusory energy acts within the abdomen as well as outside the abdomen, but the trick is that one should remain Kṛṣṇa conscious, and then the effect of such a horrible condition cannot act unfavorably upon him. In *Bhagavad-gītā* it is said that one's intelligence is his friend, and the same intelligence can also be his enemy. Here also the same idea is repeated: *suhṛdātmanaiva*, friendly intelligence. Absorption of intelligence in the personal service of Kṛṣṇa and full consciousness of Kṛṣṇa always are the path of self-realization and liberation. Without being unnecessarily agitated, if we take to the process of Kṛṣṇa consciousness by constantly chanting Hare Kṛṣṇa, Hare Kṛṣṇa, Kṛṣṇa Kṛṣṇa, Hare Hare/ Hare Rāma, Hare Rāma, Rāma Rāma, Hare Hare, the cycle of birth and death can be stopped for good.

It may be questioned herein how the child can be fully Kṛṣṇa conscious within the womb of the mother without any paraphernalia with which to execute Kṛṣṇa consciousness. It is not necessary to arrange for paraphernalia to worship the Supreme Personality of Godhead, Viṣṇu. The child wants to remain within the abdomen of its mother and at the same time wants to become free from the clutches of *māyā*. One does not need any material arrangement to cultivate Kṛṣṇa consciousness. One can cultivate Kṛṣṇa consciousness anywhere and everywhere, provided he can always think of Kṛṣṇa. The *mahā-mantra*, Hare Kṛṣṇa, Hare Kṛṣṇa, Kṛṣṇa Kṛṣṇa, Hare Hare/ Hare Rāma, Hare Rāma, Rāma Rāma, Hare Hare, can be chanted even within the abdomen of one's mother. One can chant while sleeping, while working, while imprisoned in the womb or while outside. This Kṛṣṇa consciousness cannot be checked in any circumstance. The conclusion of the child's prayer is: "Let me remain in this condition; although it is very miserable, it is better not to fall a victim to *māyā* again by going outside."

TEXT 22

कपिल उवाच

एवं कृतमतिर्गर्भे दशमास्यः स्तुवन्नृषिः ।
सद्यः क्षिपत्यवाचीनं प्रसूत्यै सूतिमारुतः ॥२२॥

kapila uvāca
evaṁ kṛta-matir garbhe
daśa-māsyaḥ stuvann ṛṣiḥ
sadyaḥ kṣipaty avācīnaṁ
prasūtyai sūti-mārutaḥ

kapilaḥ uvāca—Lord Kapila said; *evam*—thus; *kṛta-matiḥ*—desiring; *garbhe*—in the womb; *daśa-māsyaḥ*—ten-month-old; *stuvan*—extolling; *ṛṣiḥ*—the living entity; *sadyaḥ*—at that very time; *kṣipati*—propels; *avācīnam*—turned downward; *prasūtyai*—for birth; *sūti-mārutaḥ*—the wind for childbirth.

TRANSLATION

Lord Kapila continued: The ten-month-old living entity has these desires even while in the womb. But while he thus extols the

Lord, the wind that helps parturition propels him forth with his face turned downward so that he may be born.

TEXT 23

तेनावसृष्टः सहसा कृत्वावाक् शिर आतुरः ।
विनिष्क्रामति कृच्छ्रेण निरुच्छ्वासो हतस्मृतिः ॥२३॥

tenāvasṛṣṭaḥ sahasā
kṛvāvāk śira āturaḥ
viniṣkrāmati kṛcchreṇa
nirucchvāso hata-smṛtiḥ

tena—by that wind; *avasṛṣṭaḥ*—pushed downward; *sahasā*—suddenly; *kṛtvā*—turned; *avāk*—downward; *śiraḥ*—his head; *āturaḥ*—suffering; *viniṣkrāmati*—he comes out; *kṛcchreṇa*—with great trouble; *nirucchvāsaḥ*—breathless; *hata*—deprived of; *smṛtiḥ*—memory.

TRANSLATION

Pushed downward all of a sudden by the wind, the child comes out with great trouble, head downward, breathless and deprived of memory due to severe agony.

PURPORT

The word *kṛcchreṇa* means "with great difficulty." When the child comes out of the abdomen through the narrow passage, due to pressure there the breathing system completely stops, and due to agony the child loses his memory. Sometimes the trouble is so severe that the child comes out dead or almost dead. One can imagine what the pangs of birth are like. The child remains for ten months in that horrible condition within the abdomen, and at the end of ten months he is forcibly pushed out. In *Bhagavad-gītā* the Lord points out that a person who is serious about advancement in spiritual consciousness should always consider the four pangs of birth, death, disease and old age. The materialist advances in many ways, but he is unable to stop these four principles of suffering inherent in material existence.

TEXT 24

पतितो भुव्यसृङ्मिश्रः विष्ठाभूरिव चेष्टते ।
रोरूयति गते ज्ञाने विपरीतां गतिं गतः ॥२४॥

patito bhuvy asṛṅ-miśraḥ
viṣṭhā-bhūr iva ceṣṭate
rorūyati gate jñāne
viparītāṁ gatiṁ gataḥ

patitaḥ—fallen; *bhuvi*—on the earth; *asṛk*—with blood; *miśraḥ*—smeared; *viṣṭhā-bhūḥ*—a worm; *iva*—like; *ceṣṭate*—he moves his limbs; *rorūyati*—cries loudly; *gate*—being lost; *jñāne*—his wisdom; *viparītām*—the opposite; *gatim*—state; *gataḥ*—gone to.

TRANSLATION

The child thus falls on the ground, smeared with stool and blood, and plays just like a worm germinated from the stool. He loses his superior knowledge and cries under the spell of māyā.

TEXT 25

परच्छन्दं न विदुषा पुष्यमाणो जनेन सः ।
अनभिप्रेतमापन्नः प्रत्याख्यातुमनीश्वरः ॥२५॥

para-cchandaṁ na viduṣā
puṣyamāṇo janena saḥ
anabhipretam āpannaḥ
pratyākhyātum anīśvaraḥ

para-chandam—the desire of another; *na*—not; *viduṣā*—understanding; *puṣyamāṇaḥ*—being maintained; *janena*—by persons; *saḥ*—he; *anabhipretam*—into undesirable circumstances; *āpannaḥ*—fallen; *pratyākhyātum*—to refuse; *anīśvaraḥ*—unable.

TRANSLATION

After coming out of the abdomen, the child is given to the care of persons who are unable to understand what he wants, and thus he is nursed by such persons. Unable to refuse whatever is given to him, he falls into undesirable circumstances.

PURPORT

Within the abdomen of the mother, the nourishment of the child was being carried on by nature's own arrangement. The atmosphere within the abdomen was not at all pleasing, but as far as the child's feeding was concerned, it was being properly done by the laws of nature. But upon coming out of the abdomen the child falls into a different atmosphere. He wants to eat one thing, but something else is given to him because no one knows his actual demand, and he cannot refuse the undesirables given to him. Sometimes the child cries for the mother's breast, but because the nurse thinks that it is due to pain within his stomach that he is crying, she supplies him some bitter medicine. The child does not want it, but he cannot refuse it. He is put in very awkward circumstances, and the suffering continues.

TEXT 26

शायितोऽशुचिपर्यङ्के जन्तुः स्वेदजदूषिते ।
नेशः कण्डूयनेऽङ्गानामासनोत्थानचेष्टने ॥२६॥

śāyito 'śuci-paryaṅke
jantuḥ svedaja-dūṣite
neśaḥ kaṇḍūyane 'ṅgānām
āsanotthāna-ceṣṭane

śāyitaḥ—laid down; *aśuci-paryaṅke*—on a foul bed; *jantuḥ*—the child; *sveda-ja*—with creatures born from sweat; *dūṣite*—infested; *na īśaḥ*—incapable of; *kaṇḍūyane*—scratching; *aṅgānām*—his limbs; *āsana*—sitting; *utthāna*—standing; *ceṣṭane*—or moving.

TRANSLATION

Laid down on a foul bed infested with sweat and germs, the poor child is incapable of scratching his body to get relief from his itch-

ing sensation, to say nothing of sitting up, standing or even moving.

PURPORT

It should be noted that the child is born crying and suffering. After birth the same suffering continues, and he cries. Because he is disturbed by the germs in his foul bed, which is contaminated by his urine and stool, the poor child continues to cry. He is unable to take any remedial measure for his relief.

TEXT 27

तुदन्त्यामत्वचं दंशा मशका मत्कुणादयः ।
रुदन्तं विगतज्ञानं कृमयः कृमिकं यथा ॥२७॥

tudanty āma-tvacaṁ daṁśā
maśakā matkuṇādayaḥ
rudantaṁ vigata-jñānaṁ
kṛmayaḥ kṛmikaṁ yathā

tudanti—they bite; *āma-tvacam*—the baby, whose skin is soft; *daṁśāḥ*—gnats; *maśakāḥ*—mosquitoes; *matkuṇa*—bugs; *ādayaḥ*—and other creatures; *rudantam*—crying; *vigata*—deprived of; *jñānam*—wisdom; *kṛmayaḥ*—worms; *kṛmikam*—a worm; *yathā*—just as.

TRANSLATION

In his helpless condition, gnats, mosquitoes, bugs and other germs bite the baby, whose skin is tender, just as smaller worms bite a big worm. The child, deprived of his wisdom, cries bitterly.

PURPORT

The word *vigata-jñānam* means that the spiritual knowledge which the child developed in the abdomen is already lost to the spell of *māyā*. Owing to various kinds of disturbances and to being out of the abdomen, the child cannot remember what he was thinking of for his salvation. It is assumed that even if a person acquires some spiritually uplifting knowledge, circumstantially he is prone to forget it. Not only children but also elderly persons should be very careful to protect their sense of Kṛṣṇa consciousness and avoid unfavorable circumstances so that they may not forget their prime duty.

TEXT 28

इत्येवं शैशवं भुक्त्वा दुःखं पौगण्डमेव च ।
अलब्धाभीप्सितोऽज्ञानादिद्धमन्युः शुचार्पितः ॥२८॥

ity evaṁ śaiśavaṁ bhuktvā
duḥkhaṁ paugaṇḍam eva ca
alabdhābhīpsito 'jñānād
iddha-manyuḥ śucārpitaḥ

iti evam—in this way; *śaiśavam*—childhood; *bhuktvā*—having undergone; *duḥkham*—distress; *paugaṇḍam*—boyhood; *eva*—even; *ca*—and; *alabdha*—not achieved; *abhīpsitaḥ*—he whose desires; *ajñānāt*—due to ignorance; *iddha*—kindled; *manyuḥ*—his anger; *śucā*—by sorrow; *arpitaḥ*—overcome.

TRANSLATION

In this way, the child passes through his childhood, suffering different kinds of distress, and attains boyhood. In boyhood also he suffers pain over desires to get things he can never achieve. And thus, due to ignorance, he becomes angry and sorry.

PURPORT

From birth to the end of five years of age is called childhood. After five years up to the end of the fifteenth year is called *paugaṇḍa.* At sixteen years of age, youth begins. The distresses of childhood are already explained, but when the child attains boyhood he is enrolled in a school which he does not like. He wants to play, but he is forced to go to school and study and take responsibility for passing examinations. Another kind of distress is that he wants to get some things with which to play, but circumstances may be such that he is not able to attain them, and he thus becomes aggrieved and feels pain. In one word, he is unhappy, even in his boyhood, just as he was unhappy in his childhood, what to speak of youth. Boys are apt to create so many artificial demands for playing, and when they do not attain satisfaction they become furious with anger, and the result is suffering.

TEXT 29

सह देहेन मानेन वर्धमानेन मन्युना ।
करोति विग्रहं कामी कामिष्वन्ताय चात्मनः ॥२९॥

saha dehena mānena
vardhamānena manyunā
karoti vigrahaṁ kāmī
kāmiṣv antāya cātmanaḥ

saha—with; *dehena*—the body; *mānena*—with false prestige; *vardhamānena*—increasing; *manyunā*—on account of anger; *karoti*—he creates; *vigraham*—enmity; *kāmī*—the lusty person; *kāmiṣu*—towards other lusty people; *antāya*—for destruction; *ca*—and; *ātmanaḥ*—of his soul.

TRANSLATION

With the growth of the body, the living entity, in order to vanquish his soul, increases his false prestige and anger and thereby creates enmity towards similarly lusty people.

PURPORT

In *Bhagavad-gītā*, Third Chapter, verse 36, Arjuna inquired from Kṛṣṇa about the cause of a living being's lust. It is said that a living entity is eternal and, as such, qualitatively one with the Supreme Lord. Then what is the reason he falls prey to the material and commits so many sinful activities by the influence of the material energy? In reply to this question, Lord Kṛṣṇa said that it is lust which causes a living entity to glide down from his exalted position to the abominable condition of material existence. This lust circumstantially changes into anger. Both lust and anger stand on the platform of the mode of passion. Lust is actually the product of the mode of passion, and in the absence of satisfaction of lust, the same desire transforms into anger on the platform of ignorance. When ignorance covers the soul, it is the source of his degradation to the most abominable condition of hellish life.

To raise oneself from hellish life to the highest position of spiritual understanding is to transform this lust into love of Kṛṣṇa. Śrī Narottama dāsa Ṭhākura, a great *ācārya* of the Vaiṣṇava *sampradāya*, said, *kāma kṛṣṇa-karmārpaṇe:* due to our lust, we want many things for our sense gratification, but the same lust can be transformed in a purified way so that *we want everything for the satisfaction of the Supreme Personality of Godhead.* Anger also can be utilized towards a person who is atheistic or who is envious of the Personality of Godhead. As we have fallen into this material existence because of our lust and anger, the same two qualities can be utilized for the purpose of advancing in Kṛṣṇa consciousness, and one can elevate himself again to his former pure, spiritual position. Śrīla Rūpa Gosvāmī has therefore recommended that because in material existence we have so many objects of sense gratification, which we need for the maintenance of the body, we should use all of them without attachment, for the purpose of satisfying the senses of Kṛṣṇa; that is actual renunciation.

TEXT 30

भूतैः पञ्चभिरारब्धे देहे देह्यबुधोऽसकृत् ।
अहंममेत्यसद्ग्राहः करोति कुमतिर्मतिम् ॥३०॥

bhūtaiḥ pañcabhir ārabdhe
dehe dehy abudho 'sakṛt
ahaṁ mamety asad-grāhaḥ
karoti kumatir matim

bhūtaiḥ—by material elements; *pañcabhiḥ*—five; *ārabdhe*—made; *dehe*—in the body; *dehī*—the living entity; *abudhaḥ*—ignorant; *asakṛt*—constantly; *aham*—I; *mama*—mine; *iti*—thus; *asat*—nonpermanent things; *grāhaḥ*—accepting; *karoti*—he does; *ku-matiḥ*—being foolish; *matim*—thought.

TRANSLATION

By such ignorance the living entity accepts the material body, which is made of five elements, as himself. With this misunderstanding, he accepts nonpermanent things as his own and increases his ignorance in the darkest region.

PURPORT

The expansion of ignorance is explained in this verse. The first ignorance is to identify one's material body, which is made of five elements, as the self, and the second is to accept something as one's own due to a bodily connection. In this way, ignorance expands. The living entity is eternal, but because of his accepting nonpermanent things, misidentifying his interest, he is put into ignorance, and therefore he suffers material pangs.

TEXT 31

तदर्थं कुरुते कर्म यद्बद्धो याति संसृतिम् ।
योऽनुयाति ददत्क्लेशमविद्याकर्मबन्धनः ॥३१॥

tad-arthaṁ kurute karma
yad-baddho yāti saṁsṛtim
yo 'nuyāti dadat kleśam
avidyā-karma-bandhanaḥ

tat-artham—for the sake of the body; *kurute*—he performs; *karma*—actions; *yat-baddhaḥ*—bound by which; *yāti*—he goes; *saṁsṛtim*—to repeated birth and death; *yaḥ*—which body; *anuyāti*—follows; *dadat*—giving; *kleśam*—misery; *avidyā*—by ignorance; *karma*—by fruitive activities; *bandhanaḥ*—the cause of bondage.

TRANSLATION

For the sake of the body, which is a source of constant trouble to him and which follows him because he is bound by ties of ignorance and fruitive activities, he performs various actions which cause him to be subjected to repeated birth and death.

PURPORT

In *Bhagavad-gītā* it is said that one has to work to satisfy Yajña, or Viṣṇu, for any work done without the purpose of satisfying the Supreme Personality of Godhead is a cause of bondage. In the conditioned state a living entity, accepting his body as himself, forgets his eternal relationship with the Supreme Personality of Godhead and acts on the interest of his body. He takes the body as himself, his bodily expansions as his kinsmen, and the land from which his body is born as worshipable. In this way he performs all sorts of misconceived activities, which lead to his perpetual bondage in repetition of birth and death in various species.

In modern civilization, the so-called social, national and government leaders mislead people more and more, under the bodily conception of life, with the result that all the leaders, with their followers, are gliding down to hellish conditions birth after birth. An example is given in *Śrīmad-Bhāgavatam. Andhā yathāndhair upanīyamānāḥ:* when a blind man leads several other blind men, the result is that all of them fall down in a ditch. This is actually happening. There are many leaders to lead the ignorant public, but because every one of them is bewildered by the bodily conception of life, there is no peace and prosperity in human society. So-called *yogīs* who perform various bodily feats are also in the same category as such ignorant people because the *haṭha-yoga* system is especially recommended for persons who are grossly implicated in the bodily conception. The conclusion is that as long as one is fixed in the bodily conception, he has to suffer birth and death.

TEXT 32

यद्यसद्भिः पथि पुनः शिश्नोदरकृतोद्यमैः ।
आस्थितो रमते जन्तुस्तमो विशति पूर्ववत् ॥३२॥

yady asadbhiḥ pathi punaḥ
śiśnodara-kṛtodyamaiḥ
āsthito ramate jantus
tamo viśati pūrvavat

yadi—if; *asadbhiḥ*—with the unrighteous; *pathi*—on the path; *punaḥ*—again; *śiśna*—for the genitals; *udara*—for the stomach; *kṛta*—done; *udyamaiḥ*—whose endeavors; *āsthitaḥ*—associating; *ramate*—enjoys; *jantuḥ*—the living entity; *tamaḥ*—darkness; *viśati*—enters; *pūrva-vat*—as before.

TRANSLATION

If, therefore, the living entity again associates with the path of unrighteousness, influenced by sensually minded people engaged in the pursuit of sexual enjoyment and the gratification of the palate, he again goes to hell as before.

PURPORT

It has been explained that the conditioned soul is put into the Andhatāmisra and Tāmisra hellish conditions, and after suffering there he gets a hellish body like the dog's or hog's. After several such births, he again comes into the form of a human being. How the human being is born is also described by Kapiladeva. The human being develops in the mother's abdomen and suffers there and comes out again. After all these sufferings, if he gets another chance in a human body and wastes his valuable time in the association of persons who are concerned with sexual life and palatable dishes, then naturally he again glides down to the same Andhatāmisra and Tāmisra hells.

Generally, people are concerned with the satisfaction of the tongue and the satisfaction of the genitals. That is material life. Material life means eat, drink, be merry and enjoy, with no concern for understanding one's spiritual identity and the process of spiritual advancement. Since materialistic people are concerned with the tongue, belly and genitals, if anyone wants to advance in spiritual life he must be very careful about associating with such people. To associate with such materialistic men is to commit purposeful suicide in the human form of life. It is said, therefore, that an intelligent man should give up such undesirable association and should always mix with saintly persons. When he is in association with saintly persons, all his doubts about the spiritual expansion of life are eradicated, and he makes tangible progress on the path of spiritual understanding. It is also sometimes found that people are very much addicted to a particular type of religious faith. Hindus, Muslims and Christians are faithful in their particular type of religion, and they go to the church, temple or mosque, but unfortunately they cannot give up the association of persons who are too much addicted to sex life and satisfaction of the palate. Here it is clearly said that one may officially be a very religious man, but if he associates with such persons, then he is sure to slide down to the darkest region of hell.

TEXT 33

सत्यं शौचं दया मौनं बुद्धिः श्रीर्ह्रीर्यशः क्षमा ।
शमो दमो भगश्चेति यत्सङ्गाद्याति सङ्क्षयम् ॥३३॥

satyaṁ śaucaṁ dayā maunaṁ
buddhiḥ śrīr hrīr yaśaḥ kṣamā
śamo damo bhagaś ceti
yat-saṅgād yāti saṅkṣayam

satyam—truthfulness; *śaucam*—cleanliness; *dayā*—mercy; *maunam*—gravity; *buddhiḥ*—intelligence; *śrīḥ*—prosperity; *hrīḥ*—shyness; *yaśaḥ*—fame; *kṣamā*—forgiveness; *śamaḥ*—control of the mind; *damaḥ*—control of the senses; *bhagaḥ*—fortune; *ca*—and; *iti*—thus; *yat-saṅgāt*—from association with whom; *yāti saṅkṣayam*—are destroyed.

TRANSLATION

He becomes devoid of truthfulness, cleanliness, mercy, gravity, spiritual intelligence, shyness, austerity, fame, forgiveness, control of the mind, control of the senses, fortune and all such opportunities.

PURPORT

Those who are too addicted to sex life cannot understand the purpose of the Absolute Truth, nor can they be clean in their habits, not to mention showing mercy to others. They cannot remain grave, and they have no interest in the ultimate goal of life. The ultimate goal of life is Kṛṣṇa, or Viṣṇu, but those who are addicted to sex life cannot understand that their ultimate interest is Kṛṣṇa consciousness. Such people have no sense of decency, and even in public streets or public parks they embrace each other just like cats and dogs and pass it off in the name of love-making. Such unfortunate creatures can never become materially prosperous. Behavior like that of cats and dogs keeps them in the position of cats and dogs. They cannot improve any material condition, not to speak of becoming famous. Such foolish persons may even make a show of so-called *yoga*, but they are unable to control the senses and mind, which is the real purpose of *yoga* practice. Such people can have no opulence in their lives. In a word, they are very unfortunate.

TEXT 34

तेष्वशान्तेषु मूढेषु खण्डितात्मस्वसाधुषु ।
सङ्गं न कुर्याच्छोच्येषु योषित्क्रीडामृगेषु च ॥३४॥

teṣv aśānteṣu mūḍheṣu
khaṇḍitātmasv asādhuṣu
saṅgaṁ na kuryāc chocyeṣu
yoṣit-krīḍā-mṛgeṣu ca

teṣu—with those; *aśānteṣu*—coarse; *mūḍheṣu*—fools; *khaṇḍita-ātmasu*—bereft of self-realization; *asādhuṣu*—wicked; *saṅgam*—association; *na*—not; *kuryāt*—one should make; *śocyeṣu*—pitiable; *yoṣit*—of women; *krīḍā-mṛgeṣu*—dancing dogs; *ca*—and.

TRANSLATION

One should not associate with a coarse fool who is bereft of the knowledge of self-realization and who is no more than a dancing dog in the hands of a woman.

PURPORT

The restriction of association with such foolish persons is especially meant for those who are in the line of advancement in Kṛṣṇa consciousness. Advancement in Kṛṣṇa consciousness involves developing the qualities of truthfulness, cleanliness, mercy, gravity, intelligence in spiritual knowledge, simplicity, material opulence, fame, forgiveness, and control of the mind and the senses. All these qualities are to be manifested with the progress of Kṛṣṇa consciousness, but if one associates with a *śūdra*, a foolish person who is like a dancing dog in the hands of a woman, then he cannot make any progress. Lord Caitanya has advised that any person who is engaged in Kṛṣṇa consciousness and who desires to pass beyond material nescience must not associate himself with women or with persons interested in material enjoyment. For a person seeking advancement in Kṛṣṇa consciousness, such association is more dangerous than suicide.

TEXT 35

न तथास्य भवेन्मोहो बन्धश्चान्यप्रसङ्गतः ।
योषित्सङ्गाद्यथा पुंसो यथा तत्सङ्गिसङ्गतः ॥३५॥

na tathāsya bhaven moho
bandhaś cānya-prasaṅgataḥ
yoṣit-saṅgād yathā puṁso
yathā tat-saṅgi-saṅgataḥ

na—not; *tathā*—in that manner; *asya*—of this man; *bhavet*—may arise; *mohaḥ*—infatuation; *bandhaḥ*—bondage; *ca*—and; *anya-prasaṅgataḥ*—from attachment to any other object; *yoṣit-saṅgāt*—from attachment to women; *yathā*—as; *puṁsaḥ*—of a man; *yathā*—as; *tat-saṅgi*—of men who are fond of women; *saṅgataḥ*—from the fellowship.

TRANSLATION

The infatuation and bondage which accrue to a man from attachment to any other object is not as complete as that resulting from attachment to a woman or to the fellowship of men who are fond of women.

PURPORT

Attachment to women is so contaminating that one becomes attached to the condition of material life not only by the association of women but by the contaminated association of persons who are too attached to them. There are many reasons for our conditional life in the material world, but the topmost of all such causes is the association of women, as will be confirmed in the following stanzas.

In Kali-yuga, association with women is very strong. In every step of life, there is association with women. If a person goes to purchase something, the advertisements are full of pictures of women. The physiological attraction for women is very great, and therefore people are very slack in spiritual understanding. The Vedic civilization, being based on spiritual understanding, arranges association with women very cautiously. Out of the four social divisions, the members of the first order (namely *brahmacarya*), the third order (*vānaprastha*) and the fourth order (*sannyāsa*) are strictly prohibited from female association. Only in one order, the householder, is there license to mix with women under restricted conditions. In other words, attraction for woman's association is the cause of the material conditional life, and anyone interested in being freed from this conditional life must detach himself from the association of women.

TEXT 36

प्रजापतिः स्वां दुहितरं दृष्ट्वा तद्रूपधर्षितः ।
रोहिद्भूतां सोऽन्वधावदृक्षरूपी हतत्रपः ॥३६॥

prajāpatiḥ svāṁ duhitaraṁ
dṛṣṭvā tad-rūpa-dharṣitaḥ
rohid-bhūtāṁ so 'nvadhāvad
ṛkṣa-rūpī hata-trapaḥ

prajā-patiḥ—Lord Brahmā; *svām*—his own; *duhitaram*—daughter; *dṛṣṭvā*—having seen; *tat-rūpa*—by her charms; *dharṣitaḥ*—bewildered; *rohit-bhūtām*—to her in the form of a deer; *saḥ*—he; *anvadhāvat*—ran; *ṛkṣa-rūpī*—in the form of a stag; *hata*—bereft of; *trapaḥ*—shame.

TRANSLATION

At the sight of his own daughter, Brahmā was bewildered by her charms and shamelessly ran up to her in the form of a stag when she took the form of a hind.

PURPORT

Lord Brahmā's being captivated by the charms of his daughter and Lord Śiva's being captivated by the Mohinī form of the Lord are specific instances which instruct us that even great demigods like Brahmā and Lord Śiva, what to speak of the ordinary conditioned soul, are captivated by the beauty of woman. Therefore, everyone is advised that one should not freely mix even with one's daughter or with one's mother or with one's sister, because the senses are so strong that when one becomes infatuated, the senses do not consider the relationship of daughter, mother or sister. It is best, therefore, to practice controlling the senses by performing *bhakti-yoga*, engaging in the service of Madana-mohana. Lord Kṛṣṇa's name is Madana-mohana, for He can subdue the god Cupid, or lust. Only by engaging in the service of Madana-mohana can one curb the dictates of Madana, Cupid. Otherwise, attempts to control the senses will fail.

TEXT 37

तत्सृष्टसृष्टसृष्टेषु को न्वखण्डितधीः पुमान् ।
ऋषिं नारायणमृते योषिन्मय्येह मायया ॥३७॥

tat-sṛṣṭa-sṛṣṭa-sṛṣṭeṣu
ko nv akhaṇḍita-dhīḥ pumān
ṛṣiṁ nārāyaṇam ṛte
yoṣin-mayyeha māyayā

tat—by Brahmā; *sṛṣṭa-sṛṣṭa-sṛṣṭeṣu*—amongst all living entities begotten; *kaḥ*—who; *nu*—indeed; *akhaṇḍita*—not distracted; *dhīḥ*—his intelligence; *pumān*—male; *ṛṣim*—the sage; *nārāyaṇam*—Nārāyaṇa; *ṛte*—except; *yoṣit-mayyā*—in the form of a woman; *iha*—here; *māyayā*—by *māyā.*

TRANSLATION

Amongst all kinds of living entities begotten by Brahmā, namely men, demigods and animals, none but the sage Nārāyaṇa is immune to the attraction of māyā in the form of woman.

PURPORT

The first living creature is Brahmā himself, and from him were created sages like Marīci, who in their turn created Kaśyapa Muni and others, and Kaśyapa Muni and the Manus created different demigods and human beings, etc. But there is none among them who is not attracted by the spell of *māyā* in the form of woman. Throughout the entire material world, beginning from Brahmā down to the small, insignificant creatures like the ant, everyone is attracted by sex life. That is the basic principle of this material world. Lord Brahmā's being attracted by his daughter is the vivid example that no one is exempt from sexual attraction to woman. Woman, therefore, is the wonderful creation of *māyā* to keep the conditioned soul in shackles.

TEXT 38

बलं मे पश्य मायायाः स्त्रीमय्या जयिनो दिशाम् ।
या करोति पदाक्रान्तान् भ्रूविजृम्भेण केवलम् ॥३८॥

balaṁ me paśya māyāyāḥ
strī-mayyā jayino diśām
yā karoti padākrāntān
bhrūvi-jṛmbheṇa kevalam

balam—the strength; *me*—My; *paśya*—behold; *māyāyāḥ*—of *māyā; strī-mayyāḥ*—in the shape of a woman; *jayinaḥ*—conquerors; *diśām*—of all directions; *yā*—who; *karoti*—makes; *pada-ākrāntān*—following at her heels; *bhrūvi*—of her eyebrows; *jṛmbheṇa*—by the movement; *kevalam*—merely.

TRANSLATION

Just try to understand the mighty strength of My māyā in the shape of woman, who by the mere movement of her eyebrows can keep even the greatest conquerors of the world under her grip.

PURPORT

There are many instances in the history of the world of a great conqueror's being captivated by the charms of a Cleopatra. One has to study the captivating potency of woman, and man's attraction for that potency. From what source was this generated? According to *Vedānta-sūtra*, we can understand that everything is generated from the Supreme Personality of Godhead. It is enunciated there, *janmādy asya yataḥ.* This means that the Supreme Personality of Godhead, or the Supreme Person,

Brahman, the Absolute Truth, is the source from whom everything emanates. The captivating power of woman, and man's susceptibility to such attraction, must also exist in the Supreme Personality of Godhead in the spiritual world and must be represented in the transcendental pastimes of the Lord.

The Lord is the Supreme Person, the supreme male. As a common male wants to be attracted by a female, that propensity similarly exists in the Supreme Personality of Godhead. He also wants to be attracted by the beautiful features of a woman. Now the question is, if He wants to be captivated by such womanly attraction, would He be attracted by any material woman? It is not possible. Even persons who are in this material existence can give up womanly attraction if they are attracted by the Supreme Brahman. Such was the case with Haridāsa Ṭhākura. A beautiful prostitute tried to attract him in the dead of night, but since he was situated in devotional service, in transcendental love of Godhead, Haridāsa Ṭhākura was not captivated. Rather, he turned the prostitute into a great devotee by his transcendental association. This material attraction, therefore, certainly cannot attract the Supreme Lord. When He wants to be attracted by a woman, He has to create such a woman from His own energy. That woman is Rādhārāṇī. It is explained by the Gosvāmīs that Rādhārāṇī is the manifestation of the pleasure potency of the Supreme Personality of Godhead. When the Supreme Lord wants to derive transcendental pleasure, He has to create a woman from His internal potency. Thus the tendency to be attracted by womanly beauty is natural because it exists in the spiritual world. In the material world it is reflected pervertedly, and therefore there are so many inebrieties.

Instead of being attracted by material beauty, if one is accustomed to be attracted by the beauty of Rādhārāṇī and Kṛṣṇa, then the statement of *Bhagavad-gītā, paraṁ dṛṣṭvā nivartate,* holds true. When one is attracted by the transcendental beauty of Rādhā and Kṛṣṇa, he is no longer attracted by material feminine beauty. That is the special significance of Rādhā-Kṛṣṇa worship. That is testified to by Yāmunācārya. He says, "Since I have become attracted by the beauty of Rādhā and Kṛṣṇa, when there is attraction for a woman or a memory of sex life with a woman, I at once spit on it, and my face turns in disgust." When we are attracted by Madana-mohana and the beauty of Kṛṣṇa and His consorts, then the shackles of conditioned life, namely the beauty of a material woman, cannot attract us.

TEXT 39

सङ्गं न कुर्यात्प्रमदासु जातु
योगस्य पारं परमारुरुक्षुः ।
मत्सेवया प्रतिलब्धात्मलाभो
वदन्ति या निरयद्वारमस्य ॥३९॥

saṅgaṁ na kuryāt pramadāsu jātu
yogasya pāraṁ param āruruksuḥ
mat-sevayā pratilabdhātma-lābho
vadanti yā niraya-dvāram asya

saṅgam—association; *na*—not; *kuryāt*—one should make; *pramadāsu*—with women; *jātu*—ever; *yogasya*—of *yoga;* *pāram*—culmination; *param*—topmost; *āruruksuḥ*—one who aspires to reach; *mat-sevayā*—by rendering service unto Me; *pratilabdha*—obtained; *ātma-lābhaḥ*—self-realization; *vadanti*—they say; *yāḥ*—which women; *niraya*—to hell; *dvāram*—the gateway; *asya*—of the advancing devotee.

TRANSLATION

One who aspires to reach the culmination of yoga and has realized his self by rendering service unto Me should never associate with an attractive woman, for such a woman is declared in the scripture to be the gateway to hell for the advancing devotee.

PURPORT

The culmination of *yoga* is full Kṛṣṇa consciousness. This is affirmed in *Bhagavad-gītā:* a person who is always thinking of Kṛṣṇa in devotion is the topmost of all *yogīs.* And in the Second Chapter of the First Canto of *Śrīmad-Bhāgavatam,* it is also stated that when one becomes freed from material contamination by rendering devotional service unto the

Supreme Personality of Godhead, he can at that time understand the science of God.

Here the word *pratilabdhātma-lābhaḥ* occurs. *Ātmā* means "self," and *lābha* means "gain." Generally, conditioned souls have lost their *ātmā*, or self, but those who are transcendentalists have realized the self. It is directed that such a self-realized soul who aspires to the topmost platform of yogic perfection should not associate with young women. In the modern age, however, there are so many rascals who recommend that while one has genitals he should enjoy women as much as he likes, and at the same time he can become a *yogī*. In no standard *yoga* system is the association of women accepted. It is clearly stated here that the association of women is the gateway to hellish life. The association of woman is very much restricted in the Vedic civilization. Out of the four social divisions, the *brahmacārī*, *vānaprastha* and the *sannyāsī*—three orders—are strictly prohibited from the association of women; only the *gṛhasthas*, or householders, are given license to have an intimate relationship with a woman, and that relationship is also restricted for begetting nice children. If, however, one wants to stick to continued existence in the material world, he may indulge in female association unrestrictedly.

TEXT 40

योपयाति शनैर्माया योषिद्देवविनिर्मिता ।
तामीक्षेतात्मनो मृत्युं तृणैः कूपमिवावृतम् ॥४०॥

yopayāti śanair māyā
yoṣid deva-vinirmitā
tām īkṣetātmano mṛtyuṁ
tṛṇaiḥ kūpam ivāvṛtam

yā—she who; *upayāti*—approaches; *śanaiḥ*—slowly; *māyā*—representation of *māyā; yoṣit*—woman; *deva*—by the Lord; *vinirmitā*—created; *tām*—her; *īkṣeta*—one must regard; *ātmanaḥ*—of the soul; *mṛtyum*—death; *tṛṇaiḥ*—with grass; *kūpam*—a well; *iva*—like; *āvṛtam*—covered.

TRANSLATION

The woman, created by the Lord, is the representation of māyā, and one who associates with such māyā by accepting services must certainly know that this is the way of death, just like a blind well covered with grass.

PURPORT

Sometimes it happens that a rejected well is covered by grass, and an unwary traveler who does not know of the existence of the well falls down, and his death is assured. Similarly, association with a woman begins when one accepts service from her, because woman is especially created by the Lord to give service to man. By accepting her service, a man is entrapped. If he is not intelligent enough to know that she is the gateway to hellish life, he may indulge in her association very liberally. This is restricted for those who aspire to ascend to the transcendental platform. Even fifty years ago in Hindu society, such association was restricted. A wife could not see her husband during the daytime. Householders even had different residential quarters. The internal quarters of a residential house were for the woman, and the external quarters were for the man. Acceptance of service rendered by a woman may appear very pleasing, but one should be very cautious in accepting such service because it is clearly said that woman is the gateway to death, or forgetfulness of one's self. She blocks the path of spiritual realization.

TEXT 41

यां मन्यते पतिं मोहान्मन्मायामृषभायतीम् ।
स्त्रीत्वं स्त्रीसङ्गतः प्राप्तो वित्तापत्यगृहप्रदम् ॥४१॥

yāṁ manyate patiṁ mohān
man-māyām ṛṣabhāyatīm
strītvaṁ strī-saṅgataḥ prāpto
vittāpatya-gṛha-pradam

yām—which; *manyate*—she thinks; *patim*—her husband; *mohāt*—due to illusion; *mat-māyām*—My *māyā; ṛṣabha*—in the form of a man;

āyatīm—coming; *strītvam*—the state of being a woman; *strī-saṅgataḥ*—from attachment to a woman; *prāptaḥ*—obtained; *vitta*—wealth; *apatya*—progeny; *gṛha*—house; *pradam*—bestowing.

TRANSLATION

A living entity who, as a result of attachment to a woman in his previous life, has been endowed with the form of a woman, foolishly looks upon māyā in the form of a man, her husband, as the bestower of wealth, progeny, house and other material assets.

PURPORT

From this verse it appears that a woman is also supposed to have been a man in his (her) previous life, and due to his attachment to his wife, he now has the body of a woman. *Bhagavad-gītā* confirms this; a man gets his next life's birth according to what he thinks of at the time of death. If someone is too attached to his wife, naturally he thinks of his wife at the time of death, and in his next life he takes the body of a woman. Similarly, if a woman thinks of her husband at the time of death, naturally she gets the body of a man in the next life. In the Hindu scriptures, therefore, woman's chastity and devotion to man is greatly emphasized. A woman's attachment to her husband may elevate her to the body of a man in her next life, but a man's attachment to a woman will degrade him, and in his next life he will get the body of a woman. We should always remember, as it is stated in *Bhagavad-gītā*, that both the gross and subtle material bodies are dresses; they are the shirt and coat of the living entity. To be either a woman or a man only involves one's bodily dress. The soul in nature is actually the marginal energy of the Supreme Lord. Every living entity, being classified as energy, is supposed to be orginally a woman, or one who is enjoyed. In the body of a man there is a greater opportunity to get out of the material clutches; there is less opportunity in the body of a woman. In this verse it is indicated that the body of a man should not be misused through forming an attachment to women and thus becoming too entangled in material enjoyment, which will result in getting the body of a woman in the next life. A woman is generally fond of household prosperity, ornaments, furniture and dresses. She is satisfied when the husband supplies all these things sufficiently. The relationship between man and woman is very complicated, but the substance is that one who aspires to ascend to the transcendental stage of spiritual realization should be very careful in accepting the association of a woman. In the stage of Kṛṣṇa consciousness, however, such restriction of association may be slackened because if a man's and woman's attachment is not to each other but to Kṛṣṇa, then both of them are equally eligible to get out of the material entanglement and reach the abode of Kṛṣṇa. As it is confirmed in *Bhagavad-gītā*, anyone who seriously takes to Kṛṣṇa consciousness—whether in the lowest species of life or a woman or of the less intelligent classes, such as the mercantile or laborer class—will go back home, back to Godhead, and reach the abode of Kṛṣṇa. A man should not be attached to a woman, nor should a woman be attached to a man. Both man and woman should be attached to the service of the Lord. Then there is the possibility of liberation from material entanglement for both of them.

TEXT 42

तामात्मनो विजानीयात्पत्यपत्यगृहात्मकम् ।
दैवोपसादितं मृत्युं मृगयोर्गायनं यथा ॥४२॥

tām ātmano vijānīyāt
paty-apatya-gṛhātmakam
daivopasāditaṁ mṛtyuṁ
mṛgayor gāyanaṁ yathā

tām—the Lord's *māyā; ātmanaḥ*—of herself; *vijānīyāt*—she should know; *pati*—husband; *apatya*—children; *gṛha*—house; *ātmakam*—consisting of; *daiva*—by the authority of the Lord; *upasāditam*—brought about; *mṛtyum*—death; *mṛgayoḥ*—of the hunter; *gāyanam*—the singing; *yathā*—as.

TRANSLATION

A woman, therefore, should consider her husband, her house and her children to be the arrangement of the external energy of the Lord for her death, just as the sweet singing of the hunter is death for the deer.

PURPORT

In these instructions of Lord Kapiladeva it is explained that not only is woman the gateway to hell for man, but man is also the gateway to hell for woman. It is a question of attachment. A man becomes attached to a woman because of her service, her beauty and many other assets, and similarly a woman becomes attached to a man for his giving her a nice place to live, ornaments, dress and children. It is a question of attachment for one another. As long as either is attached to the other for such material enjoyment, the woman is dangerous for the man, and the man is also dangerous for the woman. But if the attachment is transferred to Kṛṣṇa, both of them become Kṛṣṇa conscious, and then marriage is very nice. Śrīla Rūpa Gosvāmī therefore recommends:

anāsaktasya viṣayān
yathārham upayuñjataḥ
nirbandhaḥ kṛṣṇa-sambandhe
yuktaṁ vairāgyam ucyate
(*Bhakti-rasāmṛta-sindhu* 1.2.255)

Man and woman should live together as householders in relationship with Kṛṣṇa, only for the purpose of discharging duties in the service of Kṛṣṇa. Engage the children, engage the wife and engage the husband, all in Kṛṣṇa conscious duties, and then all these bodily or material attachments will disappear. Since the via medium is Kṛṣṇa, the consciousness is pure, and there is no possibility of degradation at any time.

TEXT 43

देहेन जीवभूतेन लोकाल्लोकमनुव्रजन् ।
भुञ्जान एव कर्माणि करोत्यविरतं पुमान् ॥४३॥

dehena jīva-bhūtena
lokāl lokam anuvrajan
bhuñjāna eva karmāṇi
karoty aviratam pumān

dehena—on account of the body; *jīva-bhūtena*—possessed by the living entity; *lokāt*—from one planet; *lokam*—to another planet; *anuvrajan*—wandering; *bhuñjānaḥ*—enjoying; *eva*—so; *karmāṇi*—fruitive activities; *karoti*—he does; *aviratam*—incessantly; *pumān*—the living entity.

TRANSLATION

Due to his particular type of body, the materialistic living entity wanders from one planet to another, following fruitive activities. In this way, he involves himself in fruitive activities and enjoys the result incessantly.

PURPORT

When the living entity is encaged in the material body, he is called *jīva-bhūta,* and when he is free from the material body he is called *brahma-bhūta.* By changing his material body birth after birth, he travels not only in the different species of life, but also from one planet to another. Lord Caitanya says that the living entities, bound up by fruitive activities, are wandering in this way throughout the whole universe, and if by some chance or by pious activities they get in touch with a bona fide spiritual master, by the grace of Kṛṣṇa, then they get the seed of devotional service. After getting this seed, if one sows it within his heart and pours water on it by hearing and chanting, the seed grows into a big plant, and there are fruits and flowers which the living entity can enjoy, even in this material world. That is called the *brahma-bhūta* stage. In his designated condition, a living entity is called materialistic, and upon being freed from all designations, when he is fully Kṛṣṇa conscious, engaged in devotional service, he is called liberated. Unless one gets the opportunity to associate with a bona fide spiritual master by the grace of the Lord, there is no possibility of one's liberation from the cycle of birth and death in the different species of life and through the different grades of planets.

TEXT 44

जीवो ह्यस्यानुगो देहो भूतेन्द्रियमनोमयः ।
तन्निरोधोऽस्य मरणमाविर्भावस्तु सम्भवः ॥४४॥

jīvo hy asyānugo deho
bhūtendriya-mano-mayaḥ
tan-nirodho 'sya maraṇam
āvirbhāvas tu sambhavaḥ

jīvaḥ—the living entity; *hi*—indeed; *asya*—of him; *anugaḥ*—suitable; *dehaḥ*—body; *bhūta*—gross material elements; *indriya*—senses; *manaḥ*—mind; *mayaḥ*—made of; *tat*—of the body; *nirodhaḥ*—destruction; *asya*—of the living entity; *maraṇam*—death; *āvirbhāvaḥ*—manifestation; *tu*—but; *sambhavaḥ*—birth.

TRANSLATION

In this way the living entity gets a suitable body with a material mind and senses, according to his fruitive activities. When the reaction of his particular activity comes to an end, that end is called death, and when a particular type of reaction begins, that beginning is called birth.

PURPORT

From time immemorial, the living entity travels in the different species of life and the different planets, almost perpetually. This process is explained in *Bhagavad-gītā. Bhrāmayan sarva-bhūtāni yantrārūḍhāni māyayā:* under the spell of *māyā*, everyone is wandering throughout the universe on the carriage of the body offered by the material energy. Materialistic life involves a series of actions and reactions. It is a long film spool of actions and reactions, and one life-span is just a flash in such a reactionary show. When a child is born, it is to be understood that his particular type of body is the beginning of another set of activities, and when an old man dies, it is to be understood that one set of reactionary activities is finished.

We can see that because of different reactionary activities, one man is born in a rich family, and another is born in a poor family, although both of them are born in the same place, at the same moment and in the same atmosphere. One who is carrying pious activity with him is given a chance to take his birth in a rich or pious family, and one who is carrying impious activity is given a chance to take birth in a lower, poor family.

The change of body means a change to a different field of activities. Similarly, when the body of the boy changes into that of a youth, the boyish activities change into youthful activities.

It is clear that a particular body is given to the living entity for a particular type of activity. This process is going on perpetually, from a time which is impossible to trace out. Vaiṣṇava poets say, therefore, *anādi karama-phale*, which means that these actions and reactions of one's activity cannot be traced, for they may even continue from the last millennium of Brahmā's birth to the next millennium. We have seen the example in the life of Nārada Muni. In one millennium he was the son of a maidservant, and in the next millennium he became a great sage.

TEXTS 45–46

द्रव्योपलब्धिस्थानस्य द्रव्येक्षायोग्यता यदा ।
तत्पञ्चत्वमहंमानादुत्पत्तिर्द्रव्यदर्शनम् ॥४५॥
यथाक्ष्णोर्द्रव्यावयवदर्शनायोग्यता यदा ।
तदैव चक्षुषो द्रष्टुर्द्रष्टृत्वायोग्यतानयोः ॥४६॥

dravyopalabdhi-sthānasya
dravyekṣāyogyatā yadā
tat pañcatvam ahaṁ-mānād
utpattir dravya-darśanam

yathākṣṇor dravyāvayava-
darśanāyogyatā yadā
tadaiva cakṣuṣo draṣṭur
draṣṭṛtvāyogyatānayoḥ

dravya—of objects; *upalabdhi*—of perception; *sthānasya*—of the place; *dravya*—of objects; *īkṣā*—of perception; *ayogyatā*—incapability; *yadā*—when; *tat*—that; *pañcatvam*—death; *aham-mānāt*—from the misconception of "I"; *utpattiḥ*—birth; *dravya*—the physical body; *darśanam*—viewing; *yathā*—just as; *akṣṇoḥ*—of the eyes; *dravya*—of objects; *avayava*—parts; *darśana*—of seeing; *ayogyatā*—incapability;

yadā—when; *tadā*—then; *eva*—indeed; *cakṣuṣaḥ*—of the sense of sight; *draṣṭuḥ*—of the seer; *draṣṭṛtva*—of the faculty of seeing; *ayogyatā*—incapability; *anayoḥ*—of both of these.

TRANSLATION

When the eyes lose their power to see color or form due to morbid affliction of the optic nerve, the sense of sight becomes deadened. The living entity, who is the seer of both the eyes and the sight, loses his power of vision. In the same way, when the physical body, the place where perception of objects occurs, is rendered incapable of perceiving, that is known as death. When one begins to view the physical body as one's very self, that is called birth.

PURPORT

When one says, "I see," this means that he sees with his eyes or with his spectacles; he sees with the instrument of sight. If the instrument of sight is broken or becomes diseased or incapable of acting, then he, as the seer, also ceases to act. Similarly, in this material body, at the present moment the living soul is acting, and when the material body, due to its incapability to function, ceases, he also ceases to perform his reactionary activities. When one's instrument of action is broken and cannot function, that is called death. Again, when one gets a new instrument for action, that is called birth. This process of birth and death is going on at every moment, by constant bodily change. The final change is called death, and acceptance of a new body is called birth. That is the solution to the question of birth and death. Actually, the living entity has neither birth nor death, but is eternal. As confirmed in *Bhagavad-gītā, na hanyate hanyamāne śarīre:* the living entity never dies, even after the death or annihilation of this material body.

TEXT 47

तस्मान्न कार्यः सन्त्रासो न कार्पण्यं न सम्भ्रमः ।
बुद्ध्वा जीवगतिं धीरो मुक्तसङ्गश्चरेदिह ॥४७॥

tasmān na kāryaḥ santrāso
na kārpaṇyaṁ na sambhramaḥ

buddhvā jīva-gatiṁ dhīro
mukta-saṅgaś cared iha

tasmāt—on account of death; *na*—not; *kāryaḥ*—should be done; *santrāsaḥ*—horror; *na*—not; *kārpaṇyam*—miserliness; *na*—not; *sambhramaḥ*—eagerness for material gain; *buddhvā*—realizing; *jīva-gatim*—the true nature of the living entity; *dhīraḥ*—steadfast; *mukta-saṅgaḥ*—free from attachment; *caret*—one should move about; *iha*—in this world.

TRANSLATION

Therefore, one should not view death with horror, nor have recourse to defining the body as soul, nor give way to exaggeration in enjoying the bodily necessities of life. Realizing the true nature of the living entity, one should move about in the world free from attachment and steadfast in purpose.

PURPORT

A sane person who has understood the philosophy of life and death is very upset upon hearing of the horrible, hellish condition of life in the womb of the mother or outside of the mother. But one has to make a solution to the problems of life. A sane man should understand the miserable condition of this material body. Without being unnecessarily upset, he should try to find out if there is a remedy. The remedial measures can be understood when one associates with persons who are liberated. It must be understood who is actually liberated. The liberated person is described in *Bhagavad-gītā:* one who engages in uninterrupted devotional service to the Lord, having surpassed the stringent laws of material nature, is understood to be situated in Brahman.

The Supreme Personality of Godhead is beyond the material creation. It is admitted even by impersonalists like Śaṅkarācārya that Nārāyaṇa is transcendental to this material creation. As such, when one actually engages in the service of the Lord in various forms, either Nārāyaṇa or Rādhā-Kṛṣṇa or Sītā-Rāma, he is understood to be on the platform of liberation. The *Bhāgavatam* also confirms that liberation means to be situated in one's constitutional position. Since a living entity is eternally the servitor of the Supreme Lord, when one seriously and sincerely engages in the transcendental loving service of the Lord, he is situated in the position of liberation. One should try to associate with a liberated person, and then the problems of life, namely birth and death, can be solved.

While discharging devotional service in full Kṛṣṇa consciousness, one should not be miserly. He should not unnecessarily show that he has renounced this world. Actually, renunciation is not possible. If one renounces his palatial building and goes to a forest, there is actually no renunciation, for the palatial building is the property of the Supreme Personality of Godhead and the forest is also the property of the Supreme Personality of Godhead. If he changes from one property to another, that does not mean that he renounces; he was never the proprietor of either the palace or the forest. Renunciation necessitates renouncing the false understanding that one can lord it over material nature. When one renounces this false attitude and renounces the puffed-up position that he is also God, that is real renunciation. Otherwise, there is no meaning of renunciation. Rūpa Gosvāmī advises that if one renounces anything which could be applied in the service of the Lord and does not use it for that purpose, that is called *phalgu-vairāgya*, insufficient or false renunciation. Everything belongs to the Supreme Personality of Godhead; therefore everything can be engaged in the service of the Lord; nothing should be used for one's sense gratification. That is real renunciation. Nor should one unnecessarily increase the necessities of the body. We should be satisfied with whatever is offered and supplied by Kṛṣṇa without much personal endeavor. We should spend our time executing devotional service in Kṛṣṇa consciousness. That is the solution to the problem of life and death.

TEXT 48

सम्यग्दर्शनया बुद्ध्या योगवैराग्ययुक्तया ।
मायाविरचिते लोके चरेन्न्यस्य कलेवरम् ॥४८॥

samyag-darśanayā buddhyā
yoga-vairāgya-yuktayā

māyā-viracite loke
caren nyasya kalevaram

samyak-darśanayā—endowed with right vision; *buddhyā*—through reason; *yoga*—by devotional service; *vairāgya*—by detachment; *yuktayā*—strengthened; *māyā-viracite*—arranged by *māyā; loke*—to this world; *caret*—one should move about; *nyasya*—relegating; *kalevaram*—the body.

TRANSLATION

Endowed with right vision and strengthened by devotional service and a pessimistic attitude towards material identity, one should relegate his body to this illusory world through his reason. Thus one can be unconcerned with this material world.

PURPORT

It is sometimes misunderstood that if one has to associate with persons engaged in devotional service, he will not be able to solve the economic problem. To answer this argument, it is described here that one has to associate with liberated persons not directly, physically, but by understanding, through philosophy and logic, the problems of life. It is stated here, *samyag-darśanayā buddhyā:* one has to see perfectly, and by intelligence and yogic practice one has to renounce this world. That renunciation can be achieved by the process recommended in the Second Chapter of the First Canto of *Śrīmad-Bhāgavatam.*

The devotee's intelligence is always in touch with the Supreme Personality of Godhead. His attitude towards the material existence is one of detachment, for he knows perfectly well that this material world is a creation of illusory energy. Realizing himself to be part and parcel of the Supreme Soul, the devotee discharges his devotional service and is completely aloof from material action and reaction. Thus at the end he gives up his material body, or the material energy, and as pure soul he enters the kingdom of God.

Thus end the Bhaktivedanta purports of the Third Canto, Thirty-first Chapter, of the Śrīmad-Bhāgavatam, *entitled "Lord Kapila's Instructions on the Movements of the Living Entities."*

CHAPTER THIRTY-TWO

Entanglement in Fruitive Activities

TEXT 1

कपिल उवाच
अथ यो गृहमेधीयान्धर्मानेवावसन् गृहे ।
काममर्थं च धर्मान् स्वान् दोग्धि भूयः पिपर्ति तान् ॥ १ ॥

kapila uvāca
atha yo gṛha-medhīyān
dharmān evāvasan gṛhe
kāmam arthaṁ ca dharmān svān
dogdhi bhūyaḥ piparti tān

kapilaḥ uvāca—Lord Kapila said; *atha*—now; *yaḥ*—the person who; *gṛha-medhīyān*—of the householders; *dharmān*—duties; *eva*—certainly; *āvasan*—living; *gṛhe*—at home; *kāmam*—sense gratification; *artham*—economic development; *ca*—and; *dharmān*—religious rituals; *svān*—his; *dogdhi*—enjoys; *bhūyaḥ*—again and again; *piparti*—performs; *tān*—them.

TRANSLATION

The Personality of Godhead said: The person who lives in the center of household life derives material benefits by performing religious rituals, and thereby he fulfills his desire for economic development and sense gratification. Again and again he acts the same way.

PURPORT

There are two kinds of householders. One is called the *gṛhamedhī*, and the other is called the *gṛhastha.* The objective of the *gṛhamedhī* is sense gratification, and the objective of the *gṛhastha* is self-realization. Here the Lord is speaking about the *gṛhamedhī*, or the person who wants to remain in this material world. His activity is to enjoy material benefits by performing religious rituals for economic development and thereby ultimately satisfy the senses. He does not want anything more. Such a person works very hard throughout his life to become very rich and eat very nicely and drink. By giving some charity for pious activity he can go to a higher planetary atmosphere in the heavenly planets in his next life, but he does not want to stop the repetition of birth and death and finish with the concomitant miserable factors of material existence. Such a person is called a *gṛhamedhī.*

A *gṛhastha* is a person who lives with family, wife, children and relatives but has no attachment for them. He prefers to live in family life rather than as a mendicant or *sannyāsī*, but his chief aim is to achieve self-realization, or to come to the standard of Kṛṣṇa consciousness. Here, however, Lord Kapiladeva is speaking about the *gṛhamedhīs*, who have made their aim the materialistically prosperous life, which they achieve by sacrificial ceremonies, by charities and by good work. They are posted in good positions, and since they know that they are using up their assets of pious activities, they again and again perform activities of sense gratification. It is said by Prahlāda Mahārāja, *punaḥ punaś carvita-carvaṇānām:* they prefer to chew the already chewed. Again and again they experience the material pangs, even if they are rich and prosperous, but they do not want to give up this kind of life.

TEXT 2

स चापि भगवद्धर्मात्काममूढः पराङ्मुखः ।
यजते क्रतुभिर्देवान् पितॄंश्च श्रद्धयान्वितः ॥ २ ॥

sa cāpi bhagavad-dharmāt
kāma-mūḍhaḥ parāṅ-mukhaḥ
yajate kratubhir devān
pitṝṁś ca śraddhayānvitaḥ

saḥ—he; *ca api*—moreover; *bhagavat-dharmāt*—from devotional service; *kāma-mūḍhaḥ*—infatuated by lust; *parāk-mukhaḥ*—having the face turned away; *yajate*—worships; *kratubhiḥ*—with sacrificial ceremonies; *devān*—the demigods; *pitṝn*—the forefathers; *ca*—and; *śraddhayā*—with faith; *anvitaḥ*—endowed.

TRANSLATION

Such persons are ever bereft of devotional service due to being too attached to sense gratification, and therefore, although they perform various kinds of sacrifices and take great vows to satisfy the demigods and forefathers, they are not interested in Kṛṣṇa consciousness, devotional service.

PURPORT

In *Bhagavad-gītā* (7.20) it is said that persons who worship demigods have lost their intelligence: *kāmais tais tair hṛta-jñānāḥ.* They are much attracted to sense gratification, and therefore they worship the demigods. It is, of course, recommended in the Vedic scriptures that if one wants money, health or education, then he should worship the various demigods. A materialistic person has manifold demands, and thus there are manifold demigods to satisfy his senses. The *gṛhamedhīs*, who want to continue a prosperous materialistic way of life, generally worship the demigods or the forefathers by offering *piṇḍa*, or respectful oblations. Such persons are bereft of Kṛṣṇa consciousness and are not interested in devotional service to the Lord. This kind of so-called pious and religious man is the result of impersonalism. The impersonalists maintain that the Supreme Absolute Truth has no form and that one can imagine any form he likes for his benefit and worship in that way. Therefore the *gṛhamedhīs* or materialistic men say that they can worship any form of a demigod as worship of the Supreme Lord. Especially amongst the Hindus, those who are meat-eaters prefer to worship goddess Kālī because it is prescribed that one can sacrifice a goat before that goddess. They maintain that whether one worships the goddess Kālī or the Supreme Personality of Godhead Viṣṇu or any demigod, the destination is the same. This is first-class rascaldom, and such people are misled. But they prefer this philosophy. *Bhagavad-gītā* does not accept such rascaldom, and it is clearly stated that such methods are meant for persons who have lost their intelligence. The same judgment is confirmed here, and the word *kāma-mūḍha*, meaning one who has lost his sense or is infatuated by the lust of attraction for sense gratification, is used. *Kāma-mūḍhas* are bereft of Kṛṣṇa consciousness and devotional service and are infatuated by a strong desire for sense gratification. The worshipers of demigods are condemned both in *Bhagavad-gītā* and in *Śrīmad-Bhāgavatam.*

TEXT 3

तच्छ्रद्धयाक्रान्तमतिः पितृदेवव्रतः पुमान् ।
गत्वा चान्द्रमसं लोकं सोमपाः पुनरेष्यति ॥ ३ ॥

tac-chraddhayākrānta-matiḥ
pitṛ-deva-vrataḥ pumān
gatvā cāndramasaṁ lokaṁ
soma-pāḥ punar eṣyati

tat—to the demigods and forefathers; *śraddhayā*—with reverence; *ākrānta*—overcome; *matiḥ*—his mind; *pitṛ*—to the forefathers; *deva*—to the demigods; *vrataḥ*—his vow; *pumān*—the person; *gatvā*—having gone; *cāndramasam*—to the moon; *lokam*—planet; *soma-pāḥ*—drinking *soma* juice; *punaḥ*—again; *eṣyati*—will return.

TRANSLATION

Such materialistic persons, attracted by sense gratification and devoted to the forefathers and demigods, can be elevated to the moon, where they drink an extract of the soma plant. They again return to this planet.

PURPORT

The moon is considered one of the planets of the heavenly kingdom. One can be promoted to this planet by executing different sacrifices recommended in the Vedic literature, such as pious activities in worshiping the demigods and forefathers with rigidity and vows. But one cannot remain there for a very long time. Life on the moon is said to last ten thousand years according to the calculation of the demigods. The demigods' time is calculated in such a way that one day (twelve hours) is equal to six months on this planet. It is not possible to reach the moon by any material vehicle like a sputnik, but persons who are attracted by material enjoyment can go to the moon by pious activities. In spite of being promoted to the moon, however, one has to come back to this earth again when the merits of his works in sacrifice are finished. This is also confirmed in *Bhagavad-gītā* (9.21): *te taṁ bhuktvā svarga-lokaṁ viśālaṁ kṣīṇe puṇye martya-lokaṁ viśanti.*

TEXT 4

यदा चाहीन्द्रशय्यायां शेतेऽनन्तासनो हरिः ।
तदा लोका लयं यान्ति त एते गृहमेधिनाम् ॥ ४ ॥

yadā cāhīndra-śayyāyāṁ
śete 'nantāsano hariḥ
tadā lokā layaṁ yānti
ta ete gṛha-medhinām

yadā—when; *ca*—and; *ahi-indra*—of the king of snakes; *śayyāyām*—on the bed; *śete*—lies; *ananta-āsanaḥ*—He whose seat is Ananta Śeṣa; *hariḥ*—Lord Hari; *tadā*—then; *lokāḥ*—the planets; *layam*—unto dissolution; *yānti*—go; *te ete*—those very; *gṛha-medhinām*—of the materialistic householders.

TRANSLATION

All the planets of the materialistic persons, including all the heavenly planets, such as the moon, are vanquished when the Supreme Personality of Godhead, Hari, goes to His bed of serpents, which is known as Ananta Śeṣa.

PURPORT

The materially attached are very eager to promote themselves to the heavenly planets such as the moon. There are many heavenly planets to which they aspire just to achieve more and more material happiness by getting a long duration of life and the paraphernalia for sense enjoyment. But the attached persons do not know that even if one goes to the highest planet, Brahmaloka, destruction exists there also. In *Bhagavad-gītā* the Lord says that one can even go to the Brahmaloka, but still he will find the pangs of birth, death, disease and old age. Only by approaching the Lord's abode, the Vaikuṇṭhaloka, does one not take birth again in this material world. The *gṛhamedhīs*, or materialistic persons, however, do not like to use this advantage. They would prefer to transmigrate perpetually from one body to another, or from one planet to another. They do not want the eternal, blissful life in knowledge in the kingdom of God.

There are two kinds of dissolutions. One dissolution takes place at the end of the life of Brahmā. At that time all the planetary systems, including the heavenly systems, are dissolved in water and enter into the body of Garbhodakaśāyī Viṣṇu, who lies on the Garbhodaka Ocean on the bed of serpents, called Śeṣa. In the other dissolution, which occurs at the end of Brahmā's day, all the lower planetary systems are destroyed. When Lord Brahmā rises after his night, these lower planetary systems are again created. The statement in *Bhagavad-gītā* that persons who worship the demigods have lost their intelligence is confirmed in this verse. These less intelligent persons do not know that even if they are promoted to the heavenly planets, at the time of dissolution they themselves, the demigods and all their planets will be annihilated. They have no information that eternal, blissful life can be attained.

TEXT 5

ये स्वधर्मान्न दुह्यन्ति धीराः कामार्थहेतवे ।
निःसङ्गा न्यस्तकर्माणः प्रशान्ताः शुद्धचेतसः ॥५॥

ye sva-dharmān na duhyanti
dhīrāḥ kāmārtha-hetave
niḥsaṅgā nyasta-karmāṇaḥ
praśāntāḥ śuddha-cetasaḥ

ye—those who; *sva-dharmān*—their own occupational duties; *na*—do not; *duhyanti*—take advantage of; *dhīrāḥ*—intelligent; *kāma*—sense gratification; *artha*—economic development; *hetave*—for the sake of;

niḥsaṅgāḥ—free from material attachment; *nyasta*—given up; *karmāṇaḥ*—fruitive activities; *praśāntāḥ*—satisfied; *śuddha-cetasaḥ*—of purified consciousness.

TRANSLATION

Those who are intelligent and are of purified consciousness are completely satisfied in Kṛṣṇa consciousness. Freed from the modes of material nature, they do not act for sense gratification; rather, since they are situated in their own occupational duties, they act as one is expected to act.

PURPORT

The first-class example of this type of man is Arjuna. Arjuna was a *kṣatriya,* and his occupational duty was to fight. Generally, kings fight to extend their kingdoms, which they rule for sense gratification. But as far as Arjuna is concerned, he declined to fight for his own sense gratification. He said that although he could get a kingdom by fighting with his relatives, he did not want to fight with them. But when he was ordered by Kṛṣṇa and convinced by the teachings of *Bhagavad-gītā* that his duty was to satisfy Kṛṣṇa, then he fought. Thus he fought not for his sense gratification but for the satisfaction of the Supreme Personality of Godhead.

Persons who work at their prescribed duties, not for sense gratification but for gratification of the Supreme Lord, are called *niḥsaṅga,* freed from the influence of the modes of material nature. *Nyasta-karmāṇaḥ* indicates that the results of their activities are given to the Supreme Personality of Godhead. Such persons appear to be acting on the platform of their respective duties, but such activities are not performed for personal sense gratification; rather, they are performed for the Supreme Person. Such devotees are called *praśāntāḥ,* which means "completely satisfied." *Śuddha-cetasaḥ* means Kṛṣṇa conscious; their consciousness has become purified. In unpurified consciousness one thinks of himself as the Lord of the universe, but in purified consciousness one thinks himself the eternal servant of the Supreme Personality of Godhead. Putting oneself in that position of eternal servitorship to the Supreme Lord and working for Him perpetually, one actually becomes completely satisfied. As long as one works for his personal sense gratification, he will always be full of anxiety. That is the difference between ordinary consciousness and Kṛṣṇa consciousness.

TEXT 6

निवृत्तिधर्मनिरता निर्ममा निरहङ्कृताः ।
स्वधर्माप्तेन सत्त्वेन परिशुद्धेन चेतसा ॥ ६ ॥

nivṛtti-dharma-niratā
nirmamā nirahaṅkṛtāḥ
sva-dharmāptena sattvena
pariśuddhena cetasā

nivṛtti-dharma—in religious activities for detachment; *niratāḥ*—constantly engaged; *nirmamāḥ*—without a sense of proprietorship; *nirahaṅkṛtāḥ*—without false egoism; *sva-dharma*—by one's own occupational duties; *āptena*—executed; *sattvena*—by goodness; *pariśuddhena*—completely purified; *cetasā*—by consciousness.

TRANSLATION

By executing one's occupational duties, acting with detachment and without a sense of proprietorship or false egoism, one is posted in one's constitutional position by dint of complete purification of consciousness, and by thus executing so-called material duties he can easily enter into the kingdom of God.

PURPORT

Here the word *nivṛtti-dharma-niratāḥ* means "constantly engaging in executing religious activities for detachment." There are two kinds of religious performances. One is called *pravṛtti-dharma*, which means the religious activities performed by the *gṛhamedhīs* for elevation to higher planets or for economic prosperity, the final aim of which is sense gratification. Every one of us who has come to this material world has the sense of overlordship. This is called *pravṛtti*. But the opposite type of religious performance, which is called *nivṛtti*, is to act for the Supreme

Personality of Godhead. Engaged in devotional service in Kṛṣṇa consciousness, one has no proprietorship claim, nor is one situated in the false egoism of thinking that he is God or the master. He always thinks himself the servant. That is the process of purifying consciousness. With pure consciousness only can one enter into the kingdom of God. Materialistic persons, in their elevated condition, can enter any one of the planets within this material world, but all are subjected to dissolution over and over again.

TEXT 7

सूर्यद्वारेण ते यान्ति पुरुषं विश्वतोमुखम् ।
परावरेशं प्रकृतिमस्योत्पत्त्यन्तभावनम् ॥ ७ ॥

sūrya-dvāreṇa te yānti
puruṣaṁ viśvato-mukham
parāvareśaṁ prakṛtim
asyotpatty-anta-bhāvanam

sūrya-dvāreṇa—through the path of illumination; *te*—they; *yānti*—approach; *puruṣam*—the Personality of Godhead; *viśvataḥ-mukham*—whose face is turned everywhere; *para-avara-īśam*—the proprietor of the spiritual and material worlds; *prakṛtim*—the material cause; *asya*—of the world; *utpatti*—of manifestation; *anta*—of dissolution; *bhāvanam*—the cause.

TRANSLATION

Through the path of illumination, such liberated persons approach the complete Personality of Godhead, who is the proprietor of the material and spiritual worlds and is the supreme cause of their manifestation and dissolution.

PURPORT

The word *sūrya-dvāreṇa* means "by the illuminated path," or through the sun planet. The illuminated path is devotional service. It is advised in the *Vedas* not to pass through the darkness, but to pass through the sun planet. It is also recommended here that by traversing the illuminated path one can be freed from the contamination of the material modes of nature; by that path one can enter into the kingdom where the completely perfect Personality of Godhead resides. The words *puruṣaṁ viśvato-mukham* mean the Supreme Personality of Godhead, who is all-perfect. All living entities other than the Supreme Personality of Godhead are very small, although they may be big by our calculation. Everyone is infinitesimal, and therefore in the *Vedas* the Supreme Lord is called the supreme eternal amongst all eternals. He is the proprietor of the material and spiritual worlds and the supreme cause of manifestation. Material nature is only the ingredient because actually the manifestation is caused by His energy. The material energy is also His energy; just as the combination of father and mother is the cause of childbirth, so the combination of the material energy and the glance of the Supreme Personality of Godhead is the cause of the manifestation of the material world. The efficient cause, therefore, is not matter, but the Lord Himself.

TEXT 8

द्विपरार्धावसाने यः प्रलयो ब्रह्मणस्तु ते ।
तावदध्यासते लोकं परस्य परचिन्तकाः ॥ ८ ॥

dvi-parārdhāvasāne yaḥ
pralayo brahmaṇas tu te
tāvad adhyāsate lokaṁ
parasya para-cintakāḥ

dvi-parārdha—two *parārdhas; avasāne*—at the end of; *yaḥ*—which; *pralayaḥ*—death; *brahmaṇaḥ*—of Lord Brahmā; *tu*—indeed; *te*—they; *tāvat*—so long; *adhyāsate*—dwell; *lokam*—on the planet; *parasya*—of the Supreme; *para-cintakāḥ*—thinking of the Supreme Personality of Godhead.

TRANSLATION

Worshipers of the Hiraṇyagarbha expansion of the Personality of Godhead remain within this material world until the end of two parārdhas, when Lord Brahmā also dies.

PURPORT

One dissolution is at the end of Brahmā's day, and one is at the end of Brahmā's life. Brahmā dies at the end of two *parārdhas,* at which time the entire material universe is dissolved. Persons who are worshipers of Hiraṇyagarbha, the plenary expansion of the Supreme Personality of Godhead Garbhodakaśāyī Viṣṇu, do not directly approach the Supreme Personality of Godhead in Vaikuṇṭha. They remain within this universe on Satyaloka or other higher planets until the end of the life of Brahmā. Then, with Brahmā, they are elevated to the spiritual kingdom.

The words *parasya para-cintakāḥ* mean "always thinking of the Supreme Personality of Godhead," or being always Kṛṣṇa conscious. When we speak of Kṛṣṇa, this refers to the complete category of *viṣṇu-tattva.* Kṛṣṇa includes the three *puruṣa* incarnations, namely Mahā-Viṣṇu, Garbhodakaśāyī Viṣṇu and Kṣīrodakaśāyī Viṣṇu, as well as all the incarnations taken together. This is confirmed in the *Brahma-saṁhitā. Rāmādi-mūrtiṣu kalā-niyamena tiṣṭhan:* Lord Kṛṣṇa is perpetually situated with His many expansions, such as Rāma, Nṛsiṁha, Vāmana, Madhusūdana, Viṣṇu and Nārāyaṇa. He exists with all His plenary portions and the portions of His plenary portions, and each of them is as good as the Supreme Personality of Godhead. The words *parasya para-cintakāḥ* mean those who are fully Kṛṣṇa conscious. Such persons enter directly into the kingdom of God, the Vaikuṇṭha planets, or, if they are worshipers of the plenary portion Garbhodakaśāyī Viṣṇu, they remain within this universe until its dissolution, and after that they enter.

TEXT 9

क्ष्माम्भोऽनलानिलवियन्मनइन्द्रियार्थ-
भूतादिभिः परिवृतं प्रतिसञ्जिहीर्षुः ।
अव्याकृतं विशति यर्हि गुणत्रयात्मा
कालं पराख्यमनुभूय परः स्वयम्भूः ॥ ९॥

kṣmāmbho-'nalānila-viyan-mana-indriyārtha-
bhūtādibhiḥ parivṛtaṁ pratisañjihīrṣuḥ
avyākṛtaṁ viśati yarhi guṇa-trayātmā
kālaṁ parākhyam anubhūya paraḥ svayambhūḥ

kṣmā—earth; *ambhaḥ*—water; *anala*—fire; *anila*—air; *viyat*—ether; *manaḥ*—mind; *indriya*—the senses; *artha*—the objects of the senses; *bhūta*—ego; *ādibhiḥ*—and so on; *parivṛtam*—covered by; *pratisañjihīrṣuḥ*—desiring to dissolve; *avyākṛtam*—the changeless spiritual sky; *viśati*—he enters; *yarhi*—at which time; *guṇa-traya-ātmā*—consisting of the three modes; *kālam*—the time; *para-ākhyam*—two *parārdhas; anubhūya*—after experiencing; *paraḥ*—the chief; *svayambhūḥ*—Lord Brahmā.

TRANSLATION

After experiencing the inhabitable time of the three modes of material nature, known as two parārdhas, Lord Brahmā closes the material universe, which is covered by layers of earth, water, air, fire, ether, mind, ego, etc., and goes back to Godhead.

PURPORT

The word *avyākṛtam* is very significant in this verse. The same meaning is stated in *Bhagavad-gītā*, in the word *sanātana*. This material world is *vyākṛta*, or subject to changes, and it finally dissolves. But after the dissolution of this material world, the manifestation of the spiritual world, the *sanātana-dhāma*, remains. That spiritual sky is called *avyākṛta*, that which does not change, and there the Supreme Personality of Godhead resides. When, after ruling over the material universe under the influence of the time element, Lord Brahmā desires to dissolve it and enter into the kingdom of God, others then enter with him.

TEXT 10

एवं परेत्य भगवन्तमनुप्रविष्टा
ये योगिनो जितमरुन्मनसो विरागाः ।
तेनैव साकममृतं पुरुषं पुराणं
ब्रह्म प्रधानमुपयान्त्यगताभिमानाः ॥१०॥

evaṁ paretya bhagavantam anupraviṣṭā
ye yogino jita-marun-manaso virāgāḥ
tenaiva sākam amṛtaṁ puruṣaṁ purāṇaṁ
brahma pradhānam upayānty agatābhimānāḥ

evam—thus; *paretya*—having gone a long distance; *bhagavantam*—Lord Brahmā; *anupraviṣṭāḥ*—entered; *ye*—those who; *yoginaḥ*—*yogīs*; *jita*—controlled; *marut*—the breathing; *manasaḥ*—the mind; *virāgāh*—detached; *tena*—with Lord Brahmā; *eva*—indeed; *sākam*—together; *amṛtam*—the embodiment of bliss; *puruṣam*—unto the Personality of Godhead; *purāṇam*—the oldest; *brahma pradhānam*—the Supreme Brahman; *upayānti*—they go; *agata*—not gone; *abhimānāḥ*—whose false ego.

TRANSLATION

The yogīs who become detached from the material world by practice of breathing exercises and control of the mind reach the planet of Brahmā, which is far, far away. After giving up their bodies, they enter into the body of Lord Brahmā, and therefore when Brahmā is liberated and goes to the Supreme Personality of Godhead, who is the Supreme Brahman, such yogīs can also enter into the kingdom of God.

PURPORT

By perfecting their yogic practice, *yogīs* can reach the highest planet, Brahmaloka, or Satyaloka, and after giving up their material bodies, they can enter into the body of Lord Brahmā. Because they are not directly devotees of the Lord, they cannot get liberation directly. They have to wait until Brahmā is liberated, and only then, along with Brahmā, are they also liberated. It is clear that as long as a living entity is a worshiper of a particular demigod, his consciousness is absorbed in thoughts of that demigod, and therefore he cannot get direct liberation, or entrance into the kingdom of God, nor can he merge into the impersonal effulgence of the Supreme Personality of Godhead. Such *yogīs* or demigod worshipers are subjected to the chance of taking birth again when there is again creation.

TEXT 11

अथ तं सर्वभूतानां हृत्पद्मेषु कृतालयम् ।
श्रुतानुभावं शरणं व्रज भावेन भामिनि ॥११॥

atha taṁ sarva-bhūtānāṁ
hṛt-padmeṣu kṛtālayam

śrutānubhāvaṁ śaraṇaṁ
vraja bhāvena bhāmini

atha—therefore; *tam*—the Supreme Personality of Godhead; *sarva-bhūtānām*—of all living entities; *hṛt-padmeṣu*—in the lotus hearts; *kṛta-ālayam*—residing; *śruta-anubhāvam*—whose glories you have heard; *śaraṇam*—unto the shelter; *vraja*—go; *bhāvena*—by devotional service; *bhāmini*—My dear mother.

TRANSLATION

Therefore, My dear mother, by devotional service take direct shelter of the Supreme Personality of Godhead, who is seated in everyone's heart.

PURPORT

One can attain direct contact with the Supreme Personality of Godhead in full Kṛṣṇa consciousness and revive one's eternal relationship with Him as lover, as Supreme Soul, as son, as friend or as master. One can re-establish the transcendental loving relationship with the Supreme Lord in so many ways, and that feeling is true oneness. The oneness of the Māyāvādī philosophers and the oneness of Vaiṣṇava philosophers are different. The Māyāvādī and Vaiṣṇava philosophers both want to merge into the Supreme, but the Vaiṣṇavas do not lose their identities. They want to keep the identity of lover, parent, friend or servant.

In the transcendental world, the servant and master are one. That is the absolute platform. Although the relationship is servant and master, both the servant and the served stand on the same platform. That is oneness. Lord Kapila advised His mother that she did not need any indirect process. She was already situated in that direct process because the Supreme Lord had taken birth as her son. Actually, she did not need any further instruction because she was already in the perfectional stage. Kapiladeva advised her to continue in the same way. He therefore addressed His mother as *bhāmini* to indicate that she was already thinking of the Lord as her son. Devahūti is advised by Lord Kapila to take directly to devotional service, Kṛṣṇa consciousness, because without that consciousness one cannot become liberated from the clutches of *māyā*.

TEXTS 12–15

आद्यः स्थिरचराणां यो वेदगर्भः सहर्षिभिः ।
योगेश्वरैः कुमाराद्यैः सिद्धैर्योगप्रवर्तकैः ॥१२॥
भेददृष्ट्याभिमानेन निःसङ्गेनापि कर्मणा ।
कर्तृत्वात्सगुणं ब्रह्म पुरुषं पुरुषर्षभम् ॥१३॥
स संसृत्य पुनः काले कालेनेश्वरमूर्तिना ।
जाते गुणव्यतिकरे यथापूर्वं प्रजायते ॥१४॥
ऐश्वर्यं पारमेष्ठ्यं च तेऽपि धर्मविनिर्मितम् ।
निषेव्य पुनरायान्ति गुणव्यतिकरे सति ॥१५॥

ādyaḥ sthira-carāṇāṁ yo
veda-garbhaḥ saharṣibhiḥ
yogeśvaraiḥ kumārādyaiḥ
siddhair yoga-pravartakaiḥ

bheda-dṛṣṭyābhimānena
niḥsaṅgenāpi karmaṇā
kartṛtvāt saguṇaṁ brahma
puruṣaṁ puruṣarṣabham

sa saṁsṛtya punaḥ kāle
kāleneśvara-mūrtinā
jāte guṇa-vyatikare
yathā-pūrvaṁ prajāyate

aiśvaryaṁ pārameṣṭhyaṁ ca
te 'pi dharma-vinirmitam
niṣevya punar āyānti
guṇa-vyatikare sati

ādyaḥ—the creator, Lord Brahmā; *sthira-carāṇām*—of the immobile and mobile manifestations; *yaḥ*—he who; *veda-garbhaḥ*—the repository of the *Vedas; saha*—along with; *ṛṣibhiḥ*—the sages;

yoga-īśvaraiḥ—with great mystic *yogīs; kumāra-ādyaiḥ*—the Kumāras and others; *siddhaiḥ*—with the perfected living beings; *yoga-pravartakaiḥ*—the authors of the *yoga* system; *bheda-dṛṣṭyā*—because of independent vision; *abhimānena*—by misconception; *niḥsaṅgena*—nonfruitive; *api*—although; *karmaṇā*—by their activities; *kartṛtvāt*—from the sense of being a doer; *sa-guṇam*—possessing spiritual qualities; *brahma*—Brahman; *puruṣam*—the Personality of Godhead; *puruṣa-ṛṣabham*—the first *puruṣa* incarnation; *saḥ*—he; *saṁsṛtya*—having attained; *punaḥ*—again; *kāle*—at the time; *kālena*—by time; *īśvara-mūrtinā*—the manifestation of the Lord; *jāte guṇa-vyatikare*—when the interaction of the modes arises; *yathā*—as; *pūrvam*—previously; *prajāyate*—is born; *aiśvaryam*—opulence; *pārameṣṭhyam*—royal; *ca*—and; *te*—the sages; *api*—also; *dharma*—by their pious activities; *vinirmitam*—produced; *niṣevya*—having enjoyed; *punaḥ*—again; *āyānti*—they return; *guṇa-vyatikare sati*—when the interaction of the modes takes place.

TRANSLATION

My dear mother, someone may worship the Supreme Personality of Godhead with a special self-interest, but even demigods such as Lord Brahmā, great sages such as Sanat-kumāra and great munis such as Marīci have to come back to the material world again at the time of creation. When the interaction of the three modes of material nature begins, Brahmā, who is the creator of this cosmic manifestation and who is full of Vedic knowledge, and the great sages, who are the authors of the spiritual path and the yoga system, come back under the influence of the time factor. They are liberated by their nonfruitive activities and they attain the first incarnation of the puruṣa, but at the time of creation they come back in exactly the same forms and positions as they had previously.

PURPORT

That Brahmā becomes liberated is known to everyone, but he cannot liberate his devotees. Demigods like Brahmā and Lord Śiva cannot give liberation to any living entity. As it is confirmed in *Bhagavad-gītā*, only one who surrenders unto Kṛṣṇa, the Supreme Personality of Godhead, can be liberated from the clutches of *māyā*. Brahmā is called here *ādyaḥ sthira-carāṇām.* He is the original, first-created living entity, and after his own birth he creates the entire cosmic manifestation. He was fully instructed in the matter of creation by the Supreme Lord. Here he is called *veda-garbha,* which means that he knows the complete purpose of the *Vedas.* He is always accompanied by such great personalities as Marīci, Kaśyapa and the seven sages, as well as by great mystic *yogīs,* the Kumāras and many other spiritually advanced living entities, but he has his own interest, separate from the Lord's. *Bheda-dṛṣṭyā* means that Brahmā sometimes thinks that he is independent of the Supreme Lord, or he thinks of himself as one of the three equally independent incarnations. Brahmā is entrusted with creation, Viṣṇu maintains and Rudra, Lord Śiva, destroys. The three of them are understood to be incarnations of the Supreme Lord in charge of the three different material modes of nature, but none of them is independent of the Supreme Personality of Godhead. Here the word *bheda-dṛṣṭyā* occurs because Brahmā has a slight inclination to think that he is as independent as Rudra. Sometimes Brahmā thinks that he is independent of the Supreme Lord, and the worshiper also thinks that Brahmā is independent. For this reason, after the destruction of this material world, when there is again creation by the interaction of the material modes of nature, Brahmā comes back. Although Brahmā reaches the Supreme Personality of Godhead as the first *puruṣa* incarnation, Mahā-Viṣṇu, who is full with transcendental qualities, he cannot stay in the spiritual world.

The specific significance of his coming back may be noted. Brahmā and the great *ṛṣis* and the great master of *yoga* (Śiva) are not ordinary living entities; they are very powerful and have all the perfections of mystic *yoga.* But still they have an inclination to try to become one with the Supreme, and therefore they have to come back. In the *Śrīmad-Bhāgavatam* it is accepted that as long as one thinks that he is equal with the Supreme Personality of Godhead, he is not completely purified or knowledgeable. In spite of going up to the first *puruṣa-avatāra,* Mahā-Viṣṇu, after the dissolution of this material creation, such personalities again fall down or come back to the material creation.

It is a great falldown on the part of the impersonalists to think that the Supreme Lord appears within a material body and that one should therefore not meditate upon the form of the Supreme but should meditate instead on the formless. For this particular mistake, even the great mystic *yogīs* or great stalwart transcendentalists also come back again when there is creation. All living entities other than the impersonalists and monists can directly take to devotional service in full Kṛṣṇa consciousness and become liberated by developing transcendental loving service to the Supreme Personality of Godhead. Such devotional service develops in the degrees of thinking of the Supreme Lord as master, as friend, as son and, at last, as lover. These distinctions in transcendental variegatedness must always be present.

TEXT 16

ये त्विहासक्तमनसः कर्मसु श्रद्धयान्विताः ।
कुर्वन्त्यप्रतिषिद्धानि नित्यान्यपि च कृत्स्नशः ।। १६ ।।

ye tv ihāsakta-manasaḥ
karmasu śraddhayānvitāḥ
kurvanty apratiṣiddhāni
nityāny api ca kṛtsnaśaḥ

ye—those who; *tu*—but; *iha*—in this world; *āsakta*—addicted; *manasaḥ*—whose minds; *karmasu*—to fruitive activities; *śraddhayā*—with faith; *anvitāḥ*—endowed; *kurvanti*—perform; *apratiṣiddhāni*—with attachment to the result; *nityāni*—prescribed duties; *api*—certainly; *ca*—and; *kṛtsnaśaḥ*—repeatedly.

TRANSLATION

Persons who are too addicted to this material world execute their prescribed duties very nicely and with great faith. They daily perform all such prescribed duties with attachment to the fruitive result.

PURPORT

In this and the following six verses, the *Śrīmad-Bhāgavatam* criticizes persons who are too materially attached. It is enjoined in the Vedic scriptures that those who are attached to the enjoyment of material facilities have to sacrifice and undergo certain ritualistic performances. They have to observe certain rules and regulations in their daily lives to be elevated to the heavenly planets. It is stated in this verse that such persons cannot be liberated at any time. Those who worship demigods with the consciousness that each and every demigod is a separate God cannot be elevated to the spiritual world, what to speak of persons who are simply attached to duties for the upliftment of their material condition.

TEXT 17

रजसा कुण्ठमनसः कामात्मानोऽजितेन्द्रियाः ।
पितॄन् यजन्त्यनुदिनं गृहेष्वभिरताशयाः ॥१७॥

rajasā kuṇṭha-manasaḥ
kāmātmāno 'jitendriyāḥ
pitṝn yajanty anudinaṁ
gṛheṣv abhiratāśayāḥ

rajasā—by the mode of passion; *kuṇṭha*—full of anxieties; *manasaḥ*—their minds; *kāma-ātmānaḥ*—aspiring for sense gratification; *ajita*—uncontrolled; *indriyāḥ*—their senses; *pitṝn*—the forefathers; *yajanti*—they worship; *anudinam*—every day; *gṛheṣu*—in home life; *abhirata*—engaged; *āśayāḥ*—their minds.

TRANSLATION

Such persons, impelled by the mode of passion, are full of anxieties and always aspire for sense gratification due to uncontrolled senses. They worship the forefathers and are busy day and night improving the economic condition of their family, social or national life.

TEXT 18

त्रैवर्गिकास्ते पुरुषा विमुखा हरिमेधसः ।
कथायां कथनीयोरुविक्रमस्य मधुद्विषः ॥१८॥

trai-vargikās te puruṣā
vimukhā hari-medhasaḥ
kathāyāṁ kathanīyoru-
vikramasya madhudviṣaḥ

trai-vargikāḥ—interested in the three elevating processes; *te*—those; *puruṣāḥ*—persons; *vimukhāḥ*—not interested; *hari-medhasaḥ*—of Lord Hari; *kathāyām*—in the pastimes; *kathanīya*—worth chanting of; *uru-vikramasya*—whose excellent prowess; *madhu-dviṣaḥ*—the killer of the Madhu demon.

TRANSLATION

Such persons are called trai-vargika because they are interested in the three elevating processes. They are averse to the Supreme Personality of Godhead, who can give relief to the conditioned soul. They are not interested in the Supreme Personality's pastimes, which are worth hearing because of His transcendental prowess.

PURPORT

According to Vedic thought, there are four elevating principles, namely religiosity, economic development, sense gratification and liberation. Persons who are simply interested in material enjoyment make plans to execute prescribed duties. They are interested in the three elevating processes of religious rituals, economic elevation and sense enjoyment. By developing their economic condition, they can enjoy material life. Materialistic persons, therefore, are interested in those elevating processes, which are called *trai-vargika. Trai* means "three"; *vargika* means "elevating processes." Such materialistic persons are never attracted by the Supreme Personality of Godhead. Rather, they are antagonistic towards Him.

The Supreme Personality of Godhead is here described as *hari-medhaḥ*, or "He who can deliver one from the cycle of birth and death." Materialistic persons are never interested in hearing about the marvelous pastimes of the Lord. They think that they are fictions and stories and that the Supreme Godhead is also a man of material nature. They are not fit for advancing in devotional service, or Kṛṣṇa consciousness. Such materialistic persons are interested in newspaper stories, novels and imaginary dramas. The factual activities of the Lord, such as Lord Kṛṣṇa's acting in the Battle of Kurukṣetra, or the activities of the Pāṇḍavas, or the Lord's activities in Vṛndāvana or Dvārakā, are related in the *Bhagavad-gītā* and *Śrīmad-Bhāgavatam*, which are full of the activities of the Lord. But materialistic persons who engage in elevating their position in the material world are not interested in such activities of the Lord. They may be interested in the activities of a great politician or a great rich man of this world, but they are not interested in the transcendental activities of the Supreme Lord.

TEXT 19

नूनं दैवेन विहता ये चाच्युतकथासुधाम् ।
हित्वा शृण्वन्त्यसद्गाथाः पुरीषमिव विड्भुजः ॥१९॥

nūnaṁ daivena vihatā
ye cācyuta-kathā-sudhām
hitvā śṛṇvanty asad-gāthāḥ
purīṣam iva viḍ-bhujaḥ

nūnam—certainly; *daivena*—by the order of the Lord; *vihatāḥ*—condemned; *ye*—those who; *ca*—also; *acyuta*—of the infallible Lord; *kathā*—stories; *sudhām*—nectar; *hitvā*—having given up; *śṛṇvanti*—they hear; *asat-gāthāḥ*—stories about materialistic persons; *purīṣam*—stool; *iva*—like; *viṭ-bhujaḥ*—stool-eaters (hogs).

TRANSLATION

Such persons are condemned by the supreme order of the Lord. Because they are averse to the nectar of the activities of the Supreme Personality of Godhead, they are compared to stool-eating hogs. They give up hearing the transcendental activities of the Lord and indulge in hearing of the abominable activities of materialistic persons.

PURPORT

Everyone is addicted to hearing of the activities of another person, whether a politician or a rich man or an imaginary character whose activities are created in a novel. There are so many nonsensical literatures, stories and books of speculative philosophy. Materialistic persons are very interested in reading such literature, but when they are presented with genuine books of knowledge like *Śrīmad-Bhāgavatam, Bhagavad-gītā, Viṣṇu Purāṇa* or other scriptures of the world, such as the Bible and Koran, they are not interested. These persons are condemned by the supreme order as much as a hog is condemned. The hog is interested in eating stool. If the hog is offered some nice preparation made of condensed milk or ghee, he won't like it; he would prefer obnoxious, bad-smelling stool, which he finds very relishable. Materialistic persons are considered condemned because they are interested in hellish activities and not in transcendental activities. The message of the Lord's activities is nectar, and besides that message, any information in which we may be interested is actually hellish.

TEXT 20

दक्षिणेन पथार्यम्णः पितृलोकं व्रजन्ति ते ।
प्रजामनु प्रजायन्ते श्मशानान्तक्रियाकृतः ॥२०॥

dakṣiṇena pathāryamṇaḥ
pitṛ-lokaṁ vrajanti te
prajām anu prajāyante
śmaśānānta-kriyā-kṛtaḥ

dakṣiṇena—southern; *pathā*—by the path; *aryamṇaḥ*—of the sun; *pitṛ-lokam*—to Pitṛloka; *vrajanti*—go; *te*—they; *prajām*—their families; *anu*—along with; *prajāyante*—they take birth; *śmaśāna*—the crematorium; *anta*—to the end; *kriyā*—fruitive activities; *kṛtaḥ*—performing.

TRANSLATION

Such materialistic persons are allowed to go to the planet called Pitṛloka by the southern course of the sun, but they again come back to this planet and take birth in their own families, beginning again the same fruitive activities from birth to the end of life.

PURPORT

In *Bhagavad-gītā*, Ninth Chapter, verse 21, it is stated that such persons are elevated to the higher planetary systems. As soon as their lifetimes of fruitive activity are finished, they return to this planet, and thus they go up and come down. Those who are elevated to the higher planets again come back into the same family for which they had too much attachment; they are born, and the fruitive activities continue again until the end of life. There are different prescribed rituals from birth until the end of life, and they are very much attached to such activities.

TEXT 21

ततस्ते क्षीणसुकृताः पुनर्लोकमिमं सति ।
पतन्ति विवशा देवैः सद्यो विभ्रंशितोदयाः ॥२१॥

tatas te kṣīṇa-sukṛtāḥ
punar lokam imaṁ sati
patanti vivaśā devaiḥ
sadyo vibhraṁśitodayāḥ

tataḥ—then; *te*—they; *kṣīṇa*—exhausted; *su-kṛtāḥ*—results of their pious activities; *punaḥ*—again; *lokam imam*—to this planet; *sati*—O virtuous mother; *patanti*—fall; *vivaśāḥ*—helpless; *devaiḥ*—by higher arrangement; *sadyaḥ*—suddenly; *vibhraṁśita*—caused to fall; *udayāḥ*—their prosperity.

TRANSLATION

When the results of their pious activities are exhausted, they fall down by higher arrangement and again come back to this planet, just as any person raised to a high position sometimes all of a sudden falls.

PURPORT

It is sometimes found that a person elevated to a very high position in government service falls down all of a sudden, and no one can check him. Similarly, after finishing their period of enjoyment, foolish persons who are very much interested in being elevated to the position of president in higher planets also fall down to this planet. The distinction between the elevated position of a devotee and that of an ordinary person attracted to fruitive activities is that when a devotee is elevated to the spiritual kingdom he never falls down, whereas an ordinary person falls, even if he is elevated to the highest planetary system, Brahmaloka. It is confirmed in *Bhagavad-gītā* (*ābrahma-bhuvanāl lokāḥ*) that even if one is elevated to a higher planet, he has to come down again. But Kṛṣṇa confirms in *Bhagavad-gītā* (8.16), *mām upetya tu kaunteya punar janma na vidyate:* "Anyone who attains My abode never comes back to this conditioned life of material existence."

TEXT 22

तस्मात्त्वं सर्वभावेन भजस्व परमेष्ठिनम् ।
तद्गुणाश्रयया भक्त्या भजनीयपदाम्बुजम् ॥२२॥

tasmāt tvaṁ sarva-bhāvena
bhajasva parameṣṭhinam
tad-guṇāśrayayā bhaktyā
bhajanīya-padāmbujam

tasmāt—therefore; *tvam*—you (Devahūti); *sarva-bhāvena*—with loving ecstasy; *bhajasva*—worship; *parameṣṭhinam*—the Supreme Personality of Godhead; *tat-guṇa*—the qualities of the Lord; *āśrayayā*—connected with; *bhaktyā*—by devotional service; *bhajanīya*—worshipable; *pada-ambujam*—whose lotus feet.

TRANSLATION

My dear mother, I therefore advise that you take shelter of the Supreme Personality of Godhead, for His lotus feet are worth worshiping. Accept this with all devotion and love, for thus you can be situated in transcendental devotional service.

PURPORT

The word *parameṣṭhinam* is sometimes used in connection with Brahmā. *Parameṣṭhī* means "the supreme person." As Brahmā is the supreme person within this universe, Kṛṣṇa is the Supreme Personality in the spiritual world. Lord Kapiladeva advises His mother that she should take shelter of the lotus feet of the Supreme Personality of Godhead, Kṛṣṇa, because it is worthwhile. Taking shelter of demigods, even those in the highest positions, like Brahmā and Śiva, is not advised herein. One should take shelter of the Supreme Godhead.

Sarva-bhāvena means "in all-loving ecstasy." *Bhāva* is the preliminary stage of elevation before the attainment of pure love of Godhead. It is stated in *Bhagavad-gītā, budhā bhāva-samanvitāḥ:* one who has attained the stage of *bhāva* can accept the lotus feet of Lord Kṛṣṇa as worshipable. This is also advised here by Lord Kapila to His mother. Also significant in this verse is the phrase *tad-guṇāśrayayā bhaktyā.* This means that discharging devotional service unto Kṛṣṇa is transcendental; it is not material activity. This is confirmed in *Bhagavad-gītā:* those who engage in devotional service are accepted to be situated in the spiritual kingdom. *Brahma-bhūyāya kalpate:* they at once become situated in the transcendental kingdom.

Devotional service in full Kṛṣṇa consciousness is the only means for attaining the highest perfection of life for the human being. This is recommended herein by Lord Kapila to His mother. *Bhakti* is therefore *nirguṇa,* free from all tinges of material qualities. Although the discharge of devotional service appears to be like material activities, it is never *saguṇa,* or contaminated by material qualities. *Tad-guṇāśrayayā* means that Lord Kṛṣṇa's transcendental qualities are so sublime that there is no need to divert one's attention to any other activities. His behavior with the devotees is so exalted that a devotee need not try to divert his attention to any other worship. It is said that the demoniac Pūtanā came to kill Kṛṣṇa by poisoning Him, but because Kṛṣṇa was pleased to suck her breast, she was given the same position as His mother. Devotees pray, therefore, that if a demon who wanted to kill Kṛṣṇa gets such an exalted position, why should they go to anyone other than Kṛṣṇa for their worshipful attachment? There are two kinds of religious activities: one for material advancement and the other for spiritual advancement. By taking shelter under the lotus feet of Kṛṣṇa, one is endowed with both kinds of prosperity, material and spiritual. Why then should one go to any demigod?

TEXT 23

वासुदेवे भगवति भक्तियोगः प्रयोजितः ।
जनयत्याशु वैराग्यं ज्ञानं यद्ब्रह्मदर्शनम् ॥२३॥

vāsudeve bhagavati
bhakti-yogaḥ prayojitaḥ
janayaty āśu vairāgyaṁ
jñānaṁ yad brahma-darśanam

vāsudeve—unto Kṛṣṇa; *bhagavati*—the Personality of Godhead; *bhakti-yogaḥ*—devotional service; *prayojitaḥ*—discharged; *janayati*—produces; *āśu*—very soon; *vairāgyam*—detachment; *jñānam*—knowledge; *yat*—which; *brahma-darśanam*—self-realization.

TRANSLATION

Engagement in Kṛṣṇa consciousness and application of devotional service unto Kṛṣṇa make it possible to advance in knowledge and detachment, as well as in self-realization.

PURPORT

It is said by less intelligent men that *bhakti-yoga*, or devotional service, is meant for persons who are not advanced in transcendental knowledge and renunciation. But the fact is that if one engages in the devotional service of the Lord in full Kṛṣṇa consciousness, he does not have to attempt separately to practice detachment or to wait for an awakening of transcendental knowledge. It is said that one who engages unflinchingly in the devotional service of the Lord actually has all the good qualities of the demigods develop in him automatically. One cannot discover how such good qualities develop in the body of a devotee, but actually it happens. There is one instance where a hunter was taking pleasure in killing animals, but after becoming a devotee he was not prepared to kill even an ant. Such is the quality of a devotee.

Those who are very eager to advance in transcendental knowledge can engage themselves in pure devotional service, without wasting time in mental speculation. For arriving at the positive conclusions of knowledge in the Absolute Truth, the word *brahma-darśanam* is significant in this verse. *Brahma-darśanam* means to realize or to understand the Transcendence. One who engages in the service of Vāsudeva can actually realize what Brahman is. If Brahman is impersonal, then there is no question of *darśanam*, which means "seeing face to face." *Darśanam* refers to seeing the Supreme Personality of Godhead, Vāsudeva. Unless the seer and the seen are persons, there is no *darśanam. Brahma-darśanam* means that as soon as one sees the Supreme Personality of Godhead, he can at once realize what impersonal Brahman is. A devotee does not need to make separate investigations to understand the nature of Brahman. *Bhagavad-gītā* also confirms this. *Brahma-bhūyāya kalpate:* a devotee at once becomes a self-realized soul in the Absolute Truth.

TEXT 24

यदास्य चित्तमर्थेषु समेष्विन्द्रियवृत्तिभिः ।
न विगृह्णाति वैषम्यं प्रियमप्रियमित्युत ॥२४॥

yadāsya cittam artheṣu
sameṣv indriya-vṛttibhiḥ
na vigṛhṇāti vaiṣamyaṁ
priyam apriyam ity uta

yadā—when; *asya*—of the devotee; *cittam*—the mind; *artheṣu*—in the sense objects; *sameṣu*—same; *indriya-vṛttibhiḥ*—by the activities of the senses; *na*—not; *vigṛhṇāti*—does perceive; *vaiṣamyam*—difference; *priyam*—agreeable; *apriyam*—not agreeable; *iti*—thus; *uta*—certainly.

TRANSLATION

The exalted devotee's mind becomes equipoised in sensory activities, and he is transcendental to that which is agreeable and not agreeable.

PURPORT

The significance of advancement in transcendental knowledge and detachment from material attraction is exhibited in the personality of a highly advanced devotee. For him there is nothing agreeable or disagreeable because he does not act in any way for his personal sense gratification. Whatever he does, whatever he thinks, is for the satisfaction of the Personality of Godhead. Either in the material world or in the spiritual world, his equipoised mind is completely manifested. He can understand that in the material world there is nothing good; everything is bad due to its being contaminated by material nature. The materialists' conclusions of good and bad, moral and immoral, etc., are simply mental concoction or sentiment. Actually there is nothing good in the material world. In the spiritual field everything is absolutely good. There is no inebriety in the spiritual varieties. Because a devotee accepts everything in spiritual vision, he is equipoised; that is the symptom of his being elevated to the transcendental position. He automatically attains detachment, *vairāgya*, then *jñāna*, knowledge, and then actual transcendental knowledge. The conclusion is that an advanced devotee dovetails himself in the transcendental qualities of the Lord, and in that sense he becomes qualitatively one with the Supreme Personality of Godhead.

TEXT 25

स तदैवात्मनात्मानं निःसङ्गं समदर्शनम् ।
हेयोपादेयरहितमारूढं पदमीक्षते ॥२५॥

sa tadaivātmanātmānaṁ
niḥsaṅgaṁ sama-darśanam
heyopādeya-rahitam
ārūḍhaṁ padam īkṣate

saḥ—the pure devotee; *tadā*—then; *eva*—certainly; *ātmanā*—by his transcendental intelligence; *ātmānam*—himself; *niḥsaṅgam*—without material attachment; *sama-darśanam*—equipoised in vision; *heya*—to be rejected; *upādeya*—acceptable; *rahitam*—devoid of; *ārūḍham*—elevated; *padam*—to the transcendental position; *īkṣate*—he sees.

TRANSLATION

Because of his transcendental intelligence, the pure devotee is equipoised in his vision and sees himself to be uncontaminated by matter. He does not see anything as superior or inferior, and he feels himself elevated to the transcendental platform of being equal in qualities with the Supreme Person.

PURPORT

Perception of the disagreeable arises from attachment. A devotee has no personal attachment to anything; therefore for him there is no question of agreeable or disagreeable. For the service of the Lord he can accept anything, even though it may be disagreeable to his personal interest. In fact, he is completely free from personal interest, and thus anything agreeable to the Lord is agreeable to him. For example, for Arjuna at first fighting was not agreeable, but when he understood that the fighting was agreeable to the Lord, he accepted the fighting as agreeable. That is the position of a pure devotee. For his personal interest there is nothing which is agreeable or disagreeable; everything is done for the Lord, and therefore he is free from attachment and detachment. That is the transcendental stage of neutrality. A pure devotee enjoys life in the pleasure of the Supreme Lord.

TEXT 26

ज्ञानमात्रं परं ब्रह्म परमात्मेश्वरः पुमान् ।
दृश्यादिभिः पृथग्भावैर्भगवानेक ईयते ॥२६॥

jñāna-mātraṁ paraṁ brahma
paramātmeśvaraḥ pumān
dṛśy-ādibhiḥ pṛthag bhāvair
bhagavān eka īyate

jñāna—knowledge; *mātram*—only; *param*—transcendental; *brahma*—Brahman; *parama-ātmā*—Paramātmā; *īśvaraḥ*—the controller; *pumān*—Supersoul; *dṛśi-ādibhiḥ*—by philosophical research and other processes; *pṛthak bhāvaiḥ*—according to different processes of understanding; *bhagavān*—the Supreme Personality of Godhead; *ekaḥ*—alone; *īyate*—is perceived.

TRANSLATION

The Supreme Personality of Godhead alone is complete transcendental knowledge, but according to the different processes of understanding He appears differently, either as impersonal Brahman, as Paramātmā, as the Supreme Personality of Godhead or as the puruṣa-avatāra.

PURPORT

The word *dṛśy-ādibhiḥ* is significant. According to Jīva Gosvāmī, *dṛśi* means *jñāna*, philosophical research. By different processes of philosophical research under different concepts, such as the process of *jñāna-yoga*, the same Bhagavān, or Supreme Personality of Godhead, is understood as impersonal Brahman. Similarly, by the eightfold *yoga* system He appears as the Paramātmā. But in pure Kṛṣṇa consciousness, or knowledge in purity, when one tries to understand the Absolute Truth, one realizes Him as the Supreme Person. The Transcendence is realized simply on the basis of knowledge. The words used here, *paramātmeśvaraḥ pumān*, are all transcendental, and they refer to Supersoul. Supersoul is also described as *puruṣa*, but the word *Bhagavān* directly refers to the Supreme Personality of Godhead, who is full of six opulences: wealth, fame, strength, beauty, knowledge and renunciation. He is the Personality of Godhead in different spiritual skies. The various descriptions of *paramātmā*, *īśvara* and *pumān* indicate that the expansions of the Supreme Godhead are unlimited.

Ultimately, to understand the Supreme Personality of Godhead one has to accept *bhakti-yoga*. By executing *jñāna-yoga* or *dhyāna-yoga* one has to eventually approach the *bhakti-yoga* platform, and then *paramātmā*, *īśvara*, *pumān*, etc., are all clearly understood. It is recommended in the Second Canto of *Śrīmad-Bhāgavatam* that whether one is a devotee or fruitive actor or liberationist, if he is intelligent enough he should engage himself with all seriousness in the process of devotional service. It is also explained that whatever one desires which is obtainable by fruitive activities, even if one wants to be elevated to higher planets, can be achieved simply by execution of devotional service. Since the Supreme Lord is full in six opulences, He can bestow any one of them upon the worshiper.

The one Supreme Personality of Godhead reveals Himself to different thinkers as the Supreme Person or impersonal Brahman or Paramātmā. Impersonalists merge into the impersonal Brahman, but that is not achieved by worshiping the impersonal Brahman. If one takes to devotional service and at the same time desires to merge into the existence of the Supreme Lord, he can achieve that. If someone desires at all to merge into the existence of the Supreme, he has to execute devotional service.

The devotee can see the Supreme Lord face to face, but the *jñānī*, the empiric philosopher or *yogī* cannot. They cannot be elevated to the positions of associates of the Lord. There is no evidence in the scriptures stating that by cultivating knowledge or worshiping the impersonal Brahman one can become a personal associate of the Supreme Personality of Godhead. Nor by executing the yogic principles can one become an associate of the Supreme Godhead. Impersonal Brahman, being formless, is described as *adṛśya* because the impersonal effulgence of *brahmajyoti* covers the face of the Supreme Lord. Some *yogīs* see the four-handed Viṣṇu sitting within the heart, and therefore in their case also the Supreme Lord is invisible. Only for the devotees is the Lord visible. Here the statement *dṛśy-ādibhiḥ* is significant. Since the Supreme Personality of Godhead is both invisible and visible, there are different features of the Lord. The Paramātmā feature and Brahman feature are invisible, but the Bhagavān feature is visible. In the *Viṣṇu Purāṇa* this fact is very nicely explained. The universal form of the Lord and the formless Brahman effulgence of the Lord, being invisible, are inferior features. The concept of the universal form is material, and the concept of impersonal Brahman is spiritual, but the highest spiritual understanding is the Personality of Godhead. The *Viṣṇu Purāṇa* states, *viṣṇur brahma-svarūpeṇa svayam eva vyavasthitaḥ:* Brahman's real feature is Viṣṇu, or the Supreme Brahman is Viṣṇu. *Svayam eva:* that is His personal feature. The supreme spiritual conception is the Supreme Personality of Godhead. It is also confirmed in *Bhagavad-gītā: yad gatvā na nivartante tad dhāma paramaṁ mama.* That specific abode called *paramaṁ mama* is the place from which, once one attains it, one does not return to this miserable, conditional life. Every place, every space and everything belongs to Viṣṇu, but where He personally lives is *tad dhāma paramam,* His supreme abode. One has to make one's destination the supreme abode of the Lord.

TEXT 27

एतावानेव योगेन समग्रेणेह योगिनः ।
युज्यतेऽभिमतो ह्यर्थो यदसङ्गस्तु कृत्स्नशः ॥२७॥

etāvān eva yogena
samagreṇeha yoginaḥ
yujyate 'bhimato hy artho
yad asaṅgas tu kṛtsnaśaḥ

etāvān—of such a measure; *eva*—just; *yogena*—by *yoga* practice; *samagreṇa*—all; *iha*—in this world; *yoginaḥ*—of the *yogī; yujyate*—is achieved; *abhimataḥ*—desired; *hi*—certainly; *arthaḥ*—purpose; *yat*—which; *asaṅgaḥ*—detachment; *tu*—indeed; *kṛtsnaśaḥ*—completely.

TRANSLATION

The greatest common understanding for all yogīs is complete detachment from matter, which can be achieved by different kinds of yoga.

PURPORT

There are three kinds of *yoga*, namely *bhakti-yoga, jñāna-yoga* and *aṣṭāṅga-yoga.* Devotees, *jñānīs* and *yogīs* all try to get out of the material entanglement. The *jñānīs* try to detach their sensual activities from material engagement. The *jñāna-yogī* thinks that matter is false and that Brahman is truth; he tries, therefore, by cultivation of knowledge, to detach the senses from material enjoyment. The *aṣṭāṅga-yogīs* also try to control the senses. The devotees, however, try to engage the senses in the service of the Lord. Therefore it appears that the activities of the *bhaktas,* devotees, are better than those of the *jñānīs* and *yogīs.* The mystic *yogīs* simply try to control the senses by practicing the eight divisions of *yoga*—*yama, niyama, āsana, prāṇāyāma, pratyāhāra,* etc.—and the *jñānīs* try by mental reasoning to understand that sense enjoyment is false. But the easiest and most direct process is to engage the senses in the service of the Lord.

The purpose of all *yoga* is to detach one's sense activities from this material world. The final aims, however, are different. *Jñānīs* want to become one with the Brahman effulgence, *yogīs* want to realize Paramātmā, and devotees want to develop Kṛṣṇa consciousness and transcendental loving service to the Lord. That loving service is the perfect stage of sense control. The senses are actually active symptoms of life, and they cannot be stopped. They can be detached only if there is superior engagement. As it is confirmed in *Bhagavad-gītā, paraṁ dṛṣṭvā nivartate:* the activities of the senses can be stopped if they are given superior engagements. The supreme engagement is engagement of the senses in the service of the Lord. That is the purpose of all *yoga.*

TEXT 28

ज्ञानमेकं पराचीनैरिन्द्रियैर्ब्रह्म निर्गुणम् ।
अवभात्यर्थरूपेण भ्रान्त्या शब्दादिधर्मिणा ॥२८॥

jñānam ekaṁ parācīnair
indriyair brahma nirguṇam
avabhāty artha-rūpeṇa
bhrāntyā śabdādi-dharmiṇā

jñānam—knowledge; *ekam*—one; *parācīnaiḥ*—averse; *indriyaiḥ*—by the senses; *brahma*—the Supreme Absolute Truth; *nirguṇam*—beyond the material modes; *avabhāti*—appears; *artha-rūpeṇa*—in the form of various objects; *bhrāntyā*—mistakenly; *śabda-ādi*—sound and so on; *dharmiṇā*—endowed with.

TRANSLATION

Those who are averse to the Transcendence realize the Supreme Absolute Truth differently through speculative sense perception, and therefore, because of mistaken speculation, everything appears to them to be relative.

PURPORT

The Supreme Absolute Truth, the Personality of Godhead, is one, and He is spread everywhere by His impersonal feature. This is clearly expressed in *Bhagavad-gītā.* Lord Kṛṣṇa says, "Everything that is experienced is but an expansion of My energy." Everything is sustained by Him, but that does not mean that He is in everything. Sense perceptions, such as aural perception of the sound of a drum, visual perception of a beautiful woman, or perception of the delicious taste of a milk preparation by the tongue, all come through different senses and are therefore differently understood. Therefore sensory knowledge is divided in different categories, although actually everything is one as a manifestation of the energy of the Supreme Lord. Similarly, the energies of fire are heat and illumination, and by these two energies fire can display itself in many varieties, or in diversified sense perception. Māyāvādī philosophers declare this diversity to be false. But Vaiṣṇava philosophers do not accept the different manifestations as false; they accept them as nondifferent from the Supreme Personality of Godhead because they are a display of His diverse energies.

The philosophy that the Absolute is true and this creation is false (*brahma satyaṁ jagan mithyā*) is not accepted by Vaiṣṇava philosophers. The example is given that although all that glitters is not gold, this does not mean that a glittering object is false. For example, an oyster shell appears to be golden. This appearance of golden hue is due only to the perception of the eyes, but that does not mean that the oyster shell is false. Similarly, by seeing the form of Lord Kṛṣṇa one cannot understand what He actually is, but this does not mean that He is false. The form of Kṛṣṇa has to be understood as it is described in the books of knowledge such as *Brahma-saṁhitā. Īśvaraḥ paramaḥ kṛṣṇaḥ sac-cid-ānanda-vigrahaḥ:* Kṛṣṇa, the Supreme Personality of Godhead, has an eternal, blissful spiritual body. By our imperfect sense perception we cannot understand the form of the Lord. We have to acquire knowledge about Him. Therefore it is said here, *jñānam ekam. Bhagavad-gītā* confirms that they are fools who, simply upon seeing Kṛṣṇa, consider Him a common man. They do not know the unlimited knowledge, power and opulence of the Supreme Personality of Godhead. Material sense speculation leads to the conclusion that the Supreme is formless. It is because of such mental speculation that the conditioned soul remains in ignorance under the spell of illusory energy. The Supreme Person has to be understood by the transcendental sound vibrated by Him in *Bhagavad-gītā*, wherein He says that there is nothing superior to Himself; the impersonal Brahman effulgence is resting on His personality. The purified, absolute vision of *Bhagavad-gītā* is compared to the River Ganges. Ganges water is so pure that it can purify even the asses and cows. But anyone who, disregarding the pure Ganges, wishes to be purified instead by the filthy water flowing in a drain, cannot be successful. Similarly, one can successfully attain pure knowledge of the Absolute only by hearing from the pure Absolute Himself.

In this verse it is clearly said that those who are averse to the Supreme Personality of Godhead speculate with their imperfect senses about the nature of the Absolute Truth. The formless Brahman conception, however, can be received only by aural reception and not by personal experience. Knowledge is therefore acquired by aural reception. It is confirmed in the *Vedānta-sūtra, śāstra-yonitvāt:* one has to acquire pure knowledge from the authorized scriptures. So-called speculative arguments about the Absolute Truth are therefore useless. The actual identity of the living entity is his consciousness, which is always present while the living entity is awake, dreaming or in deep sleep. Even in deep sleep, he can perceive by consciousness whether he is happy or distressed. Thus when consciousness is displayed through the medium of the subtle and gross material bodies, it is covered, but when the consciousness is purified, in Kṛṣṇa consciousness, one becomes free from the entanglement of repeated birth and death.

When uncontaminated pure knowledge is uncovered from the modes of material nature, the actual identity of the living entity is discovered: he is eternally a servitor of the Supreme Personality of Godhead. The process of uncovering is like this: the rays of sunshine are luminous, and the sun itself is also luminous. In the presence of the sun, the rays illuminate just like the sun, but when the sunshine is covered by the spell of a cloud, or by *māyā*, then darkness, the imperfection of perception, begins. Therefore, to get out of the entanglement of the spell of nescience, one has to awaken his spiritual consciousness, or Kṛṣṇa consciousness, in terms of the authorized scriptures.

TEXT 29

यथा महानहंरूपस्त्रिवृत्पञ्चविधः स्वराट् ।
एकादशविधस्तस्य वपुरण्डं जगद्यतः ॥२९॥

yathā mahān ahaṁ-rūpas
tri-vṛt pañca-vidhaḥ svarāṭ
ekādaśa-vidhas tasya
vapur aṇḍaṁ jagad yataḥ

yathā—as; *mahān*—the *mahat-tattva; aham-rūpaḥ*—the false ego; *tri-vṛt*—the three modes of material nature; *pañca-vidhaḥ*—the five material elements; *sva-rāṭ*—the individual consciousness; *ekādaśa-vidhaḥ*—the eleven senses; *tasya*—of the living entity; *vapuḥ*—the material body; *aṇḍam*—the *brahmāṇḍa; jagat*—the universe; *yataḥ*—from which or from whom.

TRANSLATION

From the total energy, the mahat-tattva, I have manifested the false ego, the three modes of material nature, the five material elements, the individual consciousness, the eleven senses and the material body. Similarly, the entire universe has come from the Supreme Personality of Godhead.

PURPORT

The Supreme Lord is described as *mahat-pada*, which means that the total material energy, known as the *mahat-tattva*, is lying at His lotus feet. The origin or the total energy of the cosmic manifestation is the *mahat-tattva*. From the *mahat-tattva* all the other twenty-four divisions have sprung, namely the eleven senses (including the mind), the five sense objects, the five material elements, and then consciousness, intelligence and false ego. The Supreme Personality of Godhead is the cause of the *mahat-tattva*, and therefore, in one sense, because everything is an emanation from the Supreme Lord, there is no difference between the Lord and the cosmic manifestation. But at the same time the cosmic manifestation is different from the Lord. The word *svarāṭ* is very significant here. *Svarāṭ* means "independent." The Supreme Lord is independent, and the individual soul is also independent. Although there is no comparison between the two qualities of independence, the living entity is minutely independent, and the Supreme Lord is fully independent. As the individual soul has a material body made of five elements and the senses, the supreme independent Lord similarly has the gigantic body of the universe. The individual body is temporary; similarly, the entire universe, which is considered to be the body of the Supreme Lord, is also temporary, and both the individual and universal bodies are products of the *mahat-tattva*. One has to understand the differences with intelligence. Everyone knows that his material body has developed from a spiritual spark, and similarly the universal body has developed from the supreme spark, Supersoul. As the individual body develops from the individual soul, the gigantic body of the universe develops from the

Supreme Soul. Just as the individual soul has consciousness, the Supreme Soul is also conscious. But although there is a similarity between the consciousness of the Supreme Soul and the consciousness of the individual soul, the individual soul's consciousness is limited, whereas the consciousness of the Supreme Soul is unlimited. This is described in *Bhagavad-gītā* (13.3). *Kṣetrajñaṁ cāpi māṁ viddhi:* the Supersoul is present in every field of activity, just as the individual soul is present in the individual body. Both of them are conscious. The difference is that the individual soul is conscious of the individual body only, whereas the Supersoul is conscious of the total number of individual bodies.

TEXT 30

एतद्वै श्रद्धया भक्त्या योगाभ्यासेन नित्यशः ।
समाहितात्मा निःसङ्गो विरक्त्या परिपश्यति ॥३०॥

etad vai śraddhayā bhaktyā
yogābhyāsena nityaśaḥ
samāhitātmā niḥsaṅgo
viraktyā paripaśyati

etat—this; *vai*—certainly; *śraddhayā*—with faith; *bhaktyā*—by devotional service; *yoga-abhyāsena*—by practice of *yoga; nityaśaḥ*—always; *samāhita-ātmā*—he whose mind is fixed; *niḥsaṅgaḥ*—aloof from material association; *viraktyā*—by detachment; *paripaśyati*—understands.

TRANSLATION

This perfect knowledge can be achieved by a person who is already engaged in devotional service with faith, steadiness and full detachment, and who is always absorbed in thought of the Supreme. He is aloof from material association.

PURPORT

The atheistic mystic practitioner of *yoga* cannot understand this perfect knowledge. Only persons who engage in the practical activities of devotional service in full Kṛṣṇa consciousness can become absorbed in full *samādhi.* It is possible for them to see and understand the actual fact of the entire cosmic manifestation and its cause. It is clearly stated here that this is not possible to understand for one who has not developed devotional service in full faith. The words *samāhitātmā* and *samādhi* are synonymous.

TEXT 31

इत्येतत्कथितं गुर्वि ज्ञानं तद्ब्रह्मदर्शनम् ।
येनानुबुद्ध्यते तत्त्वं प्रकृतेः पुरुषस्य च ॥३१॥

ity etat kathitaṁ gurvi
jñānaṁ tad brahma-darśanam
yenānubuddhyate tattvaṁ
prakṛteḥ puruṣasya ca

iti—thus; *etat*—this; *kathitam*—described; *gurvi*—O respectful mother; *jñānam*—knowledge; *tat*—that; *brahma*—the Absolute Truth; *darśanam*—revealing; *yena*—by which; *anubuddhyate*—is understood; *tattvam*—the truth; *prakṛteḥ*—of matter; *puruṣasya*—of spirit; *ca*—and.

TRANSLATION

My dear respectful mother, I have already described the path of understanding the Absolute Truth, by which one can come to understand the real truth of matter and spirit and their relationship.

TEXT 32

ज्ञानयोगश्च मन्निष्ठो नैर्गुण्यो भक्तिलक्षणः ।
द्वयोरप्येक एवार्थो भगवच्छब्दलक्षणः ॥३२॥

jñāna-yogaś ca man-niṣṭho
nairguṇyo bhakti-lakṣaṇaḥ
dvayor apy eka evārtho
bhagavac-chabda-lakṣaṇaḥ

jñāna-yogaḥ—philosophical research; *ca*—and; *mat-niṣṭhaḥ*—directed towards Me; *nairguṇyaḥ*—free from the material modes of nature; *bhakti*—devotional service; *lakṣaṇaḥ*—named; *dvayoḥ*—of both; *api*—moreover; *ekaḥ*—one; *eva*—certainly; *arthaḥ*—purpose; *bhagavat*—the Supreme Personality of Godhead; *śabda*—by the word; *lakṣaṇaḥ*—signified.

TRANSLATION

Philosophical research culminates in understanding the Supreme Personality of Godhead. After achieving this understanding, when one becomes free from the material modes of nature, he attains the stage of devotional service. Either by devotional service directly or by philosophical research, one has to find the same destination, which is the Supreme Personality of Godhead.

PURPORT

It is said in *Bhagavad-gītā* that after many, many lives of philosophical research the wise man ultimately comes to the point of knowing that Vāsudeva, the Supreme Personality of Godhead, is everything, and therefore he surrenders unto Him. Such serious students in philosophical research are rare because they are very great souls. If by philosophical research one cannot come to the point of understanding the Supreme Person, then his task is not finished. His search in knowledge is still to be continued until he comes to the point of understanding the Supreme Lord in devotional service.

The opportunity for direct touch with the Personality of Godhead is given in *Bhagavad-gītā*, where it is also said that those who take to other processes, namely the processes of philosophical speculation and mystic *yoga* practice, have much trouble. After many, many years of much trouble, a *yogī* or wise philosopher may come to Him, but his path is very troublesome, whereas the path of devotional service is easy for everyone. One can achieve the result of wise philosophical speculation simply by discharging devotional service, and unless one reaches the point of understanding the Personality of Godhead by his mental speculation, all his research work is said to be simply a labor of love. The ultimate destination of the wise philosopher is to merge in the impersonal Brahman, but that Brahman is the effulgence of the Supreme Person. The

Lord says in *Bhagavad-gītā* (14.27), *brahmaṇo hi pratiṣṭhāham amṛta-syāvyayasya ca:* "I am the basis of the impersonal Brahman, which is indestructible and is the supreme bliss." The Lord is the supreme reservoir of all pleasure, including Brahman pleasure; therefore, one who has unflinching faith in the Supreme Personality of Godhead is said to be already realized in impersonal Brahman and Paramātmā.

TEXT 33

यथेन्द्रियैः पृथग्द्वारैरर्थो बहुगुणाश्रयः ।
एको नानेयते तद्वद्भगवान् शास्त्रवर्त्मभिः ॥३३॥

yathendriyaiḥ pṛthag-dvārair
artho bahu-guṇāśrayaḥ
eko nāneyate tadvad
bhagavān śāstra-vartmabhiḥ

yathā—as; *indriyaiḥ*—by the senses; *pṛthak-dvāraiḥ*—in different ways; *arthaḥ*—an object; *bahu-guṇa*—many qualities; *āśrayaḥ*—endowed with; *ekaḥ*—one; *nānā*—differently; *īyate*—is perceived; *tad-vat*—similarly; *bhagavān*—the Supreme Personality of Godhead; *śāstra-vartmabhiḥ*—according to different scriptural injunctions.

TRANSLATION

A single object is appreciated differently by different senses due to its having different qualities. Similarly, the Supreme Personality of Godhead is one, but according to different scriptural injunctions He appears to be different.

PURPORT

It appears that by following the path of *jñāna-yoga*, or empiric philosophical speculation, one reaches the impersonal Brahman, whereas by executing devotional service in Kṛṣṇa consciousness one enriches his faith in and devotion to the Personality of Godhead. But it is stated here that both *bhakti-yoga* and *jñāna-yoga* are meant for reaching the same destination—the Personality of Godhead. By the process of *jñāna-yoga* the same Personality of Godhead appears to be impersonal. As the same object appears to be different when perceived by different senses, the same Supreme Lord appears to be impersonal by mental speculation. A hill appears cloudy from a distance, and one who does not know may speculate that the hill is a cloud. Actually, it is not a cloud; it is a big hill. One has to learn from authority that the sight of a cloud is not actually a cloud but a hill. If one makes a little more progress, then instead of a cloud he sees the hill and something green. When one actually approaches the hill, he will see many varieties. Another example is in perceiving milk. When we see milk, we see that it is white; when we taste it, it appears that milk is very palatable. When we touch milk, it appears very cold; when we smell milk, it appears to have a very good flavor; and when we hear, we understand that it is called milk. Perceiving milk with different senses, we say that it is something white, something very delicious, something very aromatic, and so on. Actually, it is milk. Similarly, those who are trying to find the Supreme Godhead by mental speculation may approach the bodily effulgence, or the impersonal Brahman, and those who are trying to find the Supreme Godhead by *yoga* practice may find Him as the localized Supersoul, but those who are directly trying to approach the Supreme Truth by practice of *bhakti-yoga* can see Him face to face as the Supreme Person.

Ultimately, the Supreme Person is the destination of all different processes. The fortunate person who, by following the principles of scriptures, becomes completely purified of all material contamination, surrenders unto the Supreme Lord as everything. Just as one can appreciate the real taste of milk with the tongue and not with the eyes, nostrils or ears, one can similarly appreciate the Absolute Truth perfectly and with all relishable pleasure only through one path, devotional service. This is also confirmed in *Bhagavad-gītā. Bhaktyā mām abhijānāti:* if one wants to understand the Absolute Truth in perfection, he must take to devotional service. Of course, no one can understand the Absolute Truth in all perfection. That is not possible for the infinitesimal living entities. But the highest point of understanding by the living entity is reached by discharge of devotional service, not otherwise.

By following various scriptural paths, one may come to the impersonal effulgence of the Supreme Personality of Godhead. The transcendental pleasure derived from merging with or understanding the impersonal brahman is very extensive because Brahman is *ananta. Tad brahma niṣkalaṁ anantam: brahmānanda* is unlimited. But that unlimited pleasure can also be surpassed. That is the nature of the Transcendence. The unlimited can be surpassed also, and that higher platform is Kṛṣṇa. When one deals directly with Kṛṣṇa, the mellow and the humor relished by reciprocation of devotional service is incomparable, even with the pleasure derived from transcendental Brahman. Prabodhānanda Sarasvatī therefore says that *kaivalya*, the Brahman pleasure, is undoubtedly very great and is appreciated by many philosophers, but to a devotee, who has understood how to derive pleasure from exchanging devotional service with the Lord, this unlimited Brahman appears to be hellish. One should try, therefore, to transcend even the Brahman pleasure in order to approach the position of dealing with Kṛṣṇa face to face. As the mind is the center of all the activities of the senses, Kṛṣṇa is called the master of the senses, Hṛṣīkeśa. The process is to fix the mind on Hṛṣīkeśa, or Kṛṣṇa, as Mahārāja Ambarīṣa did (*sa vai manaḥ kṛṣṇa-padāravindayoḥ*). *Bhakti* is the basic principle of all processes. Without *bhakti*, neither *jñāna-yoga* nor *aṣṭāṅga-yoga* can be successful, and unless one approaches Kṛṣṇa, the principles of self-realization have no ultimate destination.

TEXTS 34–36

क्रियया क्रतुभिर्दानैस्तपःस्वाध्यायमर्शनैः ।
आत्मेन्द्रियजयेनापि संन्यासेन च कर्मणाम् ॥३४॥
योगेन विविधाङ्गेन भक्तियोगेन चैव हि ।
धर्मेणोभयचिह्नेन यः प्रवृत्तिनिवृत्तिमान् ॥३५॥
आत्मतत्त्वावबोधेन वैराग्येण दृढेन च ।
ईयते भगवानेभिः सगुणो निर्गुणः स्वदृक् ॥३६॥

kriyayā kratubhir dānais
tapaḥ-svādhyāya-marśanaiḥ
ātmendriya-jayenāpi
sannyāsena ca karmaṇām

yogena vividhāṅgena
bhakti-yogena caiva hi

dharmeṇobhaya-cihnena
yaḥ pravṛtti-nivṛttimān

ātma-tattvāvabodhena
vairāgyeṇa dṛḍhena ca
īyate bhagavān ebhiḥ
saguṇo nirguṇaḥ sva-dṛk

kriyayā—by fruitive activities; *kratubhiḥ*—by sacrificial performances; *dānaiḥ*—by charity; *tapaḥ*—austerities; *svādhyāya*—study of Vedic literature; *marśanaiḥ*—and by philosophical research; *ātma-indriya-jayena*—by controlling the mind and senses; *api*—also; *sannyāsena*—by renunciation; *ca*—and; *karmaṇām*—of fruitive activities; *yogena*—by *yoga* practice; *vividha-aṅgena*—of different divisions; *bhakti-yogena*—by devotional service; *ca*—and; *eva*—certainly; *hi*—indeed; *dharmeṇa*—by prescribed duties; *ubhaya-cihnena*—having both symptoms; *yaḥ*—which; *pravṛtti*—attachment; *nivṛtti-mān*—containing detachment; *ātma-tattva*—the science of self-realization; *avabodhena*—by understanding; *vairāgyeṇa*—by detachment; *dṛḍhena*—strong; *ca*—and; *īyate*—is perceived; *bhagavān*—the Supreme Personality of Godhead; *ebhiḥ*—by these; *sa-guṇaḥ*—in the material world; *nirguṇaḥ*—beyond the material modes; *sva-dṛk*—one who sees his constitutional position.

TRANSLATION

By performing fruitive activities and sacrifices, by distributing charity, by performing austerities, by studying various literatures, by conducting philosophical research, by controlling the mind, by subduing the senses, by accepting the renounced order of life and by performing the prescribed duties of one's social order; by performing the different divisions of yoga practice, by performing devotional service and by exhibiting the process of devotional service containing the symptoms of both attachment and detachment; by understanding the science of self-realization and by developing a strong sense of detachment, one who is expert in understanding the different processes of self-realization realizes the Supreme

Personality of Godhead as He is represented in the material world as well as in transcendence.

PURPORT

As it is stated in the previous verse, one has to follow the principles of the scriptures. There are different prescribed duties for persons in the different social and spiritual orders. Here it is stated that performance of fruitive activities and sacrifices and distribution of charity are activities meant for persons who are in the householder order of society. There are four orders of the social system: *brahmacarya*, *gṛhastha*, *vānaprastha* and *sannyāsa*. For the *gṛhasthas*, or householders, performance of sacrifices, distribution of charity, and action according to prescribed duties are especially recommended. Similarly, austerity, study of Vedic literature, and philosophical research are meant for the *vānaprasthas*, or retired persons. Study of the Vedic literature from the bona fide spiritual master is meant for the *brahmacārī*, or student. *Ātmendriya-jaya*, control of the mind and taming of the senses, is meant for persons in the renounced order of life. All these different activities are prescribed for different persons so that they may be elevated to the platform of self-realization and from there to Kṛṣṇa consciousness, devotional service.

The words *bhakti-yogena caiva hi* mean that whatever is to be performed, as described in verse 34, whether *yoga* or sacrifice or fruitive activity or study of Vedic literature or philosophical research or acceptance of the renounced order of life, is to be executed in *bhakti-yoga*. The words *caiva hi*, according to Sanskrit grammar, indicate that one must perform all these activities mixed with devotional service, otherwise such activities will not produce any fruit. Any prescribed activity must be performed for the sake of the Supreme Personality of Godhead. It is confirmed in *Bhagavad-gītā* (9.27), *yat karoṣi yad aśnāsi:* "Whatever you do, whatever you eat, whatever you sacrifice, whatever austerities you undergo and whatever charities you give, the result should be given to the Supreme Lord." The word *eva* is added, indicating that one *must* execute activities in such a way. Unless one adds devotional service to all activities, he cannot achieve the desired result, but when *bhakti-yoga* is prominent in every activity, then the ultimate goal is sure.

One has to approach the Supreme Personality of Godhead, Kṛṣṇa, as it is stated in *Bhagavad-gītā:* "After many, many births, one approaches the Supreme Person, Kṛṣṇa, and surrenders unto Him, knowing that He is everything." Also in *Bhagavad-gītā*, the Lord says, *bhoktāraṁ yajña-tapasām:* "For anyone who is undergoing rigid austerity or for anyone performing different kinds of sacrifices, the beneficiary is the Supreme Personality of Godhead." He is the proprietor of all planets, and He is the friend of every living soul.

The words *dharmeṇobhaya-cihnena* mean that the *bhakti-yoga* process contains two symptoms, namely attachment for the Supreme Lord and detachment from all material affinities. There are two symptoms of advancement in the process of devotional service, just as there are two processes taking place while eating. A hungry man feels strength and satisfaction from eating, and at the same time he gradually becomes detached from eating any more. Similarly, with the execution of devotional service, real knowledge develops, and one becomes detached from all material activities. In no other activity but devotional service is there such detachment from matter and attachment for the Supreme. There are nine different processes to increase this attachment to the Supreme Lord: hearing, chanting, remembering, worshiping, serving the Lord, making friendship, praying, offering everything and serving the lotus feet of the Lord. The processes for increasing detachment from material affinities are explained in verse 36.

One can achieve elevation to the higher planetary systems like the heavenly kingdom by executing one's prescribed duties and by performing sacrifices. When one is transcendental to such desires because of accepting the renounced order of life, he can understand the Brahman feature of the Supreme, and when one is able to see his real constitutional position, he sees all other processes and becomes situated in the stage of pure devotional service. At that time he can understand the Supreme Personality of Godhead, Bhagavān.

Understanding of the Supreme Person is called *ātma-tattva-avabodhena*, which means "understanding of one's real constitutional position." If one actually understands one's constitutional position as an eternal servitor of the Supreme Lord, he becomes detached from the service of the material world. Everyone engages in some sort of service. If one does not know one's constitutional position, one engages in the service of his personal gross body or his family, society or country. But as soon as one is able to see his constitutional position (the word *sva-dṛk* means "one who is able to see"), he becomes detached from such material service and engages himself in devotional service.

As long as one is in the modes of material nature and is performing the duties prescribed in the scriptures, he can be elevated to higher planetary systems, where the predominating deities are material representations of the Supreme Personality of Godhead, like the sun-god, the moon-god, the air-god, Brahmā and Lord Śiva. All the different demigods are material representations of the Supreme Lord. By material activities one can approach only such demigods, as stated in *Bhagavad-gītā* (9.25). *Yānti deva-vratā devān:* those who are attached to the demigods and who perform the prescribed duties can approach the abodes of the demigods. In this way, one can go to the planet of the Pitās, or forefathers. Similarly, one who fully understands the real position of his life adopts devotional service and realizes the Supreme Personality of Godhead.

TEXT 37

प्रावोचं भक्तियोगस्य स्वरूपं ते चतुर्विधम् ।
कालस्य चाव्यक्तगतेर्योऽन्तर्धावति जन्तुषु ॥३७॥

prāvocaṁ bhakti-yogasya
svarūpaṁ te catur-vidham
kālasya cāvyakta-gater
yo 'ntardhāvati jantuṣu

prāvocam—explained; *bhakti-yogasya*—of devotional service; *svarūpam*—the identity; *te*—to you; *catuḥ-vidham*—in four divisions; *kālasya*—of time; *ca*—also; *avyakta-gateḥ*—the movement of which is imperceptible; *yaḥ*—which; *antardhāvati*—chases; *jantuṣu*—the living entities.

TRANSLATION

My dear mother, I have explained to you the process of devotional service and its identity in four different social divisions. I have explained to you as well how eternal time is chasing the living entities, although it is imperceptible to them.

PURPORT

The process of *bhakti-yoga*, devotional service, is the main river flowing down towards the sea of the Absolute Truth, and all other processes mentioned are just like tributaries. Lord Kapila is summarizing the importance of the process of devotional service. *Bhakti-yoga*, as described before, is divided into four divisions, three in the material modes of nature and one in transcendence, which is untinged by the modes of material nature. Devotional service mixed with the modes of material nature is a means for material existence, whereas devotional service without desires for fruitive result and without attempts for empirical philosophical research is pure, transcendental devotional service.

TEXT 38

जीवस्य संसृतीर्बह्वीरविद्याकर्मनिर्मिताः ।
यास्वङ्ग प्रविशन्नात्मा न वेद गतिमात्मनः ॥३८॥

jīvasya saṁsṛtīr bahvīr
avidyā-karma-nirmitāḥ
yāsv aṅga praviśann ātmā
na veda gatim ātmanaḥ

jīvasya—of the living entity; *saṁsṛtīḥ*—courses of material existence; *bahvīḥ*—many; *avidyā*—in ignorance; *karma*—by work; *nirmitāḥ*—produced; *yāsu*—into which; *aṅga*—My dear mother; *praviśan*—entering; *ātmā*—the living entity; *na*—not; *veda*—understands; *gatim*—the movement; *ātmanaḥ*—of himself.

TRANSLATION

There are varieties of material existence for the living entity according to the work he performs in ignorance or forgetfulness of his real identity. My dear mother, if anyone enters into that forgetfulness, he is unable to understand where his movements will end.

PURPORT

Once one enters into the continuation of material existence, it is very difficult to get out. Therefore the Supreme Personality of Godhead comes

Himself or sends His bona fide representative, and He leaves behind scriptures like *Bhagavad-gītā* and *Śrīmad-Bhāgavatam,* so that the living entities hovering in the darkness of nescience may take advantage of the instructions, the saintly persons and the spiritual masters and thus be freed. Unless the living entity receives the mercy of the saintly persons, the spiritual master or Kṛṣṇa, it is not possible for him to get out of the darkness of material existence; by his own endeavor it is not possible.

TEXT 39

नैतत्खलायोपदिशेन्नाविनीताय कर्हिचित् ।
न स्तब्धाय न भिन्नाय नैव धर्मध्वजाय च ॥३९॥

naitat khalāyopadiśen
nāvinītāya karhicit
na stabdhāya na bhinnāya
naiva dharma-dhvajāya ca

na—not; *etat*—this instruction; *khalāya*—to the envious; *upadiśet*—one should teach; *na*—not; *avinītāya*—to the agnostic; *karhicit*—ever; *na*—not; *stabdhāya*—to the proud; *na*—not; *bhinnāya*—to the misbehaved; *na*—not; *eva*—certainly; *dharma-dhvajāya*—to the hypocrites; *ca*—also.

TRANSLATION

Lord Kapila continued: This instruction is not meant for the envious, for the agnostics or for persons who are unclean in their behavior. Nor is it for hypocrites or for persons who are proud of material possessions.

TEXT 40

न लोलुपायोपदिशेन्न गृहारूढचेतसे ।
नाभक्ताय च मे जातु न मद्भक्तद्विषामपि ॥४०॥

na lolupāyopadiśen
na gṛhārūḍha-cetase

nābhaktāya ca me jātu
na mad-bhakta-dviṣām api

na—not; *lolupāya*—to the greedy; *upadiśet*—one should instruct; *na*—not; *gṛha-ārūḍha-cetase*—to one who is too attached to family life; *na*—not; *abhaktāya*—to the nondevotee; *ca*—and; *me*—of Me; *jātu*—ever; *na*—not; *mat*—My; *bhakta*—devotees; *dviṣām*—to those who are envious of; *api*—also.

TRANSLATION

It is not to be instructed to persons who are too greedy and too attached to family life, nor to persons who are nondevotees and who are envious of the devotees and of the Personality of Godhead.

PURPORT

Persons who are always planning to do harm to other living entities are not eligible to understand Kṛṣṇa consciousness and cannot enter into the realm of transcendental loving service to the Lord. Also, there are so-called disciples who become submissive to a spiritual master most artificially, with an ulterior motive. They also cannot understand what Kṛṣṇa consciousness or devotional service is. Persons who, due to being initiated by another sect of religious faith, do not find devotional service as the common platform for approaching the Supreme Personality of Godhead, also cannot understand Kṛṣṇa consciousness. We have experience that some students come to join us, but because of being biased in some particular type of faith, they leave our camp and become lost in the wilderness. Actually, Kṛṣṇa consciousness is not a sectarian religious faith; it is a teaching process for understanding the Supreme Lord and our relationship with Him. Anyone can join this movement without prejudice, but unfortunately there are persons who feel differently. It is better, therefore, not to instruct the science of Kṛṣṇa consciousness to such persons.

Generally, materialistic persons are after some name, fame and material gain, so if someone takes to Kṛṣṇa consciousness for these reasons, he will never be able to understand this philosophy. Such persons take to religious principles as a social decoration. They admit themselves into some cultural institution for the sake of name only, especially in this age. Such persons also cannot understand the philosophy of Kṛṣṇa consciousness. Even if one is not greedy for material possessions but is too attached to family life, he also cannot understand Kṛṣṇa consciousness. Superficially, such persons are not very greedy for material possessions, but they are too attached to wife, children and family improvement. When a person is not contaminated by the above-mentioned faults yet at the ultimate issue is not interested in the service of the Supreme Personality of Godhead, or if he is a nondevotee, he also cannot understand the philosophy of Kṛṣṇa consciousness.

TEXT 41

श्रद्दधानाय भक्ताय विनीतायानसूयवे ।
भूतेषु कृतमैत्राय शुश्रूषाभिरताय च ॥४१॥

śraddadhānāya bhaktāya
vinītāyānasūyave
bhūteṣu kṛta-maitrāya
śuśrūṣābhiratāya ca

śraddadhānāya—faithful; *bhaktāya*—to the devotee; *vinītāya*—respectful; *anasūyave*—nonenvious; *bhūteṣu*—to all living entities; *kṛta-maitrāya*—friendly; *śuśrūṣā*—faithful service; *abhiratāya*—eager to render; *ca*—and.

TRANSLATION

Instruction should be given to the faithful devotee who is respectful to the spiritual master, nonenvious, friendly to all kinds of living entities and eager to render service with faith and sincerity.

TEXT 42

बहिर्जातविरागाय शान्तचित्ताय दीयताम् ।
निर्मत्सराय शुचये यस्याहं प्रेयसां प्रियः ॥४२॥

bahir-jāta-virāgāya
śānta-cittāya dīyatām

nirmatsarāya śucaye
yasyāhaṁ preyasāṁ priyaḥ

bahiḥ—for what is outside; *jāta-virāgāya*—to him who has developed detachment; *śānta-cittāya*—whose mind is peaceful; *dīyatām*—let this be instructed; *nirmatsarāya*—nonenvious; *śucaye*—perfectly cleansed; *yasya*—of whom; *aham*—I; *preyasām*—of all that is very dear; *priyaḥ*—the most dear.

TRANSLATION

This instruction should be imparted by the spiritual master to persons who have taken the Supreme Personality of Godhead to be more dear than anything, who are not envious of anyone, who are perfectly cleansed and who have developed detachment for that which is outside the purview of Kṛṣṇa consciousness.

PURPORT

In the beginning, no one can be elevated to the highest stage of devotional service. Here *bhakta* means one who does not hesitate to accept the reformatory processes for becoming a *bhakta.* In order to become a devotee of the Lord, one has to accept a spiritual master and inquire from him about how to progress in devotional service. To serve a devotee, to chant the holy name according to a certain counting method, to worship the Deity, to hear *Śrīmad-Bhāgavatam* or *Bhagavad-gītā* from a realized person and to live in a sacred place where devotional service is not disturbed are the first out of sixty-four devotional activities for making progress in devotional service. One who has accepted these five chief activities is called a devotee.

One must be prepared to offer the necessary respect and honor to the spiritual master. He should not be unnecessarily envious of his Godbrothers. Rather, if a Godbrother is more enlightened and advanced in Kṛṣṇa consciousness, one should accept him as almost equal to the spiritual master, and one should be happy to see such Godbrothers advance in Kṛṣṇa consciousness. A devotee should always be very kind to the general public in instructing Kṛṣṇa consciousness because that is the only solution for getting out of the clutches of *māyā.* That is really humanitarian work, for it is the way to show mercy to other people who need it very badly. The word *śuśrūṣābhiratāya* indicates a person who faithfully engages in serving the spiritual master. One should give personal service and all kinds of comforts to the spiritual master. A devotee who does so is also a bona fide candidate for taking this instruction. The word *bahir-jāta-virāgāya* means a person who has developed detachment from external and internal material propensities. Not only is he detached from activities which are not connected to Kṛṣṇa consciousness, but he should be internally averse to the material way of life. Such a person must be nonenvious and should think of the welfare of all living entities, not only of the human beings, but living entities other than human beings. The word *śucaye* means one who is cleansed both externally and internally. To become actually cleansed externally and internally, one should chant the holy name of the Lord, Hare Kṛṣṇa, or Viṣṇu, constantly.

The word *dīyatām* means that knowledge of Kṛṣṇa consciousness should be offered by the spiritual master. The spiritual master must not accept a disciple who is not qualified; he should not be professional and should not accept disciples for monetary gains. The bona fide spiritual master must see the bona fide qualities of a person whom he is going to initiate. An unworthy person should not be initiated. The spiritual master should train his disciple in such a way so that in the future only the Supreme Personality of Godhead will be the dearmost goal of his life.

In these two verses the qualities of a devotee are fully explained. One who has actually developed all the qualities listed in these verses is already elevated to the post of a devotee. If one has not developed all these qualities, he still has to fulfill these conditions in order to become a perfect devotee.

TEXT 43

य इदं शृणुयादम्ब श्रद्धया पुरुषः सकृत् ।
यो वाभिधत्ते मच्चित्तः स ह्येति पदवीं च मे ॥४३॥

ya idaṁ śṛṇuyād amba
śraddhayā puruṣaḥ sakṛt
yo vābhidhatte mac-cittaḥ
sa hy eti padavīṁ ca me

yaḥ—he who; *idam*—this; *śṛṇuyāt*—may hear; *amba*—O mother; *śraddhayā*—with faith; *puruṣaḥ*—a person; *sakṛt*—once; *yaḥ*—he who; *vā*—or; *abhidhatte*—repeats; *mat-cittaḥ*—his mind fixed on Me; *saḥ*—he; *hi*—certainly; *eti*—attains; *padavīm*—abode; *ca*—and; *me*—My.

TRANSLATION

Anyone who once meditates upon Me with faith and affection, who hears and chants about Me, surely goes back home, back to Godhead.

Thus end the Bhaktivedanta purports of the Third Canto, Thirty-second Chapter, of the Śrīmad-Bhāgavatam, *entitled "Entanglement in Fruitive Activities."*

CHAPTER THIRTY-THREE

Activities of Kapila

TEXT 1

मैत्रेय उवाच
एवं निशम्य कपिलस्य वचो जनित्री
सा कर्दमस्य दयिता किल देवहूतिः ।
विस्रस्तमोहपटला तमभिप्रणम्य
तुष्टाव तत्त्वविषयाङ्कितसिद्धिभूमिम् ॥ १ ॥

maitreya uvāca
evaṁ niśamya kapilasya vaco janitrī
sā kardamasya dayitā kila devahūtiḥ
visrasta-moha-paṭalā tam abhipraṇamya
tuṣṭāva tattva-viṣayāṅkita-siddhi-bhūmim

maitreyaḥ uvāca—Maitreya said; *evam*—thus; *niśamya*—having heard; *kapilasya*—of Lord Kapila; *vacaḥ*—the words; *janitrī*—the mother; *sā*—she; *kardamasya*—of Kardama Muni; *dayitā*—the dear wife; *kila*—namely; *devahūtiḥ*—Devahūti; *visrasta*—freed from; *moha-paṭalā*—the covering of illusion; *tam*—unto Him; *abhipraṇamya*—having offered obeisances; *tuṣṭāva*—recited prayers; *tattva*—basic principles; *viṣaya*—in the matter of; *aṅkita*—the author; *siddhi*—of liberation; *bhūmim*—the background.

TRANSLATION

Śrī Maitreya said: Thus Devahūti, the mother of Lord Kapila and wife of Kardama Muni, became freed from all ignorance concerning devotional service and transcendental knowledge. She offered her obeisances unto the Lord, the author of the basic principles of

the Sāṅkhya system of philosophy, which is the background of liberation, and she satisfied Him with the following verses of prayer.

PURPORT

The system of philosophy enunciated by Lord Kapila before His mother is the background for situation on the spiritual platform. The specific significance of this system of philosophy is stated herein as *siddhi-bhūmim*—it is the background of salvation. People who are suffering in this material world because they are conditioned by the material energy can easily get freedom from the clutches of matter by understanding the Sāṅkhya philosophy enunciated by Lord Kapila. By this system of philosophy, one can immediately become free, even though one is situated in this material world. That stage is called *jīvan-mukti.* This means that one is liberated even though one stays with his material body. That happened for Devahūti, the mother of Lord Kapila, and she therefore satisfied the Lord by offering her prayers. Anyone who understands the basic principle of Sāṅkhya philosophy is elevated in devotional service and becomes fully Kṛṣṇa conscious, or liberated, even within this material world.

TEXT 2

देवहूतिरुवाच
अथाप्यजोऽन्तःसलिले शयानं
भूतेन्द्रियार्थात्ममयं वपुस्ते ।
गुणप्रवाहं सदशेषबीजं
दध्यौ स्वयं यज्जठराब्जजातः ॥ २ ॥

devahūtir uvāca
athāpy ajo 'ntaḥ-salile śayānaṁ
bhūtendriyārthātma-mayaṁ vapus te
guṇa-pravāhaṁ sad-aśeṣa-bījaṁ
dadhyau svayaṁ yaj-jaṭharābja-jātaḥ

devahūtiḥ uvāca—Devahūti said; *atha api*—moreover; *ajaḥ*—Lord Brahmā; *antaḥ-salile*—in the water; *śayānam*—lying; *bhūta*—the material elements; *indriya*—the senses; *artha*—the sense objects; *ātma*—the mind; *mayam*—pervaded by; *vapuḥ*—body; *te*—Your; *guṇa-pravāham*—the source of the stream of the three modes of material nature; *sat*—manifest; *aśeṣa*—of all; *bījam*—the seed; *dadhyau*—meditated upon; *svayam*—himself; *yat*—of whom; *jaṭhara*—from the abdomen; *abja*—from the lotus flower; *jātaḥ*—born.

TRANSLATION

Devahūti said: Brahmā is said to be unborn because he takes birth from the lotus flower which grows from Your abdomen while You lie in the ocean at the bottom of the universe. But even Brahmā simply meditated upon You, whose body is the source of unlimited universes.

PURPORT

Brahmā is also named Aja, "he who is unborn." Whenever we think of someone's birth, there must be a material father and mother, for thus one is born. But Brahmā, being the first living creature within this universe, was born directly from the body of the Supreme Personality of Godhead who is known as Garbhodakaśāyī Viṣṇu, the Viṣṇu form lying down in the ocean at the bottom of the universe. Devahūti wanted to impress upon the Lord that when Brahmā wants to see Him, he has to meditate upon Him. "You are the seed of all creation," she said. "Although Brahmā was directly born from You, he still has to perform many years of meditation, and even then he cannot see You directly, face to face. Your body is lying within the vast water at the bottom of the universe, and thus You are known as Garbhodakaśāyī Viṣṇu."

The nature of the Lord's gigantic body is also explained in this verse. That body is transcendental, untouched by matter. Since the material manifestation has come from His body, His body therefore existed before the material creation. The conclusion is that the transcendental body of Viṣṇu is not made of material elements. The body of Viṣṇu is the source of all other living entities, as well as the material nature, which is also supposed to be the energy of that Supreme Personality of Godhead. Devahūti said, "You are the background of the material manifestation and all created energy; therefore Your delivering me from the clutches of *māyā* by explaining the system of Sāṅkhya philosophy is not so astonishing. But Your being born from my abdomen is certainly wonderful because although You are the source of all creation, You have so kindly taken birth as my child. That is most wonderful. Your body is the source of all the universe, and still You put Your body within the abdomen of a common woman like me. To me, that is most astonishing."

TEXT 3

स एव विश्वस्य भवान् विधत्ते
गुणप्रवाहेण विभक्तवीर्यः ।
सर्गाद्यनीहोऽवितथाभिसन्धि-
रात्मेश्वरोऽतर्क्यसहस्रशक्तिः ॥ ३ ॥

sa eva viśvasya bhavān vidhatte
guṇa-pravāheṇa vibhakta-vīryaḥ
sargādy anīho 'vitathābhisandhir
ātmeśvaro 'tarkya-sahasra-śaktiḥ

saḥ—that very person; *eva*—certainly; *viśvasya*—of the universe; *bhavān*—You; *vidhatte*—carry on; *guṇa-pravāheṇa*—by the interaction of the modes; *vibhakta*—divided; *vīryaḥ*—Your energies; *sarga-ādi*—the creation and so on; *anīhaḥ*—the nondoer; *avitatha*—not futile; *abhisandhiḥ*—Your determination; *ātma-īśvaraḥ*—the Lord of all living entities; *atarkya*—inconceivable; *sahasra*—thousands; *śaktiḥ*—possessing energies.

TRANSLATION

My dear Lord, although personally You have nothing to do, You have distributed Your energies in the interactions of the material modes of nature, and for that reason the creation, maintenance and dissolution of the cosmic manifestation take place. My dear Lord, You are self-determined and are the Supreme Personality of Godhead for all living entities. For them You created this material

manifestation, and although You are one, Your diverse energies can act multifariously. This is inconceivable to us.

PURPORT

The statement made in this verse by Devahūti that the Absolute Truth has many diverse energies although He personally has nothing to do is confirmed in the *Upaniṣads.* There is no one greater than Him or on an equal level with Him, and everything is completely done by His energy, as if by nature. It is understood herein, therefore, that although the modes of material nature are entrusted to different manifestations like Brahmā, Viṣṇu and Śiva, each of whom is particularly invested with different kinds of power, the Supreme Lord is completely aloof from such activities. Devahūti is saying, "Although You personally are not doing anything, Your determination is absolute. There is no question of Your fulfilling Your will with the help of anyone else besides Yourself. You are, in the end, the Supreme Soul and the supreme controller. Your will, therefore, cannot be checked by anyone else." The Supreme Lord can check others' plans. As it is said, "Man proposes and God disposes." But when the Supreme Personality of Godhead proposes, that desire is under no one else's control. He is absolute. We are ultimately dependent on Him to fulfill our desires, but we cannot say that God's desires are also dependent. That is His inconceivable power. That which may be inconceivable for ordinary living entities is easily done by Him. And in spite of His being unlimited, He has subjected Himself to being known from the authoritative scriptures like the Vedic literatures. As it is said, *śabda-mūlatvāt:* He can be known through the *śabda-brahma*, or Vedic literature.

Why is the creation made? Since the Lord is the Supreme Personality of Godhead for all living entities, He created this material manifestation for those living entities who want to enjoy or lord it over material nature. As the Supreme Godhead, He arranges to fulfill their various desires. It is confirmed also in the *Vedas*, *eko bahūnāṁ yo vidadhāti kāmān:* the supreme one supplies the necessities of the many living entities. There is no limit to the demands of the different kinds of living entities, and the supreme one, the Supreme Personality of Godhead, alone maintains them and supplies them by His inconceivable energy.

TEXT 4

स त्वं भृतो मे जठरेण नाथ
कथं नु यस्योदर एतदासीत् ।
विश्वं युगान्ते वटपत्र एकः
शेते स्म मायाशिशुरङ्घ्रिपानः ॥ ४ ॥

sa tvaṁ bhṛto me jaṭhareṇa nātha
kathaṁ nu yasyodara etad āsīt
viśvaṁ yugānte vaṭa-patra ekaḥ
śete sma māyā-śiśur aṅghri-pānaḥ

saḥ—that very person; *tvam*—You; *bhṛtaḥ*—took birth; *me jaṭhareṇa*—by my abdomen; *nātha*—O my Lord; *katham*—how; *nu*—then; *yasya*—of whom; *udare*—in the belly; *etat*—this; *āsīt*—did rest; *viśvam*—universe; *yuga-ante*—at the end of the millennium; *vaṭa-patre*—on the leaf of a banyan tree; *ekaḥ*—alone; *śete sma*—You lay down; *māyā*—possessing inconceivable powers; *śiśuḥ*—a baby; *aṅghri*—Your toe; *pānaḥ*—licking.

TRANSLATION

As the Supreme Personality of Godhead, You have taken birth from my abdomen. O my Lord, how is that possible for the supreme one, who has in His belly all the cosmic manifestation? The answer is that it is possible, for at the end of the millennium You lie down on a leaf of a banyan tree, and just like a small baby, You lick the toe of Your lotus foot.

PURPORT

At the time of dissolution the Lord sometimes appears as a small baby lying on a leaf of a banyan tree, floating on the devastating water. Therefore Devahūti suggests, "Your lying down within the abdomen of a common woman like me is not so astonishing. You can lie down on the leaf of a banyan tree and float on the water of devastation as a small baby. It is not very wonderful, therefore, that You can lie down in the abdomen of my body. You teach us that those who are very fond of children within this material world and who therefore enter into marriage to enjoy family life with children can also have the Supreme Personality of Godhead as their child, and the most wonderful thing is that the Lord Himself licks His toe."

Since all the great sages and devotees apply all energy and all activities in the service of the lotus feet of the Lord, there must be some transcendental pleasure in the toes of His lotus feet. The Lord licks His toe to taste the nectar for which the devotees always aspire. Sometimes the Supreme Personality of Godhead Himself wonders how much transcendental pleasure is within Himself, and in order to taste His own potency, He sometimes takes the position of tasting Himself. Lord Caitanya is Kṛṣṇa Himself, but He appears as a devotee to taste the sweetness of the transcendental mellow in Himself which is tasted by Śrīmatī Rādhārāṇī, the greatest of all devotees.

TEXT 5

त्वं देहतन्त्रः प्रशमाय पाप्मनां
निदेशभाजां च विभो विभूतये ।
यथावतारास्तव सूकरादय-
स्तथायमप्यात्मपथोपलब्धये ॥ ५ ॥

tvaṁ deha-tantraḥ praśamāya pāpmanāṁ
nideśa-bhājāṁ ca vibho vibhūtaye
yathāvatārās tava sūkarādayas
tathāyam apy ātma-pathopalabdhaye

tvam—You; *deha*—this body; *tantraḥ*—have assumed; *praśamāya*—for the diminution; *pāpmanām*—of sinful activities; *nideśa-bhājām*—of instructions in devotion; *ca*—and; *vibho*—O my Lord; *vibhūtaye*—for the expansion; *yathā*—as; *avatārāḥ*—incarnations; *tava*—Your; *sūkara-ādayaḥ*—the boar and other forms; *tathā*—so; *ayam*—this incarnation of Kapila; *api*—surely; *ātma-patha*—the path of self-realization; *upalabdhaye*—in order to reveal.

TRANSLATION

My dear Lord, You have assumed this body in order to diminish the sinful activities of the fallen and to enrich their knowledge in devotion and liberation. Since these sinful people are dependent on Your direction, by Your own will You assume incarnations as a boar and as other forms. Similarly, You have appeared in order to distribute transcendental knowledge to Your dependents.

PURPORT

In the previous verses, the general transcendental qualifications of the Supreme Personality of Godhead were described. Now the specific purpose of the Lord's appearance is also described. By His different energies He bestows different kinds of bodies upon the living entities, who are conditioned by their propensity to lord it over material nature, but in course of time these living entities become so degraded that they need enlightenment. It is stated in *Bhagavad-gītā* that whenever there are discrepancies in the discharge of the real purpose of this material existence, the Lord appears as an incarnation. The Lord's form as Kapila directs the fallen souls and enriches them with knowledge and devotion so that they may go back to Godhead. There are many incarnations of the Supreme Personality of Godhead, like those of the boar, the fish, the tortoise and the half-man half-lion. Lord Kapiladeva is also one of the incarnations of Godhead. It is accepted herein that Lord Kapiladeva appeared on the surface of the earth to give transcendental knowledge to the misguided conditioned souls.

TEXT 6

यन्नामधेयश्रवणानुकीर्तनाद्
यत्प्रह्वणाद्यत्स्मरणादपि क्वचित् ।
श्वादोऽपि सद्यः सवनाय कल्पते
कुतः पुनस्ते भगवन्नु दर्शनात् ॥ ६ ॥

yan-nāmadheya-śravaṇānukīrtanād
yat-prahvaṇād yat-smaraṇād api kvacit

śvādo 'pi sadyaḥ savanāya kalpate
kutaḥ punas te bhagavan nu darśanāt

yat—of whom (the Supreme Personality of Godhead); *nāmadheya*—the name; *śravaṇa*—hearing; *anukīrtanāt*—by chanting; *yat*—to whom; *prahvaṇāt*—by offering obeisances; *yat*—whom; *smaraṇāt*—by remembering; *api*—even; *kvacit*—at any time; *śva-adaḥ*—a dog-eater; *api*—even; *sadyaḥ*—immediately; *savanāya*—for performing Vedic sacrifices; *kalpate*—becomes eligible; *kutaḥ*—what to speak of; *punaḥ*—again; *te*—You; *bhagavan*—O Supreme Personality of Godhead; *nu*—then; *darśanāt*—by seeing face to face.

TRANSLATION

To say nothing of the spiritual advancement of persons who see the Supreme Person face to face, even a person born in a family of dog-eaters immediately becomes eligible to perform Vedic sacrifices if he once utters the holy name of the Supreme Personality of Godhead or chants about Him, hears about His pastimes, offers Him obeisances or even remembers Him.

PURPORT

Herein the spiritual potency of chanting, hearing or remembering the holy name of the Supreme Lord is greatly stressed. Rūpa Gosvāmī has discussed the sequence of sinful activities of the conditioned soul, and he has established, in *Bhakti-rasāmṛta-sindhu*, that those who engage in devotional service become freed from the reactions of all sinful activities. This is also confirmed in *Bhagavad-gītā*. The Lord says that He takes charge of one who surrenders unto Him, and He makes him immune to all reactions to sinful activities. If by chanting the holy name of the Supreme Personality of Godhead one becomes so swiftly cleared of all reactions to sinful activities, then what is to be said of those persons who see Him face to face?

Another consideration here is that persons who are purified by the process of chanting and hearing become immediately eligible to perform Vedic sacrifices. Generally, only a person who is born in a family of *brāhmaṇas*, who has been reformed by the ten kinds of purificatory processes and who is learned in Vedic literature is allowed to perform the Vedic sacrifices. But here the word *sadyaḥ*, "immediately," is used, and Śrīdhara Svāmī also remarks that one can *immediately* become eligible to perform Vedic sacrifices. A person born in a family of the low caste which is accustomed to eat dogs is so positioned due to his past sinful activities, but by chanting or hearing once in pureness, or in an offenseless manner, he is immediately relieved of the sinful reaction. Not only is he relieved of the sinful reaction, but he immediately achieves the result of all purificatory processes. Taking birth in the family of a *brāhmaṇa* is certainly due to pious activities in one's past life. But still a child who is born in a family of a *brāhmaṇa* depends for his further reformation upon initiation into acceptance of a sacred thread and many other reformatory processes. But a person who chants the holy name of the Lord, even if born in a family of *caṇḍālas*, dog-eaters, does not need reformation. Simply by chanting Hare Kṛṣṇa, he immediately becomes purified and becomes as good as the most learned *brāhmaṇa.*

Śrīdhara Svāmī especially remarks in this connection, *anena pūjyatvaṁ lakṣyate.* Some caste *brāhmaṇas* remark that by chanting Hare Kṛṣṇa, purification *begins.* Of course, that depends on the individual process of chanting, but this remark of Śrīdhara Svāmī's is completely applicable if one chants the holy name of the Lord without offense, for he immediately becomes more than a *brāhmaṇa.* As Śrīdhara Svāmī says, *pūjyatvam:* he immediately becomes as respectable as a most learned *brāhmaṇa* and can be allowed to perform Vedic sacrifices. If simply by chanting the holy name of the Lord one becomes sanctified instantly, then what can be said of those persons who see the Supreme Lord face to face and who understand the descent of the Lord, as Devahūti understands Kapiladeva.

Usually, initiation depends on the bona fide spiritual master, who directs the disciple. If he sees that a disciple has become competent and purified by the process of chanting, he offers the sacred thread to the disciple just so that he will be recognized as one-hundred-percent equal with a *brāhmaṇa.* This is also confirmed in the *Hari-bhakti-vilāsa* by Śrī Sanātana Gosvāmī: "As a base metal like bell metal can be changed into gold by a chemical process, any person can similarly be changed into a *brāhmaṇa* by *dīkṣā-vidhāna*, the initiation process."

It is sometimes remarked that by the chanting process one begins to purify himself and can take birth in his next life in a *brāhmaṇa* family and then be reformed. But at this present moment, even those who are born in the best *brāhmaṇa* families are not reformed, nor is there any certainty that they are actually born of *brāhmaṇa* fathers. Formerly the *garbhādhāna* reformatory system was prevalent, but at the present moment there is no such *garbhādhāna*, or seed-giving ceremony. Under these circumstances, no one knows if a man is factually born of a *brāhmaṇa* father. Whether one has acquired the qualification of a *brāhmaṇa* depends on the judgment of the bona fide spiritual master. He bestows upon the disciple the position of a *brāhmaṇa* by his own judgment. When one is accepted as a *brāhmaṇa* in the sacred thread ceremony, under the *pāñcarātrika* system, then he is *dvija*, twice-born. That is confirmed by Sanātana Gosvāmī: *dvijatvaṁ jāyate*. By the process of initation by the spiritual master, a person is accepted as a *brāhmaṇa* in his purified state of chanting the holy name of the Lord. He then makes further progress to become a qualified Vaiṣṇava, which means that the brahminical qualification is already acquired.

TEXT 7

अहो बत श्वपचोऽतो गरीयान्
यज्जिह्वाग्रे वर्तते नाम तुभ्यम् ।
तेपुस्तपस्ते जुहुवुः सस्नुरार्या
ब्रह्मानूचुर्नाम गृणन्ति ये ते ॥ ७ ॥

aho bata śva-paco 'to garīyān
yaj-jihvāgre vartate nāma tubhyam
tepus tapas te juhuvuḥ sasnur āryā
brahmānūcur nāma gṛṇanti ye te

aho bata—oh, how glorious; *śva-pacaḥ*—a dog-eater; *ataḥ*—hence; *garīyān*—worshipable; *yat*—of whom; *jihvā-agre*—on the tip of the tongue; *vartate*—is; *nāma*—the holy name; *tubhyam*—unto You; *tepuḥ tapaḥ*—practiced austerities; *te*—they; *juhuvuḥ*—executed fire sacrifices; *sasnuḥ*—took bath in the sacred rivers; *āryāḥ*—Āryans;

brahma anūcuḥ—studied the *Vedas; nāma*—the holy name; *gṛṇanti*—accept; *ye*—they who; *te*—Your.

TRANSLATION

Oh, how glorious are they whose tongues are chanting Your holy name! Even if born in the families of dog-eaters, such persons are worshipable. Persons who chant the holy name of Your Lordship must have executed all kinds of austerities and fire sacrifices and achieved all the good manners of the Āryans. To be chanting the holy name of Your Lordship, they must have bathed at holy places of pilgrimage, studied the Vedas and fulfilled everything required.

PURPORT

As it is stated in the previous verse, a person who has once offenselessly chanted the holy name of God becomes immediately eligible to perform Vedic sacrifices. One should not be astonished by this statement of *Śrīmad-Bhāgavatam.* One should not disbelieve or think, "How by chanting the holy name of the Lord can one become a holy man to be compared to the most elevated *brāhmaṇa?*" To eradicate such doubts in the minds of unbelievers, this verse affirms that the stage of chanting of the holy name of the Lord is not sudden, but that the chanters have already performed all kinds of Vedic rituals and sacrifices. It is not very astounding, for no one in this life can chant the holy name of the Lord unless he has passed all lower stages, such as performing the Vedic ritualistic sacrifices, studying the *Vedas* and practicing good behavior like that of the Āryans. All this must first have been done. Just as a student in a law class is to be understood to have already graduated from general education, anyone who is engaged in the chanting of the holy name of the Lord—Hare Kṛṣṇa, Hare Kṛṣṇa, Kṛṣṇa Kṛṣṇa, Hare Hare/ Hare Rāma, Hare Rāma, Rāma Rāma, Hare Hare—must have already passed all lower stages. It is said that those who simply chant the holy name with the tip of the tongue are glorious. One does not even have to chant the holy name and understand the whole procedure, namely the offensive stage, offenseless stage and pure stage; if the holy name is sounded on the tip of the tongue, that is also sufficient. It is said herein that *nāma*, a singular number, one name, Kṛṣṇa or Rāma, is sufficient. It is not that one has to chant all the holy names of the Lord. The holy names of the Lord are innumerable, and one does not have to chant all the names to prove that he has already undergone all the processes of Vedic ritualistic ceremonies. If one chants once only, it is to be understood that he has already passed all the examinations, not to speak of those who are chanting always, twenty-four hours a day. It is specifically said here, *tubhyam:* "unto You only." One must chant God's name, not, as the Māyāvādī philosophers say, any name, such as a demigod's name or the names of God's energies. Only the holy name of the Supreme Lord will be effective. Anyone who compares the holy name of the Supreme Lord to the names of the demigods is called *pāṣaṇḍī,* or an offender.

The holy name has to be chanted to please the Supreme Lord, and not for any sense gratification or professional purpose. If this pure mentality is there, then even though a person is born of a low family, such as a dog-eater's, he is so glorious that not only has he purified himself, but he is quite competent to deliver others. He is competent to speak on the importance of the transcendental name, just as Ṭhākura Haridāsa did. He was apparently born in a family of Muhammadans, but because he was chanting the holy name of the Supreme Lord offenselessly, Lord Caitanya empowered him to become the authority, or *ācārya,* of spreading the name. It did not matter that he was born in a family which was not following the Vedic rules and regulations. Caitanya Mahāprabhu and Advaita Prabhu accepted him as an authority because he was offenselessly chanting the name of the Lord. Authorities like Advaita Prabhu and Lord Caitanya immediately accepted that he had already performed all kinds of austerities, studied the *Vedas* and performed all sacrifices. That is automatically understood. There is a hereditary class of *brāhmaṇas* called the *smārta-brāhmaṇas,* however, who are of the opinion that even if such persons who are chanting the holy name of the Lord are accepted as purified, they still have to perform the Vedic rites or await their next birth in a family of *brāhmaṇas* so that they can perform the Vedic rituals. But actually that is not the case. Such a man does not need to wait for the next birth to become purified. He is at once purified. It is understood that he has already performed all sorts of rites. It is the so-called *brāhmaṇas* who actually have to undergo different kinds of austerities before reaching that point of purification. There are many other Vedic performances which are not described here. All such Vedic rituals have been already performed by the chanters of the holy name.

The word *juhuvuḥ* means that the chanters of the holy name have already performed all kinds of sacrifices. *Sasnuḥ* means that they have already traveled to all the holy places of pilgrimage and taken part in purificatory activities at those places. They are called *āryāḥ* because they have already finished all these requirements, and therefore they must be among the Āryans or those who have qualified themselves to become Āryans. "Āryan" refers to those who are civilized, whose manners are regulated according to the Vedic rituals. Any devotee who is chanting the holy name of the Lord is the best kind of Āryan. Unless one studies the *Vedas*, one cannot become an Āryan, but it is automatically understood that the chanters have already studied all the Vedic literature. The specific word used here is *anūcuḥ*, which means that because they have already completed all those recommended acts, they have become qualified to be spiritual masters.

The very word *gṛṇanti*, which is used in this verse, means to be already established in the perfectional stage of ritualistic performances. If one is seated on the bench of a high court and is giving judgment on cases, it means that he has already passed all legal exams and is better than those who are engaged in the study of law or those expecting to study law in the future. In a similar way, persons who are chanting the holy name are transcendental to those who are factually performing the Vedic rituals and those who expect to be qualified (or, in other words, those who are born in families of *brāhmaṇas* but have not yet undergone the reformatory processes and who therefore expect to study the Vedic rituals and perform the sacrifices in the future).

There are many Vedic statements in different places saying that anyone who chants the holy name of the Lord becomes immediately freed from conditional life and that anyone who hears the holy name of the Lord, even though born of a family of dog-eaters, also becomes liberated from the clutches of material entanglement.

TEXT 8

तं त्वामहं ब्रह्म परं पुमांसं
प्रत्यक्स्रोतस्यात्मनि संविभाव्यम् ।

स्वतेजसा ध्वस्तगुणप्रवाहं
वन्दे विष्णुं कपिलं वेदगर्भम् ॥ ८ ॥

taṁ tvām ahaṁ brahma paraṁ pumāṁsaṁ
pratyak-srotasy ātmani saṁvibhāvyam
sva-tejasā dhvasta-guṇa-pravāhaṁ
vande viṣṇuṁ kapilaṁ veda-garbham

tam—unto Him; *tvām*—You; *aham*—I; *brahma*—Brahman; *param*—supreme; *pumāṁsam*—the Supreme Personality of Godhead; *pratyak-srotasi*—turned inwards; *ātmani*—in the mind; *saṁvibhāvyam*—meditated upon, perceived; *sva-tejasā*—by Your own potency; *dhvasta*—vanished; *guṇa-pravāham*—the influence of the modes of material nature; *vande*—I offer obeisances; *viṣṇum*—unto Lord Viṣṇu; *kapilam*—named Kapila; *veda-garbham*—the repository of the *Vedas.*

TRANSLATION

I believe, my Lord, that You are Lord Viṣṇu Himself under the name of Kapila, and You are the Supreme Personality of Godhead, the Supreme Brahman! The saints and sages, being freed from all the disturbances of the senses and mind, meditate upon You, for by Your mercy only can one become free from the clutches of the three modes of material nature. At the time of dissolution, all the Vedas are sustained in You only.

PURPORT

Devahūti, the mother of Kapila, instead of prolonging her prayers, summarized that Lord Kapila was none other than Viṣṇu and that since she was a woman it was not possible for her to worship Him properly simply by prayer. It was her intention that the Lord be satisfied. The word *pratyak* is significant. In yogic practice, the eight divisions are *yama, niyama, āsana, prāṇāyāma, pratyāhāra, dhāraṇā, dhyāna* and *samādhi. Pratyāhāra* means to wind up the activities of the senses. The level of realization of the Supreme Lord evidenced by Devahūti is possible when one is able to withdraw the senses from material activities. When one is engaged in devotional service, there is no scope for his senses to be engaged otherwise. In such full Kṛṣṇa consciousness, one can understand the Supreme Lord as He is.

TEXT 9

मैत्रेय उवाच

ईडितो भगवानेवं कपिलाख्यः परः पुमान् ।
वाचाविक्लवयेत्याह मातरं मातृवत्सलः ॥ ९ ॥

maitreya uvāca
iḍito bhagavān evaṁ
kapilākhyaḥ paraḥ pumān
vācāviklavayety āha
mātaraṁ mātṛ-vatsalaḥ

maitreyaḥ uvāca—Maitreya said; *iḍitaḥ*—praised; *bhagavān*—the Supreme Personality of Godhead; *evam*—thus; *kapila-ākhyaḥ*—named Kapila; *paraḥ*—supreme; *pumān*—person; *vācā*—with words; *aviklavayā*—grave; *iti*—thus; *āha*—replied; *mātaram*—to His mother; *mātṛ-vatsalaḥ*—very affectionate to His mother.

TRANSLATION

Thus the Supreme Personality of Godhead Kapila, satisfied by the words of His mother, towards whom He was very affectionate, replied with gravity.

PURPORT

Since the Lord is all-perfect, His exhibition of affection for His mother was also complete. After hearing the words of His mother, He most respectfully, with due gravity and good manners, replied.

TEXT 10

कपिल उवाच

मार्गेणानेन मातस्ते सुसेव्येनोदितेन मे ।
आस्थितेन परां काष्ठामचिराद‍्वरोत्स्यसि ॥१०॥

kapila uvāca
mārgeṇānena mātas te
susevyenoditena me
āsthitena parāṁ kāṣṭhām
acirād avarotsyasi

kapilaḥ uvāca—Lord Kapila said; *mārgeṇa*—by the path; *anena*—this; *mātaḥ*—My dear mother; *te*—for you; *su-sevyena*—very easy to execute; *uditena*—instructed; *me*—by Me; *āsthitena*—being performed; *parām*—supreme; *kāṣṭhām*—goal; *acirāt*—very soon; *avarotsyasi*—you will attain.

TRANSLATION

The Personality of Godhead said: My dear mother, the path of self-realization which I have already instructed to you is very easy. You can execute this system without difficulty, and by following it you shall very soon be liberated, even within your present body.

PURPORT

Devotional service is so perfect that simply by following the rules and regulations and executing them under the direction of the spiritual master, one is liberated, as it is said herein, from the clutches of *māyā*, even in this body. In other yogic processes, or in empiric philosophical speculation, one is never certain whether or not he is at the perfectional stage. But in the discharge of devotional service, if one has unflinching faith in the instruction of the bona fide spiritual master and follows the rules and regulations, he is sure to be liberated, even within this present body. Śrīla Rūpa Gosvāmī, in the *Bhakti-rasāmṛta-sindhu*, has also confirmed this. *Īhā yasya harer dāsye:* regardless of where he is situated, anyone whose only aim is to serve the Supreme Lord under the direction of the spiritual master is called *jīvan-mukta*, or one who is liberated even with his material body. Sometimes doubts arise in the minds of neophytes about whether or not the spiritual master is liberated, and sometimes neophytes are doubtful about the bodily affairs of the spiritual master. The point of liberation, however, is not to see the bodily symptoms of the spiritual master. One has to see the spiritual symptoms of the spiritual master. *Jīvan-mukta* means that even though one is in the material body (there are still some material necessities, since the body is material), because one is fully situated in the service of the Lord, he should be understood to be liberated.

Liberation entails being situated in one's own position. That is the definition in the *Śrīmad-Bhāgavatam: muktir . . . svarūpeṇa vyavasthitiḥ.* The *svarūpa*, or actual identity of the living entity, is described by Lord Caitanya. *Jīvera 'svarūpa' haya—kṛṣṇera 'nitya-dāsa'*: the real identity of the living entity is that he is eternally a servitor of the Supreme Lord. If someone is one-hundred-percent engaged in the service of the Lord, he is to be understood as liberated. One must understand whether or not he is liberated by his activities in devotional service, not by other symptoms.

TEXT 11

श्रद्धत्स्वैतन्मतं मह्यं जुष्टं यद्ब्रह्मवादिभिः ।
येन मामभयं याया मृत्युमृच्छन्त्यतद्विदः ॥११॥

śraddhatsvaitan mataṁ mahyaṁ
juṣṭaṁ yad brahma-vādibhiḥ
yena mām abhayaṁ yāyā
mṛtyum ṛcchanty atad-vidaḥ

śraddhatsva—you may rest assured; *etat*—about this; *matam*—instruction; *mahyam*—My; *juṣṭam*—followed; *yat*—which; *brahma-vādibhiḥ*—by transcendentalists; *yena*—by which; *mām*—unto Me; *abhayam*—without fear; *yāyāḥ*—you shall reach; *mṛtyum*—death; *ṛcchanti*—attain; *a-tat-vidaḥ*—persons who are not conversant with this.

TRANSLATION

My dear mother, those who are actually transcendentalists certainly follow My instructions, as I have given them to you. You may rest assured that if you traverse this path of self-realization perfectly, surely you shall be freed from fearful material contamination and shall ultimately reach Me. Mother, persons who are not conversant with this method of devotional service certainly cannot get out of the cycle of birth and death.

PURPORT

Material existence is full of anxiety, and therefore it is fearful. One who gets out of this material existence automatically becomes free from all anxieties and fear. One who follows the path of devotional service enunciated by Lord Kapila is very easily liberated.

TEXT 12

मैत्रेय उवाच
इति प्रदर्श्य भगवान् सतीं तामात्मनो गतिम् ।
स्वमात्रा ब्रह्मवादिन्या कपिलोऽनुमतो ययौ ॥१२॥

maitreya uvāca
iti pradarśya bhagavān
satīṁ tām ātmano gatim
sva-mātrā brahma-vādinyā
kapilo 'numato yayau

maitreyaḥ uvāca—Maitreya said; *iti*—thus; *pradarśya*—after instructing; *bhagavān*—the Supreme Personality of Godhead; *satīm*—venerable; *tām*—that; *ātmanaḥ*—of self-realization; *gatim*—path; *sva-mātrā*—from His mother; *brahma-vādinyā*—self-realized; *kapilaḥ*—Lord Kapila; *anumataḥ*—took permission; *yayau*—left.

TRANSLATION

Śrī Maitreya said: The Supreme Personality of Godhead Kapila, after instructing His beloved mother, took permission from her and left His home, His mission having been fulfilled.

PURPORT

The mission of the appearance of the Supreme Personality of Godhead in the form of Kapila was to distribute the transcendental knowledge of Sāṅkhya philosophy, which is full of devotional service. Having imparted that knowledge to His mother—and, through His mother, to the world—Kapiladeva had no more need to stay at home, so He took permission from His mother and left. Apparently He left home for spiritual realization, although He had nothing to realize spiritually because He Himself is the person to be spiritually realized. Therefore this is an example set by the Supreme Personality of Godhead while acting like an ordinary human being so that others might learn from Him. He could, of course, have stayed with His mother, but He indicated that there was no need to stay with the family. It is best to remain alone as a *brahmacārī, sannyāsī* or *vānaprastha* and cultivate Kṛṣṇa consciousness throughout one's whole life. Those who are unable to remain alone are given license to live in household life with wife and children, not for sense gratification but for cultivation of Kṛṣṇa consciousness.

TEXT 13

सा चापि तनयोक्तेन योगादेशेन योगयुक् ।
तस्मिन्नाश्रम आपीडे सरस्वत्याः समाहिता ॥१३॥

sā cāpi tanayoktena
yogādeśena yoga-yuk
tasminn āśrama āpīḍe
sarasvatyāḥ samāhitā

sā—she; *ca*—and; *api*—also; *tanaya*—by her son; *uktena*—spoken; *yoga-ādeśena*—by the instruction on *yoga; yoga-yuk*—engaged in *bhakti-yoga; tasmin*—in that; *āśrame*—hermitage; *āpīḍe*—the flower crown; *sarasvatyāḥ*—of the Sarasvatī; *samāhitā*—fixed in *samādhi.*

TRANSLATION

As instructed by her son, Devahūti also began to practice bhakti-yoga in that very āśrama. She practiced samādhi in the house of Kardama Muni, which was so beautifully decorated with flowers that it was considered the flower crown of the River Sarasvatī.

PURPORT

Devahūti did not leave her house, because it is never recommended for a woman to leave her home. She is dependent. The very example of

Devahūti was that when she was not married, she was under the care of her father, Svāyambhuva Manu, and then Svāyambhuva Manu gave her to Kardama Muni in charity. She was under the care of her husband in her youth, and then her son, Kapila Muni, was born. As soon as her son grew up, her husband left home, and similarly the son, after discharging His duty towards His mother, also left. She could also have left home, but she did not. Rather, she remained at home and began to practice *bhakti-yoga* as it was instructed by her great son, Kapila Muni, and because of her practice of *bhakti-yoga*, the entire home became just like a flower crown on the River Sarasvatī.

TEXT 14

अभीक्ष्णावगाहकपिशान् जटिलान् कुटिलालकान् ।
आत्मानं चोग्रतपसा बिभ्रती चीरिणं कृशम् ॥१४॥

abhīkṣṇāvagāha-kapiśān
jaṭilān kuṭilālakān
ātmānaṁ cogra-tapasā
bibhratī cīriṇaṁ kṛśam

abhīkṣṇa—again and again; *avagāha*—by bathing; *kapiśān*—gray; *jaṭilān*—matted; *kuṭila*—curled; *alakān*—hair; *ātmānam*—her body; *ca*—and; *ugra-tapasā*—by severe austerities; *bibhratī*—became; *cīriṇam*—clothed in rags; *kṛśam*—thin.

TRANSLATION

She began to bathe three times daily, and thus her curling black hair gradually became gray. Due to austerity, her body gradually became thin, and she wore old garments.

PURPORT

It is the practice of the *yogī, brahmacārī, vānaprastha* and *sannyāsī* to bathe at least three times daily—early in the morning, during noontime and in the evening. These principles are strictly followed even by some *gṛhasthas*, especially *brāhmaṇas*, who are elevated in spiritual consciousness. Devahūti was a king's daughter and almost a king's wife also. Although Kardama Muni was not a king, by his yogic mystic power he accommodated Devahūti very comfortably in a nice palace with maidservants and all opulence. But since she had learned austerity even in the presence of her husband, there was no difficulty for her to be austere. Still, because her body underwent severe austerity after the departure of her husband and son, she became thin. To be too fat is not very good for spiritually advanced life. Rather, one should reduce because if one becomes fat it is an impediment to progress in spiritual understanding. One should be careful not to eat too much, sleep too much or remain in a comfortable position. Voluntarily accepting some penances and difficulties, one should take less food and less sleep. These are the procedures for practicing any kind of *yoga*, whether *bhakti-yoga, jñāna-yoga* or *haṭha-yoga.*

TEXT 15

प्रजापतेः कर्दमस्य तपोयोगविजृम्भितम् ।
स्वगार्हस्थ्यमनौपम्यं प्रार्थ्यं वैमानिकैरपि ॥१५॥

prajāpateḥ kardamasya
tapo-yoga-vijṛmbhitam
sva-gārhasthyam anaupamyaṁ
prārthyaṁ vaimānikair api

prajā-pateḥ—of the progenitor of mankind; *kardamasya*—Kardama Muni; *tapaḥ*—by austerity; *yoga*—by *yoga; vijṛmbhitam*—developed; *sva-gārhasthyam*—his home and household paraphernalia; *anaupamyam*—unequaled; *prārthyam*—enviable; *vaimānikaiḥ*—by the denizens of heaven; *api*—even.

TRANSLATION

The home and household paraphernalia of Kardama, who was one of the Prajāpatis, was developed in such a way, by dint of his mystic powers of austerity and yoga, that his opulence was sometimes envied by those who travel in outer space in airplanes.

PURPORT

The statement in this verse that Kardama Muni's household affairs were envied even by persons who travel in outer space refers to the denizens of heaven. Their airships are not like those we have invented in the modern age, which fly only from one country to another; their airplanes were capable of going from one planet to another. There are many such statements in the *Śrīmad-Bhāgavatam* from which we can understand that there were facilities to travel from one planet to another, especially in the higher planetary system, and who can say that they are not still traveling? The speed of our airplanes and space vehicles is very limited, but, as we have already studied, Kardama Muni traveled in outer space in an airplane which was like a city, and he journeyed to see all the different heavenly planets. That was not an ordinary airplane, nor was it ordinary space travel. Because Kardama Muni was such a powerful mystic *yogī*, his opulence was envied by the denizens of heaven.

TEXT 16

पयःफेननिभाः शय्या दान्ता रुक्मपरिच्छदाः ।
आसनानि च हैमानि सुस्पर्शास्तरणानि च ॥१६॥

payaḥ-phena-nibhāḥ śayyā
dāntā rukma-paricchadāḥ
āsanāni ca haimāni
susparśāstaraṇāni ca

payaḥ—of milk; *phena*—the foam; *nibhāḥ*—resembling; *śayyāḥ*—beds; *dāntāḥ*—made of ivory; *rukma*—golden; *paricchadāḥ*—with covers; *āsanāni*—chairs and benches; *ca*—and; *haimāni*—made of gold; *su-sparśa*—soft to the touch; *āstaraṇāni*—cushions; *ca*—and.

TRANSLATION

The opulence of the household of Kardama Muni is described herein. The bedsheets and mattresses were all as white as the foam of milk, the chairs and benches were made of ivory and were covered by cloths of lace with golden filigree, and the couches were made of gold and had very soft pillows.

TEXT 17

स्वच्छस्फटिककुड्येषु महामारकतेषु च ।
रत्नप्रदीपा आभान्ति ललनारत्नसंयुताः ॥१७॥

svaccha-sphaṭika-kuḍyeṣu
mahā-mārakateṣu ca
ratna-pradīpā ābhānti
lalanā ratna-saṁyutāḥ

svaccha—pure; *sphaṭika*—marble; *kuḍyeṣu*—on the walls; *mahā-mārakateṣu*—decorated with valuable emeralds; *ca*—and; *ratna-pradīpāḥ*—jewel lamps; *ābhānti*—shine; *lalanāḥ*—women; *ratna*—with jewelry; *saṁyutāḥ*—decorated.

TRANSLATION

The walls of the house were made of first-class marble, decorated with valuable jewels. There was no need of light, for the household was illuminated by the rays of these jewels. The female members of the household were all amply decorated with jewelry.

PURPORT

It is understood from this statement that the opulences of household life were exhibited in valuable jewels, ivory, first-class marble, and furniture made of gold and jewels. The clothes are also mentioned as being decorated with golden filigree. Everything actually had some value. It was not like the furniture of the present day, which is cast in valueless plastic or base metal. The way of Vedic civilization is that whatever was used in household affairs had to be valuable. In case of need, such items of value could be exchanged immediately. Thus one's broken and unwanted furniture and paraphernalia would never be without value. This system is still followed by Indians in household affairs. They keep metal utensils and golden ornaments or silver plates and valuable silk garments with gold embroidery, and in case of need, they can have some money in exchange immediately. There are exchanges for the moneylenders and the householders.

TEXT 18

गृहोद्यानं कुसुमितै रम्यं बह्वमरद्रुमैः ।
कूजद्विहङ्गमिथुनं गायन्मत्तमधुव्रतम् ॥१८॥

gṛhodyānaṁ kusumitai
ramyaṁ bahv-amara-drumaiḥ
kūjad-vihaṅga-mithunaṁ
gāyan-matta-madhuvratam

gṛha-udyānam—the household garden; *kusumitaiḥ*—with flowers and fruits; *ramyam*—beautiful; *bahu-amara-drumaiḥ*—with many celestial trees; *kūjat*—singing; *vihaṅga*—of birds; *mithunam*—with pairs; *gāyat*—humming; *matta*—intoxicated; *madhu-vratam*—with bees.

TRANSLATION

The compound of the main household was surrounded by beautiful gardens, with sweet, fragrant flowers and many trees which produced fresh fruit and were tall and beautiful. The attraction of such gardens was that singing birds would sit on the trees, and their chanting voices, as well as the humming sound of the bees, made the whole atmosphere as pleasing as possible.

TEXT 19

यत्र प्रविष्टमात्मानं विबुधानुचरा जगुः ।
वाप्यामुत्पलगन्धिन्यां कर्दमेनोपलालितम् ॥१९॥

yatra praviṣṭam ātmānaṁ
vibudhānucarā jaguḥ
vāpyām utpala-gandhinyāṁ
kardamenopalālitam

yatra—where; *praviṣṭam*—entered; *ātmānam*—unto her; *vibudha-anucarāḥ*—the associates of the denizens of heaven; *jaguḥ*—sang;

vāpyām—in the pond; *utpala*—of lotuses; *gandhinyām*—with the fragrance; *kardamena*—by Kardama; *upalālitam*—treated with great care.

TRANSLATION

When Devahūti would enter that lovely garden to take her bath in the pond filled with lotus flowers, the associates of the denizens of heaven, the Gandharvas, would sing about Kardama's glorious household life. Her great husband, Kardama, gave her all protection at all times.

PURPORT

The ideal husband-and-wife relationship is very nicely described in this statement. Kardama Muni gave Devahūti all sorts of comforts in his duty as a husband, but he was not at all attached to his wife. As soon as his son, Kapiladeva, was grown up, Kardama at once left all family connection. Similarly, Devahūti was the daughter of a great king, Svāyambhuva Manu, and was qualified and beautiful, but she was completely dependent on the protection of her husband. According to Manu, women, the fair sex, should not have independence at any stage of life. In childhood a woman must be under the protection of the parents, in youth she must be under the protection of the husband, and in old age she must be under the protection of the grown children. Devahūti demonstrated all these statements of the *Manu-saṁhitā* in her life: as a child she was dependent on her father, later she was dependent on her husband, in spite of her opulence, and she was later on dependent on her son, Kapiladeva.

TEXT 20

हित्वा तदीप्सिततममप्याखण्डलयोषिताम् ।
किञ्चिच्चकार वदनं पुत्रविश्लेषणातुरा ॥२०॥

hitvā tad īpsitatamam
apy ākhaṇḍala-yoṣitām
kiñcic cakāra vadanaṁ
putra-viśleṣaṇāturā

hitvā—having given up; *tat*—that household; *īpsita-tamam*—most desirable; *api*—even; *ākhaṇḍala-yoṣitām*—by the wives of Lord Indra; *kiñcit cakāra vadanam*—she wore a sorry look on her face; *putra-viśleṣaṇa*—by separation from her son; *āturā*—afflicted.

TRANSLATION

Although her position was unique from all points of view, saintly Devahūti, in spite of all her possessions, which were envied even by the ladies of the heavenly planets, gave up all such comforts. She was only sorry that her great son was separated from her.

PURPORT

Devahūti was not at all sorry at giving up her material comforts, but she was very much aggrieved at the separation of her son. It may be questioned here that if Devahūti was not at all sorry to give up the material comforts of life, then why was she sorry about losing her son? Why was she so attached to her son? The answer is explained in the next verse. He was not an ordinary son. Her son was the Supreme Personality of Godhead. One can give up material attachment, therefore, only when one has attachment for the Supreme Person. This is explained in *Bhagavad-gītā. Paraṁ dṛṣṭvā nivartate.* Only when one actually has some taste for spiritual existence can he be reluctant to follow the materialistic way of life.

TEXT 21

वनं प्रव्रजिते पत्यावपत्यविरहातुरा ।
ज्ञाततत्त्वाप्यभून्नष्टे वत्से गौरिव वत्सला ॥२१॥

vanaṁ pravrajite patyāv
apatya-virahāturā
jñāta-tattvāpy abhūn naṣṭe
vatse gaur iva vatsalā

vanam—to the forest; *pravrajite patyau*—when her husband left home; *apatya-viraha*—by separation from her son; *āturā*—very sorry;

jñāta-tattvā—knowing the truth; *api*—although; *abhūt*—she became; *naṣṭe vatse*—when her calf is lost; *gauḥ*—a cow; *iva*—like; *vatsalā*—affectionate.

TRANSLATION

Devahūti's husband had already left home and accepted the renounced order of life, and then her only son, Kapila, left home. Although she knew all the truths of life and death, and although her heart was cleansed of all dirt, she was very aggrieved at the loss of her son, just as a cow is affected when her calf dies.

PURPORT

A woman whose husband is away from home or has taken the renounced order of life should not be very sorry, because she still has the presence of her husband's representative, her son. It is said in the Vedic scriptures, *ātmaiva putro jāyate:* the husband's body is represented by the son. Strictly speaking, a woman is never widowed if she has a grown son. Devahūti was not very much affected while Kapila Muni was there, but upon His departure she was very afflicted. She grieved not because of her worldly relationship with Kardama Muni but because of her sincere love for the Personality of Godhead.

The example given here is that Devahūti became just like a cow who has lost her calf. A cow bereft of her calf cries day and night. Similarly, Devahūti was aggrieved, and she always cried and requested her friends and relatives, "Please bring my son home so that I may live. Otherwise, I shall die." This intense affection for the Supreme Personality of Godhead, although manifested as affection for one's son, is spiritually beneficial. Attachment for a material son obliges one to remain in material existence, but the same attachment, when transferred to the Supreme Lord, brings one elevation to the spiritual world in the association of the Lord.

Every woman can qualify herself as much as Devahūti and then can also have the Supreme Godhead as her son. If the Supreme Personality of Godhead can appear as the son of Devahūti, He can also appear as the son of any other woman, provided that woman is qualified. If one gets the Supreme Lord as a son, one can have the benefit of bringing up a nice son in this world and at the same time get promotion to the spiritual world to become the face-to-face associate of the Personality of Godhead.

TEXT 22

तमेव ध्यायती देवमपत्यं कपिलं हरिम् ।
बभूवाचिरतो वत्स निःस्पृहा तादृशे गृहे ॥२२॥

tam eva dhyāyatī devam
apatyaṁ kapilaṁ harim
babhūvācirato vatsa
niḥspṛhā tādṛśe gṛhe

tam—upon Him; *eva*—certainly; *dhyāyatī*—meditating; *devam*—divine; *apatyam*—son; *kapilam*—Lord Kapila; *harim*—the Supreme Personality of Godhead; *babhūva*—became; *aciratah*—very soon; *vatsa*—O dear Vidura; *niḥspṛhā*—unattached; *tādṛśe gṛhe*—to such a home.

TRANSLATION

O Vidura, thus always meditating upon her son, the Supreme Personality of Godhead Kapiladeva, she very soon became unattached to her nicely decorated home.

PURPORT

Here is a practical example of how one can elevate oneself in spiritual advancement by Kṛṣṇa consciousness. Kapiladeva is Kṛṣṇa, and He appeared as the son of Devahūti. After Kapiladeva left home, Devahūti was absorbed in thought of Him, and thus she was always Kṛṣṇa conscious. Her constant situation in Kṛṣṇa consciousness enabled her to be detached from hearth and home.

Unless we are able to transfer our attachment to the Supreme Personality of Godhead, there is no possibility of becoming freed from material attachment. The *Śrīmad-Bhāgavatam*, therefore, confirms that it is not possible for one to become liberated by cultivation of empiric philosophical speculation. Simply knowing that one is not matter but spirit soul, or Brahman, does not purify one's intelligence. Even if the impersonalist reaches the highest platform of spiritual realization, he falls down again to material attachment because of not being situated in the transcendental loving service of the Supreme Lord.

The devotees adopt the devotional process, hearing about the Supreme Lord's pastimes and glorifying His activities and thereby always remembering His beautiful eternal form. By rendering service, becoming His friend or His servant and offering Him everything that one possesses, one is able to enter into the kingdom of God. As it is said in *Bhagavad-gītā, tato māṁ tattvato jñātvā:* after discharging pure devotional service, one can understand the Supreme Personality of Godhead in fact, and thus one becomes eligible to enter into His association in one of the spiritual planets.

TEXT 23

ध्यायती भगवद्रूपं यदाह ध्यानगोचरम् ।
सुतः प्रसन्नवदनं समस्तव्यस्तचिन्तया ॥२३॥

dhyāyatī bhagavad-rūpaṁ
yad āha dhyāna-gocaram
sutaḥ prasanna-vadanaṁ
samasta-vyasta-cintayā

dhyāyatī—meditating; *bhagavat-rūpam*—upon the form of the Supreme Personality of Godhead; *yat*—which; *āha*—He instructed; *dhyāna-gocaram*—the object of meditation; *sutaḥ*—her son; *prasanna-vadanam*—with a smiling face; *samasta*—on the whole; *vyasta*—on the parts; *cintayā*—with her mind.

TRANSLATION

Thereafter, having heard with great eagerness and in all detail from her son, Kapiladeva, the eternally smiling Personality of Godhead, Devahūti began to meditate constantly upon the Viṣṇu form of the Supreme Lord.

TEXTS 24–25

भक्तिप्रवाहयोगेन वैराग्येण बलीयसा ।
युक्तानुष्ठानजातेन ज्ञानेन ब्रह्महेतुना ॥२४॥
विशुद्धेन तदात्मानमात्मना विश्वतोमुखम् ।
स्वानुभूत्या तिरोभूतमायागुणविशेषणम् ॥२५॥

bhakti-pravāha-yogena
vairāgyeṇa balīyasā
yuktānuṣṭhāna-jātena
jñānena brahma-hetunā

viśuddhena tadātmānam
ātmanā viśvato-mukham
svānubhūtyā tirobhūta-
māyā-guṇa-viśeṣaṇam

bhakti-pravāha-yogena—by continuous engagement in devotional service; *vairāgyeṇa*—by renunciation; *balīyasā*—very strong; *yukta-anuṣṭhāna*—by proper performance of duties; *jātena*—produced; *jñānena*—by knowledge; *brahma-hetunā*—due to realization of the Absolute Truth; *viśuddhena*—by purification; *tadā*—then; *ātmānam*—Supreme Personality of Godhead; *ātmanā*—with the mind; *viśvataḥ-mukham*—whose face is turned everywhere; *sva-anubhūtyā*—by self-realization; *tiraḥ-bhūta*—disappeared; *māyā-guṇa*—of the modes of material nature; *viśeṣaṇam*—distinctions.

TRANSLATION

She did so with serious engagement in devotional service. Because she was strong in renunciation, she accepted only the necessities of the body. She became situated in knowledge due to realization of the Absolute Truth, her heart became purified, she became fully absorbed in meditation upon the Supreme Personality of Godhead, and all misgivings due to the modes of material nature disappeared.

TEXT 26

ब्रह्मण्यवस्थितमतिर्भगवत्यात्मसंश्रये ।
निवृत्तजीवापत्तित्वात्क्षीणक्लेशाप्तनिर्वृतिः ॥२६॥

brahmaṇy avasthita-matir
bhagavaty ātma-saṁśraye
nivṛtta-jīvāpattitvāt
kṣīṇa-kleśāpta-nirvṛtiḥ

brahmaṇi—in Brahman; *avasthita*—situated; *matiḥ*—her mind; *bhagavati*—in the Supreme Personality of Godhead; *ātma-saṁśraye*—residing in all living entities; *nivṛtta*—freed; *jīva*—of the *jīva* soul; *āpattitvāt*—from the unfortunate condition; *kṣīṇa*—disappeared; *kleśa*—material pangs; *āpta*—attained; *nirvṛtiḥ*—transcendental bliss.

TRANSLATION

Her mind became completely engaged in the Supreme Lord, and she automatically realized the knowledge of the impersonal Brahman. As a Brahman-realized soul, she was freed from the designations of the materialistic concept of life. Thus all material pangs disappeared, and she attained transcendental bliss.

PURPORT

The previous verse states that Devahūti was already conversant with the Absolute Truth. It may be questioned why she was meditating. The explanation is that when one theoretically discusses the Absolute Truth, he becomes situated in the impersonal concept of the Absolute Truth. Similarly, when one seriously discusses the subject matter of the form, qualities, pastimes and entourage of the Supreme Personality of Godhead, he becomes situated in meditation on Him. If one has complete knowledge of the Supreme Lord, then knowledge of the impersonal Brahman is automatically realized. The Absolute Truth is realized by the knower according to three different angles of vision, namely impersonal Brahman, localized Supersoul and ultimately the Supreme Personality of Godhead. If one is situated, therefore, in knowledge of the Supreme Person, this implies that one is already situated in the concept of the Supersoul and impersonal Brahman.

In *Bhagavad-gītā* it is said, *brahma-bhūtaḥ prasannātmā.* This means that unless one is freed from the material entanglement and situated in Brahman, there is no question of entering into the understanding of devotional service or engaging in Kṛṣṇa consciousness. One who is engaged in devotional service to Kṛṣṇa is understood to be already realized in the Brahman concept of life because transcendental knowledge of the Supreme Personality of Godhead includes knowledge of Brahman. This is confirmed in *Bhagavad-gītā. Brahmaṇo hi pratiṣṭhāham:* the concept of the Personality of Godhead does not depend on Brahman. The *Viṣṇu Purāṇa* also confirms that one who has taken shelter of the all-auspicious Supreme Lord is already situated in the understanding of Brahman. In other words, one who is a Vaiṣṇava is already a *brāhmaṇa.*

Another significant point of this verse is that one has to observe the prescribed rules and regulations. As confirmed in *Bhagavad-gītā, yuktāhāra-vihārasya.* When one engages in devotional service in Kṛṣṇa consciousness, he still has to eat, sleep, defend and mate because these are necessities of the body. But he performs such activities in a regulated way. He has to eat *kṛṣṇa-prasāda.* He has to sleep according to regulated principles. The principle is to reduce the duration of sleep and to reduce eating, taking only what is needed to keep the body fit. In short, the goal is spiritual advancement, not sense gratification. Similarly, sex life must be reduced. Sex life is meant only for begetting Kṛṣṇa conscious children. Otherwise, there is no necessity for sex life. Nothing is prohibited, but everything is made *yukta,* regulated, with the higher purpose always in mind. By following all these rules and regulations of living, one becomes purified, and all misconceptions due to ignorance become nil. It is specifically mentioned here that the causes of material entanglement are completely vanquished.

The Sanskrit statement *anartha-nivṛtti* indicates that this body is unwanted. We are spirit soul, and there was never any need of this material body. But because we wanted to enjoy the material body, we have this body, through the material energy, under the direction of the Supreme Personality of Godhead. As soon as we are reestablished in our original position of servitorship to the Supreme Lord, we begin to forget the necessities of the body, and at last we forget the body.

Sometimes in a dream we get a particular type of body with which to work in the dream. I may dream that I am flying in the sky or that I have gone into the forest or some unknown place. But as soon as I am awake I forget all these bodies. Similarly, when one is Kṛṣṇa conscious, fully devoted, he forgets all his changes of body. We are always changing bodies, beginning at birth from the womb of our mother. But when we are awakened to Kṛṣṇa consciousness, we forget all these bodies. The bodily necessities become secondary, for the primary necessity is the engagement of the soul in real, spiritual life. The activities of devotional service in full Kṛṣṇa consciousness are the cause of our being situated in transcendence. The words *bhagavaty ātma-saṁśraye* denote the Personality of Godhead as the Supreme Soul, or the soul of everyone. In *Bhagavad-gītā* Kṛṣṇa says, *bījaṁ māṁ sarva-bhūtānām:* "I am the seed of all entities." By taking shelter of the Supreme Being by the process of devotional service, one becomes fully situated in the concept of the Personality of Godhead. As described by Kapila, *mad-guṇa-śruti-mātreṇa:* one who is fully Kṛṣṇa conscious, situated in the Personality of Godhead, is immediately saturated with love of God as soon as he hears about the transcendental qualities of the Lord.

Devahūti was fully instructed by her son, Kapiladeva, on how to concentrate her mind on the Viṣṇu form in full detail. Following the instructions of her son in the matter of devotional service, she contemplated the form of the Lord within herself with great devotional love. That is the perfection of Brahman realization or the mystic *yoga* system or devotional service. At the ultimate issue, when one is fully absorbed in thought of the Supreme Lord and meditates on Him constantly, that is the highest perfection. *Bhagavad-gītā* confirms that one who is always absorbed in such a way is to be considered the topmost *yogī.*

The real purpose of all processes of transcendental realization—*jñāna-yoga, dhyāna-yoga* or *bhakti-yoga*—is to arrive at the point of devotional service. If one endeavors simply to achieve knowledge of the Absolute Truth or the Supersoul but has no devotional service, he labors without gaining the real result. This is compared to beating the husks of wheat after the grains have already been removed. Unless one understands the Supreme Personality of Godhead to be the ultimate goal, it is valueless simply to speculate or perform mystic *yoga* practice. In the *aṣṭāṅga-yoga* system, the seventh stage of perfection is *dhyāna.* This *dhyāna* is the third stage in devotional service. There are nine stages of devotional service. The first is hearing, and then comes chanting and then contemplating. By executing devotional service, therefore, one automatically becomes an expert *jñānī* and an expert *yogī*. In other words, *jñāna* and *yoga* are different preliminary stages of devotional service.

Devahūti was expert in accepting the real substance; she contemplated the form of Viṣṇu in detail as advised by her smiling son, Kapiladeva. At the same time, she was thinking of Kapiladeva, who is the Supreme Personality of Godhead, and therefore she completely perfected her austerities, penances and transcendental realization.

TEXT 27

नित्यारूढसमाधित्वात्परावृत्तगुणभ्रमा ।
न सस्मार तदात्मानं स्वप्ने दृष्टमिवोत्थितः ॥२७॥

nityārūḍha-samādhitvāt
parāvṛtta-guṇa-bhramā
na sasmāra tadātmānaṁ
svapne dṛṣṭam ivotthitaḥ

nitya—eternal; *ārūḍha*—situated in; *samādhitvāt*—from trance; *parāvṛtta*—freed from; *guṇa*—of the modes of material nature; *bhramā*—illusion; *na sasmāra*—she did not remember; *tadā*—then; *ātmānam*—her material body; *svapne*—in a dream; *dṛṣṭam*—seen; *iva*—just as; *utthitaḥ*—one who has arisen.

TRANSLATION

Situated in eternal trance and freed from illusion impelled by the modes of material nature, she forgot her material body, just as one forgets his different bodies in a dream.

PURPORT

A great Vaiṣṇava said that he who has no remembrance of his body is not bound to material existence. As long as we are conscious of our bodily existence, it is to be understood that we are living conditionally, under the three modes of material nature. When one forgets his bodily existence, his conditional, material life is over. This forgetfulness is actually possible when we engage our senses in the transcendental loving service of the Lord. In the conditional state, one engages his senses as a member of a family or as a member of a society or country. But when one forgets all such membership in material circumstances and realizes that he is an eternal servant of the Supreme Lord, that is actual forgetfulness of material existence.

This forgetfulness actually occurs when one renders service unto the Lord. A devotee no longer works with the body for sense gratification with family, society, country, humanity and so on. He simply works for the Supreme Personality of Godhead, Kṛṣṇa. That is perfect Kṛṣṇa consciousness.

A devotee always merges in transcendental happiness, and therefore he has no experience of material distresses. This transcendental happiness is called eternal bliss. According to the opinion of devotees, constant remembrance of the Supreme Lord is called *samādhi*, or trance. If one is constantly in trance, there is no possibility of his being attacked or even touched by the modes of material nature. As soon as one is freed from the contamination of the three material modes, he no longer has to take birth to transmigrate from one form to another in this material world.

TEXT 28

तद्देहः परतःपोषोऽप्यकृशश्चाध्यसम्भवात् ।
बभौ मलैरवच्छन्नः सधूम इव पावकः ॥२८॥

tad-dehaḥ parataḥ poṣo
'py akṛśaś cādhy-asambhavāt
babhau malair avacchannaḥ
sadhūma iva pāvakaḥ

tat-dehaḥ—her body; *parataḥ*—by others (the damsels created by Kardama); *poṣaḥ*—maintained; *api*—although; *akṛśaḥ*—not thin; *ca*—and; *ādhi*—anxiety; *asambhavāt*—from not occurring; *babhau*—shone; *malaiḥ*—by dust; *avacchannaḥ*—covered; *sa-dhūmaḥ*—surrounded with smoke; *iva*—like; *pāvakaḥ*—a fire.

TRANSLATION

Her body was being taken care of by the spiritual damsels created by her husband, Kardama, and since she had no mental anxiety at that time, her body did not become thin. She appeared just like a fire surrounded by smoke.

PURPORT

Because she was always in trance in transcendental bliss, the thought of the Personality of Godhead was always carefully fixed in her mind. She did not become thin, for she was taken care of by the celestial maidservants created by her husband. It is said, according to the Āyur-vedic medical science, that if one is free from anxieties he generally becomes fat. Devahūti, being situated in Kṛṣṇa consciousness, had no mental anxieties, and therefore her body did not become thin. It is customary in the renounced order of life that one should not take any service from a servant or maid, but Devahūti was being served by the celestial maidservants. This may appear to be against the spiritual concept of life, but just as fire is still beautiful even when surrounded by smoke, she looked completely pure although it seemed that she was living in a luxurious way.

TEXT 29

स्वाङ्गं तपोयोगमयं मुक्तकेशं गताम्बरम् ।
दैवगुप्तं न बुबुधे वासुदेवप्रविष्टधीः ॥२९॥

svāṅgaṁ tapo-yogamayaṁ
mukta-keśaṁ gatāmbaram
daiva-guptaṁ na bubudhe
vāsudeva-praviṣṭa-dhīḥ

sva-aṅgam—her body; *tapaḥ*—austerity; *yoga*—*yoga* practice; *mayam*—fully engaged in; *mukta*—loosened; *keśam*—her hair; *gata*—disarrayed; *ambaram*—her garments; *daiva*—by the Lord; *guptam*—protected; *na*—not; *bubudhe*—she was aware of; *vāsudeva*—in the Supreme Personality of Godhead; *praviṣṭa*—absorbed; *dhīḥ*—her thoughts.

TRANSLATION

Because she was always absorbed in the thought of the Supreme Personality of Godhead, she was not aware that her hair was sometimes loosened or her garments were disarrayed.

PURPORT

In this verse the word *daiva-guptam,* "protected by the Supreme Personality of Godhead," is very significant. Once one surrenders unto the service of the Supreme Lord, the Lord takes charge of the maintenance of the devotee's body, and there is no need of anxiety for its protection. It is said in the Second Chapter, Second Canto, of *Śrīmad-Bhāgavatam* that a fully surrendered soul has no anxiety about the maintenance of his body. The Supreme Lord takes care of the maintenance of innumerable species of bodies; therefore, one who fully engages in His service will not go unprotected by the Supreme Lord. Devahūti was naturally unmindful of the protection of her body, which was being taken care of by the Supreme Person.

TEXT 30

एवं सा कपिलोक्तेन मार्गेणाचिरतः परम् ।
आत्मानं ब्रह्मनिर्वाणं भगवन्तमवाप ह ॥३०॥

evaṁ sā kapiloktena
mārgeṇāciratah̤ param
ātmānaṁ brahma-nirvāṇaṁ
bhagavantam avāpa ha

evam—thus; *sā*—she (Devahūti); *kapila*—by Kapila; *uktena*—instructed; *mārgeṇa*—by the path; *acirataḥ*—soon; *param*—supreme; *ātmānam*—Supersoul; *brahma*—Brahman; *nirvāṇam*—cessation of materialistic existence; *bhagavantam*—the Supreme Personality of Godhead; *avāpa*—she achieved; *ha*—certainly.

TRANSLATION

My dear Vidura, by following the principles instructed by Kapila, Devahūti soon became liberated from material bondage,

and she achieved the Supreme Personality of Godhead, as Supersoul, without difficulty.

PURPORT

Three words have been used in this connection to describe the achievement of Devahūti: *ātmānam, brahma-nirvāṇam* and *bhagavantam.* These refer to the gradual process of discovery of the Absolute Truth, mentioned herein as the *bhagavantam.* The Supreme Personality of Godhead resides in various Vaikuṇṭha planets. *Nirvāṇa* means to extinguish the pangs of material existence. When one is able to enter into the spiritual kingdom or into spiritual realization, one is automatically freed from material pangs. That is called *brahma-nirvāṇa.* According to Vedic scripture, *nirvāṇa* means cessation of the materialistic way of life. *Ātmānam* means realization of the Supersoul within the heart. Ultimately, the highest perfection is realization of the Supreme Personality of Godhead. It is to be understood that Devahūti entered the planet which is called Kapila Vaikuṇṭha. There are innumerable Vaikuṇṭha planets predominated by the expansions of Viṣṇu. All the Vaikuṇṭha planets are known by a particular name of Viṣṇu. As we understand from *Brahma-saṁhitā, advaitam acyutam anādim ananta-rūpam. Ananta* means "innumerable." The Lord has innumerable expansions of His transcendental form, and according to the different positions of the symbolical representations in His four hands, He is known as Nārāyaṇa, Pradyumna, Aniruddha, Vāsudeva, etc. There is also a Vaikuṇṭha planet known as Kapila Vaikuṇṭha, to which Devahūti was promoted to meet Kapila and reside there eternally, enjoying the company of her transcendental son.

TEXT 31

तद्वीरासीत्पुण्यतमं क्षेत्रं त्रैलोक्यविश्रुतम् ।
नाम्ना सिद्धपदं यत्र सा संसिद्धिमुपेयुषी ॥३१॥

tad vīrāsīt puṇyatamaṁ
kṣetraṁ trailokya-viśrutam
nāmnā siddha-padaṁ yatra
sā saṁsiddhim upeyuṣī

tat—that; *vīra*—O brave Vidura; *āsīt*—was; *puṇya-tamam*—most sacred; *kṣetram*—place; *trai-lokya*—in the three worlds; *viśrutam*—known; *nāmnā*—by the name; *siddha-padam*—Siddhapada; *yatra*—where; *sā*—she (Devahūti); *saṁsiddhim*—perfection; *upeyuṣī*—achieved.

TRANSLATION

The palace where Devahūti achieved her perfection, my dear Vidura, is understood to be a most sacred spot. It is known all over the three worlds as Siddhapada.

TEXT 32

तस्यास्तद्योगविधुतमार्त्यं मर्त्यमभूत्सरित् ।
स्रोतसां प्रवरा सौम्य सिद्धिदा सिद्धसेविता ॥३२॥

tasyās tad yoga-vidhuta-
mārtyaṁ martyam abhūt sarit
srotasāṁ pravarā saumya
siddhidā siddha-sevitā

tasyāḥ—of Devahūti; *tat*—that; *yoga*—by *yoga* practice; *vidhuta*—relinquished; *mārtyam*—material elements; *martyam*—her mortal body; *abhūt*—became; *sarit*—a river; *srotasām*—of all rivers; *pravarā*—the foremost; *saumya*—O gentle Vidura; *siddhi-dā*—conferring perfection; *siddha*—by persons desiring perfection; *sevitā*—resorted to.

TRANSLATION

Dear Vidura, the material elements of her body have melted into water and are now a flowing river, which is the most sacred of all rivers. Anyone who bathes in that river also attains perfection, and therefore all persons who desire perfection go bathe there.

TEXT 33

कपिलोऽपि महायोगी भगवान् पितुराश्रमात् ।
मातरं समनुज्ञाप्य प्रागुदीचीं दिशं ययौ ॥३३॥

kapilo 'pi mahā-yogī
bhagavān pitur āśramāt
mātaraṁ samanujñāpya
prāg-udīcīṁ diśaṁ yayau

kapilaḥ—Lord Kapila; *api*—surely; *mahā-yogī*—the great sage; *bhagavān*—the Supreme Personality of Godhead; *pituḥ*—of His father; *āśramāt*—from the hermitage; *mātaram*—from His mother; *samanujñāpya*—having asked permission; *prāk-udīcīm*—northeast; *diśam*—direction; *yayau*—He went.

TRANSLATION

My dear Vidura, the great sage Kapila, the Personality of Godhead, left His father's hermitage with the permission of His mother and went towards the northeast.

TEXT 34

सिद्धचारणगन्धर्वैर्मुनिभिश्चाप्सरोगणैः ।
स्तूयमानः समुद्रेण दत्तार्हणनिकेतनः ॥३४॥

siddha-cāraṇa-gandharvair
munibhiś cāpsaro-gaṇaiḥ
stūyamānaḥ samudreṇa
dattārhaṇa-niketanaḥ

siddha—by the Siddhas; *cāraṇa*—by the Cāraṇas; *gandharvaiḥ*—by the Gandharvas; *munibhiḥ*—by the *munis; ca*—and; *apsaraḥ-gaṇaiḥ*—by the Apsarās (damsels of the heavenly planets); *stūyamānaḥ*—being extolled; *samudreṇa*—by the ocean; *datta*—given; *arhaṇa*—oblations; *niketanaḥ*—place of residence.

TRANSLATION

While He was passing in the northern direction, all the celestial denizens known as Cāraṇas and Gandharvas, as well as the munis and the damsels of the heavenly planets, prayed and offered

Him all respects. The ocean offered Him oblations and a place of residence.

PURPORT

It is understood that Kapila Muni first went towards the Himalayas and traced the course of the River Ganges, and He again came to the delta of the Ganges at the sea now known as the Bay of Bengal. The ocean gave Him residence at a place still known as Gaṅgā-sāgara, where the River Ganges meets the sea. That place is called Gaṅgā-sāgara-tīrtha, and even today people gather there to offer respects to Kapiladeva, the original author of the Sāṅkhya system of philosophy. Unfortunately, this Sāṅkhya system has been misrepresented by an imposter who is also named Kapila, but that other system of philosophy does not tally with anything described in the Sāṅkhya of Kapila in the *Śrīmad-Bhāgavatam.*

TEXT 35

आस्ते योगं समास्थाय सांख्याचार्यैरभिष्टुतः ।
त्रयाणामपि लोकानामुपशान्त्यै समाहितः ॥३५॥

āste yogaṁ samāsthāya
sāṅkhyācāryair abhiṣṭutaḥ
trayāṇām api lokānām
upaśāntyai samāhitaḥ

āste—He remains; *yogam*—*yoga;* *samāsthāya*—having practiced; *sāṅkhya*—of the Sāṅkhya philosophy; *ācāryaiḥ*—by the great teachers; *abhiṣṭutaḥ*—worshiped; *trayāṇām*—three; *api*—certainly; *lokānām*—of the worlds; *upaśāntyai*—for the deliverance; *samāhitaḥ*—fixed in trance.

TRANSLATION

Even now Kapila Muni is staying there in trance for the deliverance of the conditioned souls in the three worlds, and all the ācāryas, or great teachers, of the system of Sāṅkhya philosophy are worshiping Him.

TEXT 36

एतन्निगदितं तात यत्पृष्टोऽहं तवानघ ।
कपिलस्य च संवादो देवहूत्याश्च पावनः ॥३६॥

etan nigaditaṁ tāta
yat pṛṣṭo 'haṁ tavānagha
kapilasya ca saṁvādo
devahūtyāś ca pāvanaḥ

etat—this; *nigaditam*—spoken; *tāta*—O dear Vidura; *yat*—which; *pṛṣṭaḥ*—was asked; *aham*—I; *tava*—by you; *anagha*—O sinless Vidura; *kapilasya*—of Kapila; *ca*—and; *saṁvādaḥ*—conversation; *devahūtyāḥ*—of Devahūti; *ca*—and; *pāvanaḥ*—pure.

TRANSLATION

My dear son, since you have inquired from me, I have answered. O sinless one, the descriptions of Kapiladeva and His mother and their activities are the purest of all pure discourses.

TEXT 37

य इदमनुश्रृणोति योऽभिधत्ते
कपिलमुनेर्मतमात्मयोगगुह्यम् ।
भगवति कृतधीः सुपर्णकेता-
वुपलभते भगवत्पदारविन्दम् ॥३७॥

ya idam anuśṛṇoti yo 'bhidhatte
kapila-muner matam ātma-yoga-guhyam
bhagavati kṛta-dhīḥ suparṇa-ketāv
upalabhate bhagavat-padāravindam

yaḥ—whoever; *idam*—this; *anuśṛṇoti*—hears; *yaḥ*—whoever; *abhidhatte*—expounds; *kapila-muneḥ*—of the sage Kapila; *matam*—instructions; *ātma-yoga*—based on meditation on the Lord; *guhyam*—confidential; *bhagavati*—on the Supreme Personality of Godhead;

kṛta-dhīḥ—having fixed his mind; *suparṇa-ketau*—who has a banner of Garuḍa; *upalabhate*—achieves; *bhagavat*—of the Supreme Lord; *pada-aravindam*—the lotus feet.

TRANSLATION

The description of the dealings of Kapiladeva and His mother is very confidential, and anyone who hears or reads this narration becomes a devotee of the Supreme Personality of Godhead, who is carried by Garuḍa, and he thereafter enters into the abode of the Supreme Lord to engage in the transcendental loving service of the Lord.

PURPORT

The narration of Kapiladeva and His mother, Devahūti, is so perfect and transcendental that even if one only hears or reads this description, he achieves the highest perfectional goal of life, for he engages in the loving service of the lotus feet of the Supreme Personality of Godhead. There is no doubt that Devahūti, who had the Supreme Lord as her son and who followed the instructions of Kapiladeva so nicely, attained the highest perfection of human life.

Thus end the Bhaktivedanta purports of the Third Canto, Thirty-third Chapter, of the Śrīmad-Bhāgavatam, *entitled "Activities of Kapila."*

END OF THE THIRD CANTO

Appendixes

About the Author

His Divine Grace A.C. Bhaktivedanta Swami Prabhupāda appeared in this world in 1896 in Calcutta, India. He first met his spiritual master, Śrīla Bhaktisiddhānta Sarasvatī Gosvāmī, in Calcutta in 1922. Bhaktisiddhānta Sarasvatī, a prominent religious scholar and the founder of sixty-four Gauḍīya Maṭhas (Vedic institutes), liked this educated young man and convinced him to dedicate his life to teaching Vedic knowledge. Śrīla Prabhupāda became his student, and eleven years later (1933) at Allahabad he became his formally initiated disciple.

At their first meeting, in 1922, Śrīla Bhaktisiddhānta Sarasvatī Ṭhākura requested Śrīla Prabhupāda to broadcast Vedic knowledge through the English language. In the years that followed, Śrīla Prabhupāda wrote a commentary on the *Bhagavad-gītā,* assisted the Gauḍīya Maṭha in its work and, in 1944, started *Back to Godhead,* an English fortnightly magazine. Maintaining the publication was a struggle. Singlehandedly, Śrīla Prabhupāda edited it, typed the manuscripts, checked the galley proofs, and even distributed the individual copies. Once begun, the magazine never stopped; it is now being continued by his disciples in the West and is published in over thirty languages.

Recognizing Śrīla Prabhupāda's philosophical learning and devotion, the Gauḍīya Vaiṣṇava Society honored him in 1947 with the title "Bhaktivedanta." In 1950, at the age of fifty-four, Śrīla Prabhupāda retired from married life, adopting the *vānaprastha* (retired) order to devote more time to his studies and writing. Śrīla Prabhupāda traveled to the holy city of Vṛndāvana, where he lived in very humble circumstances in the historic medieval temple of Rādhā-Dāmodara. There he engaged for several years in deep study and writing. He accepted the renounced order of life (*sannyāsa*) in 1959. At Rādhā-Dāmodara, Śrīla Prabhupāda began work on his life's masterpiece: a multivolume annotated translation of the eighteen-thousand-verse *Śrīmad-Bhāgavatam* (*Bhāgavata Purāṇa*). He also wrote *Easy Journey to Other Planets.*

After publishing three volumes of the *Bhāgavatam,* Śrīla Prabhupāda came to the United States, in September 1965, to fulfill the mission of his spiritual master. Subsequently, His Divine Grace wrote more than sixty volumes of authoritative annotated translations and summary studies of the philosophical and religious classics of India.

When he first arrived by freighter in New York City, Śrīla Prabhupāda was practically penniless. Only after almost a year of great difficulty did he establish the International Society for Krishna Consciousness, in July of 1966. Before his passing away on November 14, 1977, he guided the Society and saw it grow to a worldwide confederation of more than one hundred *āśramas,* schools, temples, institutes and farm communities.

In 1968, Śrīla Prabhupāda created New Vrindaban, an experimental Vedic community in the hills of West Virginia. Inspired by the success of New Vrindaban, now a thriving farm community of more than two thousand acres, his students have since founded several similar communities in the United States and abroad.

In 1972, His Divine Grace introduced the Vedic system of primary and secondary education in the West by founding the Gurukula school in Dallas, Texas. Since then, under his supervision, his disciples have established children's schools throughout the United States and the rest of the world, with the principal educational center now located in Vṛndāvana, India.

Śrīla Prabhupāda also inspired the construction of several large international cultural centers in India. The center at Śrīdhāma Māyāpur in West Bengal is the site for a planned spiritual city, an ambitious project for which construction will extend over many years to come. In Vṛndāvana, India, are the magnificent Kṛṣṇa-Balarāma Temple and International Guesthouse, and Śrīla Prabhupāda Memorial and Museum. There is also a major cultural and educational center in Bombay. Other centers are planned in a dozen important locations on the Indian subcontinent.

Śrīla Prabhupāda's most significant contribution, however, is his books. Highly respected by the academic community for their authority, depth and clarity, they are used as standard textbooks in numerous college courses. His writings have been translated into over fifty languages. The Bhaktivedanta Book Trust, established in 1972 to publish the works of His Divine Grace, has thus become the world's largest publisher of books in the field of Indian religion and philosophy.

In just twelve years, in spite of his advanced age, Śrīla Prabhupāda circled the globe fourteen times on lecture tours that took him to six continents. In spite of such a vigorous schedule, Śrīla Prabhupāda continued to write prolifically. His writings constitute a veritable library of Vedic philosophy, religion, literature and culture.

GLOSSARY

A

Ācārya—an ideal teacher, who teaches by his personal example; a spiritual master.

Adbhuta—the *rasa* (devotional sentiment) of wonder or amazement.

Advaita Prabhu—an incarnation of Mahā-Viṣṇu who appeared as a principal associate of Lord Caitanya Mahāprabhu.

Agni—the demigod in charge of fire.

Ahaṁ brahmāsmi—the Vedic aphorism "I am spirit."

Aja—the unborn; the Supreme Lord.

Ambarīṣa Mahārāja—a great devotee-king who perfectly executed all nine devotional practices (hearing, chanting, etc.).

Ananta—the Lord's thousand-headed serpent incarnation, who serves as the bed of Viṣṇu and sustains the planets on His hoods.

Aniruddha—one of the four original expansions of Lord Kṛṣṇa in the spiritual world; also, a grandson of Lord Kṛṣṇa.

Arjuna—one of the five Pāṇḍava brothers. Kṛṣṇa became his chariot driver and spoke the *Bhagavad-gītā* to him.

Artha—economic development.

Āśrama—one of four spiritual orders of life. *See also: Brahmacarya; Gṛhastha; Vānaprastha; Sannyāsa*

Aṣṭāṅga-yoga—the eightfold *yoga* system propounded by Patañjali.

Asura—an atheistic demon; a gross materialist.

Āyur-veda—the Vedic scriptures containing medical science.

B

Bali Mahārāja—a king who became a great devotee by surrendering everything to Vāmanadeva, the Lord's dwarf-*brāhmaṇa* incarnation.

Bhagavad-gītā—the discourse between the Supreme Lord, Kṛṣṇa, and His devotee Arjuna expounding devotional service as both the principal means and the ultimate end of spiritual perfection.

Bhagavān—the Supreme Lord, who possesses all opulences in full.

Bhāgavata Purāṇa—this scripture, *Śrīmad-Bhāgavatam.*

Bhakta—a devotee of the Supreme Lord.

Bhakti-rasāmṛta-sindhu—Rūpa Gosvāmī's definitive explanation of the science of devotional service.

References

The purports of *Śrīmad-Bhāgavatam* are all confirmed by standard Vedic authorities. The following authentic scriptures are cited in this volume. For specific page references, consult the general index.

Bhagavad-gītā

Bhakti-rasāmṛta-sindhu

Brahma-saṁhitā

Caitanya-caritāmṛta

Chāndogya Upaniṣad

Hari-bhakti-vilāsa

Īśopaniṣad

Kaṭha Upaniṣad

Nārada-pañcarātra

Patañjali-yoga-sūtra

Śrīmad-Bhāgavatam

Śvetāśvatara Upaniṣad

Varāha Purāṇa

Vedānta-sūtra

Viṣṇu Purāṇa

Bhakti-yoga—linking with the Supreme Lord by devotional service.

Bhaktisiddhānta Sarasvatī Ṭhākura—(1874-1937) the spiritual master of the author, His Divine Grace A. C. Bhaktivedanta Swami Prabhupāda, and thus the spiritual grandfather of the present-day Kṛṣṇa consciousness movement. A powerful preacher, he founded sixty-four missions in India.

Bhaktivinoda Ṭhākura—(1838-1915) the great-grandfather of the present-day Kṛṣṇa consciousness movement, the spiritual master of Śrīla Gaurakiśora dāsa Bābājī, and the father of Śrīla Bhaktisiddhānta Sarasvatī.

Bhārata-varṣa—India, named after King Bharata.

Bharata Mahārāja—a great devotee of the Lord who developed an attachment causing him to take birth as a deer. In his next life, as the *brāhmaṇa* Jaḍa Bharata, he attained spiritual perfection.

Bilvamaṅgala Ṭhākura—a great devotee-author, whose works include the *Kṛṣṇa-karṇāmṛta.*

Brahmā—the first created living being and secondary creator of the material universe.

Brahma-saṁhitā—Lord Brahmā's prayers in glorification of the Supreme Lord.

Brahmacārī—a celibate student of a spiritual master.

Brahmacarya—celibate student life; the first order of Vedic spiritual life.

Brahmajyoti—the bodily effulgence of the Supreme Lord, which constitutes the brilliant illumination of the spiritual sky.

Brahmaloka—the highest planet of the universe, that of the demigod Brahmā.

Brahman—the Absolute Truth; especially the impersonal aspect of the Absolute.

Brāhmaṇa—a member of the intellectual, priestly class; the first Vedic social order.

Bṛhaspati—the spiritual master of King Indra and chief priest for the demigods.

C

Caitanya-caritāmṛta—Śrīla Kṛṣṇadāsa Kavirāja's authorized biography of Lord Śrī Caitanya Mahāprabhu, presenting the Lord's pastimes and teachings.

Caitanya Mahāprabhu—(1486-1534) the Supreme Lord appearing as His own greatest devotee to teach love of God, especially through the process of *saṅkīrtana*.

Cāṇakya Paṇḍita—the *brāhmaṇa* advisor to King Candragupta responsible for checking Alexander the Great's invasion of India. He is a famous author of books on politics and morality.

Candra—the demigod in charge of the moon.

Cāturmāsya—the four months of the rainy season in India. Devotees take special vows of austerity during this time.

Causal Ocean—*See:* Kāraṇa Ocean.

Cintāmaṇi—a mystically potent "touchstone" described in Vedic literatures.

D

Devahūti—the daughter of Svāyambhuva Manu who was the wife of Kardama Muni and the mother of Lord Kapila.

Devakī—a wife of Vasudeva and the mother of Lord Kṛṣṇa.

Dharma—religion; duty, especially everyone's eternal service nature.

Dhṛtarāṣṭra—the uncle of the Pāṇḍavas whose attempt to usurp their kingdom for the sake of his own sons resulted in the Kurukṣetra war.

Dhruva Mahārāja—a great devotee who as a child performed severe austerities to meet the Lord and get the kingdom denied him. Thus he received an entire planet and God-realization as well.

Dhyāna—meditational *yoga*.

Diti—a wife of Kaśyapa Muni and the mother of the demons Hiraṇyākṣa and Hiraṇyakaśipu.

Durgā—the personified material energy and the wife of Lord Śiva.

Durvāsā Muni—a powerful mystic *yogī*, famous for his fearful curses.

Duryodhana—the eldest son of Dhṛtarāṣṭra and chief rival of the Pāṇḍavas.

Dvaipāyana—*See:* Vyāsadeva

Dvāpara-yuga—the third in the cycle of four ages. It lasts 864,000 years.

Dvārakā—the offshore-island kingdom of Lord Kṛṣṇa, where He performed pastimes five thousand years ago in India.

Dvārakādhīśa—the Supreme Lord, Kṛṣṇa, Lord of the city of Dvārakā.

G

Gāndhārī—the saintly and faithful wife of King Dhṛtarāṣṭra and mother of one hundred sons.

Gaṇeśa—the demigod in charge of material opulence and freedom from misfortune. He is the son of Lord Śiva and the scribe who wrote down the *Mahābhārata.*

Garbhādhāna-saṁskāra—the Vedic ceremony of purification to be performed by parents before conceiving a child.

Garbhodakaśāyī Viṣṇu—the second Viṣṇu expansion, who enters each universe and, by His glance, creates the diverse material manifestations.

Garuḍa—Lord Viṣṇu's eternal carrier, a great devotee in a birdlike form.

Gauḍīya Vaiṣṇavas—devotees of Lord Kṛṣṇa coming in disciplic succession from Lord Śrī Caitanya Mahāprabhu.

Gauracandra—the "golden moon," Lord Śrī Caitanya Mahāprabhu.

Goloka Vṛndāvana (Kṛṣṇaloka)—the highest spiritual planet, Lord Kṛṣṇa's personal abode.

Gopīs—Kṛṣṇa's cowherd girl friends, who are His most surrendered and confidential devotees.

Govinda—the Supreme Lord, Kṛṣṇa, who gives pleasure to the land, the cows and the senses.

Gṛhastha—regulated householder life; the second order of Vedic spiritual life.

Guru—a spiritual master.

H

Hanumān—the great monkey servitor of Lord Rāmacandra.

Harā—*See:* Rādhārāṇī

Hari—the Supreme Lord, who removes all obstacles to spiritual progress.

Hari-bhakti-vilāsa—Sanātana Gosvāmī's book on the rules and regulations of Vaiṣṇava life.

Haridāsa Ṭhākura—a great devotee and associate of Lord Śrī Caitanya Mahāprabhu who chanted three hundred thousand names of God a day.

Haryakṣa—*See:* Hiraṇyākṣa

Haṭha-yoga—the practice of postures and breathing exercises for achieving purification and sense control.
Hiraṇyakaśipu—a demoniac king killed by the Lord's incarnation Nṛsiṁhadeva.
Hiraṇyākṣa—the demoniac son of Kaśyapa who was killed by Lord Varāha.
Hṛṣīkeśa—the Supreme Lord, the supreme master of everyone's senses.

I

Ilāvṛta-varṣa—the original name of this earth planet, before it became known as Bhārata-varṣa.
Indra—the chief of the administrative demigods and king of the heavenly planets.
Īśopaniṣad—one of the 108 Vedic scriptures known as the *Upaniṣads.*

J

Jaḍa Bharata—Bharata Mahārāja in his final birth as the renounced *brāhmaṇa* who gave wonderful spiritual instruction to Mahārāja Rahūgaṇa.
Jagāi and Mādhāi—two great debauchees whom Lord Nityānanda converted into Vaiṣṇavas.
Janaka Mahārāja—the father of Sītā-devī, consort of Lord Rāmacandra.
Jaya and Vijaya—two doorkeepers of Vaikuṇṭha who were cursed for offending the four Kumāra Ṛṣis. After three births as demons they attained liberation.
Jīva (jīvātmā)—the living entity, who is an eternal soul, individual, but part and parcel of the Supreme Lord.
Jīva Gosvāmī—one of the six Vaiṣṇava spiritual masters who directly followed Lord Śrī Caitanya Mahāprabhu and systematically presented His teachings.
Jñāna—knowledge.
Jñāna-yoga—the process of approaching the Supreme by the cultivation of knowledge.
Jñānī—one who cultivates knowledge by empirical speculation.

K

Kalā—a form of the Lord that is an expansion of the Lord's original form.

Kālī—*See:* Durgā

Kali-yuga (Age of Kali)—the present age, characterized by quarrel. It is last in the cycle of four ages and began five thousand years ago.

Kāma—lust.

Kaṁsa—a demoniac king of the Bhoja dynasty and maternal uncle of Kṛṣṇa.

Kapila—the incarnation of the Supreme Lord who appeared as the son of Kardama Muni and Devahūti and taught the Kṛṣṇa conscious Sāṅkhya philosophy.

Kāraṇa Ocean—the corner of the spiritual universe in which Lord Mahā-Viṣṇu lies down to create the entirety of material universes.

Kāraṇodakaśāyī Viṣṇu—Mahā-Viṣṇu, the expansion of the Supreme Lord from whom all material universes emanate.

Kardama Muni—the father of Lord Kapila and one of the chief forefathers of the population of the universe.

Karma—material, fruitive activity and its reactions.

Karma-yoga—action in devotional service; also, fruitive actions performed in accordance with Vedic injunctions.

Karmī—one engaged in *karma* (fruitive activity); a materialist.

Kaśyapa—a great saint who was the father of many demigods and also of the Supreme Lord's incarnation Vāmanadeva.

Kaṭha Upaniṣad—one of the 108 Vedic scriptures known as Upaniṣads.

Keśī—a demon who attacked the inhabitants of Vṛndāvana in the form of a wild horse but was killed by Lord Kṛṣṇa.

Kīrtana—the devotional process of chanting the names and glories of the Supreme Lord.

Kṛṣṇa—the Supreme Personality of Godhead appearing in His original, two-armed form.

Kṛṣṇadāsa Kavirāja—the great Vaiṣṇava spiritual master who recorded the biography and teachings of Lord Śrī Caitanya Mahāprabhu in the *Caitanya-caritāmṛta*.

Kṛṣṇaloka—*See:* Goloka Vṛndāvana

Kṣatriya—a warrior or administrator; the second Vedic social order.

Kṣīrodakaśāyī Viṣṇu—the expansion of the Supreme Lord who enters the heart of every living being as the Supersoul.

Kumāras—four learned ascetic sons of Lord Brahmā appearing eternally as children.

Kuśa—an auspicious grass used in Vedic rituals and sacrifices.

L

Lakṣmī—the goddess of fortune and eternal consort of the Supreme Lord as Nārāyaṇa.

M

Madana—Cupid, the demigod who incites lusty desires in the living beings.

Madana-mohana—the Supreme Lord, Kṛṣṇa, who enchants even Cupid.

Mādhāi—*See:* Jagāi and Mādhāi

Madhusūdana—the Supreme Lord, Kṛṣṇa, the killer of the demon Madhu.

Mahā-lakṣmī—*See:* Lakṣmī

Mahā-mantra—the great chant for deliverance:
Hare Kṛṣṇa, Hare Kṛṣṇa, Kṛṣṇa Kṛṣṇa, Hare Hare
Hare Rāma, Hare Rāma, Rāma Rāma, Hare Hare.

Mahā-Viṣṇu—the expansion of the Supreme Lord from whom all material universes emanate.

Mahābhārata—Vyāsadeva's epic history of greater India, which includes the events of the Kurukṣetra war and the narration of *Bhagavad-gītā.*

Mahat-tattva—the original, undifferentiated form of the total material energy, from which the material world is manifest.

Mahātmā—a "great soul," an exalted devotee of Lord Kṛṣṇa.

Maheśvara—*See:* Śiva

Maitreya Muni—the great sage who spoke *Śrīmad-Bhāgavatam* to Vidura.

Makara-dhvaja—*See:* Cupid

Mantra—a transcendental sound or Vedic hymn, which can deliver the mind from illusion.

Manu—a demigod son of Brahmā who is the forefather and lawgiver of the human race. There is a succession of fourteen Manus each day of Brahmā.

Manu-saṁhitā—the scriptural lawbook for mankind, given by Manu.

Manu, Svāyambhuva—*See:* Svāyambhuva Manu

Manu, Vaivasvata—*See:* Vaivasvata Manu

Manvantara—the duration of each Manu's reign (306,720,000 years); used as a standard division of history.

Marīci—one of the great sages born directly from Lord Brahmā.

Mārkaṇḍeya Purāṇa—the Purāṇa of Mārkaṇḍeya Ṛṣi.

Mathurā—Lord Kṛṣṇa's abode, surrounding Vṛndāvana, where He took birth and to which He later returned after performing His childhood Vṛndāvana pastimes.

Māyā—the inferior, illusory energy of the Supreme Lord, which rules over this material creation; forgetfulness of one's relationship with Kṛṣṇa.

Māyāvāda—the impersonal theory of the unqualified oneness of the living entities, nature and the Supreme.

Māyāvādī—a proponent of Māyavāda philosophy.

Menakā—the famous society girl of the heavenly planets who seduced the sage Viśvāmitra.

Mohinī—the Supreme Lord's incarnation as the most beautiful woman.

Mokṣa—liberation from material bondage.

Mṛtyu—death personified.

Mukti—liberation from material bondage.

Mukunda—the Supreme Lord, who is the giver of liberation.

N

Naimiṣāraṇya—a sacred forest in central India.

Nanda Mahārāja—the king of Vraja and foster father of Lord Kṛṣṇa.

Nārada Muni—a pure devotee of the Lord who travels throughout the universes in his eternal body, glorifying devotional service. He is the spiritual master of Vyāsadeva and of many other great devotees.

Nārada-pañcarātra—Nārada Muni's book on the processes of Deity worship and *mantra* meditation.

Nārāyaṇa—Lord Kṛṣṇa's expansion as the Supreme Lord, the resting place of all living entities, in His majestic four-armed form; Lord Viṣṇu.

Narottama dāsa Ṭhākura—a Vaiṣṇava spiritual master in the disciplic succession from Lord Śrī Caitanya Mahāprabhu. A disciple of Lokanātha dāsa Gosvāmī, he wrote many Bengali songs glorifying Kṛṣṇa.

Nirguṇa-brahma—the impersonal conception of the Supreme Truth as being without any qualities.

Nirvāṇa—the cessation of material activities and existence, which, according to Vaiṣṇava philosophy, does not deny spiritual activities and existence.

Nitya-baddha—the conditioned soul, bound in the material world.

Nityānanda—the incarnation of Lord Balarāma who appeared as the principal associate of Lord Śrī Caitanya Mahāprabhu.

Niyama—restraint of the senses.

Nṛsiṁhadeva—the half-man, half-lion incarnation of the Supreme Lord, who protected Prahlāda and killed the demon Hiraṇyakaśipu.

O

Oṁkāra—the sacred sound *oṁ*, which is the beginning of many Vedic *mantras* and which represents the Supreme Lord.

P

Pāṇḍavas—Yudhiṣṭhira, Bhīma, Arjuna, Nakula and Sahadeva, the five warrior-brothers who were intimate friends and devotees of Lord Kṛṣṇa.

Paṇḍita—a scholar.

Parārdha—one half of Brahmā's lifetime of 311 trillion 40 billion years.

Paramahaṁsa—a topmost, swanlike devotee of the Supreme Lord; the highest stage of *sannyāsa.*

Paramātmā—the Supersoul, Viṣṇu as manifest in the heart of each embodied living entity and throughout material nature.

Paramparā—a disciplic succession of bona fide spiritual masters.

Parīkṣit Mahārāja—the emperor of the world who heard *Śrīmad-Bhāgavatam* from Śukadeva Gosvāmī and thus attained perfection.

Patañjali—the author of the original *yoga* system.

Pitās—forefathers; especially those departed ancestors who have been promoted to one of the higher planets.

Prabodhānanda Sarasvatī—a great Vaiṣṇava poet-philosopher and devotee of Lord Śrī Caitanya Mahāprabhu. He was the uncle of Gopāla Bhaṭṭa Gosvāmī.

Pradyumna—one of the four original expansions of Lord Kṛṣṇa in the spiritual world.

Prahlāda Mahārāja—a devotee persecuted by his demoniac father but protected and saved by the Lord in the form of Nṛsiṁhadeva.

Prāṇāyāma—breath control used in *yoga* practice, especially *aṣṭāṅga-yoga*.

Prasādam—the Lord's mercy; food or other items spiritualized by being first offered to the Supreme Lord.

Pratyāhāra—withdrawal of the senses from all unnecessary activities.

Purāṇas—the eighteen Vedic supplementary literatures, historical scriptures.

Puruṣa—the enjoyer, or male; the living entity or the Supreme Lord.

Puruṣa-avatāras—the three primary Viṣṇu expansions of the Supreme Lord who are involved in universal creation.

Pūtanā—a witch who was sent by Kaṁsa to appear in the form of a beautiful woman to kill baby Kṛṣṇa but who was killed by Him and granted liberation.

R

Rādhārāṇī—Lord Kṛṣṇa's most intimate consort, who is the personification of His internal, spiritual potency.

Rahūgaṇa Mahārāja—the king who received spiritual instruction from Jaḍa Bharata.

Rajas—the material mode of passion.

Rājasūya-yajña—the great sacrificial ceremony performed by King Yudhiṣṭhira and attended by Lord Kṛṣṇa.

Ramā—Lakṣmī, the goddess of fortune and eternal consort of the Supreme Lord, Nārāyaṇa.

Rāmacandra—an incarnation of the Supreme Lord as the perfect king.

Rāmāyaṇa—the original epic history about Lord Rāmacandra, written by Vālmīki Muni.

Rāvaṇa—a demoniac ruler who was killed by Lord Rāmacandra.

Romaharṣaṇa—the father of Sūta Gosvāmī. He was killed by Lord Balarāma for his offenses.

Ṛṣi—a sage.

Rudra—*See:* Śiva

Rukmiṇī—Lord Kṛṣṇa's principal queen in Dvārakā.

Rūpa Gosvāmī—the chief of the six Vaiṣṇava spiritual masters who directly followed Lord Śrī Caitanya Mahāprabhu and systematically presented His teachings.

S

Sāma Veda—one of the four original *Vedas.* It consists of musical settings of the sacrificial hymns.

Samādhi—trance; complete absorption in God consciousness.

Sampradāya—a disciplic succession of spiritual masters, and the followers in that tradition.

Sanātana—eternal.

Sanātana Gosvāmī—one of the six Vaiṣṇava spiritual masters who directly followed Lord Śrī Caitanya Mahāprabhu and systematically presented His teachings.

Śaṅkarācārya—the incarnation of Lord Śiva as the great philosopher who, on the order of the Supreme Lord, preached impersonalism based on the *Vedas.*

Saṅkarṣaṇa—one of the four original expansions of Lord Kṛṣṇa in the spiritual world; also, another name of Balarāma, given by Garga Muni.

Sāṅkhya—analytical discrimination between spirit and matter, and the path of devotional service described by Lord Kapila, the son of Devahūti.

Saṅkīrtana—congregational or public glorification of the Supreme Lord, Kṛṣṇa, especially through chanting of the Lord's holy names.

Sannyāsa—renounced life; the fourth order of Vedic spiritual life.

Śāstra—revealed scripture: the Vedic literature.
Sat—eternal.
Śatarūpā—the wife of Svāyambhuva Manu and mother of Devahūti.
Satya-yuga—the first and best in the cycle of the four ages of the universe. It lasts 1,728,000 years.
Saubhari Muni—a powerful mystic who accidentally fell down to sex attraction.
Śaunaka Ṛṣi—the chief of the sages assembled at Naimiṣāraṇya when Sūta Gosvāmī spoke *Śrīmad-Bhāgavatam.*
Siddhi—mystic power or perfection acquired by *yoga* practice, natural to residents of Siddhaloka.
Śikṣāṣṭaka—eight verses by Lord Śrī Caitanya Mahāprabhu glorifying the chanting of the Lord's holy name.
Sītā—the eternal consort of Lord Rāmacandra.
Śiva—the special incarnation of the Lord as the demigod in charge of the mode of ignorance and the destruction of the material manifestation.
Śivānanda Sena—a great householder devotee of Lord Śrī Caitanya Mahāprabhu.
Smārta-brāhmaṇa—a *brāhmaṇa* interested more in the external performance of the rules and rituals of the *Vedas* than in attaining Lord Kṛṣṇa, the goal of the *Vedas.*
Smṛti—revealed scriptures supplementary to the *śruti,* or original Vedic scriptures, which are the *Vedas* and *Upaniṣads.*
Śrāddha—ceremony of offerings to one's ancestors to free them from suffering.
Śrīdhara Svāmī—an early Vaiṣṇava commentator on *Bhagavad-gītā* and *Śrīmad-Bhāgavatam.*
Sudarśana cakra—the disc weapon of the Supreme Lord.
Śuddha-sattva—the spiritual platform of pure goodness.
Śūdra—a laborer; the fourth of the Vedic social orders.
Śukadeva Gosvāmī—the great devotee-sage who originally spoke *Śrīmad-Bhāgavatam* to King Parīkṣit just prior to the king's death.
Śukrācārya—the spiritual master of the demons.
Sūta Gosvāmī—the great devotee-sage who recounted the discourse between Parīkṣit and Śukadeva to the sages assembled in the forest of Naimiṣāraṇya.

Svāyambhuva Manu—the Manu who appeared first in Brahmā's day and who was the grandfather of Dhruva Mahārāja.
Śyāmasundara—the Supreme Personality of Godhead, Kṛṣṇa, who is blackish and very beautiful.

T

Tretā-yuga—the second in the cycle of the four ages of the universe. It lasts 1,296,000 years.
Tulasī—a sacred plant dear to Lord Kṛṣṇa and worshiped by His devotees.

U

Upaniṣads—the most significant philosophical sections of the *Vedas*.
Uttānapāda—the king who was a son of Svāyambhuva Manu and the father of Dhruva Mahārāja.

V

Vaikuṇṭha—the spiritual world, where there is no anxiety.
Vaiṣṇava—a devotee of the Supreme Lord, Viṣṇu, or Kṛṣṇa.
Vaiśyas—farmers and merchants; the third Vedic social order.
Vaivasvata Manu—the current Manu, the seventh of fourteen.
Vāmana—the incarnation of the Supreme Lord as a dwarf *brāhmaṇa*, to whom Bali Mahārāja surrendered everything.
Vānaprastha—one who has retired from family life; the third order of Vedic spiritual life.
Varāha—the incarnation of the Supreme Lord as a boar.
Varṇa—one of the four Vedic social-occupational divisions of society, distinguished by quality of work and situation with regard to the modes of nature (*guṇas*). *See also: Brāhmaṇa; Kṣatriya; Vaiśya; Śūdra*
Varṇāśrama-dharma—the Vedic social system of four social and four spiritual orders. *See also: Varṇa; Āśrama*
Varuṇa—the demigod in charge of the oceans.
Vasudeva—the father of Kṛṣṇa and half-brother of Nanda Mahārāja.
Vāsudeva—the Supreme Lord, Kṛṣṇa, son of Vasudeva and proprietor of everything, material and spiritual.
Vāyu—air; the demigod in charge of the wind.

Vedānta—the philosophy of the *Vedānta-sūtra* of Śrīla Vyāsadeva, containing a conclusive summary of Vedic philosophical knowledge and showing the Supreme Lord as the goal of life.

Vedānta-sūtra—Śrīla Vyāsadeva's conclusive summary of Vedic philosophical knowledge, written in brief codes.

Vedas—the original revealed scriptures, first spoken by Lord Kṛṣṇa.

Vedic literature—the original four *Vedas*, the *Upaniṣads*, the *Purāṇas* and other supplements, and also all scriptures and commentaries written in pursuance of the Vedic conclusion.

Vidura—a great devotee of Kṛṣṇa who was a son of Vyāsadeva, an incarnation of Yamarāja and an uncle of the Pāṇḍavas.

Virāṭ-puruṣa—the universal form of the Supreme Lord as the totality of all material manifestations.

Viṣṇu—the Supreme Lord; Lord Kṛṣṇa's expansions in Vaikuṇṭha and for the creation and maintenance of the material universes.

Viṣṇu-tattva—the status or category of Godhead; applies to primary expansions of the Supreme Lord.

Viṣṇu Purāṇa—one of the Vedic scriptures known as the *Purāṇas*.

Viśvanātha Cakravartī Ṭhākura—a great Vaiṣṇava spiritual master in the line of Lord Śrī Caitanya Mahāprabhu. He was a commentator on *Śrīmad-Bhāgavatam*.

Vṛndāvana—Kṛṣṇa's eternal abode, where He fully manifests His quality of sweetness; the village on this earth in which He enacted His childhood pastimes five thousand years ago.

Vṛtra—Vṛtrāsura, a great demon killed by Indra. He was actually the devotee Citraketu, who had been cursed to take a low birth.

Vyāsadeva—the incarnation of Lord Kṛṣṇa who gave the *Vedas, Purāṇas, Vedānta-sūtra* and *Mahābhārata* to mankind.

Y

Yadus—the descendants of Yadu, in which dynasty Lord Kṛṣṇa appeared.

Yajña—a Vedic sacrifice; also, the Supreme Lord, the goal and enjoyer of all sacrifices.

Yamarāja—the demigod in charge of death and of punishing the sinful.

Yāmunācārya—a great Vaiṣṇava author and spiritual master of the Śrī-sampradāya.

Yayāti—the king who, because of his lust, was cursed by Śukrācārya to prematurely accept old age.

Yoga—spiritual discipline to link oneself with the Supreme.

Yoga-siddhis—mystic powers.

Yogamāyā—the internal, spiritual energy of the Supreme Lord; also, its personification as Kṛṣṇa's younger sister.

Yogī—a transcendentalist striving for union with the Supreme.

Yojana—a Vedic unit of length equal to about eight miles.

Yugas—ages in the life of a universe, occurring in a repeated cycle of four.

Sanskrit Pronunciation Guide

Throughout the centuries, the Sanskrit language has been written in a variety of alphabets. The mode of writing most widely used throughout India, however, is called *devanāgarī*, which means, literally, the writing used in "the cities of the demigods." The *devanāgarī* alphabet consists of forty-eight characters: thirteen vowels and thirty-five consonants. Ancient Sanskrit grammarians arranged this alphabet according to practical linguistic principles, and this order has been accepted by all Western scholars. The system of transliteration used in this book conforms to a system that scholars in the last fifty years have accepted to indicate the pronunciation of each Sanskrit sound.

Vowels

अ a आ ā इ i ई ī उ u ऊ ū ऋ ṛ

ॠ ṝ ऌ ḷ ए e ऐ ai ओ o औ au

Consonants

Gutturals:	क ka	ख kha	ग ga	घ gha	ङ ṅa
Palatals:	च ca	छ cha	ज ja	झ jha	ञ ña
Cerebrals:	ट ṭa	ठ ṭha	ड ḍa	ढ ḍha	ण ṇa
Dentals:	त ta	थ tha	द da	ध dha	न na
Labials:	प pa	फ pha	ब ba	भ bha	म ma
Semivowels:	य ya	र ra	ल la	व va	
Sibilants:	श śa	ष ṣa	स sa		
Aspirate:	ह ha	Anusvāra: ं ṁ	Visarga: ः ḥ		

Numerals

० -0 १-1 २-2 ३-3 ४-4 ५-5 ६-6 ७-7 ८-8 ९-9

The vowels are written as follows after a consonant:

ा ā ि i ी ī ु u ू ū ृ ṛ ॄ ṝ े e ै ai ो o ौ au

For example: क ka का kā कि ki की kī कु ku कू kū
कृ kṛ कॄ kṝ के ke कै kai को ko कौ kau

Generally two or more consonants in conjunction are written together in a special form, as for example: क्ष kṣa त्र tra

The vowel "**a**" is implied after a consonant with no vowel symbol.

The symbol virāma (्) indicates that there is no final vowel: क्

The vowels are pronounced as follows:

a — as in **but**
ā — as in **far** but held twice as long as **a**
ai — as in **aisle**
au — as in **how**
e — as in **they**
i — as in **pin**
ī — as in **pique** but held twice as long as **i**
ḷ — as in **lree**
o — as in **go**
ṛ — as in **rim**
ṝ — as in **reed** but held twice as long as **ṛ**
u — as in **push**
ū — as in **rule** but held twice as long as **u**

The consonants are pronounced as follows:

Gutturals
(pronounced from the throat)
k — as in **kite**
kh — as in **Eckhart**
g — as in **give**
gh — as in **dig-hard**
ṅ — as in **sing**

Labials
(pronounced with the lips)
p — as in **pine**
ph — as in **up-hill** (not **f**)
b — as in **bird**
bh — as in **rub-hard**
m — as in **mother**

Cerebrals
(pronounced with tip of tongue against roof of mouth)

ṭ — as in **t**ub
ṭh — as in ligh**t-h**eart
ḍ — as in **d**ove
ḍh — as in re**d-h**ot
ṇ — as in si**n**g

Dentals
(pronounced as cerebrals but with tongue against teeth)

t — as in **t**ub
th — as in ligh**t-h**eart
d — as in **d**ove
dh — as in re**d-h**ot
n — as in **n**ut

Aspirate

h — as in **h**ome

Anusvāra

ṁ — a resonant nasal sound like in the French word *bon*

Palatals
(pronounced with middle of tongue against palate)

c — as in **ch**air
ch — as in stau**nch-h**eart
j — as in **j**oy
jh — as in he**dgeh**og
ñ — as in ca**ny**on

Semivowels

y — as in **y**es
r — as in **r**un
l — as in **l**ight
v — as in **v**ine, except when preceded in the same syllable by a consonant, then like in s**w**an

Sibilants

ś — as in the German word *s*prechen
ṣ — as in **sh**ine
s — as in **s**un

Visarga

ḥ — a final **h**-sound: **aḥ** is pronounced like **aha**; **iḥ** like **ihi**

There is no strong accentuation of syllables in Sanskrit, or pausing between words in a line, only a flowing of short and long (twice as long as the short) syllables. A long syllable is one whose vowel is long (**ā, ai, au, e, ī, o, ṝ, ū**) or whose short vowel is followed by more than one consonant (including **ḥ** and **ṁ**). Aspirated consonants (consonants followed by an **h**) count as single consonants.

Index of Sanskrit Verses

This index constitutes a complete listing of the first and third lines of each of the Sanskrit poetry verses of this volume of *Śrīmad-Bhāgavatam*, arranged in English alphabetical order. The first column gives the Sanskrit transliteration; the second, the chapter-verse reference. Apostrophes are alphabetized as *a*'s.

A

E

G

H

I

L

M

N

P

R

S

Y

Index of Verses Quoted

This index lists the verses quoted in the purports and footnotes of this volume of *Śrīmad-Bhāgavatam*. Numerals in boldface type refer to the first or third lines of verses quoted in full; numerals in roman type refer to partially quoted verses.

General Index

Numerals in boldface type indicate references to translations of the verses of *Śrīmad-Bhāgavatam*.

A

Abhavāya defined, 31
Abhaya defined, 257
Abortion, 691
Absolute Truth
  impersonalists misunderstand, 97, 176
  inquiry into, 166
  Lord as, 348, 349
  Lord reveals, **337**
  via Sāṅkhya philosophy, 345
  three features of, 349
  See also: Kṛṣṇa; Supreme Lord
Ācārya(s)
  defined, 326
  See also: Authority, spiritual; Disciplic succession; Spiritual master(s)
Ācāryopāsanam, 634
Acintya-bhedābheda, 604, 659
Activity
  body needed for, 344
  devotional service goal of, 301
  fruitive. *See:* Fruitive activities
  of God. *See:* Supreme Lord, activities of; Supreme Lord, pastimes of
  in Kṛṣṇa consciousness, 94, 175-76, 212
  Lord witnesses, 105
  material, 2, 151, 160, 161, 246
  material, compared with spiritual, 204
  sinful. *See:* Sinful activities
  spiritual
    in early morning, 132
    See also: Devotional service; *Karma;* Kṛṣṇa consciousness
Adhikāri-devatā, 423
Adhi-māsa defined, 162
Adhokṣaja defined, 73
Ādi-puruṣa, Kṛṣṇa as, 488
Advaita Ācārya, 831
Advancement, spiritual
  health & luster sign of, 193
  instruction in, 159, 297
  in Kṛṣṇa consciousness, 243
  via saintly person's association, 299, **300**
  via self-control, 307
  of society, 198, 199
  via spiritual master, 93, 257
  wife (good) helps, 156-57, 216
Africa, 140
Age (time of life)
  for marriage, 219
  for renouncing family life, 342
  for son to deliver mother, 350
Age, current. *See:* Kali-yuga
Ages, four (*yuga* cycle), 89, 244, 330
  See also: Dvāpara-yuga; Kali-yuga; Satya-yuga; Tretā-yuga
Agni, **196,** 284
Ahaṅkāra
  defined, 324
  See also: Ego, false
Ahiṁsā defined, 353
Air element, **473-**74, 483
  See also: Elements; Evolution
Air moving compared to Kardama traveling, **286**
Air of life, 474, **557-58, 561-63**
Airplane
  in ancient times, 223
  of Brahmā, 326, 327
  See also: Space travel
Aja, Brahmā as, 821
Ajña defined, 30
Akāma devotees, 170
Akṛtātmā defined, 210
Akṣaja defined, 181

Devotee(s) of Supreme Lord (*continued*)
bodily necessities of, **518**–20
Brahman realized by, 851
celibacy for, **516**–17
characteristics of, detailed, 386, **387–90**
classes of, all liberated, 410-12
compared
to calm ocean, 355
with demons, 119-20
with impersonalist(s), **406**–8, 542
with *jñānīs*, 334
to kittens, 392
to lotus, 536
with materialists, 544-45
with *munis*, 575
with *yogīs*, 287, 334
compassion for, **518,** 520
compassion of, 177-78, **616**–18, **634,** 644
& Deities, relationships between, **408**–9
Deity in box of, 72
demigods as, 34, 423
demigods' qualities develop in, 790
in demoniac families, 573
demons compared with, 119-20
demons envy, 32-33
desire devotional service, 157, 179
desirelessness of, 170, **414**
desires of, as spiritual, 598, 625
desirous & desireless, 170
detachment of, **395, 406**–7, **412–13, 417**–19, **545**–46, 550, 656
devotional service satisfies, 49
diplomacy avoided by, **636**
distinction between, 632-33, 635
enjoy all facilities, **414**
equal vision of, **516**–17, 632, 642, 646-48, **656**–57
as eternally related to Lord, **414**–17
faith of, **547**–48
false, 813
in family life, 766
foods for, 519, 630-31
free from modes of nature, **627**–28
friendship with, **387**–88, **518,** 520, 634-35
See also: Devotee(s), association with

Devotee(s) of Lord (*continued*)
Godbrothers respected by, 815
in goodness mode, **622**–23
gopīs as best, 546
gravity of, **516**–17
happiness of, 854
hearing about, **83–84**
hearing from. *See:* Devotee(s), association with
as highest *brāhmaṇa,* 653-54
householder, **333**–34
See also: Gṛhastha(s)
humility of, 637
in ignorance mode, **616**–21
impersonalists compared with, **406**–8, 542
income for, **518**–20
independence of, 43, **541**–42
initiation of, 828-29
in intermediate stage, 358
intolerant of irreligion, 91
as *īśvara*, 542
jñānīs compared with, 334
kinds of, 154-55, 170, 177-78, 341, 358
as kind to animals, 388
as kings, 139
levels of, **653**–54
as liberated souls, 183, 245-46
liberation for. *See:* Liberation
life-span of, time can't touch, **162,** 244
Lord
accepted by, 33
favors, 334, **570–84**
fulfills desires of, 145, 170, 173
in guise of, 330
known by, 334
merciful to, 168, 169
protects, 34, 115-16
relieves suffering of, **113**
seen by, **333,** 334, 794-95
as son of, 308, 310, 311, 316, 825
& Lord, relationships between. *See:* Kṛṣṇa, relationships with; Supreme Lord, relationships with
Lord's forms as preferred by, **113,** 114, 336
Lord's pastimes benefit, 88

Devotee(s) of Lord (*continued*)
Lord's pastimes relished by, **95**
as *mahātmās,* 466
maintained by Lord, 856
materialistic, Lord's kindness on, 167
materialists compared with, 544-45
material needs minimized by, 152
material world forgotten by, 853-54
material world not meant for, 164-65
meditation on, **571**-72
as mercy of Lord, **547**-48
mercy of, **387**-88, **518,** 520, 815-16
miseries unfelt by, 392
mixed, vs. pure, 545-46
in morning worship, 241
as *muni,* 519
munis compared with, 575
names of, chanting of, 572
neophyte, 358, 410-12, 632, 835
obliged to no one but Lord, 389, 423
as one with Lord's desire, 179, 416, 628, 655
opulences of, as eternal, **414**-16
in passion mode, 621
pastimes of, 84
as peaceful, **518,** 520
possessions of, 467
prayers of, 55-56
See also: Prayer(s)
preachers. *See:* Preacher(s)
preachers & nonpreachers, 341
previous qualifications for, **830**-32
protected by Lord, 587, 588, 856
pure. *See:* Pure devotee(s)
qualities of, **635**-37, 745, 814-16
recommendations for, **516-22**
rituals unnecessary for, 130
as *sādhus,* 386, **387**-90
sakāma, 170
as *sat,* 375
saved by Lord, **663**
scripture followed by, 388
scriptures understood only by, 394
seclusion for, **518**-20
see all in relation to Kṛṣṇa, 526
see Lord everywhere, 522, 525-26, **638**-39

Devotee(s) of Lord (*continued*)
self-realization from, **547**
self-realization of, 355-56, **518,** 520
as self-satisfied, 544
separatist, **619-21**
as servants eternally, 778
serve Lord spontaneously, 595, **596**-97
service to. *See:* Devotees, association with
Śiva best among, 250
speech of, 517
spiritual master chooses service for, 398
spiritual masters for. *See:* Spiritual master(s)
Śrīmad-Bhāgavatam relished by, 95
as straightforward, **636**
as "superior" to Lord sometimes, 363
symptoms of, two described, 809
third-class, liberation for, 410-12
as thoughtful, **518**-19
as tolerant, **387**-88, 418-19
as transcendental, 245, 246, **376**-77, **414**-17, **507**-8, 508, **526-27,** 540, 540, **544**-45, **599**-601, 634, **788**-89, **791**-92
wealth of, **518**-20, 701-2
as *yogīs,* 363
yogīs compared with, 287, 334
See also: Sādhus; specific devotees
Devotional service to Supreme Lord
activities of
by Ambarīṣa Mahārāja, 425-26
listed, 396-97, 399, 623, 809
recommended five, 412, 815
advantages of, 365, 387, 429-30, 790, 811
detachment as, 395, 504, **507**-8, **513**-14, 546, 791-92, 796, 809
God realization as, **396**-97, **594**-95, **638**-39, 658, 790-91, 794, **803,** 805
happiness as, 238, **363**-64, 504
knowledge as, 384, 424-25, 547, 801-2, 809
liberation as, 161, 183, 354-55, 374, 386, **393**-94, 399, **404**-5, **410**-12, 508, **536**-38, 658, **732,** 761-62, **835-36, 848**
perfection as, **376**-77, **383**-84, **425**-26, 537, 789

E

G

H

Kuśa grass, **236**
Kuśāvarta (Hardwar), 90, **92,** 93
Kuvera, Lord, **284**

L

Ladies. *See:* Women
Lake Bindu-sarovara, **181, 184, 186–90, 272, 366**
Lakṣmī, 336
as Brahmā's "mother," 579, 582
meditation on, **579**
with Viṣṇu, **583–**84
Lakṣmī-Nārāyaṇa, 113, 114
Laws of nature
conditioned souls under, 159
on interplanetary travel, 286
Lord makes, 666
as stringent, 11, 12, 106
transcendentalists surpass, 43
Leaders, government. *See:* Government(s), leader(s) of
Liberated soul(s)
compared with conditioned soul, **525–**26
detailed, **596–**601
devotee as, 183
Liberation, **536–49**
for animals, 388
austerity & penance don't give, 420, 421
from bodily identification, **596–**601
of Brahmā, **776–77**
to *brahmajyoti,* 406
via Brahmā's liberation, **777**
via chanting holy names, 243, 405
children trained for, 226
compared to maidservant, 405
of conditioned souls, 90
as constitutional position, 836
via Deity worship, **410–**12
demigod worship can't give, 783
desire for, value of, 375
detachment required for, 391
Devahūti's questions on, **531–34**
devotees', compared with impersonalists', 547-49, 628
of devotee's ancestors, 130
Liberation (*continued*)
devotees' as eternal, 548-49
devotees desireless of, **406–**7, **413, 417–**19, **625–**27
via devotional service, 183, 354-55, 374, 386, 393-94, 399, **404–**5, **410–**13, **424–**25, 508, 511, 513, **536–**38, **732,** 761-62, **835–**37, 848
devotional service as, 404-5, 508, **526–27, 536–**38, 761-62
via devotional service only, 399-400, 399-400, **420–22, 425,** 516, 533, 616, 757, 773, 789, **836**
devotional service superior to, 245-46, **403–**5
via devotional service to Lord's devotees, **385–**86
as difficult, **533**
of forefathers, 129-30
as freedom from false ego, 530
via hearing & chanting, **536–**38
via hearing from Lord, **410–**12
via hearing of Kapila & Devahūti, **862**
highest, 399-400
imperceptibly attained by devotee, 410-12, **417–**19
impersonal, devotional service required for, 794
impersonalists', compared with devotees', 547-49, 628
Kapila's benediction for, **817**
kinds of, five listed, 406, **625–**27
via knowing Lord's activities, 316
via knowledge from spiritual master, 369
via Kṛṣṇa consciousness, **385–**86, **396–**97, 660
via Kṛṣṇa only, 780
Lord
arranges, **418–**19
desires for all, 727
gives, 31
via Lord's association, 300
via Lord's mercy, **721–**22, 811-12
from material bondage, 158-59
for materially disgusted, 166
via meditating on Lord's form, **75,** 76
from modes of nature, **507–**8, 564

M

North Pole, 140
Nṛsiṁha, Lord
appeared from pillar, 311
Prahlāda &, 130

O

Occupation(s)
of eternal living entity, 346
material compared with spiritual, 204
See also: Duty; *Varṇāśrama* system
Ocean(s)
at demons' birth, **6**
devotee compared to, 355
Garbhodaka, 79, **105**
Hiraṇyākṣa harassed, **19–21**
Odor, kinds of, **480**–81
Old age
son delivers mother in, 350
See also: Age (time of life); Life, span of; Time
Omen(s)
at demons' birth, **3–11**
planetary, 10
Oṁkāra, impersonalists worship, 572
Oneness
personal, compared with impersonal, 151, 176-77, 179
See also: Brahman; Impersonalist(s); Liberation; Monists
Opportunities, intelligent person uses, 302
Opulence(s)
of Kardama's castle, **265–70,** 271
of Lord, 330, **337**–38
as Lord's mercy, 238
of planets, 288
See also: Economic development; Money; Mystic power; Perfection; Wealth
Organs for action listed, **446**
Oversoul. *See:* Supersoul

P

Pain. *See:* Suffering
Pakistan, 46
Palace(s)
of Mogul emperors, 269
in sky, Kardama created, **264–70,** 271
Pāṇḍavas, 84
See also: Arjuna; Yudhiṣṭhira
Pantheism, 176
See also: Brahman; Oneness; Supreme Lord, as all-pervading
Para defined, 357
Paradise. *See:* Heavenly planet(s); Spiritual world
Paraḥ defined, 432
Paramahaṁsa defined, 226-27
Parama-sammataḥ defined, 140
Paramātmā. *See:* Supersoul
Paramparā defined, 81
See also: Disciplic succession(s)
Parārdhas, **774–76**
Parents
begetting children, 321
children expansions of, 262
children's marriage arranged by, 172-73, 232, 320
See also: Family life; Father(s); *Gṛhastha(s);* Husband(s); Marriage; Mother(s); Wife
Parīkṣit Mahārāja, 46
Parivrāja defined, 341
Pārvatī (Bhavānī), **249**–50, 309
Passion, mode of
in begetting children, 263
Brahmā in, 117
Brahmā supervises, 105
charity in, 372
destiny according to, 245
lust & anger in, 739
twilight time for, **118**
See also: Modes of nature
Pastime defined, 439, 441, 448
Pastimes of Lord. *See:* Kṛṣṇa, pastimes of; Supreme Lord, pastimes of
Patañjali, 552
Patañjali-sūtras, 151, 152
Patañjali *yoga* system, 465
Patient in disease-material life analogy, 123
Pauganda defined, 738

Peacefulness for devotee, **518,** 520
Peace via begetting nice children, 12
Penance, 420-21, 840
  See also: Austerity; Sacrifices
Perception, sense
  knowledge beyond, 98
  See also: Speculation
Perfection
  via acting according to ability, 212-13
  via devotional service, 145, 146
  via hearing Lord's pastimes, 83
  of Kṛṣṇa consciousness, 240-42
  love for Lord as, 257-59
  in meditation, 146
  via saintly person's association, 208, 209
  of senses in Lord's service, 153
  in spiritual life, 146
  via spiritual master, 210-13, 318
  in *yoga,* 144-46, 149-52, 264, 289, 332, 333
  See also: Goal of life
Person(s). *See:* Human beings; Living entities; *specific persons*
Personalist(s). *See:* Devotee(s)
Philanthropy, 397, 510, 512-13, 543, 615, 766
Philosopher(s). *See: Brāhmaṇa(s);* Devotee(s); *Jñānī(s);* Sage(s)
Philosophy. *See:* Absolute Truth; Knowledge; *specific philosophies*
Physician in disease-material life analogy, 123
Piety, 397, **614–**15, 766
Pilgrimage places
  bathing at, 272
  charity at, 175
  at present, 93
  for purification, 92-93
Piṇḍa, 767
Piṇḍa-siddhi cited on pregnancy, 14–15
Pious persons. *See:* Devotee(s); Saintly person(s)
Pious species, 10, 187–88
Pitās, **128, 129**
Pīṭha-sthāna defined, 237
Pitṛloka, **786**
Planets
  compared to islands, 288
  differences among, 288
  disturbed at demons' birth, **3–6, 10**
  Earth. *See:* Earth planet
  as floating, **665–67**
  heavenly. *See:* Heavenly planets
  for living entities, 667
  Lord floats, 36-37
  lower, via ignorance mode, 245
  moon. *See:* Moon
  pious & impious, **10**
  as round, 288
  spiritual, 104, **414–**17, 548-49, 626
    See also: Spiritual world; Vaikuṇṭha
  three systems of, 326-27
  travel to, 286, 841
  in universal form, **487**
  See also: Material world; Universe(s); *specific planets*
Pleasure
  via devotional service, 658-59
  via God realization, 805-6
  in goodness, 153
  via hearing devotee's pastimes, **83–84**
  via hearing Lord's pastimes, 82
  See also: Enjoyment, material; Happiness; Sense gratification
Poison compared to nondevotee's words, 82
Population
  demoniac, increasing, 4, 5, 11
  in Kali-yuga, 222, 226, 343
  Prajāpatis increased, 143
  via sanctified sex life, 117, 139, 140
  Vedic culture regulates, 11, 12
  See also: Citizens; Society, human
Possessiveness. *See:* Attachment
Poverty of materialists, 467
Power
  of devotional service, 334
  of Lord & living entity compared, 289, 290
  material, 16
  mystic. *See:* Mystic power(s)
  spiritual, 151
  of *yogī,* 271, 280, 281
  See also: Energy of Supreme Lord

S

Spiritual life (*continued*)
advantage of, 375, 544
compared to razor's edge, 459
compared with material life, 123
demigods promote, 12, 17
early morning best for, 118, 132
human society meant for, 239
materialists ineligible for, 137
necessity of, 375, 544
perfection in, 146, 210-13
sense enjoyment precludes, 137
Vṛndāvana conducive to, 93
See also: Devotional service; Kṛṣṇa consciousness; Religion; Self-realization; *Yoga*
Spiritual master(s)
association with, 369
bogus, compared with bona fide, 211, 212
compared to captain, 713
Deity worship taught by, 409
devotee's service chosen by, 398
disciple asking favor from, 213
disciple's duty to, 211-13
disciple serving, 257
in disciplic succession, 634
faith in, 309, 318, 835-36
as father, 318, 321
hearing from, 81, 82, 212, 213
husband as, 309
initiation by, 816, 828-29
instructions of, execution of, 212-13, 309, 317, **318**
knowledge from, 317, 369, 470, 553, 556
knowledge via mercy of, **400–**401
as liberated, 835-36
Lord as, **414,** 416, 470
Lord known via, 257
as Lord's representative, 620
mercy of, 161, 400-401, **400–**401, 812
necessity of, 369
perfection via, 210-13
purification taught by, 466
qualifications of, 553, 654, 816
reciprocates disciple's service, 297
respect for, 813-16
spiritual advancement via, 93
trains by one's tendency, 212
Spiritual master(s) (*continued*)
worship of, **634**
See also: Pure devotee(s); *specific spiritual master(s)*
Spiritual planet(s). *See:* Planet(s), spiritual; Vaikuṇṭha planet(s)
Spiritual sky
impersonalists attain, 548–49
See also: Planet(s), spiritual; Spiritual world; Vaikuṇṭha planet(s)
Spiritual world
attaining to. *See:* Liberation
devotees attain to, 548–49
elevation to, as eternal, 788
as eternal & changeless, 776
as eternal & supreme, 795
falldown from, 400
flowers in, 568
inhabitants of, 65
Kapila Vaikuṇṭha planet in, 857
lighted by Lord's luster, 432
as Lord's internal potency, 322
material world vs., 78, 168, 314–15, 322
path to, **182,** 183
planets in, 104
in pure goodness, 78, 314–15
self-effulgent, 104
See also: Goloka Vṛndāvana; Planets, spiritual; Vaikuṇṭha; Vṛndāvana
Sports
princesses played, 223
women &, 122
Śrāddha, **328**
Śrāddha ritual, 129-30
Śrī Caitanya-caritāmṛta. See: Caitanya-caritāmṛta
Śrīdhara Svāmī cited
See also: Śrīdhara Svāmī quoted
on Brahmā giving up his body, 117
on *brāhmaṇas,* 828
on Hiraṇyākṣa addressing Lord Boar, 30, 31, 33
on Lord's form, 336
on Lord's opulences, 330
Śrīdhara Svāmī quoted
See also: Śrīdhara Svāmī cited
on purification by chanting, 828

T

U

V

W